Studies in Choice and Welfare

For further volumes:
http://www.springer.com/series/6869

Serge-Christophe Kolm

Marc Fleurbaey • Maurice Salles
John A. Weymark
Editors

Social Ethics and Normative Economics

Essays in Honour of Serge-Christophe Kolm

Springer

Editors

Marc Fleurbaey, Ph.D.
Université Paris-Descartes
CNRS and CERSES
rue des Saints-Pères 45
75006 Paris
France
marc.fleurbaey@parisdescartes.fr

Prof. Maurice Salles
Université de Caen
CREM, UMR-CNRS 6211
14032 Caen Cedex
France
maurice.salles@unicaen.fr

Prof. John A. Weymark
Vanderbilt University
Department of Economics
VU Station B #351819
2301 Vanderbilt Place
Nashville, 37235-1819
Tennessee
USA
john.weymark@vanderbilt.edu

Studies in Choice and Welfare ISSN 1614-0311
ISBN 978-3-642-17806-1 e-ISBN 978-3-642-17807-8
DOI 10.1007/978-3-642-17807-8
Springer Heidelberg Dordrecht London New York

Library of Congress Control Number: 2011924347

Cover design: eStudio Calamar Steinen

Printed on acid-free paper

Springer is part of Springer Science+Business Media (www.springer.com)

Preface

The essays in this collection were written to honour our distinguished colleague, Serge-Christophe Kolm. They were presented at a conference on "Social Ethics and Normative Economics" in honour of Serge that was held at the Université de Caen, May 18–19, 2007. This conference received generous financial support from the Association pour le Développement de la Recherche en Economie et en Statistique, the Institut d'Economie Publique, the Centre National de la Recherche Scientifique, the Centre de Recherche en Economie et Management (UMR-CNRS 6211), the Université de Caen, the région de Basse-Normandie, and the ville de Caen. We are grateful to all of these institutions for their support.

Each of the essays has been revised in light of comments received from a referee and from the editors. We would like to thank the scholars who served as referees. We are also grateful to Martina Bihn, our editor at Springer, for her support and encouragement. Last, but not least, we want to express our appreciation to Serge for the assistance he has provided in responding to our many queries about his life and scholarship.

Marc Fleurbaey
Maurice Salles
John A. Weymark

Contents

Contributors

Laurent David GDF Suez, Direction de la Stratégie et du Développement Durable, Tour 1, 1 place Samuel de Champlain, 92930 Paris La Défense cedex, France, laurent.david@gdfsuez.com

Jon Elster Collège de France, 11, place Marcelin Berthelot, 75231 Paris, cedex 05, France
and
Department of Political Science, Columbia University, 7th Floor, IAB, 420 West 118th Street, New York, NY 10027, USA, je70@columbia.edu

Marc Fleurbaey CNRS and CERSES, Université Paris-Descartes, 45 rue des Saints-Pères, 75006 Paris, France, marc.fleurbaey@parisdescartes.fr

Nicolas Gravel GREQAM-IDEP, Centre de la Vieille Charité, Université de la Méditerranée, 13002 Marseille, France, nicolas.gravel@univmed.fr

Peter J. Lambert Department of Economics, University of Oregon, Eugene, OR 97403-1285, USA, plambert@uoregon.edu

Michel Le Breton Toulouse School of Economics, GREMAQ, and IDEI, Manufacture des tabacs, Aile JJ Laffont, 21, Allée de Brienne, 31000 Toulouse, France, lebreton@cict.fr

François Maniquet CORE, Université Catholique de Louvain, 34 Voie du Roman Pays, 1348 Louvain-la-Neuve, Belgium, francois.maniquet@uclouvain.be

Thierry Marchant Department of Data Analysis, Ghent University, Henri Dunantlaan 1, 9000 Ghent, Belgium, thierry.marchant@ugent.be

Jean Mercier Ythier Université Panthéon-Assas, ERMES, and IDEP, 12 place du Panthéon, 75005 Paris, France, jean.mercier-ythier@u-paris2.fr

Olivier Merillon GDF Suez E&P, Département Acquisitions, Tour 1, 1 place Samuel de Champlain, 92930 Paris La Défense cedex, France, olivier.merillon@gdfsuez.com

Patrick Moyes GREThA (UMR CNRS 5113), Université de Bordeaux and CNRS, Avenue Léon Duguit, 33608 Pessac, France, patrick.moyes@u-bordeaux4.fr

Maurice Salles CREM, UMR-CNRS 6211, Université de Caen, 14032 Caen cedex, France, maurice.salles@unicaen.fr

Arunava Sen Indian Statistical Institute, 7 S. J. S. Sansanwal Marg, New Delhi 110016, India, asen@isid.ac.in

Jacques Silber Department of Economics, Bar-Ilan University, 52900 Ramat-Gan, Israel, jsilber_2000@yahoo.com

Laurent Simula Uppsala Center for Fiscal Studies, Department of Economics, Uppsala University, P.O. Box 513, 751 20 Uppsala, Sweden, laurent.simula@nek.uu.se

Amedeo Spadaro Paris School of Economics, 48 Bd. Jourdan, 75014 Paris, France
and
Universitat de les Illes Balears, ctra Valldemossa Km 7,5, 07122 Palma de Mallorca, Spain, spadaro@pse.ens.fr

Koichi Tadenuma Department of Economics, Hitotsubashi University, Kunitachi, Tokyo 186-8601, Japan, koichi.t@econ.hit-u.ac.jp

William Thomson Department of Economics, University of Rochester, Rochester, NY 14618, USA, wth2@mail.rochester.edu

Alain Trannoy Ecole des Hautes Etudes en Sciences Sociales, GREQAM, and IDEP, Centre de la Vieille Charité, 13236 Marseille cedex 02, France, Alain.Trannoy@eco.u-cergy.fr

John A. Weymark Department of Economics, Vanderbilt University, VU Station B #35189, 2301 Vanderbilt Place, Nashville, TN 37235-1819, USA, john.weymark@vanderbilt.edu

An Introduction to *Social Ethics and Normative Economics*

Marc Fleurbaey, Maurice Salles, and John A. Weymark

Serge-Christophe Kolm is a prominent member of the French community of *ingénieurs-économistes* (engineer-economists). Trained in the elite French *grandes écoles* (great schools), these individuals, motivated by practical problems of the public sector, have made distinguished contributions to the study of normative economics. Kolm, more so than others in this tradition, has had an ongoing interest in the philosophical foundations of normative economics, with the consequence that he has written extensively on social ethics. The essays in this volume have been written to honour Serge Kolm for his seminal research on social ethics and normative economics. In Sect. 1 of this Introduction, we provide a biographical sketch of Kolm's life and scholarship. In Sect. 2, we provide an overview of the contributions to this collection of essays.

1 Biographical Sketch

Serge Kolm was born in Paris in 1932. He spent his youth living in Paris and, during World War II, on a farm in Gascony south of Bordeaux. Kolm's early years were dominated by the German occupation of France during the war. By his own admission, this tragic period with its human suffering and lack of freedom left a profound mark on him and played a crucial role in his intellectual development.

M. Fleurbaey (✉)
CNRS and CERSES, Université Paris-Descartes, 45 rue des Saints-Pères, 75006 Paris, France
e-mail: marc.fleurbaey@parisdescartes.fr

M. Salles
CREM, UMR-CNRS 6211, Université de Caen, 14032 Caen cedex, France
e-mail: maurice.salles@unicaen.fr

J.A. Weymark
Department of Economics, Vanderbilt University, VU Station B #35189, 2301 Vanderbilt Place, Nashville, TN 37235-1819, USA
e-mail: john.weymark@vanderbilt.edu

M. Fleurbaey et al. (eds.), *Social Ethics and Normative Economics*,
Studies in Choice and Welfare, DOI 10.1007/978-3-642-17807-8_1,

Kolm was a brilliant young man. He did extremely well in the highly competitive French education system. A particular feature of French higher education is that it has two kinds of institutions operating in parallel: on one side, there are the universities and, on the other, there are the *grandes écoles*. The *grandes écoles* are mainly, but not exclusively, engineering schools. On graduation, most of the best *lycéens* (high school pupils) continue their studies in selected *lycées* in order to receive specific training to prepare for the entrance examinations for the *grandes écoles*. The top-ranked engineering school is the Ecole Polytechnique. Together with the Ecole Normale Supérieure (Higher Normal School), the Ecole Polytechnique is the most sought-after and prestigious institution for post-secondary education in France.[1] Kolm entered the Ecole Polytechnique in 1953. In spite of being an engineering school, courses there are primarily theoretical, with an emphasis on mathematics and the natural sciences.

Many well-known scholars have been associated with the Ecole Polytechnique. At the end of the nineteenth century, Henri Poincaré was a student and subsequently a professor there. Later, while Kolm was a student, Gaston Julia and Paul Lévy both taught mathematics at the Ecole Polytechnique. During that period, the Ecole Polytechnique had a small economics department under the direction of François Divisia. Divisia was a co-founder of the Econometric Society. Divisia and Lévy were Kolm's advisors for a dissertation on income distribution and redistribution, including an analysis of the effects of transfers on inequality.

After their studies, *Polytechniciens* (as students of the school are known) join the senior ranks of the French civil service, with the choice of which ministry or other government institution (such as one of the public utilities) they join determined in part on the basis of their rankings in the graduating examinations. Following a year of military service in North Africa, Kolm became a member of the *corps des ingénieurs des Ponts et Chaussées* (engineering corps of Bridges and Roads), pursuing further applied studies at the Ecole Nationale des Ponts et Chaussées (National School of Bridges and Roads). One of his teachers there was René Roy. Some other well-known economists have been *ingénieurs des Ponts et Chaussées*, such as Jules Dupuit, François Divisia, René Roy, and Pierre Massé.

In 1957, Kolm received his first appointment as a senior civil servant, the Directorship of the Senegal Development Mission. He was in particular responsible for the development of the Senegal river basin, participating in projects dealing with the construction of dams, irrigation, and agricultural experiments. As part of his duties, Kolm and his colleagues made a social and economic survey of the region. In retrospect, some of this work can be seen as an early study of multidimensional inequality. Kolm's first book in 1959, *Les Hommes du Fouta-Toro* (*Men of the Fouta-Toro*), is based on this African experience.[2]

---

[1] As its name suggests, the Ecole Normale Supérieure was founded as an institution for training teachers for secondary schools, not as an engineering school. However, it now provides training in a range of disciplines.

[2] Bibliographic details of Kolm's publications cited in this Introduction may be found in the list of his scientific publications at the end of this volume.

On Kolm's return in France in 1960, he was recruited by Edmond Malinvaud, who was at the time the Director of the Ecole Nationale de la Statistique et de l'Administration Economique (ENSAE, the National School of Statistics and Economic Management), to be a Professor and Deputy Director for Economics at ENSAE. While at ENSAE, Kolm launched a center for the training of economists and statisticians from developing countries. During this period, Kolm also designed questionnaires whose purpose was to determine the views of the sampled population on inequality and deprivation. This work was a precursor to the modern literature on the questionnaire approach to analyzing inequality.

Since 1960, Kolm has remained an academic while maintaining his links with French government ministries and agencies, for which he has undertaken several studies in applied public economics. This connection has had a major impact on his work, as exemplified by his second book, *Introduction à la Théorie Economique de l'Etat: Les Fondements de l'Economie Publique* (*Introduction to the Economic Theory of the State: The Foundations of Public Economics*), which appeared in 1964. It was with this book that the economic analysis of the public sector was first called "public economics" by an economist.[3] This book was also noteworthy for the introduction of the well-known Kolm triangle used to illustrate the optimal allocation of a public good. It was already apparent in Kolm's early publications in the 1960s that one of his main interests is in questions of social justice as related to public economics.

At Edmond Malinvaud's suggestion, Kolm accepted a position at Harvard University in 1963. He subsequently moved to Stanford University in 1967 with an arrangement that allowed him to spend half of each year in France. It was during this period that Kolm lectured on and did much of the research for his 1968 book on congestible goods, *La Théorie Economique Générale de l'Encombrement* (*The General Economic Theory of Congestion*), and what was to become a four-volume treatise on public economics known collectively as the *Cours d'Economie Publique* (*A Course on Public Economics*) that was published in 1970. The individual volumes are *La Valeur Publique* (*Public Value*), *Prix Publics Optimaux* (*Optimal Public Prices*), *La Théorie des Contraintes de Valeur et Ses Applications* (*The Theory of Value Constraints and Their Applications*), and *Le Service des Masses* (*Mass Services*).[4] The third of these four volumes provides an in-depth formal analysis of a number of issues in second-best theory such as optimal taxation and public utility pricing. It is regrettable that these books have never been translated into English because they contain ideas that are not known in the English-language literature, as well as results that have been subsequently rediscovered by other scholars.

While at Harvard, Kolm wrote his classic article, "The Optimal Production of Social Justice," for the 1966 International Economic Association conference on Public Economics held in Biarritz. The conference proceedings first appeared in

[3] Kolm subsequently discovered that Jean–Jacques Rousseau had first used this phrase.

[4] Prominent examples of a value constraint are break-even or revenue constraints applied to a public utility. Mass services are public goods and services with widespread usage, such as mass transit.

French in 1968 as *Economie Publique* and a year later in English as *Public Economics*.[5] This was Kolm's first article on normative economics and it clearly shows that his interest in the philosophical aspects of this subject were present early in his career. It was in this rather wide-ranging article that Kolm first published any of his research on normative inequality measurement. Many familiar concepts made their first appearance there. For example, in this article, we find the equally-distributed equivalent income (what Kolm called the "equal equivalent"), the relative measure of inequality obtained by first dividing the equal equivalent by the mean income and then subtracting this ratio from 1, and the absolute measure of inequality obtained by subtracting the equal equivalent from the mean income.

While on the faculty at Stanford, Kolm wrote his highly influential book, *Justice et Equité*. This book was first made available by CEPREMAP in 1971 and published by the Centre National de la Recherche Scientifique (National Center for Economic Research) a year later.[6] This volume was later translated into English in 1998 with the title *Justice and Equity*. In this book, Kolm investigated the problem of fair allocation using what is now known as the no-envy criterion.[7] In addition, Kolm also proposed using a leximin function of ordinally comparable utlities as a social welfare criterion. Note that this was the same year that John Rawls' *A Theory of Justice* (Rawls 1971) appeared, with its use of a maximin principle applied to an index of primary goods.

The time spent in the United States was also a period in which Kolm wrote on monetary economics and international finance. At Stanford, he gave a course based on his 1966 book, *Les Choix Financiers et Monétaires: Théorie et Technique Modernes* (*Financial and Monetary Choices: Modern Theory and Technique*).

For several reasons, Kolm decided to return to France in 1972 as Directeur d'Etudes (Director of Studies) at the Ecole des Hautes Etudes en Sciences Sociales (EHESS, the School for Advanced Studies in the Social Sciences) in Paris. The EHESS is basically a graduate school and research institution for the social sciences. Kolm also held joint positions at the Paris Institut d'Etudes Politiques (Institute for Political Studies), CEPREMAP, and the Ecole Nationale des Ponts et Chaussées (ENPC). At ENPC, he launched in 1982 (with Michel Deleau and Roger Guesnerie) and chaired until 1992, the Centre d'Enseignement et de Recherche en Analyse Socio-Economique (CERAS, the Teaching and Research Center in Socio-Economic Analysis).

---

[5] In Biarritz, the presentations were in English and written versions of all of the papers were made available in both English and French.

[6] CEPREMAP is an acronym for the Centre d'Etudes Prospectives d'Economie Mathématique Appliquées à la Planification (Center for Prospective Studies in Mathematical Economics Applied to Planning). The reference to mathematics, but not the acronym, was dropped when CEPREMAP became the Centre pour la Recherche Economique et Ses Applications (Center for Economic Research and Its Applications) in 2005.

[7] Kolm objects to this terminology, preferring *equité* (equity) instead. Kolm credits Jan Tinbergen for first bringing this equity concept to his attention in 1961 at a conference on development economics that was held in Paris shortly after his return from Africa.

As the 1970s progressed, the diversity of Kolm's research expanded considerably. He did research on elections, environmental economics, inequality measurement, macroeconomics, the socialist transition, and taxation theory, to name just a few of the topics that he wrote about. His 1978 book, *Les Elections Sont-elles la Démocratie?* (*Are Elections Democracy?*) was his first excursion into social choice theory. Particularly notable for the subject of this volume are his two-part 1976 *Journal of Economic Theory* article on univariate inequality and his seminal 1977 *Quarterly Journal of Economics* article on multidimensional inequality. To the best of our knowledge, the latter article is the first to be published in an economics journal about multidimensional inequality. Kolm's experience as an advisor to left-leaning governments in Chile, Portugal, and Greece informed his writings on the socialist transition in market economies, notably his 1977 book, *La Transition Socialiste: La Politique Economique de Gauche* (*The Socialist Transition: The Economic Policy of the Left*).

In the 1980s, Kolm continued to publish with some regularity on macroeconomics, including his 1984 book on macroeconomic policy, *Sortir de la Crise* (*Exit from the Crisis*). He also wrote extensively on issues related to Buddhism (based in part on time spent living and studying in Buddhist monasteries in Bhutan and Thailand) and on economic methodology, subjects on which he had not previously written much about. His thoughts on the latter subjects receive their fullest expression in his books *Le Bonheur-Liberté: Bouddhisme Profond et Modernité* (*Happiness-Freedom: Deep Buddhism and Modernity*) first published in 1982, *L'Homme Pluridimensionnel: Bouddhisme, Marxisme, Psychanalyse pour une Economie de l'Esprit* (*Pluridimensional Man: Buddhism, Marxism, and Psychoanalysis for an Economics of the Mind*) published in 1987, and *Philosophie de l'Economie* (*Economic Philosophy*) published in 1986. However, a characteristic of Kolm's research in the 1980s is that it is more and more focused on social ethics and normative economics–liberalism, social justice, altruism, reciprocity, etc., a focus that has continued to this day. This focus is exemplified by his books *La Bonne Economie: La Réciprocité Générale* (*The Good Economy: General Reciprocity*) published in 1984, *Le Libéralisme Moderne: Analyse d'une Raison Economique* (*Modern Liberalism: An Economic Analysis*) also published in 1984, and *Le Contrat Social Libéral: Philosophie et Pratique du Libéralisme* (*The Liberal Social Contract: Philosophy and Practice of Liberalism*) published in 1985.

Prior to the late 1980s, only a handful of Kolm's articles were published in English, but none of his books. His writings in English on issues related to inequality measurement appeared in the best international journals and in the widely-cited Biarritz conference volume. These ideas quickly became quite influential among the general international scholarly community. The Kolm triangle and Kolm's concept of envy-freeness also became widely known and used outside France, largely because some scholars writing in English had used his ideas in their own work. A major change in Kolm's career took place towards the end of the 1980s. At that time, Kolm decided to publish most of his work in English so as to enlarge his readership. As a consequence, for the past two decades, Kolm has received much greater recognition for his research than had previously been the case. However, the international recognition that he deserves for his earlier research that was only published in French (e.g., his monumental *Cours d'Economie Publique*) still remains largely unrealized.

For the last two decades or so, a major preoccupation of Kolm's research has been the problem of what he calls "macrojustice." By this term, Kolm means the basic principles of justice that determine the optimal distribution of resources and the specification of basic rights. He has published two major books on this subject in English: *Modern Theories of Justice* (1996) and *Macrojustice: The Political Economy of Fairness* (2005). In the first of these volumes, in just over 500 pages, one can find an introduction to Kolm's main views on normative economics, social justice, freedom, liberalism, etc. He identifies a number of ways in which theories of justice may differ (e.g., in their end values) and uses this taxonomy to compare and evaluate many of the main theories of justice that were prominent in the latter half of the last century. He also provides a preliminary account of his own solution to the problem of macrojustice. This solution has three fundamental features: (1) the satisfaction of basic needs and the alleviation of extreme suffering, (2) Kolm's now well-known and extensively discussed concept of ELIE (Equal Labor Income Equalization), and (3) process-freedom (the freedom to act without forcible interference and to enjoy the benefits of one's own actions). These ideas are developed in more detail in the second volume, in which the basic features of a theory of justice are those that would be unanimously chosen by a society of impartial and well-informed individuals.

With the ELIE proposal, each individual receives an equal share of the proceeds of the income that would be generated if everybody worked the same number of hours, with any income obtained from working more than this amount left untaxed. This proposal has the feature that it ensures that basic needs are met while respecting individual freedoms. Furthermore, it bases redistribution on a shared sense of reciprocity. In Kolm's view, reciprocity is a necessary feature of any free and equal society if it is to live together peacefully. In his most recent book, *Reciprocity: An Economics of Social Relations* (2008), Kolm provides an in-depth analysis of reciprocity, seeking to understand its origins and its implications for social relations. This book revisits and extends ideas that have appeared in Kolm's writings since the early 1980s, notably in his book, *La Bonne Economie*.

We have had to be very selective in this rather cursory overview of Serge Kolm's life and scholarship. More information about Kolm, his thoughts, and his research may be found in an interview of Kolm by Peter Lambert (Lambert 2011). Kolm is still very actively contributing to the frontiers of normative economics and social ethics, as can be seen from the list of his scientific publications at the end of this volume. We do not expect this situation to change any time soon.

2 An Overview of the Volume

The thirteen essays in this collection deal with a number of important issues in social ethics and normative economics. How should the public sector price its production and services? What are the normative foundations of criteria for comparing distributions of riches and advantages? How should intergenerational social immobility and inequality in circumstances be measured? What is a fair way to form partnerships? How vulnerable to manipulation is the Lindahl rule for allocating public goods? What are the properties of Kolm's ELIE tax proposal? Would the addition of EU-level income taxes enhance equity? How should we compare different scenarios for future societies with different population sizes? How can domain conditions in social choice theory be justified using Kolm's epistemic counterfactuals? How can Kolm's distributive liberal contract be implemented? What are the implications of norms of reciprocity for the organization of society?

Such questions have been addressed in innovative and thought-provoking ways in Serge Kolm's writings. These, and related questions, are the subject of current research by scholars interested in normative issues. Many of the issues addressed here feature in public debates and will remain on the political agenda for decades to come. The essays in this volume advance the state of knowledge and bring new perspectives to this set of issues.

In Sect. 1, we noted that Kolm's early research on the economics of the public sector remains largely unknown and unappreciated by the international scholarly community because this work is only available in French. The first essay in this volume by Laurent David, Michel Le Breton, and Olivier Merillon helps rectify this situation. They provide a much needed introduction to Kolm's early contributions to the optimal management of the public sector, discussing how the principle of marginal cost pricing was developed, criticized, and refined for second-best applications, and how the basic tools of the theory of incentives and the theory of organizations were foreshadowed in Kolm's work. This essay primarily deals with the history of ideas, arguing that Kolm provides an essential link between his French "engineer-economist" precursors who made important contributions to public sector pricing and his successors who have adopted a mechanism design approach with its emphasis on incentive constraints for the study of public sector economics. This essay is useful both for situating the main concepts employed in the normative analysis of public sector management in perspective and for shedding light on the main questions facing current decision-makers who operate in an environment in which the frontier between the public and the private sector is moving back and forth.

This essay opens with a brief overview of the contributions to public sector pricing, particularly marginal cost pricing, made by French engineer-economists such as Maurice Allais, Pierre Massé, and Marcel Boiteux, a lineage to which Kolm belongs, in the period following the end of World War II. A central issue faced by these economists is how to compute marginal cost prices. Following this discussion of Kolm's precursors, David, Le Breton, and Merillon proceed to describe how Kolm determined marginal cost prices for the case in which congestion affects the quality of the good or service provided as a function of aggregate demand.

The rest of this essay deals with the limits of the marginal cost pricing rule in second-best contexts, beginning with some of the limitations of marginal cost pricing identified in the Anglo-American literature. It then discusses how Kolm and others built on Marcel Boiteux's analysis of a public firm subject to a budget constraint to derive general principles for optimal pricing in the presence of second-best constraints. As Kolm himself noted very early on, second-best constraints may arise due to problems of asymmetric information with their associated incentive problems. For example, the government faces a principal-agent problem when a public firm that applies a marginal cost pricing rule is bailed out by the Treasury if there is a deficit. To mitigate this problem, close supervision of the managers is necessary, whereas if the managers are subjected to a balanced-budget constraint, the incentive issues may not be very severe and, hence, the managers may be left more on their own. There is therefore a tension between the decentralization of decision-making and achieving societal objectives. David, Le Breton, and Merillon conclude by discussing related considerations about the implications of second-best constraints for optimal public sector pricing and management, showing the breadth and depth of Kolm's writings on these subjects, and explaining how they have found a precise formulation in the recent literature on regulatory economics with its emphasis on incentives and asymmetric information.

The second essay, also by Laurent David, Michel Le Breton, and Olivier Merillon, considers the optimal pricing rule and the choice of the optimal capacity of a public utility facing demand uncertainty. In this essay, except for the cases considered in which only aggregate demand is known, capacity is determined by a reliability constraint imposed by the regulator, which allows the authors to focus on pricing rules. David, Le Breton, and Merillon begin by recalling the classical results obtained by Brown and Johnson for the case in which only the aggregate demand is observed and by Boiteux for the case in which the mean and standard deviation of each individual's demand is known to the utility, as well as some extensions of these results. In the Boiteux model, it is optimal to have budget balance with each consumer facing a common marginal cost price for mean demand, but personalized marginal cost prices for the standard deviation of demand. However, if the cost of the dispersion in demand is instead measured in terms of the variance, the price of this variance should not be personalized, with the consequence that the utility runs a deficit. David, Le Breton, and Merillon then describe how Kolm has modified Boiteux's model in order to consider more general cost functions and to allow for correlation in the individual demands. Kolm used this framework to revisit the issues of whether prices should be personalized and whether there should be budget balance. David, Le Breton, and Merillon also show how Kolm's pricing rule is related to the Hopkinson rate, which charges consumers in part based on peak consumption.

In the second part of this essay, a structural model is introduced in which consumers' stochastic demands are fully modelled and derived from random preferences, with incomplete markets preventing the achievement of full ex ante efficiency. The optimal pricing rule that is then obtained has some similarity to the Boiteux–Kolm pricing rules: the price for advance purchases corresponds to the price for serving the mean demand, whereas the difference between the spot and advance purchase prices corresponds to the price for the dispersion in demand.

One of the lessons of second-best analysis, as has been discussed by David, Le Breton and Merillon, is that it is impossible to separate efficiency from distributive considerations. The measurement of inequalities is therefore not just a special field in normative economics; it should be part and parcel of every policy evaluation. The next two essays explore current issues concerning inequality measurement.

In the third essay, Nicolas Gravel and Patrick Moyes study stochastic dominance criteria for the case in which every individual situation is described by two attributes. They recall the difficulty of extending to several dimensions the beautiful equivalences established in the Hardy–Littlewood–Pólya Theorem when individuals have only one attribute (such as income). This theorem shows that one univariate distribution dominates another with the same mean if and only if the following four equivalent conditions are satisfied: (1) the former distribution is obtained from the latter distribution by a sequence of elementary transformations (permutations and/or progressive transfers), (2) the dominating distribution is preferred by all additively separable, increasing, and concave social welfare functions, (3) the Lorenz curve for the first distribution dominates that of the second, and (4) the aggregate poverty gap is smaller for the dominating distribution no matter what poverty line is chosen. The first of these criteria focuses on elementary transformations, the second and the fourth on an explicit normative objective function, and the third on an empirically implementable test. Kolm has studied the extension of the first equivalence to multiple cardinal attributes, using multiplication by bistochastic matrices for the elementary transformations.

Gravel and Moyes provide normative foundations for two mutidimensional stochastic dominance criteria, one due to Atkinson and Bourguignon and the other due to Bourguignon, when there is one cardinal attribute (like income) and one ordinal attribute (like health, or family size when the unit of measurement is the household). For each of these two criteria, they provide bidimensional extensions of the Hardy–Littlewood–Pólya Theorem for both fixed-mean and variable-mean comparisons. Specifically, they identify the restrictions on the individual utility functions that ensure that all social welfare functions that exhibit inequality aversion with respect to individual utility rank distributions in the same way as the dominance criteria. They also identify the corresponding elementary transformations involving only two individuals at a time that are inequality-reducing, such as favourable permutations (a permutation of the cardinal attribute which reduces the correlation between the two attributes) and between-type progressive transfers. For the Bourguignon criteria, the sequence of elementary transformations that are used to obtain a dominating distribution from a dominated one may make use of phantom individuals in some of the intermediate steps. Gravel and Moyes raise the interesting open question of whether such phantoms are essential for their characterization.

In the fourth essay, Jacques Silber and Amedeo Spadaro address another issue that is central to the current research agenda on inequality measurement: inequality of opportunity and intergenerational mobility. They focus on the case in which the situation of individuals is depicted using discrete categories which may or may not be ranked by order of advantage (e.g., educational level, occupation, or income bracket) and which could differ between generations (e.g., educational levels for the parents and income brackets for their children). A situation is described using a social mobility matrix whose ijth entry is the number of individuals in the second generation in category j whose parents were in category i.

To ordinally compare social mobility matrices, Silber and Spadaro propose using an "immobility curve," which plots the cumulative values of m_{ij} against the cumulative values of $m_{i.}m_{.j}$, where m_{ij} is the percentage of the total population of origin i and final situation j, $m_{i.}$ is the percentage of the population with origin i, $m_{.j}$ is the percentage of the population with final situation j, and the values of both m_{ij} and $m_{i.}m_{.j}$ have been increasingly ordered in terms of their ratio. This curve coincides with the diagonal when the distribution of final situations is independent of the initial situations (in this case, one has $m_{ij}/m_{i.}m_{.j} = 1$) and lies below the diagonal otherwise. Silber and Spadaro show how the Gini and the Theil indexes of inequality can be applied to the magnitudes m_{ij} and $m_{i.}m_{.j}$ in order to construct natural cardinal measures of social immobility that are consistent with the rankings obtained using their immobility curves.

Silber and Spadaro also construct indices of inequality of opportunities or, as they call it, of inequality in "circumstances," for each of the final categories which, for concreteness, we assume are income brackets. The index for income bracket j is computed using an inequality index applied to the distributions of the actual shares $m_{ij}/m_{.j}$ of those in income bracket j from each of the originating classes. For illustrative purposes, Silber and Spadaro use the Gini and Theil inequality indices. As with Kolm's well-known procedure for constructing a normative index of relative inequality, the Silber–Spadaro indices can be interpreted as comparing the distribution of the actual shares $m_{ij}/m_{.j}$ with the distribution of the expected shares $m_{i.}$, which is the distribution that would result if there were perfect mobility. In effect, these indices measure the social loss due to social immobility. An index of inequality in circumstances is then obtained by taking a weighted average of these indices using the population shares of each of the final categories as weights. Silber and Spadaro conclude their essay with empirical illustrations of their approach using French and Israeli data.

A concern for economic equality is often motivated by considerations of fairness. Fairness is itself a multifarious concept. A number of different fairness criteria have been developed in the literature on fair allocation in concrete economic contexts. Prominent among them is the "no-envy" criterion (as it has come to be called) found in Kolm's seminal writings on this subject. An allocation exhibits no envy if no individual prefers anybody else's allocation to his or her own.

In the fifth essay, Koichi Tadenuma studies a particular and very important setting in which fairness issues naturally arise: the (one-to-one) matching problem. This matching problem consists in forming pairs out of two subgroups, such as men and women or workers and employers. For Tadenuma, the two groups are factory managers and workers. While much of the literature has focused on implementation and stability issues, often proposing rules that are biased in favour of one group, Tadenuma examines the problem of devising a matching rule that is not only stable but also equitable to both groups. The no-envy test cannot be satisfied in this application except in the unlikely situation that it is possible to match each person with his or her most preferred partner.

Tadenuma considers two kinds of equity criteria. The first seeks to minimize the total number of envy relations over the two subgroups or to minimize the greatest number of envy relations experienced by a single manager or worker. His second criterion is based on another classical fairness principle: solidarity. Tadenuma requires that when one manager or worker changes his or her preferences in such a way as to improve the ranking of his or her partner, then everybody else should benefit or everybody else should suffer from this change. Tadenuma's first result is an impossibility theorem: there is no stable rule satisfying his two fairness principles (envy minimization is computed over the set of stable matchings). However, he shows that if the larger set of individually rational and Pareto efficient matchings is considered instead of the set of stable matchings, then a possibility emerges. Tadenuma even identifies a large class of rules that satisfy both of his two equity criteria.

In the sixth essay, William Thomson studies another allocation mechanism in a classical economic context: the Lindahl rule for allocating public goods. He considers the case in which a single public good can be produced from a single private good and there are two consumers. Any of the endowment of the private good not used for production can be consumed by the two individuals. When the technology exhibits constant returns to scale, the feasibility of an allocation in such an economy can be expressed by the equation $x_1 + x_2 + y = \Omega$, where x_i is the consumption of private good of individual i, y is the quantity of public good produced and consumed by the two individuals, and Ω is the initial aggregate endowment of the private good. Kolm had the ingenious idea of representing the set of feasible allocations in such an economy by an isosceles triangle in which each component of an allocation (x_1, x_2, y) measures the distance of this point to one of the three edges of the triangle. This "Kolm triangle" has been very effectively used by Kolm, Thomson, and others to study the allocation of public goods.

Here, Thomson studies the vulnerability of the Lindahl allocation rule in "Kolm triangle economies" with respect to a specific nonmanipulability property that he calls "borrowing-proofness." He considers two versions of this property that differ depending on whether individuals in the economy are restricted to borrowing resources from each other or are permitted to borrow from outsiders. The allocation rule is not borrowing-proof if an individual can borrow some amount of the private good before the rule operates, repay the loan after receiving his allocation from the rule, and be better off as a result (the other individual must also not be worse off if he or she provided the loan). Thomson shows that the Lindahl rule is not immune to this kind of manipulation (i.e., it is not borrowing-proof) on the classical domain of continuous, monotonic, and convex preferences, but it is borrowing-proof on the subdomains in which preferences are also required to be either quasi-linear or homothetic. He then compares these results with what happens when an individual withholds some of his endowment before the Lindahl rule is applied and consumes it secretly. He shows that the Lindahl rule is not "withholding-proof" on any of his three domains. Therefore, the problem of manipulation of the Lindahl rule by withholding appears to be more serious than the problem of manipulation by borrowing.

The most obvious policy instrument for the reduction of inequalities and the achievement of some degree of fairness in the distribution of incomes is the income tax. The next two essays are devoted to an analysis of Kolm's approach to the optimal income tax problem. With Kolm's Equal Labour Income Equalization (ELIE) tax scheme, each individual contributes a fraction k of the earnings that would be received if he or she worked full time and in return receives a basic grant whose amount is the average tax paid by all individuals. For anyone who works the fraction k of a full-time job, net income is equal to the basic grant and is therefore independent of this individual's type, which here is the skill level or, equivalently, the wage rate. For anyone who works more than k, the marginal tax on labour is zero and, hence, for any given amount of work, the larger the wage, the larger is the net income and the larger is utility (for a given utility function).

In the seventh essay, Laurent Simula and Alain Trannoy assume, as in the Mirrlees formulation of the optimal income tax problem, that everyone has the same preferences for consumption and labour. They begin by noting that, in contrast to the Mirrlees model, with ELIE, the individual budget sets are type-dependent. In the rest of their essay, following Kolm, they focus on the case in which every individual chooses to work no less than the fraction k of full time and, therefore, earns enough to pay the tax. Using Cobb–Douglas preferences for illustrative purposes, Simula and Trannoy first identify the values of k for which this case applies.

Next, they show that the ELIE allocation, which is Pareto efficient, maximizes a weighted sum of utilities in which, given certain substitutability assumptions, the weights are increasing in the skill. This finding is quite intuitive because, as we have seen, with ELIE, utilities are increasing in the skill, which is only possible if larger weights are assigned to more skilled individuals. As Mirrlees has shown, maximizing an unweighted sum of utilities yields an outcome in which utility is decreasing in the skill when leisure is a normal good and everyone must face the same tax schedule (and, hence, the same budget set).

Finally, Simula and Trannoy turn to the issue of incentive compatibility. They assume that an individual is free to choose to work for a lower wage than the wage that corresponds to his or her true skill. Simula and Trannoy begin by noting that ELIE is not implementable if neither gross income nor hours worked are verifiable. However, if they are, then ELIE (with every individual working at least the fraction k of full time) is implementable because it is now possible to deduce (or observe directly) the individual skill levels. Simula and Trannoy then consider the Mirrlees case in which gross income, but not time spent working or the skill level, is observable. The ELIE allocation is not incentive-compatible in this case because individuals have an incentive to overstate the time worked, with the consequence that the inferred skill level is less than the true one. Even if it is not possible to implement the individual consumption-labour bundles of the first-best ELIE allocation, Simula and Trannoy argue that it may nevertheless be desirable to try to implement the ELIE income transfers. In an example with two individuals, they show that the allocation one obtains in this way may result in utilities that are very close to the utilities obtained with the ELIE allocation.

In the eighth essay, Marc Fleurbaey and François Maniquet also examine the issue of how to take incentive compatibility constraints into account in order to implement the ELIE proposal. Fleurbaey and Maniquet begin by extending Kolm's ELIE principle from the identification of an optimal allocation to an ordering of all allocations. The rationale for this extension is that once such an ordering is available, it can be maximized subject to any set of incentive constraints that reduces the set of attainable allocations. The ELIE ordering that they propose, on the basis of axioms inspired by the logic of Kolm's theory, ranks allocations using the leximin criterion applied to utilities defined as follows. Given the parameter k that characterizes an ELIE tax scheme, the utility assigned to individual i's consumption-labour bundle (c, ℓ) is the amount of consumption i would obtain if i worked the fraction k of full time with a specific budget set called the "implicit budget set." The implicit budget set is the budget set that is characterized by the following properties: earnings are not taxed, a lump-sum transfer is granted (or a lump-sum tax is paid), and this budget would give i the same utility as (c, ℓ) if i could freely choose from it. Thus, individual consumption-labour bundles are evaluated using a kind of money-metric utility that is conditional on the choice of k. The first-best allocation for this ordering is the standard ELIE allocation.

Fleurbaey and Maniquet then proceed to study how to maximize this ordering in the presence of different informational constraints. These constraints are similar to the ones considered by Simula and Trannoy. In the first situation that they analyze, wage rates and labour supplies are observable, but there is an incentive constraint because an individual may choose to work at less than his or her maximum possible wage. In the second situation analyzed, only earnings are observable. Unlike the standard Mirrlees model, individuals are assumed to be heterogeneous in preferences as well as in skills. Fleurbaey and Maniquet show that in both of these informational environments, it is optimal for the lowest-skilled individuals to face a zero marginal tax rate. They also show that if a special kind of allocation is Pareto efficient given the incentive constraints, then it is optimal for the ELIE ordering. In the first informational environment, this special allocation features a zero marginal tax rate for everyone who works more than the fraction k of full time, as in the ELIE allocation. In the second informational environment, this allocation is very close to a flat tax at rate k for incomes above the lowest wage.

In the ninth essay, Peter Lambert also studies income tax issues. He examines a provocative and topical idea: What would an equitable European Union income tax look like if it were added to the various national income taxes prevailing in the member states of the EU? As stressed by Lambert, the difficult question to be decided first is how to compare individual standards of living across countries. Is having €20,000 per annum net of domestic tax in Luxembourg the same as having €20,000 net in Latvia? Lambert adopts a particular method of comparison, one in which an individual resident in country A is considered to have the same living standard as an individual resident in country B if the former's ranking in country A's income distribution is the same as the latter's ranking in country B's income distribution. Therefore, €20,000 after tax in Luxembourg is a worse situation than €20,000 after tax in Latvia because the former has a lower rank in its national income distribution than the latter.

If the income distributions in two countries are described by distribution functions that in logarithms differ only in location and scale (e.g., both distributions are Pareto distributions), then there exists an isoelastic equivalent income function that matches incomes in the two countries position by position. With this as a maintained assumption about the income distributions, Lambert then proceeds to examine the implications of designing the EU-level tax so that it satisfies various equity principles. Horizontal equity is obtained when individuals who are considered equal before tax are still equal, by the same criterion, after tax. This is easy to achieve by country-specific EU tax schedules that do not alter relative positions within each country. The EU tax scheme exhibits equal progression at equal positions if individuals with the same pre-EU-tax living standards face the same degree of tax progressivity. Lambert shows that by using suitable country-specific proportional taxes, then it is possible for the EU tax scheme to satisfy both horizontal equity and equal progression at equal positions (given his maintained distributional assumption). Lambert also examines how to design the EU tax scheme so that each country makes an equal sacrifice, where equal sacrifice is defined using a social welfare function. Lambert concludes with some illustrative numerical calculations that show the effects on representative individuals of an EU tax scheme that embodies his equity principles. Using data for the year 2000, he shows, for example, that with such a tax, a Latvian with disposable income of €20,000 (roughly five times that country's mean income) would pay approximately ten times the amount of tax to the EU as someone with this income in Luxembourg (the mean income in that country)!

A social evaluation of different social situations is non-welfarist if it compares distributions of individual attributes (e.g., income, health status, or education level) directly, rather than in terms of the distributions of individual utilities obtained by each individual from his or her attribute bundle. Kolm's seminal work on multidimensional inequality helped initiate this approach to the normative evaluation of social situations. In the tenth essay, Nicolas Gravel, Thierry Marchant, and Arunava Sen extend this multidimensional-attribute approach to the comparison of social situations in which the number of individuals may differ. The comparison of social situations in which the number of individuals is not fixed is the subject of variable-population social choice theory. For the most part, the literature on this subject has been welfarist, comparing different social situations only in terms of their distributions of individual utilities.

Gravel, Marchant, and Sen provide the axiomatic foundations for a criterion that compares social situations in terms of average advantage, where the average advantage is determined by first using a common advantage function to aggregate individual attribute bundles into an overall measure of individual advantage and then averaging these values over the members of society. The societies being compared may be, for example, different countries at the same point in time or the same country at different points in time. As Gravel, Marchant, and Sen stress, the individual advantage function need not be a utility function that measures the subjective well-being that an individual obtains from an attribute bundle; it could instead reflect the value judgements of the social evaluator. The welfarist version of this average-advantage criterion has been a controversial, but much used, social objective in the debates about population ethics.

In contrast to the constructive approach to developing social objectives for the comparison of social situations that characterizes variable-population social choice theory in general and Gravel, Marchant, and Sen's essay in particular, Arrovian social choice theory for fixed populations abounds with impossibility theorems, which is hardly encouraging for policy makers interested in making concrete decisions. Kolm has been rather critical of Arrow's formulation of the social choice problem, raising concerns about many of his axioms, including the axioms relating to the domain being considered.

In its choice-theoretic formulation, Arrovian social choice identifies what should be chosen from each admissible feasible set as a function of the profile of individual preferences. Axiomatic social choice typically uses large domains of admissible feasible sets and preference profiles. A combination of a feasible set and preference profile can be thought of as being a possible world. Kolm's epistemic counterfactual principle states that while there is only one world for which a decision needs to be made, in order to justify the choice made in this world, one needs to consider the choices that would have been made in appropriate counterfactual worlds. It is these possible worlds, both real and hypothetical, that Kolm's principle identifies as the appropriate domain for an Arrovian social choice problem.

In the eleventh essay, John Weymark examines what this domain should be in order to ensure that the actual social choice is made impartially. In order to establish that impartiality is respected by what is actually chosen, one could say that if the relevant individual characteristics were permuted, then the features of the chosen alternatives (e.g., allocations of resources or benefits) should be permuted among individuals accordingly. In this way, it is possible to justify considering a specific domain of possible worlds for which social choices must be made.

Weymark suggests that the device of a veil of ignorance is useful for identifying this domain. A veil embodies the information that is morally relevant for making social decisions, with different conceptions of impartiality resulting in different specifications of the veil. He considers two kinds of impartiality. If one only requires impartiality with respect to personal identity, one obtains a thin veil of ignorance, as in the utilitarian theories of Harsanyi and Vickrey. If, however, one also wants the social choice to be impartial with respect to an individual's conception of the good and the generation he or she is a member of, Weymark argues that there is a thick veil, as in Rawls' theory of justice. Importantly, he does not consider what a self-interested observer operating behind a veil of ignorance would choose, which is an approach to determining substantive principles of justice or social ethics about which Kolm has expressed strong reservations, but only uses the idea of a veil of ignorance to eliminate morally irrelevant information from consideration. Weymark argues that the domain obtained using the thin veil can also be obtained using an ideal observer theory of the kind proposed by Adam Smith or by Hare's universal prescriptivism (which identifies substantive moral principles by examining the meaning of moral concepts) because they are both only concerned with ensuring impartiality with respect to personal identity.

Weymark shows that the domain obtained using the thin veil generates only a small domain of possible worlds, whereas the thicker veil generates a much larger domain. He further shows that the former domain is so small that some of Arrow's axioms are vacuous, but that all of the Arrovian axioms are nonvacuous on the larger domain.

The hypothetical construct of a self-interested individual acting behind a veil of interest has been used by social contract theorists such as Rawls to ground principles of justice. Kolm has proposed an alternative approach to social contract theory in which actual individuals hypothetically agree to implement an outcome that is limited in scope (e.g., an allocation of resources rather than principles of justice). They agree that the outcome identified by the social contract should be implemented because it is what would be chosen by these individuals if (1) they were free to act and benefit from these acts without coercive interference (what Kolm calls "full process-freedom") and (2) they were not subject to the impediments to implementing the terms of this contract that they are subject to in practice (e.g., verifiability of information and transaction costs). Actual implementation of this social contract may require the coercive power of the state, but the parties to this hypothetical agreement nevertheless endorse its terms because it is what would have been obtained by the actual members of society possessing full process-freedom in ideal circumstances. Kolm calls such a hypothetical agreement a "liberal social contract."

In the twelfth essay, Jean Mercier Ythier considers optimal redistribution in a liberal social contract for an exchange economy in which the impediment to achieving the ideal outcome is the presence of preference interdependencies. Interdependent preferences, particularly altruistic preferences, figure prominently in Kolm's writings. Specifically, Mercier Ythier considers a private ownership exchange economy in which each individual trades in markets in a self-centered way, but also has distributional preferences. These distributive preferences are non-paternalistic preferences over allocations (i.e., an individual ranks allocations that only differ in someone else's consumptions in the same way that person does, but may exhibit altruism, malevolence, or indifference towards him or her). Thus, when some individual i chooses a consumption bundle, this is done by maximizing i's personal "ophelimity," but i also has a utility function that has the form of a social welfare function that depends on the utility of others and which expresses i's distributive preferences.

Mercier Ythier defines a distributive optimum as a Pareto optimal allocation for the other-regarding preferences. In this set-up, a distributive liberal social contract consists of (1) a set of new individual endowments obtained by applying personalized lump-sum taxes and transfers to the actual endowments and (2) a Walrasian competitive equilibrium for an economy with the new endowments for which this equilibrium allocation is a distributive optimum that Pareto dominates (according to the other-regarding preferences) the Walrasian equilibrium allocation obtained using the initial endowments.

Mercier Ythier shows that under relatively weak assumptions, any distributive optimum (which, recall, is defined using the other-regarding preferences) can be obtained as a Walrasian equilibrium allocation using the self-centered preferences provided that suitable lump-sum transfers of the initial endowments are implemented. Furthermore, he also shows that relative to any arbitrary Walrasian equilibrium allocation (which may not be a distributive optimum), a distributive liberal social contract exists. In other words, the allocative properties of the Walrasian equilibrium do not limit the possibilities for redistribution. Thus, the rearrangement of the initial endowments called for by the distributive liberal social contract would be unanimously supported by the individuals using their other-regarding preferences even though in actuality they will make their consumption decisions based on their self-centered preferences. Therefore, in an economy that is otherwise laissez-faire in its organization of markets, a central agency that implements transfers could be fully liberal (in the sense of Kolm's liberal social contract) if it catered to the unanimous will of the society for a redistribution of initial endowments.

Issues related to reciprocity have been a major focus of Kolm's research. As we noted in Sect. 1, Kolm has argued that reciprocity is essential for harmonious social relations in a society of free and equal individuals. In the thirteenth and final essay in this volume, Jon Elster examines the relationship between reciprocity and norms, connecting Kolm's work on this topic to the recent experimental work that has developed over the last decade.

Elster distinguishes between different forms of reciprocity. He first looks at two-party reciprocity based on a shared belief that reciprocity is morally the right thing to do. Given this shared belief, it would seem that the recipient of a good or bad should reciprocate with something of equal value, but, as Elster observes, equality can mean different things. In the case of positive reciprocity (returning good with good), the possibilities include: equality of the benefits received by each of the parties from the other (equality of output), equality of the losses from their gifts (equality of input), equality of reciprocator's loss with the benefit initially received (no loss, no gain for the reciprocating party), or equality of the initiator's loss with the reciprocal benefit received (no loss, no gain for the initiator). A similar list can be made for negative reciprocity (returning bad with bad). Elster then examines how equality may be broken due to psychological mechanisms such as loss aversion or the fact that a force endured seems stronger than a force exerted. Such mechanisms contribute to explaining the risk of escalation of negative reciprocity–the *lex talionis* was conceived as a protection against such escalation.

Elster next examines how various norms (legal norms which are backed by sanctions, social norms which are backed by social approval and disapproval or ostracism, moral norms which are unconditional injunctions, and quasi-moral norms which are conditional injunctions dependent on the behaviour of others) operate to enhance reciprocity in social relations. Experiments have shown the importance of one's actions being observed or being able to observe the actions of others for generating cooperation.

Elster then turns to third-party reciprocity, which is particularly intriguing because the reciprocating act does not come from the recipient of the initial act. He distinguishes between various forms of third-party reciprocity and argues, on the basis of the experimental literature, that the spontaneous punishment of defectors (which may have different motivations) is an important mechanism that fosters cooperation and helps alleviates the free-rider problem.

As our overview of the contents of this volume demonstrates, this collection of essays covers a broad range of topics that are representative of currently active areas of research in normative economics and social ethics. Furthermore, these essays address issues about which Serge Kolm has made seminal contributions. His influence on the authors of these essays is apparent throughout this volume.

Acknowledgements We are grateful to Serge Kolm for correspondence and discussions and to Peter Lambert for making his interview with Kolm available to us, both of which have been invaluable in preparing the biographical sketch.

References

Lambert, P. J. (2011). An interview with Serge-Christophe Kolm. *Social Choice and Welfare*. Forthcoming

Rawls, J. (1971). *A theory of justice*. Cambridge, MA: Harvard University Press

Kolm as a Contributor to Public Utility Pricing, Second-Best Culture, and the Theory of Regulation

Laurent David, Michel Le Breton, and Olivier Merillon

1 Introduction

Serge-Christophe Kolm has made important contributions to many different areas of public economics. Some of his books and articles have been accessible to a large audience because they were translated from French into English, or they were published in English in international scientific journals. This is the case, for example, for most of his articles and monographs on the theory of justice and on inequality measurement. However, this part of Kolm's scientific output only represents the tip of the iceberg when it comes to research in public economics, his main research area from the mid nineteen sixties to the mid nineteen seventies. Unfortunately, this research is not that well known to the international academic community. While also normative, these contributions differ from his later contributions to public economics both in terms of motivation and objectives. As we shall show, Kolm was very much concerned and interested with the rationale(s) for public sector intervention and by the qualitative and quantitative features of optimal public policies. In particular, his research has focused primarily on the rules necessary for the efficient management of public organisations.

L. David
GDF Suez, Direction de la Stratégie et du Développement Durable, Tour 1, 1 place Samuel de Champlain, 92930 Paris La Défense cedex, France
e-mail: laurent.david@gdfsuez.com

M. Le Breton (✉)
Toulouse School of Economics, GREMAQ, and IDEI, Manufacture des tabacs, Aile JJ Laffont, 21, Allée de Brienne, 31000 Toulouse, France
e-mail: lebreton@cict.fr

O. Merillon
GDF Suez E&P, Département Acquisitions, Tour 1, 1 place Samuel de Champlain, 92930 Paris La Défense, France
e-mail: olivier.merillon@gdfsuez.com

M. Fleurbaey et al. (eds.), *Social Ethics and Normative Economics*,
Studies in Choice and Welfare, DOI 10.1007/978-3-642-17807-8_2,

The following sample of quotations from his work illustrates his perspective[1]:

> Political Economy is fundamentally a normative science. Its main aim is the provision of advice on actions. To whom? Sometimes to companies ..., sometimes to a social class ..., but most often to a State. But if one can go far enough in the positive analysis ... of the private sector just to infer at the end the public actions to be undertaken (or not to be done), most of the specific variables encountered in the analysis of the public sector are instrumental for the decision-making unit itself. Consequently, the normative view pertains much more to Public Economics as a whole than to the analysis of market mechanisms.
>
> Public Economics studies therefore the actions and the optimal organisation of the public sector. (Kolm 1971c, p. 4)

> Normative Economics is the branch of Political Economy that says what *needs* to be done. It is particularly useful for Public Economics in identifying the optimal actions of the State. (Kolm 1971b, p. 395)

> These principles first manifest themselves in the new branch of Political Economy which is Public Economics. It has the task of analysing the economic role, and to define the socially optimal behaviour, of the State, of the public sector, and of all the other institutions more or less political in nature. Because "laissez faire" is always one of the possible solutions to the "what should be done" normative problem that has been posed, Public Economics must begin by determining which activities should be undertaken by these institutions and which should be left to the market.
>
> ....
>
> While theoretical, this work has an eminently practical objective: it shows how the services being considered and the goods used to produce them should be produced and managed.[2] It is therefore a study of normative, or prescriptive, economics which looks for and identifies the optimal choice for society in diverse situations. The instrumental variables to be determined are the qualities, the quantities, the method of production, the allocation, the financing, and the institutional nature, of these activities. The allocation can be quantitative or by sales using prices or tariffs. In the latter case, they provide part of the financing, and whether there is still a deficit or not is essential for the question of the decentralisation of the management of this activity. (Kolm 1971d, pp. 20–21 and 23, footnote added)

Kolm has written many articles and monographs on public utility pricing and, more generally, on the nature and role of "public" prices in economies displaying various forms of imperfections that are likely to result in poor performance on the allocation and distribution fronts. Kolm (1971d) offers a very nice and stimulating presentation of the problems faced by public utilities and of the so-called "services publics" (public goods) problem:

---

[1] We wish that we could include more evidence of Kolm's fundamental interest in the subject of this article and of the intellectual and practical origins of his concern with this subject here. While doing so is beyond the scope of the present article, we strongly recommend reading the introduction of Kolm (1971d), which contains a complete and nice description of his approach to public economics, as well as Chap. 2 of the same book containing "le dialogue du libéral et du dirigiste" (the dialogue between a liberal and a ruler), a truly monumental piece of pedagogy.

[2] Kolm uses the terminology "services publics" or, simply, "services," to refer to goods and services supplied by the public sector. Our usage of the word "service" should also be broadly construed in this way. When capitalized, "Service" refers to the public firm or administrative agency responsible for providing the public good or service in question. Examples include the Electric Service and the Telephone Service.

> The prices of "major public services" upset the population, forcing governments into making difficult choices ...
>
> In which proportions should radio and television broadcasting, museums, orchestras, theaters, etc. ... be financed by the State, or by the spectators or listeners (entrance fees, receiving equipment taxes, or specific payment on the delivery of the service) ...
>
> Should the budget of the S.N.C.F. [the French train service and rail network provider] be balanced? Is not budget balance the criterion and the means for a "healthy management"? ... Is it not unfair that all the French taxpayers subsidies the Parisians in reducing the deficit of the R.A.T.P. [the Parisian transportation network] ... which, moreover, encourages the congestion of the capital? ... Why should higher education not be self financed by charging fees to the students who would have access to long term loans? (Kolm 1971c, pp. 5–7)

Kolm is aware of the fact that the line between private and public institutions is sometimes tiny and, in any case, difficult, if not impossible to draw:

> It is customary to contrast public and private. Actually, purely public enterprises and purely private enterprises are only two poles between which extends a continuum of varied institutions, more or less close to one or the other, intermediate between them in many ways: nationalised enterprises, public enterprises selling their services, autonomous Services, concessions, public corporations, ... (Kolm 1971c, p. 8)

Kolm's research in public economics has produced a very rich and voluminous collection of articles and books. A sample of them is included in the bibliography. The main motivation and "raison d'être" of our article is to contribute to the dissemination of Kolm's ideas, as we believe that these contributions represent at their best an intellectual tradition in public economics quite active in France by the "ingénieurs économistes" (engineer-economists). In addition to this historical exploration of one epoch of Kolm's scientific journey, we would like to emphasise the modernity and the results of his approach, his creativity, and the large spectrum of methods and concepts he was able to create and/or use on this journey.

This article presents some of Kolm's main ideas and achievements on several issues related to the optimal management of the public sector, or part of it. It has two main purposes. On the one hand, we want to show how Kolm's contributions are a continuation of the research of his precursors in the community of French "ingénieurs-économistes". These economists share several common features. The name "ingénieur-économiste" refers to the fact that they all went to major engineering schools (the "grandes écoles") and received (there and in their previous schools) a solid education in science and in engineering. In addition to this background, and as a consequence of their willingness to adopt a scientific approach to economic problems, many of them belonged to the research and executive divisions of the nationalised industries, or of the national ministries. Their interest in economics and the topics on which they were inclined to work dealt with practical concerns. The continued interaction between theory and practice has been a remarkable feature of these developments. These "ingénieurs-économistes" did not simply apply existing economic principles without creating or inventing anything on their own. In fact, many of them also wrote important articles in theoretical public economics. The point that we want to make here is that their professional activities and the various challenges, debates, and policy issues resulting from their duties were the source of inspiration for the problems they considered, and this leads to a theoretical "detour" from applied concerns to pure research, according to the usual academic standards. As employees in the public sector, these individuals had to develop responses to practical questions that arose. In doing so, however, and this is the second point that we want to stress, they looked for responses based on a solid and coherent theoretical formulation of the problems scrutinised. These practices and "culture" differ sharply from the "culture" of other civil servants who were willing to depart from these demanding principles by basing their recommendations on so-called intuitive principles. The fact that Kolm belongs to the first group is not only apparent from his work, but also from the following quotations.

> Thanks to a galaxy of famous men, Political Economy came to use the scientific method more and more throughout the nineteenth century, and it was completely converted by the end of World War II. As a consequence, Economics now stands far ahead of all the other so-called social sciences on the path of scientifisation.[3] (Kolm 1971d, p. 15–16, original footnotes omitted, new footnote added)

> Unfortunately, politicians, the press, civil servants, and businessmen, in a way so extremely superficial, only consider one aspect of the problem and neglect the rest. However, as each one of them considers a different effect, the prescribed solutions are contradictory, often extremely. And as they cannot scientifically convince each other in the dialogue of the deaf that they have established, everyone turns his idea into a "principle" so as to avoid having to discuss its foundations ... and defends his position as if it were a political choice; the power of conviction serves as a substitute for the depth of the analysis. (Kolm 1971c, p. 8)

This historical presentation is organised around the principle of marginal cost pricing. As everything could not be covered, we had to make a choice about what to discuss. This choice, of course, had to be representative of both Kolm's interests and style. We think that our focus is appropriate because, not only is this principle far more subtle than it looks at first glance, it is also a door to penetrate into the world of second-best public economics. There is no need here to remind the reader how important and useful that principle is in standard microeconomics. Implementing marginal cost pricing in the real world is controversial and raises a number of difficulties that have motivated some of Kolm's research, as well as that of some of his precursors and successors. Like many of his contemporaries, Kolm contributed to the analysis of this principle by showing how it could be used in settings different from the usual ones, and also by showing how it could be altered and/or extended when its direct application was obstructed by institutional constraints. Kolm derives the policy implications and extensions of this principle, in particular for the pricing of goods and services produced or regulated by the public sector.

As we argue, Kolm's position is in some way at the crossroad between two periods or waves in the field of public economics as practiced by the French "ingénieurs

---

[3] Kolm severely criticises the French economists appointed by universities. For Kolm, the mediocrity of these economists is however compensated by the work of the "ingénieurs économistes." Kolm (1971b, p. 15, ft. 2) writes: "While some French engineers and scientists who have converted to the field of economics have completed the best research in the world in their areas (Allais, Boiteux, Debreu–an exile–, Malinvaud, and certain others), official French academic Economics remains a laughing stock worldwide ... "

économistes." He comes after very eminent precursors who made seminal contributions to theoretical microeconomics and who were able to provide solutions to several important policy issues at the top of the agenda after World War II. But beyond his respect for this very respectable legacy, Kolm was aware of the limits and the necessity of extending their analyses. Kolm, himself, contributed to this research programme, but some of the tools from game theory and the economics of information that have subsequently proved to be so useful for this task were not yet well developed. Kolm was way ahead of his time, with some of his contributions paving the way towards the modern approach to public sector economics in terms of incentive constraints and mechanism design.

We show how Kolm's successors analysed and explored this approach. They were able to offer a deep understanding of the limits of the marginal cost pricing principle from different angles. The terminology "successors" refers to several ideas. Many of these individuals are also part of the community of French "ingénieurs-économistes" and share the methods and concerns of their predecessors. They hold a strong belief in the usefulness of microeconomics and in the necessity of founding policy recommendations on solid theoretical foundations. Some of these successors primarily focus on the theory and its extensions, while others derive applied implications of the theory. The precursors were directly confronted with management problems in the public sector; in contrast, the successors are facing a new age or period characterised by a (de)regulation process in substantial parts of the public sector. The current challenge of real world public economics is to provide helpful guidelines and principles to managers, regulators, and public policy makers to accompany the fore-mentioned process.

This article aims to offer a brief description of Kolm's scientific achievements in public economics from an historical perspective. In Sect. 2, we explain how marginal cost pricing has operated in France since World War II under the leadership of French engineers. In Sect. 3, we argue that Kolm's choice of topics, as well as his methodology, were very much a continuation of what was done by his precursors. In Sect. 4, we describe the Anglo-American contributions to marginal cost pricing and the controversies raised by the application of this principle. Then, in Sect. 5, we examine Kolm's contributions to the theory of the second best. We also show how the former tradition has been pursued in many new and important directions without any major and discontinuous change in the methodology and the agenda. In Sect. 6, we argue that Kolm has also made insightful contributions to the theory of organisations and incentives, paving the way to the new approach to optimal regulation of public agencies. Some concluding remarks are presented in Sect. 7.

To some extent, our article aims to demonstrate that Kolm's contributions lie between two periods and that they have played a major role with respect to both of them. Not only has Kolm extended the results of his precursors and applied their methods to many new areas, he also has prepared the ground for his successors through his research because he anticipated some of the questions that are, or have been, at the forefront of the more recent scientific agenda.

2 The Marginal Cost Pricing Principle and Kolm's Precursors

In many countries, the production and distribution of several important economic (private) goods and services are under the control of the public sector. In addition, the government contracts with private firms to supply goods and services, both directly for itself and for individuals. We are not going to review the list of arguments supporting the view that the government should control these specific activities. The most widely heard argument is that private firms pursue the maximisation of profits of their owners, and not the welfare of the nation. But we know that private firms, in pursuing their narrow self-interest in competitive markets, can be thought of as pursuing the public interest; there is not necessarily a conflict between the pursuit of private interests and what is in the public interest. However, when market failures occur, the pursuit of profit maximisation by firms might not result in an efficient resource allocation.

The most important kind of market failure that leads to public production arises when markets are not competitive. A common reason that markets may not be competitive is the existence of increasing returns to scale. In such a case, economic efficiency requires that there be a limited number of firms. Natural monopolies refer to industries in which increasing returns are so significant that only one firm should operate in a region.[4] In such situations, we cannot rely on competitive forces to ensure the efficiency of the industry. Efficiency requires that price equals marginal cost.[5] However, the firm will suffer a loss if it charges marginal cost because marginal cost is lower than average cost.[6]

Once it is recognised that some form of public intervention is needed, a number of questions arise: What should the principles to guide the production/investment decisions of the firms in charge of these activities be? And what pricing rules should be used? In the case of a deficit, how should the revenues required to pay for this loss be raised? When a natural monopoly produces several commodities (a multi-product monopolist), the pricing question becomes more complex. A number of new issues emerge mostly because some inputs are common to the production of all of the services. In such a setting, we may, for instance, wonder if any departure from the marginal cost pricing principle should apply uniformly to all commodities and services or, alternatively, if higher charges on some services should be used to subsidies other services.

A group of French economists faced these very questions just after World War II. As reported by Drèze (1964, pp. 4–7, footnotes omitted):

[4] In his mathematical derivation of the conditions for a Pareto optimum, Allais (1945) explicitly allows for the existence of two sectors: a competitive sector and a sector composed of natural and other monopolies.

[5] We will not reproduce here the conventional first-best defence of marginal cost pricing as an optimality principle. Most of the textbooks in microeconomic theory provide a description of the assumptions used for its derivation and contain insights on its scope of validity.

[6] Stiglitz (1988) offers a nice simple illustration of this failure, as well as the limits of the threat of entry.

> During World War II two graduates from the "Ecole Polytechnique," Maurice Allais and Pierre Massé, renewed a long tradition of contributions to mathematical economics started by Cournot and the engineer Dupuit a hundred of years before and more recently maintained by such well-known econometricians as F. Divisia and R. Roy.
>
> ....
>
> Shortly after the war, the problems of reconstruction and of management of the newly nationalized industries (electricity, gas, coal mining) gave Allais, Massé, and their colleagues, students, or followers ample opportunities for applying and developing their theories. ...
>
> By then what has sometimes been referred to as the French "marginalist" or "mathematical" school was born; an important stream of scientific activity was under way that has developed continuously ever since.
>
> This development ... has taken place largely outside the traditional professional circles and channels. Members of this school did and do belong to the staffs of the engineering schools or statistics departments, to the research as well as the executive division of the nationalized industries, or to the administration ...
>
> [T]he continued interaction between theory and practice has been another remarkable feature of these developments. While the pure theorist Allais was consulted about the management of the coal mines, Massé or Boiteux, who had executive responsibilities at EDF [Electricté de France], developed original contributions to decision or price theory. The theorists and the executives fortunately shared the view that there is no sound policy unless it is based upon a sound theory, whereas empirical relevance and verification make for sound theories. The fact that so much work has been motivated by empirical problems and that it eventually led to practical implications may partly account for the soundness of the theories.

We see the contributions of the French engineer-economists as an intellectual response to the questions raised by the public management of natural monopolies.[7] As observed by Drèze (1964, p. 8):

> Much of the success of the French marginalist school in solving difficult practical problems in this area rests ultimately upon a sound and sometimes subtle understanding of the classical marginal cost concepts.

Kolm's precursors concentrated most of their attention on pricing and investment issues. Here, we mostly focus on the pricing issue, which is not as simple as it may look at first glance. On the cost side, it is by no means clear that managers should value inputs according to market prices. If there are some distortions in the rest of the economy (in particular, if there are differences between consumption and production prices), the shadow prices reflecting the true social cost or value of these inputs may differ from the market prices. Although they were aware of these issues, it is fair to say that Kolm's precursors did not really investigate what vector of prices should be used to evaluate the cost of inputs. While implicit in various cost-benefit analyses of public projects (in particular, when deciding which rate of discount should be used), this topic was not, at that time, subject to a systematic exploration as an end in itself. Instead, the attention was focused on the determination of the total (long-term and short-term, average and marginal, etc.) cost curves of the multi-product public firm given a vector of input prices.

[7] The papers collected in Nelson (1964) and Morlat and Bessière (1971) offer a nice overview of these contributions together with their motivations.

Let $\mathbf{q} = (q_1, q_2, \ldots, q_K) \in \mathbb{R}_+^K$ denote the vector of outputs of a public firm and let C be its total (long-term or short-term, depending upon the context) cost function:

$$C = C(\mathbf{q}). \quad (1)$$

Once this function has been calculated, we are in a position to provide answers to the question raised by these economists. What are the optimal levels of investments (plant sizes and designs) and prices? In a first-best world (all markets are open, lump-sum transfers are feasible policy instruments, no distortions or "pathological" behaviour in the rest of the economy, etc.), selling each product according to its marginal cost is a necessary condition for social optimality. In the case where a pricing policy is a vector of linear prices $\mathbf{p} = (p_1, p_2, \ldots, p_K) \in \mathbb{R}_+^K$, optimal prices and quantities are therefore related by the following equations:

$$p_k = \frac{\partial C(\mathbf{q})}{\partial q_k}, \quad k = 1, \ldots, K.$$

It follows that once we are able to determine the cost function(s), we are in position to compute the optimal prices. Indeed, the work has been transferred from economics to operations research, applied mathematics, and statistics. However, the cost function is not a primitive of the problem, but is instead the result of an optimisation on the part of the firm that can turn out to be more or less complicated. The area of operations research relevant to this optimisation problem depends on the nature of the variables, linear and non-linear programming, dynamic programming, integer programming, and combinatorial optimisation, etc. In any case, the description of the variables and constraints of the problems calls for a solid understanding of the technological alternatives that should be considered and, in that respect, being an engineer certainly is a good preparation for carrying out this kind of analysis. This task has two different components:

First, we need a comprehensive description of the commodity space. What is the relevant value of K?

Second, we need an extensive analysis of the technologies from an engineering perspective.

The first task cannot be neglected. It should be recalled that from the perspective of an economist, a commodity or service is not simply described by its physical attributes and characteristics, but also by the time (or period), the place, and the contingencies of delivery. The cost of serving customers may display important differences according to the time and/or place of delivery. Distinctions based upon temporal considerations play an important role as soon as some factors are used for the production of the output(s) in different time periods, in addition to a direct concern due to investment/storage possibilities and the availability of some natural resources. Distinctions based on spatial considerations also play a critical role as soon as some transportation cost is involved in addition to production costs. Indeed, the derivations of cost functions in the case where clients are located on a geographic network are known to be among the hardest problems in operations research. Finally, as soon as uncertainty is part of the problem, the definition of a commodity/service calls for a detailed description of the conditions under which delivery will ultimately take place. The combination of the three dimensions may lead to a rather large commodity space. For instance, one unit of electricity may be priced differently according to the time of the year considered, the location of the client, and the clauses of delivery originating, for instance, in the choice of interruptibility standards.

As previously mentioned, the French engineer-economists were certainly well prepared and had the talent needed to conduct the second task. They were also successful in making their ideas operational. Their work is a perfect illustration of the derivation of what Chenery (1949) has called "engineering production functions." Instead of using statistical data, the promoters of this approach suggested using engineering data. As noted by Chenery (1949, pp. 507–510, footnote omitted):

> Industry studies have generally used statistically determined cost curves. Since these curves are based of necessity upon productive combinations which it has proved feasible to entrepreneurs to try out, they cannot usually tell us much about the broader range of productive possibilities which have been explored experimentally but not adopted commercially. The lack of this information is a great handicap in many types of economic discussion. ...
>
> Before suggesting a way of using engineering data in economic analysis, we must consider the problems which the engineer himself is trying to solve. Since his initial aim is to discover all feasible ways of making a given product or performing a given service, his first concern is not with particular inputs but with the nature of the chemical and physical transformations which are involved in the productive process. He breaks down the process of production into convenient units whose performance he attempts to describe by formulae based on the laws of physics and chemistry. Since an elementary analysis in terms of the properties of each piece of equipment is often impractical, the engineer must usually resort to testing various sizes and combinations of equipment to determine the effect of such variables as size, speed, temperature, etc. upon total performance. One basic difference between engineering analysis and economic analysis, then, is the units which are considered fundamental. While the economist deals with plants or firms or industries, the engineer must deal primarily with separate physical processes.
>
> ....
>
> If the economist wishes to use engineering data to construct a production function, he must go back to the intermediate stage in engineering calculations at which the various types of inputs are considered. These data are found in engineering textbooks .... In order to use it conveniently, the economist must abandon his convention of using one-dimensional inputs and use multi-dimensional inputs as the engineer does.

This methodology was applied by the French engineer-economists successfully in many different industries, including, for instance, coal mining, electricity, natural gas, and railways.[8]

---

[8] This article is obviously biased towards the contributions of French engineers as our priority here is to point out Kolm's lineage. We confess that a deeper investigation would have produced a more balanced evaluation of the impact of engineers on microeconomics and, in particular, on pricing and investment problems, outside our home country. Chenery (1949) is a remarkable article that should be read by anybody interested in this topic. Interestingly, he refers to an air transport analysis by Bréguet (the famous French aviator, airplane designer, and industrialist) who uses a technique to derive a cost curve based on engineering experience. Bréguet's analysis is summarised by Phelps Brown (1936). Stigler, in his contribution to Yntema et al. (1940), has also defended the

One spectacular application of marginal cost pricing is peak load pricing. The peak-load pricing problem arises when there are non-storable commodities with periodic demand fluctuations (transportation, mail, telecommunications, power supply, etc.). Peak-load pricing is based on a simple description of the commodity space. The relevant time period (say a year or a day) is divided into smaller periods (say months or day and night). Time is, therefore, considered as the relevant dimension of product differentiation. The aggregate demand facing the firm is a temporal profile of consumptions. For example, with electricity, this demand is often represented (after rearrangement) as a curve, the so-called load duration curve because time is treated as a continuous variable. The calculation of the cost curve based upon engineering data is specific to the industry considered. In the case of electricity, this task amounts to the determination of the optimal capacity configuration once the fixed and operating costs of each conceivable generating unit (coal, gas, nuclear, hydro, etc.) have been evaluated.[9]

Let us consider the simplest cost situation, namely, that defined by constant returns to scale and fixed plant capacity, with constant short-term marginal costs that do not depend on plant size. It is readily verified that the (short-term) total cost function per period is then:

$$c(q,z) = \begin{cases} \beta z + bq \text{ if } q \leq z \\ \infty \text{ if } q > z, \end{cases} \tag{2}$$

where q is the output per unit of time, z is the fixed capacity, β is a marginal capacity cost, and b is a short-term (operating) marginal cost. The long-term marginal cost is then $\beta + b$. For a temporal profile of consumptions $\mathbf{q} = (q_1, q_2, \dots, q_K)$, where K is the number of periods, we obtain the following (short-term) total cost function:

$$C(q_1, q_2, \dots, q_K; z) = \begin{cases} \beta z + b \sum_{k=1}^{K} q_k \text{ if } \sup_{1\leq k\leq K} q_k \leq z \\ \infty \text{ if } \sup_{1\leq k\leq K} q_k > z. \end{cases}$$

In this problem, total cost cannot be broken down into the sum of costs in each period because there is an input (the capacity here represents a plant or machine with a given size) that can be used repeatedly for the production in all periods. Other channels of interdependence across periods could also be considered; for instance, inventories. In the long run, capacity will be adjusted to the peak consumption.

advantages of the engineering approach, but it seems the economists at the time did not take up the suggestion. Since then, many economists have argued against the statistical approach and instead used the engineering approach. See, for example, Marsden et al. (1974) and the survey by Wibe (1984).

[9] Approaches based on engineering and financial data have also been used in settings different from cost minimisation. The application of linear programming to investment in the French electric power industry by Massé and Gibrat (1957) provides quite a remarkable illustration of this approach.

Boiteux (1949) and others have applied with success the marginal cost principle to this setting.

Another set of applications of marginal cost pricing appears when the heterogeneity dimension is spatial instead of temporal. As soon as a transportation cost is incurred prior to final consumption, the derivation of the optimal transportation network is a key feature of the cost minimisation operation (sometimes, even, transportation and production activities are closely related). Besides the combinatorial design of "roads," when pipelines are used to transport resources, the choice of the dimension of the pipe is also an important component of the transportation cost. As noted by Chenery (1949), in the case of natural gas transportation, the amount of gas transported by a pipe depends on its diameter, the pressure of the gas, and the drop in pressure along the line. Hence, enlarging the diameter, the pipe thickness, or the pumping capacity (this will depend on the spacing of compressor stations) may increase the capacity. Cheery uses an empirical relationship between these three engineering variables, known as Weymouth's formula, together with some other basic relationships to determine the cheapest transportation capacity. This is a perfect illustration of the relevance of the engineering approach. In this particular spectrum of applications, the key ingredient is an equation governing the flow of compressible fluids through pipes.

3 Kolm on Marginal Cost Pricing

Kolm has derived many ingenious and important implications from the marginal cost pricing principle for several allocation problems. This section describes his research on this issue through a sample of illustrative applications. His book *Le Service des Masses* (Kolm 1971d), which is part of his *Cours d'Economie Publique*, is a perfect illustration of the intellectual tradition of French engineer-economists that was briefly described above.[10] He has sometimes developed his own general terminology in order to show the profound unity between problems that are only different on the surface. For example, Chap. 11 of Kolm (1971d), entitled "Structures variétales," is a discussion of the commodity space: Kolm calls "variété" the specification of a commodity/service according to the period, place, or conditions of delivery. In a number of chapters in this book, he also examines issues related to the cost of production.

Le Service des Masses is devoted to a class of problems in which the joint consumption of the services by the users influences some features describing the

[10] The terminology "services des masses" (mass services) used in Kolm (1971d) refers to public goods and services used by the general population, e.g., mass transit. Kolm (1971d, p. 23) writes: "Telephone, public education, postal services, transportation by road, water, or air, water and electricity conveyance, distribution centers, radio broadcasting and television, hospital services, road systems, sewage systems, town maintenance, and most administrative services, constitute typical cases."

"quality" of one or several "variétés"/services produced by a public firm/administration. Consider the case where $K = 1$, i.e., the situation in which only one service is produced. Let i be an index that identifies any particular consumer of the service. Let q^i denote the quantity of service consumed by i, $(q^1, q^2, \ldots, q^N) \in \mathbb{R}_+^N$ denotes the vector of consumptions in the population (where N is the number of consumers), and $q \equiv \sum_{i=1}^N q^i$ denotes the aggregate consumption. In his book, Kolm introduces the key concept of a "fonction d'encombrement" (congestion function). In the case where the quality itself is one dimensional and denoted by w, this function relates the quality level w to the profile of consumptions $(q^1, q^2, \ldots, q^N)$ and to another vector $z = (z_1, z_2, \ldots, z_M)$ describing the levels of M decision variables that are often (according to Kolm) quantities of specific inputs. That is,

$$w = w(q^1, q^2, \ldots, q^N, z).$$

Kolm calls the case in which the congestion function only depends on the sum, and not the distribution, of consumptions "uniform." In this case,

$$w = w(q, z). \tag{3}$$

To illustrate how Kolm derives the pricing implications of marginal cost pricing when there are congestible goods or services, we consider the uniform case and we assume that $M = 1$. The first-order conditions for optimality are derived in Kolm (1971d, Chap. 5). Let $U^i(q^i, w)$ be a utility function describing, in monetary units, the welfare derived by consumer i when he consumes q^i units of the service with a quality equal to w and let $C(q, z)$ denote the total cost incurred by the public firm to produce a total quantity q using the input z.

Kolm demonstrates that the first-order optimality conditions are described by the following equations:

$$\frac{\partial U^i(q^i, w)}{\partial q^i} = \frac{\partial C(q, z)}{\partial q} - \frac{\partial w(q, z)}{\partial q}\left(\sum_{j=1}^{N} \frac{\partial U^j(q^j, w)}{\partial w}\right), \quad i = 1, \ldots, N, \tag{4}$$

and

$$\frac{\partial C(q, z)}{\partial z} = \frac{\partial w(q, z)}{\partial z}\left(\sum_{j=1}^{N} \frac{\partial U^j(q^j, w)}{\partial w}\right). \tag{5}$$

The first equation can be rewritten as:

$$\frac{\partial U^i(q^i, w)}{\partial q^i} + \frac{\partial w(q, z)}{\partial q}\frac{\partial U^i(q^i, w)}{\partial w} = \frac{\partial C(q, z)}{\partial q} - \frac{\partial w(q, z)}{\partial q}\left(\sum_{\substack{j=1 \\ j \neq i}}^{N} \frac{\partial U^j(q^j, w)}{\partial w}\right). \tag{6}$$

In this equation, user i's marginal willingness to pay for the consumption of the service is equal to the marginal social cost, which is the sum of the marginal cost of production and the "external" marginal social cost.

Kolm (1971d, Chap. 6) derives the pricing rules which decentralise the optimal allocation. From (4), it follows that the (linear) price p^i of the service that should be paid by user i must satisfy:

$$p^i = \frac{\partial C(q,z)}{\partial q} - \frac{\partial w(q,z)}{\partial q}\left(\sum_{\substack{j=1\\ j\neq i}}^{N} \frac{\partial U^j(q^j,w)}{\partial w}\right), \quad i = 1,\dots,N. \tag{7}$$

We deduce from (7) that optimal pricing is in general discriminatory. However, as noted by Kolm, there is an important case in which discrimination vanishes. It corresponds to the situation where the impact of a single user on aggregate consumption and, therefore, on w, can be considered as being negligible. In such a case, the optimal prices are uniform across users:

$$p^i = \frac{\partial C(q,z)}{\partial q} - \frac{\partial w(q,z)}{\partial q}\left(\sum_{j=1}^{N} \frac{\partial U^j(q^j,w)}{\partial w}\right), \quad i = 1,\dots,N. \tag{8}$$

Using (5), (8) can be equivalently written as:

$$p^i = p \equiv \frac{\partial C(q,z)}{\partial q} - \frac{\frac{\partial w(q,z)}{\partial q}}{\frac{\partial w(q,z)}{\partial z}}\frac{\partial C(q,z)}{\partial z}, \quad i = 1,\dots,N. \tag{9}$$

Besides incorporating the uniformity assumption, we note that the right-hand side of (9) consists of cost data and data on the congestion function. Each specific problem is described by a cost function c and a congestion function w. The cost function is a familiar concept, while the congestion function is not so familiar in economic analysis. It is very interesting to point out that the engineering approach, discussed extensively above, which is a trade mark of the French engineers, seems to be perfectly suited to deal with this new concept.

Kolm (1971d, Chap. 7) presents many practical problems for which the abstract model described above is very appropriate. His list of examples includes: road transportation, railway transportation, stochastic congestion, traffic accidents, pollution, and queues. Let us say a few words about some of them to show (convincingly we hope!) that engineering expertise cannot be avoided in these applications. In the case of road transportation, Kolm considers the case of a highway with z the number of lanes, q the aggregate traffic flow, and w the average speed. Under some particular assumptions, he derives the following technical relationship between the three variables:

$$w(q,z) = \frac{z - bq + \sqrt{(z-bq)^2 - 4acq^2}}{2aq},$$

where a, b, and c are parameters. This congestion function is quite special and, in fact, given a relationship between traffic density and speed, the equation describing the evolution of the traffic flow is a complicated partial differential equation. The analysis of traffic flows is a well-defined area of applied mathematics and engineering sciences, disciplines which obviously need to apply marginal cost pricing to road congestion. Lévy-Lambert (1968) produced an early analysis of optimal tolls based on these principles and the empirical congestion function.

Stochastic congestion is the topic of a companion article to this one (see David et al. 2011). In this setting, z represents the capacity of a given piece of equipment and w denotes the reliability level defined, for example, as the probability of every customer having its demand satisfied. The exact value of w depends on the details of the stochastic model. This model applies to many different industries in which the delivery of a product (e.g., electricity, gas, or water) may be interrupted or rationed due, for instance, to adverse weather conditions, a power outage, or a breakdown. For a bank, z represents the amount of total deposits of the bank and w the probability that a client is unable to withdraw some cash (see Edgeworth 1888). This case is extensively studied in the companion article mentioned above.

Queuing is a very important topic. For many public agencies and utilities, a demand that cannot be satisfied immediately can sometimes be delayed instead of being not fulfilled at all. However, waiting costs cannot be ignored and the question of an optimal organisation of the service taking into account these costs raises problems for which the framework developed by Kolm (he calls it "encombrement d'attente," i.e., waiting congestion) is very appropriate. He devotes the last third of *Le Service des Masses* to the application of marginal cost pricing to these types of problems. We are not aware of any similar systematic attempt to analyse such problems. The relationship with engineering and operations research is obvious. It is reflected, for example, by the use of the mathematics of queues when increasing demand can be expressed as a Poisson process.

Le Service des Masses contains many results on the relationships between the financial consequences of marginal cost pricing and the nature of the returns of the congestion function.[11] For instance, in Chap. 15, Kolm develops the notion of "capacité commune" (common capacity) as a key feature that is common to the cost problems considered. This concept plays a critical role in the rest of this article and has already appeared in (2). In Kolm's terminology, we have a situation of common capacity when the same input (equipment, machine, etc.) can be used to produce several varieties of the same service, as long as the input's capacity is not reached. Kolm (1971d, p. 254) writes: "Common capacity is both a private consumption between consumers of the same type and collective consumption between different types." In this chapter, Kolm also develops conditions satisfied by the optimal capacity.

[11] We do not discuss here Kolm's analysis of optimal investment policies in a truly dynamic framework.

4 Anglo-American Contributions to Marginal Cost Pricing

The previous sections dealt with marginal cost pricing. In it, we have highlighted the contributions of the French engineer-economists because we wanted to illustrate how Kolm's own contributions were positioned in the continuation of this intellectual tradition. This could leave the reader with the impression that, on the one hand, only French engineer-economists were actively participating in these developments and that, on the other hand, there was some unanimity that this pricing policy was the right one to implement when competitive markets could not be designed to produce and distribute the commodity/service in question. In this section, we briefly consider some of the Anglo-American contributions to marginal cost pricing.[12]

According to Coase (1970), Hotelling (1938) should certainly be credited for being among the first in the modern literature to suggest the use of marginal cost pricing for public utilities and enterprises. Hotelling recognises the major influence of Dupuit (1844).

In the United Kingdom, the appearance of Meade (1944) was a major event. Originally, it was circulated as a policy brief of the economic section of the Cabinet Office as part of a discussion about how state enterprises ought to be run. It was written without any thought of publication but, due to Keynes' enthusiasm, both as an adviser of the Treasury and as an editor of the *Economic Journal*, it was subsequently published as part of an *Economic Journal* symposium. Meade advocated adopting marginal cost pricing. According to Coase (1970, pp. 115–116):

> In the meantime, James Meade had become head of the economic section of the Cabinet Office and Britain had a Labor Government. A paper was prepared by the economic section setting out the policy which it was considered ought to be followed in the nationalized industries, and this included a suggestion for adopting marginal cost pricing. This proposal was not, however, accepted by the Minister concerned, Herbert Morrison, and marginal cost pricing has played no part in the pricing policies of the nationalized industries. As it happens, pricing policies in the nationalized industries have tended to develop in ways which I find very congenial, and some of the most interesting work of which I know in the field of pricing is being conducted in the nationalized electricity supply industry in Britain. The nationalized industries have in fact followed a completely different line from that suggested by the marginal cost pricing proposal as originally conceived, and in the meantime, of course, enthusiasm in the profession for marginal cost pricing has become less pronounced.

In the United States, research was also active with these ideas. Some economists expressed strong enthusiasm regarding the work accomplished by the French engineer-economists and their ability to make the marginal cost pricing principle operational. Some expressly dissented from the view that price should be equated to marginal cost.

---

[12] By no means would we like the reader to infer from our presentation that little was done on this issue in the US or the UK. Reviewing the developments in these countries goes beyond the scope of this article. In addition to the articles cited in our references and in the masterpieces of Hotelling (1938) and Vickrey (1948, 1955, 1971), the reader will find useful discussions of the early literature in Nelson (1964) and Ruggles (1949).

Among the advocates, Nelson (1963, p. 474), for example, writes:

> The word "Applications" in my title has shrunk all the way from plural to singular. For so far as I know, the only public utility enterprise in the world to proceed from the theory of marginal cost pricing to both a schedule of rates and a series of rules for investment policy is Electricité de France ...

His article outlines how Electricité de France applied marginal cost pricing.

A few years earlier, Marschak (1960) also offered a very complete and lucid analysis of the French engineer-economists' contributions. He writes:

> It is only recently that American economists have begun major efforts to apply welfare economics to the decisions of specific public enterprises. They have principally chosen the difficult field of water-resource policy, one of the very few important areas of American public enterprise where such efforts are feasible. In France, on the other hand, where the postwar public sector includes important basic industries, a major share of economists' output since the war has concerned the application of welfare-economics principles to policy-making in these industries. ...
>
> The French theoretical work on investment choice parallels recent American discussion; the work on peak-load pricing antedates recent American results; and some of the work on optimal pricing under the no-deficit constraint has no American counterpart. ... The French economists' practical success ought to encourage those American economists who have been urging American public enterprises to adopt policies closer to those which the efficiency conditions of welfare economics imply. (Marschak 1960, p. 133, footnote omitted)

It is interesting to note that Marschak identified three classes of difficulties in accepting and applying this solution. He writes:

> The many well-known difficulties in accepting and applying this solution fall roughly into three classes:
>
> 1. Deficits in the decreasing-cost enterprises of the non-competitive sector (assuming the other sector to contain only increasing-cost industries) have to be made up and surpluses in the sector's increasing-cost enterprises have to be paid out. ...
>
> 2. It may be that one of the conditions for a Pareto optimum must inevitably be severely violated.[13] ...
>
> 3. There may be enormous practical difficulties of satisfactorily defining the relevant marginal cost in the face of indivisibilities, uncertainties, joint products, the possibility of expanding or contracting various elements of plant over varying time periods, etc. (Marschak 1960, p. 143, footnote added)

While aware of the difficulties resulting from its application, Vickrey (1948, 1955) has been an important supporter of marginal cost pricing and has made important applications of these ideas to the pricing of public transportation. Among the opponents, Coase (1946) was certainly one of the most active. Clemens (1941) was an early dissenter. In his discussion of Nelson (1963), Clemens (1963, p. 482, footnote added) writes:

[13] As is well known, at least from the seminal work of Lipsey and Lancaster (1956), if there are already distortions in some sectors of the economy, it may be optimal to depart from marginal cost pricing in the controlled sector.

> I am rather skeptical of marginal cost pricing proposals as commonly put forth. In my mind, they are oversimplified. If the assumptions are granted, one cannot quarrel with the theory, but the assumptions are such as to make the applicability in practice extremely questionable. The *tarif vert* [green tariff] is a more sophisticated version of marginal cost pricing but one which is nevertheless subject to some of the usual infirmities.[14]

Clemens lists eight infirmities.

Both Marschak's three classes of difficulties and Clemens' eight infirmities (and to some extent many reservations expressed by the strongest opponents) are mostly motivated by second-best considerations. Besides these considerations, discussed more extensively in the next sections, both Clemens and Marschak allude to the enormous practical difficulties of satisfactorily defining and measuring the relevant marginal cost in the face of indivisibilities, uncertainties, joint products, the possibility of expanding a plant or expanding various elements of a plant over varying time periods, etc. In this respect, there are conflicts about the type of marginal cost that should be taken into consideration.[15] As Drèze (1995, pp. 117–118) has noted: "Vickrey ... advocates prices reflecting continuously (in time) *short run* marginal social cost. Massé ... advocates prices reflecting *long run* marginal cost."[16]

The following statement by Boiteux (1951, pp. 56–57) illustrates the French perspective at its best:

> The theory of marginal cost pricing can be interpreted in many different ways. Selling at marginal cost means setting a price equal to the cost of producing an additional unit. This cost differs obviously according to whether one plans to produce the additional unit only one time, or, on the contrary, henceforth increase the unit *flow* of goods that one has produced until now: the exceptional production of an additional unit in isolation does not justify a modification of the equipment; a definite increase in the flow of production, on the other hand, may be accompanied by a modification of the equipment to the new level of production.
>
> The concept of a tariff implies the idea of flows. One does not set a price schedule to dispose of an accidentally available stock, but to obtain a long-term equilibrium between the flow of demand and the flow of production. ...
>
> This at least is one conception of a marginal price. On the contrary, there is also the one revealed by the additional passenger story. A train is about to leave; there is a vacant seat left; a passenger presents himself who is prepared to occupy it if he does not have to pay too much. The cost of transporting this additional passenger only comprises the few extra grams of coal needed to transport his weight and the leather molecules he will extract from the seat during the duration of the journey.[17]

---

[14] The green tariff is an implementation of the marginal cost principles for Electricité de France. For a description of the historical context in which this pricing policy was introduced, the details of this policy, and an estimate of the gains resulting from this change, see Boiteux (1957), Massé (1958), and Meek (1963).

[15] Concerning peak load pricing, Joskow (1976) makes a distinction between the American, French, and British approaches. Berg and Tschirhart (1995) point out that marginal-cost pricing can be found incognito in the 1978 Public Utility Regulation Policy Act (PURPA) and that PURPA promoted six pricing standards in the name of efficiency and conservation.

[16] This kind of pricing is often referred to as spot pricing or responsive pricing. See, e.g., Vickrey (1971).

[17] See also Boiteux (1949, 1956a).

The disagreement between the two approaches pertains to the extent to which the prices of these commodities should be adjusted continuously in response to foreseeable fluctuations in either supply or demand. According to Drèze (1995, p. 118, footnote added):

> The alternatives are relatively stable prices (Massé) leading to inefficient use and occasional quantity rationing, or unpredictable price variations (Vickrey), which entail costs to users like monitoring prices and adjusting quantities.[18]

Quite interestingly, practice has evolved considerably since the early implementations of these ideas in the nineteen fifties. The green tariff was followed by major innovations at E.D.F. in the nineteen eighties and nineteen nineties. They originated from the difficulty of forecasting peak loads far ahead of time. This meant that it was desirable to adjust tariffs on short notice. We consider these and other pricing innovations in David et al. (2011).

5 Second-Best Distortions

Kolm's precursors were primarily interested in deriving the operational implications of marginal cost pricing. There is of course one important exception. Boiteux, in his seminal article (Boiteux 1956b) derives an optimal pricing rule for a public monopoly subject to a budget constraint. In Boiteux's setting, the additional constraint (i.e., in addition to the standard resource constraints) has a second-best nature and prevents the realisation of the first-best optimum. The major objective of the theory of second best is to derive general principles about the features of the optimal rules when these additional constraints are active. This theory has taught us one important lesson: Often, the first-best rules must be revised even in sectors where they can be applied due to the existence of distortions in other sectors. As such, a principle like marginal cost pricing may even have become obsolete.

We have concluded the previous section by reporting some of the criticisms that were formulated by eminent American economists against marginal cost pricing. The necessity of raising public funds to finance the deficit resulting from the application of this pricing policy is among the most important arguments supporting these dissident views. This theme is also a major concern in Kolm's work on public pricing. In Kolm (1971c), he analyses the multiple roles prices can play and the potential conflicts that can arise between these roles. Under the heading "Les Fonctions Sociales des Prix Publics" (The Social Functions of Public Prices), he

---

[18] Marschak (1960) also provides an interesting analysis of this controversy. He presented what the French engineers considered to be ideal rule and wrote:

> The view that the social cost of instability exceeds the social cost of such temporarily non-marginal pricing seems to be accepted in formulating actual pricing reforms. The prices initially approximated are those appropriate in long-run equilibrium. (p. 146)

develops a very stimulating and modern analysis of the use of public pricing as a policy instrument.[19] Kolm (1971c, pp. 31–32) writes:

> A tariff has a double direct *effect*, on the *users* and on the *budget of the Service*, which *themselves* create multiple indirect effects; one can respectively call them the *downstream* effect and the *upstream* effect or "price effect" and "budget effect."
>
> By its effect on the users, a tariff influences: their consumption of this service, their consumption of complementary and substitutable goods and services through the substitution effect, all the consumptions and productions of these individuals through the income effect, ... by the intermediary of these reactions, it also influences the production of complementary or rival goods and services ...; all these effects, in their turn, influence the degree of realisation of the social objectives.
>
> Furthermore, the tariff influences the *budget balance* of the Service .... This balance in turn operates on the public budgets and has three types of effects: (1) it influences other public receipts and expenses, and in particular tax revenues and other public services, (2) it influences therefore the *functions* of the *public finances*–public allocation, income distribution and macroeconomics effects–, and on the other hand (3) it influences the level of autonomy of several elements of the *political and administrative hierarchy* and thus the efficiency of this organisation.

The first incidence, i.e., the role of prices as signals of social costs (in the French language, this is referred to as "la vérité des prix"–the truth of prices), has been the main focus of the advocates for marginal cost pricing. While not ignored, the second incidence was considered less important. However, in all his contributions, Kolm always derives the budgetary implications of marginal cost pricing, as illustrated by the following quotations.

> Here then the fundamental dilemma of public tariff setting is posed: a price has several social functions that a certain technical structure of production renders incompatible in the sense that the best level for one is bad for the other. Therefore one contrasts the roles of prices as tools for information and coordination in the markets and as a source of revenue, in brief, its commercial and financial functions, or, one can say, its internal and external efficiencies. (Kolm 1971c, p. 11)

> The second function stems from the fact that budget equilibrium is a necessary condition of complete autonomy. ...
>
> However autonomy leads to production and service management decisions being taken by people who better know its production function and the characteristics of the demands of the users. Its advantage is thus, again, to decentralise decision-making, but instead of being between the Service and its users, now it is between the Service and its regulator. The former can be called the *downstream decentralisation of decision-making* and the latter the *upstream decentralisation of decision-making*, the reference being to the Service. (Kolm 1971d, pp. 96–97, footnote omitted)

> Compared to a state in which a balanced budget is required, on the one hand the assurance that the deficit will be made up by a public budget removes from the enterprise's management the direct incentive to satisfy the public better and at lower cost, on the other hand, the public authority that manages the budget must control the management of the service, leading to costs of administration and especially prevents decisions being taken by the better-informed individuals and quickly. (Kolm 1971c, pp. 10–11)

[19] This issue was earlier explored in Kolm (1968b).

Kolm (1971b, p. 399) points out the internal contradictions of the pricing structure.

> The rule of "selling at marginal cost" is intended to promote the decentralization of decisions by a price system. On the other hand, budget balance of an enterprise whose main interest is to assure its independence is thus also an instrument for decentralising decisions. However, when production is subject to increasing returns and the output is sold at a uniform price, selling at marginal cost results in a deficit. There is thus a contradiction between these two tools for decentralising decisions.

To understand why the existence of a deficit is perceived by Kolm and others as socially costly, it is important to remember that the virtues of marginal cost pricing rely upon a set of assumptions defining what is traditionally described as a first-best economic environment. The systematic exploration of the optimal departures from marginal cost pricing (and other first-best allocation or pricing rules) resulting from the consideration of second-best economic environments has been one of the major areas of research in theoretical public economics since the nineteen seventies.[20] The new generation of French engineer-economists, following Kolm and his precursors, has made seminal contributions to these topics, ranging from second-best modelling to the economics of regulation. In this group, Guesnerie's research agenda on general second-best environments on the one hand, and Laffont's research on the economics of regulation on the other hand, are, in many respects, the closest to follow the work of the precursors, including Kolm.

We must of course mention the pioneering contribution of Boiteux (1956b) where he derives, independently of Ramsey (1927), the optimal pricing rules of a public utility subject to a budget constraint, although this was not the main concern of the

[20] In his Presidential address to the European Economic Association, Guesnerie (1995b) considers second-best modelling as one important development of modern public economics. He notes however that

> the effects of the innovation have been slow. The earlier neoclassical tradition, a branch of which has culminated in the development of the so-called Arrow–Debreu model, had generated a coherent body of knowledge that was and remains extremely influential among economists. The ideas, models and intuitions propagated by such a tradition have deeply impregnated the profession and can still be viewed as one of its dominant theoretical 'cultures'. (p. 354)

Furthermore:

> Second-best studies have challenged a number of ideas and intuitions of the so-called first-best culture. But the body of knowledge they have generated does not have the coherency, the appeal or the clarity that would allow to build a genuine second-best culture. Consolidating a second-best body of knowledge that would truly encompass the first-best conceptions, integrating it better within the mainstream 'culture' of the profession is in my opinion a desirable aim and constitutes one of the current challenges to public economics. ...
>
> The starting point is here an education exposed, through the direct or indirect influence of Allais, Boiteux, Malinvaud, Kolm ... to the teachings of the French school of 'ingénieurs économistes', which promoted a variant of the first-best tradition." (pp. 354–355)

precursors. Kolm (1971a,b) has developed a general theory of optimal pricing that applies when some economic agents are subject to some second-best constraints that he calls "value constraints"; these constraints are either constraints on prices or on budgets (as in Boiteux). Besides the fact that Boiteux's rule appears as a corollary of Kolm's general result, it should be noted that Kolm's general theory allows for a careful analysis of many other questions. He innovatively explores the consequences of imposing balance-of-payment restrictions on international economic policies. He also provides a set of general results on optimal local departures from marginal cost prices, where "local" means a neighbourhood of the first-best allocation. In such a case, the social deadweight loss is a negative definite quadratic form with respect to the distortions, and optimal distortions are quite easy to derive. Kolm obtains results on optimal distortions for the case in which endogenous distortions correct exogenous distortions, and for the case in which the role of distortions is to raise an exogenous budget.[21]

We are not going to review here the diversity of situations and constraints leading to second-best environments, i.e., environments for which there is some rationale to depart from marginal cost pricing. According to Guesnerie (1975b, p. 127, footnotes omitted):

> Second best problems arise when the actual realization of first best optima through competitive markets–as indicated by the main theorem of welfare economics–becomes impossible. One can distinguish for the sake of simplicity three different types of reasons preventing the decentralized attainment of Pareto optima through a competitive procedure:
>
> (1) Certain markets cannot be organized (forward markets, risk markets ...), whereas others cannot be cleared (keynesian [sic] underemployment ...).
>
> (2) Lump-sum transfers postulated by the traditional welfare theory cannot be implemented in the "real world."
>
> (3) Even if all markets do exist and if any lump sum transfer is feasible, certain agents may have a noncompetitive behavior.

The second reason is often listed as the main argument to explain why public funds are costly. If the public revenue cannot be raised using this neutral tool, then it must be the case that some "imperfect" taxation devices are used to do so. Primarily among these instruments are consumption taxes: the vector of taxes is defined as the difference between the vector of consumption prices and the vector of production prices. The interested reader will find in Guesnerie (1995a) a complete analysis of several important extensions of the basic Walrasian model of general equilibrium in which these new instruments are introduced, together with the other variables and constraints describing the public sector that could be considered (production of public or private goods, pricing of public utilities, quantity controls, etc.). Clearly, the derivation of the optimal public policy cannot avoid a complete preliminary analysis of the structure of the set of tax equilibria. This is not an easy task and the set of

[21] These results also appear in Kolm (1969a). Kolm (1968a) provides a very useful application of these principles to an environment where two transportation alternatives (say, road and metro), both subject to congestion, are in competition. Given that the unit price of road services departs from its marginal social cost, what should the optimal pricing of a metro ticket be?

equilibria displays some unusual features leading to different sorts of nonconvexities that make the analysis complicated. Optimising over that set of equilibria calls for caution.

Social optimisation provides a set of social values: one for each commodity (the Lagrange multipliers attached to the scarcity constraints). A commodity's social value is the correct social valuation of an exogenous marginal increase of its endowment. One important area of research is the determination of shadow prices to guide the management of controlled firms. In contrast to first-best optimisation, shadow prices no longer coincide, in general, with market prices. The extent of the discrepancy between prices and values varies across problems.[22] In many problems, for instance the problem of optimising the production of pure public goods or private goods by the public sector, the vector of shadow prices coincides with the vector of production prices.[23] In some other problems, for instance, in the production of private goods by the public sector when the supply behaviour of the private sector is noncompetitive but lump-sum transfers are feasible, the vector of shadow prices coincides with the vector of consumption prices. In yet other problems, like the one considered by Boiteux where lump-sum transfers are also feasible (a public firm subject to a budgetary constraint), the derivation of the shadow prices shows that the vector of shadow prices is a convex combination of the vectors of market prices and social values.[24]

The implications of these considerations for the marginal cost doctrine are quite important. As pointed out by Guesnerie (1980, p. 51):

> In a first-best world, pricing policies obey a simple principle: the price of the marginal unit sold to each consumer should equate its marginal cost. Even if the implementation of such a rule may raise further problems ... it is of universal theoretical validity.
>
> In a second-best world where the absence of markets or behavioural constraints prevent the attainment of first-best Pareto optima, the prescriptions for optimal pricing policies lose both simplicity and universality. Simplicity, because prices should no longer equate marginal costs–even if marginal costs were computed on the basis of the social value of commodities rather than production price–but should take into account other elements such as demand elasticities. Universality, because the difficulty of designing piecemeal policies defining rules valid for one sector independently of government action in other sectors has been constantly emphasized by second-best theory. In particular, the pricing rules which are established from one theoretical model do depend in some sense on the whole set of policy and behavioural assumptions made in the model. Changing the policy tools available to the government not only changes the optimal prices that would emerge but also possibly the qualitative features of the optimal pricing rule and the type of information required for its implementation. It is then quite important for policy purposes to understand the logic of the derivation of pricing rules in order to evaluate their sensitivity to modifications of policy and behavioural assumptions.

[22] See Guesnerie (1979). Drèze and Stern (1990) is also an excellent reference on this topic.

[23] Guesnerie (1995a, p. 183) derives a modified Samuelson rule (see Samuelson 1954) for the provision of a public good due originally to Atkinson and Stern (1974).

[24] Guesnerie (1980) explores the nature of the shadow prices in the Boiteux model under alternative assumptions. Hagen (1988) is also an excellent reference.

This strongly suggests that we should investigate the principles governing the derivation of second-best pricing rules in a general equilibrium setting, instead of a sequential examination of the recommendations attached to any particular environment. For example, if we think that marginal cost pricing should be abandoned because it leads to a deficit, the exploration of the new pricing rules should not exclude additional instruments (unless explained otherwise) that would allow the constraints to be relaxed. For example, in a problem à la Boiteux, given the existence of an "exogenous distortion," it makes sense to use "endogenous distortions" like consumption taxes or quantity controls.[25] The shadow cost of the budgetary constraint depends on the spectrum of instruments available. We should further anticipate that pricing policies would play a distributional role, not just an allocational role.

Our discussion implies that any normative or positive exploration of the optimal pricing policies must be conducted in a general equilibrium framework, with the goal of obtaining an accurate theoretical understanding of the economic interdependencies to be taken into consideration in the design of these policies. Too often, these interdependencies as well as the difficulties resulting from this approach are partly ignored by partial equilibrium derivations based on more or less sophisticated versions of consumers' surplus. This is far from being a secondary issue, as demonstrated by Guesnerie (1975a). As already discussed, the rationale for the control by the public sector of some specific firms or industries arise from the non-convexity of production sets in a situation with high fixed costs and increasing returns to scale. As noted by Drèze (1995, p. 116):

> The presumption in this setting was that marginal cost pricing with deficits financed by lump-sum taxes would sustain a first-best efficient allocation, if such an allocation were feasible at all. In other words, the presumption was that an analogue of the first welfare theorem holds for marginal cost pricing equilibria.

Guesnerie (1975a) has demonstrated that this presumption fails as a general proposition.[26] The existence of Pareto-improving income redistributions also challenges the classical view on the separation of efficiency and equity.[27] The analysis of the set of Pareto optima in second-best environments reveals that this phenomenon occurs there too.

---

[25] In second-best environments, quantity rationing, in-kind transfers, and all sorts of instruments disqualified by the first-best culture turn out to be very valuable, as demonstrated, for example, by Guesnerie and Roberts (1987) and Wijkander (1988).

[26] Beato and Mas-Colell (1985) have produced an example in which even aggregate productive efficiency is violated. Guesnerie's seminal paper has inspired a vast literature, including Bonnisseau and Cornet (1990), Brown and Heal (1979), and Vohra (1992). The reader may refer to the special issue of the *Journal of Mathematical Economics* devoted to these questions (see Cornet 1988). The theory of general equilibrium has also been extended to cover other "correct" rules of management that differ from marginal cost pricing (Ramsey–Boiteux, two-part tariffs, etc.). The conclusions reached in these articles concerning the welfare properties of these equilibria are also negative. See, e.g., Brown and Heal (1980) and Dierker (1991). Brown and Heal (1983) offer a nice discussion of some of these issues in a simplified general equilibrium framework.

[27] This view has been expressed by many authors. Brown and Heal (1979, p. 573) write:

While devoting special attention to the problems raised by the deficit, Kolm extensively discusses many implications of acting in a second-best environment.[28] In particular, he draws attention to the distributional role of public prices. Kolm (1971c, p. 15) writes:

> Finally, the prices of public services can be used for the purpose of redistributing actual income, and hence well-being, in society, for example by requiring certain categories of users that one wants to favour to pay less. The traditional normative economist is opposed to this action: it would be better, he says, to implement this redistribution by direct transfers and to allow the beneficiaries to spend this money as they prefer rather than to subsidise their consumption of the service in question. This argument is very sound. But what happens if, in fact, the transfers are not made? Nothing justifies, then, not using the tariff for redistributive ends ...

Kolm was clearly considering as a postulate that lump-sum transfers simply do not exist. For example, Kolm (1971c, p. 73–74) writes:

> But the argument offered against the use of prices for the end of distributive justice has a more serious defect. It is that the standard transfers and poll taxes proposed as an alternative simply do not exist. Indeed, these operations must be based on objective criteria. Yet, the properties that define them can be modified, with more or less ease, by the concerned individuals ...[29]

Besides equity and justice considerations, Kolm (1971c, Chap. 3) explores in great detail the different costs of tariffs and public funds, including the macroeconomic costs that would appear if the analysis was conducted in a non-Walrasian framework in which markets do not necessarily clear through prices.

While we have limited most of the preceding discussion to linear prices, we would like to stress that Kolm has also investigated more sophisticated pricing rules involving nonlinearities. Kolm (1969b) contains very important developments on

---

> in the Arrow–Debreu model ... [e]quity and efficiency are ... independent dimensions, and much of our accepted welfare economics and cost-benefit analysis rests, explicitly or implicitly, on this fact. The examples we present demonstrate that, once one admits increasing returns, the situation is fundamentally different. Because some are efficient and others inefficient, one can no longer judge between alternative distributions purely in terms of equity. It is necessary to consider both the equity and efficiency dimensions simultaneously.

Blackorby (1990, p. 748) claims that "if second-best considerations are taken seriously, then it is much more difficult, if not impossible, to divorce efficiency from equity than one might have thought from the use of first-best economic models."

[28] In 1967, the "Rapport du Comité Interministériel des Enterprises Publiques" (known as the "Rapport Nora") was published in France. It highlighted the importance of the deficits of the main French nationalised firms and generated considerable controversy among economists.

[29] Kolm (1971b, p. 399) also claims that:

> When the theorists' unrestricted interpersonal transfers do not exist, prices have a role in income distribution. In the real world, the distribution of taxes, which is the instrument of these transfers (with some subsidies) is limited, and prices remain the main way to distribute income.

the possibilities opened up by general nonlinear price schedules.[30] In this monograph, he derives many interesting results about the properties of optimal (with respect to some social objective) nonlinear price schedules under various sets of constraints. This monograph contains a general presentation of nonlinear tariff mechanisms. It identifies the difficulties raised by the fact that the customers' preferences are privately known, which are analysed in the last two chapters of Kolm's book.

In reference to the benchmark case in which informational matters are ignored–what he calls "l'optimum" (the optimum), Kolm (1969b, p. 14) writes: "But it does not often explicitly explain why the price in general has to be the same for the many users."[31] Under the heading "La communauté" (Society), Kolm (1969b, pp. 84–87) provides a very stimulating presentation of the constraints associated with these observability issues, and he derives the properties of the optimal solution when these constraints are incorporated. Kolm's formula characterising the optimal gap between the marginal price and marginal cost is nothing less than the formula found in any modern textbook on the optimal regulation of monopolies.[32] Under the heading "discrimination," Kolm refers to the various forms of price schedules that are observed, with special attention paid to the case of two-part tariffs. More importantly, he determinates how to optimally partition the population into groups, with

---

[30] Interestingly, on many occasions (e.g., Kolm 1971c, pp. 12–14), Kolm draws attention to the fact that first-order optimality requires that the marginal price and marginal cost be equal, but not that the marginal price be constant. He calls the units preceding the marginal one, "inframarginales" (infra-marginal). These units could be sold at a different price. He immediately infers from this observation that appropriately chosen nonlinear price schedules could reconcile optimality and budget balance. But Kolm also recognises, following this good piece of news, that the implementation of such schedules raises new costs. We reach the limit of marginal analysis when, as in the case of two-part tariffs, information about the preferences of the customers in addition to the marginal valuation–what he calls "valeur d'usage" (usage value)–is required for the computation of the fixed charge. This leads, then, to a risk of suboptimal exclusion that he calls "risque d'exclusion intempestive" (ill-timed risk of exclusion).

The possibility of differential pricing is a point that is also raised by some of the opponents to marginal cost pricing. The lack of consideration for this flexibility is listed among the eight "infirmities" of marginal cost pricing considered by Clemens (1963). Clemens (1963, p. 484) writes:

> In my mind, the E.D.F. is the victim of the same fallacy that characterizes Hotelling's thesis; namely, the failure to allow for differential pricing. Optimization of social welfare does not require that all output be priced at marginal cost; all that is required is that the marginal unit be priced at marginal cost. This requirement may be met satisfactorily and without government subsidy by a well designed rate system ...

[31] Kolm (1969b, p. 48) also writes: "But all of this analysis assumes that each user can be subjected to an individualized price, and it does not explicitly take into account the costs of setting tariffs and the lack of perfect knowledge."

[32] See Kolm (1969b, p. 95). The computation of what Kolm (1969b, p. 98) calls the "forfait optimal" (optimal lump-sum payment) follows from what he has introduced under the name "droit d'abstention" (right of abstention), which is strictly similar to what is referred to today as a participation constraint.

a specific price schedule for each group.[33] Specifically, he decomposes the general problem into three nested problems:

1. "Le Problème de Complexité" (the complexity issue): How many groups?
2. "Le Problème d'Affectation" (the assignment issue): How are customers assigned to the groups?[34]
3. "Le Problème de Communauté" (the society issue): How are optimal tariffs determined in each group?

Kolm's work contains many important insights and uses advanced and sophisticated techniques. For example, he determines the qualitative features of the optimal price schedule when the number of distorted prices is a fixed exogenous finite number (this constraint being justified by the cost of administering the schedule). He provides a detailed study of the multiproduct case, incorporating constraints on prices reflecting the existence of secondary markets.[35] We were particularly strongly impressed by his treatment of the assignment problem as a linear programme with integer constraints. It is interesting to point out that in Kolm (1969b), in contrast to the books discussed earlier, the cost of public funds is introduced in a reduced form through a single parameter $1 + \lambda$, a practice completely adopted by most of the contemporary authors writing on the economics of regulation.

6 Asymmetric Information, Incentives, and Regulation

Kolm was also very interested in the theory of organisations and institutions. Kolm (1971c, p. 125) writes:

> Economists have a lot to say about markets. However they are only one of the methods used by society to produce and distribute goods and services. Another is the organisation, both in public administration and within private enterprises, and it is used for many purposes other than purely economic. But about organisations economic theory says almost nothing. It was

---

[33] Kolm (1969b, p. 114) writes: "The price discrimination can be *between the users*, *between the contingencies*, between the variations of each parameter and in particular *between the units of each quantity* or the varieties of each quantity ..."

[34] The discussion in Kolm (1969b, pp. 118–122) of the criteria to assign customers to groups is very insightful even if it is not formulated using the modern terminology of the theory of incentives. His distinction between "critère fondamental" (fundamental criterion) and "critère de reconnaissance" (recognition criterion) is very useful. Kolm (1969b, p. 121) writes:

> The search for an "objective" criterion well correlated with willingness to pay is an old problem for private monopolies. Dupuit (when considering public monopoly) suggests that passengers on his bridge should be charged according to their occupation: for the same intensity of need the middle-class with hats should accept a higher price than workers with caps!

[35] His constraints can also be reinterpreted as no cross-subsidization constraints. A contemporary analysis of the set of prices meeting these conditions appears in Faulhaber (1975).

> generally thought that this subject pertained to sociology rather than political economy. ... Everyone will agree, we think, that if one looks in this literature for tangible ideas that are not obvious, the yield is extremely poor. But one finds that the application of the economic *method* of analysis to the analysis of organisations is very fruitful ...

Kolm considered the economic theory of organisations as valid if it was able to explain why hierarchical organisations were frequently observed. He also paid a great deal of attention to the costs resulting from conflicts among the members of an organisation, and the necessity to build the appropriate incentives.

Kolm's analysis of information and incentives anticipates subsequent developments in the contemporary literature on the economics of regulation. We have introduced Kolm's distinction between the "incidence aval" and the "incidence amont" of the budget and have focused until now on the former. Kolm (1971c, Chap. 4) is, in our opinion, an extremely important and early contribution to the theory of organisations with its analysis of the agency costs arising as soon as several economic agents with rival interests interact through complicated (contractual) relationships. The lack of autonomy resulting from a budget deficit, or the limited authority of a supervisor on prices, outputs, investments, and other dimensions of the firm or administration, are central to the exploration of what he referred to as the upstream incidence. Kolm (1971c, pp. 79–80) writes:

> If the Service has a **deficit**, it must be covered by a public budget. The political and administrative authorities who choose the latter must know the usage, estimate the utility, decide on the amounts and verify the use of these funds, and, if necessary, they should be able to impose compliance with the budgetary law. They must therefore exercise a supervisory right to command the Service (this may be the threat not to renew or to lower the subsidy next time). The result is, by comparison with a state of budget balance: (**1**) administrative costs for these decisions and financial and technical controls, (**2**) a loss of information due to the fact that decisions are taken by the administrative and political authority rather than by the Service which is generally better informed about the technical possibilities and the users' needs, (**3**) a potential gain of specialisation and economies of scale due to the realisation of certain tasks of financial withholding, budgetary and accounting choices made by a central or specialised administration rather than by the Service, (**4**) an increase in the conformity of the Service with the choices of Society expressed by political means, (**5**) a possible improved coordination with the situations and choices of other public Services, (**6**) a change in the behaviour of the managers of the Service by reducing their domain of choice, (**7**) a change in the behaviour of the managers of the Service by modifying their incentives, and in particular by the loss of the *direct* incentive to maximise [the budget surplus] because however negative it is, this deficit is covered by the public budget ...

While not formulated using modern terminology, this statement of the problem echoes in many respects what is now referred to as the mechanism design or principal-agent problem.[36] He sketches the various benefits, costs, and constraints

[36] Kolm offers a very stimulating discussion of the notions of centralisation and decentralisation, although he deplores the lack of accuracy in their definitions. Kolm (1971c, p. 82) writes:

> To draw up the social balance sheet for the tariff it is necessary to estimate the gains and losses of this autonomy. Unfortunately, for this we cannot rely on a well-developed and well-known theory as we have done for market mechanisms because no such thing exists

involved in the hierarchical relationship between the central political and administrative authorities and the manager(s) of the Service. This chapter is devoted to an analysis of the issues attached to the principal-agent problem. Preliminary mathematical analyses for some of them are also included. We are not going to review the totality of this rich material, but instead we offer a brief selective discussion of a few of Kolm's key ideas and insights. These were pioneering ideas and they received a general formulation, as explained at the end of this section.

Interestingly, Kolm distinguishes between the costs of communication and organisation and the costs of incentives. He analyses the first dimension by introducing a graph-theoretical formulation, where the vertices and the edges represent, respectively, the members of the organisation and the channels of communication between them. Kolm characterises the graphs that minimise the total cost of channels and messages, and then he analyses the costs of more or less foreseeable incentives. Kolm (1971c, pp. 89–90) writes:

> Transfers of information and the organisation of work and power according to knowledge answers the problem of the members' *knowledge*. It remains to consider their desire to act: it is not sufficient that they know what to do, they must want to do it. ...
>
> To achieve its goals, an administration is driven by its members whose reasons for acting can be very different from that needed to fulfill this social function. In spite of this, to make their choices best serve this purpose is the problem of incentives.
>
> Incentives have two *factors* and public incentives two *objectives*. The former are the *motivations* of individuals and the *conditions* in which they make decisions. The latter are *productive efficiency* and the best *service of the public* on the one hand and administrative and political *conformity* on the other hand.

After discussing in turn the meaning of these concepts, Kolm compares the respective performance of the three different organisational modes he calls "Gestion Commerciale," "Gestion Autonome," and "Gestion Administrative Intégrée" (Business Administration, Autonomous Administration, and Integrated Administration). These terms are not going to be precisely defined here. The first corresponds to the pure delegation of decisions to the private sector, while the third corresponds to an organisation receiving all of its instructions from some central administrative/political authority. The second lies somewhere in between the other two.

In his comparative analysis, Kolm clearly identifies the trade-off that is a cornerstone of the modern approach to organisation theory: the organisations that perform well in terms of cost optimisation and quality of service perform relatively poorly in terms of conformity to the social objectives of society. For example, when examining the third organisational form, Kolm (1971c, p. 100) argues that it is "*a priori* best when the utility of the service is revealed by political means." But Kolm (1971c, p. 100) also asserts:

---

for administrative organisations. We must therefore build our own tools. ... [This] might seem like a digression but it is necessary to give a solid basis for a cost-benefit analysis of the degree of centralisation or decentralisation.

> However, the productive efficiency of the Service and the satisfaction of its users require the best possible knowledge of its production function and of the characteristics of demand. But the members of the Service usually have an advantage here, sometimes considerable, over those of the central administration. Direct interference from the latter is therefore very likely to be harmful from this point of view. But the Service only uses its knowledge appropriately if there is an incentive to do so. Although uninformed about the precise actions that are best, the authority often has an excellent way of achieving this incentive: it is to sell the product and choose profit as an indicator of success, attaching penalties and rewards to its level. It suffices, in particular, that the latter are simply personal remunerations that are an increasing function of this profit, which brings us back to business or, possibly, autonomous management.

Kolm (1971c, Chap. 4, Appendix 3) is devoted to an analytical formulation of this trade-off. In Kolm's analysis, the cost of public funds $1 + \lambda$ stands for the agency cost, whereas the inefficiency costs resulting from poor incentives are captured by a single number that only appears when the organisation is fully integrated.[37] While insightful, this reduced form does not provide a complete understanding of the channels through which the incentives operate. A more complete analysis has recently been provided by the new economics of regulation, which was itself built on the solid bases established in the nineteen eighties by the theory of incentives and the economics of information.

We have insisted on the historical context in presenting the contributions of Kolm's French precursors to the derivation of the optimal rules for the management of public monopolies. To some extent, the new economics of regulation is also the product of two forces: a specific social and economic demand arising in many countries, together with important developments in economic theory. In the nineteen eighties, we observed a renewed interest in the regulation of natural monopolies and oligopolies.[38] As noted by Laffont and Tirole (1993, p. xvii):

> In the policy arena discontent was expressed with the price, quality, and cost performance of regulated firms and government contractors. The remedies sought in specific industries differed remarkably: More powerful incentive schemes were proposed and implemented, deregulation was encouraged to free up competition and entry, and in some countries changes in ownership (privatization) occurred.

While different in terms of policy motivations and theoretical emphasis, the modern theory of regulation is to a large extent the continuation of the practical and theoretical construction of its predecessors.[39] Among other things, the earlier lack of focus on incentive issues by regulatory theory was perceived as a serious limitation. As noted by Laffont and Tirole (1993, p. xvii, footnote added):

---

[37] The reader can refer to Stiglitz (1988, pp. 194–210) for a stimulating presentation of the arguments and evidence concerning the comparison of efficiency in the public and private sectors, as well as an analysis of the bureaucracy.

[38] See, for example, Spulber (1989).

[39] It should be pointed out that this theory mostly employs a partial equilibrium framework.

> [T]he academic debate attempted to shed light on some shortcomings of the generally accepted theory of regulation. Regulatory theory largely ignored incentive issues. Because exogenous constraints rather than the limited access to information of regulators were the source of inefficient regulatory outcomes, the theory of regulation did not meet the standards of the newly developed principal-agent theory whose aim is to highlight the information limitations that impair agency relationships. Furthermore the considerably simplified formal models that assumed away imperfect information were less realistic in that they implied policy recommendations that require information not available to regulators in practice.[40]

The contemporary theory analyses regulation, in particular the regulation of natural monopolies, as the strategic outcome of an agency relationship. The legacy is however important and useful. Indeed, as Laffont and Tirole (1993) note:

> Academics have traditionally emphasized institutional and empirical research on regulatory issues, but there is also a substantial and useful heritage in the area. By and large, the most successful contributions refer to the normative aspects of natural monopoly pricing . . . (p. 19)

---

[40] We do not examine the "sociology" of these regulatory agencies. The French engineer-economists listed above as the precursors in this school were acting inside public firms for the general interest. There was no need for further regulation. Some of the pioneers expressed their scepticism about the social benefits to be expected from the new regulation. On electricity, Boiteux (2007, p. 6) writes:

> The mandate received by EDF was, on the one hand to produce at minimum cost and, on the other hand, to sell at cost ("long-term marginal" as defined by experts) without trying to take advantage of its monopoly to exploit the customers. This virtuous behaviour, which now raises feelings of disbelief, did not seem implausible during the "Thirty Glorious Years" [i.e., 1945–1975] and of what were called "the senior officials of the State." [The French text says "les grands commis de l'État," which implies that these officials serve the general interest.]

With nostalgia and irony, Boiteux (2007, pp. 14–15) also alludes to the "disparition" (diss-appearance) in the political economy approach of the actors defined in the traditional normative approach of our textbooks to be benevolent social planners, corresponding here to the managers of the public firms, assumed indeed to be obedient civil servants instructed to follow marginal cost pricing rules:

> To succeed in teaching the younger generations that the general interest, which is the interest of the class in power (and not the collective interest as defined by the class in power), by succeeding in explaining that anyone with power will not renounce using it for his own enrichment except in strict moderation when it is efficaceous (instead of admitting that he will use it first to complete the mission entrusted to him), . . . by succeeding in all this, the nationalised enterprise is like a bird with a lead shot in its wing.
>
> For, in such a context, why would the boss of an EDF which remains a nationalised monopoly bust his gut to reduce costs if he does not receive any benefit? . . .
>
> If the kind of person that does not give in to such easy options no longer exists, it is necessary to draw the consequences. EDF, privatized, should be left free to earn–on a long-term basis–as much money as possible, within the limits of legality and the constraints imposed on it by a "regulator." (However, either this regulator is competent and disinterested, and would thus be a person who is himself suitable to lead a still nationalised EDF, or he is incompetent and/or self interested, and this will pose some problems!)

> Despite some headway . . . on the pricing front . . . [t]he traditional theoretical approach has stalled precisely where the new regulatory economics has sprung: the incentive front. To be certain, received theory implicitly touches on incentive issues: the Ramsey–Boiteux model rules out government transfers precisely because they might be abused, and the Averch–Johnson model describes a regulated firm's self-interested input choices. But received theory can only go so far. A more rigorous and realistic approach must adhere to the discipline of the broader principal-agent theory. Modeling must include a full description of the firm's and the regulators's objectives, information structures, instruments, and constraints. Information structures and the set of feasible regulatory schemes must as much as possible reflect real-world observational and contractual costs. . . .
>
> From this perspective there are three reasons why regulation is not a simple exercise in second-best optimization theory: asymmetric information, lack of commitment, and imperfect regulators. . . . [A]symmetric information . . . limits the control the regulator can exert over the firm. The difficulty for the regulator to commit to incentive schemes, for contractual or legal reasons, also reduces the efficiency of regulation. . . . Last, the regulators or politicians may be incompetent, have their own hidden agendas, or simply be captured by interest groups; they may then not optimize social welfare.
>
> Only a thorough investigation of these limits to perfect regulation can shed light on many issues of the traditional agenda of regulatory economics. (pp. 34–35)

Any description of this sequential strategic interaction calls for a very careful examination of the regulatory environment, which must be consistent with the firm's and regulator's information structures, constraints, and feasible instruments. Constraints are often classified into three types: informational, transactional, and administrative and political. Of course, these constraints limit the efficiency of the control of government agencies, and prevent the regulator from implementing its preferred policy (whatever that may be).[41] The nature of the regulatory instruments and incentive schemes that can be used by the regulator may also vary. Accounting and demand data are typically used to monitor a firm's performance. Accounting data consists mainly of a firm's aggregate cost or profit, while the demand data, on which contracts can most easily be based, consist of prices and quantities. It is then important to know the scope of possibilities available to the regulator. According to Laffont and Tirole, current incentive schemes can be analysed along two dimensions. The first is concerned with whether the government is allowed to subsidise (or tax) regulated firms; that is, whether regulated firms can receive public funds and cover all of their costs by directly charging their private customers. The second is concerned with the power of the incentive schemes, i.e., the link between the firm's transfer from the government and/or the firm's prices and its cost or profit performance.

Laffont and Tirole (1993, Table 1, p. 11) offer a nice classification of the more important existing regulatory schemes (including cost-plus contracts, price caps, and cost of service regulation) along these two dimensions. They also revisit the received theory, in particular, Boiteux–Ramsey pricing, and marginal cost pricing and the criticisms formulated against its use by Coase and others (as discussed above).

[41] See Laffont and Tirole (1993) for a more detailed exposition of the limits to efficiency resulting from these constraints.

Interestingly, they make a clear distinction between three criticisms, also formulated by Kolm (as previously argued): the implications of a deficit, the limits of marginal analysis, and the inappropriate incentives for cost reduction.[42]

We now focus on the last point, referred to as "incidence amont" (upstream incidence) in Kolm's terminology, as it is a key concern on the agenda of the new regulatory economics. It will allow us to show how Kolm's intuitions have been explored and formulated within this new framework.

To do so, we need to depart from the assumption of an exogenous cost function C, as defined in (1). Instead, we suppose that C can be written as:

$$C = C(\beta, e, \mathbf{q}) + \varepsilon,$$

where, as before, $\mathbf{q} = (q_1, q_2, \ldots, q_K) \in \mathbb{R}_+^K$ denotes the vector of outputs of the firm, β is a technological parameter, e is the effort or cost-reducing activity, and ε is a noise term representing either forecast errors or accounting inaccuracies. This specification of C corresponds to the controlled experiment in Laffont and Tirole (1993). Letting t denote the monetary transfer from the regulator to the firm and $\psi(e)$ the disutility of effort, the firm's objective function is assumed to be:

$$U(t, e) \equiv t - \psi(e).$$

We denote by $V(\mathbf{q})$ the social value associated with the production $\mathbf{q}$. For example, in the case of private goods, $V(\mathbf{q})$ is often assumed to be the sum of the net consumer surplus $S(\mathbf{q}) - R(\mathbf{q})$ (where $S(\mathbf{q})$ is the gross consumer surplus and $R(\mathbf{q})$ is the revenue of the firm) and the social value of tax savings $(1 + \lambda)R(\mathbf{q})$ (where λ is the shadow cost of public funds). The expected (utilitarian) social welfare is then:

$$W(\beta, e, \mathbf{q}, t, \lambda) \equiv [V(\mathbf{q}) - (1 + \lambda)(t + C(\beta, e, \mathbf{q}))] + U(t, e).$$

This analytical framework captures most of the eight interactions that Kolm has listed in his approach to the upstream incidence. The regulator is assumed not to observe the variables β and e. Asymmetric information is thus two-dimensional because we simultaneously have adverse selection (lack of observability of the exogenous variable β) and moral hazard (lack of observability of the endogenous variable e). This corresponds to Channels 2 and 7 in Kolm's list. From the regulator's viewpoint, β is drawn from a cumulative distribution $F(\beta)$ on $[\underline{\beta}, \overline{\beta}]$ with density $f(\beta)$. The regulator observes C and $\mathbf{q}$ (or equivalently, prices $\overline{\mathbf{p}} = (p_1, p_2, \ldots, p_K)$). Note also that Kolm's Channel 2 is also effective because W and U do not coincide.

[42] More generally, it is important to determine how the internal structure of the firm affects the firm's decisions. For example, the effect of rate-of-return regulation on input choices are analysed in the model of Averch and Johnson (1962).

The optimal regulatory policy is derived from the maximisation of W given the incentive and participation constraints.[43] The two fundamental equations that summarize the essence of such an optimal second-best policy are the following:

$$\psi'(e) = -\frac{\partial C(\beta, e, \mathbf{q})}{\partial e} - \frac{\lambda}{1+\lambda}\frac{F(\beta)}{f(\beta)}\left[\psi''(e)\frac{\partial E(\beta, C, \mathbf{q})}{\partial \beta} + \psi'(e)\frac{\partial^2 E(\beta, C, \mathbf{q})}{\partial \beta \partial C}\frac{\partial C(\beta, e, \mathbf{q})}{\partial e}\right] \quad (10)$$

and

$$\frac{\partial V(\mathbf{q})}{\partial q_k} = (1+\lambda)\frac{\partial C(\beta, e, \mathbf{q})}{\partial q_k} + \lambda \frac{F(\beta)}{f(\beta)}\psi'(e)\frac{\partial}{\partial q_k}\left(\frac{\partial E(\beta, C, \mathbf{q})}{\partial \beta}\right), \quad k = 1, \ldots, K, \quad (11)$$

where $E(\beta, C, \mathbf{q})$ is the level of effort required for a firm of type β to produce $\mathbf{q}$ at cost C. This set of first-order conditions illustrates how this (second-best) management policy departs from the standard first-best optimality conditions. With symmetric information (i.e., when β and e are publically observable), (10) and (11) simply describe the equality between social costs and social benefits, where the social costs include a correction term if λ is different from 0.

The pricing dimension of the public policy has been our major concern in this article, so let us focus on (11) for the standard case of private goods with the assumption of linear prices. We assume that

$$V(\mathbf{q}) = S(\mathbf{q}) + \lambda R(\mathbf{q}) \text{ with } R(\mathbf{q}) = \sum_{k=1}^{K} p_k q_k.$$

Because

$$\frac{\partial S(\mathbf{q})}{\partial q_k} = p_k, \quad k = 1, \ldots, K,$$

by letting $p_l(\cdot)$ denote the inverse demand function for good l, (11) can be rewritten as:

$$p_k + \lambda\left(p_k + \sum_{l=1}^{K}\frac{\partial p_l(\mathbf{q})}{\partial q_k}q_l\right) - (1+\lambda)\frac{\partial C(\beta, e, \mathbf{q})}{\partial q_k} - \lambda\frac{F(\beta)}{f(\beta)}\psi'(e)\frac{\partial}{\partial q_k}\left(\frac{\partial E(\beta, C, \mathbf{q})}{\partial \beta}\right) = 0, \quad k = 1, \ldots, K,$$

43 This modern synthetic approach to the regulation of multiproduct natural monopolies is due to Laffont and Tirole (1990a,b).

or more compactly as:

$$L_k = R_k + I_k, \quad k = 1, \ldots, K, \tag{12}$$

where

$$L_k \equiv \frac{p_k - \frac{\partial C(\beta,e,\mathbf{q})}{\partial q_k}}{p_k}$$

is commodity k's Lerner (1934) index,

$$R_k \equiv -\frac{\lambda}{1+\lambda}\left(\sum_{l=1}^{K} \frac{\partial p_l(\mathbf{q})}{\partial q_k}\frac{q_l}{p_k}\right)$$

is commodity k's Ramsey (1927) index, and

$$I_k \equiv \left[\frac{\lambda F(\beta)\psi'(e)}{(1+\lambda)f(\beta)p_k}\right]\frac{\partial}{\partial q_k}\left(\frac{\partial E(\beta, C, \mathbf{q})}{\partial \beta}\right)$$

is commodity k's incentive correction.

We see that the Lerner index L_k, which measures the optimal departure from marginal cost pricing of good k, is decomposed into two terms, a Ramsey index and good k's incentive correction. This decomposition is enlightening because it isolates the budgetary issue from the incentive correction, and it identifies the parameters likely to shape the Lerner index with their respective effects.[44] This is, of course, a very significant advance with respect to the intuitions developed by Kolm because this general theory is structural and is constructed from basic primitives.

The decomposition in (12) yields another simple but important conclusion: incentives and the pricing of good k are disconnected if and only if $\frac{\partial}{\partial q_k}\left(\frac{\partial E(\beta,C,\mathbf{q})}{\partial \beta}\right) = 0$. Recall that, in this general setting, the regulator can use two instruments: a cost-reimbursement rule and a vector of (linear) prices. The optimal price of good k exceeds its symmetric (Ramsey) information level if and only if $\frac{\partial}{\partial q_k}\left(\frac{\partial E(\beta,C,\mathbf{q})}{\partial \beta}\right) > 0$ or equivalently:

$$\frac{\partial}{\partial q_k}\left(\frac{\frac{\partial C(\beta,e,\mathbf{q})}{\partial \beta}}{\frac{\partial C(\beta,e,\mathbf{q})}{\partial e}}\right) > 0.$$[45]

The situation where the incentive issue is solved exclusively through the appropriate design of the cost-reimbursement rule is called the "incentive-pricing dichotomy" by Laffont and Tirole (1993). In such environments, the incentive and pricing issues are separated, with a single task allocated to each instrument. This,

[44] As explained in Laffont and Tirole (1993), it also offers a new perspective on the definition of cross-subsidization.

[45] See Laffont and Tirole (1990a).

of course, implies that the cost functions exhibit specific functional structure, as demonstrated by Laffont and Tirole.

7 Conclusion

The framework adopted by Laffont and Tirole to formulate the new issues raised by the regulation of multiproduct natural monopolies extends the normative approach pioneered by Kolm and the French engineer-economists. It is more complicated than the framework adopted by their precursors because new constraints reflecting incentive constraints, lack of commitment, or political matters have been added to the optimisation problem. The optimal management rules derived in such second-best environments are precise, but are often derived in a partial equilibrium setting with specific assumptions on the primitives of the model. In contrast, the general second-best rules derived by Guesnerie (1995a) are derived in a general equilibrium setting, but often take as given the scope of the second-best instruments.

We have shown that Kolm was situated somewhere between these two epochs. On the one hand, he continued on the road paved by his precursors, enlarging the scope of application of marginal cost pricing with an engineering flavour. On the other hand, he identified and formulated many of the limits of that "doctrine," anticipating many of the developments that constitute the forefront of the contemporary approach to regulation. This article does not fully present the totality of the contributions to conventional public economics he made during this period. Obviously, his strong interest in normative and welfare economics motivated contributions in other parts of public economics including, among others, the theory of justice and its application to the determination of the optimal income tax, tax evasion, the theory of public goods, health economics, the value of human life, and cost-benefit analysis of public safety. We strongly believe that those issues that we have privileged in our exposition fairly represent his personal touch, and illustrate the connections to the interests of scholars before and after him.

To conclude, it is worthwhile to point out that, in addition to these contributions to public economics, Kolm was able to write, during the same period, several books and articles on the economics of the environment, monetary economics, macroeconomics, and welfare economics. In addition to these academic and scientific activities, he also actively participated in many policy debates and published in the main French newspapers. Serge Kolm is a distinguished citizen and scientist.

Acknowledgements We would like to express our deepest gratitude to John Weymark for his critical examination of a previous version of this article. His detailed and insightful comments and suggestions have had a major impact on the content of this article and the organisation of the main ideas. We would also like to thank an anonymous referee for his or her observations and encouragement. The translations from French sources were initially prepared by Agnès d'Artigues and Sarah Berthaud from the firm ATRATEC and subsequently revised by John Weymark. Serge Kolm and Maurice Salles kindly provided comments on the translations. Kolm's contributions had a profound impact on the desire of the second author to become an economist. It is a pleasure for him to recognise this intellectual influence and to pay his tribute.

References

Allais, M. (1945). *Economie pure et rendement social*. Paris: Sirey

Atkinson, A. B., & Stern, N. H. (1974). Pigou, taxation and public goods. *Review of Economic Studies, 41*, 119–128

Averch, H., & Johnson, L. L. (1962). Behavior of the firm under regulatory constraint. *American Economic Review, 52*, 1053–1069

Beato, P., & Mas-Colell, A. (1985). On marginal cost pricing with given tax-subsidy rules. *Journal of Economic Theory, 37*, 356–365

Berg, S. V., & Tschirhart, J. (1995). Contributions of neoclassical economics to public utility analysis. *Land Economics, 71*, 310–330

Blackorby, C. (1990). Economic policy in a second-best environment. *Canadian Journal of Economics, 23*, 748–771

Boiteux, M. (1949). La tarification des demandes en pointe: Application de la théorie de la vente au coût marginal. *Revue Générale de l'Electricité, 58*, 321–340. (Peak-load pricing. *Journal of Business, 33*, 1960, 157–179, Trans.) English trans. reprinted in Nelson, J. R. (Ed.) (1964). *Marginal cost pricing in practice* (pp. 59–89). Englewood Cliffs, NJ: Prentice-Hall.

Boiteux, M. (1951). La tarification au coût marginal et les demandes aléatoires. *Cahiers du Séminaire d'Econométrie, 1*, 56–69

Boiteux, M. (1956a). La vente au coût marginal. *Revue Française de l'Energie, 8*, 113–117. Reprinted in Morlat, G., & Bessière, F. (Eds.) (1971). *Vingt cinq ans d'économie électrique* (pp. 265–273). Paris: Dunod. (Marginal cost pricing. In Nelson, J. R. (Ed.) (1964). *Marginal cost pricing in practice* (pp. 51–58). Englewood Cliffs, NJ: Prentice-Hall, Trans.)

Boiteux, M. (1956b). Sur la gestion des monopoles publics astreints à l'équilibre budgétaire. *Econometrica, 24*, 22–40. (On the management of public monopolies subject to budgetary constraints. *Journal of Economic Theory, 3*, 1971, 219–240, Trans.)

Boiteux, M. (1957). Le tarif vert d'Electricité de France. *Revue Française de l'Energie, 8*, 137–151. Reprinted in Morlat, G., & Bessière, F. (Eds.) (1971). *Vingt cinq ans d'économie électrique* (pp. 421–445). Paris: Dunod. (The green tariff of Electricité de France. *Land Economics, 40*, 1964, 185–197, Trans. The 'tarif vert' of Electricité de France. In Nelson, J. R. (Ed.) (1964). *Marginal cost pricing in practice* (pp. 127–149). Englewood Cliffs, NJ: Prentice-Hall, Trans.)

Boiteux, M. (2007). Les ambiguïtés de la concurrence: Electricité de France et la libéralisation du marché de l'életricité. *Futuribles, 331*, 5–16

Bonnisseau, J.-M., & Cornet, B. (1990). Existence of marginal cost pricing equilibria in an economy with several nonconvex firms. *Econometrica, 58*, 661–682

Brown, D. J., & Heal, G. M. (1979). Equity, efficiency and increasing returns. *Review of Economic Studies, 46*, 571–585

Brown, D. J., & Heal, G. M. (1980). Two-part tariffs, marginal cost pricing and increasing returns in a general equilibrium model. *Journal of Public Economics, 13*, 25–49

Brown, D. J., & Heal, G. M. (1983). Marginal vs. average cost pricing in the presence of a public monopoly. *American Economic Review, Papers and Proceedings, 73*, 189–193

Chenery, H. B. (1949). Engineering production functions. *Quarterly Journal of Economics, 63*, 507–531

Clemens, E. W. (1941). Price discrimination in decreasing cost industries. *American Economic Review, 31*, 794–802

Clemens, E. W. (1963). Discussion. *American Economic Review, Papers and Proceedings, 53*, 482–485

Coase, R. H. (1946). The marginal cost controversy. *Economica, 13*, 169–182

Coase, R. H. (1970). The theory of public utility pricing and its application. *Bell Journal of Economics and Management Science, 1*, 113–128

Cornet, B. (1988). General equilibrium theory and increasing returns: Presentation. *Journal of Mathematical Economics, 17*, 103–118

David, L., Le Breton, M., & Merillon, O. (2011). Public utility pricing and capacity choice with stochastic demand. In M. Fleurbaey, M. Salles, & J. A. Weymark (Eds.) *Social ethics and normative economics: Essays in honour of Serge-Christophe Kolm* (pp. 57–99). Berlin: Springer

Dierker, E. (1991). The optimality of Boiteux–Ramsey pricing. *Econometrica, 59*, 99–121

Drèze, J., & Stern, N. (1990). Policy reform, shadow prices and market prices. *Journal of Public Economics, 42*, 1–45

Drèze, J. H. (1964). Some postwar contributions of French economists to theory and public policy: With special emphasis on problems of resource allocation. *American Economic Review, Supplement, 54*, 1–64

Drèze, J. H. (1995). Forty years of public economics: A personal perspective. *Journal of Economic Perspectives, 9*(2), 111–130

Dupuit, J. (1844). De la mesure de l'utilité des travaux publics. *Annales des Ponts et Chaussées, 8*, 332–375. (On the measurement of the utility of public works. *International Economic Papers, 2*, 1952, 83–110, Trans.)

Edgeworth, F. Y. (1888). The mathematical theory of banking. *Journal of the Royal Statistical Society, 51*, 113–127

Faulhaber, G. F. (1975). Cross-subsidization: Pricing in public enterprises. *American Economic Review, 65*, 966–977

Guesnerie, R. (1975a). Pareto-optimality in non-convex economies. *Econometrica, 43*, 1–29

Guesnerie, R. (1975b). Production of the public sector and taxation in a simple second best model. *Journal of Economic Theory, 10*, 127–156

Guesnerie, R. (1979). General statements on second best Pareto optimality. *Journal of Mathematical Economics, 6*, 169–194

Guesnerie, R. (1980). Second-best pricing rules in the Boiteux tradition. *Journal of Public Economics, 13*, 51–80

Guesnerie, R. (1995a). *A contribution to the pure theory of taxation*. Cambridge: Cambridge University Press

Guesnerie, R. (1995b). The genealogy of modern theoretical public economics: From first best to second best. *European Economic Review, 39*, 353–381

Guesnerie, R., & Roberts, K. (1987). Minimum wage legislation as a second best policy. *European Economic Review, 31*, 490–498

Hagen, K. (1988). Optimal shadow prices for public production. *Journal of Public Economics, 35*, 119–127

Hotelling, H. (1938). The general welfare in relation to problems of taxation and of railway and utility rates. *Econometrica, 6*, 242–269

Joskow, P. L. (1976). Contributions to the theory of marginal cost pricing. *Bell Journal of Economics, 7*, 197–206

Kolm, S.-C. (1968a). Le déficit optimal des transports en commun. *Revue d'Economie Politique, 78*, 658–663

Kolm, S.-C. (1968b). Le rôle social ambigu des prix publics. *Economie Appliquée, 21*, 417–516

Kolm, S.-C. (1969a). La vérité des prix dans un monde imparfait. *Revue Economique, 20*, 727–740

Kolm, S.-C. (1969b). *Prix publics optimaux*. Paris: Editions du Centre National de la Recherche Scientifique

Kolm, S.-C. (1971a). Footnotes to Marcel Boiteux's value-constained second best. *Journal of Economic Theory, 3*, 341–344

Kolm, S.-C. (1971b). *La théorie des contraintes de valeur et ses applications*. Paris: C.N.R.S. and Dunod

Kolm, S.-C. (1971c). *La valeur publique*. Paris: C.N.R.S. and Dunod

Kolm, S.-C. (1971d). *Le service des masses*. Paris: C.N.R.S. and Dunod

Laffont, J.-J., & Tirole, J. (1990a). The regulation of multiproduct firms. Part I: Theory. *Journal of Public Economics, 43*, 1–36

Laffont, J.-J., & Tirole, J. (1990b). The regulation of multiproduct firms. Part II: Applications to competitive environments and policy analysis. *Journal of Public Economics, 43*, 37–66

Laffont, J.-J., & Tirole, J. (1993). *A theory of incentives in procurement and regulation*. Cambridge, MA: MIT Press

Lerner, A. P. (1934). The concept of monopoly and the measurement of monopoly power. *Review of Economic Studies, 1*, 157–175

Lévy-Lambert, H. (1968). Tarification des services à qualité variable: Application aux péages de circulation. *Econometrica, 36*, 564–574

Lipsey, R. G., & Lancaster, K. (1956). The general theory of second best. *Review of Economic Studies, 24*, 11–32

Marschak, T. (1960). Capital budgeting and pricing in the French nationalized industries. *Journal of Business, 33*, 133–156

Marsden, J., Pingry, D., & Whinston, A. (1974). Engineering foundations of production functions. *Journal of Economic Theory, 9*, 121–140

Massé, P. (1958). Quelques incidences économiques du "tarif vert". *Revue Française de l'Energie, 9*, 392–395. Reprinted in Morlat, G., & Bessière, F., (Eds.) (1971). *Vingt cinq ans d'économie électrique* (pp. 447–452). Paris: Dunod. (Some economic effects of the "tarif vert". In Nelson, J. R. (Ed.) (1964). *Marginal cost pricing in practice* (pp. 151–156). Englewood Cliffs, NJ: Prentice-Hall, Trans.)

Massé, P., & Gibrat, R. (1957). Application of linear programming to investments in the electric power industry. *Management Science, 3*, 149–166

Meade, J. E. (1944). Price and output policy of state enterprise. *Economic Journal, 54*, 321–328

Meek, R. L. (1963). An application of marginal cost pricing: The 'green tariff' in theory and practice. *Journal of Industrial Economics, 11*, 217–236

Morlat, G., & Bessière, F. (Eds.) (1971). *Vingt cinq ans d'économie électrique*. Paris: Dunod

Nelson, J. R. (1963). Practical applications of marginal cost pricing in the public field. *American Economic Review, Papers and Proceedings, 53*, 474–481

Nelson, J. R. (Ed.) (1964). *Marginal cost pricing in practice*. Englewood Cliffs, NJ: Prentice-Hall

Phelps Brown, E. H. (1936). Cost categories and the total cost functions: Second report of the Econometrica committee on source materials for quantitative production studies. *Econometrica, 4*, 242–263

Ramsey, F. P. (1927). A contribution to the theory of taxation. *Economic Journal, 37*, 47–61

Ruggles, N. (1949). The welfare basis of the marginal cost principle. *Review of Economic Studies, 17*, 29–46

Samuelson, P. A. (1954). The pure theory of public expenditure. *Review of Economics and Statistics, 36*, 387–389

Spulber, D. F. (1989). *Regulation and markets*. Cambridge, MA: MIT Press

Stiglitz, J. E. (1988). *Economics of the public sector* (2nd ed.). New York: W. W. Norton

Vickrey, W. (1948). Some objections to marginal-cost pricing. *Journal of Political Economy, 56*, 218–238

Vickrey, W. (1955). Some implications of marginal cost pricing for public utilities. *American Economic Review, Papers and Proceedings, 45*, 605–620

Vickrey, W. (1971). Responsive pricing of public utility services. *Bell Journal of Economics and Management Science*, 2, 337–346

Vohra, R. (1992). Marginal cost pricing under bounded marginal returns. *Econometrica, 60*, 859–876

Wibe, S. (1984). Engineering production functions: A survey. *Economica, 51*, 401–411

Wijkander, H. (1988). Equity and efficiency in public sector pricing: A case for stochastic rationing. *Econometrica, 56*, 1455–1465

Yntema, T. O., Clark, J. M., Dean, J., Whitman, R. H., & Stigler, G. J. (1940). Round table on cost functions and their relations to imperfect competition. *American Economic Review, Papers and Proceedings, 30*, 400–402

Public Utility Pricing and Capacity Choice with Stochastic Demand

Laurent David, Michel Le Breton, and Olivier Merillon

1 Introduction

This article is a companion piece to David et al. (2011). In that article, we explored Serge Kolm's contributions to theoretical public economics from an historical perspective, covering a rather general range of topics and specifications. Here, in contrast, we concentrate on the implications for pricing and capacity choice of a specific aspect of the economic environment often encountered by public sector managers and regulators: the uncertainty attached to the demand for the good(s) and service(s) produced by a public utility. Following an early article by Boiteux (see Boiteux 1951), Kolm (1970, 1971) has made important contributions to this issue.

Our analysis of the economic environment considered here is, we believe, a perfect illustration of the themes and ideas discussed in our other article, particularly the issue of how to operationalize and optimally depart from the marginal cost pricing principle. Uncertain demand is clearly a real practical problem met by most public utilities with more or less acuity. Applying the marginal cost principle in such situations is not an obvious choice, mainly because the source of the demand uncertainty (not, of course, the uncertainty about primitives like preferences) lies in the impossibility of organising a complete set of Arrow–Debreu markets. These "institutional" limits on trading opportunities and, in particular, the impossibility of achieving efficient risk sharing (i.e., equality of the marginal rates of substitution of

L. David
GDF Suez, Direction de la Stratégie et du Développement Durable, Tour 1, 1 place Samuel de Champlain, 92930 Paris La Défense cedex, France
e-mail: laurent-m.david@gdfsuez.com

M. Le Breton (✉)
Toulouse School of Economics, GREMAQ, and IDEI, Manufacture des tabacs, Aile JJ Laffont, 21, Allée de Brienne, 31000 Toulouse, France
e-mail: lebreton@cict.fr

O. Merillon
GDF Suez E&P, Département Acquisitions, Tour 1, 1 place Samuel de Champlain, 92930 Paris La Défense, France
e-mail: olivier.merillon@gdfsuez.com

M. Fleurbaey et al. (eds.), *Social Ethics and Normative Economics*, Studies in Choice and Welfare, DOI 10.1007/978-3-642-17807-8_3,

income across agents and states of nature) gives rise to a second-best environment in which the determination of optimal public prices is likely to be sensitive to the details of the contractual environment ultimately considered. Indeed, as far as we know, there are no real general results on second-best rules when the second-best nature of the problem arises from incomplete markets.

In our companion article, we discussed optimal departures from marginal cost pricing to accommodate various second-best constraints, but the various uncertainties that a public utility might face were not taken into account.[1] It is worthwhile to consider such uncertainties because most utilities happen to function in such a world. However, it is important to distinguish these random features of demand from other factors influencing the variability of demand. Indeed, as pointed out by Drèze (1964, p. 18, footnote omitted):

> Short-run fluctuations in demand occur frequently in random as well as in periodic patterns. In the case of a non-storable commodity, the pricing problem raised by random fluctuations in demand is quite different from the problem of peak-load pricing. One might expect that, when the life of the equipment is long relative to the period over which demand exhibits significant fluctuations (around a known average), investment decisions would be guided by the same principles–no matter whether the fluctuations are random or periodic. As we shall see, this is not always so. As for pricing decisions, the basic difference is the following: peak load pricing calls for a *known* periodic schedule of prices, whereas pricing at short-run marginal costs under stochastic demand conditions would call for *stochastic* price variations.

These considerations lead to the following fundamental question: Why does a public utility face a stochastic demand? In these introductory remarks, we argue that the origin of this situation lies in the fact that no complete set of Arrow–Debreu markets is available to deal with the fundamental uncertainties about demand and supply. We must remember that, according to Guesnerie (1975), this fact is one (of three) of the main reasons why there is a second-best environment.[2] Many conceivable Arrow–Debreu markets for contingent commodities do not exist.[3] Kolm (1971, p. 305, footnote added) writes:

---

[1] As noted, for example, by Sherman and Visscher (1978, p. 41, parenthetical citations and footnote omitted, emphasis added):

> Ways to depart from marginal cost pricing to increase revenue and yet minimize the resulting misallocation of resources are well-accepted members of a growing family of constrained welfare-maximizing prescriptions. An important application is found in public utility pricing, where optimal peak and off-peak pricing arrangements have been modified as needed to admit second best characteristics. Second best two-part tariff schemes provide another example of pricing rules modified to satisfy budget constraints. But in all these examples, demand is assumed known with certainty. *Little attention has been given to second best solutions when demand has a random element . . .*

[2] As pointed out by Diamond (1980, p. 645): "... economies with incomplete markets can have surprising welfare properties. These examples, or counter-examples, bring out the need for further analysis of public policies in the presence of uncertainty and incomplete markets."

[3] It is now well accepted that, in many circumstances, the organisation of such markets, as well as the design of sophisticated contracts between parties involved in transactions on such markets, is simply impossible because the transaction costs attached to these hypothetical trading

> On economic analysis and practice, uncertainty has a profound impact. The extreme scarcity of futures and contingent markets, the uncertainty of future prices, are one [sic] of the most serious limitations of the regime of free enterprise and free trade. However, plans to replace this system do not face less uncertainty about the factors that would determine these prices. The effect of this ignorance is all the more important when the decisions taken are mortgaging a far distant future. It is therefore particularly important for capitalistic activities with illiquid capital. ...
>
> The uncertainties that primarily concern [large-scale public services] are those of their future costs and, often even more, their future demands. The main decisions that are affected are the choice of investments and tariffs or prices. The financial situation of these organisations, and all its institutional consequences, are therefore affected.[4]

In the first part of this article, we do not describe the menu of contractual arrangements offered to the customers of a public utility. Instead, we take as given the stochastic nature of the demand for the goods produced by it. A public utility's costs of production can be decomposed into operating costs, on the one hand, and into capacity costs, on the other. Operating costs do not raise many problems: They are concomitant to the realisation of the demand. The main questions that we ask are the following: What is the optimal level of capacity? What is the price of the good when no further information about the consumption profile of the customers is available? How can the good be priced when personal information about the consumption profile of the customers is available? How are such pricing policies implemented or how can they be implemented?

We start answering these questions for the case in which only aggregate stochastic demand is known. This framework has received considerable attention in the American literature on the regulation of utilities subject to stochastic demand. We then move to the case in which the stochastic demand of each individual customer is known, with the demand of each customer described by a random variable. If continuous observation of a customer's consumption over time, corrected for seasonal variations (if any), is possible, then knowledge of this random variable is almost equivalent to having a temporal sample of consumption observations.

In this framework, we first present the seminal contribution of Boiteux (1951). He assumes that the random variable describing each individual's consumption of the commodity in question is Gaussian (i.e., characterized by a normal distribution). Because Gaussian random variables are described by two parameters–the mean and the variance (or the standard deviation)–knowing any customer's behaviour amounts to knowing these two parameters. Both parameters influence the choice of capacity level in Boiteux's model. Boiteux determines the marginal cost of the mean (demand) and of the standard deviation (of demand).

Boiteux's contribution has been the subject of widespread discussion by Drèze, Kolm, and other scholars. We consider Drèze's analysis of the implications of the

---

arrangements are prohibitive. We return several times to this point when discussing the second-best market environments that are conceivable responses to the fact that markets are incomplete.

[4] This point has also been noted by many scholars working on public utility pricing. For example, Coate and Panzar (1989, p. 305) write: "Such is the world that most utilities find themselves in, since, in general, neither 'spot pricing' nor state-contingent contracts are possible mechanisms for the sale of their (nonstorable) services."

choice between pricing variance and pricing standard deviation. In addition, we present a detailed account of Kolm's contributions to public utility pricing in the presence of stochastic demand. Kolm's model is quite general in the sense that, on the one hand, he considers a large class of cost functions and, on the other hand, he does not assume that the individual demands are uncorrelated. Using this general framework, he determines the price for the mean and the price for the dispersion. In addition, he determines under which conditions marginal cost pricing results in discrimination between customers or a budget surplus. The contributions of Boiteux, Drèze, and Kolm are then contrasted with a popular pricing rule for large electricity and gas consumers known as the Hopkinson (1892) rate. With a Hopkinson rate, part of the amount billed is based on the largest individual peak consumption over the billing period. We show how this method is related to the pricing of the variance or the standard deviation.

In the latter part of this article, we depart from this reduced-form setting and construct a structural market environment which we then use to derive the stochastic behavioural responses of the customers of a public utility. To describe the specific market environment we consider, it is useful to first consider the benchmark case in which buying the commodity on the spot market is the only option. In such a setting, either (a) the price is unregulated and set to match demand and supply ex post or (b) the price is regulated and fixed *ex ante*, in which case some form of rationing may be needed ex post to eliminate any excess demand or supply.[5] In both cases, the public utility must form expectations about the stochastic demand in order to determine (ex ante) the optimal level of capacity. On price flexibility, Drèze (1964, p. 18, footnote omitted, new footnote added) writes:

> Stochastic short-run price variations are frequently ruled out on economic, administrative or legal grounds–and such has almost invariably been the case in the public utilities field. The combination of short-run price rigidity and short-run fluctuations in demand must then result in a combination of (1) some form of demand rationing; and (2) short-run fluctuations in output, to be met either by overloading a plant of flexible capacity or by building an adequate safety margin into a plant of fixed capacity. Both of these consequences are costly–either to the consumers or to the producers. Whenever consumers can reduce the amplitude of the short-run random fluctuations of their demand, it would obviously be desirable that the price structure induce them to do so. The question thus arises: Can some marginal cost (or "welfare loss") be attached to the random variations of an *individual* consumer's demand? If so, can a *non-stochastic* form of price discrimination reflect the marginal cost?[6]

---

[5] As demonstrated by Polemarchakis (1979) for settings involving trade under uncertainty, in the absence of markets for contingent commodities, it may be preferable for prices to be regulated and for markets to be cleared through quantity rationing instead of allowing prices to fluctuate in response to the contingency realised.

[6] Drèze (1964, pp. 18–19, footnotes omitted) also writes:

> A satisfactory answer to that question is still missing, for lack of a workable extension to uncertainty situations of the theories of efficiency and Pareto optimality. Such an extension would indeed be needed in order to specify the *kind* of market prices that could bring about an efficient allocation of resources.

Here, we consider situations in which prices are regulated (ex ante): The public utility commits to a price and sells its product at this price (resulting in a shortage if the planned capacity is insufficient, the planned capacity is sufficient but ineffective due to stochastic shocks, or if the demand is high due to, for example, adverse weather conditions). In addition to the option of buying on the spot market, consumers are offered an opportunity to buy ex ante (i.e., to reserve) some quantity of the commodity at a different price. For this setting, we determine the demand of the customers on both markets in response to the prices posted by the public utility. From the perspective of the public utility, the demand of each customer is stochastic because part of his consumption is made on the spot market. The capacity level is calculated as in Boiteux in order to meet some exogenous liability threshold. We derive the optimal prices on the advance-purchase and spot markets, and compare these prices to those derived by Boiteux and Kolm. The price differential between the advance-purchase and spot markets corresponds to the price of volatility in their model.

The rest of this article is organized as follows. In Sect. 2, we present some of the main contributions from the American literature on public utility pricing and capacity choice when demand is stochastic but not decomposed into individual stochastic demands. Then, in Sect. 3, we discuss Boiteux's seminal contribution when the questions considered in the American literature are formulated in a setting in which the customers can be differentiated according to (some of) the parameters of their stochastic demands instead of being pooled into an aggregate demand. In Sect. 4, we move to Kolm's contribution, which primarily consists of a number of important extensions of Boiteux's model. In Sect. 5, we explain how Boiteux–Kolm prices are related to the Hopkinson rate. In Sects. 6 and 7, we analyse an explicit market environment in which there are both advance-purchase and spot markets for the good supplied by the public utility. Individual stochastic demands are derived and optimal prices are calculated for this model. We then use this framework in Sect. 8 to examine the policy that the French regulatory authority implemented to price access to the natural gas transportation network. Finally, we offer some concluding remarks in Sect. 9.

We believe that Drèze was quite ahead of his time and had a complete set of markets in mind. It is quite fascinating to know that during a workshop held in Paris in 1953, discussions about these and related questions, inspired by Boiteux's seminal 1951 contribution, took place between Allais, de Finetti, Kreweras, Marschak, Wold, and Boiteux himself. As reported by Drèze (1964, p. 19, footnote 73):

> Among other things, Boiteux suggests that each customer might specify with what probability he expects his demand to be met, and what loss he would incur from lack of service; the producer would quote his price as a function of both the probability of service he is willing to guarantee and the penalty he would pay in case of shortage ...

Interestingly, Drèze concludes this sentence by remarking: "[W]hy a public utility should sell insurance (or gambles!) as well as electricity is not altogether clear to me."

2 Aggregate Stochastic Demand

Before turning to the "French" approach to public utility pricing in the following sections, we first examine how the American literature has dealt with this problem and discuss what conclusions have been reached in this literature. The American and French approaches are quite distinct from each other in many ways, the main difference being in the modelling of the demand side of the market. The American literature simply considers the aggregate stochastic demand, rather than the whole profile of individual stochastic demands.[7] This restriction may be viewed as embodying an information assumption about the public utility.

Brown and Johnson (1969) were the first to make a seminal contribution to the problem of public utility pricing when there is aggregate stochastic demand. They considered the case of a public utility that has to determine its capacity z and a vector of prices $p = (p_1, \ldots, p_t, \ldots, p_T)$ for T consecutive periods of equal duration. These periods correspond typically to time partitioning of a basic time period so as to deal with peak load issues. The cost function c for this utility depends on two arguments: the aggregate production q and the capacity z. Costs are assumed to be linear in both of these variables.[8] That is,

$$c(q,z) = \begin{cases} bq + \beta z & \text{if } q \leq z \\ \infty & \text{if } q > z. \end{cases} \tag{1}$$

We denote by $q_t(p_t, u_t)$ the aggregate demand in period t, where u_t is a continuous random variable described by the density $f_t(u_t)$.

In order to simplify the presentation, we assume that $q_t(p_t, u_t)$ exhibits the following multiplicative functional form:

$$q_t(p_t, u_t) = x_t(p_t)u_t,$$

where $x_t(p_t)$ denotes the mean demand in period t; that is,

$$\int_0^{\infty} u_t f_t(u_t) du_t = 1.$$

If we make the extra assumption that the mean demand x_t is linear with respect to p_t, we obtain the situation depicted in Fig. 1, which illustrates the case in which there are three realizations of u_t: 1, $\underline{u}_t$, and $\overline{u}_t$, where $\underline{u}_t \leq 1 \leq \overline{u}_t$.

[7] A nice illustration is provided by Berg and Tschirhart (1988).

[8] This cost specification side-steps many difficulties, the most important being economies of scale. However, we think that this "pedestrian approach"–a phrase borrowed from Drèze (1964)–is rich enough for our purposes, and is an excellent starting point for formulating some basic questions about public utility pricing. We will mostly focus on the pricing of capacity because the allocation of operating (running) costs is obvious with our linearity assumption.

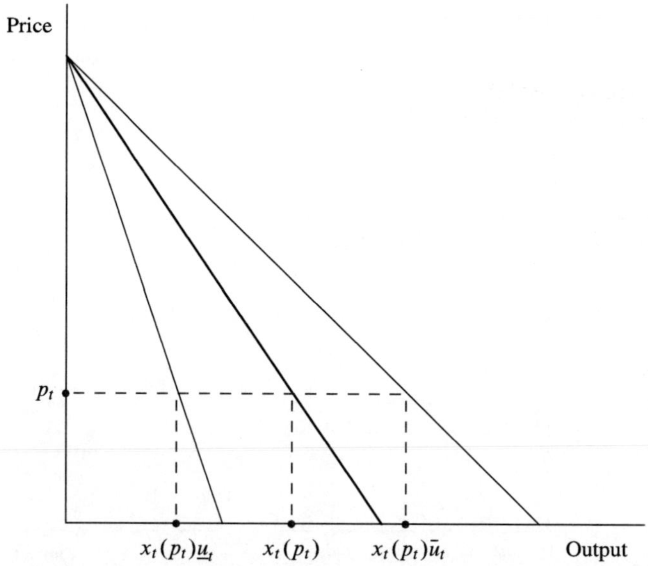

Fig. 1 Linear demand function

Because the production capacity is determined before the resolution of uncertainty, high realizations of u_t leads to a situation of rationing. In Fig. 2, we have represented a situation of excess demand (attached to the realization u_t). If we assume that the rationing is efficient, the area of the triangle L measures the loss in aggregate surplus that results when demand in the amount $x_t(p_t)u_t - z$ is not met.

We assume that the objective of the regulator is the maximisation of the expected net social surplus $E(W)$. This surplus is given by

$$E(W) = E(S - L) + E(R) - E(C),$$

where S, R, and C respectively denote the aggregate consumer surplus, the revenue, and the cost of the public utility. For the specification of cost and demand functions considered here, we obtain:

$$E(S) = \sum_{t=1}^{T}\left[\int_{0}^{\infty} f_t(u_t)\int_{p_t}^{x_t^{-1}(0)} x_t(v)u_t dv du_t\right],$$

$$E(L) = \sum_{t=1}^{T}\left[\int_{\frac{z}{x_t(p_t)}}^{\infty} f_t(u_t)\int_{p_t}^{x_t^{-1}(\frac{z}{u_t})} (x_t(v)u_t - z) dv du_t\right],$$

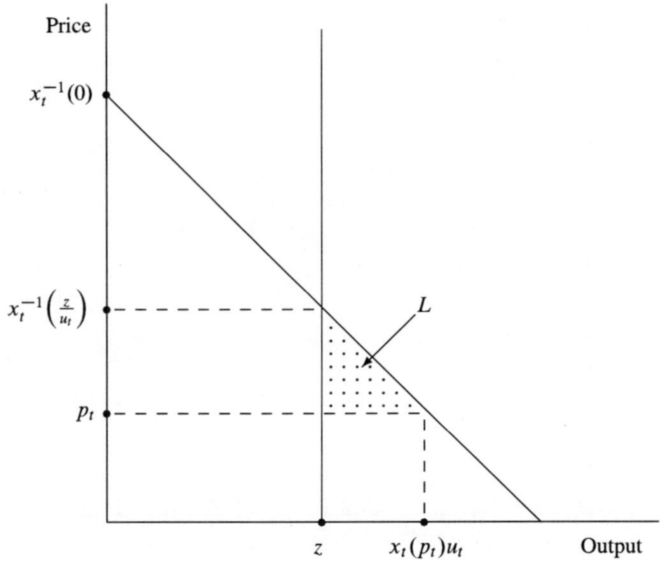

Fig. 2 Aggregate surplus loss

$$E(R) = \sum_{t=1}^{T}\left[\int_0^{\frac{z}{x_t(p_t)}} f_t(u_t)x_t(p_t)u_t p_t d u_t + \int_{\frac{z}{x_t(p_t)}}^{\infty} f_t(u_t)zu_t p_t d u_t\right],$$

and

$$E(C) = \sum_{t=1}^{T}\left[\int_0^{\frac{z}{x_t(p_t)}} f_t(u_t)x_t(p_t)u_t b d u_t + \int_{\frac{z}{x_t(p_t)}}^{\infty} f_t(u_t)zu_t b d u_t\right] + \beta z.$$

Maximisation of $E(W)$ with respect to p and z leads to the following results:

$$p_t^* = b, \quad t = 1, \ldots, T,$$

and

$$z^* > \sup_{1\leq t\leq T} x_t(b+\beta).$$

The first striking conclusion of this analysis is that the price in every period should be set equal to the short-run (i.e., the operating) marginal cost. This conclusion contrasts sharply with optimal pricing in the case of a riskless deterministic demand. This finding appears to be an important argument in defence of the American version of marginal cost pricing. The intuition underlying this result is simple. Consider a price larger than the short-run marginal cost. Either (a) the capacity constraint is not binding, in which case reducing the price is a social improvement, or (b) the capacity constraint is binding, in which case reducing the price leaves the situation unchanged because rationing has been assumed to be efficient.

In a riskless model, capacity is chosen to equal the peak demand when the price is equal to the long-run marginal cost of $b + \beta$. Thus, the second conclusion that follows from the preceding analysis is that the chosen capacity is larger than the capacity selected in the riskless model.

Although it is tempting to do so, attributing the primary responsibility for these conclusions to the random element in the demand would be misleading. Several features of the model play a critical role in the analysis.

First, consider the assumption of efficient rationing. This assumption is not easy to defend here because we have adopted an aggregate perspective and the information needed to organise the rationing of a fixed output efficiently is individual and private. The design of such a procedure is socially costly. From a more positive perspective, we could explore alternative rationing schemes. Visscher (1973) has demonstrated that if we instead suppose that the good or service is offered first to those claimants with the lowest willingness to pay, then the optimal price is equal to the long-term marginal cost and the optimal capacity can be less than the optimal capacity in the riskless case. With the more tenable assumption of purely random rationing, the optimal price lies somewhere between the two marginal costs and the optimal capacity can be smaller than the riskless optimal one, as in the preceding alternative.

The second aspect of the model that deserves to be further analysed is how events with large excess demands are treated ex ante (instead of ex post). In the formulation of Brown and Johnson (1969), there is no constraint imposed on the reliability of the system as measured, for example, by the probability of the event "the aggregate demand is larger than the available capacity."[9] When a public utility provides goods considered to be necessities, placing no constraints on the reliability of the system may be problematic.

There are many different ways to introduce constraints on the regulator in order to ensure reasonable reliability. For example, we can require that

$$P\left[x_t(p_t)u_t \leq z\right] \geq \rho_t, \quad t = 1, \ldots, T,$$

where $P[\cdot]$ denotes the probability of the event in brackets and where the thresholds ρ_t are exogenous. In such a case, the optimal prices maximise

$$E(W) + \sum_{t=1}^{T} \gamma_t \left[\int_0^{\frac{z}{x_t(p_t)}} f_t(u_t) d u_t - \rho_t \right],$$

where γ_t is the Lagrange multiplier attached to the reliability constraint for period t.

[9] We could instead introduce direct penalty costs for excess demands, as in Crew and Kleindorfer (1978).

Meyer (1975) was among the first to follow this route. He obtains the following formula for the optimal prices:

$$p_t^* = b + \gamma_t \left[\frac{\theta_t f(\theta_t)}{x_t(p_t^*)\,[1 - I_t]} \right],$$

where

$$\theta_t \equiv \frac{z}{x_t(p_t^*)} \quad \text{and} \quad I_t \equiv \int_{\frac{z}{x_t(p_t^*)}}^{\infty} u_t f_t(u_t) d u_t .$$

Optimal prices are now larger than those of Brown and Johnson. In fact, there are two ways to ensure that the reliability constraint is met. Either a larger capacity can be built or the price can be increased. Meyer's pricing formula employs a combination of these two solutions. The exact combination chosen depends on the parameters of the problem, one of which is the marginal capacity cost β, which influences the value of the prices through its impact on the value of the Lagrange multipliers.

The third aspect of the Brown–Johnson model that is subject to criticism is the assumption that the demand is independent of the service reliability. This unrealistic assumption needs to be recognised because a reliable product is certainly of higher quality than an unreliable product. This consideration is important ex ante because the level of reliability will influence the decision to invest (or not) in durables or the decision to look for commodities that are close substitutes.

Typically, when this issue is considered, a specification of the aggregate mean demand is used in which the influence of reliability on demand appears in reduced form. That is, aggregate mean demand is a function $x_t(p_t, \rho_t)$, where ρ_t denotes the level of reliability announced by the public utility for period t. With this specification of demand, the optimal prices are derived from the maximisation of $E(W)$ under the following consistency constraints:

$$\rho_t \leq P\left[x_t(p_t, \rho_t) u_t \leq z\right].$$

Thus, the announced risks are never larger than the "real" risks experienced by the customers of the public utility. The optimal prices for this specification of demand have qualitative features similar to those of Meyer.

To the best of our knowledge, only Rees (1980) and Coate and Panzar (1989) have provided structural models to explain (a) why reliability is important and (b) how reliability affects the welfare and the demands of the utility's customers, who could be either households or private firms. To simplify the following discussion, we disregard the seasonal component of demand in order to focus exclusively on the random component; that is, we assume that $T = 1$.

Coate and Panzar (1989) provide a model in which the uncertainty is on the supply side of the market. The main value added of their analysis is that it assumes that the demand behaviour incorporates reliability using rational expectations based on the price and capacity decisions of the public utility. Specifically, to each policy

(p, z), there is a unique reliability level $\rho = \rho(p, z)$ corresponding to it that meets the rational expectations test. The optimal price then satisfies

$$p^* = b + \beta \left[\frac{z}{(1-\rho)x(p^*, \rho)} \right].$$

Note that this price corresponds to the marginal cost when capacity is adjusted so as not to degrade the quality of service. The optimal price equals the sum of the marginal operating cost and the cost of adding enough capacity to serve an additional unit of demand without increasing the probability of service curtailment. The additional capacity required to satisfy this constraint is greater than one unit because adding only one unit would clearly reduce the reliability of the system. It follows that the optimal price exceeds the long-run marginal cost.[10]

Many scholars have criticized, analysed, and extended the Brown–Johnson model.[11] The Brown–Johnson solution results in a deficit, thereby necessitating price adjustments when the public utility faces a budget constraint.[12] Consumers may self ration by purchasing equipment limiting their consumption capacities, for example, by installing fuses to limit the use of electricity.[13] Among the more important extensions, there are those that explore more complicated and sophisticated ex ante contractual possibilities, like, for example, the determination of priority orderings and interruptible rates. To some extent, customers of a public utility are free to choose their own levels of probability of service, that is, their own reliability levels. Interestingly, many of the contributions to this literature depart from the aggregate framework considered up to now and instead consider the preferences of consumers as the primitives.

More complicated cost functions than the one used here might also be considered so as to capture more realistic situations. For example, Chao and Wilson (1987) examine a setting in which each consumer demands at most one unit of the good and has to select a rank in a priority ordering to which is attached two numbers: a monetary payment and a second payment conditional upon actual delivery. The technology of the utility consists of several types of equipment, each described by its own capacity, that can activated in sequence depending upon demand. This equipment is also subject to stochastic shocks. Chao and Wilson compare the solution they obtain for their model to spot pricing and stochastic rationing. Their model, as well as some of the models used to analyse some of the other extensions to the Brown–Johnson model described above, depart significantly from the "one regulated price" model considered in this section.

[10] Note, however, that with constant returns to scale, the public utility exactly breaks even.

[11] See, among others, Carlton (1977), Chao (1983), and Turvey (1970).

[12] See Sherman and Visscher (1978).

[13] See Panzar and Sibley (1978).

3 The Model of Boiteux

In 1951, Boiteux published a pioneering article (Boiteux 1951) describing a market in which each customer of a public utility has a stochastic demand. This leads to an aggregate stochastic demand from the perspective of the public utility. However, nowadays, a public utility is concerned not only with the aggregate stochastic demand, but also with how this demand is decomposed across its customers. Boiteux's model permits such a decomposition. In his model, the utility has n customers, with each customer i choosing a consumption plan over a relevant time period. In each period, customer i's demand is assumed to be a Gaussian (i.e., normal) random variable with mean μ_i and standard deviation σ_i.

As noted by Boiteux himself, the probabilistic description of a random demand depends, in general, on a large number of parameters, and each of them should be subject to a specific pricing rule that depends on its implications for total cost. Boiteux (1951, p. 62) defends his assumptions as follows:

> There can be no question, in fact, of pricing more than two characteristic parameters of the same demand. One of these parameters will be the mean demand, an important characteristic of consumption, the other will be an irregularity parameter chosen in a way to take account of safety margins required by the riskiness of this consumption. In the case of a joint demand comprising a large number of independent (in probability) individual demands, we see that it suffices to know the mean and the "standard deviation" of each individual demand to calculate the sizes to give to the facilities, including the safety margin. This safety margin is smaller when the standard deviations of the individual demands decrease, and is nullified when they are all zero. Hence, one is justified in this case, and, in fact, in most cases, to consider the standard deviation of an individual demand as the irregularity parameter.

On the cost side, Boiteux considers the cost function described by (1) and assumes that $b = 0$ because the treatment of operating costs does not raise any particular difficulty in this case. He also assumes that the public utility facing this stochastic demand must meet an exogenous reliability level ρ fixed by a regulator. The imposition of a reliability constraint has been discussed in the previous section; it is representative of current regulatory practices in some countries.

In general, the computation of these safety margins may be quite complicated. With the assumptions considered by Boiteux, it is easy to show that the capacity that is necessary to serve the profile of demands (μ_i, σ_i), $1 \leq i \leq n$, given the reliability constraint attached to ρ is equal to

$$\sum_{i=1}^{n} \mu_i + \theta(\rho) \sqrt{\sum_{i=1}^{n} \sigma_i^2},$$

where $\theta(\rho)$ is a constant that can be read from a table of the standardized normal density function. Specifically, $\theta(\rho)$ is the unique solution to

$$\int_{-\infty}^{\theta(\rho)} \frac{e^{-\frac{t^2}{2}}}{\sqrt{2\pi}} dt = \rho. \tag{2}$$

Table 1 A sample of values for $\theta(\rho)$

ρ	0.8	0.9	0.95	0.99
$\theta(\rho)$	0.845	1.285	1.645	2.325

A sample of values for $\theta(\rho)$ is shown in Table 1. The total capacity cost is then:

$$C(\boldsymbol{\mu},\boldsymbol{\sigma},\rho) = \beta\left[\sum_{i=1}^{n}\mu_i + \theta(\rho)\sqrt{\sum_{i=1}^{n}\sigma_i^2}\right], \tag{3}$$

where $\boldsymbol{\mu} = (\mu_1, \ldots, \mu_n)$ and $\boldsymbol{\sigma} = (\sigma_1, \ldots, \sigma_n)$.[14]

Boiteux applies the marginal cost pricing principle to derive the price of the mean (demand) and the price of the standard deviation (of demand). For the ith customer, the price of each unit of mean is equal to β, while the price of each unit of standard deviation is equal to

$$\beta\theta(\rho)\left[\frac{\sigma_i}{\sqrt{\sum_{i=1}^{n}\sigma_i^2}}\right].$$

Thus, the total payment made by customer i is equal to

$$\beta\left[\mu_i + \frac{\sigma_i^2}{\sqrt{\sum_{i=1}^{n}\sigma_i^2}}\theta(\rho)\right].$$

Boiteux's prices call for several comments. First, we note that, with these prices, the public utility breaks even.[15] Second, the prices are personalized: The price paid by customer i for one unit of standard deviation depends on his own standard deviation. This conclusion should not come as a surprise because the total cost function for the dispersion in demand is

$$C(\sigma_1, \ldots, \sigma_n) = \beta\theta(\rho)\left[\sqrt{\sum_{i=1}^{n}\sigma_i^2}\right] \tag{4}$$

and, in this equation, the quantity of standard deviation "supplied" to customer i is multiplied by itself.[16] Consequently, once uncertainty has been introduced, the

[14] A lower case c is used for a cost function whose arguments are quantity and capacity, whereas an upper case C is used when the arguments are the stochastic demands, which are characterized by their means and standard deviations. In some cases, an extra argument, which can be capacity or reliability, is also used.

[15] The cost function is homogeneous of degree 1.

[16] Note that (4) is obtained from (3) by subtracting the cost of serving the aggregate mean demand.

commodity supplied by the public utility, which previously was homogeneous, is no longer homogeneous. The marginal cost of supplying customer i is not the same as the marginal cost of supplying customer j whenever $\sigma_i \neq \sigma_j$. We now have a truly multiproduct firm, as in David et al. (2011), with a one-to-one correspondence between each product in their model and each customer here. In terms of their notation, we have $K = n$ and $q_k = \sigma_k$. These idiosyncratic marginal costs are responsible for the personalized prices.

Suppose now that instead of applying the marginal cost pricing principle to derive the price of standard deviation, we use it to derive the price of variance. In this case, the price per unit of variance is the same for each customer and is equal to

$$\beta\theta(\rho)\left[\frac{1}{2\sqrt{\sum_{i=1}^{n}\sigma_i^2}}\right]. \tag{5}$$

The total payment made by customer i is now equal to

$$\beta\left[\mu_i + \frac{\sigma_i^2}{2\sqrt{\sum_{i=1}^{n}\sigma_i^2}}\theta(\rho)\right].$$

The part of his expenditure related to the dispersion or "irrégularité" (irregularity) has been divided by 2 and, hence, the public utility now experiences a budget deficit. Using the multiproduct analogy developed above, we note that with this change of variables, that is, with $q_k = \sigma_k^2$ instead of $q_k = \sigma_k$, the total cost function for the dispersion in demand is now

$$C\left(q_1, q_2, \ldots, q_n\right) = \beta\theta(\rho)\left[\sqrt{\sum_{i=1}^{n} q_i}\right] \tag{6}$$

instead of (4). The cost function given in (6) is not homogeneous of degree 1, but instead exhibits decreasing returns to scale.[17] However, the marginal cost of each product is the same and, for this reason, the prices are now anonymous.

This discussion may create some confusion about what to do. Can we compare the implications from the point of view of allocative efficiency of the two ways of pricing the randomness of demand–either through the standard deviation, as in Boiteux (1951), or through the variance? On this issue, Drèze (1964, p. 21) writes:

[17] Drèze (1964, p. 22, emphasis and footnotes omitted) offers a very lucid explanation of this observation that complements what is said here. After some algebra, he concludes that: "...uncertainty about demand will typically transform (technologically) constant returns to scale into (economically) increasing returns to scale!" This issue highlights the necessity of carefully defining the commodity space, a point discussed extensively in our companion article, David et al. (2011).

> This situation may seem to involve an element of ambiguity; indeed it looks as if the *principle* of marginal cost pricing leaves room for indeterminacy when we come to *applications*. The ambiguity might be obviated by claiming that the combination of marginal cost pricing *and* constant returns to scale should result in a break-even situation–so that [the standard deviation] provides the right pricing formula. ...
>
> Surprisingly enough, a closer look at the problem reveals this choice to be erroneous.

While equally acceptable from the point of view of allocative efficiency, the two solutions differ in terms of whether there is a budget deficit or if there is price discrimination.[18] We could certainly explore further solutions along these lines. For example, multiplying the quadratic pricing formula in (5) by 2 restores budget balance while preserving the anonymity of prices. If we want to price standard deviation subject to an anonymity constraint or to price variance subject to a budget constraint, the application of the general principles presented in David et al. (2011) would lead to a new set of prices.

While simple, the Boiteux model is very instructive and paves the way for many useful generalisations. Boiteux was aware of the limitations of his own work and, as we shall see, has suggested many interesting generalisations himself. One issue that has not yet been dealt with explicitly is the ex post treatment of unsatisfied demands. As already discussed in the previous section, any welfare evaluation needs to obtain some information about consumer preferences. In the Boiteux model, we start with the Gaussian demands without paying attention to the behavioural responses of the customers to variations in prices. Drèze (1964) points out the necessity of considering this response. He formulates the Gaussian demand functions as functions of the two prices and also of the reliability level ρ. Drèze (1964, p. 23, footnotes omitted and using our notation) writes:

> ... questions of existence and uniqueness of the solution remain to be examined. In principle a solution may exist for any [ρ], so that [ρ] must be determined on independent grounds. Indeed, a reduction in [$1-\rho$] may be viewed as an improvement of the quality of the product. ... A market solution would probably exist if the probability of shortage [$1-\rho$] could be varied [together with the price ... attached to variance] from one individual to the next. Short of achieving such flexibility, some estimate of the consumer's surplus associated with variations of [$1-\rho$] would be needed in order to choose a probability of shortage.

The first important extension proposed by Boiteux concerns what he calls the "fourniture non garantie" (interruptible supply). Boiteux (1951, p. 63) writes:

> But, we have neglected a full category of customers, those who, not demanding a guaranteed supply, do not require to be served in all circumstances. Particularly valuable as customers because, ready to stand aside at the time of a random peak in demand, they can, however, contribute to a better use of the safety margin when it is partially unemployed. It is known that particularly beneficial tariffs can be offered to them.

---

[18] Kolm (1970, p. 271) reports that several scholars have reached similar conclusions:

> ... successively Edmond Malinvaud (in a personal letter to Marcel Boiteux) then Jacob Marshak [sic] (in a talk at the Paris conference on risk in 1951), and Jacques Drèze (in his remarkable study of French economists' contributions since the war, for the *American Economic Review*), have observed that pricing dispersion in terms of the variance rather than in terms of the standard deviation, yields an optimal nondiscriminatory price but leads to a budget deficit.

Boiteux (1951, pp. 63–64) offers a very insightful analysis of the pricing issues raised by the introduction of this category of customers in answer to the following question: Should these customers contribute to the financing of the capacity cost and, if so, what is the optimal price for this new service? He was aware that the answer is closely related to the intensity of the demand for the "fourniture non garantie," but he admits that his reasoning and results are not completely rigorous.

Marchand (1974) has extended Boiteux's model in this direction. He assumes that each customer of the public utility selects a consumption plan described by two variables: the mean (as previously discussed) and the maximal consumption (instead of the variance). Each customer can subscribe ex ante to a maximum level of demand (say, individual capacity) and an average demand. Thus, Marchand considers the more complicated situation in which there are a finite number of consumption levels possible ordered in sequence instead of a single reliability level. This sequence describes a priority order of the customers. Interruption of service can happen, but the order must be respected. The allocation of the capacity follows the following ordering: Whenever some capacity is available and customers with priorities up to a particular priority have been served, we move on to the customers with the next highest priority. The aggregate demand for this level of priority is confronted with the residual capacity. If the capacity suffices to cover this demand, we proceed to the next priority level. Otherwise, there is a shortage accompanied with rationing. Of course, given the announced levels of reliability, the public utility invests in a capacity consistent with its announcement. Marchand determines and interprets the optimal prices for this model of interruptible supply.

Aside from the important and natural extension discussed above, Boiteux asserts that his results are robust to some generalisations of his model. On the one hand, the Gaussian assumption about the distribution of the demands could be relaxed without changing substantially the calculation of the capacity. On the other hand, the assumption that individual demands are independent (which is quite unrealistic in many applications) can also be relaxed. However, he does not provide a detailed analysis of these extensions. They are examined in the following sections.

4 Kolm's Generalisations

Kolm (1970, 1971) provides several generalisations of the Boiteux model.[19] Like Boiteux, he considers a public utility with a finite number n of customers, with the demand q^i of customer i being a random variable described by two parameters: its

---

[19] Kolm (1970), while speaking very highly of Boiteux, describes the model of Boiteux (1951) as being a special case of his own general model. Kolm (1970, p. 270) writes:

> In 1950 [sic], Marcel Boiteux, one of the greatest French economists of all time (of whom, having engaged in the process of creating economic science, we cannot refrain from regretting that his talents are now devoted to the production of electricity rather than to economic theory) presented a model that is a particular case [of Kolm's general model].

As an aside, we endorse this complimentary statement.

mean μ_i and its standard deviation σ_i. Kolm (1971, pp. 327–328) defends his point of view as follows:

> A producer generally does not know what demand for his product will present itself to him. This uncertainty is costly because it prevents making the best adjustment of his decisions, and in particular of equipment, to the demand which will be effectively served. The pricing of this product (called "the service") must therefore present to consumers or customers (called users) a bill for their contribution to this uncertainty. This raises the problem of measuring the uncertainty of the quantities demanded. A unique measure of the uncertainty of an uncertain variable is a measure of the dispersion of its potential realisations; it is null when the uncertainty disappears and is positive otherwise. Assuming that this uncertainty is probabilistic, a "natural" measure of this dispersion, and of this uncertainty, is the standard deviation or its square, the variance. Of course, the covariances between the individual consumptions (which is to say of each user) must also generally be taken into account because they affect the dispersion of the global production, which is their sum. Finally, the cost will obviously also depend on the mean values of these quantities.
>
> This chapter [i.e., Chap. 21] and the interpretation of the preceding one for uncertainty differ from the point of view of price setting in that the price paid (or the shadow price considered) is no longer specified according to the contingency but depends on the set of demands in all the contingencies by means of certain functions of this set (these are means or dispersions) less specific in general than the contingent demands themselves. In practice, the price may be fixed according to certain types of consumption to which correspond specific values of these functions. In fact, we consider probabilistic contingencies and these functions are parameters of the probability distribution of the demands. Often, in such a case, these parameters are estimated in practice from observed time series of consumptions at dates in which their joint distributions are assumed to be identical and independent. One can thus estimate the parameters of the different types of consumption sold. But often this calculation takes place for consumptions that are themselves priced, the sum to be paid being calculated, according to a rule known by the customers, after observing these quantities; knowing that his consumptions are recorded and that these parameters are calculated and from them the price he must pay, taking into account, finally, his needs, the user chooses his temporal profile of consumption.

Quite clearly, Kolm acknowledges that the market and pricing environment that he considers is second best. A "first-best" consumption plan would consist of a vector describing the demand for each contingency, "éventualité" in Kolm's terminology. Subsequently, Kolm has shown that such actions are legitimately called for in some circumstances.

Given an ex ante decision z (which can be a capacity as before, but can also receive alternative interpretations), any realisation of the aggregate demand q leads to a total cost equal to $c(q, z)$. If we consider the expected cost as the cost criterion to be considered by the public utility, then, given z, the ex ante total cost is equal to

$$C(\boldsymbol{\mu}, \boldsymbol{\sigma}, z) = \int_{\Omega} c\left(\sum_{i=1}^{n} q^i(\omega), z\right) d\omega,$$

where Ω denotes the set of possible states of the world. Each state $\omega \in \Omega$ is understood to be a complete description of the world once the uncertainty is resolved.

Optimisation with respect to z leads to a function $C(\boldsymbol{\mu}, \boldsymbol{\sigma})$. This function can be expressed as a function $C(\mu, \sigma)$ where μ and σ are, respectively, the mean and the standard deviation of the aggregate demand if, for example, $c(q, z)$ is quadratic or if the aggregate demand only depends on these two parameters. The mean μ is simply the sum of the μ_i, and so only depends on $\boldsymbol{\mu}$. The standard deviation σ depends exclusively on $\boldsymbol{\sigma}$ if the random variables q^i are independent or perfectly correlated. The first of these two situations was the one considered by Boiteux (1951).

When the preceding conditions are satisfied, the marginal cost of mean and the marginal cost of standard deviation (or variance) are well defined. For example, when

$$c(q, z) = c(q) = k_0 + k_1 q + k_2 q^2,$$

where k_0, k_1, and k_2 are parameters depending on z with $k_2 > 0$, we obtain

$$\frac{\partial C(\mu, \sigma)}{\partial \mu} = k_1 + 2k_2\mu, \quad \frac{\partial C(\mu, \sigma)}{\partial \sigma} = 2k_2\sigma, \text{ and } \frac{\partial C(\mu, \sigma)}{\partial \sigma^2} = k_2.$$

Alternatively, we could consider the cost function:

$$c(q, z) = \begin{cases} bq + \beta z & \text{if } q \leq z \\ bq + \beta z + k\,(q - z) & \text{if } q > z, \end{cases} \tag{7}$$

which for $k > 0$ sufficiently large is approximately the cost function (1) used by Boiteux (1951). With this cost function,

$$C(\mu, \sigma, z) = b\mu + \beta z + k \int_z^{\infty} (q - z)\,\phi(q) dq,$$

where $\phi(q)$ is the density function of the aggregate demand. Optimisation with respect to z yields

$$\begin{aligned} C(\mu, \sigma) &= b\mu + \beta z(\mu, \sigma) + k \int_{z(\mu,\sigma)}^{\infty} (q - z(\mu, \sigma))\,\phi(q) dq \qquad (8) \\ &= b\mu + k \int_{z(\mu,\sigma)}^{\infty} q\phi(q) dq, \end{aligned}$$

where $z = z(\mu, \sigma)$ is determined by solving

$$1 - \Phi(z) = \frac{\beta}{k} \equiv 1 - \rho$$

and where Φ is the cumulative distribution function associated with ϕ. The cost function in (8) differs from that of Boiteux because of the presence of the third term.[20] The main differences between this model and the one in Boiteux (1951) are that Boiteux does not optimise with respect to z and he does not assume that the demand must be served *ex post*. Instead, the value of $z(\mu, \sigma)$ is deduced from an exogenous value of ρ.

Kolm (1970) does not consider the cost function given in (7), but instead implicitly uses the following variant:

$$c(q, z) = \begin{cases} bq + \beta z & \text{if } q \leq z \\ bq + \beta z + k & \text{if } q > z, \end{cases}$$

where again k is positive parameter assumed to be very large. Kolm does not compute the expected cost resulting from this technology, but we easily obtain:

$$C(\mu, \sigma, z) = b\mu + \beta z + k(1 - \Phi(z)).$$

Optimisation with respect to z yields

$$C(\mu, \sigma) = b\mu + \beta z(\mu, \sigma) + k(1 - \Phi(z(\mu, \sigma))),$$

where $z = z(\mu, \sigma)$ is determined by solving

$$\Phi(z) = \frac{\beta}{k}.$$

In the Gaussian case, we obtain:

$$z(\mu, \sigma) = \mu + \sigma \sqrt{\ln \left[\frac{k^2}{2\sigma^2 \beta^2 \pi} \right]}.$$

Once the cost function $C(\mu, \sigma)$ is determined, knowledge of the values of $\frac{\partial \mu}{\partial \mu_i}$, $\frac{\partial \sigma}{\partial \sigma_i}$, and $\frac{\partial \sigma^2}{\partial \sigma_i^2}$ is all that is required to apply marginal cost pricing. Of course, $\frac{\partial \mu}{\partial \mu_i} = 1$. In the case of independent demands considered by Boiteux, we obtain:

$$\frac{\partial \sigma}{\partial \sigma_i} = \frac{\sigma_i}{\sigma} \quad \text{and} \quad \frac{\partial \sigma^2}{\partial \sigma_i^2} = 1.$$

In the case of perfect correlation, because $\sigma = \sum_{i=1}^{n} \sigma_i$ when the demands are perfectly correlated, we instead obtain:

$$\frac{\partial \sigma}{\partial \sigma_i} = 1 \quad \text{and} \quad \frac{\partial \sigma^2}{\partial \sigma_i^2} = \frac{\sigma}{\sigma_i}.$$

[20] The second term corresponds to the capacity cost given by (3) in Boiteux's model.

After all of this information has been collected, we can derive the optimal (unit) prices for customer i for the mean, standard deviation, and variance:

$$p_{\mu_i} = \frac{\partial C(\mu,\sigma)}{\partial \mu},$$

$$p_{\sigma_i} = \frac{\partial C(\mu,\sigma)}{\partial \sigma}\frac{\partial \sigma}{\partial \sigma_i},$$

and

$$p_{\sigma_i^2} = \frac{\partial C(\mu,\sigma)}{\partial \sigma^2}\frac{\partial \sigma^2}{\partial \sigma_i^2} = \frac{1}{2\sigma}\frac{\partial C(\mu,\sigma)}{\partial \sigma}\frac{\partial \sigma^2}{\partial \sigma_i^2}.$$

We note immediately that the customers of the public utility face no price discrimination when the utility prices uncertainty using the variance in the case of independent demands and using the standard deviation in the case of perfectly correlated demands. Kolm (1970) should be credited for being the first to make this important observation. Further, as he cleverly observed, the payment of any customer for uncertainty using variance pricing is equal to half the payment using standard deviation pricing when demands are either independent or perfectly correlated. When demands are independent, customer i pays the fraction $\frac{\sigma_i}{\sigma}$ (which is less than 1) of what he pays when demands are perfectly correlated. We deduce that when the public utility prices uncertainty according to the standard deviation of demand, its revenues are twice what it would receive if it instead priced according to the variance when demands are independent or perfectly correlated.

From these observations, it is easy to deduce the implications for the budget of the public utility of these alternative pricing policies for the two demand regimes being considered. Kolm (1970) uses these observations to derive general results when the cost function exhibits constant returns to scale: When standard deviation pricing is used, the public utility breaks even, whereas when variance pricing is used, only half of the total cost resulting from uncertainty is recouped. Kolm provides an exact calculation for the net revenue of the public utility in the quadratic case. He also provides some insights for the case in which the uncertainty is moderate. In such a case, Kolm considers a Taylor expansion of $c(q)$ to the second order around the mean μ as an approximation of $c(q)$. He deduces that:

$$C(\mu,\sigma) = C'(\mu) + \frac{1}{2}C''(\mu)\sigma^2,$$

from which the marginal cost prices follow immediately.

Kolm (1971) provides further analysis of public utility pricing when demand is stochastic. In Chap. 7, he examines this issue when there is what he calls "encombrement stochastique" (stochastic congestion), while Chaps. 19, 20, and 21 contain a more detailed presentation and interpretation of the environment considered in Kolm (1970), which is the environment that has been considered in the preceding discussion. To conclude this section, we would like to briefly comment on these related contributions.

The environment that Kolm calls "encombrement stochastique" is a special case of his general theory. It is discussed extensively in our companion article (David et al. 2011) and calls for the explicit construction of the "fonction d'encombrement" (congestion function). In our companion article, the quality of the service w is measured by the reliability level and we assume that the mean and dispersion parameters of the individual demands are identical and fixed (and therefore beyond the scope of the analysis). It is as if the behaviour of a customer is known to be random with fixed parameters of randomness once he accesses the service. Here, the question is not to price uncertainty, but, instead, to price access to the service.

Consider the case in which the public utility has q customers, where q is treated as a continuous variable, with each customer characterised by a Gaussian demand with mean μ and standard variation σ. The aggregate demand is then a Gaussian random variable with mean μq and standard deviation s equal to σq in the case of perfectly correlated demands and to $\sigma\sqrt{q}$ when the demands are independent. The "fonction d'encombrement" is then:

$$w(q,z) = \Phi\left(\frac{z-\mu q}{s}\right),$$

where, as before, $\Phi(\rho)$ is a constant that can be read from a table of the standardized normal density function. It follows immediately that in the case of perfect correlation, the "fonction d'encombrement" exhibits constant qualitative returns. The situation is more complicated in the case of independence. Straightforward calculations show that

$$\frac{\frac{\partial w(q,z)}{\partial q}}{\frac{\partial w(q,z)}{\partial z}} = -\frac{1}{2}\left(\frac{z}{q}+\mu\right).$$

From this formula, we easily deduce as in Kolm (1971, pp. 121–122) that the qualitative returns depend on the sign of $z - \mu q$. Given the realistic assumption that $z > \mu q$, we infer that in the case of independent demands, the qualitative returns are likely increasing. These calculations, together with the general results obtained by Kolm that are presented in our companion article, provide very sharp predictions about the budget of the public utility. If the marginal cost of z is constant, then a public utility that prices optimally according to marginal cost breaks even in the case of perfectly correlated demands and experiences a deficit equal to half the cost of the capacity safety margin in the case of independent demands.

The ideas discussed by Boiteux, Drèze, and Kolm can certainly be extended in various other directions. We have already mentioned Marchand's analysis of the case in which different levels of liability are offered by the public utility. We could also consider the case of a public utility that is not risk neutral and derive the optimal prices of the first two moments of the stochastic demand in this new context.

5 Implementation: Hopkinson Rates and Related Matters

While discussing Boiteux (1951), we have been very careful to make a distinction between the fluctuations considered here and the seasonal (or daily) periodic fluctuations that motivate traditional peak load pricing, which usually takes the form of time-of-use (TOU) pricing.[21] The implementation of the pricing formulas discussed by Boiteux, Drèze, and Kolm requires the first two moments of the random demand of each customer of the public utility over a given period of time as inputs. We could consider that this period, say a month, is divided into T very small intervals, say quarter-hour intervals, and that the actual consumption of each customer is recorded for each of these T subperiods.[22] For each customer i, let us assume that the consumptions q_t^i in each subperiod $t = 1, \ldots, T$ are identically distributed and independent Gaussian random variables with parameters (μ_i, σ_i). Then, the first two empirical moments constitute good estimates of the true ones. In practice, this raises a number of questions.

First, we must be able to measure the quantities used in the calculation of these parameters because they are used to determine how much the utility bills each of its customers. As noted by Drèze (1995, p. 122):

> ... implementation of efficient economic schemes sometimes requires sophisticated technology. ... [T]his can require unique ways of taking tolls in subways, metering industrial electricity, or charging for road use. Although some of these difficulties have been addressed, research and development in the area have been pursued erratically ...

Boiteux (1951, p. 63) himself has pointed out that the solution could depend on the type of commodity considered:

> Some markets, such as electricity, lend themselves fairly easily to a very detailed invoicing according to the level of irregularity of each individual demand: meters recording the square of the power requested moment by moment, provide the standard deviation, while regular meters indicate the average power. This is, however, an exceptional case. Most markets do not lend themselves, in general, to a differentiation between any categories of subscription, and the regular tariff.

Second, regarding the optimal capacity, Veall (1983) makes the important observation that using the Gaussian distribution when the Gumbel distribution would be more appropriate results in the utility constructing insufficient capacity. This is so because it has not allowed for skewness of the peak demand. To take this skewness into account, instead of considering the standard deviation or the variance of consumption, we could consider the maximal quarter-hour consumption, that is, the individual peak during the month. Veall (1983) investigates this approach.

---

[21] See, for example, Seeto et al. (1997), Woo et al. (1995), Woo et al. (1996), and Woo et al. (2002).

[22] De la Vallée Poussin (1968) adopts this framework and examines the allocation problem in which there are only two prices available to decentralise the decisions of the customers in spite of the fact that there are T different Arrow–Debreu commodities. He derives and interprets the solution of this second-best market environment.

Consider the sequence of aggregate consumptions $(q_1, q_2, \ldots, q_T)$. Then, it can established that the limiting distribution of $q^{\max} \equiv \max_{1 \leq t \leq T} q_t$ for large T is described by the cumulative distribution function G defined by:

$$G(q) = e^{-e^{-\left(\frac{q-l_T}{s_T}\right)}},$$

where

$$l_T = \mu + b_T \sigma \text{ with } b_T \equiv \sqrt{2\ln(T)} - \frac{\ln(\ln(T)) + \ln(4\pi)}{2\sqrt{2\ln(T)}}$$

and

$$s_T = a_T \sigma \text{ with } a_T \equiv \frac{1}{\sqrt{2\ln(T)}}.$$ [23]

Given an exogenous level of reliability ρ, we deduce from $G(z) = \rho$ the capacity

$$z = \mu + k\sigma \text{ with } k \equiv b_T - a_T \ln(-\ln(\rho)).$$

This capacity is different from the mathematical expectation of the peak, which is given by

$$E\left(q^{\max}\right) = \mu + k^e \sigma \text{ with } k^e \equiv b_T + \gamma a_T,$$

where $\gamma \simeq 0.577$ is Euler's constant.

If we take into account a possible correlation η across individual demands, the Boiteux–Kolm prices of customer i are

$$p_{\mu_i} = \beta \quad \text{and} \quad p_{\sigma_i} = \beta k \frac{(\sigma_i + \eta\sigma_{-i})}{\sigma},$$

where $\sigma_{-i} \equiv \sum_{j \neq i} \sigma_j$. Veall characterizes the optimal prices when $q_i^{\max}$ is used instead of σ_i. More precisely, he derives the price $p_{q_i^{\max}}$ to be paid for the peak consumption and the price $\overline{p}_i$ to be paid for mean consumption:

$$p_{q_i^{\max}} = \beta \frac{k}{k^e} \frac{(\sigma_i + \eta\sigma_{-i})}{\sigma} \quad \text{and} \quad \overline{p}_i = \frac{\beta - p_{q_i^{\max}}}{T}.$$

Up to a change in variables, these prices are those derived from the marginal cost pricing principle by Boiteux and Kolm. The key observation is that the pair of Boiteux–Kolm prices resulting from this change of variables corresponds to a rate almost universally used by electric and gas utilities for both large-volume sales on wholesale markets and to their industrial customers, the so-called Hopkinson (1892) rate or tariff. With a Hopkinson rate, each customer is charged both for mean

[23] This distribution is called the double exponential or Gumbel distribution.

(or total) consumption and for peak consumption, as is the case with the prices derived by Veall.

How can we explain that popularity? Veall (1983, p. 428, footnote omitted) suggests that:

> The most likely answer is that it seemed to be a simple method of dividing the capacity costs according to one view of each customer's capacity requirement. The problem, of course, is that the maximum demand charge is based on individual peak demand, which may not be related to the peak system. For example, consider a user whose peak demand is normally at 7:00 A.M. when the system peak is at 7:00 P.M. This user faces an incorrect incentive to use less electricity when there is idle generation capacity, but has no special incentive to reduce usage during the peak period when capacity may be strained.

Suppose, however, that coincident demand (consumption at the time of the system peak) and each customer's peak demand are all outcomes of the same stochastic process. Then, because an individual's peak demand is a function of his variance demand, the Hopkinson rate's maximum demand charge would then be a variance charge used to price each marginal user's effect on system variance and, hence, on optimal capacity. As noted by Veall (1983, p. 428, emphasis omitted, footnote added):

> Although this argument does not provide convincingly support for the Hopkinson rate as commonly applied, it may justify its use in combination with TOU rates when the demand charge is for maximum quarter-hour usage during the "on-peak" period.[24]

The Hopkinson rate has been named after the pioneering British engineer, John Hopkinson, who described this way of pricing electricity in his Presidential Address to the Junior Engineering Society in 1892 (see Hopkinson 1892). He was the very first person to articulate the distinction between fixed and operating costs, and to state explicitly that a customer should pay for both his share of fixed costs and his actual consumption. Charges for fixed costs in his scheme are assessed according to the "connected load," which is the amount of equipment that a customer is connected to. But Hopkinson's equating of maximum demand with the connected load for electricity consumption discouraged customers from installing more lamps than absolutely necessary because they would be forced to pay for this load even if used only rarely. Therefore, electric utility managers turned their attention to the Wright rate introduced by Arthur Wright of the Brooklyn Edison Company. This rate defines maximal demand as a customer's actual maximum during the billing period. A special meter was provided to measure this maximum.[25]

---

[24] Interestingly, this remark appears already in Boiteux (1951, p. 69, emphasis added), who points out in concluding his article that:

> ... extending the preceding results to the case of periodic stochastic demands only introduces expositional difficulties. *Safety margins, as such, are only needed at the time of peak demand, thus what has just been said about constant stochastic demands is no longer valid except in the neighbourhood of peaks, with some qualifications.*

[25] We refer the reader to the fascinating article of Yakubovich et al. (2005), which provides an historical perspective on the development of pricing systems for electricity. The Barstow rate (named

It should be noted that, in both the Boiteux–Kolm–Hopkinson and the "demand" settings, the customers are "invited" to send a signal to the public utility about their real or potential "needs." The lack of coincidence between the two quantities lies in the fact that uncertainty has not been resolved when this signal is requested. Quite sophisticated pricing methods have been proposed to deal with this issue.[26] As an illustration, in Sect. 8, we discuss how the French authority in charge of regulating energy markets has implemented a pricing system for transporting natural gas.

6 Advance-Purchase and Spot Markets: Demand Behaviour

In this and the next two sections, we explore an imperfect market environment that provides a useful description of many existing (regulated or not) industries. Specifically, we consider a setting in which a consumer can buy a good from a public utility in an advance-purchase market and can then supplement this quantity by purchasing more of this good in a spot market in the following period. We assume that prices on both markets are regulated and examine this market environment from a normative perspective. In this section, we develop a simple structural model to analyse consumer demand behaviour in such an environment. In the next section, we derive the prices that maximise the aggregate net social surplus. These prices have a definite flavour of the Boiteux–Kolm prices discussed above: The discount offered for advance purchases is analogous to the premium offered to less volatile consumers in the Boiteux–Kolm setting. Our model is, however, fully specified. The basic primitives of the model are the consumer preferences and information. We then turn to more practical matters in Sect. 8, where we explain why and how these theoretical developments may be useful in analysing the policy implemented by the French regulatory authority for accessing the natural gas pipeline network.

We suppose that at time $t = 0$, a customer of a public utility plans his time $t = 1$ consumption of the good supplied by the utility. For concreteness, and with a view to the application in Sect. 8, we interpret this good as being natural gas. The customer is offered the opportunity to purchase some quantity of this good at $t = 0$ at some unit price $\underline{p}$ and/or to purchase some extra quantity of this good at $t = 1$ at some unit price $\overline{p}$.[27] A customer may prefer to buy part (possibly all) of his total

after William Barstow of the New York Edison Company), a time-of-use rate, was the main alternative considered to the Hopkinson and Wright rates in the 1890s. It is quite interesting to observe that the Wright rate was widely and rapidly adopted at the expense of the Barstow rate.

[26] An interesting overview of the current pricing practices for electricity may be found in Energy and Environmental Economics, Inc. (2006).

[27] The model developed here when applied to the market for natural gas applies exclusively to households. A different model is needed for natural gas demand by firms. See David et al. (2007) for the extension to firm demand.

consumption at time 1 in advance.[28] We assume here that both prices are regulated. As a consequence, for the case in which there is only one ex post regulated price, clearing the market may call for some rationing. In determining the behavioural responses of the customers to a given a pair of prices $(\underline{p}, \overline{p})$, we ignore the risk of rationing on these decisions. Unless $\underline{p} < \overline{p}$, there is no reason for anyone to make an advance purchase (i.e., to reserve some of the good), so we assume that $\underline{p} < \overline{p}$. When $\underline{p} < \overline{p}$, the trade-off for any customer is rather straightforward: He must balance the financial gain attached to reserving some quantity of the good in advance with the informational gain from delaying his decision. The consumption plan of customer i at $t = 0$ consists of two quantities: a quantity $\underline{q}_i$ bought in an advance-purchase market and a quantity $\overline{q}_i$ bought later on a spot market when his needs are properly estimated. This second quantity is a random variable from the ex ante perspective. Henceforth, we assume that the public utility forms perfect expectations about demand.

Our simple model aims not only at explaining what the volume of gas demanded by a consumer will be in reaction to the menu of prices offered, but also how the total demand will be shared between advance-purchase and spot markets. These decisions will depend, of course, on his needs/preferences/values for gas consumption in comparison with other commodities. The key assumption is that the valuation of a consumer depends on information not disclosed at time $t = 0$.

Specifically, we suppose that the public utility has n customers, $i = 1, \ldots, n$, whose behaviour is described as follows. As above, uncertainty is described through a set of states of the world Ω. We now assume that the stochastic influence of the state of the world ω for each client i is binomial: Either the state of the world is favourable to gas consumption at time $t = 1$ or it is not. Thus,

$$\Omega = \prod_{i=1}^{n} \{\underline{\omega}_i, \overline{\omega}_i\},$$

where for all $i = 1, \ldots, n$, $\underline{\omega}_i$ and $\overline{\omega}_i$ are two real numbers such that $\underline{\omega}_i < \overline{\omega}_i$. Without loss of generality, we suppose henceforth that $\underline{\omega}_i = 0$. The state $\overline{\omega}_i$ refers to circumstances unfavourable to gas consumption at time $t = 1$ from the perspective of customer i. The probability of the event $\{\omega_i = 0\}$ is π_i.

Finally, in order to make our partial equilibrium approach meaningful, we assume that the preferences of customer i for gas consumption at time $t = 1$ are described by the quasi-linear utility function

$$v_i(q_i + \omega_i) + M,$$

where v_i is an increasing and strictly concave continuously differentiable function and M denotes the expenditure on other goods. In adopting this specification for the

[28] We can also imagine that the regulator offers service priority to those who make advance purchases but, henceforth, we ignore this dimension of differentiation.

indirect utility function, we are supposing that units can be chosen for describing the state of the world so that the state and gas consumption are perfect substitutes.

In this contractual environment, a consumption plan is a three-dimensional vector $(\underline{q}_i, \overline{q}_i(\underline{\omega}_i), \overline{q}_i(\overline{\omega}_i)) = (\underline{q}_i, \overline{q}_i(0), \overline{q}_i(\overline{\omega}_i))$. With the assumption that customer i is risk neutral, his expected utility for this plan is

$$\pi_i v_i(\underline{q}_i + \overline{q}_i(0)) + (1-\pi_i) v_i(\underline{q}_i + \overline{q}_i(\overline{\omega}_i) + \overline{\omega}_i) - \underline{p}\,\underline{q}_i - \bar{p}(\pi_i \bar{q}_i(0) + (1-\pi_i)\overline{q}_i(\overline{\omega}_i)).$$

We obtain the following first-order conditions for i's optimisation problem:

$$v_i'(\underline{q}_i + \overline{q}_i(0)) = \overline{p} \leftrightarrow v_i'(\underline{q}_i) \geq \overline{p}, \tag{9}$$

$$v_i'(\underline{q}_i + \overline{q}_i(\overline{\omega}_i) + \overline{\omega}_i) = \overline{p} \leftrightarrow v_i'(\underline{q}_i + \overline{\omega}_i) \geq \overline{p}, \tag{10}$$

and

$$\pi_i v_i'(\underline{q}_i + \overline{q}_i(0)) + (1-\pi_i)\, v_i'(\underline{q}_i + \overline{q}_i(\overline{\omega}_i) + \overline{\omega}_i) = \underline{p} \text{ if } \underline{q}_i > 0. \tag{11}$$

If $v_i'(\underline{q}_i) < \overline{p}$ (respectively, $v_i'(\underline{q}_i + \overline{\omega}_i) < \overline{p}$), then $\overline{q}_i(0) = 0$ (respectively, $\overline{q}_i(\overline{\omega}_i) = 0$). Because v_i has been assumed to be strictly concave, it follows that if $v_i'(\underline{q}_i) < \overline{p}$, then $v_i'(\underline{q}_i + \overline{\omega}_i) < \overline{p}$. Therefore, from (9) and (10), if $\overline{q}_i(\overline{\omega}_i) > 0$, then $\overline{q}_i(0) > 0$.

We deduce from these equations that necessarily

$$\overline{q}_i(\overline{\omega}_i) = 0.$$

Indeed, if on the contrary $\overline{q}_i(\overline{\omega}_i) > 0$, because then $\overline{q}_i(0) > 0$, we infer from (9) and (10) that

$$\pi_i v_i'(\underline{q}_i + \overline{q}_i(0)) + (1-\pi_i)\, v_i'(\underline{q}_i + \overline{q}_i(\overline{\omega}_i) + \overline{\omega}_i) = \overline{p},$$

which contradicts (11) because $\overline{p} > \underline{p}$.

The intuition behind this result is fairly simple. Any circumstance that is adverse to gas consumption leads to a decrease in the marginal utility of gas consumption with respect to a reference consumption. In our binary setting, this happens when $\omega_i = \overline{\omega}_i$ and, in this case, it is optimal to purchase the contingent optimal quantity of gas at the lowest possible price, that is, in advance. If, in contrast, the state is such that it favours gas consumption, then the spot market will (likely) be used to make additional purchases.

A direct implication of the preceding observations is that the consumption plan of customer i reduces to a two-dimensional vector $(\underline{q}_i, \overline{q}_i(0))$, that we simply denote by $(\underline{q}_i, \overline{q}_i)$. The first-order conditions are then:

$$\pi_i v_i'(\underline{q}_i + \overline{q}_i) + (1-\pi_i)\, v_i'(\underline{q}_i + \overline{\omega}_i) = \underline{p} \text{ if } \underline{q}_i > 0 \tag{12}$$

and

$$v_i'(\underline{q}_i + \overline{q}_i) = \overline{p} \text{ if } \overline{q}_i > 0. \tag{13}$$

Consumer i finds it optimal to purchase all of his gas in advance if the unique solution $\underline{q}_i$ of

$$\pi_i v_i'(\underline{q}_i) + (1 - \pi_i)\, v_i'(\underline{q}_i + \overline{\omega}_i) = \underline{p} \tag{14}$$

satisfies

$$v_i'(\underline{q}_i) \leq \overline{p}. \tag{15}$$

Similarly, customer i finds optimal to purchase all of its gas on the spot market if

$$\pi_i v_i'(\overline{q}_i) + (1 - \pi_i)\, v_i'(\overline{\omega}_i) \leq \underline{p}, \tag{16}$$

where $\overline{q}_i$ is the unique solution of

$$v_i'(\overline{q}_i) = \overline{p}. \tag{17}$$

Hence, all gas is purchased on the spot market if and only if

$$v_i'(\overline{\omega}_i) \leq \frac{\underline{p} - \pi_i \overline{p}}{1 - \pi_i}. \tag{18}$$

For example, when $\underline{p}$ is smaller than $\pi_i \overline{p}$, we conclude that this cannot happen. The inequality in (18) is less likely to hold when $\underline{p}$ is small, $\overline{p}$ is large, and $v_i'(\overline{\omega}_i)$ is large. In contrast, the effect of π_i is ambiguous.

Finally, consumer i will not purchase gas at all if

$$\pi_i v_i'(0) + (1 - \pi_i)\, v_i'(\overline{\omega}_i) \leq \underline{p} \text{ and } v_i'(0) \leq \overline{p}.$$

Let $\underline{q}_i(\underline{p})$ be the unique solution to equation (14). Inequality (15) then becomes:

$$\overline{p} \geq \frac{\underline{p} - (1 - \pi_i)\, v_i'(\underline{q}_i(\underline{p}) + \overline{\omega}_i)}{\pi_i} \equiv \varphi_i\left(\underline{p}\right). \tag{19}$$

From the implicit function theorem, we deduce that

$$\underline{q}_i'(\underline{p}) = \frac{1}{\pi_i v_i''(\underline{q}_i) + (1 - \pi_i)\, v_i''(\underline{q}_i + \overline{\omega}_i)}$$

and, hence, that

$$\varphi_i'\left(\underline{p}\right) = \frac{1 - \frac{(1-\pi_i) v_i''(\underline{q}_i + \overline{\omega}_i)}{\pi_i v_i''(\underline{q}_i) + (1-\pi_i) v_i''(\underline{q}_i + \overline{\omega}_i)}}{\pi_i} = \frac{v_i''(\underline{q}_i)}{\pi_i v_i''(\underline{q}_i) + (1 - \pi_i)\, v_i''(\underline{q}_i + \overline{\omega}_i)}.$$

It should be noted that if $v_i'(x)$ tends to 0 when x tends to $+\infty$, then $\varphi_i\left(\underline{p}\right)$ tends to 0 when $\underline{p}$ tends to 0. Moreover, rearranging (18) yields the inequality:

$$\overline{p} \leq \frac{\underline{p} - (1 - \pi_i)\, v_i'(\overline{\omega}_i)}{\pi_i} \equiv \psi_i(\underline{p}). \tag{20}$$

The functions φ_i and ψ_i defined in (19) and (20) make it easier to identify the four potential groups of customers: those who do not consume gas, those who consume gas exclusively in advance, those who purchase their gas exclusively on the spot market, and those who use both markets. It is useful to note that these functions intersect at $\underline{p} = \pi_i v_i'(0) + (1 - \pi_i)\, v_i'(\overline{\omega}_i)$, in which case $\varphi_i\left(\underline{p}\right) = \psi_i\left(\underline{p}\right) = v_i'(0)$. The curvature of the function φ_i depends on the monotonicity properties of the coefficient $-\frac{v_i'''(x)}{v_i''(x)}$. The derivation of the functions φ_i and ψ_i is straightforward. For example, when $v_i(x) = -e^{-\lambda_i x}$ with $\lambda_i > 0$, we obtain:

$$\varphi_i\left(\underline{p}\right) = \frac{\underline{p} - (1 - \pi_i)\, \lambda_i e^{-\lambda_i [\underline{q}_i(\underline{p}) + \overline{\omega}_i]}}{\pi_i} \quad \text{and} \quad \psi_i(\underline{p}) = \frac{\underline{p} - (1 - \pi_i)\, \lambda_i e^{-\lambda_i \overline{\omega}_i}}{\pi_i}.$$

At time $t = 1$, the total gas consumption of customer i is the realization of a Bernouilli random variable with mean $\underline{q}_i\left(\underline{p}, \overline{p}\right) + \pi_i \overline{q}_i\left(\underline{p}, \overline{p}\right)$ and standard deviation $\sqrt{\pi_i (1 - \pi_i)}\overline{q}_i\left(\underline{p}, \overline{p}\right)$. If this customer purchases natural gas on both markets, then the determination of his demands can be computed quite simply from the first-order conditions (12) and (13) using the inverse function of v_i', which is henceforth denoted by Ψ_i.

To obtain a complete description of the aggregate demand behaviour, the structure of uncertainty remains to be described. We have assumed that the uncertainty each consumer i faces is described by a Bernouilli model in which the marginal distribution associated with him is characterised by a single number π_i. The aggregate behaviour depends on the joint distribution across customers. For example, in the case of two customers ($n = 2$), a state of the world is described by a vector $\omega \in \{0, \overline{\omega}_1\} \times \{0, \overline{\omega}_2\}$. The joint distribution is defined by the contingency table shown in Table 2.[29] The last row and last column correspond to the marginals. Complete information about the correlation across states is contained in the coefficient r. The circumstances influencing the demand for gas of the two customers

[29] An alternative simple way of modelling the correlation would be to add an extra component to the product space $\prod_{i=1}^{n} \{\underline{\omega}_i, \overline{\omega}_i\}$ (e.g., by letting $\Omega = \{\underline{\theta}, \overline{\theta}\} \times \prod_{i=1}^{n} \{\underline{\omega}_i, \overline{\omega}_i\}$) and then assuming that the joint distribution is the product of the marginals. In such a setting, the uncertainty affecting customer i would consist of two terms: a macroeconomic or climatic term θ together with an idiosyncratic term ω_i. The analysis of the customer i's demand for gas could be conducted as before with $v_i(q_i + \omega_i)$ replaced by $v_i(q_i + \theta + \omega_i)$. However, there are now four distinct states of the world for each customer and the analytics are quite tedious.

Table 2 The joint distribution function when $n = 2$

	0	ϖ_2	
0	$r\pi_1\pi_2$	$\pi_1(1 - r\pi_2)$	π_1
ϖ_1	$\pi_2(1 - r\pi_1)$	$1 - \pi_1 - \pi_2 + r\pi_1\pi_2$	$1 - \pi_1$
	π_2	$1 - \pi_2$	

are independent when $r = 1$, as in Boiteux (1951). In contrast, they are perfectly correlated when $r = \frac{1}{\pi_1} = \frac{1}{\pi_2}$, which is one of the cases considered by Kolm (1970).

In the rest of this article, we limit our attention to the case of independent shocks, that is, only the idiosyncratic risk is taken into consideration. From the perspective of the public utility serving its n customers, the stochastic aggregate demand for gas consumption at time $t = 1$ is therefore the sum of n independent (but not identically distributed) Bernouilli random variables $\widetilde{q}_i$, where

$$\widetilde{q}_i = \begin{cases} \underline{q}_i\left(\underline{p}, \overline{p}\right) + \overline{q}_i\left(\underline{p}, \overline{p}\right) & \text{with probability } \pi_i \\ \underline{q}_i\left(\underline{p}, \overline{p}\right) & \text{with probability } 1 - \pi_i. \end{cases}$$

The aggregate demand consists of a deterministic term $\sum_{i=1}^{n} \underline{q}_i\left(\underline{p}, \overline{p}\right)$ and a random term $\sum_{i=1}^{n} \overline{q}_i\left(\underline{p}, \overline{p}\right)$. The first term is the aggregate advance purchase, while the second term is the aggregate purchase on the spot market. Both terms depend on the two dimensional price policy $\left(\underline{p}, \overline{p}\right)$.

Henceforth, we assume that n is a large number and we replace the exact aggregate demand by its Gaussian approximation.[30] If for some $\delta > 0$,

$$\frac{\sum_{i=1}^{n} \pi_i (1 - \pi_i)\left(\pi_i^{1+\delta} + (1 - \pi_i)^{1+\delta}\right)(\overline{q}_i(\varpi_i))^{2+\delta}}{\left(\sqrt{\sum_{i=1}^{n} \sigma_i^2}\right)^{2+\delta}} \underset{n\to\infty}{\to} 0,$$

we deduce from Lyapounov's central limit theorem that if n is sufficiently large, then

$$q\left(\underline{p}, \overline{p}\right) \equiv \sum_{i=1}^{n} \left(\underline{x}_i\left(\underline{p}, \overline{p}\right) + \overline{x}_i\left(\underline{p}, \overline{p}\right)\right)$$

behaves approximately as a Gaussian random variable $N(\mu, \sigma)$, where

$$\mu = \sum_{i=1}^{n} \mu_i \text{ with } \mu_i = \underline{q}_i\left(\underline{p}, \overline{p}\right) + \pi_i \overline{q}_i\left(\underline{p}, \overline{p}\right), \quad i = 1, \ldots, n, \tag{21}$$

[30] As pointed out by a referee, the use of such approximation calls for further mathematical analysis that is not provided here.

and

$$\sigma = \sqrt{\sum_{i=1}^{n} \sigma_i^2} \text{ with } \sigma_i = \sqrt{\pi_i(1-\pi_i)}\overline{q}_i\left(\underline{p}, \overline{p}\right), \quad i = 1, \ldots, n. \tag{22}$$

7 Advance-Purchase and Spot Markets: Optimal Public Utility Pricing

We are now in a position to derive the optimal "Gaussian" prices for our model. By optimal, here we mean prices that maximise the social objective function defined as the sum of the aggregate net surplus of the customers and the net revenue of the public utility. We do not consider here the issues raised by a budget deficit or the cost of public funds.[31] On the cost side, we proceed as in Boiteux (1951); that is, we assume that there is an exogenous level of reliability ρ and that the capacity z is determined so as to provide this quality of service.

Substituting (21) and (22) into (3), the total capacity cost is

$$\beta\left[\sum_{i=1}^{n}\left(\underline{q}_i\left(\underline{p}, \overline{p}\right) + \pi_i \overline{q}_i\left(\underline{p}, \overline{p}\right)\right) + \theta(\rho)\sqrt{\sum_{i=1}^{n} \pi_i(1-\pi_i)\overline{q}_i^2\left(\underline{p}, \overline{p}\right)}\right].$$

The public utility's optimisation problem is then:

$$\max_{\underline{p}, \overline{p}} \sum_{i=1}^{n}\left[\pi_i v_i(\underline{q}_i\left(\underline{p}, \overline{p}\right) + \overline{q}_i\left(\underline{p}, \overline{p}\right)) + (1-\pi_i)v_i(\underline{q}_i\left(\underline{p}, \overline{p}\right) + \overline{\omega}_i)\right]$$
$$-\beta\left[\sum_{i=1}^{n}\left(\underline{q}_i\left(\underline{p}, \overline{p}\right) + \pi_i \overline{q}_i\left(\underline{p}, \overline{p}\right)\right)\right] - \beta\theta(\rho)\left[\sqrt{\sum_{i=1}^{n} \pi_i(1-\pi_i)\overline{q}_i^2\left(\underline{p}, \overline{p}\right)}\right].$$

With the symmetry assumption that $\pi_i = \pi$ for all $i = 1, \ldots, n$, it can be demonstrated that the optimal pricing policy $(\underline{p}^*, \overline{p}^*)$ is the solution of the following pair of equations:

$$\underline{p}^* = \beta + (1-\pi)\left(\overline{p}^* - \beta\right) - \left[\frac{\beta\theta(\rho)\sqrt{\pi(1-\pi)}A(\underline{p}^*, \overline{p}^*)}{B(\underline{p}, \overline{p})\sqrt{\sum_{i=1}^{n}(\overline{q}_i(\overline{\omega}_i)(\underline{p}, \overline{p}))^2}}\right] \tag{23}$$

[31] The calculation of the Ramsey–Boiteux prices in this context can be obtained from the authors upon request.

and

$$\overline{p}^* = \beta + \left[\frac{\pi\beta\theta(\rho)}{\sqrt{\pi(1-\pi)}}\right]\left[\frac{C(\underline{p}^*, \overline{p}^*)}{D(\underline{p}^*, \overline{p}^*)\sqrt{\sum_{i=1}^{n}(\overline{q}_i(\overline{\omega}_i)(\underline{p}^*, \overline{p}^*))^2}}\right], \tag{24}$$

where

$$A(\underline{p}, \overline{p}) \equiv \sum_{i=1}^{n} \Psi_i'\left(\frac{\underline{p} - (1-\pi)\overline{p}}{\pi}\right)\overline{q}_i(\overline{\omega}_i)(\underline{p}, \overline{p}),$$

$$B(\underline{p}, \overline{p}) \equiv \sum_{i=1}^{n} \Psi_i'\left(\frac{\underline{p} - (1-\pi)\overline{p}}{\pi}\right),$$

$$C(\underline{p}, \overline{p}) \equiv \sum_{i=1}^{n} \Psi_i'(\overline{p})\overline{q}_i(\overline{\omega}_i)(\underline{p}, \overline{p}),$$

and

$$D(\underline{p}, \overline{p}) \equiv \sum_{i=1}^{n} \Psi_i'(\overline{p}).$$ [32]

The price equations in (23) and (24) are complicated and not easy to interpret in this general framework in which no limits on the heterogeneity across consumers have been imposed.

In the fully symmetric case, that is, with the extra assumption that for all $p > 0$,

$$\Psi_i'(p) = \Psi_j'(p) \text{ and } \overline{\omega}_i = \overline{\omega}_j, \quad i, j = 1, \ldots, n,$$

from (23) and (24), we obtain the following simple formulas for the optimal prices:

$$\underline{p}^* = \beta \tag{25}$$

and

$$\overline{p}^* = \beta + \frac{\sqrt{\pi}\beta\theta(\rho)}{\sqrt{n}\sqrt{(1-\pi)}}. \tag{26}$$

Formula (25) is transparent: The capacity component of the price of gas on the advance-purchase market is exactly equal to the marginal cost of capacity. Therefore, (25) and (26) imply that the price differential between the advance-purchase and spot markets (expressed in ratio form) is

$$\frac{\overline{p}^*}{\underline{p}^*} = 1 + \frac{\theta(\rho)}{\sqrt{n}}\sqrt{\frac{\pi}{1-\pi}}.$$

[32] The details of the proof are available from the authors upon request. In earlier sections, π stood for the number π. It shall always be clear from the context whether π is this number or a common probability.

The second term reflects the premium offered to a consumer who buys his gas on the advance-purchase market. By (2), $\theta(\rho)$ is an increasing function. Thus, the magnitude of this premium increases with the safety margin ρ and with the probability π that the true state is one that is unfavourable to gas consumption. However, this premium declines with the number of customers.[33] This finding is not surprising because when shocks are independent, the case considered here, the uncertainty decreases when the number of observations increases.

These second-best prices inherit some of the features of marginal cost prices. In fact, they are quite similar to Boiteux–Kolm prices. To some extent, $\underline{p}^*$ is analogous to the price of average consumption, whereas $\overline{p}^* - \underline{p}^*$ is analogous to the price of dispersion.

Our general pricing formulas (23) and (24) have been derived using the weak symmetry assumption that π_i is independent of i in order to eliminate ex ante differences across clients other than their tastes. Nevertheless, the pricing formulas are not simple in spite of this step towards homogeneity in the customer base of the public utility. This complexity is due to the idiosyncratic impacts of the ex post realizations of the states ω_i on the public utility's costs. Because the price $\overline{p}$ is uniform, by assumption, it cannot accommodate differences in costs arising in this way.[34] It follows from (23) and (24) that

$$\overline{p}^* - \underline{p}^* = \left[\frac{\beta\theta(\rho)}{\sqrt{\sum_{i=1}^{n}(\overline{q}_i(\overline{\omega}_i)(\underline{p}^*,\overline{p}^*))^2}}\right] \times \left[\frac{\sqrt{\pi(1-\pi)}A(\underline{p}^*,\overline{p}^*)}{B(\underline{p}^*,\overline{p}^*)} + \frac{\pi^2 C(\underline{p}^*,\overline{p}^*)}{D(\underline{p}^*,\overline{p}^*)\sqrt{\pi(1-\pi)}}\right].$$

Thus, the difference between the price of gas on the spot market and the corresponding price on the advance-purchase market captures the idiosyncratic costs described above.

To get a better understanding of the parameters that have an influence on the determination of these prices, consider the following simple asymmetric setting. There are two groups of customers, with n^l identical individuals ($l = 1, 2$) in each group. That is,

$$\pi_i \equiv \pi^1,\ v_1 \equiv v^1,\ \overline{\omega}_i \equiv \overline{\omega}^1, \quad i = 1, \ldots, n^1.$$
$$\pi_j \equiv \pi^2,\ v_j \equiv v^2,\ \overline{\omega}_j \equiv \overline{\omega}^2, \quad j = 1, \ldots, n^2.$$

---

[33] We could also interpret this premium in the context of the pricing of transport services (e.g., airlines or railways). A discount is offered to a consumer buying his ticket well in advance compared with the price paid by him for buying his ticket at the last minute.

[34] It is common in the literature to adopt this uniformity or nondiscrimination constraint as a second-best constraint (e.g., Kolm 1970). The optimal price is obtained from the minimisation of a weighted average of the distortions.

For an interior solution, the first-order conditions for the public utility's optimisation problem imply that

$$\left(\underline{p}-\beta\right)\left[\gamma e^1+e^2\right]-\left(\overline{p}-\beta\right)\left[\gamma\pi^1 e^1+\pi^2 e^2\right]$$
$$=-\beta\theta(\rho)\left[\frac{\gamma^2\pi^1 n^2(1-\pi^1)\beta_1 e^1+\pi^2\beta_2 n^1(1-\pi^2)e^2}{\sqrt{n^1\left(n^2\right)^2\pi^1(1-\pi^1)\left(\beta_1\right)^2\gamma^2+n^2\left(n^2\right)^2\pi^2\left(\beta_2\right)^2(1-\pi^2)}}\right]$$
$$=-\beta\theta(\rho)\left[\frac{\frac{\gamma^2\pi^1(1-\pi^1)\beta_1 e^1}{n^1}+\frac{\pi^2\beta_2(1-\pi^2)e^2}{n^2}}{\sqrt{\frac{\pi^1(1-\pi^1)(\beta_1)^2\gamma^2}{n^1}+\frac{\pi^2(\beta_2)^2(1-\pi^2)}{n^2}}}\right]$$

and

$$\left(\underline{p}-\beta\right)\left[\gamma f^1+f^2\right]+\left(\overline{p}-\beta\right)\left[\gamma\pi^1\alpha^1 g^1+\pi^2\alpha^2 g^2\right]$$
$$=\beta\theta(\rho)\left[\frac{\gamma n^2\pi^1(1-\pi^1)\left(\alpha^1\right)^2 g^1+\pi^2 n^1(1-\pi^2)\left(\alpha^2\right)^2 g^2}{\sqrt{n^1\left(n^2\right)^2\pi^1(1-\pi^1)\left(\alpha^1\right)^2\gamma^2+n^2\left(n^2\right)^2\pi^2\left(\alpha^2\right)^2(1-\pi^2)}}\right]$$
$$=\beta\theta(\rho)\left[\frac{\frac{\gamma^2\pi^1(1-\pi^1)\left(\alpha^1\right)^2 g^1}{n^1}+\frac{\pi^2\left(\alpha^2\right)^2(1-\pi^2)g^2}{n^2}}{\sqrt{\frac{\pi^1(1-\pi^1)\left(\alpha^1\right)^2\gamma^2}{n^1}+\frac{\pi^2\left(\alpha^2\right)^2(1-\pi^2)}{n^2}}}\right],$$

where for $i=1,2,$

$$\gamma\equiv\frac{n^1\underline{q}^1\left(\underline{p},\overline{p}\right)}{n^2\underline{q}^2\left(\underline{p},\overline{p}\right)},\quad \alpha^i\equiv\frac{\overline{q}^i\left(\underline{p},\overline{p}\right)}{\underline{q}^i\left(\underline{p},\overline{p}\right)},\quad e^i\equiv\frac{\partial\underline{q}^i\left(\underline{p},\overline{p}\right)}{\partial\underline{p}}\frac{\underline{p}}{\underline{q}^i\left(\underline{p},\overline{p}\right)},$$
$$f^i\equiv\frac{\partial\underline{q}^i\left(\underline{p},\overline{p}\right)}{\partial\overline{p}}\frac{\overline{p}}{\underline{q}^i\left(\underline{p},\overline{p}\right)}\partial\overline{p},\quad\text{and}\quad g^i\equiv\frac{\partial\overline{q}^i\left(\underline{p},\overline{p}\right)}{\partial\overline{p}}\frac{\overline{p}}{\overline{q}^i\left(\underline{p},\overline{p}\right)}\partial\overline{p}.$$

David et al. (2007) refer to these equations as the fundamental price equations because they provide the optimal second-best distorsions between the prices and the marginal capacity cost. They highlight the relevant parameters: γ, which measures the market shares of the two groups; α^1 and α^2, which measure the ratio of the volumes of transactions on the two markets for the two groups of customers; the different cross and direct price elasticities e^1, e^2, f^1, f^2, g^1, and g^2; and the volatility of the demands of the two groups as measured by the parameters π^1 and π^2.

It is important to observe that the parameters in these equations are not all logically independent because they are related through the first-order conditions of the customers' optimisation problems. For example, we always have

$$f^i = -\pi^i e^i, \quad i = 1, 2.$$

Furthermore, these equations do not provide us with a closed-form analytic solution because the parameters may depend on the prices $\underline{p}$ and $\overline{p}$. As a consequence, these nonlinear equations may be quite complex.

If $\pi^1 = \pi^2 \equiv \pi$, $\alpha^1 = \alpha^2 \equiv \alpha$, $e^1 = e^2 \equiv e$, and $g^1 = g^2 \equiv g$, then the only source of asymmetry is the market shares of the two groups. In this case, the system of price equations simplifies as follows:

$$\begin{pmatrix} e\,(\gamma+1) & -\pi e\,(\gamma+1) \\ -\pi f\,(\gamma+1) & \pi\alpha g\,(\gamma+1) \end{pmatrix} \begin{pmatrix} \underline{p}-\beta \\ \overline{p}-\beta \end{pmatrix} = \beta\theta(\rho) \begin{pmatrix} -\sqrt{\pi(1-\pi)}e \left[\dfrac{\frac{\gamma^2}{n^1}+\frac{1}{n^2}}{\sqrt{\frac{\gamma^2}{n^1}+\frac{1}{n^2}}} \right] \\ \alpha\sqrt{\pi(1-\pi)}g \left[\dfrac{\frac{\gamma^2}{n^1}+\frac{1}{n^2}}{\sqrt{\frac{\gamma^2}{n^1}+\frac{1}{n^2}}} \right] \end{pmatrix},$$

from which we obtain:

$$\underline{p} = \beta$$

and

$$\overline{p} = \beta + \beta\theta(\rho)\sqrt{\frac{(1-\pi)}{\pi}}\,\frac{\sqrt{\frac{\gamma^2}{n^1}+\frac{1}{n^2}}}{(\gamma+1)}.$$

The latter expression can be alternatively expressed as

$$\overline{p} = \beta + \beta\theta(\rho)\sqrt{\frac{(1-\pi)}{\pi}}\,\frac{\sqrt{n^1E^2+n^2}}{n^1E+n^2},$$

where $E \equiv \underline{q}^1\left(\underline{p},\overline{p}\right)/\underline{q}^2\left(\underline{p},\overline{p}\right)$. That is, $\overline{p}$ is expressed in terms of the ratio E of the average consumptions in each group instead of the ratio γ of the aggregate consumptions in each group.

The second-best environment considered here is complex because there are some contingent markets missing. Furthermore, the impossibility of employing price discrimination between customers provides an additional constraint on the regulator. As a consequence of the general second-best principle, the creation of additional distortions may be optimal. Thus, the derived departures from marginal cost pricing should not come as a surprise.

The market environment considered in this and the preceding section could be augmented in several directions.[35] If we consider, for example, airline bookings, consumers are typically offered a large spectrum of options beyond the simple binary choice considered here. This specific market incompleteness and the issues raised by the assumption that demand is stochastic have received significant attention in the industrial organisation literature. When there are only spot markets, many suppliers face stochastic demand but are forced to precommit on price and capacity.[36] For such situations, several concepts of competitive equilibrium have been developed that predict price dispersion in equilibrium: Firms with high prices sell their capacity only in the event of large demand, while firms with low prices sell their capacity in all circumstances.[37] The same environment has been analysed using various models of imperfect competition, including the limiting case of a monopoly.[38] The consequences of permitting advance-purchase discounts have also been examined in situations of perfect and imperfect competition.[39]

8 Some Lessons for the Regulation of the French Natural Gas Transportation Industry

In this article, we have often alluded to the practical concerns and issues that have motivated theoretical developments on public utility pricing and regulation. In this section, we consider some of the practical lessons that emerge from our theoretical analysis by discussing the regulation of the natural gas pipeline transportation industry in France.

With the liberalisation of markets, a significant transformation of the natural gas industry has occurred worldwide in recent decades. According to Doane et al. (2004), this process has been primarily facilitated by the issuance of two orders from the Federal Energy Regulatory Commission (FERC) in the United States.[40]

[35] Diamond (1980), for example, mentions the use of a futures market when he analyses what institutions could improve the inefficiency resulting from the fact that trades are not contingent on the state of nature.

[36] Both precommitment to prices and capacities and demand uncertainty are central features of many industries in addition to the regulated industries considered in this article.

[37] The key equilibrium concept is due to Prescott (1976). For further analysis, the reader may consult, for example, Carlton (1978, 1979, 1991), Dana (1999), and Eden (1990).

[38] See, for example, Dana (2001), Deneckere and Peck (1995), and Wilson (1988).

[39] See, for example, Dana (1998) and Gale and Holmes (1992, 1993).

[40] Several studies had already analysed the U.S. regulatory policy for natural gas pipeline companies that was in force in the 1960s and 1970s. See, for example, Callen (1978), McAvoy and Noll (1973), and Wellisz (1963). Among its other provisions, under the Natural Gas Act of 1938, sales to public utilities are treated differently from industrial sales. The regulatory policy calls for an allocation of the overhead cost between these two categories of users. The studies cited above have examined the behavioural implications for pipeline operators of the empirical rule (the Atlantic Seaboard Formula) selected for this purpose.

FERC Order No. 436, released in 1985, encouraged pipeline companies to separate their sales and transportation functions; this order also established rules to govern open access. FERC Order No. 636, released in 1992, required operators of interstate pipelines to unbundle their gas and transportation functions, to cease selling bundled gas supplies, and to provide comparable transportation to all shippers, regardless of whether the shipper had also purchased gas from them. In the European Union, following the 1998 directive, a similar deregulation process was initiated.[41] Unsurprisingly, the accounting issues related to unbundling and issues related to providing access to the pipeline network have attracted most of the attention of regulators. Questions dealing with pricing and investing in capacity are the most prominent. While not specific to this industry, the determination of the structure of prices imposed by a regulator on the "authorised" users to obtain access to the pipeline network raises some specific difficulties that call for an appropriate analysis.

One of our main concerns has been to provide a normative framework for evaluating some features of the policy implemented by the Commission de Régulation de l'Energie (CRE), which is the French agency regulating energy markets, for allocating and pricing access to the existing pipeline capacity across the different firms permitted to deliver natural gas to customers located on French territory.[42] The CRE has implemented "un tarif d'utilisation des réseaux de distribution de gaz naturel" (a user's tariff for local natural gas distribution networks). There are several such local networks, but only one global distribution network. A local network is used by a public utility to deliver natural gas to wholesale customers who are served by this network or by large end users who may get direct access to it. The CRE's policy is multidimensional. We examine one of these dimensions, one that is related to the theoretical framework developed in this article. Henceforth, we abusively identify capacity with transportation capacity ("capacité de liaison" in French), ignoring for the moment entry, exchange, exit, and storage capacities, and consider the case of a single local network.

---

[41] In contrast to the regulatory policy of the United States, no market-based rate proposals submitted by natural gas pipeline companies have been considered in the European Union. For an analysis of the theoretical consequences of the role of excess capacity in such a regulatory setting, see McAfee and Reny (2007).

The European market is active: The growth rate in consumption of natural gas is about 2% per year and the total consumption in the European Union was about 493 Gm^3 in 2005. More data about the relative weight of natural gas consumption in aggregate energy consumption by residential, commercial, and industrial customers; about trends for the coming decade; and policy statements about the effectiveness of the current regulations may be found on the websites of the various regulators.

[42] The reader who wishes to gain more detail about the financial and institutional aspects of the current system may consult the website of the CRE (http://www.cre.fr), as well as that of the public utility that is the main operator of the pipeline network (http://www.gazdefrance-reseau-transport.com). A detailed description of the regulatory process and its evolution may be found in Commission de Régulation de l'Energie (2006).

Any supplier of natural gas who wants to use this capacity faces a menu consisting of several tariffs for pricing the use of a local network.[43] The menu mostly consists of traditional two-part tariffs, but it includes one three-part tariff. When an supplier makes its decisions, it must determine how much daily capacity is "needed" in order to deliver natural gas to its customers. Besides deciding on the capacity needed, the supplier must decide on whether to reserve transportation capacity on an annual ("terme de souscription annuelle de capacité journalière"), monthly ("souscription mensuelle de capacité journalière"), or daily basis. The regulated prices specify how much it costs to reserve a unit of daily capacity for the term of the contract. These prices differ according to the length of the reservation selected. On average, the price charged for a monthly reservation is equal to 1/8 of the corresponding price for an annual reservation.[44] Similarly, the price for a daily reservation is equal to 1/20 of the corresponding price for a monthly reservation. In both cases, the price for a unit of daily capacity increases by 50% when the length of the contract decreases, that is, using our notation: $\overline{p}/\underline{p} = 3/2$.

A supplier may be reluctant to make advance reservations when the consumption of many of its customers exhibits great volatility, preferring instead to delay reserving capacity and to wait until its exact demand is known. The trade-off between the advance-purchase and spot contractual arrangements is the one described in the theoretical model developed in the preceding two sections, except for the fact that there are actually three markets, not two. In our theoretical model, we have not accounted for contracts that allow for service to be interrupted. There are some sophisticated rules to sequentially allocate the existing capacity given the reservations made.

The basic payment described above is subject to adjustment because a customer's consumption is not limited to the amount reserved. Each month, the operator of the distribution network (a public utility) records the daily differential between the actual consumption and the amount reserved if this differential exceeds 5% of the reserved capacity. The differential for a month is the sum of (a) the largest daily differential and (b) 10% of the sum of the recorded daily differentials. The network operator imposes a penalty on a customer whenever this number exceeds 5% of the reserved daily capacity, calculated as follows. The penalty per unit of capacity is equal to twice the monthly reservation price for the part of the differential between 5 and 15% of the reserved capacity and to four times the monthly reservation price for the part of the differential above 15% of the reserved capacity.

It would be of interest to contrast the choice of prices by the CRE with the optimal prices derived using our theoretical normative approach. To do so requires estimating the main parameters in our formulas. However, as should be obvious, our whole theory is based on competitive price-taking behaviour by the users of the network. However, the current market situation is imperfectly competitive, with the regulated prices for access to the transportation network serving as costs for the

[43] In December 2005, the French government approved the tariffs proposed by the CRE. See Commission de Régulation de l'Energie (2006) for a detailed discussion of these tariffs.

[44] The price for a unit of daily capacity reserved on a monthly basis varies with the time of year. For example, the monthly rate in December is 4/12 times the annual rate.

suppliers delivering natural gas to end users. Understanding the consequences of the market power of these suppliers on final prices is important for deriving optimal prices that take account of the extra distortions introduced by the noncompetitive nature of the markets.

9 Concluding Remarks

Further research on public utility pricing and capacity choice when there is stochastic demand should examine the implications of allowing for more sophisticated contractual arrangements, such as different forms of contingent contracts. For example, in 1985, Electricité de France (EDF), the French electric company, decided to propose contracts that stipulated the number of days (actually 22 days) when peak-load prices would be charged to its large customers. This policy left open the actual dates, which were announced by EDF on short notice based on prevailing conditions. As noted by Drèze (1995, p. 118):

> From a theoretical viewpoint, these developments correspond to state-contingent pricing, with an implicit insurance contract limiting the frequency of peak prices. ... However, I am not aware of a theoretical analysis validating *precisely* that arrangement, as opposed to alternative second-best candidates.

Another form of contingent forward delivery contracts, priority service (Chao and Wilson 1987) specifies the customer's service order of priority: In each contingency, the public utility rations supplies by serving customers in order of their selected priorities until the supply is exhausted or all customers are served. Theorists and practitioners have discussed other types of contractual arrangements, but as Drèze (1995, p. 119, footnote added) has noted:

> These analyses are still in infancy: the papers that I know do partial equilibrium analysis under assumptions of risk neutrality. Some day, these papers will be viewed as early illustrations of a general equilibrium analysis that includes uncertainty and incomplete markets.[45]

Kolm (1971, Chap. 19) offers a very insightful classification of pricing schemes under the heading "Taxonomie de la Tarification de l'Incertitude" (Taxonomy of the Pricing of Uncertainty). He provides a comparison of the variety of pricing environments that could be considered (or are used) when demand is stochastic. In particular, Kolm (1971, p. 308, footnote added and using our notation) writes:

> It is interesting to note that the nature of the agent whose information is tainted by the uncertainty being considered (particularly the Service or some user) does not matter in order to describe the logic of price setting in all cases in which it is sufficient for that [purpose] to consider *contingent* services, that is, linked in their definition to contingencies.[46] ...

---

[45] See, for example, Spulber (1992a,b) and Wilson (1993) for more theory and examples.

[46] "Service" refers to the organisation that provides the service in question (e.g., the Electric Service).

> The objects of the price setting are the quantities $[q^i_j]$ of the service consumed by the users i in the contingencies j. A price schedule offered to user i is a function of these quantities for this i, representing the amount that he must pay if he chooses this consumption. However this price setting can be accomplished in different ways.

Kolm discusses nine different pricing schemes. The first simply modifies the complete set of markets à la Arrow–Debreu by allowing for personalised non-linear prices. The next three are variants of it. Kolm's second scheme forbids ex ante sales: The effective payment takes place ex post once the actual consumption q^i_j is known. However, the function T^i_j specifying the price to the ith user in the jth contingency as a function of the quantity q^i_j can be defined *ex ante*. Kolm's fifth scheme introduces the possibility of purchasing a specific quantity, or an upper bound ξ^i on that quantity, regardless of the contingency that is realized; the pricing function is then simply a function T^i.[47] Comparing the optimal regulated prices for the different ways of pricing uncertainty considered by Kolm is a promising area of research.

We have seen that the literature on public utilities has explored the principles and rules for optimally investing in capacity in various market environments. Indeed, a public utility has to decide ex ante how much to invest in different kinds of equipment, which determine what capacities are possible and, more generally, what it costs to meet the different possible realisations of demand. Given the multi-product nature of a public utility, arising from qualitative as well as temporal, locational, and contingent characteristics, these capacities are used in the production of several (if not all) of its products. Choosing these joint inputs is a key decision. As pointed out by Kolm (1970, pp. 244–245):

> One of our main interests will be to determine the optimal choice between the costs that serve the production of several varieties, which are shared, and others that are specifically associated with each of them. ... When a model of uncertainty is applied, a shared cost is chosen *ex ante*, before the demand is known, and a specific production cost is a cost chosen *ex post*, knowing the demand to be served.

Once these decisions have been made, the situation (ex post) may be unsatisfactory, either because there is an excess capacity at the given price or because there is an excess demand resulting in the need for rationing.[48] In any case, the existence of excess capacity should not be interpreted as a sign of poor management, but instead as the optimal response of a public utility to the stochastic demand given the constraints on its pricing instruments.

It would be misleading to consider demand randomness as the only rationale for maintaining excess capacity. Boiteux (1951, pp. 57–61) provides a very insightful

---

[47] We refer the reader to Kolm (1971) for a complete presentation of these alternative pricing schemes.

[48] The concept of "capacity" refers to the limiting case in which there is a tight upper bound on production. More generally, it could consist of heterogeneous equipment, with each piece of equipment described by its size and capacity. See, for example, Oren et al. (1985) and Wilson (1993).

discussion of this issue after decomposing the demand into three components, each requiring its own pricing treatment:

> These assertions appear to us to be based on a certain number of confusions. Various reasons can motivate excess production capacities ... It would be absurd to conclude that the peak rate should be calculated as if it constituted a systematic production capacity surplus.
>
> ....
>
> We have, in the course of this quick analysis of demand regimes, identified three reasons for why production capacities that are perfectly adapted to demand can appear to be in surplus, and to justify a low marginal cost:
>
> *periodicity of demand* renders superfluous, off-peak, investments needed for the peak,
>
> *trend of the demand* justifies investments temporarily in surplus, either while waiting for a later expansion of consumption, or while waiting for the natural disappearance of investments that a decline in demand has rendered superfluous,
>
> *randomness of demand* necessitates safety margins which, by their very nature, are rarely fully utilized.

It would be of interest to reconsider the optimal pricing of dispersion in such a general setting.

Acknowledgements We would like to express our deepest gratitude to John Weymark for his very careful reading of an earlier version of this article. His detailed and insightful comments and suggestions have had a major impact on its content and on the exposition of its main ideas. The translations from French sources were initially prepared by Agnès d'Artigues and Sarah Berthaud from the firm ATRATEC and subsequently revised by John Weymark. We are grateful to Serge Kolm for his comments on the translations from his work. We also thank an anonymous referee for his or her observations and encouragement. The contributions of Serge Kolm have had a profound impact on the desire of the second author to become an economist. It is a pleasure for him to recognize this intellectual influence and to pay his tribute.

References

Berg, S. V., & Tschirhart, T. (1988). *Natural monopoly regulation: Principles and practice.* Cambridge University Press, Cambridge

Boiteux, M. (1951). La tarification au coût marginal et les demandes aléatoires. *Cahiers du Séminaire d'Econométrie, 1*, 56–69.

Brown, G. Jr., & Johnson, M. B. (1969). Public utility pricing and output under risk. *American Economic Review, 59*, 119–128

Callen, J. L. (1978). Production, efficiency, and welfare in the natural gas transmission industry. *American Economic Review, 68*, 311–323

Carlton, D. W. (1977). Peak load pricing with stochastic demand. *American Economic Review, 67*, 1006–1010

Carlton, D. W. (1978). Market behavior with demand uncertainty and price inflexibility. *American Economic Review, 68*, 571–587

Carlton, D. W. (1979). Contracts, price rigidity, and market equilibrium. *Journal of Political Economy, 87*, 1034–1062

Carlton, D. W. (1991). The theory of market allocation and its implications for marketing and industrial organization: Why rationing is efficient. *Journal of Law and Economics, 34*, 231–262

Chao, H.-P. (1983). Peak load pricing and capacity planning with demand and supply uncertainty. *Bell Journal of Economics, 14*, 179–190

Chao, H.-P., & Wilson, R. (1987). Priority service: Pricing, investment, and market organization. *American Economic Review, 77*, 899–916.

Coate, S., & Panzar, J. (1989). Public utility pricing and capacity choice under risk: A rational expectations approach. *Journal of Regulatory Economics, 1*, 305–317

Commission de Régulation de l'Energie (2006). La régulation du marché du gaz naturel. Rapport d'Activité of the French Commission de Régulation de l'Energie, June 2006

Crew, M. A., & Kleindorfer, P. R. (1978). Reliability and public utility pricing. *American Economic Review, 68*, 31–40

Dana, J. D. Jr. (1998). Advance-purchase discounts and price descrimination in competitive markets. *Journal of Political Economy, 106*, 395–422

Dana, J. D. Jr. (1999). Equilibrium price dispersion under demand uncertainty: The roles of costly capacity and market structure. *RAND Journal of Economics, 30*, 632–660

Dana, J. D. Jr. (2001). Monopoly price dispersion under demand uncertainty. *International Economic Review, 42*, 649–670

David, L., Le Breton, M., & Merillon, O. (2007). Regulating the natural gas transportation industry: Optimal pricing policy of a monopolist with advance-purchase and spot markets. Working Paper No. 488, Institut d'Economie Industrielle, University of Toulouse 1

David, L., Le Breton, M., & Merillon, O. (2011). Kolm as a contributor to public utility pricing, second-best culture, and the theory of regulation. In M. Fleurbaey, M. Salles, & J. A. Weymark (Eds.), *Social ethics and normative economics: Essays in honour of Serge-Christophe Kolm* (pp. 19–56). Berlin: Springer

De la Vallée Poussin, D. (1968). Tarification de l'électricité selon la moyenne et la variance de la consommation individuelle. *Recherches Economiques de Louvain, 34*, 53–72

Deneckere, R., & Peck, J. (1995). Competition over price and service rate when demand is stochastic: A strategic analysis. *RAND Journal of Economics, 26*, 148–162

Diamond, P. (1980). Efficiency and uncertain supply. *Review of Economic Studies, 47*, 645–651

Doane, M. J., McAfee, R. P., & Williams, M. A. (2004). Evaluating and enhancing competition in the interstate natural gas transportation industry. *Natural Resources Journal, 44*, 761–808

Drèze, J. H. (1964). Some postwar contributions of French economists to theory and public policy: With special emphasis on problems of resource allocation. *American Economic Review, Supplement, 54*, 1–64

Drèze, J. H. (1995). Forty years of public economics: A personal perspective. *Journal of Economic Perspectives, 9*(2), 111–130

Eden, B. (1990). Marginal cost pricing when spot markets are complete. *Journal of Political Economy, 98*, 1293–1306

Energy and Environmental Economics, Inc. (2006). A survey of time-of-use (TOU) pricing and demand-response (DR) programs. Report prepared for the United States Environmental Protection Agency by Energy and Environmental Economics, Inc., San Francisco, July 2006

Gale, I. L., & Holmes, T. J. (1992). The efficiency of advance-purchase discounts in the presence of aggregate demand uncertainty. *International Journal of Industrial Organization, 10*, 413–437

Gale, I. L., & Holmes, T. J. (1993). Advance-purchase discounts and monopoly allocation of capacity. *American Economic Review, 83*, 135–146

Guesnerie, R. (1975). Production of the public sector and taxation in a simple second best model. *Journal of Economic Theory, 10*, 127–156

Hopkinson, J. (1892). On the cost of electricity supply. *Transactions of the Junior Engineering Society, 3*, 1–14. Reprinted in B. Hopkinson (Ed.) (1901). *Original Papers by the Late John Hopkinson, D.Sc., F.R.S. Volume I: Technical Papers* (pp. 254–268). Cambridge: Cambridge University Press

Kolm, S.-C. (1970). Service optimal d'une demande variable et prix de l'incertitude. *Revue Economique, 21*, 243–271

Kolm, S.-C. (1971). *Le Service des Masses*. Paris: C.N.R.S. and Dunod

Marchand, M. G. (1974). Pricing power supplied on an interruptible basis. *European Economic Review*, *5*, 263–274

McAfee, R. P., & Reny, P. J. (2007). The role of excess capacity in determining market power in natural gas transportation markets. *Journal of Regulatory Economics*, *32*, 209–223

McAvoy, P. W., & Noll, R. (1973). Relative prices on regulated transactions of the natural gas pipelines. *Bell Journal of Economics and Mangement Science*, *4*, 212–234

Meyer, R. A. (1975). Monopoly pricing and capacity choice under uncertainty. *American Economic Review*, *65*, 326–337

Oren, S., Smith, S., & Wilson, R. (1985). Capacity pricing. *Econometrica*, *53*, 545–566

Panzar, J. C., & Sibley, D. S. (1978). Public utility pricing under risk: The case of self-rationing. *American Economic Review*, *68*, 888–895

Polemarchakis, H. M. (1979). Incomplete markets, price regulation, and welfare. *American Economic Review*, *69*, 662–669

Prescott, E. C. (1976). Efficiency of the natural rate. *Journal of Political Economy*, *83*, 1229–1236

Rees, R. (1980). Consumer choice and non-price rationing in public utility pricing. In B. M. Mitchell & P. R. Kleindorfer (Eds.), *Regulated industries and public enterprise: European and United States perspectives* (pp. 207–228). Lexington, MA: D. C. Heath

Seeto, D., Woo, C.-K., & Horowitz, I. (1997). Time-of-use rates vs. Hopkinson tariffs redux: An analysis of the choice of rate structures in a regulated electricity distribution company. *Energy Economics*, *19*, 169–185

Sherman, R., & Visscher, M. (1978). Second best pricing with stochastic demand. *American Economic Review*, *68*, 41–53

Spulber, D. F. (1992a). Capacity-contingent nonlinear pricing by regulated firms. *Journal of Regulatory Economics*, *4*, 299–319

Spulber, D. F. (1992b). Optimal nonlinear pricing and contingent contracts. *International Economic Review*, *33*, 747–772

Turvey, R. (1970). Public utility pricing and output under risk: Comment. *American Economic Review*, *60*, 485–486

Veall, M. R. (1983). Industrial electricity demand and the Hopkinson rate: An application of the extreme value distribution. *Bell Journal of Economics*, *14*, 427–440

Visscher, M. L. (1973). Welfare-maximizing price and output with stochastic demand: Comment. *American Economic Review*, *63*, 224–229

Wellisz, S. H. (1963). Regulation of natural gas pipeline companies: An economic analysis. *Journal of Political Economy*, *71*, 30–43

Wilson, C. A. (1988). On the optimal pricing policy of a monopolist. *Journal of Political Economy*, *96*, 164–176.

Wilson, R. (1993). *Nonlinear pricing*. New York: Oxford University Press

Woo, C.-K., Orans, R., Horii, B., & Chow, P. (1995). Pareto-superior time-of-use rate option for industrial firms. *Economic Letters*, *49*, 267–272

Woo, C.-K., Chow, P., & Horowitz, I. (1996). Optional real-time pricing of electricity for industrial firms. *Pacific Economic Review*, *1*, 79–92.

Woo, C.-K., Horii, B., & Horowitz, I. (2002). The Hopkinson tariff alternative to TOU rates in the Israel Electric Corporation. *Managerial and Decision Economics*, *23*, 9–19

Yakubovich, V., Granovetter, M., & McGuire, P. (2005). Electric charges: The social construction of rate systems. *Theory and Society*, *34*, 579–612

Bidimensional Inequalities with an Ordinal Variable

Nicolas Gravel and Patrick Moyes

1 Introduction and Motivation

The normative foundations of the comparison of distributions of a single attribute between a given number of individuals are by now well-established. They originate in the equivalence between four plausible answers to the question of when a distribution **x** can be considered normatively better than a distribution **y** with the same mean. These answers, the equivalence of which was first established by Hardy et al. (1952) and popularized later on among economists by Kolm (1969), Dasgupta et al. (1973), Sen (1997), and Fields and Fei (1978), among others, are the following:

1. Distribution **x** can be obtained from distribution **y** by means of a finite sequence of progressive (or equivalently Pigou–Dalton) transfers.
2. All utilitarian ethical observers who assume that individuals convert the attribute into well-being by means of the same non-decreasing concave utility function rank distribution **x** above distribution **y**.
3. The poverty gap is lower in distribution **x** than in distribution **y** whatever the poverty line.
4. The Lorenz curve of distribution **x** lies above that of **y**.

This important result, henceforth referred to as the Hardy–Littlewood–Pólya (HLP) Theorem, can be generalized in a number of ways.[1] It shows the congruence

[1]Dasgupta et al. (1973) have shown that the equivalence remains valid when more general social welfare functionals than the utilitarian one are used. It is also easy to extend the equivalence to situations in which the distributions under comparison have different means (see, e.g., Kolm 1969; Shorrocks 1983).

N. Gravel (✉)
GREQAM-IDEP, Université de la Méditerranée, Centre de la Vieille Charité, 13002 Marseille, France
e-mail: nicolas.gravel@univmed.fr

P. Moyes
GREThA (UMR CNRS 5113), Université de Bordeaux and CNRS, Avenue Léon Duguit, 33608 Pessac, France
e-mail: patrick.moyes@u-bordeaux4.fr

M. Fleurbaey et al. (eds.), *Social Ethics and Normative Economics*, Studies in Choice and Welfare, DOI 10.1007/978-3-642-17807-8_4,

of four a priori distinct robust approaches to inequality measurement. The first of these focuses on the *elementary operations* that intuitively capture the very notion of inequality reduction. The second approach links inequality measurement to a set of explicit normative principles and seeks for *unanimity* over all principles in this set. The last two approaches provide *empirically implementable tests*–in terms of poverty or Lorenz dominance–for checking whether one distribution dominates another. These tests have been shown in numerous studies to be quite useful in conclusively comparing several distributions. Moreover, when the Lorenz domination criterion fails to conclusively rank some distributions and when ethically more demanding indices are used in a second stage in order to obtain clear-cut conclusions, it is common to require that these summary indices be compatible with at least one of the conditions of the HLP Theorem (see, e.g., Foster 1985).

Remarkable as they are, the foundations for inequality measurement provided by the HLP Theorem only concern distributions of a *single attribute*, typically identified with individual income. Yet, the ability of income alone to capture all normatively relevant aspects of a person's situation has been seriously challenged in the last 30 years. The focus on income is to a large extent justified on the assumption that it provides a good measure of the level of well-being achieved by an individual who behaves rationally in a comprehensive and fully competitive market environment. This neglects the fact that a number of commodities that contribute to a person's well-being are not given market values. Typical instances are amenities like recreational areas or publicly provided services like education or health care, for which markets are imperfect or even do not exist. Also, attributes like family circumstances or health status affect a person's well-being but are not immediately connected to income. The multidimensional nature of human beings is also at the heart of the capability approach developed by Sen (1985), where the functionings are generally associated with attributes such as health and educational levels, but in no way with income alone.

While the last 30 years have witnessed a number of contributions that have proposed dominance criteria for comparing distributions of several attributes, one has to admit that the theory has not attained a degree of achievement comparable to that of the unidimensional approach. Three directions for generalizing the HLP Theorem to multi-attribute distributions have been explored in the literature. The first of these, illustrated by Atkinson and Bourguignon (1982), starts from the second statement of the HLP Theorem and imposes plausible conditions on the individual utility functions, now assumed to depend upon many attributes. The objective is then to find empirically implementable tests that permit one to check whether one distribution of attributes dominates the other for all social welfare functionals in the class considered. Building on the results of Hadar and Russell (1974) in the multidimensional risk literature, Atkinson and Bourguignon (1982) have shown that first- and second-order multidimensional stochastic dominance imply unanimity of judgements among all utilitarians for specific classes of utility functions. Atkinson and Bourguignon (1987) have proposed a nice interpretation of these criteria in the specific case in which there are only two attributes, one of which is income and the other is an ordinal index of needs like household size. Bourguignon (1989) has proposed an interesting empirically implementable criterion that lies in between the first- and second-order criteria of Atkinson and Bourguignon (1982). He further identified the restrictions that have to be placed on the utility functions in order that the ranking of distributions agreed to by all utilitarians coincides with that implied by his criterion. Interesting as it is, this line of research does not identify the elementary operations that intuitively capture the nature of the equalization process corresponding to the criteria.

The second route consists in proposing elementary operations that generalize one-dimensional Pigou–Dalton transfers and in identifying the individual utility functions that guarantee that the utilitarian principle provides a ranking of distributions equivalent to that obtained from performing a finite number of such transformations. This is the strategy chosen by Kolm (1977), who proves that a distribution of attributes $\mathbf{x}$ results from applying a bistochastic matrix to a distribution of attributes $\mathbf{y}$ if and only if $\mathbf{x}$ would be ranked above $\mathbf{y}$ by all utilitarian rankings based on non-decreasing concave individual utility functions. Kolm's approach has the merit of providing a precise elementary operation that captures a possible meaning of an inequality reduction in a multidimensional setting and of identifying the class of utilitarian normative judgements that is consistent with it. Yet, the elementary operation that he considers, and which consists of transferring an *identical fraction* of each attribute between two individuals, is rather specific. Moreover, Kolm did not produce an empirically implementable test that corresponds to utilitarian unanimity over the class of non-decreasing concave utility functions.

The third route, based this time on the last statement of the HLP Theorem, has been taken by Koshevoy (1995), who proposed the use of the *Lorenz zonotope* as an appropriate generalization of the Lorenz curve in the multidimensional framework. Kosehevoy proved, among other things, that a sufficient condition for one distribution to dominate another according to his criterion is that the former can be obtained from the latter through multiplication by a bistochastic matrix. This obviously does not tell us much about the implicit equalization process embedded in the Lorenz zonotope criterion because the converse implication does not hold. Furthermore, Koshevoy did not provide any indication about what the properties of the utility function are that guarantee that the ranking of distributions generated by unanimity among all utilitarian ethical observers will coincide with that implied by the Lorenz zonotope criterion. While the utilitarian unanimity considered by Kolm implies Koshevoy's quasi-ordering, the converse implication does not hold, and it is therefore difficult to justify the use of the Lorenz zonotope from a normative standpoint.

It is fair to recognize that the elementary transformations that were believed to lie behind the Atkinson and Bourguignon (1982) and Bourguignon (1989) criteria have been discussed by various authors, including Atkinson and Bourguignon (1982) themselves, Ebert (2000), and Moyes (1999). However, none of these authors has succeeded in proving that if one distribution is ranked above another distribution by a criterion, then it is possible to obtain the dominating distribution from the dominated one by successive applications of the considered transformations. Hence, despite the relative wealth of attempts made in this direction during the last 30 years, there seems to be no multidimensional analogue to the HLP Theorem. In this article, and building on work detailed elsewhere (see Gravel and Moyes 2006), we provide a step towards establishing such an equivalence for the case in which there are only two attributes to be distributed and in which only one of the attributes is cardinally measurable.

Restricting attention to distributions of two attributes might look restrictive, but it provides a simple enough structure in which the basic problem can be addressed. Our asymmetric treatment of the two attributes is certainly more disputable. Yet, there are a number of instances in which only ordinal information is available about the value of attributes. For instance, one may be interested in the evaluation of income distributions for households, who differ in size and composition, as in Atkinson and Bourguignon (1987) or Bourguignon (1989). Even though precise information is provided on household composition, such as the number and ages of the family's members, one may be reluctant to assign a cardinal meaning to it. A similar situation arises when one has to compare the well-being of different populations on the basis of the joint distributions of income and health status of their members. Indicators like infant mortality or life expectancy are routinely used for measuring individuals' health status and, here again, it may be argued that the information provided by these indicators is only ordinal in nature (see, e.g., Allison and Foster 2004). On the other hand, there is a wide agreement among economists about the fact that individual income–at least when used in a specific price configuration–is a cardinally meaningful attribute. It is therefore not unrealistic to consider two attributes that cannot be defined with the same degree of precision and which therefore require a different treatment in a normative analysis.[2]

Our approach focuses on three types of elementary operations, each of which captures a specific feature of the equalizing process. The first of these operations is simply a Pigou–Dalton transformation, where the transfer is now required to take place between two individuals with the same endowment of the ordinal attribute. In order to avoid confusion with the usual concept of a progressive transfer in the unidimensional case, we refer to this elementary operation as a *within-type progressive transfer*. The second elementary operation–which we refer to as a *favorable permutation*–consists of permuting the cardinal attribute endowments of two individuals who can be unambiguously ordered in terms of the two attributes. This permutation actually amounts to reducing the pairwise correlation–or positive association–between the two attributes. A *between-type progressive transfer* is the third elementary operation we consider. It consists of transferring an amount of the cardinal attribute from a better-off individual in both attributes to a worse-off individual in both attributes in such a way that the beneficiary of the transfer

[2] Additional arguments for considering an asymmetric treatment of attributes may be found in the survey of the dominance approach to multidimensional inequality measurement by Trannoy (2006).

is not made richer than the donor in the cardinal attribute.[3] These three operations are described as *elementary* in the sense that it seems difficult to think of simpler inequality-reducing operations into which they could be decomposed. Yet, as will be seen below, this is not perfectly true as far as between-type progressive transfers are concerned. It is indeed always possible under some conditions to decompose a between-type progressive transfer into a within-type progressive transfer and a favorable permutation.

In so far as the normative foundation of inequality measurement is concerned, we adopt a somewhat more prudent approach than the utilitarian one. It is indeed well-known that the utilitarian rule is a rather particular method for making normative judgements that shows little concern for inequality in well-being. As argued by Sen (1997), it might be preferable to use more flexible aggregation rules that allow for such an aversion to utility inequality. Accepting this argument, we adopt the view that unanimity should be looked for over the large family of all utility-inequality averse welfarist social welfare functionals. The utilitarian rule clearly belongs to this family, as do the maximin and the leximin ones. As we will show in this article, our prudent approach is not as restrictive as it might seem at first sight. Indeed, for a large class of individual utility functions, the application of unanimity among all utility-inequality averse welfarist ethical observers criterion provides the same ranking of distributions as unanimity using the utilitarian rule.

Turning finally to the issue of designing implementable tests for comparing distributions of attributes, we focus on two criteria that have aroused contrasting interests in the profession. The first of these, proposed by Atkinson and Bourguignon (1982), is the one that has received the greatest attention in the literature. It declares that a situation dominates another situation if the proportion of the population that is poor in the two attributes is lower in the former situation than in the latter for all pairs of poverty lines (one such line for each attribute). The second criterion that is examined is a generalization of the ordered poverty gap quasi-ordering due to Bourguignon (1989). This criterion ranks a distribution above another if the poverty gap in the cardinal attribute in the dominating distribution is lower than that in the dominated one for all poverty lines assigned to individuals that are a non-increasing function of the endowment of the ordinal attribute.

The organization of the rest of this article is as follows. We introduce in Sect. 2 our bidimensional model along with our notation and preliminary definitions. Section 3 presents the normative criteria used by the ethical observer in order to rank the distributions being compared. We show that unanimity of the value judgements among all utilitarian ethical observers and among all welfarist ones coincide if the individual utility functions possess an appropriate *closedness* property that is satisfied by the utility functions considered here. Section 4 provides the analogue of the HLP Theorem for the first criterion of Atkinson and Bourguignon (1982).

[3] In contrast to the bistochastic transformation considered in Kolm (1977), where the same equalizing process is applied to both attributes, a between-type progressive transfer entails redistribution in only one dimension.

In a similar spirit, Sect. 5 examines the normative foundations of the ordered poverty gap dominance criterion of Bourguignon (1989). While the analogue of the HLP Theorem is established for this criterion as well, this result depends to a significant extent on the possibility of adding dummy individuals to the original population. Finally, Sect. 6 concludes this article by summarizing the main results and hinting at possible avenues for future research.

2 Notation and Preliminary Definitions

We consider finite *societies* in which each individual is endowed with two attributes: the first attribute is cardinal and transferable between individuals, while the second is ordinal and cannot be transferred between them. To make things simple, we find it convenient to associate the first attribute with *income* and the second with *ability*. The latter term, however, should not be taken too literally; it may represent the ordering of households in terms of decreasing size (Atkinson and Bourguignon 1987), or of individuals in terms of health (Allison and Foster 2004), or of individuals in terms of consumption of local public goods (Gravel et al. 2009).

A *bidimensional distribution*, or more compactly a *situation*, for a population of n individuals is a $n \times 2$ matrix

$$\mathbf{s} \equiv (\mathbf{x};\mathbf{a}) := \begin{bmatrix} x_1 & a_1 \\ \vdots & \vdots \\ x_i & a_i \\ \vdots & \vdots \\ x_n & a_n \end{bmatrix} = \begin{bmatrix} \mathbf{s}_1 \\ \vdots \\ \mathbf{s}_i \\ \vdots \\ \mathbf{s}_n \end{bmatrix}, \tag{1}$$

such that $\mathbf{s}_i = (x_i, a_i)$ fully describes individual i, where $x_i \in \mathscr{D} := [\underline{v}, \overline{v}] \subset \mathbb{R}$ and $a_i \in \mathscr{A} := \left[\underline{h}, \overline{h}\right] \subset \mathbb{R}$ are respectively the income and the ability of individual i. The marginal *distributions of income* and *ability* in situation $\mathbf{s} \equiv (\mathbf{x};\mathbf{a})$ are indicated respectively by $\mathbf{x} := (x_1, \dots, x_n)^{\mathrm{T}} \in \mathscr{D}^n$ and $\mathbf{a} := (a_1, \dots, a_n)^{\mathrm{T}} \in \mathscr{A}^n$, where the superscript T denotes the transposed vector. The general set of situations for a population of n individuals is denoted by

$$\mathbb{S}_n := \{\mathbf{s} \equiv (\mathbf{x};\mathbf{a}) \mid (x_i, a_i) \in \mathscr{D} \times \mathscr{A},\ \forall\, i = 1, 2, \dots, n\}. \tag{2}$$

We let $\mu(\mathbf{x})$ represent the *mean income* in situation $\mathbf{s} \equiv (\mathbf{x};\mathbf{a})$.

We will make extensive use in what follows of the representation of the bidimensional distributions by means of their associated joint, marginal, and conditional cumulative distribution functions. Given the situation $\mathbf{s} \equiv (\mathbf{x};\mathbf{a}) \in \mathbb{S}_n$, we denote by $N(v,h) = \{i \mid x_i = v \text{ and } a_i = h\}$ the set of individuals who receive an income equal to v and who have an ability equal to h. The *joint density function* of $\mathbf{s} \equiv (\mathbf{x};\mathbf{a})$

is given by

$$f(v, h) = n(v, h)/n, \tag{3}$$

where $n(v, h) = \#N(v, h)$. Similarly, the set of individuals who receive an income no greater than v and whose ability is no greater than h is indicated by $Q(v, h) = \{i \mid x_i \leq v \text{ and } a_i \leq h\}$. Letting $q(v, h) = \#Q(v, h)$, the *joint cumulative distribution function* is defined by

$$F(v, h) = q(v, h)/n. \tag{4}$$

The set of individuals whose income is equal to v is denoted by $N_1(v) = \{i \mid x_i = v\}$, while $N_2(h) = \{i \mid a_i = h\}$ indicates the set of individuals whose ability is equal to h. The *marginal density functions of income* and *ability* are respectively defined by

$$f_1(z) = n_1(v)/n \text{ and } f_2(h) = n_2(h)/n, \tag{5}$$

where $n_1(v) = \#N_1(v)$ and $n_2(h) = \#N_2(h)$. The set of individuals whose income in situation $\mathbf{s} \equiv (\mathbf{x}; \mathbf{a})$ is no greater than v is indicated by $Q_1(v) = \{i \mid x_i \leq v\}$, while the set of individuals whose ability is no greater than h is denoted by $Q_2(h) = \{i \mid a_i \leq h\}$. The *marginal distribution functions of income* and *ability* are respectively defined by

$$F_1(z) = q_1(v)/n \text{ and } F_2(h) = q_2(h)/n, \tag{6}$$

where $q_1(v) = \#Q_1(v)$ and $q_2(h) = \#Q_2(h)$. The *conditional density functions of income* and *ability* are indicated by

$$f_1(v \mid h) = n(v, h)/n_2(h) \text{ and } f_2(h \mid v) = n(v, h)/n_1(v), \tag{7}$$

respectively. Let $Q_1(v \mid h) = \{i \mid x_i \leq v \text{ and } a_i = h\}$ represent the set of individuals whose ability is equal to h and whose income is no greater than v. Similarly, we denote by $Q_2(h \mid v) = \{i \mid a_i \leq h \text{ and } x_i = v\}$ the set of individuals whose income is equal to v and whose ability is no greater than h. Then the *conditional distribution functions of income* and *ability* are defined by

$$F_1(v \mid h) = q_1(v \mid h)/n_2(h) \text{ and } F_2(h \mid v) = q_2(h \mid v)/n_1(v), \tag{8}$$

respectively, where $q_1(v \mid h) = \#Q_1(v \mid h)$ and $q_2(h \mid v) = \#Q_2(h \mid v)$.

Throughout this article, we are interested in the comparison of situations $\mathbf{s}^\circ \equiv (\mathbf{x}^\circ; \mathbf{a}^\circ), \mathbf{s}^* \equiv (\mathbf{x}^*; \mathbf{a}^*) \in \mathbb{S}_n$ $(n \geq 2)$. The associated joint, marginal, and conditional density functions and distribution functions of $\mathbf{s}^*$ and $\mathbf{s}^\circ$ will be identified by means of the same superscripts. In practice, it is not necessary to consider the range of all possible values for our two attributes; it is sufficient to make computations using the values of income and ability that actually occur in the situations under comparison. To this aim, we define:

$$M_1(\mathbf{s}) := \{v_j \in \mathscr{D} \mid \exists i : x_i = v_j\}, \tag{9a}$$

$$M_2(\mathbf{s}) := \{h_j \in \mathscr{A} \mid \exists i : a_i = h_j\}, \tag{9b}$$

$$M_1(\mathbf{s}^*, \mathbf{s}^\circ) := \{v_j \in \mathscr{D} \mid \exists i : x_i^* = v_j \text{ or } x_i^\circ = v_j\}, \tag{9c}$$

$$M_2(\mathbf{s}^*, \mathbf{s}^\circ) := \{h_j \in \mathscr{A} \mid \exists i : a_i^* = h_j \text{ or } a_i^\circ = h_j\}, \tag{9d}$$

$$m_1(\mathbf{s}) := \# M_1(\mathbf{s}), \tag{9e}$$

$$m_2(\mathbf{s}) := \# M_2(\mathbf{s}), \tag{9f}$$

$$m_1(\mathbf{s}^*, \mathbf{s}^\circ) := \# M_1(\mathbf{s}^*, \mathbf{s}^\circ), \tag{9g}$$

$$m_2(\mathbf{s}^*, \mathbf{s}^\circ) := \# M_2(\mathbf{s}^*, \mathbf{s}^\circ). \tag{9h}$$

We label the distinct elements in $M_1(\mathbf{s})$, $M_2(\mathbf{s})$, $M_1(\mathbf{s}^*, \mathbf{s}^\circ)$, and $M_2(\mathbf{s}^*, \mathbf{s}^\circ)$ so that $v_1 < v_2 < \cdots < v_{m_1(\mathbf{s})}$, $h_1 < h_2 < \cdots < h_{m_2(\mathbf{s})}$, $v_1 < v_2 < \cdots < v_{m_1(\mathbf{s}^*,\mathbf{s}^\circ)}$, and $h_1 < h_2 < \cdots < h_{m_2(\mathbf{s}^*,\mathbf{s}^\circ)}$, respectively.

Example 1. For the sake of illustration, we introduce the following four situations, in which, for graphical convenience, we permit ability to take on only two possible values:

$$\mathbf{s}^1 = \begin{bmatrix} 1 & 1 \\ 2 & 2 \\ 4 & 1 \\ 5 & 2 \\ 5 & 2 \end{bmatrix}, \quad \mathbf{s}^2 = \begin{bmatrix} 2 & 1 \\ 1 & 2 \\ 5 & 1 \\ 4 & 2 \\ 5 & 2 \end{bmatrix}, \quad \mathbf{s}^3 = \begin{bmatrix} 3 & 1 \\ 1 & 2 \\ 5 & 1 \\ 4 & 2 \\ 4 & 2 \end{bmatrix}, \quad \text{and } \mathbf{s}^4 = \begin{bmatrix} 4 & 1 \\ 1 & 2 \\ 4 & 1 \\ 3 & 2 \\ 5 & 2 \end{bmatrix}.$$

For later reference, we note that all four situations have the same marginal distribution of ability.

On some occasions, we will restrict attention to situations with the same mean income. In the particular case in which the joint distribution function of one situation lies nowhere above the joint distribution function of the other situation, the equal mean income assumption implies that the situations under comparison have identical marginal distribution functions of income. This result is precisely stated in the following lemma proved–as well as all formal results in this article–in Gravel and Moyes (2006).

Lemma 1. *Let* $\mathbf{s}^*, \mathbf{s}^\circ \in \mathbb{S}_n$ $(n \geq 2)$ *and suppose that* $\mu(\mathbf{x}^*) = \mu(\mathbf{x}^\circ)$. *Then* $F^*(v,h) \leq F^\circ(v,h)$ *for all* $v \in \mathscr{D}$ *and all* $h \in \mathscr{A}$ *implies that* $F_1^*(v) = F_1^\circ(v)$ *for all* $v \in \mathscr{D}$.

3 The Welfare Criteria

Following the usual practice in the dominance approach, we assume (a) that all individuals transform their endowments of the two attributes into well-being by means of the same utility function and (b) that the distribution of the individual utilities in a situation provide all the relevant information for appraising this situation from a normative point of view. It is convenient to think of an ethical observer who is in charge of evaluating the different situations under comparison on the basis of the distributions of utilities they generate. There are at least two interpretations that can be given to this way of proceeding. The first is the *welfarist* approach according to which the utility function is the one actually used by the individuals in order to convert their endowments of the attributes into well-being.[4] It is assumed that well-being is a cardinally measurable and interpersonally comparable variable that summarizes all the aspects of an individual's situation that are deemed relevant for normative evaluation. The other interpretation–the *non-welfarist* approach–is to view the utility function as reflecting the assessment of the individual's situation by the ethical observer. There is no presumption in the latter approach that utility is connected to the individual's actual well-being and one must rather interpret the utility function as a predefined *social norm*. In either interpretation, the *symmetry* assumption according to which individuals are assigned the same utility function may be defended (see, e.g., Gravel and Moyes 2006; Trannoy 2006).

The utility achieved by individual i in situation $\mathbf{s} \equiv (\mathbf{x}; \mathbf{a})$ as envisaged by the ethical observer–be it welfarist or not–is indicated by $U(\mathbf{s}_i) = U(x_i, a_i)$. To simplify the exposition, we assume throughout that the *utility function* $U\colon \mathscr{D} \times \mathscr{A} \to \mathbb{R}$ is twice differentiable in income and we denote by $\mathbb{U}$ the set of all such functions. We use $U(\mathbf{s}) \equiv U(\mathbf{x}; \mathbf{a}) := (U(x_1, a_1), \ldots, U(x_n, a_n))$ to indicate the *distribution of utility* generated by the situation $\mathbf{s} \equiv (\mathbf{x}; \mathbf{a}) \in \mathbb{S}_n$ when the utility function is $U \in \mathbb{U}$. The *utilitarian rule* ranks the situations under comparison on the basis of the sum of the utilities they generate. More precisely, from the point of view of a utilitarian ethical observer endowed with the utility function $U \in \mathbb{U}$, the social welfare in situation $\mathbf{s} \equiv (\mathbf{x}; \mathbf{a}) \in \mathbb{S}_n$ is equal to $\sum_{i=1}^{n} U(x_i, a_i)$, and the situation $\mathbf{s}^*$ is considered to be no worse than situation $\mathbf{s}^\circ$ if and only if

$$\sum_{i=1}^{n} U\left(x_i^*, a_i^*\right) \geq \sum_{i=1}^{n} U\left(x_i^\circ, a_i^\circ\right). \tag{10}$$

The utility function U captures the utilitarian ethical observer's normative judgement and it is the only parameter by which such ethical observers can be distinguished. In order to rule out as much arbitrariness as possible, we require all utilitarian ethical observers whose utility functions U belong to a given class $\mathbb{U}^* \subset \mathbb{U}$ to agree on the ranking of the situations under comparison.

---

[4] We refer the reader to Blackorby et al. (2005) and Griffin (1986) for discussions of the welfarist approach in economics and philosophy, respectively.

Utilitarian Unanimity Rule. Situation $\mathbf{s}^*$ is no worse than situation $\mathbf{s}^\circ$ for the utilitarian unanimity rule over the class $\mathbb{U}^* \subset \mathbb{U}$ if and only if

$$\sum_{i=1}^{n} U\left(x_i^*, a_i^*\right) \geq \sum_{i=1}^{n} U\left(x_i^\circ, a_i^\circ\right), \ \forall\, U \in \mathbb{U}^*. \tag{11}$$

The following obvious result, which originates in the additive separability of the utilitarian social welfare function, expresses the independence of the utilitarian rule with respect to the unconcerned individuals.

Lemma 2. *Let $U \in \mathbb{U}$ and consider arbitrary situations $\mathbf{s}^*, \mathbf{s}^\circ \in \mathbb{S}_n$ ($n \geq 2$), $\mathbf{s} \in \mathbb{S}_q$, where $q \geq 1$. Then the following two statements are equivalent:*

(a) $\sum_{i=1}^{n} U\left(x_i^*, a_i^*\right) + \sum_{i=1}^{q} U\left(x_i, a_i\right) \geq \sum_{i=1}^{n} U\left(x_i^\circ, a_i^\circ\right) + \sum_{i=1}^{q} U\left(x_i, a_i\right)$.

(b) $\sum_{i=1}^{n} U\left(x_i^*, a_i^*\right) \geq \sum_{i=1}^{n} U\left(x_i^\circ, a_i^\circ\right)$.

The utilitarian unanimity rule allows us to encompass different value judgements whose spectrum is fully captured by the subset $\mathbb{U}^*$ of admissible utility functions. Much of the discussion in this article will address the question of what constitutes the relevant set of utility functions over which one is looking for unanimity.

However, the utilitarian rule is just one among many other possible principles that can be used for aggregating individual utility levels. It has been criticized on the grounds that it pays no attention to the way that utilities are distributed among the individuals. One might prefer to appeal to principles that express some aversion to the inequality in the distribution of individual utilities, such as Maximin or Leximin. More precisely, we are interested in those social welfare functionals that incorporate a concern for both efficiency and equity considerations. Formally, the social welfare in situation $\mathbf{s} \in \mathbb{S}$ is given by $G(U(\mathbf{x}; \mathbf{a})) := G\left(U\left(x_1, a_1\right), \ldots, U\left(x_n, a_n\right)\right)$, where $G: \mathbb{R}^n \to \mathbb{R}$ is the social welfare functional. We will say that situation $\mathbf{s}^*$ is no worse than situation $\mathbf{s}^\circ$ for an ethical observer endowed with the utility function $U \in \mathbb{U}$ and the social welfare functional G if and only if

$$G\left(U\left(\mathbf{x}^*; \mathbf{a}^*\right)\right) \geq G\left(U\left(\mathbf{x}^\circ; \mathbf{a}^\circ\right)\right). \tag{12}$$

Inequality aversion is typically captured by the property of Schur-concavity. We indicate by $\mathbb{G}_{SC}$ the set of all social welfare functionals that are monotone and Schur-concave (see Kolm 1969; Dasgupta et al. 1973).[5] A particularly cautious–but on the other hand definitively uncontroversial–position consists in declaring that social welfare improves if and only if condition (12) holds whatever the social welfare functional and the utility function, provided the former expresses a concern for efficiency and equity considerations.

[5] The mapping $G: \mathbb{R}^n \to \mathbb{R}$ is *monotone* if $G(\mathbf{u}) \geq G(\mathbf{v})$ for all $\mathbf{u} = (u_1, \ldots, u_n)$ and $\mathbf{v} = (v_1, \ldots, v_n)$ such that $u_i \geq v_i$ for all $i = 1, 2, \ldots, n$. It is *Schur-concave* if $G(B\mathbf{u}) \geq G(\mathbf{u})$ for all $\mathbf{u} = (u_1, \ldots, u_n)$ and all bistochastic matrices B (see Marshall and Olkin 1979).

Welfarist Unanimity Rule. Situation $\mathbf{s}^*$ is no worse than situation $\mathbf{s}^\circ$ for the welfarist unanimity rule over the class of utility functions $\mathbb{U}^* \subset \mathbb{U}$ and the class of social welfare functionals $\mathbb{G}^* \subset \mathbb{G}$ if and only if

$$G\left(U\left(\mathbf{x}^*;\mathbf{a}^*\right)\right) \geq G\left(U\left(\mathbf{x}^\circ;\mathbf{a}^\circ\right)\right), \ \forall U \in \mathbb{U}^*, \ \forall G \in \mathbb{G}^*. \tag{13}$$

Interestingly, the utilitarian and welfarist unanimity rules coincide on a particular subset of the utility functions. Before we proceed to a precise statement of this result, we first need to introduce some additional notation and a definition. Let $\mathbf{u}^* := \left(u_1^*, \ldots, u_n^*\right)$ and $\mathbf{u}^\circ := \left(u_1^\circ, \ldots, u_n^\circ\right)$ be two distributions of individual utilities. Denote respectively as $\mathbf{u}_{()}^*$ and $\mathbf{u}_{()}^\circ$ the non-decreasing rearrangements of $\mathbf{u}^*$ and $\mathbf{u}^\circ$ defined by $u_{(1)}^* \leq u_{(2)}^* \leq \cdots \leq u_{(n)}^*$ and $u_{(1)}^\circ \leq u_{(2)}^\circ \leq \cdots \leq u_{(n)}^\circ$. Then we will say that $\mathbf{u}^*$ *generalised Lorenz dominates* $\mathbf{u}^\circ$, which we write as $\mathbf{u}^* \geq_{\mathrm{GL}} \mathbf{u}^\circ$, if and only if

$$\frac{1}{n}\sum_{i=1}^{k} u_{(i)}^* \geq \frac{1}{n}\sum_{i=1}^{k} u_{(i)}^\circ, \ \forall k = 1, 2, \ldots, n \tag{14}$$

(see Kolm 1969; Shorrocks 1983). An interesting result for our purpose is the fact that the rankings of the distributions of utilities by the welfarist unanimity rule and the generalised Lorenz quasi-ordering prove to be identical under certain conditions.

Lemma 3 (see, e.g., Marshall and Olkin 1979). *Let* $\mathbf{u}^*, \mathbf{u}^\circ \in \mathbb{R}^n$. *Then the following two statements are equivalent:*

(*a*) $\mathbf{u}^* \geq_{\mathrm{GL}} \mathbf{u}^\circ$.

(*b*) $G\left(\mathbf{u}^*\right) \geq G\left(\mathbf{u}^\circ\right)$ *for all* $G \in \mathbb{G}_{\mathrm{SC}}$.

Given the above result, it is now possible to identify the restrictions to be imposed on the class of utility functions that guarantee that the rankings of situations implied by the utilitarian and welfarist unanimities are identical.

Proposition 1. *Let* $\mathbb{U}^* \subseteq \mathbb{U}$, $\mathbb{G}^* \subseteq \mathbb{G}_{\mathrm{SC}}$, *and* $\mathbf{s}^*, \mathbf{s}^\circ \in \mathbb{S}_n$ $(n \geq 2)$. *Then a sufficient condition for* (11) *and* (13) *to be equivalent is that* $\Psi \circ U \in \mathbb{U}^*$ *whenever* $\Psi\colon \mathbb{R} \to \mathbb{R}$ *is non-decreasing and concave.*

The preceding result indicates that in order to obtain an equivalence between utilitarian and welfarist unanimities, it is sufficient that the class of utility functions under consideration be closed under the operation of applying monotonic and concave–but still identical for each individual–transformations. Because the classes of utility functions that we will consider in the next two sections possess this property, Proposition 1 will make things simpler by allowing us to focus on the utilitarian unanimity rule without loss of generality.

4 Bidimensional Headcount Poverty Dominance

As we emphasized above, the influential contribution of Atkinson and Bourguignon (1982) is silent about the elementary equalizing transformations of situations that result in welfare improvements in terms of the dominance criteria they introduced. Because we are primarily interested in the way that the attributes are distributed among the individuals, we will first restrict our attention to comparisons of situations whose marginal distribution functions of income and ability are identical.

We will say that situation $\mathbf{s}^*$ is obtained from situation $\mathbf{s}^\circ$ by means of an income *favorable permutation*–or equivalently that $\mathbf{s}^\circ$ is obtained from situation $\mathbf{s}^*$ by means of an income *unfavorable permutation*–if there exist two individuals i and j such that:

$$x_j^* = x_i^\circ < x_j^\circ = x_i^*;\ a_i^* = a_i^\circ < a_j^\circ = a_j^*; \text{ and} \tag{15a}$$

$$s_g^* = s_g^\circ,\ \forall\, g \neq i, j. \tag{15b}$$

A favorable permutation consists in exchanging the cardinal attribute endowment of the better-off individual in both attributes with that of the worse-off individual in both attributes. Such a transformation involving two individuals i and j whose initial situations are respectively $\mathbf{s}_i^\circ = (x_i^\circ, a_i^\circ) = (u, h)$ and $\mathbf{s}_j^\circ = \left(x_j^\circ, a_j^\circ\right) = (v, k)$ with $u < v$ and $h < k$ is represented in Fig. 1. The permutation of the endowments in the cardinal attribute actually reduces the correlation–or equivalently the positive association–existing between the two attributes. The resulting situation may be considered less unequal than the original situation in the sense that

$$U\left(x_i^\circ, a_i^\circ\right) < U\left(x_i^*, a_i^*\right) \leq U\left(x_j^*, a_j^*\right) < U\left(x_j^\circ, a_j^\circ\right) \text{ or} \tag{16a}$$

$$U\left(x_i^\circ, a_i^\circ\right) < U\left(x_j^*, a_j^*\right) < U\left(x_i^*, a_i^*\right) < U\left(x_j^\circ, a_j^\circ\right) \tag{16b}$$

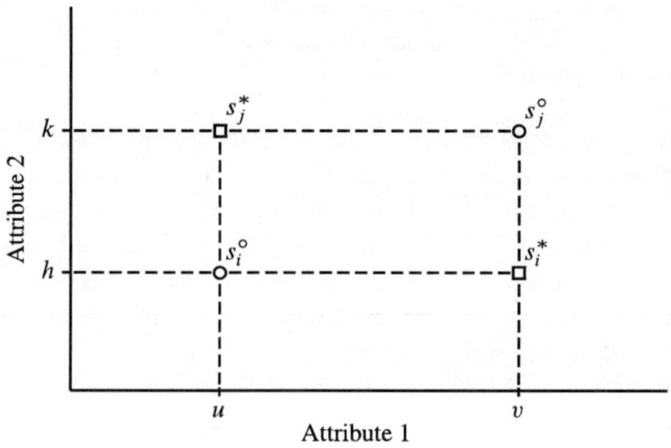

Fig. 1 A favorable permutation

for all monotone increasing utility functions U. On the other hand, a favorable permutation has no impact on the distribution of each attribute in the population: the marginal distribution functions of income and ability are left unchanged and so is mean income.

Let $U_v(v,h)$ denote the first derivative of $U(v,h)$ with respect to income. The next result, the proof of which is obvious, identifies the conditions to be imposed on the utility function in order for social welfare as measured by the utilitarian rule to improve as the result of a favorable permutation.

Lemma 4. *For all* $\mathbf{s}^*, \mathbf{s}^\circ \in \mathbb{S}_n$ $(n \geq 2)$: $\sum_{i=1}^n U\left(x_i^*, a_i^*\right) \geq \sum_{i=1}^n U\left(x_i^\circ, a_i^\circ\right)$ *whenever* $\mathbf{s}^*$ *is obtained from* $\mathbf{s}^\circ$ *by means of a favorable permutation if and only if*

$$U_v(v,h) \geq U_v(v,k), \; \forall\, v \in \mathscr{D}, \; \forall\, h,k \in \mathscr{A} \; (h < k). \tag{C1}$$

According to Lemma 4, non-increasing marginal utility of income is necessary and sufficient for a utilitarian ethical observer to consider that a favorable permutation results in a weak welfare improvement. We denote as

$$\mathbb{U}_1 := \{U \in \mathbb{U} \mid U \text{ satisfies (C1)}\} \tag{17}$$

the class of utility functions with non-increasing marginal utility of income.

Atkinson and Bourguignon (1982) have shown that the ranking of situations by the utilitarian unanimity rule over the class $\mathbb{U}_1$ is actually implied by the ranking obtained by comparing the graphs of their joint cumulative distribution functions. Precisely, we will say that situation $\mathbf{s}^*$ *first-order stochastic dominates* situation $\mathbf{s}^\circ$, which we write as $\mathbf{s}^* \geq_{\mathrm{FSD}} \mathbf{s}^\circ$, if and only if

$$F^*(v,h) \leq F^\circ(v,h), \; \forall\, v \in \mathscr{D}, \; \forall\, h \in \mathscr{A}. \tag{18}$$

Using (4), (7), and (8), upon substitution, condition (18) can be equivalently rewritten as

$$\sum_{g=1}^{h} f_2^*(g)\, H^*(z \mid g) \leq \sum_{g=1}^{h} f_2^\circ(g)\, H^\circ(z \mid g), \; \forall\, z \in \mathscr{D}, \; \forall\, h \in M_2\left(\mathbf{s}^*, \mathbf{s}^\circ\right), \tag{19}$$

where

$$H(z \mid h) := \frac{q_1(z \mid g)}{n_2(g)} \tag{20}$$

is the *headcount poverty* of the subpopulation of individuals having ability h in situation $\mathbf{s}$. Condition (19) expresses the fact that there is less poverty in situation $\mathbf{s}^*$ than in situation $\mathbf{s}^\circ$ for all possible values of the bidimensional poverty line (z,h), where poverty is measured by the percentage of individuals whose income and ability fall strictly below z and h, respectively. More precisely, we will say that situation $\mathbf{s}^*$ *headcount poverty dominates* situation $\mathbf{s}^\circ$, which we write as $\mathbf{s}^* \geq_{\mathrm{HP}} \mathbf{s}^\circ$, when condition (19)–equivalently condition (18)–holds.

Lemma 4 in conjunction with the result of Atkinson and Bourguignon (1982) suggests that favorable permutations might be the elementary transformations that lie behind first-order stochastic–equivalently headcount poverty–dominance. The following result shows that this intuition is correct with certain qualifications.

Lemma 5. *Let* $\mathbf{s}^*, \mathbf{s}^\circ \in \mathbb{S}_n$ $(n \geq 2)$ *be such that* $\mathbf{a}^* = \mathbf{a}^\circ$ *and* $\mu(\mathbf{x}^*) = \mu(\mathbf{x}^\circ)$. *Then:*

(*a*) $F^*(v,h) \leq F^\circ(v,h)$ *for all* $v \in \mathscr{D}$ *and all* $h \in \mathscr{A}$ $\left(v \neq v_{m_1(\mathbf{s}^*,\mathbf{s}^\circ)}\right.$ *and* $\left.h \neq h_{m_2(\mathbf{s}^*,\mathbf{s}^\circ)}\right)$

implies that

(*b*) $\mathbf{s}^*$ *is obtained from* $\mathbf{s}^\circ$ *by means of a finite sequence of favorable permutations of income.*

Making use of Proposition 1 and Lemmas 4 and 5, we obtain the following result, which constitutes the analogue to the HLP Theorem for first-order stochastic–equivalently headcount poverty–dominance.

Theorem 1. *Let* $\mathbf{s}^*, \mathbf{s}^\circ \in \mathbb{S}_n$ $(n \geq 2)$ *be such that* $\mathbf{a}^* = \mathbf{a}^\circ$ *and* $\mu(\mathbf{x}^*) = \mu(\mathbf{x}^\circ)$. *Then statements (a), (b), (c), and (d) below are equivalent:*

(*a*) $\mathbf{s}^*$ *is obtained from* $\mathbf{s}^\circ$ *by means of a finite sequence of permutations of individuals and/or favorable permutations.*

(*b*) $\sum_{i=1}^{n} U\left(x_i^*, a_i^*\right) \geq \sum_{i=1}^{n} U\left(x_i^\circ, a_i^\circ\right)$ *for all* $U \in \mathbb{U}_1$.

(*c*) $U(\mathbf{x}^*; \mathbf{a}^*) \geq_{\mathrm{GL}} U(\mathbf{x}^\circ; \mathbf{a}^\circ)$ *for all* $U \in \mathbb{U}_1$.

(*d*) 1. $F^*(v,h) \leq F^\circ(v,h)$ *for all* $v \in \mathscr{D}$ *and all* $h \in M_2(\mathbf{s}^*, \mathbf{s}^\circ)$ $\left(v \neq v_{m_1(\mathbf{s}^*,\mathbf{s}^\circ)}\right.$ *and* $\left.h \neq h_{m_2(\mathbf{s}^*,\mathbf{s}^\circ)}\right)$.

2. $F_1^*(v) = F_1^\circ(v)$ *for all* $v \in \mathscr{D}$.

3. $F_2^*(h) = F_2^\circ(h)$ *for all* $h \in M_2(\mathbf{s}^*, \mathbf{s}^\circ)$.

Sketch of Proof. The fact that statement (a) implies statement (b) follows from Lemma 4. Proposition 1 and the fact that the class of utility functions $\mathbb{U}_1$ is closed under composition by a non-decreasing and concave function guarantee the equivalence between statements (b) and (c). The fact that (d) is necessary for (b) to hold can be easily shown by suitably choosing degenerate utility functions in the class $\mathbb{U}_1$. Finally, Lemma 5 establishes that statement (d) implies statement (a). □

Theorem 1 confirms the intuition that what we call favorable permutations are the elementary transformations that lie behind the bidimensional headcount poverty criterion. It is fair to note that Epstein and Tanny (1980) have proven a similar result using a different argument. Theorem 1, in conjunction with the fact that headcount poverty dominance is a necessary condition for a situation to be ranked above another one by all utilitarian ethical observers whose marginal utility of income is non-increasing with ability, fills the gaps in Atkinson and Bourguignon (1982,

Prop. 2). A byproduct of Theorem 1 is the recognition that the aforementioned result of Atkinson and Bourguignon (1982) goes far beyond utilitarianism and actually holds for all monotone social welfare functionals exhibiting inequality aversion towards the distribution of individual utilities.

Application of the headcount poverty criterion to the comparison of the situations of Example 1 indicates that $\mathbf{s}^2 \geq_{\text{HP}} \mathbf{s}^1$, which does not come as a surprise because situation $\mathbf{s}^2$ is derived from situation $\mathbf{s}^1$ by means of two favorable permutations. These are actually the only situations that can be ranked by the headcount poverty criterion, which means that for no other pair of situations is it possible to find a general agreement among the welfarist ethical observers whose marginal utility of income is non-increasing in ability.

So far, we have restricted our attention to the case in which the situations under comparison have identical marginal distributions of income and ability. While this allows us to focus on equity considerations, the practical relevance of the results we have obtained is limited. Theorem 1 can be easily extended to the general case in which the marginal distributions are no longer fixed provided one is willing to introduce further restrictions on the utility functions.

We will say that situation $\mathbf{s}^*$ is obtained from situation $\mathbf{s}^\circ$ by means of an *income increment* if there exists an individual i such that:

$$x_i^* > x_i^\circ;\ a_i^* = a_i^\circ;\ \text{and} \tag{21a}$$

$$s_g^* = s_g^\circ,\ \forall\, g \neq i. \tag{21b}$$

We will equally say that situation $\mathbf{s}^\circ$ is obtained from situation $\mathbf{s}^*$ by means of an *income decrement*. Contrary to a favorable permutation, which leaves the marginal distribution of income unchanged, an income increment moves the graph of the marginal distribution function of income downwards. Although it is immediately obvious, we find it convenient for later purposes to state the following result.

Lemma 6. *For all* $\mathbf{s}^*, \mathbf{s}^\circ \in \mathbb{S}_n$ $(n \geq 2)$: $\sum_{i=1}^n U\left(x_i^*, a_i^*\right) \geq \sum_{i=1}^n U\left(x_i^\circ, a_i^\circ\right)$ *whenever* $\mathbf{s}^*$ *is obtained from* $\mathbf{s}^\circ$ *by means of an income increment if and only if*

$$U_v(v,h) \geq 0,\ \forall\, v \in \mathcal{D},\ \forall\, h \in \mathcal{A}. \tag{C2}$$

Similarly we will say that situation $\mathbf{s}^*$ is obtained from situation $\mathbf{s}^\circ$ by means of an *ability increment* if there exists an individual i such that:

$$x_i^* = x_i^\circ;\ a_i^* > a_i^\circ;\ \text{and} \tag{22a}$$

$$s_g^* = s_g^\circ,\ \forall\, g \neq i. \tag{22b}$$

Clearly, the graph of the marginal distribution of ability will go down as the result of an ability increment. For later use, we state the following result.

Lemma 7. *For all* $\mathbf{s}^*, \mathbf{s}^\circ \in \mathbb{S}_n$ $(n \geq 2)$: $\sum_{i=1}^n U\left(x_i^*, a_i^*\right) \geq \sum_{i=1}^n U\left(x_i^\circ, a_i^\circ\right)$ *whenever* $\mathbf{s}^*$ *is obtained from* $\mathbf{s}^\circ$ *by means of an ability increment if and only if*

$$U(v,h) \leq U(v,k), \ \forall\, v \in \mathscr{D}, \ \forall\, h,k \in \mathscr{A} \ (h < k). \tag{C3}$$

According to Lemmas 6 and 7, the monotonicity in both arguments of the utility function is necessary and sufficient for a utilitarian ethical observer to record income and ability increments as welfare-improving. We use

$$\mathbb{U}_1^* := \{U \in \mathbb{U} \mid U \text{ satisfies (C1), (C2), and (C3)}\} \tag{23}$$

to indicate the class of monotone utility functions whose marginal utility of income is non-increasing in ability. We therefore obtain:

Theorem 2. *Let* $\mathbf{s}^*, \mathbf{s}^\circ \in \mathbb{S}_n$ $(n \geq 2)$. *Then statements (a), (b), (c), and (d) below are equivalent:*

(*a*) $\mathbf{s}^*$ *is obtained from* s° *by means of a finite sequence of permutations of individuals, income increments, ability increments, and/or favorable permutations.*

(*b*) $\sum_{i=1}^n U\left(x_i^*, a_i^*\right) \geq \sum_{i=1}^n U\left(x_i^\circ, a_i^\circ\right)$ *for all* $U \in \mathbb{U}_1^*$.

(*c*) $U\left(\mathbf{x}^*; \mathbf{a}^*\right) \geq_{\mathrm{GL}} U\left(\mathbf{x}^\circ; \mathbf{a}^\circ\right)$ *for all* $U \in \mathbb{U}_1^*$.

(*d*) $F^*(v,h) \leq F^\circ(v,h)$ *for all* $v \in \mathscr{D}$ *and all* $h \in M_2\left(\mathbf{s}^*, \mathbf{s}^\circ\right)$.

5 Bidimensional Ordered Poverty Gap Dominance

Here, we again proceed in two steps by first examining the case in which the situations to be compared have identical marginal distributions of income and ability. We will say that situation $\mathbf{s}^*$ is obtained from situation $\mathbf{s}^\circ$ by means of a *within-type progressive transfer* of income if there exist two individuals i and j such that:

$$x_i^\circ < x_i^* \leq x_j^* < x_j^\circ; \ a_i^\circ = a_i^* = a_j^* = a_j^\circ; \tag{24a}$$

$$x_i^* - x_i^\circ = x_j^\circ - x_j^*; \text{ and} \tag{24b}$$

$$s_g^* = s_g^\circ, \ \forall\, g \neq i,j. \tag{24c}$$

The marginal distribution function of ability is left unchanged by a within-type progressive transfer while the distribution of income conditional on ability is made more equal.

Let $U_{vv}(v,h)$ denote the second derivative of $U(v,h)$ with respect to income. Using this second derivative, one can easily identify the property of the utility function that guarantees that social welfare as measured by the utilitarian rule improves as the result of a within-type progressive transfer.

Lemma 8. *For all* $\mathbf{s}^*, \mathbf{s}^\circ \in \mathbb{S}_n$ $(n \geq 2)$: $\sum_{i=1}^n U\left(x_i^*, a_i^*\right) \geq \sum_{i=1}^n U\left(x_i^\circ, a_i^\circ\right)$ *whenever* $\mathbf{s}^*$ *is obtained from* $\mathbf{s}^\circ$ *by means of a within-type progressive transfer if and only if*

$$U_{vv}(v,h) \leq 0,\ \forall\, v \in \mathscr{D},\ \forall\, h \in \mathscr{A}. \tag{C4}$$

The multidimensional nature of the situations under comparison actually plays no role in the concept of a within-type progressive transfer, which is merely a restatement of the usual Pigou–Dalton transfer in our framework. The next transformation, which fully exploits the bidimensionality of a situation, constitutes in our model a very natural generalisation of a unidimensional progressive transfer. We will say that situation $\mathbf{s}^*$ is obtained from situation $\mathbf{s}^\circ$ by means of a *between-type progressive transfer* of income if there exist two individuals i and j such that:

$$x_i^\circ < x_i^* \leq x_j^* < x_j^\circ;\ a_i^\circ = a_i^* < a_j^* = a_j^\circ; \tag{25a}$$

$$x_i^* - x_i^\circ = x_j^\circ - x_j^*;\ \text{and} \tag{25b}$$

$$s_g^* = s_g^\circ,\ \forall\, g \neq i, j. \tag{25c}$$

A between-type progressive transfer resembles a Pigou–Dalton transfer but there is a major difference: the beneficiary of the transfer must be poorer than the donor and she must also have a lower ability. Put differently, the transfer recipient must be deprived in both dimensions–income and ability–compared to the donor. Such a transfer is illustrated in Fig. 2, where individual i receives an additional income of $v - u$ while individual j gives away an amount of income equal to $t - w$, where $u < v < w < t$, $v - u = t - w$, and $h < k$.

Both within-type and between-type progressive transfers leave the marginal distribution of ability unchanged. But contrary to a within-type progressive transfer, which has an unambiguous effect on the conditional distribution of income, here the graph of the conditional distribution function of income of the ability group to which the receiver belongs moves downwards, while the opposite situation arises for the ability group of the donor. The overall effect on the joint distribution function of income and ability is ambiguous and the bidimensional headcount poverty criterion

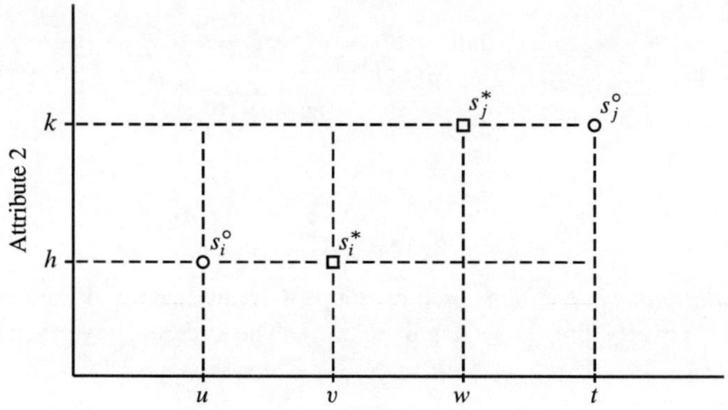

Fig. 2 A between-type progressive transfer

does not allow one to sign the overall welfare impact of a between-type progressive transfer. Somewhat surprisingly, no condition in addition to the ones we have considered up to now need to be imposed on the utility function for a between-type progressive transfer to imply a welfare improvement.

Lemma 9. *For all* $\mathbf{s}^*, \mathbf{s}^\circ \in \mathbb{S}_n$ $(n \geq 2)$: $\sum_{i=1}^n U\left(x_i^*, a_i^*\right) \geq \sum_{i=1}^n U\left(x_i^\circ, a_i^\circ\right)$ *whenever* $\mathbf{s}^*$ *is obtained from* $\mathbf{s}^\circ$ *by means of a between-type progressive transfer if conditions* (C1) *and* (C4) *are satisfied.*

According to Lemma 9, it is sufficient for welfare as conceived by a utilitarian ethical observer to increase as the result of a between-type progressive transfer that the marginal utility of income be non-increasing in income and in ability. The corresponding class of utility functions is indicated by

$$\mathbb{U}_2 := \{U \in \mathbb{U} \mid U \text{ satisfies (C1) and (C4)}\}. \tag{26}$$

Contrary to what happens with the elementary transformations that we introduced previously–in particular, the favorable permutations of income–it is not clear whether the conditions we obtain here are also necessary for a between-type progressive transfer to result in a welfare improvement.[6]

Bourguignon (1989) introduced a dominance criterion that coincides with the one that requires unanimity over all utilitarian ethical observers who use a utility function that is non-decreasing and concave in income and whose marginal utility of income is non-increasing in ability. In order to define Bourguignon's criterion, we first need to introduce some additional notation and technicalities.

An *ordered poverty line* is a non-decreasing mapping $\mathbf{z}: \mathscr{A} \to \mathscr{D}$ such that $\mathbf{z}(h) \in \mathscr{D}$ is the poverty line assigned to all the individuals whose abilities are equal to h. The poverty line faced by an individual is no longer exogenously given as in the standard unidimensional framework; it now depends on her personal situation. The *ordered poverty gap* in situation $\mathbf{s} \equiv (\mathbf{x}; \mathbf{a}) \in \mathbb{S}_n$ when the ordered poverty line is $\mathbf{z}$ is given by

$$\mathbb{P}(\mathbf{z}; \mathbf{s}) = \sum_{h \in M_2(\mathbf{s})} f_2(h) \int_{\underline{v}}^{\mathbf{z}(h)} F_1(t \mid h)\, dt = \sum_{h \in M_2(\mathbf{s})} f_2(h)\, P\left(\mathbf{z}(h) \mid h\right), \tag{27}$$

where

$$P\left(\mathbf{z}(h) \mid h\right) = \frac{1}{n_2(h)} \sum_{i \in Q_1(\mathbf{z}(h) \mid h)} \left(\mathbf{z}(h) - x_i\right) \tag{28}$$

is the *conditional poverty gap* of the group of individuals with ability equal to h when the poverty line is set equal to $\mathbf{z}(h)$. The ordered poverty gap inherits

[6] Ebert (2000) makes use of a continuity argument to show that requiring marginal utility of income to be decreasing in ability and utility to be concave with respect to income are also necessary for the sum of utilities to increase as the result of a between-type progressive transfer.

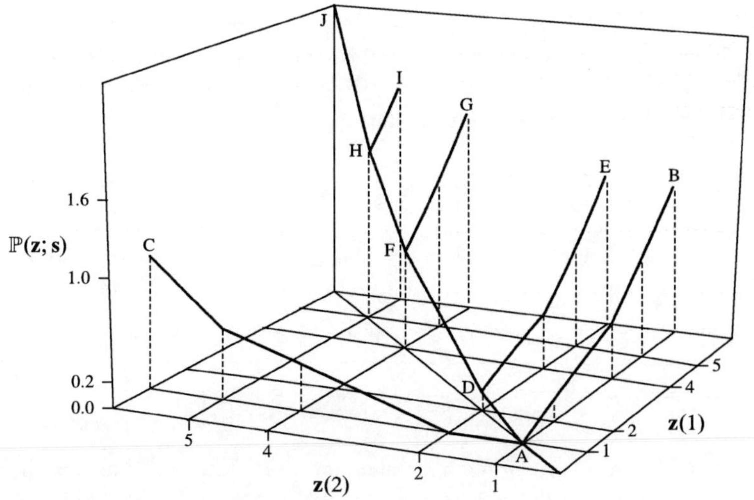

Fig. 3 Ordered poverty gap curves

all the properties of the usual poverty gap: $\mathbb{P}(\mathbf{z};\mathbf{s})$ is non-decreasing and convex on the income range $\left[v_1, v_{m_2(\mathbf{s})}\right]$, and linear on the intervals $\left[v_j, v_{j+1}\right)$, $j = 1, 2, \ldots, m_2(\mathbf{s}) - 1$, and $\left[v_{m_2(\mathbf{s})}, +\infty\right)$.

In order to illustrate the preceding definition, in Fig. 3, we have represented the ordered poverty gap curves of situation $\mathbf{s}^1$ in Example 1. There are two ability groups–say the handicapped ($h = 1$) and the healthy ($h = 2$)–and thus two poverty lines $\mathbf{z}(1)$ and $\mathbf{z}(2)$. Given the properties of the poverty gap curves, because $\mathbf{z}(1) \geq \mathbf{z}(2)$ there are four ordered poverty gap curves corresponding to the convex piecewise linear lines AB, DE, EG, and HI. Actually, the curve AB is nothing but the conditional poverty gap curve of the group of handicapped individuals weighted by their corresponding population share. Similarly, the piecewise linear line AC represents the weighted conditional poverty gap curve of the group of healthy individuals. Summing the curves AB and AC we obtain the curve AJ, which is the integral of the marginal distribution of income or, equivalently, the poverty gap for the whole population of individuals irrespective of their type.

We will say that situation $\mathbf{s}^*$ *ordered poverty gap dominates* situation $\mathbf{s}^\circ$, which we write as $\mathbf{s}^* \geq_{\mathrm{OPG}} \mathbf{s}^\circ$, if and only if

$$\mathbb{P}\left(\mathbf{z};\left(\mathbf{x}^*;\mathbf{a}^*\right)\right) \leq \mathbb{P}\left(\mathbf{z};\left(\mathbf{x}^\circ;\mathbf{a}^\circ\right)\right), \ \forall\, \mathbf{z} \text{ non-increasing in } h. \tag{29}$$

Definition (27) makes clear that the ordered poverty gap is the weighted sum of the conditional poverty gaps, where the weights are equal to the marginal densities of ability. For later reference, we will say that situation $\mathbf{s}^*$ *conditional poverty gap dominates* situation $\mathbf{s}^\circ$, which we write as $\mathbf{s}^* \geq_{\mathrm{CPG}} \mathbf{s}^\circ$, if and only if

$$P^*\left(z\,|\,h\right) \leq P^\circ\left(z\,|\,h\right), \ \forall\, z \in \mathscr{D}, \ \forall\, h \in M_2\left(\mathbf{s}^*, \mathbf{s}^\circ\right). \tag{30}$$

When the situations under comparison have identical marginal distributions of ability, it is immediately clear that conditional poverty gap dominance implies ordered poverty gap dominance, while the converse implication does not hold. Straightforward computations indicate that

$$\mathbb{P}\left(\mathbf{z}; \left(\mathbf{s}^*; \mathbf{s}^\circ\right)^{\mathrm{T}}\right) = \mathbb{P}\left(\mathbf{z}; \mathbf{s}^*\right) + \mathbb{P}\left(\mathbf{z}; \mathbf{s}^\circ\right), \; \forall\, \mathbf{s}^* \in \mathbb{S}_n, \; \forall\, \mathbf{s}^\circ \in \mathbb{S}_q \; (n, q \geq 1). \quad (31)$$

The next result, which is a direct consequence of the additive separability of the ordered poverty gap, will play a crucial role in subsequent developments.

Lemma 10. *For all* $\mathbf{s}^*, \mathbf{s}^\circ \in \mathbb{S}_n$ $(n \geq 2)$ *and all* $\mathbf{s} \in \mathbb{S}_q$ $(q \geq 1)$, *we have:*

$$\mathbf{s}^* \geq_{\mathrm{OPG}} \mathbf{s}^\circ \iff \left(\mathbf{s}^*; \mathbf{s}\right)^{\mathrm{T}} \geq_{\mathrm{OPG}} \left(\mathbf{s}^\circ; \mathbf{s}\right)^{\mathrm{T}}. \quad (32)$$

The following result is simply a restatement of well-known results in the unidimensional case (see Berge 1963; Hardy et al. 1952; Marshall and Olkin 1979).

Lemma 11. *Let* $\mathbf{s}^*, \mathbf{s}^\circ \in \mathbb{S}_n$ $(n \geq 2)$ *be such that* $\mathbf{a}^* = \mathbf{a}^\circ$ *and* $\mu(\mathbf{x}^*) = \mu(\mathbf{x}^\circ)$. *Then* $\mathbf{s}^* \geq_{\mathrm{CPG}} \mathbf{s}^\circ$ *implies that* $\mathbf{s}^*$ *is obtained from* $\mathbf{s}^\circ$ *by means of a finite sequence of within-type progressive transfers of income.*

Our last lemma will play a decisive role in the proof of our main result. It is a separation result, which states that ordered poverty gap domination can always be decomposed into headcount poverty and conditional poverty gap dominations.[7]

Lemma 12. *Let* $\mathbf{s}^*, \mathbf{s}^\circ \in \mathbb{S}_n$ $(n \geq 2)$ *be such that* $\mathbf{a}^* = \mathbf{a}^\circ$, $\mu(\mathbf{x}^*) = \mu(\mathbf{x}^\circ)$, *and* $\mathbf{s} \in \mathbb{S}_q$ $(q \geq 1)$. *Then*

$$\left(\mathbf{s}^*; \mathbf{s}\right)^{\mathrm{T}} \geq_{\mathrm{OPG}} \left(\mathbf{s}^\circ; \mathbf{s}\right)^{\mathrm{T}} \quad (33)$$

if and only if there exist two situations $\tilde{\mathbf{s}} \in \mathbb{S}_n$ *and* $\hat{\mathbf{s}} \in \mathbb{S}_q$ *such that*

$$\left(\mathbf{s}^*; \mathbf{s}\right)^{\mathrm{T}} \geq_{\mathrm{HP}} \left(\tilde{\mathbf{s}}; \hat{\mathbf{s}}\right)^{\mathrm{T}} \geq_{\mathrm{CPG}} \left(\mathbf{s}^\circ; \mathbf{s}\right)^{\mathrm{T}}. \quad (34)$$

Making use of Lemma 2, Proposition 1, Lemmas 4 and 5, and Lemmas 8–12, we obtain the following theorem, which reveals the normative foundations of the Bourguignon (1989) ordered poverty gap quasi-ordering.

Theorem 3. *Let* $\mathbf{s}^*, \mathbf{s}^\circ \in \mathbb{S}_n$ $(n \geq 2)$ *be such that* $\mathbf{a}^* = \mathbf{a}^\circ$ *and* $\mu(\mathbf{x}^*) = \mu(\mathbf{x}^\circ)$. *Then statements (a), (b), (c), and (d) below are equivalent:*

(*a*) *There exist* $q \geq 1$ *and a situation* $\mathbf{s} \in \mathbb{S}_q$ *such that* $(\mathbf{s}^*; \mathbf{s})^{\mathrm{T}}$ *is obtained from* $(\mathbf{s}^\circ; \mathbf{s})^{\mathrm{T}}$ *by means of a finite sequence of permutations of individuals, favorable permutations, and/or within-type progressive transfers.*

[7] Analogous results are well-known in the unidimensional setting, where generalised Lorenz domination is decomposed into first order stochastic domination and Lorenz domination (see, e.g., Marshall and Olkin 1979).

(b) $\sum_{i=1}^{n} U\left(x_i^*, a_i^*\right) \geq \sum_{i=1}^{n} U\left(x_i^\circ, a_i^\circ\right)$ *for all* $U \in \mathbb{U}_2$.

(c) $U\left(\mathbf{x}^*; \mathbf{a}^*\right) \geq_{\mathrm{GL}} U\left(\mathbf{x}^\circ; \mathbf{a}^\circ\right)$ *for all* $U \in \mathbb{U}_2$.

(d) 1. $\mathbb{P}\left(\mathbf{z}; \left(\mathbf{x}^*; \mathbf{a}^*\right)\right) \leq \mathbb{P}\left(\mathbf{z}; \left(\mathbf{x}^\circ; \mathbf{a}^\circ\right)\right)$ *for all* $\mathbf{z}$ *non-increasing in* h;

2. $F_2^*(h) = F_2^\circ(h)$ *for all* $h \in M_2\left(\mathbf{s}^*, \mathbf{s}^\circ\right)$.

Sketch of Proof. Invoking Lemmas 4 and 8, we deduce from statement (a) that

$$\sum_{i=1}^{n} U\left(x_i^*, a_i^*\right) + \sum_{i=1}^{q} U\left(x_i, a_i\right) \geq \sum_{i=1}^{n} U\left(x_i^\circ, a_i^\circ\right) + \sum_{i=1}^{q} U\left(x_i, a_i\right) \qquad (35)$$

for all $U \in \mathbb{U}_2$, which by Lemma 2 is equivalent to statement (b). Proposition 1 and the fact that the class of utility functions $\mathbb{U}_2$ is closed under composition by a non-decreasing and concave function guarantee the equivalence between statements (b) and (c). The fact that (d) is necessary for (b) to hold can be easily shown by suitably choosing degenerate utility functions in the class $\mathbb{U}_2$. Invoking the separability of the ordered poverty gap dominance criterion (see Lemma 10), we deduce from statement (d) that

$$\left(\mathbf{s}^*; \mathbf{s}\right)^{\mathrm{T}} \geq_{\mathrm{OPG}} \left(\mathbf{s}^\circ; \mathbf{s}\right)^{\mathrm{T}}, \ \forall\, \mathbf{s} \in \bigcup_{q=1}^{\infty} \mathbb{S}_q. \qquad (36)$$

Using Lemma 12, we deduce from (36) that there exists a situation $(\tilde{\mathbf{s}}\,; \hat{\mathbf{s}})^{\mathrm{T}}$ such that

$$\left(\mathbf{s}^*; \mathbf{s}\right)^{\mathrm{T}} \geq_{\mathrm{HP}} (\tilde{\mathbf{s}}\,; \hat{\mathbf{s}})^{\mathrm{T}} \geq_{\mathrm{CPG}} \left(\mathbf{s}^\circ; \mathbf{s}\right)^{\mathrm{T}}. \qquad (37)$$

Finally, Lemmas 5 and 11 establish that (37) implies statement (a), which makes the argument complete. □

The equivalence between unanimous agreement among all utilitarian ethical observers whose marginal utility of income is non-increasing in both attributes and ordered poverty gap dominance was first established by Bourguignon (1989). However, the normative meaning of this result is somewhat obscured by the fact that the nature of the underlying elementary transformations that are needed to transform the dominated situation into the dominating one was not revealed. Also, the ingenious proof technique employed by Bourguignon relied on the introduction of auxiliary functions whose meaning is unclear. Theorem 3 is motivated by these critiques, but we have to admit that the answer it provides is not totally satisfactory. Indeed, in order to identify the elementary transformations, successive applications of which allow one to derive the dominating situation from the dominating one, it may be the case that we have to introduce a virtual situation–namely, the situation $\mathbf{s}$ in statement (a). Actually, it is not always necessary to have recourse to such a fictitious situation to prove the equivalence between statements (a) and (d). Thanks to the separability of the different normative criteria we appeal to, the virtual situation plays only an instrumental role in the derivation of our result. There is a strong presumption that this instrumental situation actually mirrors the auxiliary functions used by Bourguignon in his proof.

Leaving aside the fact that we do not provide a means for identifying with precision the virtual situation, the main limitation of Theorem 3 is that it is silent as far as between-type progressive transfers are concerned. Indeed, we know from Lemma 9 that all utilitarian ethical observers whose marginal utility of income is non-increasing in income and ability will consider that a between-type progressive transfer results in improvement in social welfare. However, we have not succeeded in showing that a finite sequence of such transformations enables the dominated situation to be transformed into the dominating one, nor have we been able to prove that this is impossible. All we have shown is that it is possible to transform the dominated situation into the dominating situation–with *both situations augmented by the virtual situation*–by means of favorable permutations and within-type progressive transfers. This is a challenging question because a between-type progressive transfer can always be decomposed into a within-type progressive transfer followed by a favorable permutation provided that one adds a fictitious individual endowed with the income of the beneficiary and the ability of the donor prior to the transfer. Figure 4 illustrates the three steps involved in this decomposition process.

To simplify matters, suppose that the population consists of two individuals i and j and consider two situations $\mathbf{s}^* = (\mathbf{s}_i^*, \mathbf{s}_j^*)^{\mathrm{T}}$ and $\mathbf{s}^\circ = (\mathbf{s}_i^\circ, \mathbf{s}_j^\circ)^{\mathrm{T}}$ for which

$$\mathbf{s}_i^\circ = (x_i^\circ, a_i^\circ) = (u, h), \quad \mathbf{s}_j^\circ = (x_j^\circ, a_j^\circ) = (t, k), \tag{38a}$$

$$\mathbf{s}_i^* = (x_i^*, a_i^*) = (u, k), \quad \mathbf{s}_j^* = (x_j^*, a_j^*) = (t, h), \tag{38b}$$

where $u < v \leq w < t$, $v - u = t - w = \Delta$, and $h < k$. Thus, situation $\mathbf{s}^* = (\mathbf{s}_i^*, \mathbf{s}_j^*)^{\mathrm{T}}$ is obtained from situation $\mathbf{s}^\circ = (\mathbf{s}_i^\circ, \mathbf{s}_j^\circ)^{\mathrm{T}}$ by means of a single between-type progressive transfer. Consider now an individual g whose situation is given by

$$\mathbf{s}_g^\circ = (x_g^\circ, a_g^\circ) = (u, k). \tag{39}$$

Adding individual g to the initial population $\{i, j\}$, we obtain the augmented situation $(\mathbf{s}_i^\circ, \mathbf{s}_j^\circ; \mathbf{s}_g^\circ)^{\mathrm{T}}$. Individuals g and j have the same ability, but individual j is richer than individual g. Taking an income amount $\Delta > 0$ from individual j and giving it to individual g we obtain the new situation $(\mathbf{s}_i^\circ, \mathbf{s}_j^*; \mathbf{s}_g^*)^{\mathrm{T}}$, which is obtained from $(\mathbf{s}_i^\circ, \mathbf{s}_j^\circ; \mathbf{s}_g^\circ)^{\mathrm{T}}$ by means of a within-type progressive transfer. Observe that individual i is deprived in both income and ability compared to individual g. By exchanging the incomes of individuals i and g, we obtain the situation $(\mathbf{s}_i^*, \mathbf{s}_j^*; \mathbf{s}_g^\circ)^{\mathrm{T}}$, which is obtained from situation $(\mathbf{s}_i^\circ, \mathbf{s}_j^*; \mathbf{s}_g^*)^{\mathrm{T}}$ by means of a favorable permutation. Individual g is back to her initial situation, so she actually played only an instrumental role in the decomposition. We could have equally well proceeded by choosing $\mathbf{s}_g^\circ = (x_g^\circ, a_g^\circ) = (t, h)$, which would have led to a within-type progressive transfer from individual g to individual i followed by a favorable permutation of income between individuals g and j.

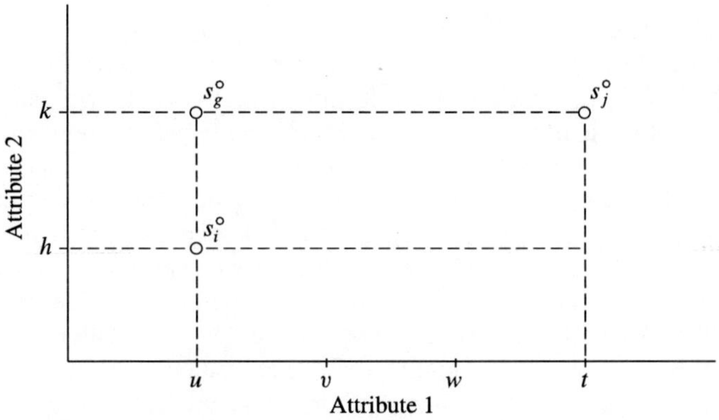

(a) Step 1. Addition of the dummy individual

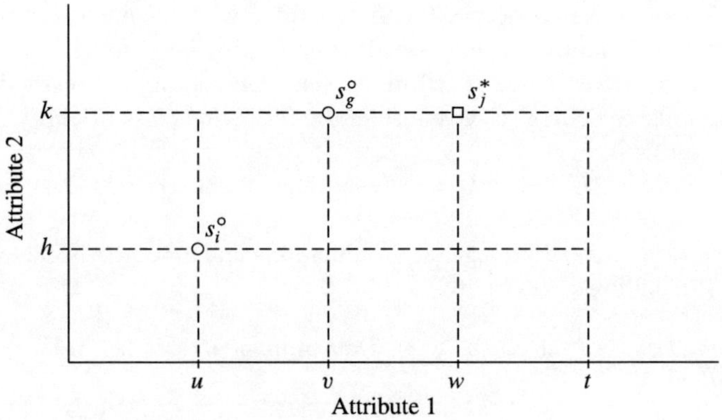

(b) Step 2. Within-type progressive transfer

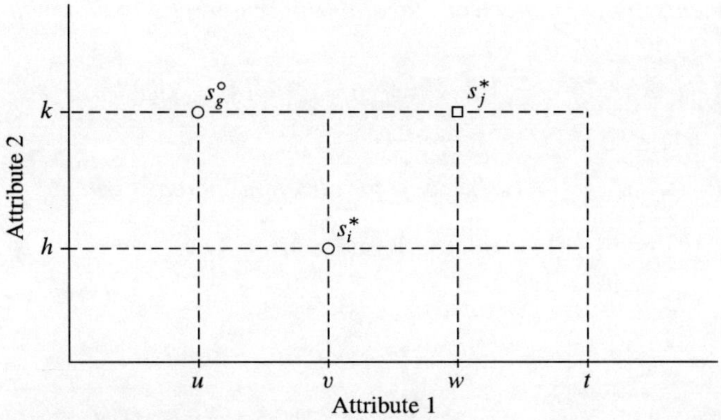

(c) Step 3. Favorable permutation

Fig. 4 Decomposition of a between-type progressive transfer

Application of condition (d.1) of Theorem 3 to the situations of Example 1 allows us to obtain a decisive verdict in all possible pairs of situations but one, namely $\{\mathbf{s}^3, \mathbf{s}^4\}$. That $\mathbf{s}^3 \geq_{\mathrm{OPG}} \mathbf{s}^2$ can readily be anticipated from the fact that situation $\mathbf{s}^3$ is obtained from situation $\mathbf{s}^2$ by means of a favorable permutation involving individuals 1 and 5. Similarly, it is not a surprise that $\mathbf{s}^3 \geq_{\mathrm{OPG}} \mathbf{s}^1$ because ordered poverty gap dominance is compatible with headcount poverty dominance. On the other hand, the fact that $\mathbf{s}^4 \geq_{\mathrm{OPG}} \mathbf{s}^2$ is at first sight unexpected given the way the situations in Example 1 have been constructed.[8] However, close inspection reveals that $\mathbf{s}^4$ can be directly obtained from $\mathbf{s}^2$ by means of a within-type progressive transfer involving individuals 1 and 3 followed by a favorable permutation of the incomes of individuals 1 and 4. This example provides an instance where there is no need to introduce an auxiliary situation in order to derive the dominating situation from the dominated one by means of favorable permutations and within-type progressive transfers.

While Theorem 3 is concerned with situations with identical income and ability marginal distributions, it is easy to extend it to the general case of variable marginal distributions if one is willing to introduce additional restrictions on the utility functions. Specifically, we consider the following class of utility functions:

$$\mathbb{U}_2^* := \{U \in \mathbb{U} \mid U \text{ satisfies (C1), (C2), (C3), and (C4)}\}. \tag{40}$$

Dispensing with the restrictions that the situations under comparison have identical marginal distributions, we obtain:

Theorem 4. *Let* $\mathbf{s}^*, \mathbf{s}^\circ \in \mathbb{S}_n$ $(n \geq 2)$. *Then statements (a), (b), (c), and (d) below are equivalent:*

(*a*) *There exist* $q \geq 1$ *and a situation* $\tilde{\mathbf{s}} \in \mathbb{S}_q$ *such that* $(\mathbf{s}^*; \tilde{\mathbf{s}})^{\mathrm{T}}$ *is obtained from* $(\mathbf{s}^\circ; \tilde{\mathbf{s}})^{\mathrm{T}}$ *by means of a finite sequence of permutations of individuals, income increments, ability increments, favorable permutations, and/or within-type progressive transfers.*

(*b*) $\sum_{i=1}^n U\left(x_i^*, a_i^*\right) \geq \sum_{i=1}^n U\left(x_i^\circ, a_i^\circ\right)$ *for all* $U \in \mathbb{U}_2^*$.

(*c*) $U(\mathbf{x}^*; \mathbf{a}^*) \geq_{\mathrm{GL}} U(\mathbf{x}^\circ; \mathbf{a}^\circ)$ *for all* $U \in \mathbb{U}_2^*$.

(*d*) 1. $\mathbb{P}(\mathbf{z}; (\mathbf{x}^*; \mathbf{a}^*)) \leq \mathbb{P}(\mathbf{z}; (\mathbf{x}^\circ; \mathbf{a}^\circ))$ *for all* $\mathbf{z}$ *non-increasing in* h;

2. $F_2^*(h) = F_2^\circ(h)$ *for all* $h \in M_2(\mathbf{s}^*, \mathbf{s}^\circ)$.

[8] Actually, two transformations of equal magnitude whose impacts on social welfare go in opposite directions are needed to convert situation $\mathbf{s}^4$ into situation $\mathbf{s}^3$. The favorable permutation consisting of exchanging the incomes of individuals 1 and 4 results in a welfare improvement, while the unfavorable permutation between individuals 3 and 5 of the same amount unambiguously decreases welfare. The net effect on social welfare of these two transformations is therefore ambiguous unless one is prepared to impose additional restrictions on the utility functions.

6 Concluding Remarks

The aim of this article has been to investigate the normative foundations of two implementable criteria–the so-called headcount poverty and ordered poverty gap quasi-orderings–designed for comparing distributions of two attributes, one of which–income–is cardinally measurable, while the other–ability–is ordinal. Our ambition has been to provide in each of the cases considered, an equivalence result analogous to the celebrated HLP Theorem in the unidimensional framework. More precisely, we have wanted (a) to identify the class of utility functions for which all welfarist ethical observers whose value judgements belong to this class rank the situations under comparison in the same way as the dominance criterion and (b) to uncover the elementary transformations whose finite application permits one to derive the dominating situation from the dominated one.

A marginal utility of income that is non-increasing in ability ensures that the welfarist unanimity rule and the headcount poverty quasi-ordering rank situations in the same way, while a favorable permutation is the transformation which, if applied a finite number of times, allows one to derive the dominating situation from the dominated one. As far as the headcount poverty–equivalently first-order stochastic dominance–criterion is concerned Theorem 1 provides the desired equivalence. Matters are far less satisfactory in the case of the ordered poverty gap dominance criterion because we did not manage to establish an equivalence in Theorem 3 without resorting to the adjunction of a virtual situation. Using this technical device, we were able to show that repeated applications of favorable permutations and within-type progressive transfers allow one to transform the dominated situation into the dominating one. On the other hand, we know that all welfarist ethical observers whose marginal utilities of income is non-increasing in both income and ability will record as welfare-improving a between-type progressive transfer. However, it is still an open question whether it is possible to obtain the dominating situation from the dominated one by means of between-type progressive transfers *without* resorting to dummy individuals.

Other limitations of the present analysis concern the number of attributes considered and also the informational assumptions we have made. Focusing on just two attributes is certainly restrictive and does not allow us to capture all the relevant dimensions of a person's well-being. The *Human Development Index* (HDI) is a good example of an aggregate measure focusing on three essential factors that contribute to a person's well-being: income, life expectancy, and literacy. Increasing the number of dimensions is certainly one direction to go, but such an extension is likely to become quite involved very quickly. To give but one example, the meaning of correlation, which lies at the heart of the concept of a favorable permutation, needs to be substantially reformulated when more than two attributes are considered. Suppose, for example, there are three attributes, as in the HDI case, then the welfare impact of a favorable permutation involving the first and second attributes will depend on the quantity of the third attribute received by the individuals involved in the transformation.[9] The question also arises of knowing if it could be possible to adapt the approach of Bourguignon (1989) in order to rank situations involving only cardinal attributes, as is done in Kolm (1977) and Atkinson and Bourguignon (1982).

There is a general skepticism concerning the ability of the dominance approach to provide relevant information because of the incomplete nature of the quasi-orderings it relies on. The non-decisiveness of this approach is accentuated in the multi-attribute case and it is expected to be more serious as the number of dimensions increases. The criteria we have investigated in this article are no exception. To some extent, they may be considered as a first step that has to supplemented by the use of multidimensional cardinal indices, like those characterized in Ebert (1995) for instance. However, to conclude on a more positive note, it is worth mentioning that the criteria we have examined provide a conclusive verdict in a non-negligible number of cases, as the evidence in Gravel et al. (2009) shows.

Acknowledgements We thank Stephen Bazen, Marc Fleurbaey, and an anonymous referee whose useful comments helped us to improve this article. In particular, the critical examination of an earlier version of this article by Marc Fleurbaey led us to reconsider significantly some of our original positions. Needless to say, the authors bear the entire responsibility for remaining errors and deficiencies.

References

Allison, R. A., & Foster, J. E. (2004). Measuring health inequality using qualitative data. *Journal of Health Economics*, *23*, 503–524

Atkinson, A. B., & Bourguignon, F. (1982). The comparison of multidimensioned distributions of economic status. *Review of Economic Studies*, *49*, 183–201

Atkinson, A. B., & Bourguignon, F. (1987). Income distributions and differences in needs. In G. R. Feiwel (Ed.), *Arrow and the foundations of the theory of economic policy* (pp. 350–370). London: Macmillan

Berge, C. (1963). *Topological spaces: Including a treatment of multi-valued functions, vector spaces and convexity*. Edinburgh: Oliver and Boyd

Blackorby, C., Bossert, W., & Donaldson, D. (2005). *Population issues in social choice theory, welfare economics, and ethics*. Cambridge: Cambridge University Press

Bourguignon, F. (1989). Family size and social utility: Income distribution dominance criteria. *Journal of Econometrics*, *42*, 67–80

Dasgupta, P., Sen, A., & Starrett, D. (1973). Notes on the measurement of inequality. *Journal of Economic Theory*, *6*, 180–187

Ebert, U. (1995). Income inequality and differences in household size. *Mathematical Social Sciences*, *30*, 37–53

[9] One possibility for avoiding this difficulty is to make the extra value judgement that some attributes are separable from each other, which rules out the possibility of using one attribute to compensate for the other. This is the route followed, for instance, by Muller and Trannoy (2011), who assume separability between life expectancy at birth and educational attainment, but maintain the possibility of using income to compensate for poor health and low education.

Ebert, U. (2000). Sequential generalized Lorenz dominance and transfer principles. *Bulletin of Economic Research*, *52*, 113–123

Epstein, L. G., & Tanny, S. M. (1980). Increasing generalized correlation: A definition and some economic consequences. *Canadian Journal of Economics*, *13*, 16–34

Fields, G. S., & Fei, J. C. H. (1978). On inequality comparisons. *Econometrica*, *46*, 305–316

Foster, J. E. (1985). Inequality measurement. In H. P. Young (Ed.), *Fair allocation* (pp. 38–61). Providence, RI: American Mathematical Society

Gravel, N., & Moyes, P. (2006). Ethically robust comparisons of distributions of two individual attributes. Document de Travail No. 06-05, Institut d'Economie Publique.

Gravel, N., Moyes, P., & Tarroux, B. (2009). Robust international comparisons of distributions of disposable income and regional public goods. *Economica*, *76*, 432–461

Griffin, J. (1986). *Well-being: Its meaning, measurement and moral importance*. Oxford: Clarendon

Hadar, J., & Russell, W. R. (1974). Stochastic dominance in choice under uncertainty. In M. S. Balch, D. L. McFadden, & S. Y. Wu (Eds.), *Essays on economic behavior under uncertainty* (pp. 135–150). Amsterdam: North-Holland

Hardy, G. H., Littlewood, J. E., & Pólya, G. (1952). *Inequalities* (2nd ed.). Cambridge: Cambridge University Press

Kolm, S.-C. (1969). The optimal production of social justice. In J. Margolis & H. Guitton (Eds.), *Public economics: An analysis of public production and consumption and their relations to the private sector* (pp. 145–200). London: Macmillan

Kolm, S.-C. (1977). Multidimensional egalitarianisms. *Quarterly Journal of Economics*, *91*, 1–13

Koshevoy, G. (1995). Multivariate Lorenz majorization. *Social Choice and Welfare*, *12*, 93–102

Marshall, A. W., & Olkin, I. (1979). *Inequalities: Theory of majorization and its applications*. New York: Academic Press

Moyes, P. (1999). Comparaisons de distributions hétérogènes et critères de dominance. *Economie et Prévision*, *138–139*, 125–146

Muller, C., & Trannoy, A. (2011). A dominance approach to the appraisal of the distribution of well-being across countries. *Journal of Public Economics*, *95*, 239–246

Sen, A. K. (1985). *Commodities and capabilities*. Amsterdam: North-Holland

Sen, A. K. (1997). *On Economic Inequality. Expanded edition with a substantial annexe by James E. Foster and Amartya Sen* (2nd ed.). Oxford: Clarendon

Shorrocks, A. F. (1983). Ranking income distributions. *Economica*, *50*, 3–17

Trannoy, A. (2006). Multidimensional egalitarianism and the dominance approach: A lost paradise? In F. Farina & E. Savaglio (Eds.), *Inequality and economic integration* (pp. 284–302). London: Routledge

Inequality of Life Chances and the Measurement of Social Immobility

Jacques Silber and Amedeo Spadaro

1 Introduction

The topic of intergenerational mobility measurement has been increasingly popular among economists in recent years. For interesting surveys, see, for example, Solon (1999) and Corak (2004). In a recent article, Van de gaer et al. (2001) have made a distinction between three meanings of intergenerational mobility, stressing respectively the idea of movement, the inequality of opportunity, and the inequality of life chances.

When mobility is viewed as movement, the goal is usually to measure the degree to which the position of children is different from that of their parents. Those adopting such an approach tend to work with transition matrices whose typical element p_{ij} refers to the probability that a child has position j given that his or her parents had position i. These matrices are square matrices and it should be clear that mobility in this sense will be higher the smaller the value of the probabilities p_{ii}.

The second approach to mobility attempts to measure the degree to which the income prospects of children are equalized so that these prospects do not depend on the social origin of the parents. What is often done in such types of analyses when comparing, for example, two groups of parents (e.g., differentiated by educational level or occupation) is to check whether the distribution of the outcomes (incomes) of the children of one group of parents stochastically dominates the distribution of the second category of parents. See, for example, Peragine (2004) and Lefranc et al. (2009).

J. Silber (✉)
Department of Economics, Bar-Ilan University, 52900 Ramat-Gan, Israel
e-mail: jsilber_2000@yahoo.com

A. Spadaro
Paris School of Economics, 48 Bd. Jourdan, 75014 Paris, France and Universitat de les Illes Balears, ctra Valldemossa Km 7,5, 07122 Palma de Mallorca, Spain
e-mail: spadaro@pse.ens.fr

M. Fleurbaey et al. (eds.), *Social Ethics and Normative Economics*,
Studies in Choice and Welfare, DOI 10.1007/978-3-642-17807-8_5,

The third approach emphasizes the concept of inequality of life chances so that "the only thing that matters here is that children get equal lotteries. The prizes do not matter." (Van de gaer et al. 2001, p. 522). Such an approach is particularly relevant when one analyzes the movement between socio-economic categories which cannot always be ranked in order of importance.

In this article, we focus most of our attention on the third approach. In Sect. 2, we first propose an ordinal approach to measuring inequality in life chances based on the use of what we call social immobility curves. We then suggest two cardinal measures of social immobility that do not require the social mobility matrix that is to be analyzed to be a square matrix. This allows us to study the transition from the original social category (educational level or occupation) of the parents to the income class to which the children belong. These measures could also be applied to an analysis of the transition from one type of social category (e.g., educational level of the parents) to another type of social category (e.g., profession of the children), assuming that there is no specific ordering of these categories.

In Sect. 3, we stress the importance of the marginal distributions when comparing social immobility in two populations. More precisely, when these populations are parents and children, we recommend neutralizing the differences between the distribution of the parents by social category (e.g., occupation or educational level) and the distribution of the children by income. We suggest borrowing ideas that have appeared, for example, in the literatures on occupational segregation and horizontal inequity measurement, so that when comparing two populations a distinction can be made between differences in gross and net social immobility, the latter concept assuming that the marginal distributions of the two populations being compared are identical.

In Sect. 4, borrowing some concepts from the literature on equality of opportunity (e.g., Roemer 1998; Kolm 2001; Ruiz-Castillo 2003; Villar 2005), we define an inequality-in-circumstances curve and relate it to the social immobility curve previously presented.

Two empirical illustrations are provided in Sect. 5 to demonstrate the usefulness of the concepts previously defined. The data for the first illustration comes from a survey conducted in France in 1998 and allows us to measure the degree of social immobility and of inequality in circumstances on the basis of information on the occupation of fathers or mothers and of the income class to which sons or daughters belong. Using a second set of data, based on a social survey conducted in Israel in 2003, we then measure social immobility and inequality in circumstances by studying the transition from the educational level of the fathers to the income class to which the children belong. Both illustrations confirm that tools that had previously been used in the field of occupational segregation and horizontal inequity measurement are also relevant for the study of equality of opportunity.

Concluding comments are given in Sect. 6. In the Appendix, we show how to decompose variations over time in the extent of social mobility.

2 Measuring Social Immobility

2.1 *Social Immobility Curves*

Let M be a data matrix whose rows i correspond to the social origins of the individuals being considered (e.g., occupation or the educational level of the father or mother) and whose columns j correspond to the income brackets to which these individuals belong. For example, a typical element M_{ij} of M could be the number of individuals whose incomes belong to income bracket j and whose father had educational level i.

Let m_{ij}, $m_{i.}$, and $m_{.j}$ be defined as:

$$m_{ij} = \frac{M_{ij}}{\sum_{i=1}^{I} \sum_{j=1}^{J} M_{ij}}, \tag{1}$$

$$m_{i.} = \sum_{j=1}^{J} m_{ij}, \tag{2}$$

and

$$m_{.j} = \sum_{i=1}^{I} m_{ij}. \tag{3}$$

Then perfect social mobility may be said to exist when the probability that an individual belongs to a specific income bracket k is independent of his social origin h, that is, when $m_{hk} = m_{h.}m_{.k}$.

Let $(m_{i.}m_{.j})$ denote a vector in which the products $m_{i.}m_{.j}$ of the elements $m_{i.}$ and $m_{.j}$ are increasingly ordered according to the values of the ratios $\frac{m_{ij}}{m_{i.}m_{.j}}$. Similarly, let (m_{ij}) denote the vector in which the shares m_{ij} are also increasingly ordered by the values of these ratios. By plotting the cumulative values of the products $m_{i.}m_{.j}$ on the horizontal axis and the cumulative values of the shares m_{ij} on the vertical axis, one obtains a *social immobility curve*. This curve is in fact what is known in the literature as a relative concentration curve and is an illustration of what Chakravarty and Silber (2007) have called a "dependence curve." Clearly, its slope is non-decreasing. In the specific case in which $m_{ij} = m_{i.}m_{.j}$ for each i and j, the corresponding social immobility curve is the diagonal line going from $(0, 0)$ to $(1, 1)$. Social immobility curves can be used to provide an ordinal approach to the measurement of social immobility.

Now assume that $\frac{m_{fh}}{m_{f.}m_{.h}} > \frac{m_{fk}}{m_{f.}m_{.k}}$ and $\frac{m_{lk}}{m_{l.}m_{.k}} > \frac{m_{lh}}{m_{l.}m_{.l}}$. Consider two "transfers" of size δ, one from m_{fh} to m_{fk} and one from m_{lk} to m_{lh}. The combination of these two transfers implies that there is no change in the marginal shares of h and k. These two margin-preserving transfers have been called an "independence-increasing margins-preserving composite transfer" (IIMPCT) by Chakravarty and

Silber (2007), who have established the link between IIMPCT and the concept of independence domination (a stochastic dominance relation for dependence curves). The latter is checked using the social immobility curves.[1]

2.2 Cardinal Measures of Social Mobility

Chakravarty and Silber (2007) have derived the link between the ordering of dependence curves and the values taken by dependence indices that have the following two properties. First, they obey the property of symmetry, implying, for example, that the exact label of the social status of the parent or the child does not matter. Second, their value decreases when there is a IIMPCT. Chakravarty and Silber also stress that the two indices introduced below, which are derived using the Theil and Gini indices, belong to this family of indices.

The first index we have selected is directly related to one of the famous indices of Theil (1967). Theil's index may be interpreted as comparing prior probabilities with posterior probabilities. In our case, the "prior probabilities" are the products $m_{h.}m_{.k}$, while the "posterior probabilities" are the proportions m_{hk}. Such a formulation then leads to the following *Theil index of social immobility*:

$$T_{sim} = \sum_{i=1}^{I}\sum_{j=1}^{J} m_{i.}m_{.j} \ln\left(\frac{m_{i.}m_{.j}}{m_{ij}}\right). \tag{4}$$

Note that the value of this index equals 0 when there is perfect independence between the social origin and income brackets.

Another possibility is to use a Gini-related index, as suggested originally by Flückiger and Silber (1994). As stressed by Silber (1989b), the Gini index may be also used to measure the degree of dissimilarity between a set of prior probabilities and a set of posterior probabilities. In the case of inequality measurement, the "prior probabilities" are the population shares and the "posterior probabilities" are the income shares. Let $[m_{i.}m_{.j})]'$ be a row vector of the "prior probabilities"

[1] This type of transfer has been mentioned before in the literature under the name of a "marginal preserving swap" (MPS). To the best of our knowledge, most of this literature has dealt, however, with the idea of an ordering on discrete bivariate distributions (e.g., Tchen 1980), the derivation of a measure of dependence for pairs of random variables with continuous distribution functions (e.g., Schweizer and Wolff 1981), or the concept of (positive quadrant) dependence in two-way tables with ordered margins (e.g., Bartolucci et al. 2001). The assumption that the margins may be ordered was also made by Epstein and Tanny (1980), Atkinson and Bourguignon (1982), and Dardanoni and Lambert (2001). In this case, use can be made of L-superadditive evaluation functions (see Marshall and Olkin 1979), which are increasing in an MPS. We are indeed very thankful to an anonymous referee for drawing our attention to some of these studies. We want, however, to stress that our analysis does not require that the margins can be ordered. For each cell of a contingency table, we derive a variable measuring the degree of dependence between its corresponding margins. This variable is the ordering criterion, as shown by Chakravarty and Silber (2007).

corresponding to the $I \times J$ cells (i, j) and let $[m_{ij}]$ be a column vector of the "posterior probabilities" (the actual probabilities) for these cells, where, as in Silber (1989a), the elements of these row and column vectors have both been ranked so that they are decreasing in the ratio $\frac{m_{ij}}{m_{i.}m_{.j}}$. The *Gini index of social immobility* is expressed as:

$$G_{sim} = [m_{i.}m_{.j}]' G[m_{ij}]. \tag{5}$$

The operator G in (5), called the *G-matrix* (see Silber 1989a), is an $I \times J$ by $I \times J$ square matrix whose typical element g_{pq} is equal to 0 if $p = q$, to $+1$ if $p > q$, and to -1 if $p < q$. Note that the index G_{sim} is also equal to 0 when the "prior probability" $m_{i.}m_{.j}$ equals the "posterior probability" m_{ij} for all i and j.

3 Comparing Two Social Mobility Matrices

Suppose that we want to compare two social mobility matrices M and V. Such matrices may refer to two different periods or to two population subgroups at a given time, such as ethnic groups, regions, etc. On the basis of each of these two matrices, we could compute social immobility indices, such as those defined in expressions (4) and (5), and determine in which case social immobility is higher. This may, however, be too hasty a way to draw firm conclusions, as will now be shown.

Suppose that the social mobility matrices M and V correspond to two different time periods, with the rows showing the social orgins of the parents and the columns showing the income brackets of the children. Social mobility may vary over time for various reasons. First, there may have been a change in the distribution of parents by social origin. Second, there may have been a change in the income distribution of the children. These two possibilities correspond to a variation in one of the margins of the social mobility matrix. There may, however, be a third reason for a variation in the degree of social mobility. Even if there was no change over time in the margins of the social mobility matrix, there may have been a change in the degree of independence between the rows (social origins of the parents) and columns (shares of various income brackets of the children) of this matrix. This distinction between the impact of a change in the margins of a matrix and a change in the *internal structure* of this matrix (the degree of independence between the rows and columns of a matrix) was pointed out by Karmel and MacLachlan (1988) in the framework of an analysis of changes over time in occupational segregation by gender.[2]

In the Appendix, we show how it is possible to apply the methodology proposed by Karmel and MacLachlan (1988) to decompose the change over time in the degree

[2] The idea of making a distinction between changes in the internal structure and in the margins of a matrix is not a novel idea. In the literature on social mobility, there is a long tradition of making a distinction between what is called exchange and structural mobility. We thank Marc Fleurbaey for this observation.

of social mobility (or to decompose the change in the degree of social mobility of two population subgroups) into changes in the margins and in the internal structure of the social mobility matrix. This methodology uses an algorithm originally proposed by Deming and Stephan (1940).[3] In addition, as has already been observed by Deutsch et al. (2009) in the framework of occupational segregation analysis, it will be shown that it is possible to generalize this methodology using the concept of a Shapley decomposition (see Chantreuil and Trannoy 1999; Shorrocks 1999; Sastre and Trannoy 2002). An elementary presentation of this approach is given in the Appendix.

4 Measures of Social Immobility Versus Measures of Inequality in Circumstances

Assuming that the rows of the social mobility matrix to be analyzed correspond to the social origins of the individuals and the columns to the income classes to which they belong, one can adopt the terminology used in the literature on equality of opportunity and call the rows "types" or "circumstances." Under certain conditions, it is also possible to use the term "levels of effort" for the columns, although such an extension implies quite strong assumptions concerning the link between income and effort.

Our definition of inequality in circumstances is adapted from ideas presented in Kolm (2001). We define *inequality in circumstances* to be the weighted average of the inequalities within each income class (effort level), the weights being the population shares of the various income classes. Inequality is measured in the way that Kolm (2001) has suggested by comparing the average level of income for a given level of effort with what he calls the "equal equivalent" level of income for this same level of effort. We measure inequality within a given income class (effort level) by comparing the distribution of the "actual shares" $\frac{m_{ij}}{m_{.j}}$ for each income class j with what could be considered to be the "expected shares" $m_{i.}$.

Using one of Theil's inequality measures, this approach results in the following *Theil measure of inequality in circumstances within income class* j:

$$T_j = \sum_{i=1}^{I} m_{i.} \ln \left(\frac{m_{i.}}{m_{ij}/m_{.j}} \right). \tag{6}$$

[3] The distinction between variations in the margins and in the internal structure of a matrix also has a long tradition in mathematical statistics. In this literature, the term "copula" is used instead of "internal structure." We thank an anonymous referee for drawing our attention to this point. Note also that the algorithm proposed by Deming and Stephan is not the only one that can be used. Little and Wu (1991) mention three other methods.

The *Theil measure of overall inequality in circumstances* T_{circ} is then defined as:

$$\begin{aligned} T_{circ} &= \sum_{j=1}^{J} m_{.j} T_j \\ &= \sum_{j=1}^{J} m_{.j} \sum_{i=1}^{I} m_{i.} \ln\left(\frac{m_{i.}}{m_{ij}/m_{.j}}\right) \\ &= \sum_{j=1}^{J} \sum_{i=1}^{I} m_{i.} m_{.j} \ln\left(\frac{m_{i.} m_{.j}}{m_{ij}}\right), \end{aligned} \tag{7}$$

which is in fact identical to the measure T_{sim} of social immobility in (4).

Let us now measure inequality in circumstances on the basis of the Gini index. We will again measure inequality within a given income class (effort level) by comparing the distribution of the actual shares $\frac{m_{ij}}{m_{.j}}$ for each income class j with the expected shares $m_{i.}$. Using the Gini-matrix that was defined in (5), we derive the following *Gini measure of inequality in circumstances within income class* j:

$$G_j = [m_{i.}]' G \left[\frac{m_{ij}}{m_{.j}}\right] = \frac{[m_{i.}]' G [m_{ij}]}{m_{.j}}, \tag{8}$$

where the two vectors (of dimension I) on both sides of the G-matrix in (8) are ranked according to decreasing values of the ratios $\frac{m_{ij}}{m_{i.}}$.

To derive an overall Gini index of inequality of circumstances G_{circ}, we will have to weight the indices given in (8) by the weights of the income classes j. We should, however, remember that in defining such an overall within-groups Gini inequality index, the sum of the weights will not be equal to 1. Each weight will in fact be equal to $(m_{.j})^2$ because, as with the traditional within-groups Gini index, the weights are equal to the product of the population and income shares. Therefore, the *Gini measure of overall inequality in circumstances* G_{circ} is defined as:

$$\begin{aligned} G_{circ} &= \sum_{j=1}^{J} \frac{(m_{.j})^2}{m_{.j}} [m_{i.}]' G [m_{ij}] \\ &= \sum_{j=1}^{J} (m_{.j}) [m_{i.}]' G [m_{ij}] \\ &= \sum_{j=1}^{J} [m_{.j} m_{i.}]' G [m_{ij}]. \end{aligned} \tag{9}$$

Note that the formulation for G_{circ} in (9) is not identical to that of G_{sim} in (5). To see the difference between these two formulations, the following graphical interpretation may be given. As was done when drawing a social immobility curve, we put on the horizontal and vertical axes, respectively, the expected shares $m_{i.}$ and the actual shares $\frac{m_{ij}}{m_{.j}}$, starting with income class 1 and ranking both sets of shares according to increasing values of the ratios $\frac{m_{ij}}{m_{i.}m_{.j}}$. We then do the same for income class 2 and continue with the other classes until income class J is reached. What we have then obtained is a curve which could be called an *inequality-in-circumstances curve*. It comprises J sections, one for each income class. Clearly, the slope of this curve is not always non-decreasing. It is non-decreasing within each income class, but reaches the diagonal each time we come to the end of an income class.

We should however note that the shares used to draw an inequality-in-circumstances curve are the same as those used in constructing a social immobility curve, as can be seen by comparing both sides of the G-matrix in (5) and (9). In drawing the curve measuring inequality in circumstances, we have simply reshuffled the sets of shares used in drawing a social immobility curve. Rather than ranking both sets of shares–the cumulative shares $m_{i.}m_{.j}$ on the one hand and the cumulative shares m_{ij} on the other hand–according to increasing values of the ratios $\frac{m_{ij}}{m_{i.}m_{.j}}$ working with all $I \times J$ shares, we have first collected the shares corresponding to the first (poorest) income class and ranked them according to increasing values of the ratios $\frac{m_{i1}}{m_{i.}m_{.1}}$ and then have successively done the same for all of the other income classes.

An illustration of the difference between an inequality-in-circumstances curve and a social immobility curve is given in Fig. 1, which will be analyzed in the empirical section. Note that whereas the index G_{circ} is equal to twice the area lying between the inequality-in-circumstances curve and the diagonal, the index G_{sim} is equal to twice the area lying between the social immobility curve and the diagonal. The area lying between the inequality-in-circumstances curve and the social immobility curve may then be considered to be a measure of the degree of overlap between the various income classes in terms of the gaps between the expected and actual shares.

5 The Empirical Analysis

5.1 The Data Sources

We have analyzed two sets of data, one for France and one for Israel.

The first data set is a survey of 2000 individuals conducted in France by Thomas Piketty in the year 1998 with financial support from the McArthur Foundation (Piketty 1998). This data set contains 65 variables and includes income, many socio-demographic characteristics, and answers to questions on social, political, ethical, and cultural issues.

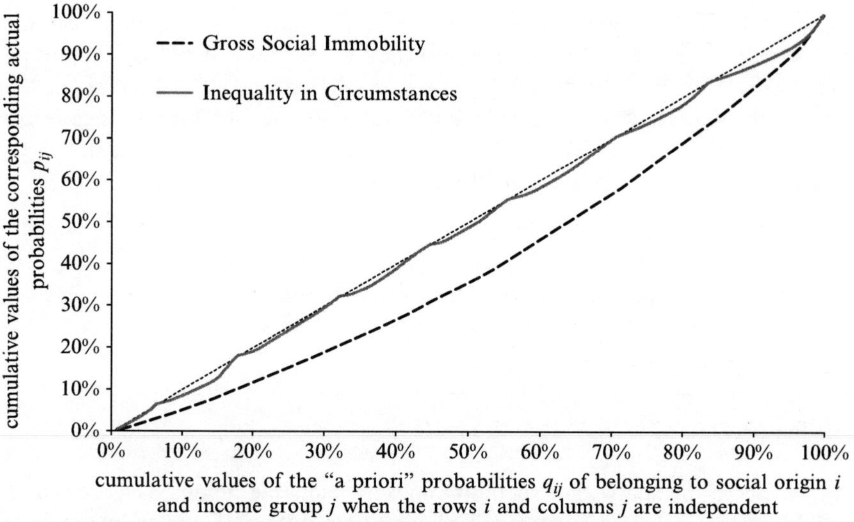

Fig. 1 Gross social immobility and inequality-in-circumstances curves for France: Father's occupation versus daughter's income

Two types of variables were drawn from this database. To measure the social origin of the parents, we used information on the profession of either the father or the mother.[4] The social status of the children's generation was measured by monthly income classified into eight categories.[5] On the basis of these two variables, we have constructed the social mobility matrix M defined previously, with row i corresponding to the profession of either the father or the mother, depending on the case considered, and with column j corresponding to the income group to which the individual (the child, either the son or the daughter, depending on the case examined) belongs.[6]

The second data set is the Social Survey that was conducted in Israel in 2003. The social origin of an individual was measured by the highest educational certificate or degree his or her father received.[7] The social status of the children was

---

[4] Eight professions were distinguished: farmer (i.e., head of agricultural enterprise), businessman, store owner or artisan, manager or independent professional, technician or middle rank manager, employee, blue collar worker (including salaried persons working in agriculture), not working outside of the household, and retired.

[5] The range of these income classes is given in Tables 10 and 11.

[6] In our empirical analysis and in the Appendix, all social mobility matrices are defined in terms of shares (i.e., the sum of all of their elements is equal to 1).

[7] Seven educational categories were distinguished: elementary school completion, secondary school completion without a baccalaureate, a baccalaureate certificate, post-secondary level with a non-academic certificate, a B.A. or a similar academic certificate, an M.A. or a similar diploma, an M.D. or a similar certificate, and a Ph.D. or a similar diploma.

measured by the total gross income of all members of the household to which the individual belongs, whatever the source of the income (work, pensions, support payments, rents, etc.). Ten income classes were distinguished.[8] On the basis of these two variables, we have constructed a social mobility matrix M whose definition is similar to that defined previously for the French data, with the educational level of the father replacing the profession of the parents.[9]

5.2 *The Results of the Empirical Investigation*

5.2.1 Measuring Social Immobility

The French Data

The results of the analysis of social immobility using the French data are reported in Tables 1–6, each of which examines one of six different comparisons based on demographic characteristics. In each comparison, we give the value of the Gini social immobility index and decompose the difference between the values taken by this index in two different cases (distinguished by the genders of a parent and child) into the three components of social immobility mentioned previously. For each index and component, we also give confidence intervals based on a bootstrap analysis. It is easy to observe that in all six of these tables (Tables 1–6), the two Gini indices of social immobility being compared are always significantly different one from the other. Moreover, each of the components of social immobility in all six of the tables is always significantly different from 0.

The first striking result that emerges from these tables is that the degree of social immobility is significantly higher when comparing fathers and daughters (a Gini social immobility index equal to 0.202) or fathers and sons (a Gini social immobility index equal to 0.193) than when comparing mothers and sons (a Gini social immobility index equal to 0.143) or even mothers and daughters (a Gini social immobility index equal to 0.166). We also observe when comparing, for example, the degree of social immobility from fathers to sons with that from mothers to sons that the difference (a lower degree of social immobility in the latter case) is much higher once we control for the margins. In other words, the difference in the degree of net social immobility is in this case much higher than the difference in gross social immobility

[8] The range of these income classes is given in Table 12.

[9] Note that in both empirical illustrations, while we have data on incomes ("prizes"), we ignore these values. We are well aware of the fact that the value of the "prizes" matter (see Van de gaer et al. 2001). Because the methodological section of this article has emphasized the concept of dependence between the margins (which are nonordered categorical variables), we have preferred here to concentrate our analysis on the measurement of inequality of life chances. In future work, we hope to integrate "prizes" into the analysis, an extension that should allow us to measure not only inequality in life chances, but also inequality of opportunities.

Table 1 Comparing social mobility in France from fathers to daughters with social mobility from fathers to sons using the Gini social immobility index

Components of the difference	Value of the Gini social immobility index	Bootstrap standard deviation	Conf. int. lower bound (95%)	Conf. int. upper bound (95%)
Social immobility from fathers to daughters (G1)	0.20237	0.0047	0.1947	0.2101
Social immobility from fathers to sons (G2)	0.19261	0.0045	0.1852	0.2000
Difference (G2−G1)	−0.00976	0.0002	−0.0101	−0.0094
Net difference in social immobility	−0.00083	0.0000	−0.0009	−0.0008
Difference due to differences in the margins of the social mobility matrix	−0.00892	0.0002	−0.0093	−0.0086
Difference due to differences in the professional composition of the fathers' generation	−0.00780	0.0002	−0.0081	−0.0075
Difference due to differences in the income distribution of the children (daughters versus sons)	−0.00112	0.0000	−0.0012	−0.0011

Table 2 Comparing social mobility in France from fathers to daughters with social mobility from mothers to sons using the Gini social immobility index

Components of the difference	Value of the Gini social immobility index	Bootstrap standard deviation	Conf. int. lower bound (95%)	Conf. int. upper bound (95%)
Social immobility from fathers to daughters (G1)	0.20237	0.0047	0.1947	0.2101
Social immobility from mothers to sons (G2)	0.14332	0.0033	0.1380	0.1487
Difference (G2−G1)	−0.05905	0.0014	−0.0613	−0.0568
Net difference in social immobility	0.03358	0.0008	0.0323	0.0349
Difference due to differences in the margins of the social mobility matrix	−0.09263	0.0021	−0.0961	−0.0891
Difference due to differences in the professional composition of the parents (fathers versus mothers)	−0.08731	0.0020	−0.0906	−0.0840
Difference due to differences in the income distribution of the children (daughters versus sons)	−0.00532	0.0001	−0.0055	−0.0051

Table 3 Comparing social mobility in France from fathers to sons with social mobility from mothers to daughters using the Gini social immobility index

Components of the difference	Value of the Gini social immobility index	Bootstrap standard deviation	Conf. int. lower bound (95%)	Conf. int. upper bound (95%)
Social immobility from fathers to sons (G1)	0.19261	0.0045	0.1852	0.2000
Social immobility from mothers to daughters (G2)	0.16609	0.0038	0.1598	0.1724
Difference (G2−G1)	−0.02652	0.0006	−0.0275	−0.0255
Net difference in social immobility	0.09566	0.0022	−0.0993	−0.0920
Difference due to differences in the margins of the social mobility matrix	0.06913	0.0016	0.0665	0.0718
Difference due to differences in the professional composition of the parents (fathers versus mothers)	0.07993	0.0018	0.0769	0.0830
Difference due to differences in the income distribution of the children (sons versus daughters)	−0.01080	0.0002	−0.0112	−0.0104

Table 4 Comparing social mobility in France from fathers to daughters with social mobility from mothers to daughters using the Gini social immobility index

Components of the difference	Value of the Gini social immobility index	Bootstrap standard deviation	Conf. int. lower bound (95%)	Conf. int. upper bound (95%)
Social immobility from fathers to daughters (G1)	0.20237	0.0047	0.1947	0.2101
Social immobility from mothers to daughters (G2)	0.16609	0.0039	0.1598	0.1724
Difference (G2−G1)	−0.03628	0.0008	−0.0377	−0.0349
Net difference in social immobility	0.04479	0.0010	0.0431	0.0465
Difference due to differences in the margins of the social mobility matrix	−0.08107	0.0019	−0.0842	−0.0780
Difference due to differences in the professional composition of the parents (fathers versus mothers)	−0.08163	0.0019	−0.0847	−0.0785
Difference due to differences in the income distribution of the daughters	0.00056	0.0000	0.0005	0.0006

Table 5 Comparing social mobility in France from fathers to sons with social mobility from mothers to sons using the Gini social immobility index

Components of the difference	Value of the Gini social immobility index	Bootstrap standard deviation	Conf. int. lower bound (95%)	Conf. int. upper bound (95%)
Social immobility from fathers to sons (G1)	0.19261	0.0045	0.1852	0.2000
Social immobility from mothers to sons (G2)	0.14332	0.0033	0.1380	0.1487
Difference (G2−G1)	−0.04929	0.0012	−0.0512	−0.0474
Net difference in social immobility	−0.13980	0.0032	−0.1451	−0.1345
Difference due to differences in the margins of the social mobility matrix	0.09051	0.0021	0.0871	0.0940
Difference due to differences in the professional composition of the parents (fathers versus mothers)	0.09097	0.0021	0.0875	0.0944
Difference due to differences in the income distribution of the sons	−0.00046	0.0000	−0.0005	−0.0004

Table 6 Comparing social mobility in France from mothers to daughters with social mobility from mothers to sons using the Gini social immobility index

Components of the difference	Value of the Gini social immobility index	Bootstrap standard deviation	Conf. int. lower bound (95%)	Conf. int. upper bound (95%)
Social immobility from mothers to daughters (G1)	0.16609	0.0039	0.1598	0.1724
Social immobility from mothers to sons (G2)	0.14332	0.0033	0.1380	0.1487
Difference (G2−G1)	−0.02277	0.0005	−0.0236	−0.0219
Net difference in social immobility	−0.01413	0.0003	−0.0147	−0.0136
Difference due to differences in the margins of the social mobility matrix	−0.00864	0.0002	−0.0090	−0.0083
Difference due to differences in the professional composition of the mothers	−0.00535	0.0001	−0.0056	−0.0051
Difference due to differences in the income distribution of the children (daughters versus sons)	−0.00329	0.0001	−0.0034	−0.0032

(0.140 rather than 0.049). Note also that the impact of the margins is mainly related to differences in the occupational structure of the parents.

As an illustrative example, in Fig. 1 (see above), we have drawn the gross social immobility curve for the case in which the transition analyzed is that from father's occupation to daughter's income.

The Israeli Data

The results of the analysis of social immobility for the Israeli data are presented in Tables 7–9, with bootstrap confidence intervals again provided. In these tables, the comparisons are based on the geographic origins of the fathers. Specifically, differences in the degree of social mobility between three groups are analyzed: those individuals whose father was born in Asia or Africa, those whose father was born in Europe or America, and those whose father was born in Israel. Note that it is also the case here that in the three comparisons being considered, the Gini indices of social immobility are significantly different one from the other and that each of the components of social immobility is always significantly different from 0.

The most striking result here is certainly the fact that social immobility is much higher among those whose fathers were born in Asia or Africa (a Gini social immobility index of 0.233) than among those whose fathers were born in Europe or America (a Gini social immobility index of 0.124) or even among those whose fathers were born in Israel (a Gini social immobility index of 0.147).

The results are even more striking when we compare gross with net social immobility. When looking at the results given in Table 7, we observe that whereas the gross difference between the Gini indices of social immobility of those whose fathers were born in Asia or Africa and those whose fathers were born in Europe or America is equal to 0.110, the net difference (net of changes in the margins) is equal to 0.310. Note also that the impact of the margins is essentially due to differences in the education levels of the fathers of the two groups being compared. Quite similar conclusions may be drawn when comparing individuals whose fathers were born in Asia or Africa and in Israel (Table 8).

In Fig. 2, we compare gross and net social immobility curves for Israel. The gross curves are shown for two groups, individuals whose fathers were born in Europe or America (EA) and individuals whose fathers were born in Asia or Africa (AA). The net social immobility curve was drawn based on a matrix that has the margins of the matrix of those whose fathers were born in Europe or America but the internal structure of the matrix of those whose fathers were born in Asia or Africa. This evidence shows that the gap in social immobility is bigger when comparing the EA and AA groups once we control for the margins.

Table 7 Comparing the degree of social immobility in Israel using the Gini social immobility index based on the father's birthplace: Europe or America versus Asia or Africa

Components of the difference	Value of the Gini social immobility index	Bootstrap standard deviation	Conf. int. lower bound (95%)	Conf. int. upper bound (95%)
Social immobility when father was born in Asia or Africa (G1)	0.23276	0.0054	0.2239	0.2416
Social immobility when father was born in Europe or America (G2)	0.12357	0.0028	0.1189	0.1282
Difference (G2−G1)	−0.10919	0.0025	−0.1133	−0.1050
Net difference in social immobility	−0.31028	0.0072	−0.3220	−0.2985
Difference due to differences in the margins of the social mobility matrix	0.20109	0.0047	0.1934	0.2088
Difference due to differences in the educational composition of the parents' generation	0.19625	0.0045	0.1889	0.2036
Difference due to differences in the income distribution of the children's generation	0.00484	0.0001	0.0047	0.0050

Table 8 Comparing the degree of social immobility in Israel using the Gini social immobility index based on the father's birthplace: Asia or Africa versus Israel

Components of the difference	Value of the Gini social immobility index	Bootstrap standard deviation	Conf. int. lower bound (95%)	Conf. int. upper bound (95%)
Social immobility when father was born in Asia or Africa (G1)	0.23276	0.0054	0.2239	0.2416
Social immobility when father was born in Israel (G2)	0.14696	0.0033	0.1415	0.1525
Difference (G2−G1)	−0.08580	0.0020	−0.0891	−0.0825
Net difference in social immobility	−0.16360	0.0038	−0.1699	−0.1573
Difference due to differences in the margins of the social mobility matrix	0.07780	0.0018	0.0748	0.0808
Difference due to differences in the educational composition of the parents' generation	0.07953	0.0018	0.0765	0.0825
Difference due to differences in the income distribution of the children's generation	−0.00173	0.0000	−0.0018	−0.0017

Table 9 Comparing the degree of social immobility in Israel using the Gini social immobility index based on the father's birthplace: Europe or America versus Israel

Components of the difference	Value of the Gini social immobility index	Bootstrap standard deviation	Conf. Int. lower bound (95%)	Conf. Int. upper bound (95%)
Social immobility when father was born in Europe or America (G1)	0.12357	0.0028	0.1189	0.1282
Social immobility when father was born in Israel (G2)	0.14696	0.0033	0.1415	0.1525
Difference (G2−G1)	0.02338	0.0005	0.0225	0.0243
Net difference in social immobility	0.04875	0.0011	0.0469	0.0506
Difference due to differences in the margins of the social mobility matrix	−0.02537	0.0006	−0.0263	−0.0244
Difference due to differences in the educational composition of the parents' generation	−0.02041	0.0005	−0.0212	−0.0196
Difference due to differences in the income distribution of the children's generation	−0.00496	0.0001	−0.0051	−0.0048

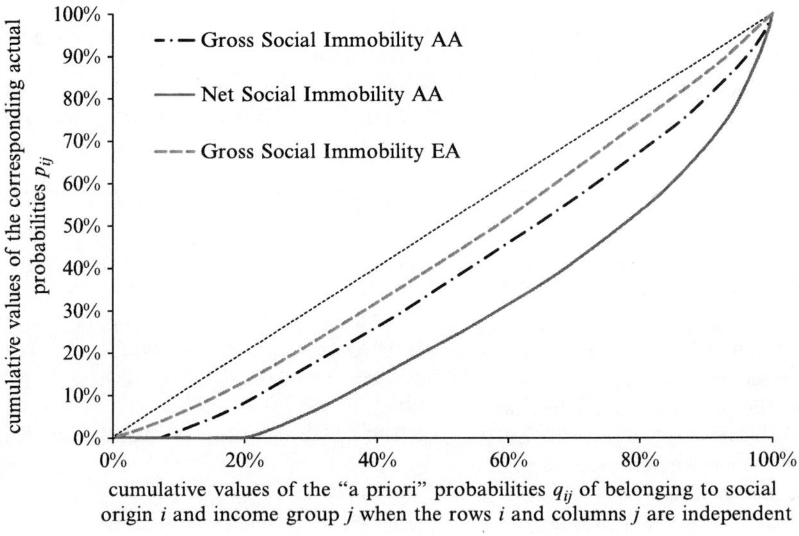

Fig. 2 Gross and net social immobility curves for Israel: Fathers born in Europe or America (EA) versus fathers born in Asia or Africa (AA)

5.2.2 Inequality in Circumstances

The French Data

In Tables 10–12, we give two examples of the use of the Theil or Gini indices of inequality in circumstances. The first example uses French data related to the transition from the occupation of the fathers to the income class to which their daughters belong (see Tables 10 and 11). First, we may note (see Table 10) that, as expected, the sum of the contributions of the various income classes to the overall Theil index of inequality in circumstances is indeed equal to the value of this index. Second, according to both the Theil and the Gini indices, the two income classes in which inequality in circumstances is highest are the income classes corresponding to the income ranges 4,000FF–5,999FF and 20,000FF or more. As far as the largest relative contributions of the income classes to the overall Theil or Gini indices of inequality in circumstances are concerned (remember that the weights of the income classes are not the same for the Theil and the Gini indices), the results are quite similar. In both cases, the largest relative contribution is that of the richest income class. The second largest is that of the class with an income range of 4,000FF–5,999FF for the Theil index and that of the classes 4,000FF–5,999FF and 12,000FF–14,999FF (the results are almost identical for these two income classes) for the Gini index.

As mentioned previously, the gross social immobility curve for the case in which the transition analyzed is that from father's occupation to daughter's income is shown in Fig. 1. On this same graph, we have plotted the inequality-in-circumstances curve for this case. The large area lying between both curves clearly indicates that the gap between the expected shares $m_{i.}m_{.j}$ and the actual shares m_{ij} is not a function of income. Hence, there is a large amount of overlap between the income classes when the ranking is based on the ratio of actual to expected shares.

The Israeli Data

The second illustration is based on Israeli data concerning individuals whose fathers were born in Asia or Africa. Unfortunately, we could not compute Theil indices because some of the cells in the data matrix were empty. For the Gini index (see Table 12), the two income classes with the highest values of this index are those corresponding to the income ranges NIS 3,001–4,000 and NIS 4,001–5,000. We also observe in this table that the two income classes that contribute the most to the overall value of the Gini index of inequality in circumstances are those corresponding to the income ranges NIS 7,001–9,000 and NIS 9,001–12,000.

Table 10 Measuring inequality in circumstances in France using the Theil Index based on the social mobility from fathers to daughters

Income class (FF)	Theil index of income class and overall Theil index of inequality in circumstances	Bootstrap standard deviation	Conf. int. lower bound (95%)	Conf. int. upper bound (95%)	Share of each income class in overall population analyzed	Contribution of each income class to overall Theil index of inequality in circumstances	Percentage contribution of each income class to overall Theil index of inequality in circumstances
< 4,000	0.07427	0.0017	0.0714	0.0771	0.0636	0.00472	0.0711
4,000–5,999	0.12520	0.0029	0.1204	0.1300	0.1136	0.01423	0.2142
6,000–7,999	0.03017	0.0007	0.0290	0.0313	0.1422	0.00429	0.0646
8,000–9,999	0.04145	0.0009	0.0399	0.0430	0.1425	0.00516	0.0777
10,000–11,999	0.05072	0.0012	0.0488	0.0526	0.1083	0.00549	0.0827
12,000–14,999	0.03633	0.0008	0.0349	0.0377	0.1534	0.00557	0.0839
15,000–19,999	0.05963	0.0014	0.0573	0.0619	0.1312	0.00782	0.1178
≥ 20,000	0.11720	0.0027	0.1127	0.1217	0.1632	0.01913	0.2880
All income classes	0.06642	0.0015	0.0639	0.0689		0.06642	

Table 11 Measuring inequality in circumstances in France using the Gini Index based on the social mobility from fathers to daughters

Income class (FF)	Gini index of income class and overall Gini index of inequality in circumstances	Bootstrap standard deviation	Conf. int. lower bound (95%)	Conf. int. upper bound (95%)	Share of each income class in overall population analyzed	Contribution of each income class to overall Gini index of inequality in circumstances	Percentage contribution of each income class to overall Gini index of inequality in circumstances
< 4,000	0.1957	0.0045	0.1882	0.2032	0.0636	0.00079	0.0328
4,000–5,999	0.2653	0.0061	0.2553	0.2753	0.1136	0.00342	0.1420
6,000–7,999	0.1221	0.0028	0.1175	0.1267	0.1422	0.00247	0.1024
8,000–9,999	0.1461	0.0033	0.1406	0.1516	0.1425	0.00226	0.0939
10,000–11,999	0.1632	0.0038	0.1569	0.1695	0.1083	0.00191	0.0794
12,000–14,999	0.1463	0.0034	0.1407	0.1519	0.1534	0.00344	0.1428
15,000–19,999	0.1848	0.0042	0.1779	0.1917	0.1312	0.00318	0.1320
≥ 20,000	0.2485	0.0058	0.2390	0.2580	0.1632	0.00662	0.2746
All income classes	0.02411	0.0006	0.0232	0.0250		0.02411	

Table 12 Measuring inequality in circumstances in Israel using the Gini Index based on the social mobility among those whose father was born in Asia or Africa

Income class (NIS)	Gini index of income class and overall Gini index of inequality in circumstances	Bootstrap standard deviation	Conf. int. lower bound (95%)	Conf. int. upper bound (95%)	Share of each income class in overall population analyzed	Contribution of each income class to overall Gini index of inequality in circumstances	Percentage contribution of each income class to overall Gini index of inequality in circumstances
≤ 2,000	0.2112	0.0049	0.2032	0.2192	0.0435	0.00040	0.0177
2,001–3,000	0.1957	0.0045	0.1883	0.2031	0.0621	0.00075	0.0335
3,001–4,000	0.2758	0.0064	0.2652	0.2864	0.0932	0.00239	0.1062
4,001–5,000	0.3002	0.0070	0.2887	0.3117	0.0745	0.00167	0.0740
5,001–7,000	0.1231	0.0028	0.1184	0.1278	0.1677	0.00346	0.1536
7,001–9,000	0.2413	0.0056	0.2321	0.2505	0.1304	0.00411	0.1822
9,001–12,000	0.2325	0.0054	0.2237	0.2413	0.1366	0.00396	0.1755
12,001–15,000	0.1618	0.0037	0.1557	0.1679	0.1118	0.00302	0.1341
15,001–20,000	0.1784	0.0041	0.1716	0.1852	0.0497	0.00223	0.0990
> 20,000	0.2205	0.0050	0.2122	0.2288	0.1305	0.00054	0.0242
All income classes	0.02253	0.0005	0.0217	0.0234		0.02253	

6 Concluding Comments

This article has suggested applying the tools of analysis that have been used previously in the field of occupational segregation and horizontal inequity to the study of intergenerational social immobility. The concept of a social immobility curve was introduced and two indices of social immobility, related to the Theil and Gini indices, have been proposed. The empirical results confirmed the need to make a distinction between the concepts of gross and net social immobility. Finally, this article has introduced two measures of inequality in circumstances, also derived from the Theil and Gini indices. Whereas the Theil index of inequality in circumstances turns out to be identical to the Theil index of social immobility, we have shown that the Gini index of inequality in circumstances differs from the Gini index of social immobility, and these differences were indeed confirmed by our empirical illustrations.

Acknowledgements This article was written when Jacques Silber was visiting the Levy Economics Institute of Bard College. He wishes to thank this Institute for its very warm hospitality. The authors wish to thank an anonymous referee as well as Marc Fleurbaey for their extremely useful comments. They also acknowledge the help of Adi Lazar in preparing the revised version of this article. Amedeo Spadaro acknowledges financial support from the Spanish Government (SEJ2005-08783-C04-03/ECON) and from the French Government (ANR BLAN06-2_139446).

Appendix: Decomposing Variations Over Time in the Extent of Social Mobility

The purpose of this Appendix is to show how it is possible to derive the specific contributions to the overall variation in the extent of intergenerational social immobility due to changes in the income distribution of the children and in the distribution of the parents by social category (these two changes correspond to variations in the margins of the social mobility matrix), as well as in the "pure" variation in the extent of social immobility (changes in the degree of independence between the rows and columns of the social mobility matrix itself).

Neutralizing the Specific Impacts of Changes in the Margins of the Social Mobility Matrix

The methodology used to isolate the specific effects of changes in the margins is borrowed from the literature on the measurement of occupational segregation (see Karmel and MacLachlan 1988) and is extended here to the measurement of variations in the extent of social mobility.

Suppose that the population under scrutiny is divided into I social origin categories and J income brackets. We define a matrix Q in such a way that its typical element q_{ij} is equal to the product $m_{i.}m_{.j}$ of the margins i and j of the social mobility matrix M. Clearly, if m_{ij} is equal to q_{ij} for all i and j, then there is independence between the social origins (the rows of the matrix M) and the incomes of the individuals (the columns of the matrix M). If m_{ij} is not equal to q_{ij} for at least some i and j, then the rows and the columns of M are at least partially dependent. Such a link between the income of an individual and his or her social origin should help us measure the extent of social immobility.

Let us now suppose that we wish to decompose the variation over time in the extent of social mobility. In order to do so, we will adopt a technique originally proposed by Deming and Stephan (1940) and used by Karmel and MacLachlan (1988). The idea, when comparing two matrices of proportions M and V, is to construct a third matrix S that has, for example, the internal structure of the matrix M but the margins of the matrix V. To construct S, one first multiplies all the cells (i, j) of M by the ratios $\frac{v_{i.}}{m_{i.}}$, where $v_{i.}$ and $m_{i.}$ are respectively the horizontal margins of the matrices V and M. Let R be the matrix obtained after such a multiplication. Next multiply all the cells (i, j) of the matrix R by the ratios $\frac{v_{.j}}{r_{.j}}$, where $v_{.j}$ and $r_{.j}$ are now the vertical margins of the matrices V and R. Let U be this new matrix.

As shown by Deming and Stephan (1940), if this procedure is repeated several times, then the matrix obtained quickly converges to a matrix S that has the margins of the matrix V but the internal structure of the matrix M. In other words, the degree of social immobility corresponding to the matrix S is identical to that corresponding to the original matrix M, but the matrix S has the same income distribution for the individuals and the same internal structure of social origins for these individuals as that of the matrix V. One could naturally have proceeded in the reverse order by starting with the matrix V and ending up with a matrix W that has the margins of the matrix M but the internal structure of the matrix V.

Decomposing Variations Over Time in the Extent of Social Mobility

We have just shown how the transformation of the matrix M into the matrix V can be carried out in two stages: one in which the margins are changed and one in which the internal structure of the matrix is modified. Let $\Delta SM = SM(V) - SM(M)$ denote the overall variation in the extent of social mobility. In fact, ΔSM may be expressed as the sum of a contribution $C_{\Delta ma}$ of differences in the margins and a contribution $C_{\Delta is}$ of differences in the internal structure of the two social mobility matrices being compared. By applying the idea of a *nested Shapley decomposition* (see Sastre and Trannoy 2002), we show that it is possible to further decompose the contribution $C_{\Delta ma}$ into the sum of the contributions C_h and C_t of the horizontal and vertical margins.

Using a nested Shapley decomposition and the definitions of the matrices S and W given previously, the contribution $C_{\Delta ma}$ of a change in the margins to the overall variation ΔSM may be defined as:

$$\begin{aligned} C_{\Delta ma} &= (1/2)[SM(S) - SM(M)] + (1/2)\{[SM(V) - SM(M)] \\ &\quad - [SM(W) - SM(M)]\} \\ &= (1/2)\{[SM(S) - SM(M)] + [SM(V) - SM(W)]\} \end{aligned} \tag{A.1}$$

and the contribution $C_{\Delta is}$ of the change in the internal structure of the matrix to the overall variation ΔSM may be defined as:

$$\begin{aligned} C_{\Delta is} &= (1/2)[SM(W) - SM(M)] + (1/2)\{[SM(V) - SM(M)] \\ &\quad - [SM(S) - SM(M)]\} \\ &= (1/2)\{[SM(W) - SM(M)] + [SM(V) - SM(S)]\}. \end{aligned} \tag{A.2}$$

Note that $C_{\Delta ma} + C_{\Delta is} = \Delta SM$.

It is possible to further decompose the contribution $C_{\Delta ma}$. We previously defined the matrix R that was obtained by multiplying the cells (i, j) of M by the ratios $\frac{v_{i.}}{m_{i.}}$, where $v_{i.}$ and $m_{i.}$ are respectively the horizontal margins of the matrices M and V. Let N denote the matrix that is obtained by multiplying the cells (i, j) of M by the ratios $\frac{v_{.j}}{m_{.j}}$, where $v_{.j}$ and $m_{.j}$ are respectively the vertical margins of the matrices M and V. We now apply a nested Shapley decomposition to the difference D_{ma1} defined as:

$$D_{ma1} = [SM(S) - SM(M)]. \tag{A.3}$$

Letting Δh and Δt denote respectively the changes in the horizontal and vertical margins, using the definitions of R and N given previously, the contributions $C_{\Delta h1}$ and $C_{\Delta t1}$ to the difference D_{ma1} may be defined as:

$$\begin{aligned} C_{\Delta h1} &= (1/2)[SM(R) - SM(M)] + (1/2)\{[SM(S) - SM(M)] \\ &\quad - [SM(N) - SM(M)]\} \\ &= (1/2)\{[SM(R) - SM(M)] + [SM(S) - SM(N)]\} \end{aligned} \tag{A.4}$$

and

$$\begin{aligned} C_{\Delta t1} &= (1/2)[SM(N) - SM(M)] + (1/2)\{[SM(S) - SM(M)] \\ &\quad - [SM(R) - SM(M)]\} \\ &= (1/2)\{[SM(N) - SM(M)] + [SM(S) - SM(R)]\}. \end{aligned} \tag{A.5}$$

Let us now decompose in a similar way the difference D_{ma2} defined as:

$$D_{ma2} = [SM(V) - SM(W)]. \tag{A.6}$$

We define two additional matrices C and F as follows. The elements c_{ij} of the matrix C are obtained by multiplying the elements v_{ij} of the matrix V by the ratios $\frac{w_{i.}}{v_{i.}}$, where $w_{i.}$ and $v_{i.}$ are the horizontal margins of the matrices W and V. Similarly, the elements f_{ij} of the matrix F are obtained by multiplying the elements v_{ij} of the matrix V by the ratios $\frac{w_{.j}}{v_{.j}}$, where $w_{.j}$ and $v_{.j}$ are the vertical margins of the matrices W and V. We may therefore define the contributions $C_{\Delta h2}$ and $C_{\Delta t2}$ to the difference D_{ma2} as:

$$\begin{aligned} C_{\Delta h2} &= (1/2)[SM(V) - SM(C)] + (1/2)\{[SM(V) - SM(W)] \\ &\quad - [SM(V) - SM(F)]\} \\ &= (1/2)\{[SM(V) - SM(C)] + [SM(F) - SM(W)]\} \end{aligned} \tag{A.7}$$

and

$$\begin{aligned} C_{\Delta t2} &= (1/2)[SM(V) - SM(F)] + (1/2)\{[SM(V) - SM(W)] \\ &\quad - [SM(V) - SM(C)]\} \\ &= (1/2)\{[SM(V) - SM(F)] + [SM(C) - SM(W)]\}. \end{aligned} \tag{A.8}$$

Now combining (A.1), (A.3), (A.4), (A.5), (A.6), (A.7), and (A.8), we conclude that the contribution $C_{\Delta ma}$ may be written as:

$$C_{\Delta ma} = C_h + C_t, \tag{A.9}$$

where

$$\begin{aligned} C_h &= (1/2)C_{\Delta h1} + (1/2)C_{\Delta h2} \\ &= (1/4)\{[(SM(R) - SM(M)) + (SM(S) - SM(N))] \\ &\quad + [(SM(V) - SM(C)) + (SM(F) - SM(W)]\} \end{aligned} \tag{A.10}$$

and

$$\begin{aligned} C_t &= (1/2)C_{\Delta t1} + (1/2)C_{\Delta t2} \\ &= (1/4)\{[(SM(N) - SM(M)) + (SM(S) - SM(R))] \\ &\quad + [(SM(V) - SM(F)) + (SM(C) - SM(W)]\}. \end{aligned} \tag{A.11}$$

Combining (A.10) and (A.11), as expected, we observe that

$$C_h + C_t = (1/2)\{[(SM(S) - SM(M)] + [SM(V) - SM(W)]\} = C_{\Delta ma}. \tag{A.12}$$

References

Atkinson, A. B., & Bourguignon, F. (1982). The comparison of multi-dimensioned distributions of economic status. *Review of Economic Studies*, *49*, 183–201

Bartolucci, F., Forcina, A., & Dardanoni, V. (2001). Positive quadrant dependence and marginal modeling in two-way tables with ordered margins. *Journal of the American Statistical Association*, *96*, 1497–1506

Chakravarty, S. R., & Silber, J. (2007). On independence ordering and its measurement. Unpublished manuscript, Economics Research Unit, Indian Statistical Institute, Kolkata and Department of Economics, Bar-Ilan University

Chantreuil, F., & Trannoy, A. (1999). Inequality decomposition values: The trade-off between marginality and consistency. Document de Travail No. 99-24, THEMA

Corak, M. (2004). *Generational income mobility in North America and Europe*. Cambridge: Cambridge University Press

Dardanoni, V., & Lambert, P. (2001). Horizontal inequity comparisons. *Social Choice and Welfare*, *18*, 799–816

Deming, W. E., & Stephan, F. F. (1940). On a least squares adjustment of a sampled frequency table when the expected marginal totals are known. *Annals of Mathematical Statistics*, *11*, 427–444

Deutsch, J., Flückiger, Y., & Silber, J. (2009). Analyzing changing occupational segregation: The case of Switzerland (1970–2000). In Y. Flückiger, S. F. Reardon, & J. Silber (Eds.), *Occupational and residential segregation. Research in Economic Inequality*, (Vol. 17, pp. 171–202). Bingley, UK: Emerald Group Publishing

Epstein, L. G., & Tanny, S. M. (1980). Increasing generalized correlation: A definition and some economic consequences. *Canadian Journal of Economics*, *13*, 16–34

Flückiger, Y., & Silber, J. (1994). The Gini index and the measurement of multidimensional inequality. *Oxford Bulletin of Economics and Statistics*, *56*, 225–228

Karmel, T., & MacLachlan, M. (1988). Occupational sex segregation–Increasing or decreasing? *Economic Record*, *64*, 187–195

Kolm, S.-C. (2001). To each according to her work? Just entitlement from action: Desert, merit, responsibility, and equal opportunities. A review of John Roemer's *Equality of Opportunity*. Document de Travail No. 01-07, IDEP

Lefranc, A., Pistolesi, N., & Trannoy, A. (2009). Equality of opportunity and luck: Definitions and testable conditions, with an application to income in France. *Journal of Public Economics*, *93*, 1189–1207

Little, R. J. A., & Wu, M.-M. (1991). Models for contingency tables with known margins when target and sampled populations differ. *Journal of the American Statistical Association*, *86*, 87–95

Marshall, A. W., & Olkin, I. (1979). *Inequalities: Theory of majorization and its applications*. New York: Academic Press

Peragine, V. (2004). Ranking income distributions according to equality of opportunity. *Journal of Economic Inequality*, *2*, 11–30

Piketty, T. (1998). Attitudes toward income inequality in France: Do people really disagree? Document de Travail No. 9918, CEPREMAP

Roemer, J. E. (1998). *Equality of opportunity*. Cambridge, MA: Harvard University Press

Ruiz-Castillo, J. (2003). The measurement of inequality of opportunities. In J. A. Bishop & Y. Amiel (Eds.), *Inequality, welfare and poverty: Theory and measurement. Research in Economic Inequality* (Vol. 9, pp. 1–34). Oxford: JAI Press

Sastre, M., & Trannoy, A. (2002). Shapley inequality decomposition by factor components: Some methodological issues. In P. Moyes, C. Seidl, & A. Shorrocks (Eds.), *Inequalities: Theory, experiments and applications. Journal of Economics,* supplement 9 (pp. 51–89). Vienna: Springer

Schweizer, B., & Wolff, E. F. (1981). On nonparametric measures of dependence for random variables. *Annals of Statistics*, *9*, 879–885

Shorrocks, A. F. (1999). Decomposition procedures for distributional analysis: A unified framework based on the Shapley value. Unpublished manuscript, Department of Economics, University of Essex and Institute for Fiscal Studies

Silber, J. (1989a). Factor components, population subgroups and the computation of the Gini index of inequality. *Review of Economics and Statistics*, *71*, 107–115

Silber, J. (1989b). On the measurement of employment segregation. *Economic Letters*, *30*, 237–243

Solon, G. (1999). Intergenerational mobility in the labor market. In O. Ashenfelter & D. E. Card (Eds.), *Handbook of labor economics* (Vol. 3A, pp. 1761–1800). Amsterdam: North-Holland

Tchen, A. H. (1980). Inequalities for distributions with given marginals. *Annals of Probability*, *8*, 814–827

Theil, H. (1967). *Economics and information theory*. Amsterdam: North-Holland

Van de gaer, D., Schokkaert, E., & Martinez, M. (2001). Three meanings of intergenerational mobility. *Economica*, *68*, 519–537

Villar, A. (2005). On the welfare evaluation of income and opportunity. *Contributions to Theoretical Economics*, *5*, Issue 1, Article 3

Partnership, Solidarity, and Minimal Envy in Matching Problems

Koichi Tadenuma

1 Introduction

Consider a firm that has several factories. The firm must assign workers to these factories. Each factory manager has preferences over the workers, while each worker has preferences over which factory he works at. What is a desirable rule to match workers to factories?

Allocation problems such as the above example are called *two-sided matching problems*. They were first studied by Gale and Shapley (1962), who defined a matching to be *stable* if (a) no matched agent would rather be unmatched and (b) there does no exist a pair of agents (one from each group, in our example, a worker and a manager) who would both prefer to be matched to each other than to whom they are matched. They also presented an algorithm to find a stable matching.[1] However, the matching is only optimal *to one side* among all the stable matchings.

In this article, we search for rules that select a matching in a socially desirable way. A *matching rule* is a mapping that associates with each preference profile a matching. In addition to stability and related principles, we consider two properties that a socially desirable matching rule should satisfy, one based on envy minimization and one based on a solidarity principle that applies to particular kinds of preference changes.

For each profile, a rule should recommend an equitable matching. Here, our notion of equity is the concept of *no-envy*, which has played a central role in the theory of fair allocation since it was introduced and studied by Foley (1967) and Kolm (1972). However, a difficulty immediately arises. Unless there exists a matching in which every agent is matched to his first choice, someone must envy another agent. Hence, in general there are no envy-free matchings. When this is the case, we can instead employ a quantitative measure of aggregate envy and seek to

[1]A good reference to the subsequent extensive analyses of this subject is Roth and Sotomayor (1990).

K. Tadenuma
Department of Economics, Hitotsubashi University, Kunitachi, Tokyo 186-8601, Japan
e-mail: koichi.t@econ.hit-u.ac.jp

M. Fleurbaey et al. (eds.), *Social Ethics and Normative Economics*,
Studies in Choice and Welfare, DOI 10.1007/978-3-642-17807-8_6,

minimize its value. Several such measures of envy have been proposed. Feldman and Kirman (1974) advocated the total number of instances of envy as the measure of envy. Counting the instances of envy of each agent, Suzumura (1983) proposed to minimize the maximal number over all agents. In this article, we consider envy minimization according to each of these two social measures of envy, namely, *total envy minimization* and *maximal envy minimization*.

In our factory example, workers usually acquire factory-specific skills in the long-run, and thereby become higher ranked in the preference orders of the managers they are currently matched with. At the same time, workers also prefer working at their current places of employment to working elsewhere after obtaining such skills. Thus, it is natural to consider preference changes such that for each agent i, his current partner in a matching chosen by the rule is preferred to more of his potential partners after the preference change, holding the relative rankings of the other possible partners fixed. Such a transformation of preferences is called a *rank-enhancement of partners*.

The *solidarity principle*, a fundamental principle in normative economics, requires that, when some data in the problem (preferences, the amount of resources, and so on) change, all the agents in the same situation with respect to the change should be affected in the same direction: They should all be better off or they should all be worse off at the new allocation chosen by the rule. One form of this principle is *solidarity under preference changes*: When the preferences of some agents change, the agents *whose preferences are fixed* should be affected in the same direction. This version of the solidarity principle was first studied by Moulin (1987) in the context of quasi-linear binary social choice. Thomson (1993, 1997, 1998) extensively analyzed this property in classes of resource allocations problems with single-peaked preferences and with indivisible goods. Sprumont (1996) considered a class of general choice problems and formulated a solidarity property that applies when the feasibility constraints and the preferences can change simultaneously. All of these authors have considered *arbitrary changes* of preferences. However, to require solidarity for arbitrary changes of preferences is often too demanding.

Here, we restrict our attention to "natural" or "simple" changes of preferences, namely rank-enhancements of partners. We look for matching rules that satisfy *Solidarity under Rank-Enhancement of Partners*. Moreover, we consider a weak version of this solidarity property, which says that if *only one* agent increases the rank of his original partner, then the other agents should be either all better off or all worse off in the new matching chosen by the rule. This version of the solidarity principle is called *Solidarity under Single Rank-Enhancement of Partner*.

We examine the existence of a matching rule that selects an envy-minimizing matching in the set of stable matchings and satisfies Solidarity under Single Rank-Enhancement of Partner. Unfortunately, when there are at least five potential pairs, these properties are incompatible.

Faced with this impossibility result, we weaken the requirement that matching rules be stable to the requirement that they be *individually rational* and *Pareto efficient*. This weakening drastically changes the result: There exists a rule that both selects an envy-minimizing matching in the set of individually rational and

Pareto-efficient matchings and satisfies Solidarity under Rank-Enhancement of Partners. Moreover, any such selection rule meeting a certain separability condition satisfies the solidarity property.

The organization of the rest of this article is as follows. The next section gives basic definitions and notation. Section 3 introduces our concept of equity as envy minimization. Section 4 introduces the solidarity properties. It also presents the impossibility and possibility results on the compatibility of these solidarity principles with envy minimization. The final section contains some concluding remarks.

2 Basic Definitions and Notation

Let $F = \{f_1, f_2, \ldots, f_n\}$ and $W = \{w_1, w_2, \ldots, w_n\}$ be two fixed disjoint finite sets such that $|F| = |W| = n$. We call F *the set of factory managers* and W *the set of workers*. For each $i \in F \cup W$, let $X_i \in \{F, W\}$ be the set with $i \notin X_i$ and $Y_i \in \{F, W\}$ the set with $i \in Y_i$. We call X_i *the set of possible partners for agent* i. For each $i \in F \cup W$, a *preference relation of agent* i, denoted by R_i, is a linear order on $X_i \cup \{i\}$.[2] An alternative $j \in X_i$ indicates that agent i is matched to agent j in X_i and the alternative i that agent i is not matched to any agent in X_i (i.e., he is "matched to himself"). Let $\mathcal{R}_i$ be the set of all possible preference relations for agent i. Given $R_i \in \mathcal{R}_i$, we define the relation P_i on $X_i \cup \{i\}$ as follows: For all $x, x' \in X_i \cup \{i\}$, xP_ix' if and only if xR_ix' holds but $x'R_ix$ does not hold.[3]

To concisely express a preference relation $R_i \in \mathcal{R}_i$, we represent it, as in Roth and Sotomayor (1990), by an ordered list of the members of $X_i \cup \{i\}$. For example, the list

$$R_{f_2} = w_3 \; w_1 \; f_2 \; w_2 \; \ldots$$

indicates that manager f_2 prefers being matched to worker w_3 to being matched to w_1, and prefers being matched to w_1 to being unmatched, and so on.

A *preference profile* is a list $R = (R_i)_{i \in F \cup W}$. Let $\mathcal{R} = \prod_{i \in F \cup W} \mathcal{R}_i$ be the class of all preference profiles. We also consider the subclass $\mathcal{R}^*$ of preference profiles such that being unmatched is the worst situation for every agent:

$$\mathcal{R}^* = \{R \in \mathcal{R} \mid \forall i \in F \cup W, \; \forall j \in X_i, \; jP_ii\}.$$

A *matching* μ is a one-to-one function from $F \cup W$ onto itself such that for all $i \in F \cup W$, $\mu^2(i) = i$ and if $\mu(i) \notin X_i$, then $\mu(i) = i$. Let $\mathcal{M}$ be the set of all matchings.

Following Roth and Sotomayor (1990), we represent a matching as a list of matched pairs. For example, the matching

[2] Note that we exclude indifference between any two distinct elements in $X_i \cup \{i\}$.

[3] Because R_i is a linear order, xP_ix' if and only if xR_ix' and $x' \neq x$.

$$\mu = \begin{cases} f_1 & f_2 & f_3 & (w_2) \\ w_3 & w_1 & (f_3) & w_2 \end{cases}$$

has two matched pairs (f_1, w_3) and (f_2, w_1) with f_3 and w_2 unmatched (i.e., self matched).

Let $R \in \mathscr{R}$ be given. A matching $\mu \in \mathscr{M}$ is *individually rational for* R if for all $i \in F \cup W$, $\mu(i) R_i i$. It is *Pareto efficient for* R if there is no $\mu' \in \mathscr{M}$ such that for all $i \in F \cup W$, $\mu'(i) R_i \mu(i)$ and for some $i \in F \cup W$, $\mu'(i) P_i \mu(i)$. It is *stable for* R if it is individually rational for R and there is no pair $(f, w) \in F \times W$ such that $w P_f \mu(f)$ and $f P_w \mu(w)$.

Let $\mathscr{R}_0 \subseteq \mathscr{R}$. A *matching rule*, or simply a *rule, on* $\mathscr{R}_0$, denoted by φ, is a function from $\mathscr{R}_0$ to $\mathscr{M}$. For each $R \in \mathscr{R}_0, \varphi(R)$ is interpreted as being a desirable matching for the preference profile R. If $\varphi(R) = \mu$, we write $\varphi_i(R) = \mu(i)$ for each $i \in F \cup W$. Given a correspondence Ψ from $\mathscr{R}_0$ to $\mathscr{M}$, we say that a rule φ on $\mathscr{R}_0$ is a *selection rule from* Ψ if for all $R \in \mathscr{R}_0$, $\varphi(R) \in \Psi(R)$. Let I, P, IP, and S denote the correspondences on $\mathscr{R}_0$ that associate with each $R \in \mathscr{R}_0$ the set of individually rational matchings for R, the set of Pareto-efficient matchings for R, the set of individually rational and Pareto-efficient matchings for R, and the set of stable matchings for R, respectively.

3 Envy Minimization

A fundamental concept of equity in the theory of fair allocation is *no-envy*. In our model, a matching is *envy-free* if no agent prefers being matched to another agent's partner to being matched to his present partner. However, except for the rare case in which every agent can be matched to his first choice, there exists no envy-free matching. Thus, following Feldman and Kirman (1974) and Suzumura (1983), we introduce a social measure of envy, and look for matchings in which the measure of envy is minimized.

Let a preference profile $R \in \mathscr{R}$ and a matching $\mu \in \mathscr{M}$ be given. For each agent $i \in F \cup W$, define

$$e_i(\mu, R_i) = \#\{j \in X_i \mid j = \mu(k) \text{ for some } k \in Y_i \text{ and } j P_i \mu(i)\}.$$[4]

The integer $e_i(\mu, R_i)$ is the number of instances of envy that agent i has in μ. Let $e(\mu, R) = (e_i(\mu, R_i))_{i \in F \cup W} \in \mathbb{R}^{2n}$.[5] Summing up the $2n$ numbers $e_i(\mu, R_i)$ over all of the agents, we obtain the number of total instances of envy in μ. Define

$$t(\mu, R) = \sum_{i \in F \cup W} e_i(\mu, R_i),$$

[4] Given a set A, we denote by $\#A$ the cardinality of A.

[5] We denote by $\mathbb{R}$ the set of real numbers.

which is the "social measure of envy" due to Feldman and Kirman (1974). They proposed to minimize this number.

Let Ψ be a correspondence from $\mathcal{R}$ to $\mathcal{M}$. Define the correspondence T^{Ψ} from $\mathcal{R}$ to $\mathcal{M}$ by setting

$$T^{\Psi}(R) = \{\mu \in \Psi(R) \mid \forall \mu' \in \Psi(R),\ t(\mu', R) \geq t(\mu, R)\}$$

for each $R \in \mathcal{R}$. The set $T^{\Psi}(R)$ is the set of matchings that minimize the total instances of envy in $\Psi(R)$.

Suzumura (1983) considered agents with the largest $e_i(\mu, R_i)$ as being the "worst off" agents in μ and proposed to minimize the maximal element in $e(\mu, R) = (e_i(\mu, R_i))_{i \in F \cup W}$. This idea is based on the maximin principle due to Rawls (1971). Define the correspondence E^{Ψ} by setting

$$E^{\Psi}(R) = \{\mu \in \Psi(R) \mid \forall \mu' \in \Psi(R),\ \max_{i \in F \cup W}(e_i(\mu', R_i)) \geq \max_{i \in F \cup W}(e_i(\mu, R_i))\}$$

for each $R \in \mathcal{R}$. The set $E^{\Psi}(R)$ is the set of matchings that minimize the maximal individual instances of envy in $\Psi(R)$.

Further refinements of $\Psi(R)$ can be obtained by using the lexicographic order (see Schmeidler 1969; Sen 1970). Let $\theta\colon \mathbb{R}^{2n} \to \mathbb{R}^{2n}$ be a function that rearranges the coordinates of each vector in $\mathbb{R}^{2n}$ in nonincreasing order. We denote by $\geq_L$ the lexicographic order on $\mathbb{R}^{2n}$.[6] Define the correspondence L^{Ψ} by setting

$$L^{\Psi}(R) = \{\mu \in \Psi(R) \mid \forall \mu' \in \Psi(R),\ \theta(e(\mu', R)) \geq_L \theta(e(\mu, R))\}$$

for each $R \in \mathcal{R}$. The set $L^{\Psi}(R)$ is the set of matchings that lexicographically minimize the maximal individual instances of envy in $\Psi(R)$.

Note that none of the social measures of envy defined above use any cardinal "utilities" or "intensities of preferences." Rather, they depend only on ordinal preferences (rankings).

4 Solidarity

In this section, we formulate the solidarity properties of matching rules for certain "natural" changes of preferences. In the following definitions, $\mathcal{R}_0$ denotes the domain of a matching rule φ.

Let an agent $i \in F \cup W$, a preference relation $R_i \in \mathcal{R}_i$, and a matching $\mu \in \mathcal{M}$ be given. We say that *a preference relation $R_i' \in \mathcal{R}_i$ is obtained from R_i by rank-enhancement of the partner in μ* if (a) for all $j \in X_i \cup \{i\}$, $\mu(i) R_i j$ implies

[6] For all $x, y \in \mathbb{R}^{2n}$, $x >_L y$ if and only if there is $k \in \{1, \ldots, 2n\}$ such that for all $i < k$, $x_i = y_i$ and $x_k > y_k$. For all $x, y \in \mathbb{R}^{2n}$, $x \geq_L y$ if and only if $x >_L y$ or $x = y$.

$\mu(i)R'_i j$ and (b) for all $j, k \in X_i \cup \{i\}$ with $j, k \neq \mu(i)$, $jR'_i k$ if and only if $jR_i k$. Let $Q(R_i, \mu)$ be the set of preference relations that are obtained from R_i by rank-enhancements of the parters in μ. Given $R \in \mathscr{R}$ and $\mu \in \mathscr{M}$, let $Q(R, \mu) = \{R' \in \mathscr{R} \mid \forall i \in F \cup W,\ R'_i \in Q(R_i, \mu)\}$.

With rank-enhancements of the partners in μ, only the current partners in the matching μ can be preferred to more agents; the preferences over any other agents are unchanged. See the Introduction for some motivation for considering this kind of change in preferences.

The solidarity principle requires that when some agents change their preferences, then every other agent whose preferences are unchanged should be affected in the same direction. Given $R, R' \in \mathscr{R}$, let $K(R, R') = \{i \in F \cup W \mid R_i = R'_i\}$ denote the set of agents whose preferences are the same in R and R'.

Solidarity under Rank-Enhancement of Partners. For all $R, R' \in \mathscr{R}_0$, if $R' \in Q(R, \varphi(R))$, then either $\varphi_i(R')R_i\varphi_i(R)$ for all $i \in K(R, R')$ or $\varphi_i(R)R_i\varphi_i(R')$ for all $i \in K(R, R')$.

A weaker version of the above property is obtained if we apply the requirement only when *one* agent changes his preferences.

Solidarity under Single Rank-Enhancement of Partner. For all $R, R' \in \mathscr{R}_0$, if $R'_i \in Q(R_i, \varphi(R))$ for some $i \in F \cup W$ and $R'_k = R_k$ for all $k \in F \cup W$ with $k \neq i$, then either $\varphi_k(R')R_k\varphi_k(R)$ for all $k \in K(R, R')$ or $\varphi_k(R)R_k\varphi_k(R')$ for all $k \in K(R, R')$.

We now examine whether there exist rules that always select an envy-minimizing matching in the set of stable matchings and that satisfy Solidarity under Single Rank-Enhancement of Partner. Our first result is an impossibility theorem when $n \geq 5$: Even on the restricted domain $\mathscr{R}^*$ (the class of preference profiles such that being unmatched is the worst alternative for each agent), if a rule always selects an envy-minimizing matching in the set of stable matchings, then it cannot satisfy Solidarity under Single Rank-Enhancement of Partner. As defined above, E^S is the correspondence that associates with each preference profile the set of matchings that minimize the maximal individual instances of envy in the set of stable matchings and T^S is the correspondence that associates with each profile the set of matchings that minimize the total instances of envy in the set of stable matchings.

Theorem 1. *Suppose that $n \geq 5$. Then:*

(i) No selection rule from the correspondence E^S on $\mathscr{R}^*$ satisfies Solidarity under Single Rank-Enhancement of Partner.
(ii) No selection rule from the correspondence T^S on $\mathscr{R}^*$ satisfies Solidarity under Single Rank-Enhancement of Partner.

Proof. (i) Let φ be a selection rule from E^S. Let $R \in \mathscr{R}^*$ be a preference profile such that

$$\begin{aligned} R_{f_1} &= w_1\ w_4\ w_5\ w_2\ \ldots \\ R_{f_2} &= w_2\ w_4\ w_5\ w_1\ \ldots \\ R_{f_3} &= w_1\ w_3\ \ldots \\ R_{w_1} &= f_2\ f_3\ f_1\ \ldots \\ R_{w_2} &= f_1\ f_2\ \ldots \\ R_{w_3} &= f_3\ \ldots \end{aligned}$$

and for all $i > 3$, $w_i P_{f_i} w$ for all $w \in W \setminus \{w_i\}$ and $f_i P_{w_i} f$ for all $f \in F \setminus \{f_i\}$. Then, the unique stable matching for R is

$$\mu = \begin{cases} f_1 & f_2 & f_3 & f_4 & \ldots & f_n \\ w_2 & w_1 & w_3 & w_4 & \ldots & w_n \end{cases}.$$

Hence, $\varphi(R) = \mu$.

Let $R' \in \mathscr{R}^*$ be such that

$$R'_{f_3} = w_3\ w_1\ \ldots$$

and for all $i \in F \cup W$ with $i \neq f_3$, $R'_i = R_i$. There are exactly two stable matchings for R': μ and

$$\mu' = \begin{cases} f_1 & f_2 & f_3 & f_4 & \ldots & f_n \\ w_1 & w_2 & w_3 & w_4 & \ldots & w_n \end{cases}.$$

Because $\max_{i \in F \cup W}(e_i(\mu', R'_i)) = 2 < 3 = \max_{i \in F \cup W}(e_i(\mu, R'_i))$, $E^S(R') = \{\mu'\}$. Hence, $\varphi(R') = \mu'$. Observe that $R' \in Q(R, \mu)$ and $f_1, w_1 \in K(R, R')$. But $\mu'(f_1) = w_1$, $\mu(f_1) = w_2$, and $w_1 P_{f_1} w_2$, while $\mu(w_1) = f_2$, $\mu'(w_1) = f_1$, and $f_2 P_{w_1} f_1$. Thus, φ violates Solidarity under Single Rank-Enhancement of Partner.

(ii) Let φ be a selection rule from T^S. Let $R, R' \in \mathscr{R}^*$ be the preference profiles as defined above. Notice that $t(\mu', R') = 3 < 6 = t(\mu, R')$ and, hence, $\varphi(R') = \mu'$. Thus, by the same argument as above, the rule φ violates Solidarity under Single Rank-Enhancement of Partner. □

It is clear that the impossibility result in Theorem 1 extends to any domain $\mathscr{R}_0$ such that $\mathscr{R}_0 \supseteq \mathscr{R}^*$, and in particular, to $\mathscr{R}$.

Theorem 1 shows a trade-off, under the requirement of stability, between envy minimization and solidarity, at least if $n \geq 5$. On the one hand, a rule should always choose an equitable matching in the set of stable matchings. On the other hand, a rule should satisfy an appealing solidarity property given a natural class of preference changes. But these requirements are incompatible, so we have to give up one of these properties.

We weaken the requirement of stability and consider selection rules from the set of individually rational and Pareto-efficient matchings. However, among envy-minimizing selection rules from the set of individually rational and Pareto-efficient matchings, there exist rules that violate Solidarity under Single Rank-Enhancement of Partner. Consider the following example.

Example. Let $n = 4$ and $R \in \mathscr{R}^*$ be given by

$$\begin{aligned} R_{f_1} &= w_1\ w_2\ w_3\ w_4\ f_1 \\ R_{f_2} &= w_1\ w_2\ w_3\ w_4\ f_2 \\ R_{f_3} &= w_4\ w_3\ w_1\ w_2\ f_3 \\ R_{f_4} &= w_4\ w_3\ w_1\ w_2\ f_4 \end{aligned}$$

$$\begin{aligned} R_{w_1} &= f_1\ f_2\ f_3\ f_4\ w_1 \\ R_{w_2} &= f_1\ f_2\ f_3\ f_4\ w_2 \\ R_{w_3} &= f_3\ f_4\ f_1\ f_2\ w_3 \\ R_{w_4} &= f_4\ f_3\ f_1\ f_2\ w_4. \end{aligned}$$

Assume that $\varphi(R) = \mu$, where

$$\mu = \begin{cases} f_1 & f_2 & f_3 & f_4 \\ w_1 & w_2 & w_3 & w_4 \end{cases}.$$

Note that $\mu \in T^{IP}(R)$ and $\mu \in L^{IP}(R)$; that is, μ is an envy-minimizing matching in the set of individually rational and Pareto-efficient matchings. Let $R' \in \mathscr{R}$ be given by

$$R'_{f_3} = w_3\ w_4\ w_1\ w_2\ f_3$$

and for all $i \neq f_3$, $R'_i = R_i$. Notice that $R' \in Q(R, \mu)$. Now assume that $\varphi(R') = \mu'$, where

$$\mu' = \begin{cases} f_1 & f_2 & f_3 & f_4 \\ w_2 & w_1 & w_3 & w_4 \end{cases}.$$

We have $\mu' \in T^{IP}(R')$ and $\mu' \in L^{IP}(R')$. However, because $\mu(f_1) P_{f_1} \mu'(f_1)$, whereas $\mu'(f_2) P_{f_2} \mu(f_2)$, the rule φ violates Solidarity under Single Rank-Enhancement of Partners.

The rule φ in the above example looks peculiar. With the matching $\varphi(R) = \mu$, the agents are separated into two groups, $A_1 = \{f_1, f_2, w_1, w_2\}$ and $A_2 = \{f_3, f_4, w_3, w_4\}$, in which every agent is matched to another agent in the same group as himself. In going from R to R', only agent f_3 increases the rank of his partner in μ, namely agent w_3. This change in the preferences of f_3 should be "irrelevant" to group A_1, and it should not affect the matching of the members within A_1.

The following property formalizes the above idea.

Separability. For all $R, R' \in \mathscr{R}_0$ and all $A \subseteq F \cup W$, if $\varphi(R) = \mu$, $\mu(A) = A$, $R' \in Q(R, \mu)$, and $R'_i = R_i$ for all $i \in A$, then $\varphi_i(R') = \mu(i)$ for all $i \in A$.

The next result shows that, on the domain $\mathscr{R}^*$ of profiles such that being unmatched is the worst situation for every agent, *any* separable rule that minimizes envy (in the sense of leximin or total number) in the set of individually rational and Pareto-efficient matchings satisfies Solidarity under Rank-Enhancement of Partners.

Recall that L^{IP} is the correspondence that associates with each profile the set of matchings that lexicographically minimize individual instances of envy in the set of individually rational and Pareto efficient matchings and T^{IP} is the correspondence that associates with each profile the set of matchings that minimize total instances of envy in the set of individually rational and Pareto efficient matchings, respectively.

Theorem 2. *Suppose that $n \geq 2$. Then:*

(i) Any selection rule from the correspondence L^{IP} on $\mathscr{R}^*$ that satisfies Separability also satisfies Solidarity under Rank-Enhancement of Partners.
(ii) Any selection rule from the correspondence T^{IP} on $\mathscr{R}^*$ that satisfies Separability also satisfies Solidarity under Rank-Enhancement of Partners.

Proof. (i) Assume that φ is a selection rule from L^{IP} defined on $\mathscr{R}^*$ that satisfies Separability. Let $R \in \mathscr{R}^*$ and $\varphi(R) = \mu$. Then, μ lexicographically minimizes envy in the set $I(R) \cap P(R)$. Let $R' \in Q(R, \mu)$. Note that because $R \in \mathscr{R}^*$ and $\mu \in I(R) \cap P(R)$, we have $\mu(i) \neq i$ for all $i \in F \cup W$. Hence, $R' \in \mathscr{R}^*$.

We will first show that μ lexicographically minimizes envy in the set $I(R') \cap P(R')$ as well. It is clear that μ is individually rational and Pareto efficient for R' because $R' \in Q(R, \mu)$. It remains to show that for all $\mu' \in I(R') \cap P(R')$, $\theta(e(\mu, R')) \leq_L \theta(e(\mu', R'))$. Notice that because $R, R' \in \mathscr{R}^*$, we have $I(R) = I(R')$. However, in general, there is no inclusion relation between $P(R)$ and $P(R')$ even if $\mu \in P(R)$ and $R' \in Q(R, \mu)$. Hence, we distinguish two cases. Let $\mu' \in I(R') \cap P(R')$.

Case 1. $\mu' \in I(R) \cap P(R)$.
Because μ lexicographically minimizes envy in $I(R) \cap P(R)$, we have

$$\theta(e(\mu, R)) \leq_L \theta(e(\mu', R)). \tag{1}$$

We now show that because $R' \in Q(R, \mu)$, we also have

$$e_i(\mu, R'_i) - e_i(\mu, R_i) \leq e_i(\mu', R'_i) - e_i(\mu', R_i) \tag{2}$$

for all $i \in F \cup W$. Clearly, if $\mu(i) = \mu'(i)$, then (2) holds with equality. If, however, $\mu(i) \neq \mu'(i)$, because $R, R' \in \mathscr{R}^*$ and $R' \in Q(R, \mu)$, it follows that the left-hand side of (2) is nonpositive and the right-hand side is nonnegative, so again (2) is satisfied. An implication of (2) is that the lexicographic order of $e(\mu, R)$ and $e(\mu', R)$ is preserved if $[e(\mu, R') - e(\mu, R)]$ is added to the former and $[e(\mu', R') - e(\mu', R)]$ is added to the latter. Thus, it follows from (1) and (2) that $\theta(e(\mu, R')) \leq_L \theta(e(\mu', R'))$.

Case 2. $\mu' \notin I(R) \cap P(R)$.
Because $\mu' \in I(R') = I(R)$, we have $\mu' \notin P(R)$. Thus, there exists $\mu'' \in I(R) \cap P(R)$ that Pareto dominates μ' at R. Then,

$$\theta(e(\mu'', R)) \leq_L \theta(e(\mu', R)) \tag{3}$$

because in μ'' no agent is matched to an agent with a lower rank in his preference order than in μ' and, hence, no agent has more instances of envy in μ'' than in μ'. Because μ lexicographically minimizes envy in $I(R) \cap P(R)$, it follows that

$$\theta(e(\mu, R)) \leq_L \theta(e(\mu'', R)). \tag{4}$$

By (3) and (4), we have $\theta(e(\mu, R)) \leq_L \theta(e(\mu', R))$. The rest of the argument is as in Case 1.

We have shown that μ lexicographically minimizes envy in the set $I(R') \cap P(R')$. Let $\varphi(R') = \hat{\mu}$. We now show that $\hat{\mu} = \mu$.

Suppose, on the contrary, that $\hat{\mu}(i^*) \neq \mu(i^*)$ for some $i^* \in F \cup W$. Note that $\hat{\mu}(i^*) \neq i^*$ and $\mu(i^*) \neq i^*$ because $R, R' \in \mathscr{R}^*$ and $\mu, \hat{\mu} \in I(R') \cap P(R')$. Let $J(R, R') = \{i \in F \cup W \mid R'_i \neq R_i\}$. By Separability, for all $i \in F \cup W$ with $i \notin J(R, R') \cup \mu(J(R, R'))$, $\hat{\mu}(i) = \mu(i)$. Hence, $i^* \in J(R, R') \cup \mu(J(R, R'))$. Let $j \in F \cup W$ be defined by $j = i^*$ if $i^* \in J(R, R')$ and $j = \mu(i^*)$ if $i^* \notin J(R, R')$. Then, necessarily, $\hat{\mu}(j) \neq \mu(j)$ and $R'_j \neq R_j$. Now partition the set $F \cup W$ into the following three sets:

$$A = \{i \in F \cup W \mid \hat{\mu}(i) \neq \mu(i) \text{ and } R'_i \neq R_i\}$$
$$B = \{i \in F \cup W \mid \hat{\mu}(i) \neq \mu(i) \text{ and } R'_i = R_i\}$$
$$C = \{i \in F \cup W \mid \hat{\mu}(i) = \mu(i)\}.$$

Notice that $A \neq \varnothing$ because $j \in A$. Let $i \in A$. Because $R, R' \in \mathscr{R}^*$, $R' \in Q(R, \mu)$, $\hat{\mu}(i) \neq \mu(i)$, and $R'_i \neq R_i$, we have $e_i(\mu, R_i) > e_i(\mu, R'_i)$ and $e_i(\hat{\mu}, R_i) \leq e_i(\hat{\mu}, R'_i)$. Hence,

$$e_i(\mu, R_i) - e_i(\mu, R'_i) > 0 \geq e_i(\hat{\mu}, R_i) - e_i(\hat{\mu}, R'_i). \tag{5}$$

Let $i \in B$. Then, obviously, $e_i(\mu, R_i) = e_i(\mu, R'_i)$ and $e_i(\hat{\mu}, R_i) = e_i(\hat{\mu}, R'_i)$. Thus,

$$e_i(\mu, R_i) - e_i(\mu, R'_i) = 0 = e_i(\hat{\mu}, R_i) - e_i(\hat{\mu}, R'_i). \tag{6}$$

Let $i \in C$. Then, $e_i(\mu, R_i) = e_i(\hat{\mu}, R_i)$ and $e_i(\mu, R'_i) = e_i(\hat{\mu}, R'_i)$. Hence,

$$e_i(\mu, R_i) - e_i(\mu, R'_i) = e_i(\hat{\mu}, R_i) - e_i(\hat{\mu}, R'_i). \tag{7}$$

Because both μ and $\hat{\mu}$ lexicographically minimize envy in the set $I(R') \cap P(R')$, we have

$$\theta(e(\mu, R')) = \theta(e(\hat{\mu}, R')). \tag{8}$$

Reasoning as in Case 1, it then follows from (5) to (8) that

$$\theta(e(\mu, R)) >_L \theta(e(\hat{\mu}, R)). \tag{9}$$

Now, if $\hat{\mu} \in I(R) \cap P(R)$, then (9) implies that μ does not lexicographically minimize envy in $I(R) \cap P(R)$, which is a contradiction. If $\hat{\mu} \notin I(R) \cap P(R)$, then by the same argument as in Case 2 above, there exists $\tilde{\mu} \in I(R) \cap P(R)$ that Pareto dominates $\hat{\mu}$ for which $\theta(e(\tilde{\mu}, R)) \leq_L \theta(e(\hat{\mu}, R))$. Hence, we have $\theta(e(\tilde{\mu}, R)) <_L \theta(e(\mu, R))$, which is again a contradiction. Thus, we must have $\hat{\mu} = \mu$.

(ii) The proof of (ii) is essentially the same as that of (i). Simply replace $\theta(e(\cdot, \cdot))$ with $t(\cdot, \cdot)$, as well as $\leq_L$ with $\leq$. □

The proof of Theorem 2 has actually shown that any separable selection rule from the correspondence L^{IP} (or T^{IP}) on $\mathscr{R}^*$ satisfies *Invariance under Rank-Enhancement of Partners*, the property that requires the selected matching to be unchanged after rank-enhancement of partners. It is clear that Invariance under Rank-Enhancement of Partners implies Solidarity under Rank-Enhancement of Partners.

An example of a separable selection rule from L^{IP} (or from T^{IP}) is as follows. For all $R \in \mathscr{R}^*$, all $i \in F \cup W$, and all $Z \subseteq \mathscr{M}$, let $G_i^R(Z) = \{\mu \in Z \mid \forall \mu' \in Z, \mu(i) R_i \mu'(i)\}$. Define the rule φ^* by setting $\varphi^*(R) = G_{f_n}^R \circ G_{f_{n-1}}^R \circ \cdots \circ G_{f_1}^R(L^{IP}(R))$ for all $R \in \mathscr{R}^*$. It can be checked that $\# \varphi^*(R) = 1$ for all $R \in \mathscr{R}^*$. Indeed, if $\mu, \mu' \in \varphi^*(R)$, then $\mu(i) I_i \mu'(i)$ for all $i \in F$. Because any R_i is a linear order on $W \cup \{i\}$, we have $\mu(i) = \mu'(i)$ for all $i \in F$ and, hence, $\mu = \mu'$. It is clear that φ^* satisfies Separability and, by Theorem 2, it also satisfies Solidarity under Rank-Enhancement of Partners.

Note that φ^* is not *anonymous*, the requirement that the rule should not depend on the "names" $(f_1, f_2, \ldots)$ of the agents in each group, nor on the "names" $(F$ and $W)$ of the groups. However, searching for an anonymous rule would lead us to a dead end. As Masarani and Gokturk (1989) have shown, there exists no rule that selects a Pareto-efficient matching that is also anonymous.[7]

5 Conclusion

In this article, we have formulated a principle of equity as envy minimization on the one hand, and a principle of solidarity on the other hand, for the class of two-sided matching problems. The former requires that a rule should always select an envy-minimizing matching in the set of matchings meeting some basic conditions. The latter requires that when the preferences of some agents change in a natural way, all of the agents whose preferences are fixed should be affected in the same way; either

[7] Strictly speaking, Masarani and Gokturk (1989) suggested that in order for a matching rule to be "fair," it should be anonymous, stable, and satisfy a property that they called "maximin optimality." They showed that no rule can satisfy all of these properties simultaneously. In order to establish the impossibility result, however, the last property is not necessary and stability can be weakened to Pareto efficiency.

all better off or all worse off. We have shown that when matchings are required to be stable, the two principles are incompatible, but with the weaker requirements of individual rationality and Pareto efficiency, they are fully compatible. What we have done in this article is to draw a line between the cases in which we can obtain a rule satisfying all of the desirable properties we have considered and the cases in which we cannot.

Our analysis has been confined to the case of one-to-one matchings. However, our impossibility results straightforwardly extend to the more general class of many-to-one matching problems if we do not impose any constraints on the number of workers that each factory should accommodate because the class of one-to-one matching problems is a subclass of this general class. It may be of interest to examine whether our impossibility and possibility results extend to the case of many-to-one matchings with some constraints such that there is a minimum number of workers that each factory must have. To consider other desirable properties of matching rules under some "natural" changes of the data and examine their compatibility may also be an interesting topic for future research.

Acknowledgements I would like to thank B. Klaus, M. Fleurbaey, W. Thomson, and the participants in the Conference on Social Ethics and Normative Economics in honour of Serge-Christophe Kolm held in Caen, May 18–19, 2007, for helpful comments and discussions. I have also benefited from insightful comments and useful suggestions from two anonymous referees of this article. I am especially grateful to the editor, John Weymark, for making numerous comments, suggestions, and corrections that have greatly improved the content and exposition of this article. Financial support from the Ministry of Education, Culture, Sports, Science and Technology, Japan, through its grant for the Twenty-First Century Center of Excellence Program on the Normative Evaluation and Social Choice of Contemporary Economic Systems and the Grant-in-Aid for Scientific Research (B) No. 18330036 is gratefully acknowledged.

References

Feldman, A. M., & Kirman, A. (1974). Fairness and envy. *American Economic Review*, *64*, 996–1005

Foley, D. (1967). Resource allocation and the public sector. *Yale Economic Essays*, *7*, 45–98

Gale, D., & Shapley, L. S. (1962). College admissions and the stability of marriage. *American Mathematical Monthly*, *69*, 9–15

Kolm, S.-C. (1972). *Justice et équité*. Editions du Centre National de la Recherche Scientifique, Paris (Trans. as: *Justice and equity*). Cambridge, MA: MIT Press (1997)

Masarani, F., & Gokturk, S. S. (1989). On the existence of fair matching algorithms. *Theory and Decision*, *26*, 305–322

Moulin, H. (1987). The pure compensation problem: Egalitarianism versus laissez-fairism. *Quarterly Journal of Economics*, *101*, 769–783

Rawls, J. (1971). *A theory of justice*. Cambridge, MA: Harvard University Press

Roth, A., & Sotomayor, M. (1990). *Two-sided matching: A study in game-theoretic modeling and analysis*. Cambridge: Cambridge University Press

Schmeidler, D. (1969). The nucleolus of a characteristic function game. *SIAM Journal of Applied Mathematics*, *17*, 1163–1170

Sen, A. K. (1970). *Collective choice and social welfare*. San Francisco: Holden-Day

Sprumont, Y. (1996). Axiomatizing ordinal welfare egalitarianism when preferences may vary. *Journal of Economic Theory*, *68*, 77–110

Suzumura, K. (1983). *Rational choice, collective decisions, and social welfare*. Cambridge: Cambridge University Press

Thomson, W. (1993). The replacement principle in public good economies with single-peaked preferences. *Economics Letters*, *42*, 31–36

Thomson, W. (1997). The replacement principle in economies with single-peaked preferences. *Journal of Economic Theory*, *76*, 145–168

Thomson, W. (1998). The replacement principle in economies with indivisible goods. *Social Choice and Welfare*, *15*, 57–66

Borrowing-Proofness of the Lindahl Rule in Kolm Triangle Economies

William Thomson

1 Introduction

Allocation rules can be manipulated in a variety of ways. Agents may misrepresent their preferences, a possibility that has been extensively studied. They can also take advantage of the control they have over resources, and different kinds of stratagems of this type have been identified. For instance, in a classical exchange economy in which resources are allocated by means of the Walrasian rule, an agent may benefit from withholding some of his endowment. He may even benefit from destroying some of it. Also, he may benefit from transferring some of his endowment to someone else (of course without this second agent being hurt, thereby having no reason not to accept the transfer). For a discussion of these phenomena, see Gale (1974), Aumann and Peleg (1974), Postlewaite (1979), and Thomson (1987a,b). Additional manipulation opportunities are discussed in Thomson (2007).

We consider here the following form of manipulation. Suppose that prior to the operation of the chosen rule, an agent borrows resources so as to augment his endowment. The rule is then applied; he receives the consumption bundle the rule assigns to him, and he returns what he had borrowed. In the end, he may be better off than if he had not borrowed. Our objective is to study the requirement on a rule that it not be subject to this kind of manipulation. We call it "borrowing-proofness." The requirement is formulated and studied in the context of classical economies by Thomson (2009).

We have in mind two possible scenarios. First, an agent may have access to resources outside of the group of agents with whom he normally trades. There is a growing literature concerning situations of this kind, when an agent may exploit the particular place he holds in the social network. Here, we imagine that an agent who is part of some community is also involved with another community where he can borrow resources. This other community is not explicitly modeled. We then have an "open-economy" model, and we refer to the property

---

W. Thomson
Department of Economics, University of Rochester, Rochester, NY 14618, USA
e-mail: wth2@mail.rochester.edu

M. Fleurbaey et al. (eds.), *Social Ethics and Normative Economics*,
Studies in Choice and Welfare, DOI 10.1007/978-3-642-17807-8_7,

of immunity to manipulation through borrowing from the outside world as "open-economy borrowing-proofness." Alternatively, the agent could simply exaggerate the resources he owns, without the social planner being able to verify these claims of ownership. This virtual augmentation is mathematically equivalent to actual borrowing from the outside, but for simplicity we will mainly refer to one story, the borrowing story.

The second scenario pertains to situations in which an agent borrows from one of his fellow traders. He should of course provide the lender the incentive to do so: after the borrower has returned what he borrowed, the lender should be at least as well off as he would have been if he had not lent. We now have a "closed-economy" model and we refer to the property of immunity to borrowing from within as "closed-economy borrowing-proofness."

The resource allocation problem we consider is standard: there are two goods, one private good and one public good; the private good can be either consumed as such, or it can be used as input in the production of the public good. At what level should the public good be produced, and how much should each agent contribute to its production? These are the questions addressed in the literature on public good provision.

We investigate the manipulability through borrowing of a rule that is central to this literature, the "Lindahl rule" (Lindahl 1919). Characterizing the equilibria of manipulation games associated with this rule when agents can either withhold part of their endowments or exaggerate them is the object of Thomson (1979) and Sertel and Sanver (1999). We study the borrowing-proofness of the Lindahl rule on three standard preference domains, when only the "classical" assumptions of continuity, monotonicity, and convexity of preferences are made and when, in addition, preferences are either quasi-linear or homothetic. (We add assumptions that guarantee its single-valuedness.) We show that on both the quasi-linear and the homothetic domains, the Lindahl rule is borrowing-proof under either scenario (Propositions 1 and 2 and Propositions 3 and 4). In fact, as long as the public good is a normal good, this conclusion holds. However, on the classical domain, it does not (Examples 1 and 4).

It is interesting to relate open-economy borrowing-proofness to the requirement of immunity to manipulation through withholding of some of one's endowment, called "withholding-proofness" (Postlewaite 1979 introduces this property for private good economies). It is known that the Lindahl rule is not withholding-proof on the classical domain (Thomson 1979, 1987b). We show that this negative result also holds on either the quasi-linear domain or the homothetic domain (Examples 2 and 3). Altogether then, manipulation through open-economy borrowing should be less of a concern than manipulation through withholding.

Another reason why it should be less of a concern is of course that borrowing requires an agent to have access to external resources under the first scenario, and to convince one of his fellow traders to go along with his scheme under the second scenario, whereas withholding can be carried out entirely on one's own. When manipulation is interpreted as exaggeration, asking agents to provide proof of ownership is a practical way to deal with the behavior.

Yet, for our negative results, we place a bound on the amount borrowed, and in fact, we prove stronger claims: no matter how small that bound is, borrowing-proofness fails.

Why should we worry about agents manipulating through borrowing? For the same reason we should worry about them manipulating by misrepresenting their preferences, or by transferring their endowments among one another, or by withholding or destroying part of their endowments. An allocation rule is chosen because of the properties it enjoys. If an agent does not behave as specified by the rule, the allocations the rule is supposed to reach are less likely to be reached. In most cases, the first consequence of manipulation, be it misrepresentation of preferences or endowment manipulation in any of its forms, is that a rule designed to produce efficient allocations will be prevented from doing so. Also, a rule is usually specified so as to satisfy some distributional or participation requirements. These too may not be satisfied if agents manipulate.

Ours is not an intertemporal model of a monetary economy. Borrowing financial resources is of course a very convenient means of achieving intertemporal efficiency and there is no reason to object to it in that context.[1]

To establish most of our results, we use the so-called Kolm triangle, the very ingenious geometric representation of public good economies with two agents, two goods, one private good and one public good, and a linear technology, developed by Kolm (1971). Throughout this exposition we adopt the didactic style that this device makes possible.[2]

This article is organized as follows. In Sect. 2, we introduce the model. In Sect. 3, we define and discuss the open-economy version of borrowing-proofness. In Sect. 4, we study the manipulability of the Lindahl rule through withholding and provide some insight into the reasons why it is more vulnerable to this sort of behavior than to manipulation through open-economy borrowing. In Sect. 5, we consider the closed-economy version of borrowing-proofness. In Sect. 6, we offer concluding comments and list open questions.

2 Notation and Definitions

There are two goods, one private good and one public good, and $n \in \mathbb{N}$ agents. Let $N \equiv \{1, \ldots, n\}$ be the set of agents. Each agent $i \in N$ is equipped with a preference relation defined on $\mathbb{R}^2_+$, denoted by R_i. Let P_i denote the strict preference

[1] Unfortunately, in describing the phenomenon in which we are interested, we could not find a term that would not bring to mind allocation over time.

[2] Other geometric representations have been proposed. The Dolbear (1967) triangle allows one to keep standard rectangular axes for one of the agents but not for both. Thus, it breaks the symmetry between them. The Kolm triangle has the advantage of treating both agents symmetrically. The representation used by Sertel (1994) uses standard rectangular axes for both agents, but a feasible allocation is mapped into two points in $\mathbb{R}^2_+$.

relation associated with R_i and I_i the corresponding indifference relation. Let $R \equiv (R_1, \ldots, R_n)$ denote the profile of preferences. Each agent $i \in N$ is endowed with an amount $\omega_{ix} \geq 0$ of the private good. Let $\omega_x \equiv (\omega_{1x}, \ldots, \omega_{nx}) \in \mathbb{R}^N_+$ denote the profile of these endowments.[3] The private good can be consumed as such or it can be used in the production of the public good. Initially, there is no public good, so we set $\omega_y \equiv 0$. Let $\omega \equiv (\omega_x, \omega_y) \in \mathbb{R}^N_+ \times \mathbb{R}_+$. The production set is a subset of $\mathbb{R}^2$ denoted Y, with inputs measured negatively and outputs measured positively. An *economy with agent set* N is a list (R, ω, Y) in some domain $\mathscr{E}^N$ defined by imposing restrictions on preferences (such as continuity and convexity) and on the production set (such as convexity). A (feasible) *allocation for* $(R, \omega, Y) \in \mathscr{E}^N$ is a list $z \equiv (x, y) \in \mathbb{R}^N_+ \times \mathbb{R}_+$ such that $(-\sum(\omega_{ix} - x_i), y) \in Y$. *Agent i's consumption at* z is the pair $z_i \equiv (x_i, y)$. Let $Z(\omega, Y)$ denote the set of feasible allocations of (R, ω, Y). We work with a linear technology: there is $\alpha \in \mathbb{R}_+$ such that the production of each unit of the public good requires α units of input. We choose units of measurement of the goods so that $\alpha = 1$.

Our results pertain to the *classical domain*, when preferences are continuous, convex, and monotonic (an increase in the consumption of any of the goods makes an agent better off), and two important subdomains, defined as follows. The preference relation R_i is *quasi-linear* if indifference between bundles is preserved under translations of these bundles parallel to the private good axis by any non-negative amount: for each pair $\{z_i, z'_i\} \in \mathbb{R}^2_+$ and each $t \in \mathbb{R}_+$, if $z_i \; I_i \; z'_i$, then $(z_i + (t, 0)) \; I_i \; (z'_i + (t, 0))$.[4] The preference relation R_i is *homothetic* if indifference between bundles is preserved under homothetic transformations of these bundles: for each pair $\{z_i, z'_i\} \in \mathbb{R}^2_+$ and each $\lambda \in \mathbb{R}_+$, if $z_i \; I_i \; z'_i$, then $(\lambda z_i) \; I_i \; (\lambda z'_i)$. Let $\mathscr{R}_{cl}$ denote the domain of classical preferences. Let $\mathscr{R}_{ql}$ and $\mathscr{R}_{hom}$ denote the domain of preferences, that, in addition to satisfying the classical assumptions, are quasi-linear and homothetic respectively. Let $\mathscr{E}^N_{cl}$, $\mathscr{E}^N_{ql}$, and $\mathscr{E}^N_{hom}$ be the corresponding domains of economies. Let $\mathscr{E}^N$ be a generic domain of economies.

Given a domain $\mathscr{E}^N$, *a solution on* $\mathscr{E}^N$ is a mapping φ associating with each $(R, \omega, Y) \in \mathscr{E}^N$ a non-empty subset of $Z(\omega, Y)$, denoted $\varphi(R, \omega, Y)$. We use the term *rule* when the mapping is *single-valued*. A solution φ is *essentially single-valued* if for each $(R, \omega, Y) \in \mathscr{E}^N$, each pair $\{z, z'\} \subseteq \varphi(R, \omega, Y)$, and each $i \in N$, $z_i \; I_i \; z'_i$.[5] The *Pareto solution, P*, associates with each economy its set of allocations such that there is no other allocation that each agent finds at least as desirable, and at least one agent prefers: $z \in P(R, \omega, Y)$ if $z \in Z(\omega, Y)$ and there is no $z' \in Z(\omega, Y)$ such that for each $i \in N$, $z'_i \; R_i \; z_i$, and for at least one $i \in N$, $z'_i \; P_i \; z_i$.

---

[3] The notation $\mathbb{R}^N$ and $\mathbb{R}^N_+$ designates the cross-product of $|N|$ copies of $\mathbb{R}$ and $\mathbb{R}_+$ respectively indexed by the elements of N.

[4] A common alternative specification of the quasi-linearity assumption is obtained by dropping the requirement that the consumption of the private good be non-negative, and in fact, letting it be unbounded below. Then, the Pareto set is invariant under arbitrary (in sign and magnitude) transfers of the private good. This makes working with this model particularly easy.

[5] We could also speak of a rule being *single-valued* up to Pareto-indifference.

Given $a^1, a^2 \in \mathbb{R}^2_+$, **seg[$a^1, a^2$]** designates the segment connecting these two points. Given $a^1, \ldots, a^k \in \mathbb{R}^2_+$, **bro.seg[$a^1, \ldots, a^k$]** designates the broken segment $\text{seg}[a^1, a^2] \cup \cdots \cup \text{seg}[a^{k-1}, a^k]$.

3 Open-Economy Borrowing-Proofness

Next is a formal statement of our requirement of immunity to manipulation through borrowing from the outside. Agent i is the borrower and he augments his endowment of the private good from ω_{ix} to ω'_{ix} by borrowing. (Obviously, one cannot borrow a public good.) Given $\omega_x \in \mathbb{R}^N_+$ and $i \in N$, we denote by ω_{-ix} the vector obtained from ω_x by dropping its i-th coordinate. Let φ be a solution.

Open-Economy Borrowing-Proofness. For each $e \equiv (R, \omega, Y) \in \mathscr{E}^N$, each $i \in N$, and each $\omega' \in \mathbb{R}^N_+ \times \mathbb{R}_+$, if $\omega'_{ix} > \omega_{ix}$, $\omega'_{-ix} = \omega_{-ix}$, and $\omega'_y = 0$, then it is not the case that for some $z \in \varphi(R, \omega, Y)$ and for some $z' \in \varphi(R, \omega', Y)$, $[z'_i - (\omega'_{ix} - \omega_{ix}, 0)]\ P_i\ z_i$.

For an agent to want to borrow, he should first be able to return what he borrowed. Thus, the property is written in the negative. We should worry about him borrowing only if he is able to return what he borrowed and after doing so, ends up better off.

We could have stated the definition for *single-valued* solutions. In the strategic analysis of allocation correspondences, each strategy has an associated set of outcomes, and the question comes up how a player bases his choice of a strategy on comparisons of sets of outcomes. This question does not arise for a *single-valued* solution, that is, for what we called a "rule." We wrote our definition with existential quantifiers on the allocations chosen before and after the manipulation. This means that no matter what choice would be made if he did not borrow, an agent would evaluate optimistically the choice that would be made if he did borrow. However, our results are proved in situations in which the solution that interests us here is *single-valued*.[6]

An alternative definition is obtained by imagining that the borrower obtains resources from one of his fellow traders, instead of from an unspecified outside world. In general, the bundle the rule assigns to the lender will change when the rule is operated from the reshuffled endowments, and he may find his new bundle worse than the bundle he would have received if he had not lent. For him to accept lending, it should be the case that after getting back the resources he lent, he does

[6] One could allow for *essential single-valuedness*, but Pareto-indifference of the allocations chosen for the reported profile of endowments would not necessarily imply Pareto-indifference after the amounts borrowed have been returned. Thus, the problem of specifying how an agent compares sets of allocations would still have to be faced. The issue is discussed by Thomson (1979). A concept of immunity to manipulation for correspondences is studied by Ching and Zhou (2002) but other formulations have been proposed.

end up at least as well off as if he had not lent. The possibility of improving one's welfare by borrowing "from within" is discussed in Sect. 5.

We prove our negative results and illustrate our positive ones concerning *open-economy borrowing-proofness* by means of two-agent examples. Then, we can use the geometric device known as the *Kolm triangle* (Kolm 1971). We assume familiarity with this device (for a didactic exposition, see Thomson 1999). The essential features are as follows. Let $N \equiv \{1, 2\}$ and $e \equiv (R, \omega, Y) \in \mathcal{E}^N$ be an economy with a linear (normalized) technology. An allocation $z \equiv (x_1, x_2, y) \in Z(\omega, Y)$ is represented as a point in an equilateral triangle of height $\omega_{1x} + \omega_{2x}$. The lower left and lower right corners, labeled 0_1 and 0_2, are origins. The two agents' consumptions are measured from these points. Their consumptions x_1 and x_2 of the private good are measured by the distances from z to the left and right sides of the triangle (and *not* by the horizontal distances from z to these sides); their common consumption of the public good is measured by the vertical distance from z to the base of the triangle.

On either the quasi-linear domain or the homothetic domain, the Pareto set has a simple structure, even more so if in fact preferences are strictly convex, as depicted in our figures.

The key implication of quasi-linearity for convex preferences, in either the standard rectangular axes or in the slanted axes of the Kolm triangle representation, is that for each agent $i \in N$ and each pair of bundles $z_i \equiv (x_i, y)$ and $z'_i \equiv (x'_i, y')$, the line(s) of support to his upper contour set at z_i is (are) at least as steep as the line(s) of support to his upper contour set at z'_i if and only if $y \geq y'$. If preferences are strictly convex and z is an efficient allocation, no other allocation is Pareto-indifferent to it. Then, in the Kolm triangle, under quasi-linearity, the Pareto set has three parts, which to save space, we do not show on a separate figure, but in Fig. 3, used later to prove one of our results. Consider the triangle with origins 0_1 and 0_2 in that figure. The true endowment profile corresponds to the point marked ω. For each $i \in N$, z^i designates the most preferred allocation for agent i in that triangle. The three parts then are (a) a horizontal segment from the left side of the triangle to the right side, seg$[a^1, a^2]$, at each point of which indifference curves admit a common line of support; (b) a segment lying in the left side of the triangle, seg$[z^2, a^1]$, and (c) a segment lying in its right side, seg$[z^1, a^2]$.

Given $z_i \in \mathbb{R}^2_+ \setminus \{0_i\}$, we designate by $\boldsymbol{\rho(0_i, z_i)}$ the ray emanating from agent i's origin 0_i and passing through z_i. The key implication of homotheticity for convex preferences is that for each agent $i \in N$ and each pair of bundles $z_i \equiv (x_i, y)$ and $z'_i \equiv (x'_i, y')$, the line(s) of support to his upper contour set at z_i is (are) at least as steep as the line(s) of support to his upper contour set at z'_i if and only if $\rho(0_i, z_i)$ is at least as steep as $\rho(0_i, z'_i)$. In the Kolm triangle, under strict convexity and homotheticity, the Pareto set is a curve connecting the slanted sides of the triangle that satisfies the following property. If z is an efficient allocation, the rest of the

Pareto set lies entirely in the bow-tie shaped area between the rays emanating from the two origins and passing through z, $\rho(0_1, z_1)$ and $\rho(0_2, z_2)$.[7]

The solution defined by Lindahl (1919) can be considered as a counterpart for public good economies of the Walrasian rule, as it calls for each agent to maximize his preferences on a budget line. The main difference is that prices for public goods (in terms of the private good) are individualized. The producer faces a price for the public good that is the sum of the prices faced by the consumers. Profits made in production are distributed according to a vector $\theta \in \Delta^N$ of profit shares. The *Lindahl solution*, $\boldsymbol{L}$, associates with each economy its set of allocations that can be supported by prices: $z \equiv (x, y) \in L(R, \omega, Y)$ (here, the technology Y does not have to be linear) if $z \in Z(\omega, Y)$ and there is $p \equiv (p_i)_{i \in N} \in \mathbb{R}^N_+$ such that for each $i \in N$, $x_i + p_i y \leq \omega_{ix}$, and for each $z'_i \equiv (x'_i, y') \in \mathbb{R}^2_+$ such that $x'_i + p_i y' \leq \omega_{ix} + \theta_i(-1, \sum p_i)z^*$, where $z^* \in Y$ is a production plan maximizing $(-1, \sum p_i)z$ for $z \in Y$, we have $z_i \; R_i \; z'_i$. The prices p are called "equilibrium prices." An agent's "offer curve" is defined as in Walrasian analysis by tracing out the agent's maximizing bundle as a function of the prices he faces. Let agent i's offer curve from endowment ω_i be denoted $\boldsymbol{oc(R_i, \omega_i)}$ (preferences being fixed, in the figures, we use the more compact notation $\boldsymbol{oc(\omega_i)}$). In the Kolm triangle, the Lindahl allocations are obtained in the same way that Walrasian allocations are in the Edgeworth box–by intersecting offer curves.

We specify the counterexamples used for our negative results geometrically, introducing them in such a way as to make it as intuitive as possible how we arrived at them. We do not give explicit analytical expressions for representations of preferences. Such expressions would often be quite complicated without shedding any additional light on the nature of the results.

Figure 1 shows how to accommodate borrowing. We always consider borrowing by agent 1, calling $\beta > 0$ the amount he borrows. We need to enlarge the triangle by this amount. We keep his origin fixed at 0_1, and translate agent 2's origin to the right by the vector $\left(\frac{2}{\sqrt{3}}\beta, 0\right)$, denoting his new origin $0'_2$. We also translate the endowment profile and any data that pertains to agent 2 in the original triangle (indifference curves, consumptions) by this vector, because all of these objects have to be re-measured from $0'_2$. Let $\mathbf{tr}(\boldsymbol{\omega}, \boldsymbol{\omega'})$ be this horizontal translation. In the figure, the segments seg$[a, \omega']$, seg$[b, 0'_2]$, and seg$[c, z']$ all have length β. Suppose a rule selects z for (R, ω, Y) and z' for (R, ω', Y). Agent 1's final consumption, once he has returned what he borrowed, is the pair consisting of the first and third components of the allocation $\tilde{z}$ obtained by translating z' by the vector $\left(-\frac{2}{\sqrt{3}}\beta, 0\right)$ (this is the translation $-\text{tr}(\omega, \omega')$). We now compare z_1 to $\tilde{z}_1 \equiv z'_1 - (\beta, 0)$. For the rule to

[7] The proof is simple. Let $z \in P(e)$. In the Kolm triangle, the lines of support to the two agents' indifference curves at z coincide. Let z' be another feasible allocation. If z' is above $\rho(0_1, z_1)$, agent 1's line(s) of support at z'_1 is (are) steeper than its line(s) of support at z_1. If z' is also above $\rho(0_2, z_2)$, agent 2's line(s) of support at z'_2 is (are) flatter than its line(s) of support at z_2. Thus, the lines of support at z'_1 and z'_2 cross. The same argument can be made about any point that is below both $\rho(0_1, z_1)$ and $\rho(0_2, z_2)$. The remaining points are between $\rho(0_1, z_1)$ and $\rho(0_2, z_2)$, as claimed.

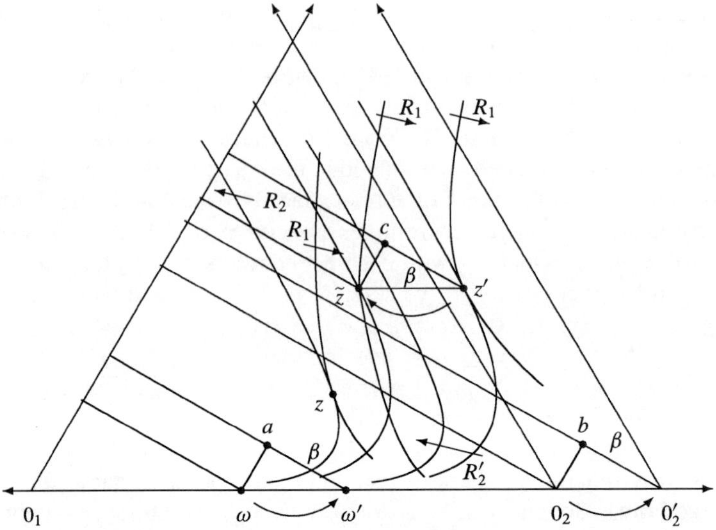

Fig. 1 Enlarging a Kolm triangle so as to accommodate borrowing

be *open-economy borrowing-proof*, z_1 should always be at least as desirable as $\tilde{z}_1$ according to R_1. In Fig. 1, that is not the case, so the property is violated.

The figure shows that even if a rule is designed to select efficient allocations (note that indifference curves are tangent at z in the original triangle and also at z' in the enlarged triangle), the allocation that results after the borrower has returned the resources he borrowed may not be efficient. Indeed, the indifference curves through $\tilde{z}$ are typically not tangent there. This is of course one of the reasons why we should be concerned about borrowing.

We show that on both the quasi-linear domain and on the homothetic domain, the Lindahl rule is *open-economy borrowing-proof*.

On the quasi-linear domain, we may think that if an allocation is efficient, so is any other allocation obtained by horizontal translation to the left or to the right, and that translation invariance of any rule would imply its *open-economy borrowing-proofness*. However, one should be careful about boundaries, and even on its subdomain on which it selects interior allocations, a rule need not be translation invariant. The Lindahl rule does satisfy this property whenever it selects interior allocations, but other appealing rules exist that do not.

Figure 2 shows what happens to an agent's offer curve as his endowment decreases. As we will soon embed agent 1's map into a Kolm triangle, let us work within slanted axes. For the endowment ω_1^1, agent 1's offer curve never reaches the slanted axis and that is also the case for any endowment to the right of ω_1^1 and for

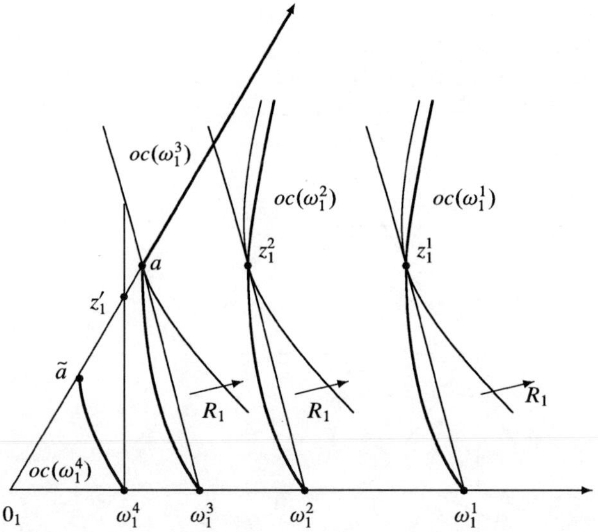

Fig. 2 Offer curves for quasi-linear preferences

a range of endowments to the left of ω_1^1, such as ω_1^2.[8] The bundles maximizing his preferences on two parallel price lines, if both bundles are interior, are related by a horizontal translation. Examples are the points z_1^1 and z_1^2, which maximize his preferences on two parallel budget lines emanating from ω_1^1 and ω_1^2. His offer curve for the endowment ω_1^3 is obtained by translating his offer curve for ω_1^1 and truncating it by the slanted axis: in the figure, it consists of the arc from ω_1^3 to a and the part of that axis that is above a. For the even smaller endowment ω_1^4, the truncation is more significant and the offer curve consists of the arc from ω_1^4 to $\tilde{a}$ and the part of the left slanted axis that is above $\tilde{a}$. The point z_1' is a maximizer of the agent's preferences on a price line emanating from ω_1^4.

On the quasi-linear domain with strictly convex and smooth preferences, the Lindahl correspondence is *single-valued*. This conclusion holds because each agent's demand for the public good is a monotonic function of the price of that good (relative to that of the private good) that he faces.

Proposition 1. *On the domain of strictly convex, smooth, and quasi-linear preferences, the Lindahl rule is open-economy borrowing-proof.*

Proof. The proof is illustrated in Fig. 3 for a strictly convex and smooth economy $(R, \omega, Y) \in \mathscr{E}_{ql}^N$, where $N \equiv \{1, 2\}$. The proof for more than two agents is essentially the same and we omit it. Let $z \equiv (x_1, x_2, y) \equiv L(R, \omega, Y)$. Agent 1 borrows

[8] For some preference relations, all offer curves reach the slanted axis.

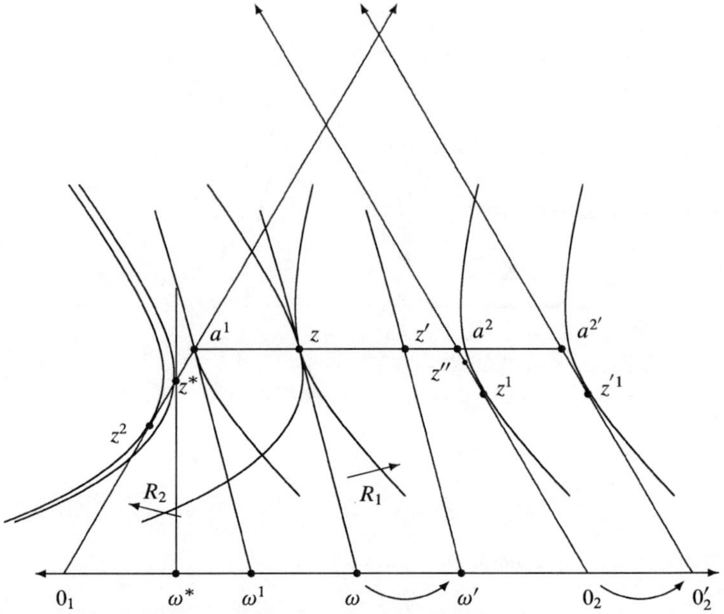

Fig. 3 On the domain of strictly convex, smooth, and quasi-linear preferences, the Lindahl rule is open-economy borrowing-proof (Proposition 1)

the amount β of the private good. Let ω' be the new endowment profile in the enlarged Kolm triangle and $z' \equiv L(R, \omega', Y)$. If $x_1 > 0$ (as illustrated in the figure), then $z'_1 = z_1 + (\beta, 0)$. Indeed, by the translation invariance of indifference curves, the price line that makes z a Lindahl allocation in the original economy, when translated by the amount borrowed, is a price line that makes the translate of z by $\text{tr}(\omega, \omega')$ a Lindahl allocation in the augmented economy: the allocation chosen by the Lindahl rule moves in a co-variant way with agent 1's borrowing. After returning the amount borrowed, he ends up with the same bundle as he would have received had he not borrowed. (If agent 2's consumption of the private good is zero initially, such as at z'' in the figure, the argument is the same as for interior Lindahl allocations.)

For an endowment profile sufficiently close to 0_1, such as ω^* in the figure, the resulting Lindahl allocation $z^* \equiv L(R, \omega^*, Y)$ is a boundary allocation ($x_1^* = 0$). If agent 1 borrows an amount that brings the endowment allocation to a point such as ω^1, the new Lindahl allocation is a^1, a boundary allocation too ($x_1 = 0$). Agent 1 is obviously unable to return what he borrowed. The same observation holds for any borrowed amount that brings the endowment allocation to a point of $\text{seg}[\omega^*, \omega^1]$, the resulting Lindahl allocation being a point of $\text{seg}[z^*, a^1]$. If he borrows enough for the resulting Lindahl allocation to be interior–for instance, if the new endowment allocation is ω, the Lindahl allocation is z–but he ends up paying more per unit of the public good than he did initially, and he receives less of the private good than he borrowed. Thus, his new assignment is still insufficient for him to return what he borrowed. □

On the homothetic domain with strictly convex preferences, the Lindahl rule is *single-valued*. Just like for the quasi-linear case, this is because each agent's demand for the public good is a strictly decreasing function of the price of that good (relative to that of the private good) that he faces.

Proposition 2. *On the domain of strictly convex and homothetic preferences, the Lindahl rule is open-economy borrowing-proof.*

Proof. The proof is illustrated in Fig. 4 for a strictly convex economy $(R, \omega, Y) \in \mathcal{E}^N_{hom}$, where $N \equiv \{1, 2\}$. The proof for more than two agents is essentially the same. Let $z \equiv L(R, \omega, Y)$. Agent 1 borrows the amount β of the private good. Let ω' be the new endowment profile in the enlarged Kolm triangle and $z' \equiv L(R, \omega', Y)$. Agent 1's offer curve from ω'_1, $oc(\omega'_1)$, goes through the point a obtained by subjecting z to the same homothetic expansion centered at 0_1 that takes ω to ω'. Also, agent 2's offer curve measured from $0'_2$ is obtained by subjecting $oc(\omega_2)$ to $\text{tr}(\omega, \omega')$. The point b is the image of z under that translation. It follows from these facts that $oc(\omega'_1)$ and $oc'(\omega_2)$ cross at a point z' to the left of the line obtained by subjecting the initial equilibrium price line to $\text{tr}(\omega, \omega')$. Agent 1's final consumption is obtained by

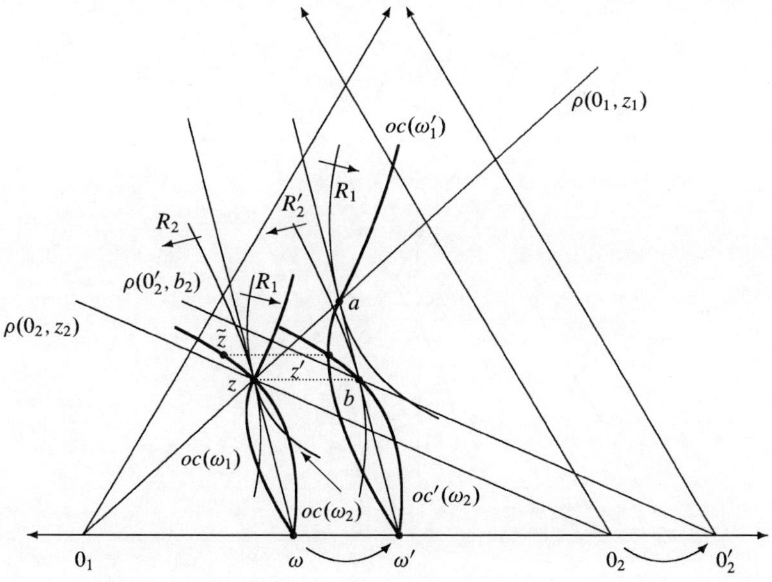

Fig. 4 On the domain of strictly convex and homothetic preferences, the Lindahl rule is open-economy borrowing-proof (Proposition 2)

subjecting z_1' to the inverse translation, $-\text{tr}(\omega, \omega')$, and it is therefore to the left of the initial equilibrium price line. Agent 1 does not benefit from borrowing. □

It is not difficult to see that as long as the public good is a normal good, the reasoning just made applies. In their analysis of the endowment misrepresentation game associated with the Lindahl rule, Sertel and Sanver (1999) note that if the public good is a normal good, then at equilibrium, agents do not exaggerate their endowments. This result implies the conclusions that we have reached by means of our graphical analysis.

Finally, we consider the classical domain and show by means of an economy with strictly convex preferences (Example 1) that, now, *open-economy borrowing-proofness* fails.

Example 1. On the strictly convex and classical domain, the Lindahl rule is not open-economy borrowing-proof.

The proof is by means of a strictly convex economy $(R, \omega, Y) \in \mathscr{E}_{cl}^N$, where $N \equiv \{1, 2\}$, illustrated in Figs. 5 and 6. Agent 1's intended offer curve from ω_1, $oc(\omega_1)$, consists of a backward-bending arc from ω_1 to a point z on the vertical line through ω, followed by a half-line parallel to the left side of the triangle. Agent 2's preferences are the same, so his offer curve from ω_2 is the symmetric image of $oc(\omega_1)$ with respect to the vertical line through ω. The offer curves $oc(\omega_1)$ and $oc(\omega_2)$ intersect at ω and z. Thus, $\{z\} = L(R, \omega, Y)$.

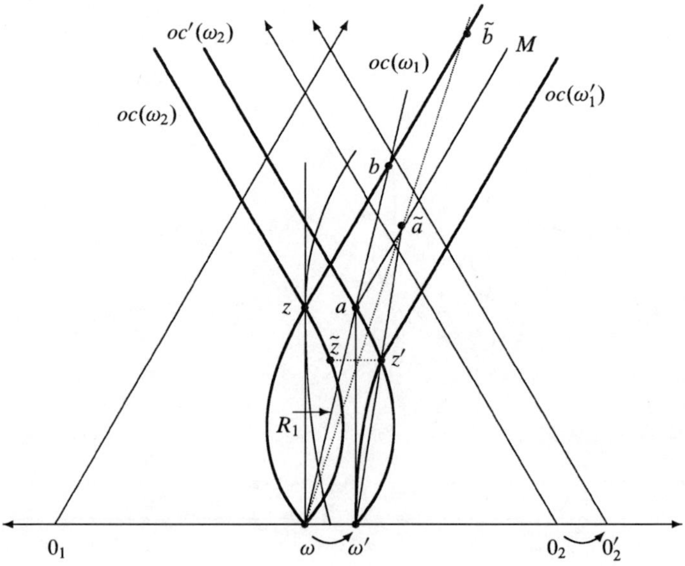

Fig. 5 On the classical domain, the Lindahl rule is not open-economy borrowing-proof (Example 1)

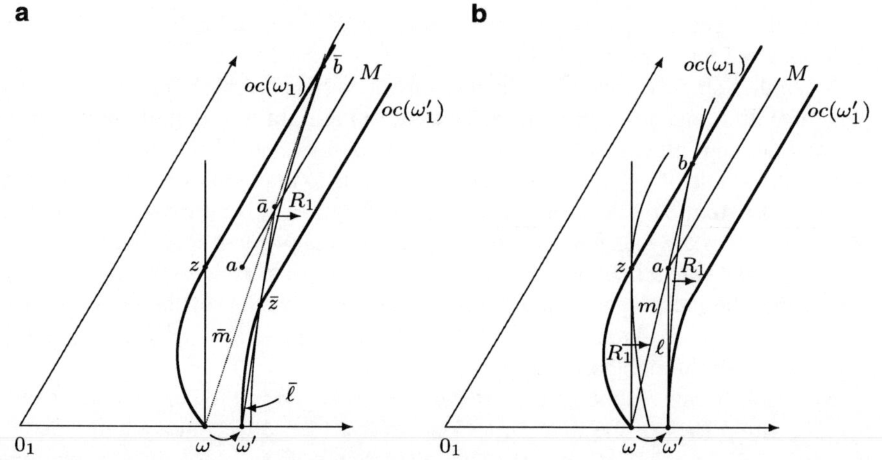

Fig. 6 Generating agent 1's map for Example 1

Let $\beta > 0$. Agent 1 borrows the amount β of the private good. We enlarge the Kolm triangle so as to accommodate the increase in his endowment. Let ω' be the new endowment profile. In the enlarged Kolm triangle, let $oc'(\omega_2)$ be agent 2's offer curve redrawn from ω_2'. It is the translate of $oc(\omega_2)$ by $\text{tr}(\omega, \omega')$. Let z' be a point of $oc'(\omega_2)$ whose public good component is smaller than the public good component of z. Agent 1's intended offer curve from ω_1', $oc(\omega_1')$, consists of a backward-bending arc from ω_1' to z', also followed by a half-line parallel to the left side of the triangle. It admits a vertical tangency line at ω_1'. Our objective is to specify preferences for agent 1 rationalizing $oc(\omega_1)$ as his offer curve from ω_1 and $oc(\omega_1')$ as his offer curve from ω_1'.

We show in Fig. 6 how to construct agent 1's indifference curve through ω_1' as well as all of his higher indifference curves. Let a be obtained from z by $\text{tr}(\omega, \omega')$ and M be the half-line emanating from a that is parallel to the left side of the triangle. Let $\bar{\ell}$ be any line emanating from ω' whose slope is positive and greater than the slope of the left side of the triangle (Fig. 6a). We will associate with it a point of $oc(\omega_1)$ and a point of $oc(\omega_1')$. Let $\bar{z}$ be the point of intersection of $\bar{\ell}$ with $oc(\omega_1')$. The line $\bar{\ell}$ intersects M at $\bar{a}$. Next, we draw the line $\bar{m}$ from ω passing through $\bar{a}$. This line intersects $oc(\omega_1)$ at $\bar{b}$. We now draw an indifference curve for agent 1 that is tangent to $\bar{\ell}$ at $\bar{z}$ and to $\bar{m}$ at $\bar{b}$. We have rationalized $\bar{z}$ as a point of $oc(\omega_1')$ and $\bar{b}$ as a point of $oc(\omega_1)$.

As $\bar{\ell}$ becomes steeper and steeper, the point $\bar{z}$ gets closer and closer to ω'. At the limit, $\bar{\ell}$ is vertical and $\bar{z} = \omega'$ (Fig. 6b). Let us refer to $\bar{\ell}$ when it assumes this vertical position as ℓ. Then, it intersects M at a and the line m from ω passing through a intersects $oc(\omega_1)$ at b. Now, we draw an indifference curve for agent 1 that is tangent to ℓ at ω_1' and tangent to m at b. This is the left-most indifference curve that we generate for agent 1 in this manner. We have rationalized ω' as a point of $oc(\omega_1')$ and b as a point of $oc(\omega_1)$.

All of these indifference curves can be drawn without crossing, and we have now generated all of agent 1's indifference curves to the right of the indifference curve through ω', and in the process rationalized the part of $oc(\omega_1)$ that lies above b as well as the whole of $oc(\omega_1')$. Note that because z' is to the right of ℓ, its translate by $-\text{tr}(\omega, \omega')$ is to the right of the vertical line through ω. It is now easy to complete R_1 to the left of the indifference curve through ω' that we just specified for him so as to rationalize the remainder of $oc(\omega_1)$ (the arc from ω to z and the segment $[z, b]$), and so that the indifference curve through z passes to the left of the translate of z' by $-\text{tr}(\omega, \omega')$. Then, agent 1 prefers his final bundle, $\tilde{z}_1 \equiv z_1' - (\beta, 0)$, to z_1. He is made better off through borrowing.

Note that because none of the offer curves involved in the construction bends back down, in each of the two economies we consider, the economy with endowment profile ω and the economy with endowment profile (ω_1', ω_2), there is a unique Lindahl allocation. □

Remark 1. In the construction of Example 1, we fix ω and then specify β to be an arbitrary positive number. Thus, the example shows that no matter how small the amount is that agent 1 is allowed to borrow in relation to his endowment, his preferences may be such that he can benefit from doing so.

4 Borrowing Versus Withholding

Another form of manipulation has been considered in the literature. It involves withholding of some of one's endowment for private consumption later. A rule is *withholding-proof* if no agent ever benefits from such behavior.

Withholding-Proofness. For each $e \equiv (R, \omega, Y) \in \mathcal{E}^N$, each $i \in N$, and each $\omega' \in \mathbb{R}_+^N \times \mathbb{R}_+$, if $\omega_{ix}' < \omega_{ix}$, $\omega_{-ix}' = \omega_{-ix}$, and $\omega_y' = 0$, then it is not the case that for some $z \in \varphi(R, \omega, Y)$ and some $z' \in \varphi(R, \omega', Y)$, $[z_i' + (\omega_{ix} - \omega_{ix}', 0)]\ P_i\ z_i$.

It is known that the Lindahl rule is not *withholding-proof* on the classical domain (Thomson 1979, 1999). The examples described next show that this negative result still holds on either the strictly convex, smooth, and quasi-linear domain, or on the strictly convex and homothetic domain. Thus, in the light of Sect. 3, it appears that *open-economy borrowing-proofness* is satisfied more generally than *withholding-proofness*.

Example 2. On the domain of strictly convex, smooth, and quasi-linear preferences, the Lindahl rule is not withholding-proof.

The proof is by means of a strictly convex and smooth economy $(R, \omega, Y) \in \mathcal{E}_{ql}^N$, where $N \equiv \{1, 2\}$, illustrated in Fig. 7. Let $z \equiv L(R, \omega, Y)$. Agent 1 withholds the amount β of the private good. Let ω' be the new endowment profile in the reduced

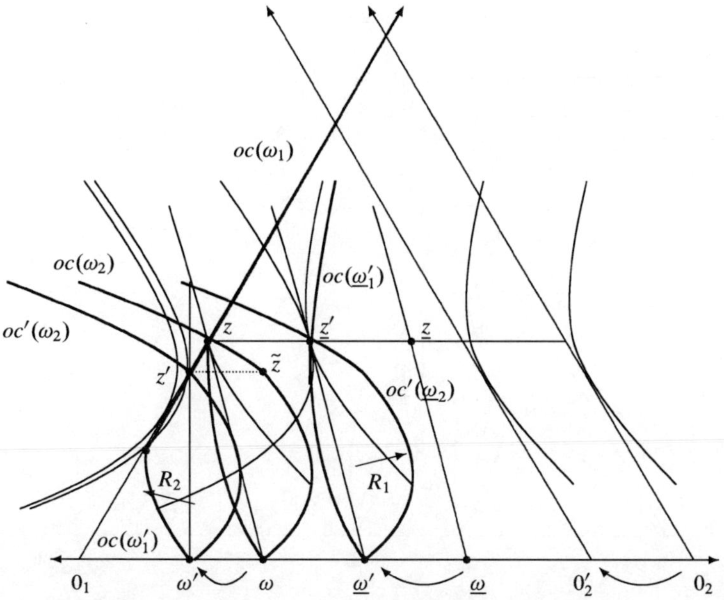

Fig. 7 On the strictly convex, smooth, and quasi-linear domain, the Lindahl rule is not withholding-proof (Example 2)

Kolm triangle. Let $z' \equiv L(R, \omega', Y)$. This allocation is the intersection of $oc(\omega_1')$, which is truncated, and $oc'(\omega_2)$. The price faced by agent 1 for the public good at equilibrium has turned in his favor. After adding to z_1' the vector agent 1 withheld, we obtain $z_1' + (\beta, 0)$. To show a violation of *withholding-proofness*, it now suffices to draw agent 1's indifference curve through z_1 sufficiently close to the line passing through ω and z to ensure that agent 1 prefers $z_1' + (\beta, 0)$ to z_1. Then, he benefits from withholding.

If we had started from the endowment profile $\underline{\omega}$, for which the resulting Lindahl allocation is interior, then for a range of values of the amount withheld, the new endowment profile would have resulted in an interior Lindahl allocation. In the figure, an endowment profile that achieves this is $\underline{\omega}'$. Then the Lindahl allocation from this new endowment, $\underline{z}'$ in the figure, would be obtained from the Lindahl allocation from $\underline{\omega}$ by $\text{tr}(\underline{\omega}, \underline{\omega}')$, and agent 1 would not have benefitted from withholding. □

Example 3. On the domain of strictly convex and homothetic preferences, the Lindahl rule is not withholding-proof.

The proof is by means of a strictly convex economy $(R, \omega, Y) \in \mathscr{E}^N_{hom}$, where $N \equiv \{1, 2\}$, illustrated in Fig. 8. Let $z \equiv L(R, \omega, Y)$. Agent 1 withholds the amount β of the private good. Let ω' be the new endowment profile in the reduced Kolm triangle and $z' \equiv L(R, \omega', Y)$. The essential characteristic of agent 1's offer curve from his new endowment, $oc(\omega_1')$, is that on each price line that he may face,

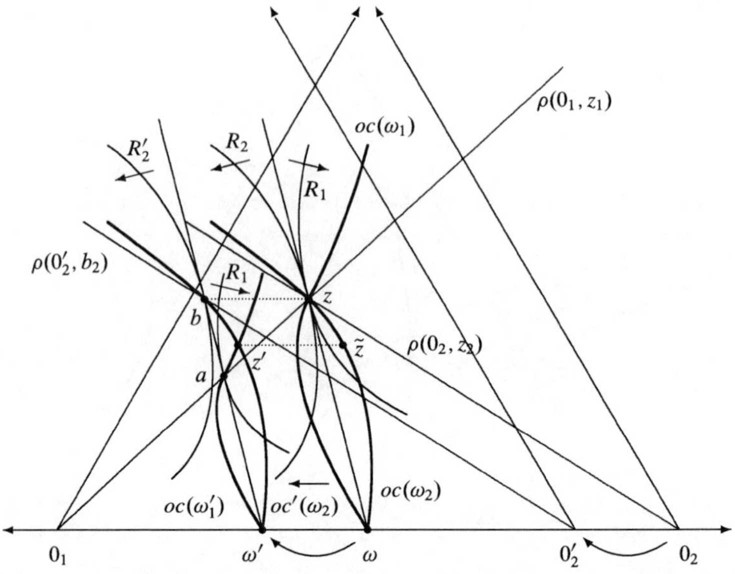

Fig. 8 On the strictly convex and homothetic domain, the Lindahl rule is not withholding-proof (Example 3)

agent 1's most preferred trade is smaller than it was from his initial endowment. Agent 2's offer curve measured from the new origin $0'_2$ in the reduced triangle, $oc'(\omega_2)$, is obtained by subjecting his initial offer curve $oc(\omega_2)$ to $\text{tr}(\omega, \omega')$. The two offer curves from ω' cross to the right of the line obtained by subjecting the initial equilibrium price line to $\text{tr}(\omega, \omega')$. Thus, $z'_1 + (\beta, 0)$ is to the right of the initial equilibrium price line. It now suffices to draw agent 1's indifference curve through z_1 sufficiently close to the line passing through ω and z to ensure that agent 1 benefits from withholding. □

Remark 2. A parallel observation to one made in connection to Example 1 holds: Examples 2 and 3 show that no matter how small the amount is that agent 1 withholds in relation to his endowment, his preferences may be such that he could benefit from doing so.

Both borrowing and withholding have the effect of "bringing the attention of the rule" to a different part of the manipulating agent's consumption space. An examination of the proofs of our results concerning the two behaviors reveals that the difference in the conclusions comes from the fact that for the classes of preferences on which we have focused, quasi-linear preferences and homothetic preferences, augmenting one's endowment through borrowing and decreasing it through withholding have predictably opposite effects on offer curves; in the borrowing case, demand for the public good increases at every price, and in the withholding case, demand decreases at every price. Because the other agent has a well-behaved map, this leads to a predictably more favorable individualized price for the manipulating agent in the case of withholding, and a predictably less favorable individualized price for him in the case of borrowing.

5 Closed-Economy Borrowing-Proofness

Let us now imagine that an agent borrows from some other agent present in the economy, not from outside sources; after the rule is applied, and the agent has returned what he borrowed, he may be better off, but in order to guarantee the participation of the agent from whom he borrowed, this agent should be made at least as well off as he would have been otherwise. (Of course, the borrower could borrow from several agents. Then each of them should end up at least as well off as if he had not borrowed.) The property of immunity to behavior of this kind is formulated in Thomson (2009) under the name of "closed-economy borrowing-proofness." For a selection from the Pareto correspondence, this property is automatically met if there are only two agents, so we need to consider economies with a least three agents, and the Kolm triangle is not available anymore. Formally, the requirement is the following:

Closed-Economy Borrowing-Proofness. For each $e \equiv (R, \omega, Y) \in \mathcal{E}^N$, each $\{i, j\} \subseteq N$, and each $\omega' \in \mathbb{R}^N_+ \times \mathbb{R}_+$, if $\omega'_{ix} > \omega_{ix}$, $\omega'_{ix} + \omega'_{jx} = \omega_{ix} + \omega_{jx}$, for each $k \in N \setminus \{i, j\}$, $\omega'_{kx} = \omega_{kx}$, and $\omega'_y = 0$, then it is not the case that for some $z \in \varphi(R, \omega, Y)$ and some $z' \in \varphi(R, \omega', Y)$, we have $[z'_i - (\omega'_{ix} - \omega_{ix}, 0)]\ P_i\ z_i$ and $[z'_j + (\omega'_{ix} - \omega_{ix}, 0)]\ R_j\ z_j$.

We start with two positive results.

Proposition 3. *On the domain of strictly convex, smooth, and quasi-linear preferences, the Lindahl rule is closed-economy borrowing-proof.*

Proof. Consider a strictly convex and smooth economy $(R, \omega, Y) \in \mathcal{E}^N_{ql}$, and let $z \in L(R, \omega, Y)$. Let $\{i, j\} \subset N$ and suppose that agent i borrows the amount β of the private good from agent j. Let $\omega'_{ix} \equiv \omega_{ix} + \beta$, $\omega'_{jx} \equiv \omega_{jx} - \beta$, and for each $k \in N \setminus \{i, j\}$, $\omega'_{kx} \equiv \omega_{kx}$, and $\omega'_y = 0$. Let $z' \equiv L(R, \omega', Y)$. Agent i's final bundle is $z'_i - (\beta, 0)$. For him to benefit, he should face a lower price for the public good (his budget line should become steeper). By quasi-linearity, this implies that $y' > y$. For each $k \in N \setminus \{i\}$, if z'_k is a maximizing consumption bundle in agent k's budget set, the price he should face for the public good should be at most as large as it was initially. However it is incompatible with feasibility that every agent faces a lower price. □

Proposition 4. *On the domain of strictly convex and homothetic preferences, the Lindahl rule is closed-economy borrowing-proof.*

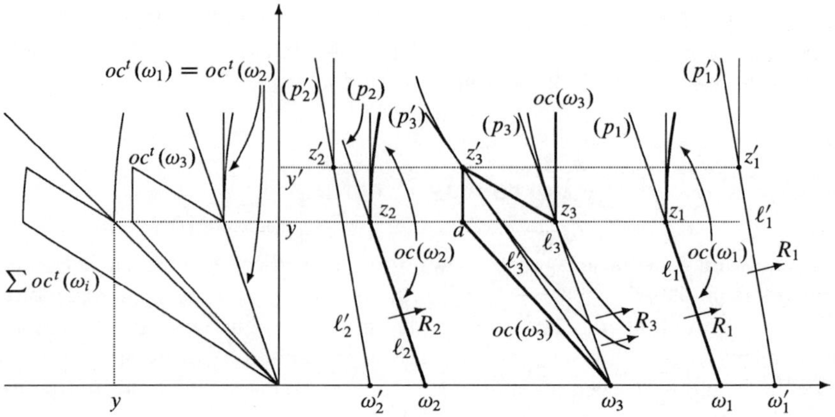

Fig. 9 On the strictly convex, smooth, and classical domain, the Lindahl rule is not closed-economy borrowing-proof (Example 4)

Proof. The proof is the same as the proof of Proposition 3 until the sentence beginning with "By quasi-linearity." However, the same conclusion is reached by invoking homotheticity. The proof concludes as does the previous one. □

The proofs of the two previous propositions make it clear that what underlies them is, once again, normality of the public good. On the classical domain, this property is not necessarily met, and we have the following negative result.

Example 4. On the strictly convex, smooth, and classical domain, the Lindahl rule is not closed-economy borrowing-proof.

Let $N \equiv \{1, 2, 3\}$. The proof is by means of an economy in $\mathscr{E}_{cl}^N$ with strictly convex and smooth preferences (Figs. 9 and 10). The initial endowment profile is denoted $\omega \in \mathbb{R}_+^N \times \mathbb{R}_+$. Agent 1 borrows resources from agent 2, the resulting endowment profile being denoted ω'. The production technology is linear, each unit of input yielding one unit of output, and as before, the production set is denoted Y. The initial economy is (R, ω, Y) and after agent 1 borrows, it is (R, ω', Y). There is a unique Lindahl allocation, both initially and after the change in endowments.

Let $\omega_{1x}, \omega'_{1x}, \beta \in \mathbb{R}_+$ be such that $\omega'_{1x} = \omega_{1x} + \beta$. Let $y, y' > 0$ be such that $y < y'$. Let $\omega_{2x}, \omega'_{2x} > 0$ be such that $\omega'_{2x} = \omega_{2x} - \beta$. Let $p_2, p'_2 \in \mathbb{R}_+$ be such that (i) $0 < p'_2 < p_2 < 1$, (ii) the point z'_2 of ordinate y' on the line ℓ'_2 emanating from ω'_2 and normal to $(1, p'_2)$ has a positive abscissa, and (iii) the point z_2 of ordinate y on the line ℓ_2 emanating from ω_2 and normal to $(1, p_2)$ is to the right of ℓ'_2. These conditions imply that z_2 has a positive abscissa.

Let $p_1, p'_1 \in \mathbb{R}_+$ be such that (i) $0 < p'_1 < p_1$ and $p_3 \equiv 1 - p_1 - p_2 < 1$ and (ii) the point z_1 of ordinate y on the line ℓ_1 emanating from ω_1 and normal to $(1, p_1)$ and the point z'_1 of ordinate y' on the line ℓ'_1 emanating from ω'_1 and normal to $(1, p'_1)$ have positive abscissas. Let $p'_3 \equiv 1 - p'_1 - p'_2$. Because $p'_1 < p_1$ and

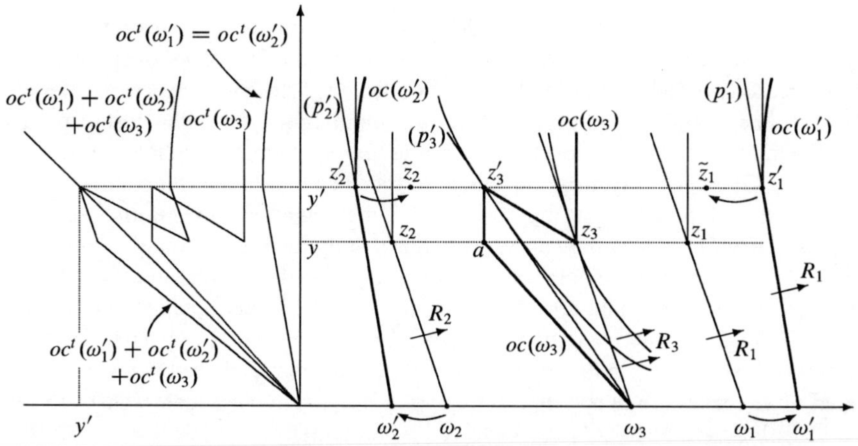

Fig. 10 On the strictly convex, smooth, and classical domain, the Lindahl rule is not closed-economy borrowing-proof (Example 4 continued)

$p_2' < p_2$, then $p_3' > p_3$. Let $\omega_{3x} \in \mathbb{R}_+$ be such that the point z_3' of ordinate y' on the line ℓ_3' emanating from ω_3 and normal to $(1, p_3')$ has a positive abscissa. (The figures depict an economy for which $p_1 = p_2 = p_3$ and $p_1' = p_2'$.) Because $y < y'$ and $p_3 < p_3'$, the point z_3 of ordinate y on the line ℓ_3 emanating from ω_3 and normal to $(1, p_3)$ also has a positive abscissa. Next, we specify offer curves, at first not insisting on either strict convexity or smoothness of preferences.

Let R_1 be such that (i) the indifference curve through ω_1 consists of seg$[\omega_1, z_1]$ and the vertical half-line emanating from z_1, and (ii) the indifference curve through ω_1' consists of seg$[\omega_1', z_1']$ and the vertical half-line emanating from z_1'. It follows from (i) that $oc(\omega_1)$ contains seg$[\omega_1, z_1]$ and that above the horizontal line of ordinate y, it continues to the right of the half-line emanating from z_1. Similarly, it follows from (ii) that $oc(\omega_1')$ contains seg$[\omega_1', z_1']$ and that above the horizontal line of ordinate y', it continues to the right of the half-line emanating from z_1'.

Let R_2 be such that (i) the indifference curve through ω_2 consists of seg$[\omega_2, z_2]$ and the vertical half-line emanating from z_2, and (ii) the indifference curve through ω_2' consist of seg$[\omega_2', z_2']$ and the vertical half-line emanating from z_2'. It follows from (i) that $oc(\omega_2)$ contains seg$[\omega_2, z_2]$ and that above the horizontal line of ordinate y, it continues to the right of the half-line emanating from z_2. Similarly, it follows from (ii) that $oc(\omega_2')$ contains seg$[\omega_2', z_2']$ and that above the horizontal line of ordinate y', it continues to the right of the half-line emanating from z_2'.

Let $a \equiv (a_1, a_2) \in \mathbb{R}^2_+$ be such that $a_1 = x_3'$ and $a_2 < y'$ (say $a_2 = y$). Let R_3 be such that $oc_3(\omega_3)$ consists of bro.seg$[\omega_3, a, z_3', z_3]$, followed by the vertical half-line emanating from z_3.

Let $\omega_x \equiv (\omega_{1x}, \omega_{2x}, \omega_{3x})$, $\omega_{3x}' = \omega_{3x}$, and $\omega_x' \equiv (\omega_{1x}', \omega_{2x}', \omega_{3x}')$. Let $z \equiv (x_1, x_2, x_3, y)$ and $z' \equiv (x_1', x_2', x_3', y')$. We have $z \in L(R, \omega, Y)$ and $z' \in L(R, \omega', Y)$. We claim that, in fact, z and z' are the only Lindahl allocations for ω and ω'

respectively. For each $\tilde{y} \in \mathbb{R}_+$, we identify the individualized prices for the public good at which each of the three agents would demand this level of the public good. From these, we deduce the total amount collected if the public good is offered at level $\tilde{y}$. For a Lindahl equilibrium, this total should be equal to the cost of producing the public good at that level. Given our assumptions on the technology, this cost is also $\tilde{y}$. Geometrically, it is convenient to translate the three offer curves horizontally to the origin, add them up horizontally, then check if the resulting aggregate demand curve and the supply curve, which is simply the line of slope -1 emanating from the origin, cross at a point of ordinate $\tilde{y}$. If this is the only point of intersection, we have a unique Lindahl allocation. In Figs. 9 and 10, the translated offer curves of the initial economy are denoted $oc^t(\omega_1)$, $oc^t(\omega_2)$, and $oc^t(\omega_3)$. Their aggregate is denoted $\sum oc^t(\omega_i)$. After agent 1 borrows from agent 2, these two agents' translated offer curves are denoted $oc^t(\omega_1')$ and $oc^t(\omega_2')$. The aggregate translated offer curve is then written as $oc^t(\omega_1') + oc^t(\omega_2') + oc^t(\omega_3)$.

In Figs. 9 and 10, uniqueness of the points of intersection of the aggregate demand curve and the supply curve can be verified.

The Lindahl allocation z' for the endowment profile ω' is such that, defining $\tilde{z} \equiv (z_1' - (\beta, 0), z_2' + (\beta, 0))$, we have $\tilde{z}_1 \; P_1 \; z_1$ and $\tilde{z}_2 \; R_2 \; z_2$. To conclude the proof, it suffices to take strictly convex and smooth approximations to the preferences just defined. This can easily be done, but once again we dispense with analytical expressions.[9] □

Remark 3. Here too, a similar observation to Remark 1 made in connection to Example 1 holds: Example 4 can be specified, and we have constructed it with that objective in mind, to show that no matter how small the amount that agent 1 is allowed to borrow in relation to his endowment and in relation to the endowment of the lender (we may require for instance that the ratio of the amount borrowed over either of these endowments not exceed a certain value), there are economies such that he could benefit from borrowing. When introducing ω_{1x} and β, it suffices to add the requirement that $\frac{\beta}{\omega_{1x}}$ be no greater than the desired value; then, in introducing ω_{2x}, to add the requirement that $\frac{\beta}{\omega_{2x}}$ also be no greater than the desired value.

6 Conclusion

We close by relating our study to the existing literature, and by stating some open questions. The present article is indeed only a first step in the study of the opportunity through manipulation of endowments that we envision.

1. *More than one private good.* In a related article in which we examine *borrowing-proofness* in the context of classical private good economies (Thomson 2009), we obtain a number of negative results concerning the compatibility of this

[9] The preferences of both agents 1 and 2 can in addition be specified to be homothetic.

requirement with efficiency and one or the other of several distributional requirements. We prove these results for economies with two goods. Such conclusions are easily extendable to economies in which public goods are also present. It suffices to specify preferences so that, at all efficient allocations, the public goods are not produced because the demand does not justify the expense. Thus, we have limited ourselves here to economies with only one private good. Because the public goods themselves cannot be borrowed, manipulation opportunities through borrowing are more limited in the present context than they are in economies with only private goods. Our results are somewhat more positive than in such economies, as we have found a number of natural preference domains on which the Lindahl solution is immune to manipulation through borrowing.

2. *Other rules*. In a companion article (Thomson 2008), we study the *borrowing-proofness* of other allocation rules in the context of the same model. These rules are inspired by the literature on fairness.
3. *Introducing a cost of borrowing*. To be able to borrow, an agent should in general pay a fee.[10] The higher the fee, the less likely will borrowing be worthwhile. Thus, it would be interesting to obtain results describing the extent to which introducing a cost of borrowing will prevent the sort of manipulation with which we are concerned. However, results independent of the preference profile and of the particular initial endowment profile are unlikely.
4. *Manipulation involving groups of agents*. Other, more sophisticated, forms of borrowing than the one we have analyzed can be defined involving groups of agents.

   First, several agents may coordinate their borrowing and, after each of them has returned what he borrowed, each of them ends up with a bundle that he prefers.

   Second, their opportunities to gain may be enhanced if, instead of each of them returning exactly what he borrowed, they jointly return what they borrowed in total.

   Third, they may obtain additional improvements in their welfares if, after returning what they borrowed, they carry out transfers among themselves.

   Fourth, in a closed economy, as long as a lender's welfare ends up at least as high at what it would have been if he had not lent, he should be willing to lend; thus, one could argue that the obligation of the borrowers should simply be to return a bundle that allows the lender to achieve the welfare he would achieve if he had not lent. The idea can be applied to borrowing by a group from some other group.

   We leave the analysis of these behaviors to future study, limiting ourselves to noting that for each of the negative results we have obtained by focusing on manipulation by one agent only, the situation is of course worsened when agents may coordinate their manipulation.

[10] We do not want to use the expression "interest rate" because, as we noted earlier, our model is not an intertemporal one.

5. *Borrowing games*. Once it is known that a rule is not immune to manipulation, one may want to understand what happens when all agents attempt separately to manipulate to their own advantage. Full-fledged game theoretic analysis of a rule requires that a manipulation game be associated with the rule, and its equilibrium allocations identified and compared to the allocations the rule would recommend under truthful behavior. Local conditions for a list of strategies to be an equilibrium of the game of endowment misrepresentation associated with the Lindahl rule are derived by Thomson (1979), who also calculates simple examples. This question is addressed in the case of economies with normal goods by Sertel and Sanver (1999).
6. *Other classes of problems*. On the basis of this article and Thomson (2008, 2009), some understanding of the strength of *borrowing-proofness* is emerging. A more definitive assessment will have to wait until other classes of problems are studied. Economies with indivisible goods, both when these are the only goods available and when, in addition, there is an infinitely divisible good that can be used to perform compensations, are investigated by Atlamaz and Thomson (2007), who report a combination of positive and negative results. The withholding issue is considered for economies with indivisible goods by Atlamaz and Klaus (2007).

Acknowledgements I thank a referee, Tarık Kara, Yoichi Kasajima, and John Weymark for their comments, and the NSF for its support under grant No. SES 0214691. This article was prepared for presentation at a conference honoring Serge-Christophe Kolm held at the University of Caen in May 2007.

References

Atlamaz, M., & Klaus, B. (2007). Manipulation via endowments in exchange markets with indivisible goods. *Social Choice and Welfare*, *28*, 1–18

Atlamaz, M., & Thomson, W. (2007). Borrowing-proofness in economies with indivisible goods. Unpublished manuscript, Department of Economics, University of Rochester

Aumann, R., & Peleg, B. (1974). A note on Gale's example. *Journal of Mathematical Economics*, *1*, 209–211

Ching, S., & Zhou, L. (2002). Multi-valued strategy-proof social choice rules. *Social Choice and Welfare*, *19*, 569–580

Dolbear, F. T. (1967). On the theory of optimal externality. *American Economic Review*, *57*, 90–103

Gale, D. (1974). Exchange equilibrium and coalitions: An example. *Journal of Mathematical Economics*, *1*, 63–66

Kolm, S.-C. (1971). *La valeur publique*. Paris: C.N.R.S. and Dunod

Lindahl, E. (1919). *Die gerechtichkeit der besteurung*. Gleerup, Lund. (Trans. in part as: Just taxation–A positive solution. In R. A. Musgrave & A. T. Peacock (Eds.) (1958). *Classics in the theory of public finance* (pp. 168–176). London: Macmillan.)

Postlewaite, A. (1979). Manipulation via endowments. *Review of Economic Studies*, *46*, 255–262

Sertel, M. (1994). Manipulating Lindahl equilibrium via endowments. *Economics Letters*, *46*, 167–171.

Sertel, M., & Sanver, R. (1999). Equilibrium outcomes of Lindahl-endowment pretension games. *European Journal of Political Economy*, *15*, 149–162

Thomson, W. (1979). The equilibrium allocations of Walras and Lindahl manipulation games. Discussion Paper No. 111, Center for Economic Research, University of Minnesota
Thomson, W. (1987a). Monotonic allocation rules. Working Paper No. 116, Rochester Center for Economic Research, University of Rochester. Revised 1995
Thomson, W. (1987b). Monotonic allocation rules in economies with public goods. Working Paper No. 117, Rochester Center for Economic Research, University of Rochester. Revised 1995
Thomson, W. (1999). Economies with public goods: An elementary geometric exposition. *Journal of Public Economic Theory*, *1*, 139–176
Thomson, W. (2007). New variable-population paradoxes for resource allocation. Unpublished manuscript, Department of Economics, University of Rochester
Thomson, W. (2008). Borrowing-proofness in economies with public goods. In preparation
Thomson, W. (2009). Borrowing-proofness. Working Paper No. 545, Rochester Center for Economic Research, University of Rochester

When Kolm Meets Mirrlees: ELIE

Laurent Simula and Alain Trannoy

1 Introduction

Since the work by Mirrlees (1971, 1974, 1986), the second-best approach to welfarist optimal taxation has been widely adopted. This approach discards *personalized* lump-sum transfers and taxes because they are not implementable when the exogenous parameters on which they depend are private information. In contrast, in his recent book *Macrojustice* (Kolm 2004), Serge-Christophe Kolm proposes a tax scheme derived from fundamental principles of justice that corresponds in essence to providing everyone with a common lump-sum subsidy and then taxing productivity linearly. The lump-sum subsidy is common to everyone, and so does not depend on private information. Nevertheless, because productivity is taxed in addition to the lump-sum transfer, the tax scheme proposed by Kolm depends on knowing an individual's productivity. Kolm claims that this schedule achieves justice without resulting in losses in efficiency. The practicality of this proposal is likely to be received with scepticism by the common public economist for whom it is like claiming to have solved the problem of squaring the circle.

However, the tax scheme derived by Kolm (2004) has many attractive features that make it worth further study. First, it turns out to have a remarkable structure when every individual to whom it applies provides a quantity of labour in excess of what is needed for him to pay his net tax. In this case, everyone transfers the income from the same time spent working to society in return for which they each receive the average amount transferred. In other words, each citizen works a fixed fraction

L. Simula (✉)
Uppsala Center for Fiscal Studies, Department of Economics, Uppsala University, P.O. Box 513, SE-751 20 Uppsala, Sweden
e-mail: laurent.simula@nek.uu.se

A. Trannoy
Ecole des Hautes Etudes en Sciences Sociales, GREQAM, and IDEP, Centre de la Vieille Charité, 13236 Marseille cedex 02, France
e-mail: Alain.Trannoy@eco.u-cergy.fr

M. Fleurbaey et al. (eds.), *Social Ethics and Normative Economics*, Studies in Choice and Welfare, DOI 10.1007/978-3-642-17807-8_8,

of his time with a view to paying his contribution to the rest of society and is then free to devote his remaining time either to labour or leisure. This structure is referred to as *Equal-Labour Income Equalization* or ELIE by Kolm (2004, p. 112). ELIE is a very simple way of equally distributing among citizens contributions from them based on their means: "from each, to each other, the product of the same labour" and "from each, to each other, according to her capacities." From an economic policy perspective, the idea that time worked above some threshold, like the legal working hours per week, must be free of taxes has recently been defended by some economists (e.g., Godet 2007) and has been partially implemented in France by President Sarkozy.

Formally, an *ELIE tax scheme* consists of (a) a tax based on labour productivity and also (b) an *endogeneity* condition on individual labour supply. Therefore, to be as clear and precise as possible, the tax in (a) should be distinguished from the ELIE tax scheme itself. The former consists of a lump-sum tax paid to the government that is proportional to productivity combined with a transfer from the government of the average amount paid by all individuals. The net taxes paid by all of the individuals is necessarily budget balanced when the social objective is purely redistributive. The formula specifying the net tax in (a) is referred to as *Kolm's formula*. Given this definition, any ELIE tax scheme must belong to the family of Kolm formula tax schemes. That is why studying Kolm formula tax schemes in conjunction with ELIE tax schemes seems interesting to us. Nevertheless, it should be clearly emphasized that Kolm (2004) only argues in favour of ELIE, which consists of both (a) and (b).

Given these caveats, this article aims at casting light on Kolm's formula and ELIE from the viewpoint of Mirrleesian welfarist optimal taxation so as to address some issues that are not fully embraced in Kolm's work. It endeavours to understand how ELIE tax schemes can be interpreted in this standard framework. We focus on three issues:

(1) The endogeneity condition (b) that must be added to a Kolm formula tax scheme to obtain ELIE basically depends on the labour responses of the utility maximizing individuals. Therefore, it needs to be checked that, when ELIE is put into practice, individuals have the incentive to work no less than the time required to pay the common contribution. As a consequence, some conditions have to be met to obtain ELIE, and it is thus worthwhile to determine if these conditions are restrictive. More specifically, it is shown that the range of possible redistributions is significantly reduced when the endogeneity condition is taken into account.

(2) Kolm's formula corresponds to a first-best solution to the problem of wealth redistribution within the population. Any Kolm formula tax scheme gives rise to a Pareto optimal allocation that can be obtained as the outcome of the maximization of a social welfare function for appropriate social weights. Uncovering the weights that generate Kolm's formula and ELIE is thus of crucial importance for the understanding of these redistributive mechanisms. The shape of the distribution of these weights proves to be very specific and in sharp contrast with what is normally assumed about the weight distribution in the standard approach to optimal taxation. In particular, it is shown that these social weights must be strictly increasing with

ability for the set of working individuals provided that some very weak conditions are satisfied. This result remains valid when there are two parameters of heterogeneity in the population: productivities on the one hand and the taste for consumption (or leisure) on the other.

(3) It is argued by Kolm (2011, p. 95) that ELIE is incentive-compatible in the sense that "it induces individuals to work with their capacities that are the most highly remunerated." This raises the question of whether these abilities are observable or can be inferred from publicly verifiable information, that is, whether the problem is first- or second-best. In his seminal article, Mirrlees (1971) popularized the idea that gross income (or total product) is observable, but that neither the time spent working nor ability (which is equal to the wage in his model) is observable. He says that "the government can observe the total product of each individual, that is the product of the wage rate and the amount worked, but is unable to observe either of these alone" (Mirrlees 1997, p. 1316). It is the inability of the policy-maker to determine an individual's ability that accounts for the second-best nature of his problem. However, as emphasized by Mirrlees (1971, p. 208) himself in the conclusion of his article: "It would be good to devise taxes complementary to the income-tax, designed to avoid the difficulties that tax is faced with." Such a tax could be based on the ratio between the gross income and the hours worked by an individual if both of these variables are verifiable and can thus be included in the contract between the taxpayer and the policy-maker. The basic difference between the latter tax and a Mirrleesian income tax is thus the variables that are verifiable. Nevertheless, if an individual's gross income and hours worked are both observable, as pointed out by Dasgupta and Hammond (1980), it does not follow that one can infer her ability because this individual may choose to not work to the best of her ability.

We mainly consider two informational frameworks, those of Dasgupta and Hammond (1980) and Mirrlees (1971). In both cases, gross incomes are observable. In the former, hours worked are also observable, whereas in the latter, they are not. One might expect that the incentive-compatibility of ELIE is likely to depend on whether gross incomes and hours worked are verifiable by the tax authorities. When they are, ELIE is incentive compatible. Specifically, we show how the first-best net transfers of ELIE can be implemented by means of a truthful direct mechanism in weakly dominant strategies. In effect, these informational assumptions justify leaving the second best for the first best, with the consequence that ELIE resolves the fundamental trade-off between equity and efficiency. However, for individuals engaged in what we call "brainwork," tracking the time worked and work attendance is irrelevant. In this case, it is established that individuals have an incentive to misreport their productivities through the gross-income/labour combinations they choose.

Related work by Fleurbaey and Maniquet (2011) has also considered the incentive-compatibility of ELIE in both of the above-mentioned informational settings. A major difference between their analysis and ours is that they assume that individuals exhibit a diversity of preferences for leisure. Kolm regards this diversity as a private matter and not as a legitimate ground for redistribution, in contrast to productivity differences which are. Therefore, from an ethical viewpoint, it seems justified–as a first pass–to focus on the latter and to consider, as we do here, the restrictive framework in which all individuals have the same preferences. The other advantage of this approach is obviously that it avoids introducing a second source of heterogeneity into the Mirrlees model, which is well known to make it difficult to solve the optimal tax problem. To cope with this additional source of heterogeneity, Fleurbaey and Maniquet employ a different social welfare function from the utilitarian one used here, one that is less demanding in terms of the interpersonal utility comparisons that it requires. Using their framework, Fleurbaey and Maniquet provide an axiomatic foundation for ELIE to serve as a basic flat tax.

The rest of this article is organized as follows. Section 2 clarifies the difference between a Kolm formula tax scheme and ELIE. Section 3 investigates the restrictions under which the former coincides with the latter. Section 4 tackles the problem of deriving ELIE as a first-best tax scheme in the standard framework of optimal taxation. Section 5 focuses on the implementability of ELIE. Section 6 offers concluding comments.

2 ELIE: Type-Dependent Budget Sets and Corvée Labour

The population consists of a continuum of individuals who only differ in productivity θ. Hence, an individual whose productivity is θ is referred to as a "θ-individual." The technology exhibits constant returns to scale. There are two commodities, consumption $x \in \mathbb{R}_+$ and labour $\ell \in [0,1]$, where the time endowment of each individual has been normalized to equal 1. The consumption good is chosen as the numeraire. A θ-individual working ℓ units of time has gross income $z := \theta\ell$.

Individual productivity θ belongs to $\Theta \equiv \left[\underline{\theta}, \overline{\theta}\right] \subseteq \mathbb{R}_+$. Its cumulative distribution function $F : \Theta \to [0,1]$, assumed to be continuously differentiable with derivative $f(\theta) > 0$, is common knowledge.

The tax policy can now be introduced formally. As stressed in the introduction, we are interested in two kinds of tax schedules:

- With a *Kolm formula tax scheme of degree* k, every θ-individual is required to transfer $k\theta$ to society in exchange for which he receives $k\mathbf{E}[\theta]$, where $\mathbf{E}[\cdot]$ denotes the expectation over Θ. Hence, the tax function is $T : \Theta \times [0,1] \to \mathbb{R}$, where
$$T(\theta, k) = k(\theta - \mathbf{E}[\theta]). \tag{1}$$
- The *ELIE tax scheme of degree* k combines (a) a Kolm formula tax scheme of degree k with (b) a condition on the endogenous individual labour supply. In the absence of involuntary unemployment, this condition states that all productive individuals must provide $\ell \geq k$ to take part in the overall redistributive mechanism (Kolm 2011, p. 102). Because it can be argued that a redistributive tax schedule should be universal with the same schedule applied to everyone, special

attention will also be paid below to the case in which all citizens face the ELIE tax scheme of degree k.[1]

Given the tax function T, the *budget constraint* of a θ-individual is

$$0 \le x \le \theta\ell - T(\theta,k) = \theta(\ell - k) + k\mathbf{E}[\theta]. \tag{2}$$

Because a θ-individual cannot spend more on consumption than the maximum net income he obtains when devoting his whole time endowment to labour, his maximum possible consumption is equal to

$$x_{\max}(\theta,k) := \theta(1-k) + k\mathbf{E}[\theta] \tag{3}$$

in the absence of exogenous wealth. For $k \ne 1$, this upper bound on individual consumption, $x_{\max}(\theta,k)$, is strictly increasing in θ: the more productive an individual, the wider the range of consumption levels available to him. In addition, because net income cannot be negative, a θ-individual chooses his labour supply in $[\ell_{\min}(\theta,k), 1]$, where

$$\ell_{\min}(\theta,k) := \max\left\{0, k\left(1 - \frac{\mathbf{E}[\theta]}{\theta}\right)\right\}. \tag{4}$$

Note that $\ell_{\min}(\theta,k)$ is always less than k. Given (2), (3), and (4), the budget set of a θ-individual is defined as

$$\mathscr{B}(\theta) := \{(x,\ell) \in \mathbb{R}_+ \times [\ell_{\min}(\theta,k), 1] : x \le \theta\ell + k\,(\mathbf{E}[\theta] - \theta)\}. \tag{5}$$

By definition, the budget set of a θ-individual is independent of any endogeneity condition. It is thus the same with a Kolm formula tax scheme of degree k and the corresponding ELIE tax scheme of degree k. Consequently, except in the laissez-faire case in which $k = 0$ and, thus, $\ell_{\min}(\theta,k) = 0$ for all θ, the geometry of a Kolm formula tax scheme and ELIE basically depends on whether an individual's productivity is less than the average. This observation is illustrated in Fig. 1 for a population consisting of three individuals whose productivities are chosen so that $\theta_1 < \mathbf{E}[\theta]$, $\theta_2 = \mathbf{E}[\theta]$, and $\theta_3 > \mathbf{E}[\theta]$. The fact that an individual budget set is type-dependent with a *positive lower bound on labour supply* for the more productive part of the population (i.e., for $\theta > \mathbf{E}[\theta]$) is a fundamental feature of a Kolm formula tax scheme and ELIE.

The type-dependency of the individual budget sets distinguishes Kolm formula and ELIE tax schemes from the usual tax schedules considered in the second-best optimal income tax literature. Indeed, in this literature, all individuals make their

[1] These desiderata are incorporated in the actual tax schedules in many developed countries. In France, for instance, the 13th article of the Declaration of the Rights of Man and of the Citizen, which has a constitutional status, states that the common contribution should be equitably distributed among *all* the citizens in proportion to their means.

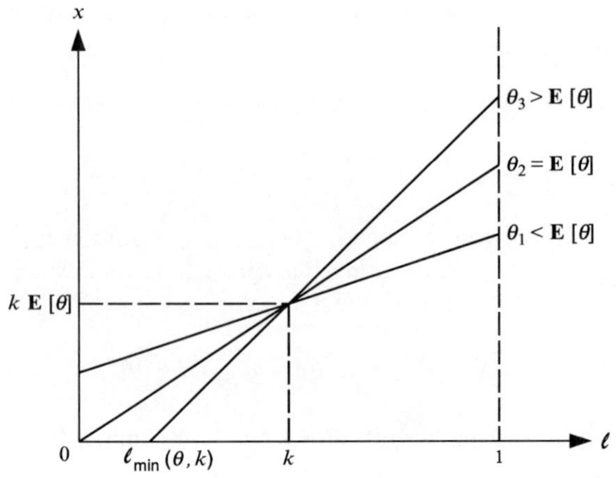

Fig. 1 Budget sets

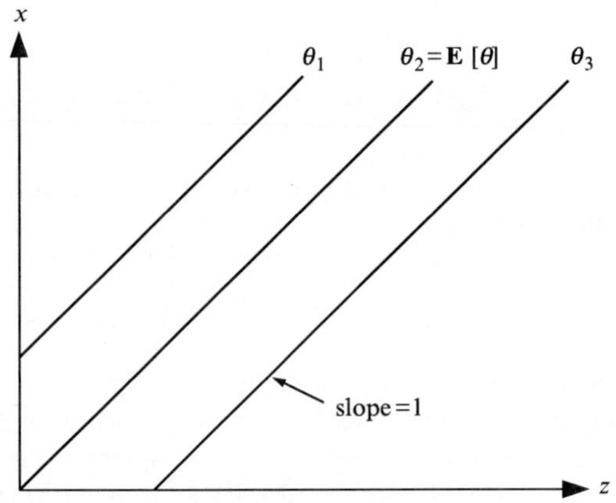

Fig. 2 Inclusion of budget sets in the gross-income/consumption space

choices from the same budget set in the gross income/consumption space. In contrast, Kolm's formula and ELIE gives rise to *inclusion of budget sets*, as illustrated in Fig. 2.[2] In this diagram, the opportunity set of an individual of type θ_i, $i = 1, 2, 3$, with $\theta_1 < \theta_2 < \theta_3$ consists of all the points in the nonnegative quadrant lying on or below the line marked θ_i.

With regard to labour supply, a Kolm formula tax scheme and ELIE constrain every individual whose productivity is above the average to work at least $\ell_{\min}(\theta, k) > 0$ in order to pay the strictly positive tax $T(\theta, k) = k\,(\theta - \mathbf{E}[\theta])$. So,

[2] Kolm has shown that ELIE nevertheless exhibits equality of opportunity for some well-defined indexes of equality of opportunity.

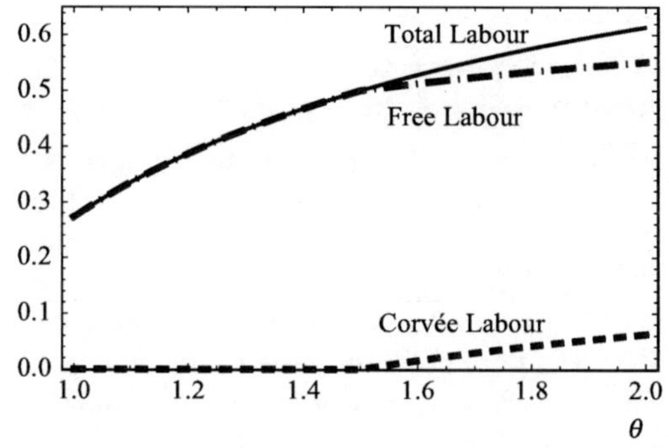

Fig. 3 Corvée labour, free labour, total labour

contrary to the situation of individuals in the less productive part of the population, highly skilled individuals do not have the *freedom of being idle*. This assertion must be qualified. Its validity rests on the assumption that highly skilled individuals have no assets and cannot borrow. If this assumption were relaxed, the model would no longer be static and intertemporal aspects should be taken into account.

In the absence of intertemporal considerations, $\ell_{\min}(\theta, k)$ is increased from 0 to $1 - \mathbf{E}[\theta]/\overline{\theta}$ when k goes from 0 to 1. Thus, $\ell_{\min}(\theta, k)$ can be regarded as the unpaid amount of labour required by Kolm's formula in lieu of taxes, i.e., as "*corvée labour*," with k corresponding to the degree of "serfdom" of the talented.

An example is provided in Fig. 3 for the case in which individuals have preferences represented by the log-transform of the Cobb–Douglas utility function

$$U(x, \ell) = \alpha \log x + (1 - \alpha) \log(1 - \ell). \tag{6}$$

We assume that $\alpha = 0.5$, productivity levels are uniformly distributed between 1 and 2, and $k = 0.25$. In this example, everyone provides an amount of labour $\ell(\theta, k)) > k$, which consists of corvée labour in the amount of $\ell_{\min}(\theta, k)$ and free labour in the amount of $\ell(\theta, k) - \ell_{\min}(\theta, k)$.

3 The Requirements of ELIE

Because the definition of ELIE includes a condition on the endogenous labour supply, it is difficult to see what the necessary conditions are for it to hold without using a microeconomic model. That is why it is worth examining the utility maximization programme of the individuals facing a Kolm formula tax scheme. It is maintained, in this section, that all individuals have the same preferences over consumption and leisure. They are represented by a twice continuously differentiable and strictly concave utility function $U : \mathbb{R}_+ \times [0, 1] \to \mathbb{R}$, with $U'_x > 0$, $U'_\ell < 0$, and $U(x, \ell) \to -\infty$ when $x \to 0$ or $\ell \to 1$. The *utility maximization programme* of a given θ-individual is thus

$$\max_{(x,\ell)\in\mathscr{B}(\theta)} U(x,\ell). \tag{7}$$

Let $\ell(\theta,k)$ denote the individual labour supply.

There are at least three ways of dealing with the endogeneity condition involved in the definition of the ELIE tax scheme of degree k: (a) the class of individual preferences could be restricted, (b) each individual who would voluntarily choose to work less than the required common contribution could be excluded from the redistributive scheme, or (c) the values of equalization labour k could be restricted to those that are feasible. The third possibility seems the most natural to us. Formally, it amounts to determining *which values of k are compatible with the requirement that every individual provides at least k hours of labour.*

In order to cast light on the necessary restrictions on k for this to be the case, it is assumed that all individuals have the same Cobb–Douglas preferences represented by (6) with $0<\alpha<1$. This utility specification is purely illustrative; other utility functions could naturally be considered. A θ-individual chooses the consumption/labour bundle that solves the maximization problem in (6). The necessary and sufficient first-order condition implies that

$$\ell(\theta)=\max\left\{0,\alpha+(1-\alpha)\frac{T(\theta,k)}{\theta}\right\}, \tag{8}$$

$$x(\theta)=\begin{cases}\alpha(\theta-T(\theta,k)) & \text{if } \theta>\theta_0,\\ -T(\theta,k) & \text{if } \theta\le\theta_0,\end{cases} \tag{9}$$

where

$$\theta_0:=\frac{k}{\left[k+\frac{\alpha}{1-\alpha}\right]}\mathbf{E}[\theta] \tag{10}$$

is the productivity threshold at which individuals are idle, provided that $\theta_0\ge\underline{\theta}$. The proportion of non-working individuals in the population is equal to $F(\theta_0)$ and all of these individuals are necessarily less productive than the average. ELIE requires that $\ell(\theta)\ge k$, $\forall\theta\in\Theta$, and $\underline{\theta}\neq 0$, or, equivalently,

$$k\le\frac{\theta}{\left[\theta+\frac{1-\alpha}{a}\right]\mathbf{E}[\theta]},\quad\forall\theta\in\Theta,\ \text{and } \underline{\theta}\neq 0. \tag{11}$$

Because the RHS of the inequality in (11) is increasing in θ, Proposition 1 follows.

Proposition 1. *With Cobb–Douglas preferences, ELIE is obtained if and only if*

$$k\le\frac{\underline{\theta}}{\underline{\theta}+\left[\frac{1-\alpha}{\alpha}\right]\mathbf{E}[\theta]}=:k_m \text{ and } \underline{\theta}\neq 0. \tag{12}$$

By (10), there are *no idle individuals in the population* if $\theta_0<\underline{\theta}$, i.e., if

$$k<\min\left\{1,\left(\frac{\alpha}{1-\alpha}\right)\left(\frac{\underline{\theta}}{\mathbf{E}[\theta]-\underline{\theta}}\right)\right\}=:k_0. \tag{13}$$

Both threshold values of k, k_0 and k_m, are useful in the subsequent analysis. Because $k_m < k_0 \leq 1$, the individual labour response to Kolm's formula imposes restrictions on the values of equalization labour k that are compatible with ELIE. Because $1 - \alpha$ corresponds to the share of the full income any individual devotes to leisure, it seems reasonable to expect α not to exceed 0.5. If so, k_m is less than 0.5. The condition that $k \leq k_m$ might thus be regarded as restrictive. In addition, if there are individuals whose ability is zero in the population (i.e., if $\underline{\theta} = 0$), an impossibility result is obtained.

4 Kolm's Formula and ELIE as First-Best Tax Schemes

In essence, a Kolm formula tax scheme of degree k and, thus, the ELIE tax scheme of degree k can be regarded as linear taxes based on productivity, with a marginal tax rate of k accompanied by a lump-sum subsidy chosen so that the tax scheme is budget balanced. Indeed, by construction,

$$\mathbf{E}[T(\theta, k)] = k(\mathbf{E}[\theta] - \mathbf{E}[\theta]) = 0. \tag{14}$$

Provided that productivity is exogenous and publicly known, both tax schemes are examples of first-best tax schemes. The purpose of this section is to shed light on the social weights that generate these first-best tax schemes. We consider a social planner with a Bergson–Samuelson social welfare function. We are thus departing from the ethical framework considered by Kolm. However it is interesting to determine what kind of social welfare function the "Kolmian" social planner is trying to maximize.

With respect to Kolm's tax formula, the polar situations in which $k = 0$ and $k = 1$ are well-known in the literature. When $k = 0$, laissez-faire is obtained. When $k = 1$, all individuals have the same full income $\mathbf{E}[\theta]$. Note that this corresponds to the outcome of the maximization of a pure utilitarian social welfare function if all individuals have the utility function defined in (6). In this case, there is a curse of the highly-skilled: the optimal indirect utility function is strictly decreasing in productivity provided that leisure is a normal good (Mirrlees 1971, 1974). That is why it is henceforth assumed that $k \in (0, 1)$. In each step of our analysis, we first derive general results for Kolm's tax formula and then restrict the range of feasible k to apply them to ELIE.

4.1 Statement of the Problem

The standard viewpoint of optimal income taxation is adopted. Individual social weights are given by the function $\lambda: \Theta \to \mathbb{R}_{++}$, which is assumed to be $\mathscr{C}^1$ almost everywhere. An *allocation* is a pair of functions $x: \Theta \to \mathbb{R}_+$ and $\ell: \Theta \to [0, 1]$

that describes how consumption and labour supply vary with productivity. The corresponding tax schedule is the function $\tau\colon \Theta \to \mathbb{R}$ given by $\tau(\theta) = \theta\ell(\theta) - x(\theta)$. The policy-maker chooses the allocations that maximize social welfare

$$W = \int_{\Theta} \lambda(\theta) U(x, \ell) dF(\theta) \tag{15}$$

subject to the tax revenue constraint

$$\int_{\Theta} \tau(\theta) dF(\theta) \geq 0. \tag{16}$$

Because W is homogeneous of degree one in λ, $\mathbf{E}[\lambda] = \int_{\Theta} \lambda(\theta) dF(\theta)$ can be normalized without loss of generality. It is convenient to choose

$$\mathbf{E}[\lambda] = 1. \tag{17}$$

The first-best tax scheme is solution to the following optimization programme:

Problem 1. Choose $x\colon \Theta \to \mathbb{R}_+$ and $\ell\colon \Theta \to [0, 1]$ to maximize W subject to the tax revenue constraint (16).

Letting γ denote the Lagrange multiplier associated with the tax revenue constraint (16), Problem 1 amounts to maximizing

$$\int_{\Theta} \{\lambda(\theta) U(x, \ell) + \gamma[\theta\ell - x]\} dF(\theta). \tag{18}$$

The question addressed in this section can thus be summarized as follows:

Problem 2. For $k \in (0, 1)$, find $\lambda\colon \Theta \to \mathbb{R}_{++}$ such that the optimal tax scheme $\tau(\theta)$ at a solution to Problem 1 is given by Kolm's formula for this value of k.

4.2 Social Welfare Weights for Kolm's Tax Formula and ELIE: The Cobb–Douglas Case

For simplicity, it is first assumed that the individual utility function is given by (6). Note that $\alpha \in (0, 1)$ is the common taste parameter for consumption. Because Problem 1 is concave and $f > 0$, the necessary and sufficient first-order conditions for the solution to Problem 1 are:

$$x(\theta) = \frac{\alpha}{\gamma} \lambda(\theta), \ \forall \theta \in \Theta, \tag{19}$$

$$\ell(\theta) = \max\left\{0, 1 - \left(\frac{1-\alpha}{\gamma}\right)\left(\frac{\lambda(\theta)}{\theta}\right)\right\}, \ \forall \theta \in \Theta. \tag{20}$$

In addition, the tax revenue constraint (16) must be binding at the social optimum. For the given α, the first-order condition (19) shows that consumption is increasing in productivity if and only if the individual social weights are themselves increasing in productivity. By (19) and (20),

$$\theta\ell(\theta) - x(\theta) = \begin{cases} \theta - \frac{\lambda(\theta)}{\gamma} & \text{if } \lambda(\theta) \leq \frac{\gamma}{1-\alpha}\theta, \\ -\alpha\frac{\lambda(\theta)}{\gamma} & \text{if } \lambda(\theta) > \frac{\gamma}{1-\alpha}\theta. \end{cases} \tag{21}$$

The tax function τ at a solution to Problem 1 corresponds to Kolm's tax formula of degree k if and only if $T(\theta, k) \equiv \theta\ell(\theta) - x(\theta)$. That is,

$$\lambda(\theta) = \begin{cases} \gamma[\theta(1-k) + k\mathbf{E}(\theta)] & \text{if } \dfrac{k\mathbf{E}(\theta)}{(k + \frac{\alpha}{1-\alpha})} \leq \theta, \\ -\frac{\gamma}{\alpha}k[\theta - \mathbf{E}(\theta)] & \text{otherwise.} \end{cases} \tag{22}$$

Because $\mathbf{E}[\lambda] = 1$,

$$\gamma = \left[\mathbf{E}(\theta)\Pr\left(\frac{k\mathbf{E}(\theta)}{(k + \frac{\alpha}{1-\alpha})} \leq \theta\right)\right]^{-1}, \tag{23}$$

where the probability expression is the proportion of working individuals, which only depends on the exogenous parameters of the economy.

For our Cobb–Douglas example, the previous results allow us to characterize the social weights under which Kolm's tax formula is obtained as a first-best tax scheme for $k \in (0, 1)$.

Proposition 2. *Suppose that the individual utility function is given by* (6) *with* $0 < \alpha < 1$. *Then, for* $k \in (0, 1)$, *the first-best solution to Problem 1 generates a transfer scheme corresponding to Kolm's tax formula for k if and only if the social weights are given by*

$$\lambda(\theta, \alpha) = \begin{cases} \gamma[\theta(1-k) + k\mathbf{E}(\theta)] & \textit{if } \dfrac{k\mathbf{E}(\theta)}{(k + \frac{\alpha}{1-\alpha})} \leq \theta, \\ -\frac{\gamma}{\alpha}k[\theta - \mathbf{E}(\theta)] & \textit{otherwise.} \end{cases} \tag{24}$$

The contribution of this proposition is to cast light on the *shape* of the distribution of the social weights that generate a tax scheme corresponding to Kolm's tax formula. Given the preference specification, it can first be noted that the social weights $\lambda(\theta)$ are (piecewise) linear in productivity. Moreover, if there are idle individuals in the population, these social weights must be V-shaped. Otherwise, they are strictly increasing for the whole population. This particular pattern for the social weights is in sharp contrast with what is usually considered in the optimal income tax literature. Indeed, the standard view is that the social weights are decreasing in ability; the rationale for this monotonicity restriction being based on the idea that the policy-maker is adverse to income inequality. Consequently, Proposition 2 demonstrates that Kolm's tax formula has a fundamentally different normative basis than does Mirrleesian optimal income tax theory.

The V-shape of the social weights with respect to productivity can be explained as follows. On the one hand, because $T(\theta, k) = k(\theta - \mathbf{E}[\theta])$, the more productive an idle individual, the smaller the transfer he receives. As a result, the consumption level is strictly decreasing in θ below θ_0. By (19), this is only possible if the social weights are strictly decreasing. On the other hand, by (9), consumption increases with ability above θ_0. Therefore, (19) implies that the social weights must be strictly increasing in productivity for the more productive part of the population. All individuals work at least k units of time under the ELIE tax scheme of degree k. Hence, the probability in (23) is equal to 1. Therefore, in this case, Proposition 2 reduces to:

Corollary 1. *Suppose that the individual utility function is given by* (6) *with* $0 < \alpha < 1$. *Then, the first-best solution to Problem 1 generates a transfer scheme corresponding to ELIE for the given value of k if and only if the social weights are given by*

$$\lambda(\theta) = (1-k)\frac{\theta}{\mathbf{E}[\theta]} + k. \tag{25}$$

4.3 Social Weights for ELIE: The General Case

Further insights into the shape of the distribution of the social weights that generate an ELIE tax scheme are now provided for well-behaved preferences parameterized by α. Every Pareto optimal allocation maximizes a weighted sum of utilities subject to the resource and technological constraints. The solution of such a maximization problem is assumed to be *interior* for the ELIE tax scheme of degree k, with every individual providing more than k units of labour.

For the utility maximization programme (7), the indirect utility of a θ-individual is

$$V(\theta, k) := U(\theta\ell(\theta, k) - T(\theta, k), \ell(\theta, k)), \tag{26}$$

where $\ell(\theta, k)$ denotes the labour supply of a θ-individual. Let $\beta(\theta)$ be the Lagrange multiplier for the budget constraint (2) of a θ-individual. The first-order condition with respect to consumption is

$$U'_x(x, \ell) = \beta(\theta). \tag{27}$$

By the envelope theorem,

$$\beta(\theta) = -\frac{\partial V(\theta, k)}{\partial T(\theta, k)}. \tag{28}$$

The social policy-maker maximizes W subject to the tax revenue constraint (16). Recall that γ is the Lagrange multiplier of this constraint. Thus, the first-order condition with respect to consumption is

$$U'_x(x,\ell) = \frac{\gamma}{\lambda(\theta)}. \tag{29}$$

Combining (27), (28), and (29), one obtains

$$\begin{aligned}\lambda(\theta) &= \gamma\left(-\frac{\partial V(\theta,k)}{\partial T(\theta,k)}\right)^{-1}\\ &= \frac{\gamma}{U'_x(\theta(\ell(\theta,k)-k)+k\mathbf{E}[\theta],\ell(\theta,k))}.\end{aligned} \tag{30}$$

This equation states that the weight of the utility of a θ-individual in the social objective function equals the reciprocal of his marginal utility of wealth evaluated at the support prices $(1,\theta)$ and imputed lump-sum wealth $kE[\theta]$. Consequently,

$$\lambda'(\theta) = -\frac{\gamma(U'_x)^2}{\left[\left(\theta\frac{d\ell(\theta,k)}{d\theta}+\ell(\theta,k)-k\right)U''_{xx}+\frac{d\ell(\theta,k)}{d\theta}U''_{x\ell}\right]}, \tag{31}$$

where all derivatives are evaluated at $(\theta(\ell(\theta,k)-k)+k\mathbf{E}[\theta],\ell(\theta,k))$.

Using the Slutsky equation,

$$\frac{d\ell(\theta,k)}{d\theta} = \frac{\partial h(\theta,k)}{\partial\theta} - (\ell(\theta,k)-k)\frac{\partial\ell(\theta,k)}{\partial T(\theta,k)}, \tag{32}$$

where $h(\theta,k)$ is the Hicksian labour supply. By the law of compensated demand, the first term of the Slutsky equation–which captures the substitution effect of changing θ–is positive. Because $\ell(\theta,k)-k \geq 0$, the second term–which captures the income effect–is non-positive provided that leisure is a normal good, i.e., if $\partial\ell(\theta,k)/\partial T(\theta,k) > 0$. Recalling that $U''_{xx} < 0$ and that there is *ALEP complementarity* between consumption and labour (or *ALEP substitutability* between consumption and leisure) if and only if $U''_{x\ell} > 0$ (see Allen 1934; Auspitz and Lieben 1889; Edgeworth 1925; Pareto 1906), Proposition 3 follows from (31) and (32).

Proposition 3. *Assume* (i) *that there is ALEP substitutability between consumption and leisure and* (ii) *that the substitution effect on labour supply is larger than the income effect. Then, the social weights that generate ELIE are strictly increasing in productivity.*

5 Implementation of ELIE

This section focuses on the implementability of the ELIE tax schemes. Following Mirrlees (1971), we assume that productivity differences are the only source of heterogeneity.

5.1 The Implementation Issue

Mirrlees (1971, p. 208) notes in the conclusion of his seminal article on optimal income taxation that "it would be good to devise taxes complementarity to the income tax, designed to avoid the difficulties that the tax is faced with ... [T]his could be achieved by introducing a tax schedule that depends upon time worked as well as upon labour-income." In fact, once the government knows both variables in the Mirrlees framework, it is capable of inferring the productivity level of each individual because gross income is the product of productivity and time worked. Thus, there seems to be no reason not to design a tax based on individual skills. Accordingly, Kolm (2004, p. 175) considers that "scholars who let their thinking be directed by casual superficial remarks about difficulties of implementation and in particular information are bound to run in the wrong direction."

There are however different arguments that temper the idea that there has been a misplaced emphasis on implementation. The starting point is to distinguish occupations according to whether or not the labour time is verifiable by an employer.

On the one hand, there are jobs for which an employer can precisely record the hours that people work, thanks to a time clock for instance. In this case, the labour time $\ell(\theta)$ can be obtained by the policy-maker, possibly at some cost. The extraction of this information belongs to the economics of tax evasion (Cowell 1990). However, it would be incorrect to conclude from the fact that the labour supply of a θ-individual is observable that the ratio of his gross income to the number of hours worked necessarily is his correct productivity level θ. This point has been made clear by Dasgupta and Hammond (1980). Any θ-individual has the possibility to provide labour at a lower productivity level θ'. In other words, θ is the maximum productivity level of a θ-individual. Formally, let $\ell(\theta';\theta)$ be the labour supply of a θ-individual at productivity θ'. Then, his total labour supply is $\int_{\underline{\theta}}^{\theta} \ell(\theta';\theta)d\theta'$. The computed productivity θ^c is obtained as the ratio of his total gross income $\int_{\underline{\theta}}^{\theta} \ell(\theta';\theta)\theta' d\theta'$ to his total labour supply, i.e., $\theta^c = \int_{\underline{\theta}}^{\theta} \ell(\theta';\theta)\theta' d\theta' / \int_{\underline{\theta}}^{\theta} \ell(\theta';\theta)d\theta'$. It is equal to θ if and only the tax scheme gives a θ-individual an incentive to provide all labour using his actual skill so that his labour supply is $\ell(\theta;\theta)$. In all other cases, taxing the computed productivity can no longer be considered as a lump-sum tax because the computed productivity is endogenous to the tax scheme. In other words, it is incorrect to conclude from the absence of cheating on time worked that the best productivity level of an individual is public knowledge. *For this type of labour, work-time evasion and implementation are both meaningful issues.*

On the other hand, there are other occupations for which it proves difficult to separate time worked from leisure. This observation notably applies to individuals involved in "brainwork" occupations for which the use of a time clock would be completely irrelevant. Because the time spent working is not verifiable, nobody can establish that a given individual in this kind of occupation is cheating. So, *the problem of work-time evasion does not exist for this second type of labour, whilst the implementation issue must still be taken into account.* This last issue is particularly important because the individuals involved in these kinds of occupations are likely to belong to the more productive part of the population and to pay positive taxes.

Of course, in a more general framework in which productivity is the product of innate talent and effort, the knowledge of time worked would not be sufficient to identify productivity either. We deliberately place ourselves in the simplest case, where effort is not taken into account, to examine if ELIE is incentive compatible.

5.2 *Incentive Compatibility of ELIE*

Incentive compatibility of ELIE basically depends on the verifiability of gross income and time worked, i.e., on *which variables can be included in the contract between the policy-maker and an individual worker*. By definition, a variable is verifiable if a contract that depends on it can be enforced by a third party (e.g., an arbitrator or court) who can verify the value of the variable and make the parties fulfill the contract. Hence, a contract can only depend on verifiable variables. This subsection clarifies key points regarding incentive-compatibility; its contribution is mainly pedagogical.

Let us consider individuals who are faced with the ELIE tax scheme of degree k ($k \neq 0$). Three cases need to be distinguished.

5.2.1 Non-Verifiability of Gross Income and Hours Worked

In the first case, neither gross income z nor time worked ℓ are verifiable. Thus, the government has no means of recovering the true productivity level of an individual from knowledge of z and ℓ. Consequently, *the tax base is purely declaratory*. Every individual thus has an incentive to claim that his gross income z and his labour time ℓ are such that $z/\ell = \underline{\theta}$. Indeed, he then obtains the maximum transfer $-T(\underline{\theta}, k)$, which maximally relaxes his budget constraint. As a consequence,

$$\int_{\Theta} T(\underline{\theta}, k) dF(\theta) = k(\underline{\theta} - \mathbf{E}[\theta]) < 0, \tag{33}$$

which implies that the tax revenue constraint (2) is necessarily violated. Therefore, in this case, *the ELIE tax scheme is not incentive compatible*.

5.2.2 Verifiability of Gross Income and Hours Worked

The polar case is now considered: gross income and hours worked are verifiable and included in the contract between the policy-maker and the taxpayer. In this case, it is known from Dasgupta and Hammond (1980) that a tax schedule is incentive-compatible if indirect utility is non-decreasing in productivity.

To gain further insight into this finding, it is worth describing the timing of the game between the taxpayers and the policy-maker. Let $\hat{\theta}$ be the productivity level at which labour is actually supplied:

1. First, the tax authority announces a tax schedule

$$T(\hat{\theta}, k) = k(\hat{\theta} - \mathbf{E}[\hat{\theta}]). \tag{34}$$

2. Second, for all $\theta \in \Theta$, each θ-individual chooses at which productivity level $\hat{\theta} = z/\ell$ (with $\hat{\theta} \leq \theta$) he wants to provide his labour. He then pays a common contribution $k\hat{\theta}$ and receives $k\mathbf{E}[\hat{\theta}]$ from society.

As is standard in optimal income taxation theory, we are interested in implementation in weakly dominant strategies. In this context, the tax schedule (34) is implementable if each individual cannot increase his well-being by hiding his true productivity level θ.

For convenience, it is assumed that a θ-individual can only provide labour at *one* skill level $\hat{\theta} \leq \theta$. When his gross income is z and his time worked is ℓ, his observed skill is given by $\hat{\theta} = z/\ell$. Therefore, his utility level when he chooses $z/\ell = \hat{\theta}$ is given by

$$\max_{\ell_{\min}(\hat{\theta}) \leq \ell \leq 1} U(\hat{\theta}\ell - T(\hat{\theta}, k), \ell) =: V(\hat{\theta}), \tag{35}$$

where $V(\hat{\theta})$ is the indirect utility of a $\hat{\theta}$-individual. Hence, a θ-individual chooses to work with the skill level $\hat{\theta}$ that solves

$$\max_{\hat{\theta} \leq \theta} V(\hat{\theta}). \tag{36}$$

Accordingly, *every individual maximizes his utility when working at his best skill if $V(\hat{\theta})$ is non-decreasing in productivity*. Applying the envelope theorem to

$$V(\hat{\theta}) \equiv U(\hat{\theta}(\ell(\hat{\theta}) - k) + k\mathbf{E}[\hat{\theta}], \ell(\hat{\theta})), \tag{37}$$

one obtains

$$V'(\hat{\theta}) = U'_x(\hat{\theta}(\ell(\hat{\theta}) - k) + k\mathbf{E}[\hat{\theta}], \ell(\hat{\theta}))[\ell(\hat{\theta}) - k]. \tag{38}$$

Hence, because $U'_x > 0$, the indirect utility $V(\hat{\theta})$ is non-decreasing in $\hat{\theta}$ if and only if

$$\ell(\hat{\theta}) \geq k, \tag{39}$$

which is satisfied with the ELIE tax scheme of degree k. In summary:

Proposition 4. *The ELIE tax scheme of degree k is implementable as a direct truthful mechanism in weakly dominant strategies if both gross income and time worked are observable by the policy-maker and verifiable by a third party.*

In this sense "the individuals choose to work with their best skills and thus to 'reveal' their capacities and to exhibit their economic value." (Kolm 2011, p. 118, emphasis omitted) Hence, *ELIE is incentive compatible for all individuals in occupations for which a "time clock" can be used.*

5.2.3 Verifiability of Gross Income and Non-Verifiability of Hours Worked

It remains to examine if the preceding result extends to the numerous individuals working in occupations for which the use of a time clock is irrelevant. In this case, time worked is no longer verifiable, so that it would be useless to include it in the contract between the policy-maker and a taxpayer. Hence, a θ-individual no longer needs to spend the same time working as a $\hat{\theta}$-individual if he chooses to earn the same gross income as the latter.

A natural solution in this case is to refer to some legal definition of the time worked, like the average working time $\overline{\ell}$, for example. The policy-maker infers that the productivity of a θ-individual with gross income z is $z/\overline{\ell}$. If this ratio is used as a tax base, then a Kolm formula tax scheme of degree k becomes

$$T\left(\frac{z}{\overline{\ell}},k\right)=k\left(\frac{z}{\overline{\ell}}-\mathbf{E}[z/\overline{\ell}]\right)=\frac{k}{\overline{\ell}}(z-\mathbf{E}[z]). \tag{40}$$

The tax function in (40) is a linear tax on gross income, with marginal tax rate $k/\overline{\ell}$ and basic income $k\mathbf{E}[z/\overline{\ell}]$. It is budget balanced because, by construction, $\mathbf{E}\left[T(z/\overline{\ell},k)\right]=0$. Moreover, it is incentive compatible if $k/\overline{\ell}<1$. However, although this function is linear in gross income, it does not correspond to a first-best ELIE tax scheme, which is linear in labour productivity.

An alternative solution to the implementation problem is to ask every individual to report his non-verifiable time worked $\hat{\ell}$ in conjunction with his verifiable gross income $\hat{z}$. The inferred productivity level $\hat{\theta}=\hat{z}/\hat{\ell}$ is then used as a tax base. The hidden productivity level is $\theta=\hat{z}/\ell$, where ℓ is the actual time worked. In this case, a θ-individual chooses

$$(\hat{z}^*(\theta),\hat{\ell}^*(\theta))=\underset{\substack{\hat{z}-T\left(\frac{\hat{z}}{\hat{\ell}},k\right)\geq 0,\\ 0\leq\hat{\ell}\leq 1}}{\arg\max}\; U\left(\hat{z}-T\left(\frac{\hat{z}}{\hat{\ell}},k\right),\frac{\hat{z}}{\theta}\right). \tag{41}$$

Hence, every θ-individual claims that he works $\hat{\ell}^*(\theta)=1$ in order to maximize his utility provided that T is increasing in gross income. Because he never chooses to work 24 hours a day, it follows that he *overstates* his labour time in such a way that the policy-maker *underestimates* his productivity. That is, he chooses $\hat{\theta}$ so that $\hat{\theta}=\hat{z}^*(\theta)<\theta$.

Proposition 5. *Suppose that gross income is verifiable and that time worked is non-verifiable. Then, if the ELIE tax scheme of degree k is based on the inferred productivity level $\hat{\theta}$, everybody has an incentive to overstate his time worked so as to understate his true productivity level θ. Therefore, this tax scheme is not implementable as a direct truthful mechanism in weakly dominant strategies.*

Recall from Proposition 2 that in order for an ELIE tax scheme to be optimal when there is no private information, the social weights must be strictly increasing in productivity. However, even with this restriction on the weights, Proposition 5 demonstrates that ELIE is not sufficiently favourable to the highly-skilled individuals to prevent every individual from *understating* his productivity level when hours worked are non-verifiable.

5.3 Implications

In practice, there are many occupations in which labour time is not verifiable by the employer. Moreover, individuals in these occupations are on average highly skilled and, by Proposition 5, understate their true productivity level when we depart from the first-best setting. Thus, there is a difficulty in implementing ELIE when hours worked are non-verifiable.

There are different routes to construct a second-best alternative to the ELIE tax scheme of degree k. A first route would retain the social weights (24) that generate Kolm's tax formula as a solution to Problem 1 and use them to solve the second-best problem which takes incentive-compatibility into account. However, there seems to be no reason why a welfarist objective that coincides with Kolm's scheme in the first-best context would be relevant to Kolm's philosophy in the second-best. A second route, which is followed in this article and that does not rest on welfarism, aims at implementing the *first-best* transfers of ELIE in a second-best setting.

For illustrative purposes, it is henceforth assumed that the population consists of two types of individuals who are involved in brainwork occupations, with respective productivities $\underline{\theta}$ and $\overline{\theta}$ ($\underline{\theta} < \overline{\theta}$).

5.3.1 A Second-Best Alternative to ELIE: Principles

Given the usual results of contract theory (see, e.g., Laffont and Martimort 2002), one expects that when a second-best alternative to ELIE is implemented that (a) the optimal tax schedule will not involve any distortion of the labour supply of the high-type individual and (b) the only binding incentive-compatibility constraint will be that of the high-type individual. Therefore, in a two-type population, the basic idea is to examine to what extent the utility of the low type must be decreased to make the high type indifferent between his own bundle and that of the low type. For this purpose, it is sufficient to introduce a linear tax, faced by the low type $\underline{\theta}$, that distorts his labour supply and that ensures budget balancedness through an increase in the lump-sum subsidy to this type. For convenience, it is assumed that there are only two individuals in the population, one for each ability level. The construction of a budget-balanced and incentive-compatible allocation proceeds in four steps.

First, when the low-skilled individual faces a distortionary tax rate t on gross income and a second-best lump-sum transfer $\widetilde{T}(\underline{\theta}, k)$, his budget constraint is

$$x(\underline{\theta}) = (1-t)z(\underline{\theta}) - \widetilde{T}(\underline{\theta}, k). \tag{42}$$

The first-order condition for the utility maximization programme of the low type states that his marginal rate of substitution at the optimal bundle is equal to his net-of-tax wage rate, i.e.,

$$-\frac{U_z'(x(\underline{\theta}), z(\underline{\theta})/\underline{\theta})}{U_x'(x(\underline{\theta}), z(\underline{\theta})/\underline{\theta})} = 1 - t. \tag{43}$$

Second, the high type has no incentive to mimic the low type if the utility the former obtains at his own bundle $\left(x\left(\overline{\theta}\right), z\left(\overline{\theta}\right)\right)$ is not less than what he receives from the bundle $(x(\underline{\theta}), z(\underline{\theta}))$ of the latter, i.e., if $V\left(\overline{\theta}; \overline{\theta}\right) \geq V\left(\underline{\theta}; \overline{\theta}\right)$, where

$$V(\theta', \theta) := U\left(x(\theta'), \frac{z(\theta')}{\theta}\right). \tag{44}$$

In order to minimize the loss in efficiency, this inequality must be binding at the optimum. Therefore, the second-best allocation must satisfy

$$V\left(\overline{\theta}; \overline{\theta}\right) = V\left(\underline{\theta}; \overline{\theta}\right). \tag{45}$$

Third, the net transfer to the low-skilled individual must be the same as in the first best $T(\underline{\theta}, k)$, which ensures that the high-skilled individual pays the same tax as in the first best. Formally,

$$\widetilde{T}(\underline{\theta}, k) + tz(\underline{\theta}) = T(\underline{\theta}, k). \tag{46}$$

As a consequence,

$$\widetilde{T}(\underline{\theta}, k) < T(\underline{\theta}, k), \tag{47}$$

implying that the second-best lump-sum transfer $-\widetilde{T}(\underline{\theta}, k)$ must be greater than the first best transfer $-T(\underline{\theta}, k)$.

The fourth step consists in checking that the low type has no incentive to mimic the high type, i.e., that

$$V(\underline{\theta}; \underline{\theta}) > V\left(\overline{\theta}; \underline{\theta}\right). \tag{48}$$

The second-best problem is therefore:

Problem 3. Choose $\widetilde{T}(\underline{\theta}, k)$ and $t \in (0, 1)$ such that (42), (43), (45), (46), and (48) are satisfied.

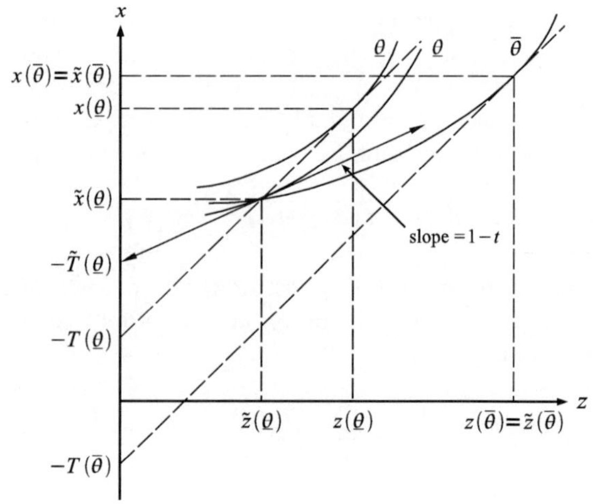

Fig. 4 Geometric construction

Figure 4 shows the logic of the construction of the solution to Problem 3. (In this figure, k is suppressed from the notation; x, z, and T correspond to first-best levels; $\tilde{x}$, $\tilde{z}$, and $\widetilde{T}$ to second-best levels; and the indifference curves are labelled by productivity levels.) The two budget lines for the low-skilled individual cross at the new equilibrium for this individual. A simple example is now provided to show the practicality of this approach.

5.3.2 A Second-Best Alternative to ELIE: An Example

A complete solution to Problem 3 is now provided for the case in which both individuals have the same Cobb–Douglas utility function

$$U(x,\ell) = x^{\alpha}(1-\ell)^{1-\alpha}. \tag{49}$$

For illustrative purposes, it is assumed that $k = 1/4$, $\alpha = 1/2$, $\underline{\theta} = 1$, and $\overline{\theta} = 3/2$.

In the first-best setting, the ELIE tax scheme of degree k is such that

$$T(\underline{\theta},k) = \frac{1}{4}\left(1 - \frac{1}{2}\left(1 + \frac{3}{2}\right)\right) = -\frac{1}{16} \tag{50}$$

and $T\left(\overline{\theta},k\right) = 1/16$. Because $k < k_m \simeq 0.44$, it is known from Proposition 1 that every individual provides labour in excess of the common contribution k. Table 1 gives the corresponding first-best labour supply, consumption, and utility levels. Although $V(\underline{\theta};\underline{\theta}) < V\left(\overline{\theta};\overline{\theta}\right)$ at the first-best solution, it can be verified that the high-skilled individual has an incentive to misreport his productivity, while the low-skilled individual reveals his type truthfully. The mimicking behaviour of

Table 1 First-best and second-best allocations corresponding to ELIE

θ	x	ℓ	z	$V(\underline{\theta};\theta)$	$V(\overline{\theta};\theta)$
First-best					
$\underline{\theta}$	0.531	0.469	0.469	0.531	0.397
$\overline{\theta}$	0.719	0.521	0.781	0.604	0.587
Second-best					
$\underline{\theta}$	0.475	0.413	0.413	0.528	0.397
$\overline{\theta}$	0.719	0.521	0.781	0.587	0.587

the high-skilled individual results in a public deficit equal to $T(\underline{\theta}, k) \times 2 = 1/8$. The budget-balance constraint is thus violated. This observation illustrates the result obtained in Proposition 5: *the high-skilled individual does not choose to work with his best possible skill thereby "revealing" his capacity and exhibiting his economic value*.

The second-best Problem 3 amounts to finding t and $T(\underline{\theta}, k)$ that solve the following system of four equations before checking that the low-skilled individual has no incentive to overstate his productivity level:

$$V(\overline{\theta};\overline{\theta}) = x^{\alpha}(\underline{\theta})\left(1 - \frac{\underline{\theta}\ell(\underline{\theta})}{\overline{\theta}}\right)^{1-\alpha}, \tag{51}$$

$$\left[\frac{1-\alpha}{\alpha}\right]\left[\frac{x(\underline{\theta})}{1-\ell(\underline{\theta})}\right] = (1-t)\underline{\theta}, \tag{52}$$

$$x(\underline{\theta}) = (1-t)\underline{\theta}\ell(\underline{\theta}) - \widetilde{T}(\underline{\theta}, k), \tag{53}$$

$$\widetilde{T}(\underline{\theta}, k) + t\underline{\theta}\ell(\underline{\theta}) = T(\underline{\theta}, k), \tag{54}$$

where $x(\overline{\theta}) \simeq 0.719$, $\ell(\overline{\theta}) \simeq 0.521$, and $T(\underline{\theta}) = -1/16$. Using (52), (53), and (54)), one obtains

$$x(\underline{\theta}) = \alpha\left[\frac{1-t}{1-\alpha t}\right](\underline{\theta} - T(\underline{\theta}, k)), \tag{55}$$

$$\ell(\underline{\theta}) = \frac{1}{1-\alpha t}\left[\alpha(1-t) + \left(\frac{1-\alpha}{\underline{\theta}}\right)T(\underline{\theta}, k)\right], \tag{56}$$

which are substituted in (51) to get

$$V(\overline{\theta};\overline{\theta}) = \left[\alpha\left(\frac{1-t}{1-\alpha t}\right)(\underline{\theta} - T(\underline{\theta}, k))\right]^{\alpha} \times \left(1 - \frac{\alpha\underline{\theta}(1-t) + (1-\alpha)T(\underline{\theta}, k)}{\overline{\theta}(1-\alpha t)}\right)^{1-\alpha}. \tag{57}$$

It then remains to solve (57) for t and substitute the obtained value in (55) and (56). It is found that $t = 19.12\%$ and, hence, that $\widetilde{T}(\underline{\theta}, k) = -0.1414$ instead of $T(\underline{\theta}, k) = -0.0625$. Table 1 provides the other second-best results. As expected, the low-skilled individual has no incentive to mimic the high-skilled one, which confirms that it was not necessary to take his incentive-compatibility constraint (48) explicitly into account. In addition, his second-best indirect utility is only slightly reduced compared to the first-best one ($\simeq -0.56\%$). This is a very modest price to pay for the ELIE tax scheme to induce individual truth-telling.

The basic idea is to worsen the position of the low-skilled individual compared to the first-best allocation in such a way that this worsening is seen to be more painful to the high-skilled individual than to the low-skilled individual. It is possible to do this because the two types of individuals do not value a reduction in gross income in the same way. The adjustment proceeds as follows. First, the introduction of the distorting tax gives rise to a substitution effect that induces the low-skilled individual to reduce his labour supply. He is impoverished by the associated income effect and is thus encouraged to work more. In general, the variation in labour supply is ambiguous, whereas consumption is reduced. However, in the example, the substitution effect prevails because the income effect is partially compensated for by the increase in the lump-sum transfer to the low-skilled individual. Thus, the low-skilled individual chooses to increase his leisure to the detriment of consumption. Second, both individuals value the reduction in consumption in the same way because they have the same utility function. However, they do not equally value the impact of the decrease in gross income required from the low-type individual. This reduction translates into a smaller increase in leisure for the high-skilled individual than for the low-skilled individual because the former is more productive than the latter.

6 Concluding Comments

ELIE has some very attractive and striking features. It corresponds to the idea that laissez-faire should be implemented over a certain threshold of labour time, with the income from this equal labour being given by everyone to share among all citizens. However, it must be conceded that the ELIE tax scheme derived by Kolm is not without its shortcomings.

First, its definition involves an endogeneity condition whose satisfaction requires some qualifications. Second, it subjects the more productive part of the population to "corvée labour" and embodies, therefore, some troubling "feudalistic" features. Third, in the first-best framework and under weak assumptions, it is generated by social weights that are strictly increasing in productivity for all working individuals. If Kolm's proposal should get credit for expanding the set of ethically acceptable social weights, it could nevertheless encounter stiff opposition from some normative economists because of the gross income and consumption profiles it is associated with. Fourth, it is only implementable as a truthful mechanism in weakly dominant strategies when both gross income and time worked are observable and

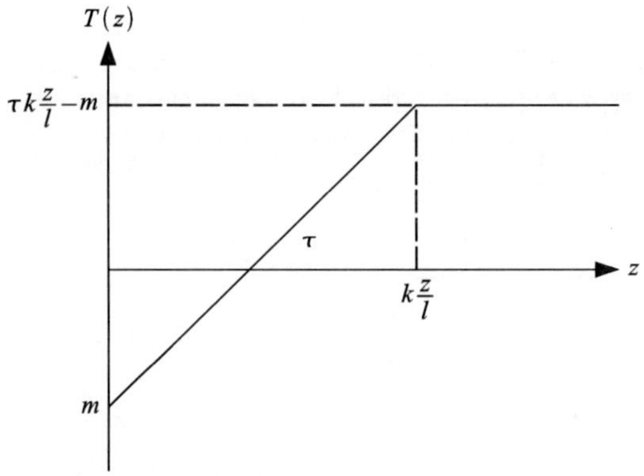

Fig. 5 Overtime exemption flat tax

verifiable. Because we believe that non-verifiability of time worked is a key feature of brainwork occupations, it seems to us that the implementation issue must be fully addressed. A simple method has been proposed when there are only two skill levels so as to obtain the first-best transfers of ELIE in a second-best world in which time worked is not verifiable. This method constitutes the first step of a more complete investigation of the implementation issue for a larger number of types that is carried out in a companion article (see Simula and Trannoy 2011).

More generally, it seems to us that the endogeneity condition included in the definition of ELIE raises difficulties. For instance, it is argued by Kolm that, under ELIE, individuals benefit from a basic income $k\mathbf{E}[\theta]$ (see Kolm 2011, p. 111). Because a basic income is by definition the income received by an individual who is not working, this assertion seems problematic, at least for the more productive part of the population. For this reason, it may be promising to study an income tax schedule that combines a flat tax at rate τ with an exemption for overtime labour. If m denotes the basic income, this "overtime exemption flat tax schedule" is defined by setting

$$T(z, \ell; \tau, k) = \tau \min\left\{z, k\frac{z}{\ell}\right\} - m. \tag{58}$$

This tax schedule allows us to distinguish two regimes depending on whether an individual has earnings below or above a threshold income. This threshold corresponds to the earnings of an individual who works k hours at his apparent productivity z/ℓ. It is obviously supposed that both gross income and time worked are verifiable. When the labour income is smaller than this level, the tax formula reduces to a regular flat tax; when the labour income is higher, the tax liability is capped by the threshold, as shown in Fig. 5. This overtime exemption flat tax is incentive compatible provided that τ is less than 1. A more thorough study of such a tax schedule is left for future research.

Acknowledgements Very helpful comments from Serge-Christophe Kolm, Antoine d'Autume, Gareth Myles, two anonymous referees and, in particular, the co-editor, John Weymark, are gratefully acknowledged. We have also benefited from discussions with the participants in the Conference on Social Ethics and Normative Economics held in honour of Serge-Christophe Kolm at the University of Caen, May 2007, in the Public Economics Seminar of CES–Paris 1 and ENS Cachan, and in the Economics Seminar of the University of Verona. The usual caveat applies.

References

Allen, R. G. D. (1934). A comparison between different definitions of complementary and competitive goods. *Econometrica, 2*, 168–175.

Auspitz, R., & Lieben, R. (1889). *Untersuchungen über die theorie des preises*. Leipzig: Verlag von Duncker und Humbolt

Cowell, F. A. (1990). *Cheating the government: The economics of evasion*. Cambridge, MA: MIT Press

Dasgupta, P., & Hammond, P. J. (1980). Fully progressive taxation. *Journal of Public Economics, 13*, 141–154

Edgeworth, F. Y. (1925). The pure theory of monopoly. In *Papers relating to political economy*, (Vol. I, pp. 111–142). London: Macmillan

Fleurbaey, M., & Maniquet, F. (2011). Kolm's tax, tax credit, and the flat tax. In M. Fleurbaey, M. Salles, & J. A. Weymark (Eds.), *Social ethics and normative economics: Essays in honour of Serge-Christophe Kolm* (pp. 217–239). Berlin: Springer

Godet, M. (2007). *Le courage du bon sens: Pour construire l'avenir autrement*. Paris: Odile Jacob

Kolm, S.-C. (2004). *Macrojustice: The political economy of fairness*. Cambridge: Cambridge University Press

Kolm, S.-C. (2011). Economic macrojustice: Fair optimum income distribution, taxation and transfers. In C. Gamel & M. Lubrano (Eds.), *On Kolm's theory of macrojustice: A pluridisciplinary forum of exchange* (pp. 69–130). Berlin: Springer

Laffont, J.-J., & Martimort, D. (2002). *The theory of incentives: The principal-agent model*. Princeton: Princeton University Press

Mirrlees, J. A. (1971). An exploration in the theory of optimum income taxation. *Review of Economic Studies, 38*, 175–208

Mirrlees, J. A. (1974). Notes on welfare economics, information and uncertainty. In M. Balch, D. McFadden, & S.-Y. Wu (Eds.), *Essays in economic behavior under uncertainty* (pp. 243–258). Amsterdam: North-Holland

Mirrlees, J. A. (1986). The theory of optimal taxation. In K. J. Arrow & M. D. Intriligator (Eds.), *Handbook of mathematical economics* (Vol. III, pp. 1197–1249). Amsterdam: North-Holland

Mirrlees, J. A. (1997). Information and incentives: The economics of carrots and sticks. *Economic Journal, 107*, 1311–1329

Pareto, V. (1906). *Manuele di economia politica, con una introduzione alla scienza sociale*. Milan: Società Editrice Libraria

Simula, L., & Trannoy, A. (2011). An exploration of incentive-compatible ELIE transfers. In C. Gamel & M. Lubrano (Eds.), *On Kolm's theory of macrojustice: A pluridisciplinary forum of exchange* (pp. 207–231). Berlin: Springer

Kolm's Tax, Tax Credit, and the Flat Tax

Marc Fleurbaey and François Maniquet

1 Introduction

In several of his recent contributions, most notably Kolm (2004), Serge-Christophe Kolm has developed a solution to the macro-justice problem which he calls Equal Labor Income Equalization (ELIE). It consists in a particular labor income taxation scheme that he advocates as the ideal compromise between freedom and equality requirements.

The ELIE proposal is, in essence, a first-best taxation scheme involving a parameter, k, which can be thought of as being the share of every individual's labor time which is equally shared within society. At an ELIE allocation, earning ability is taxed in such a way that the net income an individual would get should he choose to work precisely k is equalized among individuals. If an individual's earning ability is s, he pays the tax ks and receives a universal grant g. Therefore, if he works exactly k at the wage rate s, his net income is g, independently of s. Individuals choosing to work more than k are paid marginally at their wage rate; that is, the marginal tax on earnings is zero. Individuals choosing to work less than k have to "buy" their leisure, and have to do so at its marginal value as well.

Implementing the ELIE scheme requires the earning ability of each individual to be observable. If the earning ability is not observable, then Kolm's proposal needs to be adapted into a second-best version. This is what we study in this article.

In order to refine the ELIE scheme for the second-best context, we will begin by defining a social ordering function compatible with ELIE. A social ordering function defines a complete ranking of the set of allocations for each profile of the population characteristics. The social ordering function, which we define below and which

M. Fleurbaey (✉)
CNRS and CERSES, Université Paris-Descartes, 45 rue des Saints-Pères, 75006 Paris, France
e-mail: marc.fleurbaey@parisdescartes.fr

F. Maniquet
CORE, Université Catholique de Louvain, 34 Voie du Roman Pays, 1348 Louvain-la-Neuve, Belgium
e-mail: francois.maniquet@uclouvain.be

M. Fleurbaey et al. (eds.), *Social Ethics and Normative Economics*, Studies in Choice and Welfare, DOI 10.1007/978-3-642-17807-8_9,

we axiomatize, rationalizes ELIE in the sense that the ELIE allocations maximize the social ordering function in the special case in which the information is complete. Moreover, we believe it incorporates the basic fairness principles underlying ELIE and thereby extends the thrust of the ELIE idea to the comparison of arbitrary allocations.

Then, we use this social ordering function to derive taxation schemes under different information settings. First, we look at the case in which the earning ability cannot be observed but incomes and labor times are observable. Consequently, the wage rate can be deduced from the observables, but individuals may still decide to take jobs at wage rates lower than their actual earning ability. This is the same informational framework as in Dasgupta and Hammond (1980). We prove that under certain conditions, the resulting taxation scheme is similar to Kolm's proposal regarding incomes earned by individuals working more than k, but differs substantially for the other individuals.

Second, we look at the case in which only income, but not labor time nor the wage rate, is observable. This is the typical case considered in the optimal income taxation literature, following Mirrlees (1971). We derive some insights about the optimal income tax scheme, in particular that taxation of incomes at a constant marginal tax rate equal to k appears as an important benchmark. We therefore establish a surprising connection between ELIE and the flat tax.

This connection is loose, however, for low incomes. Indeed, we also show that in both of the informational contexts studied here, one feature of the first-best version of ELIE is preserved at the optimal second-best tax: low incomes up to the lowest earning ability should have a marginal tax of zero. This is a notable result in the light of recent reforms of the welfare state in which efforts have been made to reduce the marginal tax on low incomes.[1]

A related analysis is made by Simula and Trannoy (2011), who observe that if all individuals work more than k at the ELIE first-best allocation, then ELIE is incentive-compatible when labor time is observable. For the case in which only income is observable, they suggest seeking an incentive-compatible allocation that is as close as possible to ELIE. There are three main differences with our approach. First, we study economies with heterogeneity in skills and preferences, whereas Simula and Trannoy examine economies with heterogeneity in skills only. Second, we use a different social welfare function (more specifically a different social ordering function), to which we give axiomatic foundations. Third, we do not restrict attention to situations in which all individuals work more than k. When some individuals work less than k, the first-best ELIE allocation is not always incentive-compatible even when labor time is observable, as we will show below.

In Sect. 2, we present the model and define our social ordering function. In Sect. 3, we provide an axiomatic justification for it. In Sect. 4, we study the optimal tax scheme when both labor times and incomes are observable. In Sect. 5, we

[1] This practical evolution has already found echoes in economic theory. See, e.g., Choné and Laroque (2005), Boadway, Marchand, Pestieau, and del Mar Racionero (2002), and Fleurbaey and Maniquet (2006, 2007).

examine the optimal tax scheme when only incomes are observable. Section 6 offers concluding comments.

2 The Model

Our model is identical to the one Kolm used to develop his ELIE proposal. This model was introduced in the axiomatic literature on fairness by Pazner and Schmeidler (1974). It generalizes the model of Mirrlees (1971) by allowing individuals to have different preferences, not only different earning abilities. There are two goods, labor time (l) and consumption (c). The population of an economy is finite. If the set of individuals in an economy is N, each individual $i \in N$ has a *production skill* $s_i \geq 0$, which enables him to produce the quantity $s_i l_i$ of the consumption good with labor time l_i. This individual can also choose to work at a lower productivity (wage rate) $w_i \leq s_i$, in which case his earnings are equal to $w_i l_i$. Individual i also has *preferences* represented by an ordering R_i over bundles $z_i = (l_i, c_i)$, where $0 \leq l_i \leq 1$ and $c_i \geq 0$. Let $X = [0,1] \times \mathbb{R}_+$ denote an individual's labor-consumption set. We assume that the wage rate w_i does not directly affect an individual's satisfaction.

We study the domain $\mathscr{E}$ of economies defined as follows. Let $\mathscr{N}$ denote the set of non-empty finite subsets of the set of positive integers $\mathbb{N}_+$ and $\mathscr{R}$ denote the set of continuous, convex, and strictly monotonic (negatively in labor, positively in consumption) orderings over X. An *economy* $e = (s_N, R_N)$ belongs to the domain $\mathscr{E}$ if $N \in \mathscr{N}$, $s_N \in \mathbb{R}_+^N$, and $R_N \in \mathscr{R}^N$; that is,

$$\mathscr{E} = \bigcup_{N \in \mathscr{N}} (\mathbb{R}_+^N \times \mathscr{R}^N).$$

Let $e = (s_N, R_N) \in \mathscr{E}$. An *allocation* is a vector $x_N = (w_i, z_i)_{i \in N} \in \mathbb{R}_+^N \times X^N$. It is *feasible* for e if $w_i \leq s_i$ for all $i \in N$ and

$$\sum_{i \in N} c_i \leq \sum_{i \in N} w_i l_i.$$

Because w_i does not affect i's satisfaction, we will generally restrict attention to bundle allocations $z_N = (z_i)_{i \in N} \in X^N$ in the context of social evaluation.[2] Bundle allocations will also be called allocations for short when there is no risk of confusion. Let $Z(e)$ be the subset of X^N for which $l_i = 0$ for all $i \in N$ such that $s_i = 0$. We will restrict attention to this subset, as it does not make sense in any first-best or second-best context to make an individual work when his productivity is nill. This restriction is useful because it simplifies the presentation of our social ordering.

[2] At the cost of heavier notation, we could always deal with allocations x_N and deduce from the Pareto principle the fact that only z_N really matters.

A *social ordering* for an economy $e = (s_N, R_N) \in \mathscr{E}$ is a complete ordering over the set $Z(e)$ of (bundle) allocations. A *social ordering function* (SOF) $\mathbf{R}$ associates a social ordering $\mathbf{R}(e)$ to each economy $e \in \mathscr{E}$. We write $z_N \, \mathbf{R}(e) \, z'_N$ to denote that allocation z_N is at least as good as z'_N in e. The corresponding strict social preference and social indifference relations are denoted $\mathbf{P}(e)$ and $\mathbf{I}(e)$, respectively. Following the social choice tradition initiated by Arrow (1951), we require a social ordering to rank all allocations in $Z(e)$, not just the feasible allocations.[3] We depart, however, from Arrow's legacy by letting the social ordering depend on s_N, not just on R_N. We do this because fairness principles may recommend treating individuals differently depending on their earning ability. As it turns out, this happens with ELIE.

Our next objective in this section is to define the social ordering function that we consider to be associated with Kolm's ELIE proposal. To do so requires introducing some terminology. Let $e = (s_N, R_N) \in \mathscr{E}$ and let $i \in N$. For $A \subseteq X$, let $m(R_i, A) \subseteq A$ denote the set of bundles (if any) that are the best in A for the preferences R_i; that is,

$$m(R_i, A) = \left\{z_i \in A \mid \forall z'_i \in A,\ z_i \, R_i \, z'_i\right\}.$$

For $z_i = (l_i, c_i) \in X$ and $s_i \in \mathbb{R}_+$, let $B(z_i, s_i) \subseteq X$ denote the *budget set* obtained with s_i for which z_i is on the budget frontier:

$$B(z_i, s_i) = \{(l'_i, c'_i) \in X \mid c'_i - s_i l'_i \leq c_i - s_i l_i\}.$$

In the special case in which $s_i = 0$ and $c_i = 0$, we adopt the convention that

$$B(z_i, s_i) = \{(l'_i, c'_i) \in X \mid c'_i = 0,\ l'_i \geq l_i\}.$$

Let ∂B denote the upper frontier of the set B. Also, let $IB(z_i, s_i, R_i) \subseteq X$ denote the *implicit budget* at z_i, which is defined to be the budget set with slope s_i having the property that i is indifferent between z_i and his preferred bundle in that budget set:

$$IB(z_i, s_i, R_i) = B(z'_i, s_i) \text{ for any } z'_i \text{ such that } z'_i \, I_i \, z_i \text{ and } z'_i \in m(R_i, B(z'_i, s_i)).$$

By the strict monotonicity of preferences, this definition is unambiguous. See Fig. 1 for an illustration of this construction. Notice that the bundle z_i need not belong to the implicit budget. Also note that implicit budgets provide a set representation of the preferences of individual i in e in the sense that

$$z_i \, R_i \, z'_i \Leftrightarrow IB(z_i, s_i, R_i) \supseteq IB(z'_i, s_i, R_i).$$

[3] Although we think that it is less justified, we could have restricted the definition of a social ordering function to feasible allocations and still derive the same results.

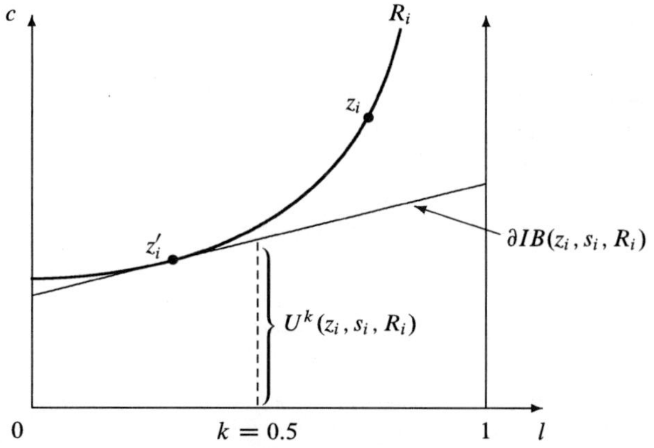

Fig. 1 Implicit budget and utility function

We are now equipped to define the SOFs that will be used in the subsequent discussion. We consider a family of SOFs, parameterized by a coefficient $k \in [0, 1]$. For each $k \in [0, 1]$, the corresponding SOF will be denoted $\mathbf{R}^k$. Each SOF in the family is based on a specific utility representation of the preferences, and it compares allocations by applying the leximin aggregation rule to the utility vectors derived from these numerical representations.

Assuming that a parameter $k \in [0, 1]$ has been chosen, let us begin by defining the utility functions. Let $e = (s_N, R_N) \in \mathcal{E}$ and let $i \in N$. The utility function $U^k(\cdot, s_i, R_i)$ is constructed as follows: $U^k(z_i, s_i, R_i)$ is the vertical coordinate of the bundle with abscissa k on the frontier of the implicit budget of individual i at z_i. Formally,

$$U^k(z_i, s_i, R_i) = u \Leftrightarrow (k, u) \in \partial IB(z_i, s_i, R_i).$$

This construction is illustrated in Fig. 1 for the case $k = 0.5$. Observe that this construction works only for bundles such that $(k, 0) \in IB(z_i, s_i, R_i)$ when $s_i > 0$. Let $Y^k(e)$ denote the subset of $Z(e)$ for which this condition is satisfied for all $i \in N$.

Such utility indexes depend on k and also on s_i, not just on R_i. This dependence is justified by the fact that the philosophy of ELIE is not welfarist. These utility indexes in fact measure how well-off an individual is in terms of budget opportunities, not in terms of subjective satisfaction or happiness. Even though these indexes are ordinally consistent with each individual's preferences, the interpersonal comparisons they generate are basically resourcist, not welfarist. Moreover, the principles underlying ELIE stipulate that individuals are partly (depending on k) entitled to enjoy the benefits of their own productivity, so it is normal for the corresponding indexes to be sensitive to k and to individual skills. It must be emphasized that the axiomatic justification that is offered in the next section provides a joint derivation of the social aggregation rule and of these utility indexes from basic principles.

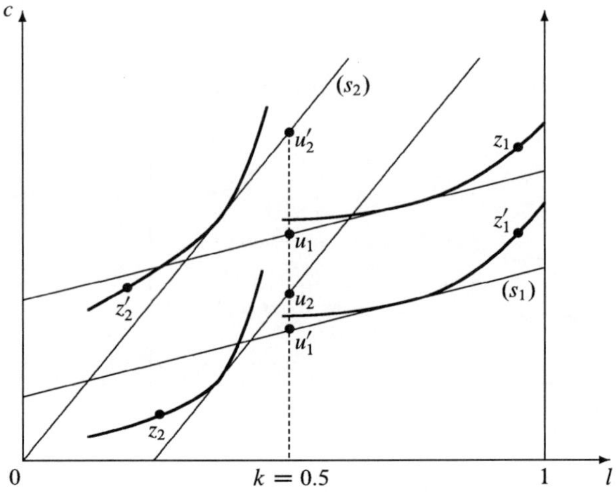

Fig. 2 Illustration of the k-Leximin social ordering function (SOF)

The social ordering $\mathbf{R}^k(e)$ on $Y^k(e)$ is obtained by applying the leximin criterion to vectors of U^k utility levels. The definition of the leximin criterion is the following. For two vectors of real numbers u_N, u'_N, one says that u_N is weakly better than u'_N for the leximin criterion, which will be denoted here by

$$u_N \geq_{lex} u'_N,$$

when the smallest component of u_N is not lower than the smallest component of u'_N, and if they are equal, the second smallest component is not lower, and so forth.

k-Leximin ($\mathbf{R}^k$). For all $e = (s_N, R_N) \in \mathscr{E}$ and all $z_N, z'_N \in Y^k(e)$,

$$z_N \, \mathbf{R}^k(e) \, z'_N \Leftrightarrow u_N \geq_{lex} u'_N,$$

where, for all $i \in N$, $u_i = U^k(z_i, s_i, R_i)$ and $u'_i = U^k(z'_i, s_i, R_i)$.

This SOF is illustrated in Fig. 2 for a two-individual economy $e = ((s_1, s_2), (R_1, R_2)) \in \mathscr{E}$. We see in the figure that $s_1 < s_2$ and that the preferences R_1 are less leisure oriented preferences than R_2. The allocations $z_N = (z_1, z_2)$ and $z'_N = (z'_1, z'_2)$ have to be compared. First, the implicit budgets associated with the four bundles are identified. Then, on the frontier of each budget, the bundle with abscissa k is identified. The vertical coordinates of these bundles are denoted by u_1, u_2, u'_1, and u'_2 in the figure (corresponding respectively to $U^{0.5}(z_1, s_1, R_1)$, $U^{0.5}(z_2, s_2, R_2)$, $U^{0.5}(z'_1, s_1, R_1)$, and $U^{0.5}(z'_2, s_2, R_2)$). We observe that $u'_1 < u_2 < u_1 < u'_2$. These inequalities imply that $z_N \, \mathbf{P}^{0.5}(e) \, z'_N$.

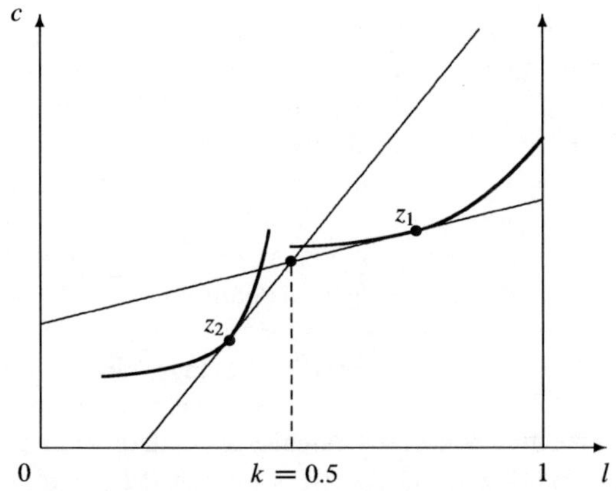

Fig. 3 First-best allocation for k-Leximin

We do not study the extension of $\mathbf{R}^k(e)$ to $Z(e) \setminus Y^k(e)$, as this is of little consequence for the study of taxation. It is easy to find reasonable extensions. For instance, when $(k,0) \notin IB(z_i, s_i, R_i)$ and $s_i > 0$, one can define

$$U^k(z_i, s_i, R_i) = u \Leftrightarrow (k-u, 0) \in \partial IB(z_i, s_i, R_i),$$

which yields $u < 0$. With this extended definition of U^k, $\mathbf{R}^k$ satisfies the axioms introduced in the next section over $Z(e)$.

The aim of a SOF is to give precise policy recommendations as a function of the informational conditions describing the set of tools available to the policy maker. If the informational conditions are those of a first-best world, then maximizing the social ordering $\mathbf{R}^k(e)$ on the set of feasible allocations leads to the ELIE allocations corresponding to parameter k. Indeed, at a (first-best) Pareto-efficient allocation, one has $w_i = s_i$ and $B(z_i, s_i) = IB(z_i, s_i, R_i)$ for all $i \in N$. A best allocation for $\mathbf{R}^k(e)$ is such that, in addition, the U^k utility levels are equalized, which implies that all budget set frontiers cross at a bundle with abscissa k. An example is given in Fig. 3, for the same economy as above.

In the next section, we provide axiomatic foundations for this family of SOFs.

3 Axiomatic Foundations

The family of SOFs inspired by Kolm's ELIE proposal, which we call the k-Leximin SOFs, satisfy a set of axioms that we define in this section. We also show that every SOF satisfying this set of axioms must satisfy a maximin property, which makes the SOF close to a k-Leximin SOF. The material in this section draws on previous work in which we have provided a similar axiomatic characterization of a family of SOFs containing the $\mathbf{R}^k$.[4] We present a variant of that characterization here in order to highlight the relationship between the k-Leximin SOF on the one hand and Kolm's fairness principles and his justification of ELIE on the other.

We begin with the key axiom establishing this relationship. This axiom is consistent with Kolm's idea that incomes should be equal among individuals working k. Let $e = (s_N, R_N) \in \mathscr{E}$ and $z_N, z'_N \in Z(e)$. Assume that z_N and z'_N differ only in the bundles of two individuals, say $p, q \in N$, and that in both allocations, p and q each freely choose to work k in a budget set determined by a lump-sum transfer and his own skill level. Using the notation of the preceding section, it follows that for $j = p, q$, one has $l_j = l'_j = k, z_j \in m(R_j, B(z_j, s_j))$, and $z'_j \in m(R_j, B(z'_j, s_j))$. Assume, moreover, that p and q do not have the same consumption level in z_N, for instance, $c_p > c_q$. We then regard individual p as relatively richer than individual q. The social situation is not worsened, the axiom says, if $c_p > c'_p > c'_q > c_q$, so that the inequality in consumption between p and q is reduced in z'_N.[5]

k-Equal Labor Consumption Equalization. For all $e = (s_N, R_N) \in \mathscr{E}$, all $p, q \in N$, and all $z_N, z'_N \in Z(e)$ for which $z_i = z'_i$ for all $i \neq p, q$, if

(i) $l_p = l'_p = l_q = l'_q = k$;
(ii) $c_p > c'_p > c'_q > c_q$;
(iii) for all $j \in \{p, q\}, z_j \in m(R_j, B(z_j, s_j))$ and $z'_j \in m(R_j, B(z'_j, s_j))$,

then $z'_N \mathbf{R}(e) z_N$.

Our next axiom captures the idea that individuals should be held responsible for their preferences and that society should not treat them differently – which, in this context, means that it should not tax them differently – on the sole basis that they have different preferences. This idea is also an important tenet of Kolm's conception of fairness. Consequently, if two individuals have the same skill but possibly different preferences, then they should be given the same treatment, which we interpret as requiring the social evaluation to focus on the opportunities available to them rather than their particular choice of consumption and labor.

Consider two individuals p and q endowed with the same skill s and facing different budget sets $B(z_p, s)$ and $B(z_q, s)$. One set contains the other, so the corresponding individual can be regarded as being relatively richer than the other. Assume, now, that we permute their budget sets. By doing so, we may have increased or decreased the observed inequality in consumption or in labor time, depending on these individuals' preferences. Nevertheless, the axiom states that the

[4] See Fleurbaey and Maniquet (2005). For first-best allocation rules, see also Fleurbaey and Maniquet (1996) and Maniquet (1998).

[5] This kind of inequality reduction principle can be traced back to Hammond (1976, 1979). What is specific here is that it is applied to consumption rather than welfare, and for special amounts of labor.

resulting allocation is equally fair (or equally unfair) as the initial one, because the distribution of budget sets is unchanged.[6] Formally,

Budget Anonymity. For all $e = (s_N, R_N) \in \mathscr{E}$, all $p, q \in N$ for which $s_p = s_q$, and all $z_N, z'_N \in Z(e)$ for which $z_i = z'_i$ for all $i \neq p, q$, if

(i) $B(z'_p, s_p) = B(z_q, s_q)$ and $B(z'_q, s_q) = B(z_p, s_p)$;
(ii) for all $j \in \{p, q\}$, $z_j \in m(R_j, B(z_j, s_j))$ and $z'_j \in m(R_j, B(z'_j, s_j))$,

then $z'_N \, \mathbf{I}(e) \, z_N$.

The third axiom is the classical Strong Pareto axiom.

Strong Pareto. For all $e = (s_N, R_N) \in \mathscr{E}$ and all $z_N, z'_N \in Z(e)$, (i) if $z_i \, R_i \, z'_i$ for all $i \in N$, then $z_N \, \mathbf{R}(e) \, z'_N$ and (ii) if, in addition, $z_j \, P_j \, z'_j$ for some $j \in N$, then $z_N \, \mathbf{P}(e) \, z'_N$.

The last axiom is a separability condition. It states that when an individual has the same bundle in two allocations, the ranking of these two allocations should remain the same if this individual were simply absent from the economy. Let $|N|$ denote the cardinality of N.

Separation. For all $e = (s_N, R_N) \in \mathscr{E}$ with $|N| \geq 2$ and all $z_N, z'_N \in Z(e)$, if there exists a $j \in N$ such that $z_j = z'_j$, then

$$z_N \, \mathbf{R}(e) \, z'_N \Rightarrow z_{N \setminus \{j\}} \, \mathbf{R}(e') \, z'_{N \setminus \{j\}},$$

where $e' = (s_{N \setminus \{j\}}, R_{N \setminus \{j\}}) \in \mathscr{E}$.

As can be easily checked, the k-Leximin SOFs presented in the previous section satisfy our four axioms. Moreover, any SOF satisfying these axioms must rank allocations exactly like a k-Leximin SOF whenever the lowest levels of utility U^k differ in the allocations being compared.

Proposition 1. *For all $k \in [0, 1]$:*

(i) On $Z(e)$, the k-Leximin SOF satisfies k-Equal Labor Consumption Equalization, Budget Anonymity, Strong Pareto, and Separation.
(ii) If a SOF satisfies k-Equal Labor Consumption Equalization, Budget Anonymity, Strong Pareto, and Separation, then it satisfies the following property: for all $e = (s_N, R_N) \in \mathscr{E}$ and all $z_N, z'_N \in Y^k(e)$, if

$$\min_{i \in N} U^k(z_i, s_i, R_i) > \min_{i \in N} U^k(z'_i, s_i, R_i),$$

then $z_N \, \mathbf{P}(e) \, z'_N$.

The proof of (ii) is provided in the Appendix.

[6] We could as well formulate an axiom that requires inequality reduction in budget sets for agents with the same skill. The rest of the analysis would follow with little modification.

4 Second Best: Observable Labor Time

We now turn to second-best situations. In this section, we assume that the planner only observes earnings $w_i l_i$ and labor time l_i, so that she can deduce wage rates w_i, but she does not observe the individuals' earning abilities s_i. Any individual can choose to work at a lower wage rate than his maximum possible, $w_i < s_i$, if this is in his interest.[7] Observe that, in Fig. 4 (a variant of Fig. 3 with two more individuals), individual 2 would prefer to have individual 3's bundle rather than his own. It would be advantageous for him to work at the same wage rate as individual 3 because this would give him access to individual 3's bundle. Therefore, the ELIE first-best allocation is not, in general, incentive-compatible in this context.[8]

Because the wage rates w_i are (indirectly) observed, the planner can offer a tax function on earnings, $\tau_w \colon [0, w] \to \mathbb{R}$, that is specific to each value of w. Individual i will then choose w_i and (l_i, c_i) to maximize his satisfaction subject to the constraints that $w_i \leq s_i$ and $c_i \leq w_i l_i - \tau_{w_i}(w_i l_i)$. One can have $\tau_{w_i}(w_i l_i) < 0$, in which case the tax turns into a subsidy. When $c_i = w_i l_i - \tau_{w_i}(w_i l_i)$ for all $i \in N$, the allocation is feasible if and only if $\sum_{i \in N} \tau_{w_i}(w_i l_i) \geq 0$.

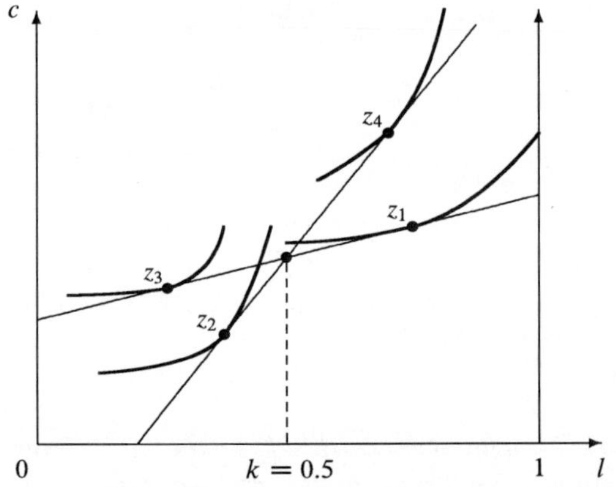

Fig. 4 An Equal labor income equalization (ELIE) allocation that is not incentive compatible

[7] Observe that the first-best ELIE allocation can be implemented when s_i is observable, even if individual preferences are private information.

[8] In anticipation of concepts to be introduced in this section, we may note that the allocation depicted in Fig. 3 is incentive-compatible because neither individual would want to mimic the other. But this allocation cannot be implemented by the menu of budget sets shown in Fig. 3 because individual 2 would like to be able to choose from individual 1's budget set and can work at $w_2 = s_1$ (in contrast, individual 1 is unable to work at $w_1 = s_2$). Another menu must be offered in order to implement the allocation (e.g., offer a menu such that for the two skill levels of these individuals, the post-tax budget set is the same and coincides with the intersection of the budget sets in the figure).

In this context, an *incentive-compatible* allocation $x_N = (w_N, z_N)$ is obtained when no individual envies the bundle of any other individual working at a wage rate he could earn: for all $i, j \in N$, if $s_i \geq w_j$, then $(l_i, c_i)\ R_i\ (l_j, c_j)$. This definition does not refer to tax menus, but there is a classical connection between incentive-compatibility and taxes which takes the following form in the current context. First, every allocation obtained by offering a menu $\{\tau_w\}$ and letting the individuals choose their wage rate and bundle subject to the skill constraint $w_i \leq s_i$ and the budget constraint $c_i \leq w_i l_i - \tau_{w_i}(w_i l_i)$ is incentive-compatible.

Conversely, every incentive-compatible allocation can be obtained by offering a menu of tax functions $\{\tau_w\}$ and letting the individuals choose their wage rate and bundle subject to the skill constraint $w_i \leq s_i$ and the budget constraint $c_i \leq w_i l_i - \tau_{w_i}(w_i l_i)$. For instance, the tax function τ_w can be defined so that the graph of $f_w(l) = wl - \tau_w(wl)$ in the (l, c)-space is the lower envelope of the indifference curves of all individuals i such that $w_i \geq w$. For future reference, let this menu of taxes be called the "envelope menu". Note the following fact: when $w > w'$, the set of individuals i for whom $w_i \geq w'$ contains the set of individuals for whom $w_i \geq w$, so that the lower envelope of the indifference curves of the former set is nowhere above the lower envelope for the latter set. In other words, the envelope menu $\{\tau_w\}$ satisfies the following "nesting property": for all $w > w'$ and all $l \in [0, 1]$, $wl - \tau_w(wl) \geq w'l - \tau_{w'}(w'l)$. In conclusion, every incentive-compatible allocation can be implemented by a tax menu $\{\tau_w\}$ satisfying the nesting property.

Because w_i does not affect i's satisfaction directly, it is inefficient to let him work at a wage $w_i < s_i$. Fortunately, it is always possible to replace an incentive-compatible allocation $x_N = (w_N, z_N)$ by another allocation $x'_N = (s_N, z_N)$ in which every individual works at his potential and obtains the same bundle as in x_N. This is possible because for all $i, j \in N$, $s_i \geq s_j$ implies $s_i \geq w_j$, so that if for all $i, j \in N$, $(l_i, c_i)\ R_i\ (l_j, c_j)$ whenever $s_i \geq w_j$, then one also has $(l_i, c_i)\ R_i\ (l_j, c_j)$ whenever $s_i \geq s_j$, which is equivalent to saying that x'_N is incentive-compatible. Therefore, from now on we will focus on bundle-allocations z_N and simply assume that $w_i = s_i$ for all $i \in N$.

Let us now fix $e = (s_N, R_N) \in \mathcal{E}$. Let $\underline{s}$ denote the lowest component in s_N. Our first result is that an optimal allocation for $\mathbf{R}^k(e)$ can be obtained by a menu $\{\tau_w\}$ such that the individuals with the lowest skill face a zero marginal tax. This result is obtained with the following assumption.

Restriction 1. For all $i \in N$, there exists a $j \in N$ such that $s_j = \underline{s}$ and $R_j = R_i$.

This restriction is quite natural for large populations. It is satisfied when preferences and skills are independently distributed, but it is much weaker than that.

Proposition 2. *Assume that earnings and labor times (but not skills) are observable. Let $e = (s_N, R_N) \in \mathcal{E}$ satisfy Restriction 1. Then, every second-best optimal allocation for $\mathbf{R}^k(e)$ can be obtained by a menu $\{\tau_w\}$ for which $\tau_{\underline{s}}$ is a non-positive constant-valued function.*

Proof. At a laissez-faire allocation, z^L_N, $U^k(z^L_i, s_i, R_i) = ks_i$ for all $i \in N$. Therefore, at this allocation, $\min_{i \in N} U^k(z^L_i, s_i, R_i) = k\underline{s}$.

Let z_N^* be an optimal allocation for $\mathbf{R}^k(e)$. The structure of the argument is the following. If z_N^* cannot be obtained by a menu $\{\tau_w\}$ for which $\tau_{\underline{s}}$ is a non-positive constant-valued function, then it is possible to define a new menu $\{\hat{\tau}_w\}$ for which $\hat{\tau}_{\underline{s}}$ is a non-positive constant-valued function, with a corresponding allocation $\hat{z}_N$ such that $\min_{i \in N} U^k(\hat{z}_i, s_i, R_i) \geq \min_{i \in N} U^k(z_i^*, s_i, R_i)$ and such that there is a budget surplus, which proves that z_N^* is not optimal (because the budget surplus can be redistributed so as to increase the welfare of all agents).

Because $z_N^* \, \mathbf{R}^k(e) \, z_N^L$, necessarily $\min_{i \in N} U^k(z_i^*, s_i, R_i) \geq k\underline{s}$. Let $\{\tau_w\}$ be the envelope menu implementing z_N^*. By construction, the graph of $f_{\underline{s}}(l) = \underline{s}l - \tau_{\underline{s}}(\underline{s}l)$ is the lower envelope of the indifference curves of all $i \in N$ at z_N^*. Consider now the lower envelope of the indifference curves of individuals $i \in N$ for which $s_i = \underline{s}$ and suppose that it lies above $f_{\underline{s}}(l)$ for some $l \in [0, 1]$. By Restriction 1, this implies that there are i, j such that $R_i = R_j$, $s_i = \underline{s}$, $s_j > \underline{s}$, and the indifference curve of i at z_i^* is above that of j at z_j^*, which contradicts incentive-compatibility. Therefore, the graph of $f_{\underline{s}}(l)$ is also the lower envelope of the indifference curves of the individuals $i \in N$ for which $s_i = \underline{s}$.

Let $a = \max \tau_{\underline{s}}$. One must have $a \leq 0$ for the following reason. For any individual $i \in N$,

$$U^k(z_i^*, s_i, R_i) = \min \{c - s_i l \mid (l, c) \, R_i \, z_i^*\} + k s_i.$$

Because the graph of $f_{\underline{s}}$ is the envelope curve of the indifference curves of the individuals i for which $s_i = \underline{s}$, necessarily there is one such i for whom

$$\min \{c - s_i l \mid (l, c) \, R_i \, z_i^*\} = -\max \tau_{\underline{s}}.$$

For this individual, then, $U^k(z_i^*, s_i, R_i) = -a + k\underline{s}$. Recall that $U^k(z_i^*, s_i, R_i) \geq k\underline{s}$. Therefore, $a \leq 0$.

Let $\hat{\tau}_{\underline{s}}(\underline{s}l) = a$ for all $l \in [0, 1]$. The menu $\{\tau_w \mid w > \underline{s}\} \cup \{\hat{\tau}_{\underline{s}}\}$ (i.e., $\hat{\tau}_{\underline{s}}$ replaces $\tau_{\underline{s}}$) still satisfies the nesting property. In every allocation $\hat{z}_N$ obtained with this new menu, all $i \in N$ for which $s_i = \underline{s}$ receive the subsidy $-a$ and have $U^k(\hat{z}_i, s_i, R_i) = -a + k\underline{s}$. For $i \in N$ for which $s_i > \underline{s}$, $U^k(\hat{z}_i, s_i, R_i) = U^k(z_i^*, s_i, R_i)$. Therefore, $\min_{i \in N} U^k(\hat{z}_i, s_i, R_i) \geq \min_{i \in N} U^k(z_i^*, s_i, R_i)$. Suppose that for some $i \in N$ for which $s_i = \underline{s}$, z_i^* is no longer in the budget set. This implies that $\tau_{\underline{s}}(s_i l_i^*) < a$ and that when choosing from the new menu, i gets a lower subsidy (namely, $-a$). If there is such an individual, then the new menu generates a budget surplus. This budget surplus can be redistributed so as to increase $\min_{i \in N} U^k(z_i^*, s_i, R_i)$, in contradiction to the assumption that z_N^* was optimal for $\mathbf{R}^k(e)$.[9] In conclusion, z_N^* must still be implementable with the new menu. □

[9] For the proof that a budget surplus always makes it possible to obtain another incentive-compatible allocation in which every individual is strictly better-off, see Fleurbaey and Maniquet (2006, Lemma 3).

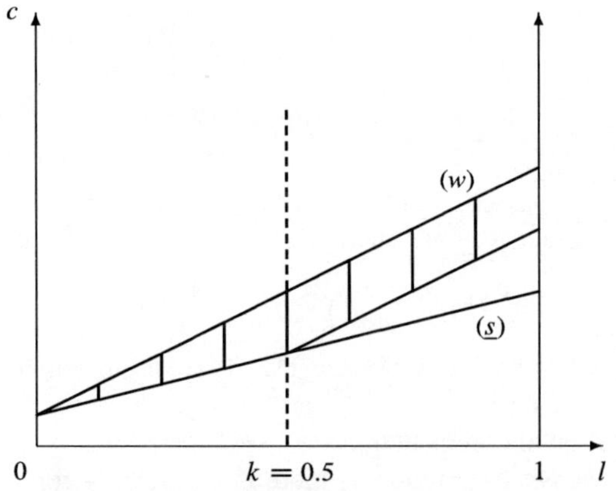

Fig. 5 The dashed area contains optimal budget curves for w

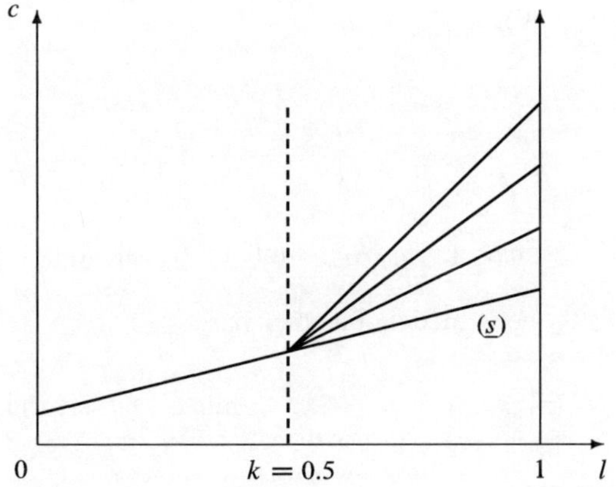

Fig. 6 Illustration of Proposition 3

By a similar argument, one can show that every optimal allocation can be obtained by a tax menu for which the graph of $f_w(l) = wl - \tau_w(wl)$ lies in the dashed area depicted in Fig. 5.

Our next result focuses on the case in which the lower bound of such areas is binding. Such a situation makes the configuration of budget lines the closest possible, given the incentive-compatibility constraints, to the first-best ELIE configuration that was shown in Figs. 3 and 5. This case is illustrated in Fig. 6.

Proposition 3. *Assume that earnings and labor times (but not skills) are observable. Let $e = (s_N, R_N) \in \mathcal{E}$ satisfy Restriction 1 and let $b \geq 0$. For each w, let τ_w be defined by: $\tau_w(wl) = (w - \underline{s})\, l - b$ for $l \leq k$ and $\tau_w(wl) = (w - \underline{s})\, k - b$ for $l \geq k$. If an allocation obtained with the menu $\{\tau_w\}$ is second-best Pareto-efficient, then it is second-best optimal for $\mathbf{R}^k(e)$.*

Proof. Let z_N^* be an allocation obtained with $\{\tau_w\}$. By construction, one has

$$\min_{i \in N} U^k(z_i^*, s_i, R_i) = b + k\underline{s}.$$

Assume that z_N^* is Pareto-efficient among all incentive-compatible feasible allocations. Let z_N be another feasible and incentive-compatible allocation for which for some $i \in N$,

$$U^k(z_i, s_i, R_i) > U^k(z_i^*, s_i, R_i).$$

This inequality implies that $z_i \; P_i \; z_i^*$. Because z_N^* is Pareto-efficient, there is another $j \in N$ for whom $z_j^* \; P_j \; z_j$.

Two cases must be distinguished.

Case 1: $l_j^* < k$. By Restriction 1, there is an $i_0 \in N$ for which $s_{i_0} = \underline{s}$ and $R_{i_0} = R_j$. Because $l_j^* < k$, z_j^* is in i_0's budget set (see Fig. 6) and $z_{i_0}^* \; I_{i_0} \; z_j^*$. The fact that $z_j^* \; P_j \; z_j$ and that, by incentive-compatibility, $z_j \; R_j \; z_{i_0}$ implies that $z_{i_0}^* \; P_{i_0} \; z_{i_0}$ or, equivalently,

$$U^k(z_{i_0}, s_{i_0}, R_{i_0}) < U^k(z_{i_0}^*, s_{i_0}, R_{i_0}).$$

Because $U^k(z_{i_0}^*, s_{i_0}, R_{i_0}) = b + k\underline{s} = \min_{i \in N} U^k(z_i^*, s_i, R_i)$, this inequality implies that

$$\min_{i \in N} U^k(z_i, s_i, R_i) < \min_{i \in N} U^k(z_i^*, s_i, R_i).$$

Case 2: $l_j^* \geq k$. By construction, one then has

$$U^k(z_j^*, s_j, R_j) = b + k\underline{s} = \min_{i \in N} U^k(z_i^*, s_i, R_i),$$

which again implies that

$$\min_{i \in N} U^k(z_i, s_i, R_i) < \min_{i \in N} U^k(z_i^*, s_i, R_i).$$

In conclusion, z_N cannot be better than z_N^* for $\mathbf{R}^k(e)$. □

This result may seem to have limited scope because it is generally unlikely that the menu $\{\tau_w\}$ as defined in the proposition generates a second-best efficient allocation. But one can safely conjecture that if the allocation obtained with this menu is not too inefficient, then the optimal tax menu is close to $\{\tau_w\}$. Note that for $k = 0$, this menu corresponds to the laissez-faire policy (one must then have $b = 0$), which yields an efficient allocation and is indeed optimal for $\mathbf{R}^0(e)$. The likelihood that the optimal menu is close to $\{\tau_w\}$ therefore increases as k gets smaller.

In practice, a menu like $\{\tau_w\}$ is easy to enforce (assuming that labor time or wage rates are observable), and one can then proceed to check if it generates large inefficiencies.

5 Second Best: Unobservable Labor Time

We now turn to a different second-best context in which we assume that the planner only observes earned incomes $y_i = w_i l_i$ and is unable to identify the individuals' wage rates, as in the classical literature following Mirrlees (1971). Therefore, redistribution is now made via a single tax function τ. Observe that, in this context, it is always best for every individual $i \in N$ to earn any given gross income by working at his maximal wage rate $w_i = s_i$ because with the tax only depending on y_i and not on w_i or l_i, doing so minimizes l_i for a fixed level of consumption. We can therefore focus on bundle-allocations z_N and simply assume that $w_i = s_i$ for all $i \in N$.

With this kind of redistribution, individual i's budget set is defined by (see the left-hand panel in Fig. 7):

$$B^{\tau}(s_i) = \{(l, c) \in X \mid c \leq s_i l - \tau(s_i l)\}.$$

It is convenient to focus on the earnings-consumption space in which the budget set is defined by (see the right-hand panel of Fig. 7; we retain the same notation B^{τ} as no confusion is possible):

$$B^{\tau}(s_i) = \{(y, c) \in [0, s_i] \times \mathbb{R}_+ \mid c \leq y - \tau(y)\}.$$

In the right-hand panel of Fig. 7, the indifference curve has been rescaled so that the choice of labor time in $[0, 1]$ is equivalent to a choice of earnings in $[0, s_i]$.

An incentive-compatible allocation z_N, in this context, is obtained when no individual envies the *earnings*-consumption bundle of any other individual earning a level of gross income that he could earn: for all $i, j \in N$, if $s_i \geq y_j$, then $(l_i, c_i)\, R_i\, (y_j/s_i, c_j)$.

Every allocation obtained by offering budget sets defined by a tax function τ is incentive-compatible. Conversely, every incentive-compatible allocation can be obtained by offering a tax function τ and letting every individual $i \in N$ choose his bundle in the budget set $B^{\tau}(s_i)$. For instance, the tax function τ can be defined

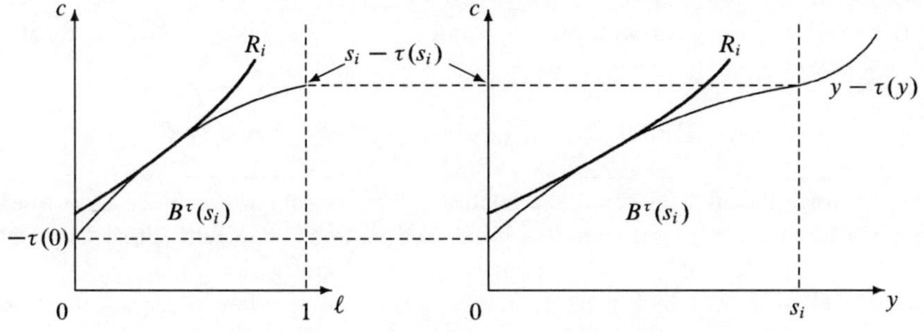

Fig. 7 Preferences over consumption-leisure and over consumption-earnings

so that the graph of $f(y) = y - \tau(y)$ in the (y, c)-space is the lower envelope of the indifference curves of all individuals in this space at the allocation under consideration.

For any $e = (s_N, R_N) \in \mathcal{E}$, let $S = \{s_i \mid i \in N\}$, $\underline{s} = \min S$, and $\overline{s} = \max S$. As in the previous section, our reasoning below does not require a specific number of individuals, but it is clear that we think of economies with a finite but large number of individuals. In particular, we will impose a restriction on the population of individuals so that the pre-tax income cannot be too informative a signal. According to this restriction, over any interval of earnings $[0, s]$, it is impossible by only looking at preferences over *earnings* and consumption restricted to that interval of earnings to identify individuals with greater productivity than s and to distinguish them, on the basis of their preferences, from individuals with productivity s.

Restriction 2. For all $i \in N$ and all $s \in S$ for which $s < s_i$, there exists a $j \in N$ such that $s_j = s$ and for all $(y, c), (y', c') \in [0, s] \times \mathbb{R}_+$:

$$\left(\frac{y}{s_j}, c\right) R_j \left(\frac{y'}{s_j}, c'\right) \Leftrightarrow \left(\frac{y}{s_i}, c\right) R_i \left(\frac{y'}{s_i}, c'\right).$$

Our next result is that with this restriction, the zero marginal tax result still holds for low-skilled individuals when labor time is unobservable.

Proposition 4. *Assume that only earnings are observable. Let* $e = (s_N, R_N) \in \mathcal{E}$ *satisfy Restriction 2. Then, every second-best optimal allocation for* $\mathbf{R}^k(e)$ *can be obtained by a tax function* τ *that is constant over* $[0, \underline{s}]$.

Proof. This proposition is a corollary of Theorem 3 in Fleurbaey and Maniquet (2007) because the preferences $\mathbf{R}^k(e)$ coincide with "Equivalent-Budget" social preferences (defined in that article) for reference preferences $\tilde{R}$ with indifference curves having cusps when $\ell = k$ and a marginal rate of substitution at any point $(l, c) \neq (k, c)$ that is lower than $\underline{s}$ if $l < k$ and greater than $\overline{s}$ if $l > k$. □

We now focus on a particular kind of tax function which satisfies this property, what will be called a *k-type tax*. It is defined as follows:

(i) for all $y \in [0, \underline{s}]$, $\tau(y) = \tau(0) \leq 0$;
(ii) for all $s, s' \in S$ for which $s < s'$ and $s < s_i < s'$ for no $i \in N$ and for all $y \in [s, s']$,

$$\tau(y) = \min\{\tau(0) + k(s - \underline{s}) + (y - s), \tau(0) + k(s' - \underline{s})\}.$$

This formula calls for some explanation. This tax function is piece-wise linear. For low incomes in the segment $[0, \underline{s}]$, the tax function is constant with a fixed subsidy of $-\tau(0)$. Then comes a segment $\left[\underline{s}, y^1\right]$ for some y^1 between $\underline{s}$ and the next element s^1 of S on which the rate of taxation is one hundred percent. Of course, no individual is expected to earn an income in this interval. The next segment is the interval $[y^1, s^1]$ on which there is a zero marginal tax rate. Then, the function continues with successive pairs of intervals, one with a one hundred percent marginal tax and the other with a zero marginal tax. The key feature of this tax function is that the points $(s, \tau(s))$, for $s \in S$, are colinear and the slope of this line is precisely k; that is, for all $s, s' \in S$,

$$\frac{\tau(s) - \tau(s')}{s - s'} = k.$$

When S is a large set with elements spread over the interval $[\underline{s}, \overline{s}]$, the tax function is therefore approximately a flat tax (constant marginal tax rate) except for the $[0, \underline{s}]$ interval on which it is constant.

The corresponding budget set, whose upper boundary is given by $y - \tau(y)$, is illustrated in Fig. 8, where the indifference curves of five individuals (rescaled so as to fit into (y, c)-space) are also depicted.

An interesting property of a k-type tax function τ is that for all $i \in N$, if i chooses a bundle that is on the segment with slope 1 (zero marginal tax) just below s_i, then

$$U^k(z_i, s_i, R_i) = -\tau(0) + k\underline{s}.$$

Let us prove this fact (called *Property P* for future reference) by focusing, for clarity but without loss of generality, on individual 4 in Fig. 8, assuming that $s_4 = s^2$. From the second term in the definition of τ, one has

$$\tau(y_4) = \tau(0) + k(s^2 - \underline{s}).$$

Bundle z_4 is optimal for R_4 in the budget set for which this level of tax is lump-sum. Therefore, one simply has

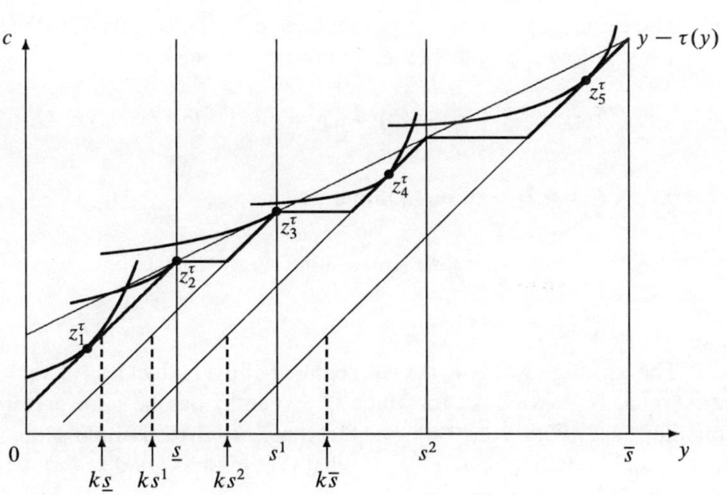

Fig. 8 Illustration of a k-type tax

$$U^k(z_4, s_4, R_4) = -\tau(y_4) + ks^2$$
$$= -\tau(0) + k\underline{s},$$

which shows that Property P holds. Note that the quantity $-\tau(0)+k\underline{s}$ is independent of s_i. This tax function therefore equalizes U^k across individuals who work full time or just below full time. This equality can be seen in Fig. 8 by observing that the vertical lengths at $k\underline{s}$, ks^1, ks^2, and $k\overline{s}$ between the horizontal axis and the lines of slope 1 corresponding to each of these values of s are all the same.

From Fig. 8, it is also clear that an individual who chooses a bundle on a lower segment of the budget set must have a greater implicit budget and, hence, that $-\tau(0) + k\underline{s}$ is a lower bound for $U^k(z_i, s_i, R_i)$ for all $i \in N$. Note that this lower bound is attained at least by all $i \in N$ for which $s_i = \underline{s}$. Therefore, every allocation z_N obtained with a k-type tax is such that $\min_{i \in N} U^k(z_i, s_i, R_i) = -\tau(0) + k\underline{s}$.

This observation is important in order to obtain the next result.

Proposition 5. *Assume that only earnings are observable. Let $e = (s_N, R_N) \in \mathcal{E}$ satisfy Restriction 2. If an allocation obtained with a k-type tax is second-best Pareto-efficient, then it is second-best optimal for $\mathbf{R}^k(e)$.*

Proof. Let z_N be an allocation obtained by a k-type tax function τ. The value of $\min_{i \in N} U^k(z_i, s_i, R_i)$ is $-\tau(0) + k\underline{s}$, as explained in the paragraph preceding the proposition. Assume that z_N is Pareto-efficient in the set of incentive-compatible feasible allocations.

Let z'_N be another feasible and incentive-compatible allocation (not necessarily obtained by a k-type tax function) for which not all individuals are indifferent between z_i and z'_i. By the Pareto-efficiency of z_N, there must be some $i \in N$ for which $z_i \ P_i \ z'_i$ or, equivalently, $U^k(z_i, s_i, R_i) > U^k(z'_i, s_i, R_i)$.

Two cases must be distinguished.

Case 1. The earnings y_i are on the last segment of i's budget set (i.e., the segment with slope 1 just below s_i). In this case, by Property P, one has

$$U^k(z_i, s_i, R_i) = -\tau(0) + k\underline{s} = \min_{i \in N} U^k(z_i, s_i, R_i),$$

so that $U^k(z_i, s_i, R_i) > U^k(z'_i, s_i, R_i)$ implies

$$\min_{i \in N} U^k(z_i, s_i, R_i) > \min_{i \in N} U^k(z'_i, s_i, R_i)$$

and, therefore, $z_N \ \mathbf{P}^k(e) \ z'_N$.

Case 2. The earnings y_i are on the last segment of the budget set for some $s < s_i$. By Restriction 2, there exists a j for which $s_j = s$ and j has the same preferences as i over bundles (y, c) with $y \in [0, s]$. The fact that $z_i \ P_i \ z'_i$ then implies that $z_j \ P_j \ z'_j$ because if j could obtain a bundle (y', c') that is at least as good as (y_j, c_j), then i could also have it. As a consequence,

$$U^k(z_j, s_j, R_j) = -\tau(0) + k\underline{s} > U^k(z'_j, s_j, R_j),$$

implying that

$$\min_{i \in N} U^k(z_i, s_i, R_i) > \min_{i \in N} U^k(z_i', s_i, R_i)$$

and, therefore, $z_N \, \mathbf{P}^k(e) \, z_N'$.

In conclusion, z_N is optimal for $\mathbf{R}^k(e)$. □

Determining the conditions under which a k-type tax is actually second-best Pareto-efficient is beyond the scope of this article. It is clear that this is more likely to be the case for low values of k. Let us, nevertheless, mention the example provided in Fleurbaey and Maniquet (1998) of a Pareto-efficient flat tax of 50% in a model of double heterogeneity with quasi-linear preferences and a uniform distribution of tastes.

Even if no allocation obtained with a k-type tax function is efficient, the k-type tax functions are nonetheless interesting benchmarks because of the property that individuals working full time have the minimum value of $U^k(z_i, s_i, R_i)$, whatever their skill. Because two different k-type tax functions (for the same k) define nested budget sets (one function always dominates the other), it is a valuable exercise to seek the lowest feasible k-type tax function, and we conjecture that the optimal tax function is often close to it for low values of k. (For $k = 0$, the lowest feasible k-type tax function is the laissez-faire policy $\tau \equiv 0$, which is optimal for $\mathbf{R}^0(e)$.)

6 Concluding Comments

Kolm's ELIE proposal strikes the imagination because it yields a simple configuration of budget sets. Such a configuration, however, is not compatible with incentives in general when individuals' potential earnings are not observable (even when, as Kolm assumes, labor time is observable). Our purpose in this article has been to extend the ELIE concept into a full social ordering that can serve to rank all allocations, and to examine the optimal tax that one derives from this ordering in the two prominent second-best contexts studied in the optimal taxation literature.

We have seen that one feature of the ELIE first-best configuration is preserved in the two second-best contexts studied here: the low-skilled individuals should face a zero marginal tax rate. This is a rather striking feature of a tax rule. It contrasts markedly with classical results obtained with standard social welfare functions in the optimal taxation literature when individuals are assumed to have the same preferences over labor and consumption and to differ only in their skills.[10] But it is consonant with recent reforms of income tax and income support institutions in countries like the United States and the United Kingdom.

Another, perhaps more surprising, result is the connection between ELIE and the flat tax proposal. For tax functions that depend only on total earnings (and do not depend on labor time or the wage rate), ELIE can be roughly summarized as "a zero

[10] See, e.g., Diamond (1998).

marginal tax up to the lowest wage and a constant marginal tax rate k beyond that". When the lowest wage rate is zero (for instance, because of unemployment), this description boils down to a flat tax at rate k.

A full description of the optimal tax has not been provided in this article because it is extremely difficult to provide a precise description of the set of feasible taxes in a model with multi-dimensional heterogeneity of individuals. This leaves opportunities for future research. But it may be worth stressing that the social ordering function proposed in this article can easily be used to evaluate any feasible allocation when the distribution of the population characteristics is known, and in previous works we have shown how to make evaluations directly from the budget set generated by the tax function.[11] This evaluation can be done as well with $\mathbf{R}^k$. For instance, in the framework of the previous section, one can evaluate an arbitrary tax function by seeking the lowest k-type tax function that lies nowhere below it. When political constraints make the optimal tax out of reach, this kind of criterion can serve to evaluate piecemeal reforms of suboptimal tax functions.

It is also possible to evaluate taxes in the case in which different industries or types of jobs display different informational constraints, so that for some individuals s_i is observable, for others only y_i and w_i (or l_i) are observable, and for the rest only y_i is observable. The evaluation then consists in computing the minimum of $U^k(z_i, s_i, R_i)$ for each category of individuals, using the results of this article, and then maximizing the smallest of these three values.

Acknowledgements We would like to thank participants in the conference organised in Caen in honor of Serge-Christophe Kolm and Serge Kolm himself for numerous stimulating discussions. This article has also benefited from comments by Maurice Salles, John Weymark, and a referee.

Appendix

In this Appendix, we prove Proposition 1.(ii). That is, we show that if a SOF satisfies k-Equal Labor Consumption Equalization, Budget Anonymity, Strong Pareto, and Separation, then it satisfies the following property: for all $e = (s_N, R_N) \in \mathscr{E}$ and all $z_N, z'_N \in Y^k(e)$, if

$$\min_{i \in N} U^k(z_i, s_i, R_i) > \min_{i \in N} U^k(z'_i, s_i, R_i),$$

then $z_N \, \mathbf{P}(e) \, z'_N$.

Step 1. We first prove that for all $e = (s_N, R_N) \in \mathscr{E}$, $p, q \in N$, and $z_N, z'_N \in Y^k(e)$ for which $z_i = z'_i$ for all $i \neq p, q$, if

$$U^k(z_p, s_p, R_p) < U^k(z'_p, s_p, R_p) < U^k(z'_q, s_q, R_q) < U^k(z_q, s_q, R_q),$$

[11] See Fleurbaey (2006) and Fleurbaey and Maniquet (2006).

then $z'_N\,\mathbf{R}(e)\,z_N$. Let $z^1_N, z^2_N \in Y^k(e)$ be defined as follows. For all $j \in \{p,q\}$: $z^1_j\, I_j\, z_j$, $z^2_j\, I_j\, z'_j$, $z^1_j \in IB(z_j, s_j, R_j)$, and $z^2_j \in IB(z'_j, s_j, R_j)$; whereas for all $j \notin \{p,q\}$: $z^1_j = z_j$ and $z^2_j = z'_j$. By Strong Pareto,

$$z_N\,\mathbf{I}(e)\,z^1_N \text{ and } z'_N\,\mathbf{I}(e)\,z^2_N.$$

We now define $M = \{a,b\} \in \mathcal{N}$ with $a, b \notin N$, $s_a = s_p$, $s_b = s_q$, and $R_a = R_b \in \mathcal{R}$ such that when facing budget sets with slope s_p and s_q, respectively, the two individuals in M choose a labor time equal to k. Let $z^1_a, z^1_b, z^2_a, z^2_b \in X$ be defined by

$$\begin{aligned} z^1_a &\in m(R_a, B(z^1_p, s_a)),\\ z^1_b &\in m(R_b, B(z^1_q, s_b)),\\ z^2_a &\in m(R_a, B(z^2_p, s_a)),\\ z^2_b &\in m(R_b, B(z^2_q, s_b)). \end{aligned}$$

We must prove that $z'_N\,\mathbf{R}(e)\,z_N$. On the contrary, assume that $z_N\,\mathbf{P}(e)\,z'_N$. Then, by Strong Pareto,

$$\left(z_{N\setminus\{p,q\}}, z^1_p, z^1_q\right)\mathbf{P}(e)\,(z'_{N\setminus\{p,q\}}, z^2_p, z^2_q).$$

By Separation,

$$\left(z_{N\setminus\{p,q\}}, z^1_p, z^1_q, z^2_a, z^2_b\right)\mathbf{P}(e')\,(z'_{N\setminus\{p,q\}}, z^2_p, z^2_q, z^2_a, z^2_b),$$

where $e' = ((s_N, s_a, s_b), (R_N, R_a, R_b))$.[12] By Budget Anonymity, swapping the budgets of individuals p and a, as well as those of q and b, one gets

$$(z_{N\setminus\{p,q\}}, z^2_p, z^2_q, z^1_a, z^1_b)\,\mathbf{I}(e')\,\left(z_{N\setminus\{p,q\}}, z^1_p, z^1_q, z^2_a, z^2_b\right).$$

Observe that $c^1_a < c^2_a < c^2_b < c^1_b$ and $\ell^1_a = \ell^2_a = \ell^1_b = \ell^2_b = k$. By k-Equal Labor Consumption Equalization,

$$(z_{N\setminus\{p,q\}}, z^2_p, z^2_q, z^2_a, z^2_b)\,\mathbf{R}(e')\,(z_{N\setminus\{p,q\}}, z^2_p, z^2_q, z^1_a, z^1_b).$$

---

[12] If z_N and z'_N are feasible, then so are z^1_N and z^2_N, but $\left(z_{N\setminus\{p,q\}}, z^1_p, z^1_q, z^2_a, z^2_b\right)$ and $(z'_{N\setminus\{p,q\}}, z^2_p, z^2_q, z^2_a, z^2_b)$ need not be. This is, therefore, where the proof needs to be changed if we want to restrict the definition of SOF to feasible allocations. But the required change is minor: an agent c should be added who has a sufficiently large skill, a sufficiently large labor time, and a sufficiently low consumption that the resulting allocation is feasible.

By transitivity, if we gather the above relations, we get

$$(z_{N\setminus\{p,q\}}, z_p^2, z_q^2, z_a^2, z_b^2)\, \mathbf{P}(e')\, (z'_{N\setminus\{p,q\}}, z_p^2, z_q^2, z_a^2, z_b^2),$$

an obvious contradiction.[13]

Step 2. Let $e = (s_N, R_N) \in \mathscr{E}$ and $z_N, z'_N \in Y^k(e)$. Assume that

$$\min_{i \in N} U^k(z_i, s_i, R_i) > \min_{i \in N} U^k(z'_i, s_i, R_i)$$

and $z'_N\, \mathbf{R}(e)\, z_N$. Choose $p \in N$ so that $U^k(z'_p, s_p, R_p) = \min_{i \in N} U^k(z'_i, s_i, R_i)$. Let $z_N^1 \in Y^k(e)$ be such that $U^k(z_p^1, s_p, R_p) = U^k(z'_p, s_p, R_p)$ and for all $j \in N \setminus \{p\}$,

$$U^k(z_j^1, s_j, R_j) > \max\left\{U^k(z_j, s_j, R_j), U^k(z'_j, s_j, R_j)\right\}.$$

By Strong Pareto, $z_N^1\, \mathbf{P}(e)\, z'_N$. Choose $z_N^2 \in Y^k(e)$ so that for all $j \in N \setminus \{p\}$,

$$\min_{i \in N} U^k(z_i, s_i, R_i) > U^k(z_j^2, s_j, R_j) > U^k(z_p^2, s_p, R_p) > U^k(z_p^1, s_p, R_p).$$

By an iterative application of Step 1, we can prove that $z_N^2\, \mathbf{R}(e)\, z_N^1$. That is, for each $j \in N \setminus \{p\}$, we apply the argument in Step 1 to individuals j and p, decreasing the index of j to $U^k(z_i^2, s_i, R_i)$ while at the same time slightly increasing that of individual p, calibrating such increases so that p's index reaches $U^k(z_p^2, s_p, R_p)$ when p is paired with the last individual from $N \setminus \{p\}$. By transitivity, we get $z_N^2\, \mathbf{P}(e)\, z_N$, contradicting Strong Pareto.

References

Arrow, K. J. (1951). *Social choice and individual values*. New York: Wiley.

Boadway, R., Marchand, M., Pestieau, P., & del Mar Racionero, M. (2002). Optimal redistribution with heterogeneous preferences for leisure. *Journal of Public Economic Theory*, *4*, 475–498.

Choné, P., & Laroque, G. (2005). Optimal incentives for labor force participation. *Journal of Public Economics*, *89*, 395–425.

Dasgupta, P., & Hammond, P. J. (1980). Fully progressive taxation. *Journal of Public Economics*, *13*, 141–154.

Diamond, P. A. (1998). Optimal income taxation: An example with a U-shaped pattern of optimal marginal tax rates. *American Economic Review*, *88*, 83–95.

Fleurbaey, M. (2006). Social welfare, priority to the worst-off and the dimensions of individual well-being. In F. Farina & E. Savaglio (Eds.), *Inequality and economic integration* (pp. 225–268). London: Routledge.

[13] Recall that $z_{N\setminus\{p,q\}} = z'_{N\setminus\{p,q\}}$.

Fleurbaey, M., & Maniquet, F. (1996). Fair allocation with unequal production skills: The no-envy approach to compensation. *Mathematical Social Sciences*, *32*, 71–93.

Fleurbaey, M., & Maniquet, F. (1998). Optimal income taxation: An ordinal approach. Discussion Paper No. 9865, CORE, Université Catholique de Louvain.

Fleurbaey, M., & Maniquet, F. (2005). Fair orderings with unequal production skills. *Social Choice and Welfare*, *24*, 93–128.

Fleurbaey, M., & Maniquet, F. (2006). Fair income tax. *Review of Economic Studies*, *73*, 55–83.

Fleurbaey, M., & Maniquet, F. (2007). Help the low-skilled or let the hardworking thrive? A study of fairness in optimal income taxation. *Journal of Public Economic Theory*, *9*, 467–500.

Hammond, P. J. (1976). Equity, Arrow's conditions, and Rawls' difference principle. *Econometrica*, *44*, 793–804.

Hammond, P. J. (1979). Equity in two-person situations. *Econometrica*, *47*, 1127–1136.

Kolm, S.-C. (2004). *Macrojustice: The political economy of fairness*. Cambrdige: Cambridge University Press.

Maniquet, F. (1998). An equal-right solution to the compensation-responsibility dilemma. *Mathematical Social Sciences*, *35*, 185–202.

Mirrlees, J. A. (1971). An exploration in the theory of optimum income taxation. *Review of Economic Studies*, *38*, 175–208.

Pazner, E., & Schmeidler, D. (1974). A difficulty in the concept of fairness. *Review of Economic Studies*, *41*, 441–443.

Simula, L., & Trannoy, A. (2011). When Kolm meets Mirrlees: ELIE. In M. Fleurbaey, M. Salles, & J. A. Weymark (Eds.), *Social ethics and normative economics: Essays in honour of Serge-Christophe Kolm* (pp. 193–216). Berlin: Springer.

Positional Equity and Equal Sacrifice: Design Principles for an EU-Wide Income Tax?

Peter J. Lambert

1 Introduction

The prospect – or, in the UK at least, the spectre – of an EU income tax occasionally looms, both in the popular press and also in the European Parliament. To whit, consider the old headline "Now Britain faces single European tax system: France and Germany spearhead plan to control revenue and social security" in *The Independent* newspaper of 16th January 1997, and the article, nine years on, entitled "Now EU wants a £510 income tax" in *The Daily Express* newspaper of December 31st 2006, which was prompted, no doubt, by the opinion expressed at a recent EU summit by M. Jose Maria Gil-Robles, President of the European Parliament, that "the direct taxation of the people would more closely involve individual citizens with the European government." A certain UK web blogger noted, in reaction to this news, "Oh Brilliant. We already shell out billions of pounds for an organisation we don't want to be in as well as having to put up with stupid laws that they shove on us .... When will it end? If they do manage to get a European income tax I will refuse to pay it. Even if it means jail time." It is worth noting, however, that economists do not, as yet at any rate, advocate an EU-wide income tax.[1]

[1]See, e.g., Cnossen (2002) on this issue. An exception of sorts is provided by Atkinson (2002), where an EU-wide income tax to fund the Official Development Assistance (ODA) to the tune of 1% of EU gross national product is proposed. The total EU GNP in 2002 amounted to €10,000 billion (using the American definition of a billion as a thousand million). The implied €100 billion in ODA would have been more than double the existing level, and still only account for one third of the value of spending on agricultural subsidies. Atkinson proposed that each EU country's tax base for a flat rate levy would comprise household disposable incomes in excess of a threshold set at 60% of the EU median per household, adjusted for family size and differences in purchasing power. Atkinson did not specify how each EU country's tax bill should be distributed across households, however. The design of a putative EU income tax, at the household or individual level, is the focus of the present article. We return to Atkinson's proposal later.

P.J. Lambert
Department of Economics, University of Oregon, Eugene, OR 97403-1285, USA
e-mail: plambert@uoregon.edu

M. Fleurbaey et al. (eds.), *Social Ethics and Normative Economics*, Studies in Choice and Welfare, DOI 10.1007/978-3-642-17807-8_10,

In this article, we consider the putative introduction of an EU-wide layer of income tax, additional to the national income taxes of the Member States, whose revenue would go directly to the center. The tax would be levied on disposable income in each country, i.e., on income net of domestic income tax. One can imagine the new tax being levied at a universal flat rate on all disposable incomes throughout the EU in order not to interfere with relative income differentials between and within countries. It is a small leap from there to suppose that a concessionary rate for the poorest countries might be instituted, and another small leap to a plethora of flat rates, negotiated country-by-country by the politicians, and perhaps to the introduction of progression.

For systematic analysis, the question of an EU-wide social welfare function (henceforth, SWF) arises, in which a person's domicile may or may not be a relevant factor. However, as shown by Cubel and Lambert (2002a,b), if domicile is not relevant to social welfare, and a common income tax were devised, applicable in all countries, then both overall welfare and inequality could potentially be improved by allowing an element of differentiation into this tax – thereby, at least on the face of it, admitting horizontal inequity.[2]

If allowance is made for differences in the taxable capacities of citizens of the different Member States, then of course horizontal inequity does not automatically follow from different within-country tax treatments. Recent research shows that, depending on the mechanism that identifies the equals across countries, an extended equal treatment characteristic, that of equal progression among equals, which could be said to supplement both the vertical and horizontal aspects, may also be achievable – alongside both vertical equity and classical horizontal equity (see Ebert and Lambert 2004).

How should we identify the equals across the EU countries? Ought we to admit of differences in need or social desert based on domicile? As between an income unit in Luxembourg having €20,000 p.a. net of domestic tax and an income unit in Latvia also having €20,000 p.a. net of domestic tax, which is socially the more deserving of an additional euro? Arguably the one in Luxembourg suffers more relative deprivation than the one in Latvia, being further down its country-specific distribution of living standards (see Runciman 1966); but would this merit a more lenient income tax in Luxembourg? Does not one's intuition go the other way? There is an interesting issue here for income tax design.

In what follows, we explore the possibilities for equitable income taxation across EU member countries under the assumption that *the equals in the different countries are those at the same percentile points in their within-country net income distributions*, and under the additional assumption that the within-country net income distributions differ in logarithms only by location and scale – as would be the case,

---

[2] In the case of proportional taxes, for a group of countries that can be divided into poorer and richer subgroups in a specific sense (see Cubel and Lambert 2002a,b), relative to taxing everybody at a common flat rate, vertical equity is enhanced by taxing people in the poorer subgroup at a lower flat rate and in the richer subgroup of countries at a higher flat rate.

for example, in a world of lognormal income distributions.[3] Clearly this "positional" method of identifying the equals, which has echoes of Roemer's (1998) argument that those who supply equivalent effort are at the same percentile position in their respective distributions, would result in the different tax treatment of an income unit in Luxembourg having €20,000 p.a. net and an income unit in Latvia also having €20,000 p.a. net.[4] We shall be able to examine the appropriate differences in tax treatment of such income units shortly. Later, when the model has been fully developed, we shall broaden the question of redistribution within the EU, and consider how an EU income tax might evolve through time, and what the limitations of the positional approach may be.

The structure of this article is as follows. In Sect. 2, we explain the procedure for identifying the equals in different EU countries and define the appropriate criteria for both classical horizontal equity and an extended equity principle, equal progression among equals, in an EU-wide layer of income tax. In Sect. 3, we introduce the positional equity concept, and identify the criterion for achieving positional equity across the EU under the assumption that the member countries' income distributions differ in logarithms only by location and scale. In Sect. 4, we divert to briefly discuss equal sacrifice taxation when the social evaluation function takes a mixed utilitarian and rank-dependent form, in which case one's tax liability is a function of both one's income and one's percentile in the income distribution. In Sect. 5, we explore normative conditions under which the positionally equitable EU income tax could be regarded as engendering equal sacrifices within each EU country. Section 6 considers what such a tax system would look like in practice, while Sect. 7 contains some final remarks about the EU as a community of redistribution.

2 A Putative EU-Wide Income Tax: Equity Criteria

For simplicity, let us confine attention to two countries, A and B say, and let us assume that a person's domicile enters into the SWF as well as his or her net income level. Then, following Ebert's (2000) approach, set in the general context of social heterogeneity in a population, we may introduce an *equivalent income function* to conduct the business of identifying the equals across countries in terms of their living standards. For country A, we express the living standard in terms of net money income. For country B, a function $S: \mathbb{R}_+ \to \mathbb{R}_+$ is invoked, to express as $S(x)$ the equivalent living standard in country A of a citizen of country B who has a

[3] These assumptions were articulated in Lambert (2004b) and briefly explored there.

[4] See Roemer (2006, p. 235) for a nice encapsulation: "In measuring an individual's effort, we should attempt to sterilize out that aspect of effort which is attributable to circumstance. A simple way of doing so is to identify an individual's degree of effort with the quantile which he or she occupies on the distribution of advantage of his or her type." In the present context, we can think of positional equity in terms of "sterilizing out" the effects of circumstance qua birthplace/domicile from peoples' fortunes.

nominal net income level of x. The function $S(x)$ need only be continuous and strictly increasing (Ebert 2000). For $n > 2$ countries, say A and $B_1, B_2, \ldots, B_{n-1}$, $n-1$ such functions would be needed.

A citizen of country A with net income x_A and a citizen of country B with net income x_B will be equals if and only if $S(x_B) = x_A$. Let the putative EU tax schedules for A and B be $t_A(x)$ and $t_B(x)$ respectively, and let

$$v_A(x) = x - t_A(x) \quad \text{and} \quad v_B(x) = x - t_B(x)$$

be the respective post-EU-tax income functions. If by equal treatment we mean that those with the same pre-EU-tax living standard should also have the same post-EU-tax living standard, which is the usual criterion for classical horizontal equity, this requires the following property:

$$S(x_B) = x_A \Rightarrow v_A(x_A) = S(v_B(x_B));$$

or writing x_B as x and substituting,

$$S(v_B(x)) = v_A(S(x)). \tag{1}$$

That is, the living standard after tax of a citizen of country B having x before the EU tax should be the same as that of a citizen of A having $S(x)$ before the EU tax.[5] Setting $t_A(x)$ as the "reference" tax schedule in country A, which can embody any chosen degree of vertical equity, $t_B(x)$ would have to be designed to satisfy (1) in order that both horizontal and vertical equity be achieved by the overall income tax.

The result of Ebert and Lambert (2004) already referred to shows that if the equivalent income function takes the isoelastic form

$$S(x) = \left(\frac{x}{b}\right)^a, \tag{2}$$

where $a > 0$ and $b > 0$ are constants, then when $t_B(x)$ is constructed so that the tax system $\{t_A(x), t_B(x)\}$ obeys (1), citizens of country B with a given pre-EU-tax living standard will face the same degree of progression as citizens of country A with that living standard. Thus, an extended concept of equity, *equal progression among equals*, is attainable in this case (and, in fact, in only the isoelastic case).[6]

[5] If, on the other hand, "equal treatment" means that pre-tax equals should experience equal average tax rates, the criterion would be $t_A(S(x))/S(x) = t_B(x)/x$. If equal treatment were taken to mean equal tax payments, then $t_A(S(x)) = t_B(x)$ would be the criterion. For more on these alternative criteria, see Lambert (2004a).

[6] See Ebert and Lambert (2004) for further details, and also Dardanoni and Lambert (2002). The progression measure is residual progression, defined for a schedule $t(x)$ as the elasticity of post-tax income $v(x) = x - t(x)$ with respect to pretax income, i.e., as $xv'(x)/v(x)$.

3 Lognormality and Positional Equity

It is perhaps an heroic assumption to make that country-specific net income distributions within the EU are all lognormal. In fact, for what follows, the EU member income distributions may belong to some other family of distributions which in logarithms differ only by location and scale – such as the Pareto and Singh-Maddala families, for example. Again restricting attention expositionally to the case of two countries A and B, under the location and scale assumption, an isoelastic function $x_A = S(x_B)$ exists that matches the incomes in A and B position by position.[7] Taking the equals in the different EU countries to be those at the same percentile points, (1) can be used to specify an EU-wide layer of additional income tax that both assures equal treatment by percentile in the classical sense and also equal progression by percentile.

Putting $S(x) = (x/b)^a$ from (2) into (1), and taking $t_A(x)$ as given, the following formula for $v_B(x)$ in terms of $v_A(x)$ results:

$$v_B(x) = b\left[v_A\left(\left(\frac{x}{b}\right)^a\right)\right]^{\frac{1}{a}}. \tag{3}$$

In one special case, that in which $t_A(x)$ is proportional, $v_A(x) = (1 - g_A)x$ say, it is clear from (3) that for equity, $t_B(x)$ should also be proportional:

$$v_B(x) = (1 - g_B)x, \quad g_B = 1 - (1 - g_A)^{1/a}. \tag{4}$$

An EU-wide layer of differentiated proportional tax surcharges could thus be supported as fully equitable if $a \neq 1$. Proportional EU taxes would have the advantage of not interfering with relative income differentials within countries. They would have to be differentiated to the extent that inequality differed between countries. In the lognormal case, the flat tax rate would have to be higher in more unequal countries, and lower in less unequal countries.[8]

Whatever tax schedule is selected for country A, proportional or not, so long as it expresses the desired degree of vertical equity in country A, the tax for B is dictated by the equity requirement in (3), and this guarantees not only equal treatment by percentile in the classical sense but also equal progression by percentile across countries.

[7] If $\ln(x_A) \sim N(\theta_A, \sigma_A^2)$ and $\ln(x_B) \sim N(\theta_B, \sigma_B^2)$ then, as the reader may verify, $S(x) = (x/b)^a$ matches incomes position by position for $a = \sigma_A/\sigma_B$ and $b = \exp\{\theta_B - a^{-1}\theta_A\}$.

[8] From (4), $g_B > g_A$ if $a < 1$ and $g_B < g_A$ if $a > 1$. The case $a = 1$ would yield a common proportional tax in both countries; see footnote 2. Under the lognormality assumption, the Lorenz curves for A and B do not intersect if $\sigma_A \neq \sigma_B$, i.e., if $a \neq 1$. Setting $a = \sigma_A/\sigma_B$ as in footnote 7, we have $g_B > g_A$ if $\sigma_A < \sigma_B$ and $g_B < g_A$ if $\sigma_A > \sigma_B$. A minor error in Lambert (2004b) led to this relationship being incorrectly described there.

4 Positional Social Welfare and Equal Sacrifice

If the tax schedule chosen for country A by the EU tax designers is such that it engenders equal sacrifices within that country, according to a local (country A) social decision-maker's imposed value judgement, does the tax schedule required by (3) to hold in country B also engender equal sacrifices as perceived within country B? This would be very pleasant, as it would allow the politicians in country B to assure their country-folk that the tax they will have to pay has been well thought-out, but condition (3), for equity, is paramount; the answer to the equal sacrifice question depends entirely on the evaluation functions attributed by the social decision-makers in each country. We investigate this question now.

Despite the avowedly utilitarian nature of equal sacrifice analysis, Yaari (1988) has shown that the principle can also be articulated in terms of a rank-dependent (linear) social welfare function, in which case one's tax liability becomes a function of one's *position* in the distribution of income rather than one's income *per se*. Lambert and Naughton (2009) extend the equal sacrifice prescription to a class of "hybrid" utilitarian and rank-dependent social welfare functions, which invoke a social utility-of-income function and also attribute weights giving systematically differing social importance to different people's positions in the income distribution. In such a case, tax liability is a function of *both* one's income *and* one's position. This model seems to be worth investigating in the EU context, given the positional equity criterion already articulated.

The Lambert and Naughton (2009) analysis is based upon a doubly parametric family of social evaluation functions of the form

$$Z_X(e,\upsilon) = \int_0^\infty U_e(x)\varphi'_\upsilon(F(x))f(x)dx, \tag{5}$$

where

$$U_e(x) = \alpha\left[\frac{x^{1-e}}{1-e}\right], \quad \text{if } 0 \le e \ne 1,$$

$$U_1(x) = \alpha \ln(x),$$

and

$$\varphi_\upsilon(p) = 1-(1-p)^\upsilon, \quad \text{with } 0 \le p \le 1 \text{ and } \upsilon \ge 1,$$

where $\alpha > 0$ is an arbitrary constant (in the sequel, α will be allowed to differ between countries) and $F(x)$ is the distribution function for taxable income. These are "hybrid" utilitarian and rank-dependent social welfare functions which were originally introduced by Berrebi and Silber (1981) and further developed by Duclos and Araar (2003, 2005).[9] The special case $\upsilon = 1$ generates the utilitarian SWF

[9] See also Ebert (1988, pp. 155–156), where rank-dependent SWFs are developed that are concave in incomes. In Ebert and Welsch (2004), the "Atkinson–Gini family" of SWFs is also considered, the aim being to fit parameter estimates to the preferences of a "representative European

popularized by Atkinson in his 1970 article and presaged in the work of Kolm (1968, 1969); see also Kolm (1999, pp. 59–61). The special case $e = 0$ is that of the Yaari (1988) linear and rank-dependent SWF.

An equal sacrifice tax function $t(x)$ for this social evaluation function is such that the individual welfare reductions caused, in the transition from the pre-tax income x to post-tax income $x - t(x)$, are all equal. Assuming that the application of the tax does not change people's positions in the distribution (i.e., that the tax $t(x)$ is incentive-preserving), from (5), the welfare reduction accounted for by a person with pre-tax income x and position p is proportional to

$$[U_e(x) - U_e(x - t(x))]\varphi'_\upsilon(p).$$

(The utility gap alone does *not* measure the sacrifice in the positional model; it is the losses from $Z_X(e, \upsilon)$ that must be equalized. For more on this point, see Lambert and Naughton (2009).) That is, the equal sacrifice tax function $t(x)$ takes the form

$$t(x) = x - \left[x^{1-e} - \frac{c(1-e)}{\upsilon[1 - F(x)]^{\upsilon-1}}\right]^{\frac{1}{1-e}}, \quad \forall x \in [x_0, x_1], \quad \text{if } e \neq 1 \tag{6a}$$

and

$$t(x) = \left[1 - \exp\left\{\frac{-c}{\upsilon[1 - F(x)]^{\upsilon-1}}\right\}\right]x, \quad \forall x \in [x_0, x_1], \quad \text{if } e = 1, \tag{6b}$$

for some $x_0 \geq 0$ and, unless $\upsilon = 1$, for some x_1 such that $F(x_1) \neq 1$ (if $\upsilon = 1$, then $x_1 \to \infty$), where the per-person sacrifice is αc. Unless $\upsilon = 1$, this tax depends on both income and percentile. When $\upsilon = 1$, (6a) and (6b) yield the well-known solution to the classical equal sacrifice criterion:

$$U_e(x) - U_e(x - t(x)) \equiv \alpha c, \quad \forall x \geq x_0,$$

(see, for example, Young 1990) and when $e = 0$, (6a) reduces to

$$t(x) = \frac{c}{\upsilon[1 - F(x)]^{\upsilon-1}}, \quad \forall x \in [x_0, x_1] \text{ with } x_0 > \frac{c}{\upsilon},$$

which is in fact the Yaari (1988) prescription.[10]

individual" on the basis of happiness data in the Eurobarometer survey series. For the genesis of a more general class of "rank-dependent expected utility" (RDEU) evaluation functions of the form $Z = \int U(x)\varphi'(F(x))f(x)dx$ where $U(x)$ and $\varphi(p)$ are both concave, the reader may consult Quiggin (1993, Chaps. 5 and 14).

[10] As e and υ increase, the interval between the two cut-offs x_0 and x_1 dictated by admissibility of the equal sacrifice prescription becomes smaller and smaller. The cut-offs x_0 and x_1 provide a "floor" and a "ceiling" for the average tax rate profile, but bring "cusps" into the tax level/income

5 Value Judgements for Positional Equity and Equal Sacrifice

Let the social evaluation function in country A be $Z_A(e, \upsilon)$ defined as in (5), in which the utility function is

$$U_A(x) = \alpha_A \left[\frac{x^{1-e}}{1-e}\right] \quad \text{if } 0 \leq e \neq 1,$$

$$U_A(x) = \alpha_A \ln(x) \quad \text{if } e = 1,$$

and the distribution function for taxable incomes is $F_A(\cdot)$. Let the tax schedule $t_A(x)$ in country A be defined by (6a) or (6b). As already explained, for equity, the tax schedule $t_B(x)$ in country B is defined by substituting $t_A(x)$ into (3), obtaining:

$$v_B(x_B) = b\,[v_A(x_A)]^{1/a} = b\,[x_A - t_A(x_A)]^{1/a},$$

or, from (6),

$$v_B(x_B) = b\left[x_A^{1-e} - \frac{c(1-e)}{\upsilon[1-F_A(x_A)]^{\upsilon-1}}\right]^{\frac{1}{a(1-e)}} \quad \text{if } e \neq 1$$

and

$$v_B(x_B) = b\exp\left\{\frac{-c}{a\upsilon[1-F_A(x_A)]^{\upsilon-1}}\right\} x_A^{1/a} \quad \text{if } e = 1.$$

Because of the percentile matching criterion, if $F_B(\cdot)$ is the distribution function for pre-tax incomes in country B, then

$$F_A(x_A) = F_B(x_B), \quad \text{where } x_A = S(x_B) = \left(\frac{x_B}{b}\right)^a.$$

It follows that t_B(x) is defined as follows:

$$t_B(x_B) = x_B - \left[x_B^{a(1-e)} - \frac{b^{a(1-e)}c(1-e)}{\upsilon[1-F_B(x_B)]^{\upsilon-1}}\right]^{\frac{1}{a(1-e)}} \quad \text{if } e \neq 1 \qquad (7a)$$

relationships: see Lambert and Naughton (2009) for further details. The presence of these cut-offs does not mean that tax liabilities will be zero at the bottom and top. Some prescription other than equal sacrifice would have to guide such taxes, and would, of course, have to be taken into account in determining the revenue consequences of the tax system. Early writers, from Carver (1895) onwards, were content to have the equal sacrifice principle applied over a bounded range. Young (1990) found that his equal sacrifice model did not fit in the tails of the US income distribution. If $e < 1$, the restriction $x_0[1 - F(x_0)]^{(\upsilon-1)/(1-e)} > [\frac{c}{\upsilon}(1-e)]^{1/(1-e)}$ on x_0 is implied.

and

$$t_B(x_B) = \left[1 - \exp\left\{\frac{-c}{a\upsilon[1 - F_B(x_B)]^{\upsilon-1}}\right\}\right] x_B \quad \text{if } e = 1. \tag{7b}$$

The per capita sacrifice in country A is $\alpha_A c$.

What does it take in order that this "induced" tax $t_B(x)$ also be an equal sacrifice tax for a social evaluation function in country B like the one in country A, but with parameters $\tilde{c}$, $\tilde{e}$, and $\tilde{\upsilon}$, say?

For equal sacrifices of $\alpha_B \tilde{c}$ per capita in country B, according to the evaluation function $Z_B(\tilde{e}, \tilde{\upsilon})$ defined as in (5), but with utility-of-income function

$$U_B(x) = \alpha_B \left[\frac{x^{1-\tilde{e}}}{1-\tilde{e}}\right] \quad \text{if } 0 \le \tilde{e} \neq 1$$

and

$$U_B(x) = \alpha_B \ln(x) \quad \text{if } \tilde{e} = 1,$$

from (6) we must have:

$$t_B(x_B) = x_B - \left[x_B^{1-\tilde{e}} - \frac{\tilde{c}(1-\tilde{e})}{\tilde{\upsilon}[1 - F_B(x_B)]^{\tilde{\upsilon}-1}}\right]^{\frac{1}{1-\tilde{e}}} \quad \text{if } \tilde{e} \neq 1 \tag{8a}$$

and

$$t_B(x_B) = \left[1 - \exp\left\{\frac{-\tilde{c}}{\tilde{\upsilon}[1 - F_B(x_B)]^{\tilde{\upsilon}-1}}\right\}\right] x_B \quad \text{if } \tilde{e} = 1, \tag{8b}$$

with end-of-range restrictions that we shall simply assume from now on. Comparing (7) with (8), the following result is fairly immediate.

Theorem 1. *If* $\upsilon = \tilde{\upsilon}$, $1 - \tilde{e} = a(1 - e)$, *and* $\tilde{c} = c\left[\frac{b^{1-\tilde{e}}}{a}\right]$, *then (7) and (8) are equivalent.*

Under the conditions on social evaluation functions expressed in this theorem, the rank weighting scheme in country B is the same as that in country A ($\upsilon = \tilde{\upsilon}$), the inequality aversion parameters of the respective utility of income functions differ, and the per capita sacrifice levels $\alpha_A c$ and $\alpha_B \tilde{c}$ are related in this way:

$$\frac{\alpha_A c}{\alpha_B \tilde{c}} = \frac{U_A(x_A)}{U_B(x_B)} = \frac{U_A(S(x_B))}{U_B(x_B)}, \quad \forall x_B.$$

Hence, the proportional sacrifice is the same for equals in the two countries. If $a = b = 1$, the income distributions in A and B are identical and so are the tax functions. In general, the relationship between the tax schedules $t_A(x)$ and $t_B(x)$, and the per capita sacrifice levels $\alpha_A c$ and $\alpha_B \tilde{c}$, depends on both the shift in location and the shift in scale of the distribution of income in B (in logarithms) away from that in A.[11]

A restriction must apply in order that the $\tilde{e}$ of Theorem 1 be nonnegative when $e < 1$. It is that

$$a < \left(\frac{1}{1-e}\right). \tag{9}$$

If inequality is very low in region B, so that $a = \sigma_A/\sigma_B$ is very large, then (9) may be violated for some values of $e < 1$. In fact, given σ_A and $\sigma_B < \sigma_A$,

$$e > 1 - \frac{1}{a} = \frac{(\sigma_A - \sigma_B)}{\sigma_A}$$

is required. This inequality tells us that the equal sacrifice model cannot apply in both countries if inequality aversion in the relatively very low inequality country B is not sufficiently close to unity. In the case of n countries, A and B_i, $i = 1, 2, \ldots, n-1$, in the analogue of Theorem 1, the inequality aversions $\tilde{e}_i$ should satisfy

$$1 - \tilde{e}_i = a_i(1-e), \quad \text{where } a_i = \frac{\sigma_A}{\sigma_{B_i}}. \tag{10}$$

This model fails to prescribe equal sacrifice taxes in all countries unless

$$e > \max\left\{1 - \frac{1}{a_1}, 1 - \frac{1}{a_2}, \ldots, 1 - \frac{1}{a_{n-1}}\right\}. \tag{11}$$

If (11) does hold, then the following is implied by (10): if $0 < e < 1$, then inequality aversion $\tilde{e}_i$ (< 1) will be lower the higher is a_i (i.e., the lower is inequality in country B_i), whilst if $e > 1$, inequality aversion $\tilde{e}_i$ (> 1) will be higher the higher is a_i (i.e., the lower is inequality in country B_i). We have not seen such links suggested between inequality and inequality aversion in any other literature.[12]

[11] As Lambert and Naughton (2009) show for this equal sacrifice model, there is a one-to-one relationship between the per capita sacrifice level and the revenue raised by the tax.

[12] One might wish that the model would validate a lower concern for inequality in countries where inequality is lower, but this is clearly not the case: a positive association between $|1-\tilde{e}_i|$ and σ_{B_i} is suggested, given σ_A. Atkinson (1970, p. 251) argues for higher inequality aversion in richer counties: "...it might quite reasonably be argued that as the general level of income rises we are more concerned about inequality ...," whilst Lambert, Millimet, and Slottje (2003, p. 1072) find a tendency for inequality aversion and inequality to move in opposite directions between countries: "... the inference that relatively inequality averse countries have lower levels of objective inequality appears robust ...." See also Harvey (2005) on this issue.

6 Positionally Equitable Equal Sacrifice Taxes in the EU: Some Illustrative Calculations

Let p be the rank of a person in country A with income x_A, and let the income of a person in country B with rank p be x_B, where, of course, $x_A = \left(\frac{x_B}{b}\right)^a$ and $p = F_A(x_A) = F_B(x_B)$. Let

$$\mathrm{ATR}_A(p) = \frac{t_A(x_A)}{x_A} \quad \text{and} \quad \mathrm{ATR}_B(p) = \frac{t_B(x_B)}{x_B}$$

be the average tax rates at percentile p in the two countries. It follows either from (3) or by substituting parameter values from Theorem 1 into (8) and comparing with (6) that

$$[1 - \mathrm{ATR}_A(p)] = [1 - \mathrm{ATR}_B(p)]^a. \tag{12}$$

Therefore, if $a \neq 1$, average tax rates are not the same at corresponding positions in the two distributions (recall footnote 8 on this point).

Equation (12) can be used to compute average tax rates at given percentile points in B from information about distribution A and its tax schedule (this is not necessary if $e = 1$, as the average tax rate in each country is constant in this case). Thus, let $u(p)$ denote the value in $N(0, 1)$ at percentile point p, so that

$$x_A = \exp\{\theta_A + u(p)\sigma_A\}$$

is the income level at percentile p in country A. Assuming that $e \neq 1$, from (6a) we have

$$\mathrm{ATR}_A(p) = 1 - \left[1 - \frac{c(1-e)}{\upsilon \exp\{(1-e)(\theta_A + u(p)\sigma_A)\}(1-p)^{\upsilon-1}}\right]^{\frac{1}{1-e}}. \tag{13}$$

Then, $\mathrm{ATR}_B(p)$ follows from (12). If we set c such that the average tax rate on the median income in country A is λ, say, then (13) requires that

$$c = \frac{\upsilon \exp\{(1-e)(\theta_A + u(\frac{1}{2})\sigma_A)\} \left(\frac{1}{2}\right)^{\upsilon-1}}{(1-e)}[1 - (1-\lambda)^{1-e}],$$

where, of course, $u\left(\frac{1}{2}\right) = 0$. Consequently, (13) itself becomes

$$\mathrm{ATR}_A(p) = 1 - \left[1 - \frac{1 - (1-\lambda)^{1-e}}{\exp\{(1-e)\sigma_A u(p)\}[2(1-p)]^{\upsilon-1}}\right]^{\frac{1}{1-e}} \quad \text{if } e \neq 1, \tag{14a}$$

Table 1 Approximate lognormal parameters θ and σ^2 for the distributions of net annual incomes and the mean incomes μ in six EU countries for the year 2000

Luxembourg	$\theta = 9.771$	$\sigma^2 = 0.296$	$\mu = 20,312$
Denmark	$\theta = 9.566$	$\sigma^2 = 0.245$	$\mu = 16,131$
UK	$\theta = 9.448$	$\sigma^2 = 0.399$	$\mu = 15,483$
Spain	$\theta = 8.698$	$\sigma^2 = 0.346$	$\mu = 7,122$
Greece	$\theta = 8.400$	$\sigma^2 = 0.375$	$\mu = 5,364$
Portugal	$\theta = 8.289$	$\sigma^2 = 0.377$	$\mu = 4,805$

which is readily computed in terms of p, e, υ, and λ, along with the lognormal parameter σ_A. If $e = 1$, then from (6b),

$$c = \frac{\upsilon\left(\frac{1}{2}\right)^{\upsilon-1}}{(1-\lambda)}$$

is required. Thus,

$$\text{ATR}_A(p) = 1 - (1-\lambda)^{\frac{1}{[2(1-p)]^{\upsilon-1}}} \quad \text{if } e = 1. \tag{14b}$$

In order to compute the average tax rate in B at percentile p we use (12); the only additional information we need is the relativity parameter $a = \sigma_A/\sigma_B$. To compute the average tax rate in A or B at a fixed income level, $\tilde{x}$ say, first we identify the relevant percentile points for that income level in A and B, call them $\tilde{p}_A$ in A and $\tilde{p}_B$ in B.[13] We then use (14) to compute $\text{ATR}_A(\tilde{p}_A)$ and $\text{ATR}_A(\tilde{p}_B)$) and (12) to obtain $\text{ATR}_B(\tilde{p}_B)$ in terms of $\text{ATR}_A(\tilde{p}_B)$).

We now give some illustrative calculations to show how the additional layer of income tax might impact upon income units in countries of the old EU with high and low mean incomes and high and low inequality, and upon new member countries and candidate countries too.

The first two columns of Table 1 show the mean of logarithms θ and variance of logarithms σ^2 for the distributions of household disposable income *per capita* in six EU countries for the year 2000.[14] The last column of this table shows the

[13] These points can be identified from the equations

$$u(\tilde{p}_A) = \frac{[\ln(\tilde{x}) - \theta_A]}{\sigma_A} \quad \text{and} \quad u(\tilde{p}_B) = \frac{[\ln(\tilde{x}) - \theta_B]}{\sigma_B},$$

and the $N(0,1)$ distribution. Notice that $u(\tilde{p}_B) = au(\tilde{p}_A) + [(a-1)\theta_A - a\ln(b)]/\sigma_A$.

[14] In Cholezas and Tsakloglou (2009), the mean and the variance of logarithms of hourly net earnings in 2000 in 13 of the original 15 EU countries can be found, computed from the final wave of the European Community Household Panel (ECHP) for 2001, where the income reference year is 2000. These summary statistics do not relate to overall net incomes, however, on account of missing components such as unearned incomes, and also because hours worked vary between countries (see Cholezas and Tsakloglou 2009). The figures quoted in Table 1 are for disposable incomes

mean incomes μ for those countries in nominal euros, computed according to the lognormality assumption as $\mu = \exp\{\theta + \frac{1}{2}\sigma^2\}$.[15]

In order to proceed with stylized calculations, representing putative member countries of the EU, but not actual ones dependent on these specific estimates, we select representative "high" and "low" values for the lognormal parameters, namely:

$$\theta_L = 8.3, \quad \theta_H = 9.8, \quad \sigma_L^2 = 0.25, \quad \sigma_H^2 = 0.40.$$

Taking combinations of these parameters, we obtain four putative distributions exhibiting respectively high (H) and low (L) mean of logarithms and high (H) and low (L) variance of logarithms, which we may call HH, HL, LH, LL (clearly, Luxembourg and Denmark could be represented by HL, and the UK by HH, but low inequality does not always occur along with a low mean in this data; the other three countries cited are much closer to LH than LL).[16] New and candidate countries of the EU generally have lower per capita income levels, but similar inequality experiences as the older member states.[17] An "ultra-low" θ-value, in combination with the already-set high and low σ^2-values can be used to represent such countries. We chose

$$\theta_U = 8.0$$

for this purpose, giving rise to two new constellations UL and UH (which could represent Croatia and Latvia, respectively, for example) to join the existing four.

---

from all sources, but excluding households whose total such income is less than €1,000 per year (because the variance of logarithms is very sensitive to extremely low income values). We thank Panos Tsakloglou for supplying the tabulations from which these estimates are drawn.

[15] The ranking of the countries in Table 1 in terms of means accords with that of the OECD for real GDP per head in 2002. See Stapel, Pasanen, and Reinecke (2004), in which Luxembourg is characterized as a high income country, Denmark is near the top of the high-middle income group, the UK is a little further down in that group, Spain is at the top of the low-middle income group, and Greece and Portugal are in the middle of that group.

[16] Interestingly, Luxembourg belongs in the HH (rather than the HL) category, with no other changes of category, in terms of both hourly net earnings and personal (rather than household) net incomes. In Lambert (2007), similar illustrative calculations to those given here are undertaken in terms of net hourly earnings. Kolm's (2004) *equal labour income equalization* (ELIE) proposal, to exempt overtime earnings from income tax, would boil down effectively to a tax on the hourly wage rate. ELIE is under active consideration for the French income tax at the time of writing. We base our calculations here on household disposable income per capita, rather than personal net income. These calculations illustrate the effect of the proposed EU tax on households rather than on individuals within households; the alternative could also be explored.

[17] Take Latvia and Croatia as examples of new and candidate EU countries. In World Bank (2006), GDP per capita and Gini coefficient values can be found for very many countries including these two and, of course, all of the countries of the old EU. Variances of logs are absent from these statistics unfortunately, but the Ginis suggest that Latvia's inequality lies between that of Portugal and the UK, and that Croatia's is close to that of Denmark. In respect of the means, and broadly in accord with Stapel, Pasanen, and Reinecke (2004), Latvia in 2003 had a real GDP per head of about one fifth of that in Luxembourg, and Croatia fared slightly better.

Taking HH as country A, the parameters $a_i = \sigma_A/\sigma_{B_i}$ and $b_i = \exp\{\theta_{B_i} - a_i\theta_A\}$ for i = HH, LH, HL, LL, UH, UL can now be calculated. Here are the relevant values:

HH: $a_{\mathrm{HH}} = 1,\ b_{\mathrm{HH}} = 1$

LH: $a_{\mathrm{LH}} = 1,\ b_{\mathrm{LH}} = \exp\{\theta_{\mathrm{L}} - a_{\mathrm{LH}}^{-1}\theta_{\mathrm{H}}\} = \exp\{8.3 - 9.8\} = 0.22$

HL: $a_{\mathrm{HL}} = 1.6,\ b_{\mathrm{HL}} = \exp\{\theta_{\mathrm{H}} - a_{\mathrm{HL}}^{-1}\theta_{\mathrm{H}}\} = \exp\{9.8 - (1.6^{-1} \times 9.8)\} = 39.45$

LL: $a_{\mathrm{LL}} = 1.6,\ b_{\mathrm{LL}} = \exp\{\theta_{\mathrm{L}} - a_{\mathrm{LL}}^{-1}\theta_{\mathrm{H}}\} = \exp\{8.3 - (1.6^{-1} \times 9.8)\} = 8.80$

UH: $a_{\mathrm{UH}} = 1,\ b_{\mathrm{UH}} = \exp\{\theta_{\mathrm{U}} - a_{\mathrm{UH}}^{-1}\theta_{\mathrm{H}}\} = \exp\{8.0 - 9.8\} = 0.17$

UL: $a_{\mathrm{UL}} = 1.6,\ b_{\mathrm{UL}} = \exp\{\theta_{\mathrm{U}} - a_{\mathrm{UL}}^{-1}\theta_{\mathrm{H}}\} = \exp\{8.0 - (1.6^{-1} \times 9.8)\} = 6.52$

We shall not need the b_i-values for the calculation of average tax rates at percentiles (recall (12) and (14)). We set $\upsilon = 1, 2$ (representing the utilitarian and Gini-based mixed SWF respectively), and choose $e = \frac{1}{2}, 1, 2$ as the inequality aversion parameter in country HH, which from (10) is equal to that in the other high-inequality countries, from which it also follows that inequality aversion in the low-inequality countries has to be respectively $\tilde{e} = 0.2, 1, 2.6$ for coherence with the model.

Table 2 presents the average tax rates by percentile in each of the six constellations for the case in which $\lambda = 0.01$, i.e., when the average tax rate at median income in country HH is set at 1%. As shown in this table, the utilitarian equal sacrifice tax is regressive when $e = \frac{1}{2}$. In fact, this would be so for any $e < 1$ (see Young 1990). Also the tax is regressive when $e = 1$ in the Gini-based case (see Lambert and Naughton 2009). Notice that in all cases, the average tax rate at the median is 1% in high inequality constellations, and 0.54% in low inequality constellations (and these are the flat rates at all percentiles if $\upsilon = e = 1$). The tax rate at given percentiles depends *only* on inequality – there is no discrepancy between these tax rates in the high, low, and ultra-low mean constellations – for example Luxembourg (HL) experiences lower average tax rates than Latvia (UH) *at given percentiles*. For $\upsilon = 2$, the average tax rate rises much faster along the income parade when $e = 2$ than when $e = \frac{1}{2}$, but starts from a lower base.

Table 3 shows average tax rates in the six constellations *at fixed income levels* (for which the b_i-values are used to compute the appropriate positions $\tilde{p}_i$, as described in footnote 13). The fixed income levels chosen for these comparisons are those to be found at the 20th to 80th percentile points in constellation HH. Comparing HH with HL, we see that among the richer countries of the EU, those with less inequality have lower tax rates at any given income level. The constellations LH and UH could represent poorer old EU countries and new ones, for example Portugal and Latvia. Taxpayers in these countries can expect to pay higher taxes than those living in the richer countries *at the same income level* (though not at the same percentile, as we have already observed). We do not presently have LL countries in the EU, though Croatia is a candidate EU member that may enter in the UL category. The tax rates shown in Table 3 for LL and UL are extraordinarily high and would clearly

Table 2 Percentage average tax rates at given percentiles for the six constellations

Percentile	20th	30th	40th	50th	60th	70th	80th
$\upsilon = 1$ (utilitarian)							
$e = \frac{1}{2}$							
HH, LH, UH	1.30	1.18	1.08	1.00	0.92	0.85	0.77
HL, LL, UL	0.70	0.63	0.58	0.54	0.49	0.45	0.41
$e = 1$							
HH, LH, UH	1.00	1.00	1.00	1.00	1.00	1.00	1.00
HL, LL, UL	0.54	0.54	0.54	0.54	0.54	0.54	0.54
$e = 2$							
HH, LH, UH	0.59	0.72	0.85	1.00	1.17	1.39	1.69
HL, LL, UL	0.32	0.39	0.46	0.54	0.63	0.74	0.91
$\upsilon = 2$ (Gini-based)							
$e = \frac{1}{2}$							
HH, LH, UH	0.82	0.84	0.90	1.00	1.15	1.41	1.91
HL, LL, UL	0.44	0.45	0.48	0.54	0.62	0.76	1.03
$e = 1$							
HH, LH, UH	1.59	1.40	1.20	1.00	0.80	0.60	0.40
HL, LL, UL	0.86	0.75	0.64	0.54	0.43	0.32	0.21
$e = 2$							
HH, LH, UH	0.37	0.52	0.71	1.00	1.46	2.29	4.12
HL, LL, UL	0.20	0.28	0.38	0.54	0.78	1.23	2.23

be grossly inefficient, entailing major disincentive effects. In fact, as indicated by the parentheses, these tax rates should be discounted. The combination of a low or ultra-low mean and low inequality implies that the income values in constellations LL and UL that correspond to many of the decile values in Table 3 for HH will be right at the top – where the density of taxpayers is extremely thin – and the equal sacrifice model in any case breaks down at very high percentiles (see equations (6) and footnote 10).[18]

Finally, we turn to the Luxembourg/Latvia question in terms of which we opened this whole discussion. A net annual income of €20,000 is close to the mean in Luxembourg and at approximately the 65th percentile on the basis of the figures in Table 1, and at approximately the 75th percentile in the UK (our representative

[18] It is interesting to compare these findings with the pattern of overall average tax rates in EU countries derived by Atkinson (2002) according to his proposal for an overall 1% EU income tax to fund development assistance. Using a tax base for each country as described in footnote 1 and EUROMOD calculations, Atkinson found that, inter alia, Portugal, Greece, and Spain would have contribution rates of around 0.7%, whilst for the UK and Denmark, the rate would be about 1% (the same as for a proportional tax system on all income), and for Luxembourg, it would be about 1.35% (see Atkinson 2002, especially Fig. 16.2).

Table 3 Percentage average tax rates at given income values (expressed in terms of HH percentile) for the six constellations

Income value, by percentile, in HH	Percentage average tax rate at that income value					
	HH	HL	LH	LL	UH	UL
$\upsilon = 1, e = 2$						
20th	0.59	0.32	2.59	(35.45)	3.47	(99.89)
30th	0.72	0.38	3.15	(39.53)	4.21	(99.91)
40th	0.85	0.44	3.72	(43.15)	4.96	(99.92)
50th	1.00	0.50	4.33	(46.60)	5.77	(99.93)
60th	1.17	0.57	5.04	(50.07)	6.70	(99.94)
70th	1.39	0.66	5.94	(53.81)	7.86	(99.95)
80th	1.69	0.77	7.16	(58.09)	9.44	(99.96)
$\upsilon = 2, e = 2$						
20th	0.37	0.20	1.64	(25.56)	2.20	(99.82)
30th	0.52	0.27	2.27	(31.83)	3.04	(99.87)
40th	0.71	0.37	3.12	(38.75)	4.17	(99.91)
50th	1.00	0.50	4.33	(46.60)	5.77	(99.93)
60th	1.46	0.71	6.23	(55.63)	8.24	(99.99)
70th	2.29	1.05	9.52	(66.00)	12.45	(99.99)
80th	4.12	1.73	16.16	(77.60)	20.67	(99.99)

of constellation HH). Taking Latvia to be represented by θ_{U} and σ_{H}, a net annual income of €20,000 would be more than five times the Latvian mean and in the very top percentile. We see from Table 3 that the additional layer of income tax across the EU, if designed to satisfy positional equity and equal sacrifice, could lead to tax rates of the order of $1\frac{1}{2}\%$–3% in the UK, 0.7%–$1\frac{1}{2}\%$ in Luxembourg, and 8%–15% in Latvia on an annual disposable income of €20,000 (depending on parameter values and assuming a 1% tax on the median UK income).

7 Concluding Remarks

A much-debated issue in present-day political philosophy is whether redistribution should be kept within nations or go beyond. The debate was started by Rawls (1993), who argued that it should be kept within Nation-States. The European Union is of course not a Nation-State, but is acquiring some of the features of one. Citizens who believe they are being treated fairly will be more likely to consent to their own taxation. In the model of this article, tax fairness should be seen as both an instrumental and an ultimate objective. By invoking utility functions defined over own income and rank, we suggest that citizens can think empathetically, with one's own country providing the social perception of reality, which provides the basis for extending the boundary to empathy to include one's peers (similarly placed individuals) in other countries. For a recent paper concerning subjective dimensions of equity, see Osberg and Smeeding (2006).

Would the EU become effectively a Nation-State, then it could be seen as a "community of redistribution" in Kolm's (2004) language, a "federal polity" in Buchanan's (1950) terms. For Buchanan, similarly situated individuals in different EU member countries should have equivalent overall "fiscal residua" (p. 568), i.e., the value of public services provided by the EU, as well as by the member countries, would have to be taken into account in formulating an equal treatment criterion (which our criterion (3) does not attempt to do). For Kolm (2004), a degree of redistribution would be established across the EU reflecting what is politically and socially possible and desired in this community. Kolm would foresee a process according to which, as a European sense of community progressively develops, a degree of redistribution in between full equalization and no redistribution at all would emerge and evolve dynamically. The parameter λ, which in our model specifies the percentage tax rate on the median income in the reference country A (constellation HH in the empirical illustration) and fully determines the entire profile of taxes given the value judgement and distributional parameters, could be adjusted upwards from a much lower starting point than the 1% we have assumed to reflect such an evolution. In the longer term, when the EU will have become fully a community of redistribution, it will be the differences in absolute income levels (in euros), both between and within countries, that will be the focus of concern for policymakers.[19] Our model – in which the inequalities which exist between countries are taken as given and condition the tax functions – may well be inappropriate at such a time (and rather as in the USA, the federal income tax may become the major one and the State income taxes take on minor roles). If fiscal equity across the EU called for equal average tax rates on equal net incomes across member countries, rather than equal treatment in the sense of (3), then of course none of the analysis of this paper would apply (as we said in footnote 5). We have conditioned the analysis on a positional equity criterion, according to which the equals in different EU countries are those at the same percentile points in the country-specific income distributions. We also assumed that the country-specific income distributions differ in logarithms by location and scale only. Our illustrative calculations have shown that, under these assumptions, it would be feasible to design an EU income tax which would engender both equal progression among equals and equal sacrifices from the citizens of each country in terms of rank-dependent and utilitarian social evaluation functions. Moreover, under the scheme advocated, each person experiences the same proportionate utility-of-income sacrifice as his or her peers in the other EU countries. The way is now open for a deeper and more careful study should the issue of the direct taxation of EU citizens actually reach the political agenda.

[19] As a referee pointed out, the positional approach, which draws upon Roemer's ideas on equality of opportunity, clearly puts the emphasis on within-country inequality. Another approach in the equality of opportunity literature aims at equalizing opportunity sets. Such an approach would more naturally focus upon inter-country differences, and could lead to a model in which the tax rate paid by an individual should be a function of the country to which he or she belongs.

Acknowledgements This article was drafted whilst I was a Visiting Professor in the Department of Economics at the University of Otago. I am most grateful for the hospitality provided. I also thank Serge Kolm, Tony Atkinson, Panos Tsakloglou, Udo Ebert, Lars Osberg, Helen Naughton, Mark Chandler, Ivica Urban, Marc Fleurbaey, and an anonymous referee for helpful comments.

References

Atkinson, A. B. (1970). On the measurement of inequality. *Journal of Economic Theory, 2*, 244–263

Atkinson, A. B. (2002). 1% of €10,000 billion. In P. Townsend & D. Gordon (Eds.), *World poverty: New policies to defeat an old enemy* (pp. 401–411). Bristol: Policy Press

Berrebi, Z. M., & Silber, J. (1981). Weighting income ranks and levels: A multi-parameter generalization for absolute and relative inequality indices. *Economics Letters, 7*, 391–397

Buchanan, J. M. (1950). Federalism and fiscal equity. *American Economic Review, 40*, 583–599

Carver, T. N. (1895). The ethical basis of distribution and its application to taxation. *Annals of the American Academy of Political and Social Science, 6*, 79–99

Cholezas, I., & Tsakloglou, P. (2009). Earnings inequality in Europe: Structure and patterns of intertemporal changes. In P. Dolton, R. Asplund, & E. Barth (Eds.), *Education and inequality across Europe* (pp. 122–146). Cheltenham: Edward Elgar

Cnossen, S. (2002). Tax policy in the European Union: A review of issues and options. *FinanzArchiv: Public Finance Analysis, 58*, 466–558

Cubel, M., & Lambert, P. J. (2002a). Progression-neutral income tax reforms and horizontal inequity. *Journal of Economics, Supplement, 9*, 1–8. Special issue on *Inequalities: Theory, experiments and applications*, P. Moyes, C. Seidl, & A. F. Shorrocks (Eds.)

Cubel, M., & Lambert, P. J. (2002b). A regional approach to income tax policy. *Public Finance Review, 30*, 124–143

Dardanoni, V., & Lambert, P. J. (2002). Progressivity comparisons. *Journal of Public Economics, 86*, 124–143

Duclos, J.-Y., & Araar, A. (2003). An Atkinson–Gini family of social evaluation functions. *Economics Bulletin, 3*(19), 1–16

Duclos, J.-Y., & Araar, A. (2005). An Atkinson–Gini class of social evaluation functions: Theory and illustration using data from the Luxembourg Income Study. LIS Working Paper No. 416, Luxembourg Income Study

Ebert, U. (1988). Measurement of inequality: An attempt at unification and generalization. *Social Choice and Welfare, 5*, 147–169

Ebert, U. (2000). Equivalizing incomes: A normative approach. *International Tax and Public Finance, 7*, 619–640

Ebert, U., & Lambert, P. J. (2004). Horizontal equity and progression when equivalence scales are not constant. *Public Finance Review, 32*, 426–440

Ebert, U., & Welsch, H. (2004). The social evaluation of income distribution: An assessment based on happiness surveys. LIS Working Paper No. 381, Luxembourg Income Study

Harvey, J. (2005). A note on the "natural rate of subjective inequality" hypothesis and the approximate relationship between the Gini coefficient and the Atkinson index. *Journal of Public Economics, 89*, 1021–1025

Kolm, S.-C. (1968). La production optimale de justice sociale. In J. Margolis & H. Guitton (Eds.), *Economie Publique* (pp. 109–177). Paris: Editions du Centre National de la Recherche Scientifique

Kolm, S.-C. (1969). The optimal production of social justice. In J. Margolis & H. Guitton (Eds.), *Public economics: An analysis of public production and consumption and their relations to the private sector* (pp. 145–200). London: Macmillan. Reprinted with corrections in K. J. Arrow & G. Debreu (Eds.), *Landmark papers in general equilibrium, social choice and welfare*

(pp. 606–653). Cheltenham: Edward Elgar, 2001. Relevant sections reprinted with an editorial introduction by P. J. Lambert in *Journal of Economic Inequality*, *5*, 2007, 216–234
Kolm, S.-C. (1999). The rational foundations of income inequality measurement. In J. Silber (Ed.), *Handbook of income inequality measurement* (pp. 19–100). Boston: Kluwer
Kolm, S.-C. (2004). *Macrojustice: The political economy of fairness*. Cambridge: Cambridge University Press
Lambert, P. J. (2004a). Equivalence scales, horizontal equity and horizontal inequity. In C. Dagum & G. Ferrari (Eds.), *Household behaviour, equivalence scales, welfare and poverty* (pp. 75–84). Heidelberg: Physica-Verlag
Lambert, P. J. (2004b). Income taxation and equity. *Baltic Journal of Economics*, *4*(4), 39–54
Lambert, P. J. (2007). Positional equity and equal sacrifice: Design principles for an EU-wide income tax? Discussion Paper No. 0706, Department of Economics, University of Otago
Lambert, P. J., & Naughton, H. T. (2009). The equal sacrifice principle revisited. *Journal of Economic Surveys*, *23*, 328–349
Lambert, P. J., Millimet, D. L., & Slottje, D. (2003). Inequality aversion and the natural rate of subjective inequality. *Journal of Public Economics*, *87*, 1061–1090
Osberg, L., & Smeeding, T. (2006). "Fair" inequality? Attitudes toward pay differentials: The United States in comparative perspective. *American Sociological Review*, *71*, 450–473
Quiggin, J. (1993). *Generalized expected utility theory: The rank-dependent model*. Boston: Kluwer
Rawls, J. (1993). The law of peoples. *Critical Inquiry*, *20*, 36–68
Roemer, J. E. (1998). *Equality of opportunity*. Cambridge, MA: Harvard University Press
Roemer, J. E. (2006). Review essay, "The 2006 World Development Report: Equity and Development". *Journal of Economic Inequality*, *4*, 233–244
Runciman, W. G. (1966). *Relative deprivation and social justice*. London: Routledge
Stapel, S., Pasanen, J., & Reinecke, S. (2004). Purchasing power parities and related economic indicators for EU, candidate countries and EFTA. Statistics in Focus No. 53, Eurostat, Luxembourg
World Bank (2006). *World development indicators*. Washington: World Bank
Yaari, M. (1988). A controversial proposal concerning inequality measurement. *Journal of Economic Theory*, *44*, 381–397
Young, H. P. (1990). Progressive taxation and equal sacrifice. *American Economic Review*, *80*, 253–266

Comparing Societies with Different Numbers of Individuals on the Basis of Their Average Advantage

Nicolas Gravel, Thierry Marchant, and Arunava Sen

1 Introduction

At an abstract level, one can view the various theories of justice that have been discussed in economics and philosophy in the last 50 years or so, including of course that of Serge-Christophe Kolm (2005), as attempts at providing criteria for comparing alternative *societies* on the basis of their "ethical goodness." The compared societies can be truly distinct societies, such as India and China. They can also be the same society examined at two different points of time (say India today and India 20 years ago) or, more counterfactually, before and after a tax reform or demographic shock.

In many theories, societies are described by lists of *attribute bundles*, as many bundles as there are individuals in the society. However, existing theories and approaches differ markedly with respect to the choice of the individual attributes that are deemed normatively relevant to describe a society. In classical social choice theory, developed along the lines of the famous impossibility theorem of Arrow (1950), the only considered attribute is an individual's ordinal preference ordering over social alternatives, in which case a society can be considered as being a list of preference orderings. The scope of classical Arrovian theory is, however, restricted to normative comparisons involving societies with the same number of individuals. In the welfarist approach, defended forcefully by Blackorby et al. (2005), among

N. Gravel (✉)
GREQAM-IDEP, Université de la Méditerranée, Centre de la Vieille Charité, 13002 Marseille, France
e-mail: nicolas.gravel@univmed.fr

T. Marchant
Department of Data Analysis, Ghent University, Henri Dunantlaan 1, 9000 Ghent, Belgium
e-mail: thierry.marchant@ugent.be

A. Sen
Indian Statistical Institute, 7 S. J. S. Sansanwal Marg, New Delhi 110016, India
e-mail: asen@isid.ac.in

M. Fleurbaey et al. (eds.), *Social Ethics and Normative Economics*,
Studies in Choice and Welfare, DOI 10.1007/978-3-642-17807-8_11,

many others, the relevant attribute is an individual's utility, in which case a society can be summarized by the list of utility numbers achieved by the individuals. The welfarist tradition has explored the problems raised by comparing societies with different numbers of people in considerable detail. See, for example, Parfit (1984), Blackorby et al. (2005), Broome (2004), and the literature surveyed therein for examples of welfarist approaches to variable population ethics. As another example of a normative approach for comparing societies, there is the multidimensional functioning and capabilities theory of Sen (1985), in which the individual attributes are taken to be various functionings (nutrition, education, health, etc.). As far as we are aware, there have not been many attempts to apply Sen's theory to societies involving different numbers of individuals.

In this article, we discuss a general method for comparing *all* logically conceivable finite lists of attribute bundles without entering into the (philosophically important) matter of identifying what these attributes are. Taking the relevant individual attributes as given, we formulate several principles that can be used for comparing alternative lists of attribute bundles and we show that these principles characterize a rather specific method for comparing societies. The criterion characterized herein can be thought of as comparing societies on the basis of their *average advantage* for some advantage function defined on the set of attribute bundles.

If one takes the view that utility is the *only* relevant individual attribute, then this article may be seen as providing an alternative characterization of the family of social orderings called *average generalized utilitarianism* by Blackorby et al. (2005, pp. 171–172, 198). With average general utilitarianism, individual utilities are first transformed by some function – here called an advantage function – before being averaged.

Yet, the main interest of the characterization provided in this article is that it applies as well to *non-welfarist* multidimensional contexts in which the situation of an individual is described by a bundle of attributes. In any such context, the properties that we impose on the ranking of all societies force one to aggregate these attributes into a measure of individual *advantage* and to compare different societies on the basis of their average advantage. Of course, when interpreted from this perspective, the *advantage function* that aggregates the bundles of attributes need *not* be that which corresponds to an individual's subjective well-being. It could, rather, be thought of as being the value assigned to the individual attributes by the social planner or, more generally, by the theoretician of justice. While the main theorem in this article does not impose any restrictions on the advantage function other than monotonicity and continuity, it is quite easy to require it to satisfy additional properties by imposing further assumptions on the social ordering. An example of such a property is aversion to attribute inequality which, if imposed on the social ordering, places additional restrictions on the individual advantage function.

The rest of this article is organized as follows. In Sect. 2, we introduce the formal model, the main axioms, and the criterion used to compare societies. Section 3 provides our main result and Sect. 4 indicates how some additional restrictions on the advantage function can be obtained by imposing additional properties on the social ordering. Section 5 concludes.

2 Notation and Basic Definitions

2.1 Notation

The sets of integers, non-negative integers, strictly positive integers, real numbers, non-negative real numbers, and strictly positive real numbers are denoted by $\mathbb{N}$, $\mathbb{N}_+$, $\mathbb{N}_{++}$, $\mathbb{R}$, $\mathbb{R}_+$, and $\mathbb{R}_{++}$ respectively. The cardinality of any set A is denoted by $\#A$ and the k-fold Cartesian product of a set A with itself is denoted by A^k. Our notation for vector inequalities is $\geqq$, $\geq$, and $>$.

The k-dimensional unit vector is denoted by 1^k. The inner product of an $n \times m$ matrix a by an $m \times r$ matrix b is denoted by $a \cdot b$. A *permutation matrix* π is a square matrix whose entries are either 0 or 1 and sum to 1 in every row and every column.

Given a vector v in $\mathbb{R}^k$ and a positive real number ε, we denote by $N_\varepsilon(v)$ the *ε-neighborhood around v* defined by $N_\varepsilon(v) = \{x \in \mathbb{R}^k : |x_h - v_h| < \varepsilon \text{ for all } h = 1, \ldots, k\}$. If Φ is a function from a subset A of $\mathbb{R}^k$ to $\mathbb{R}$ and $\mathbf{a}$ is a vector in A, for every strictly positive real number Δ such that $(a_1, \ldots, a_j + \Delta, \ldots, a_k) \in A$, we denote by $\Phi_j^\Delta(a)$ its (discrete right-hand-side) jth *derivative* defined by:

$$\Phi_j^\Delta(\mathbf{a}) = \frac{\Phi(a_1, \ldots, a_j + \Delta, \ldots, a_k) - \Phi(\mathbf{a})}{\Delta}. \tag{1}$$

A *binary relation* $\succsim$ on a set Ω is a subset of $\Omega \times \Omega$. Following the convention in economics, we write $x \succsim y$ instead of $(x, y) \in \succsim$. Given a binary relation $\succsim$, we define its *symmetric factor* $\sim$ by $x \sim y \iff [x \succsim y$ and $y \succsim x]$ and its *asymmetric factor* $\succ$ by $x \succ y \iff [x \succsim y$ and $\neg(y \succsim x)]$. A binary relation $\succsim$ on Ω is *reflexive* if the statement $x \succsim x$ holds for every $x \in \Omega$, is *transitive* if $x \succsim z$ always follows from $[x \succsim y$ and $y \succsim z]$ for any $x, y, z \in \Omega$, and is *complete* if $x \succsim y$ or $y \succsim x$ holds for every distinct $x, y \in \Omega$. A reflexive, transitive, and complete binary relation is called an *ordering*.

2.2 The Framework

We assume that the situation of an individual can be described – at least for the purpose of normative evaluation – by a bundle of k (with $k \in \mathbb{N}_{++}$) attributes. Accordingly, we view a society s as a finite ordered list of vectors in $\mathbb{R}^k$, every such vector being interpreted as the bundle of attributes that describes the situation of the individual to which it corresponds. Let $n(s)$ denote the number of individuals living in society s. Then, we can depict any society s as an $n(s) \times k$ matrix:

$$s = \begin{bmatrix} s_{11} & \dots & s_{1k} \\ \vdots & \vdots & \vdots \\ s_{n(s)1} & \dots & s_{n(s)k} \end{bmatrix},$$

where s_{ij}, for $i = 1, \dots, n(s)$ and $j = 1, \dots, k$, is interpreted as the amount of attribute j received by individual i in society s. Denote by s_i the vector of attributes received by i in s. A society s with $n(s)$ individuals is therefore an element of $\mathbb{R}^{n(s)k}$ and the set of all logically conceivable societies is $\cup_{l \in \mathbb{N}_{++}} \mathbb{R}^{lk}$. If s is a society in $\mathbb{R}^{mk}$ and s' is a society in $\mathbb{R}^{nk}$, we denote by (s, s') the society in $\mathbb{R}^{(m+n)k}$ in which the first m individuals get, in the same order, the bundles obtained by the corresponding individuals in s and the last n individuals get the bundles obtained, in the same order, by the n individuals in s'. To alleviate notation, we write, for any attribute bundle x in $\mathbb{R}^k$, the one-individual society (x) as x.

We note that depicting societies as ordered lists of attribute bundles makes sense only if one adopts an *anonymity* postulate that "the names of the individuals do not matter." We adopt this postulate throughout, even though we are fully aware that it rests on an implicit assumption that the attribute bundle received by an individual constitutes the *only* information about this individual's situation that is deemed normatively relevant. It is therefore important for the interpretation of our framework that one adopts an extensive list of attributes, which could include many consumptions goods, health, education levels, and, possibly, Rawlsian primary goods such as the "social bases of self respect." Perhaps, one should also view these bundles of goods and primary goods as being distinguished by the time at which they are made available if one wants to adopt a lifetime perspective. A clear discussion about the explicit modeling of this anonymity postulate within a richer – albeit welfarist – formal framework is provided in Blackorby et al. (2005, Chap. 3.9).

We should also mention that our framework leads one to consider all conceivable societies, including societies consisting of a single individual. While these kinds of "societies" may be considered to lie outside the realm of theories of justice, there are several instances in which normative comparisons of small communities are made. For instance, it is not uncommon in applied welfare economics to compare the well-being of an individual with that of a family. Of course, we are doing much more than that here because we also normatively compare a family of three persons with, say, the whole People's Republic of China. Note, too, that we rank all single-individual societies and thus, implicitly, all bundles of attributes from a social point of view. We believe that this is acceptable only if the ethical importance of the attributes commands widespread support.

We compare all societies on the basis of a social ordering $\succsim$, with asymmetric and symmetric factors $\succ$ and $\sim$ respectively. We interpret the statement $s \succsim s'$ as meaning that "the distribution of the k attributes in society s is at least as just as the corresponding distribution in society s'." A similar interpretation is given to the statements $s \succ s'$ ("strictly more just") and $s \sim s'$ ("equally just").

2.3 The Axioms

In this article, we identify the properties (axioms) of the ordering $\succsim$ that are necessary and sufficient for the existence of a monotonically increasing and continuous *advantage function* $u: \mathbb{R}^k \to \mathbb{R}$ such that, for all societies s and s' in $\cup_{l\in\mathbb{N}_{++}}\mathbb{R}^{lk}$, one has:

$$s \succsim s' \Longleftrightarrow \sum_{i=1}^{n(s)} \frac{u(s_i)}{n(s)} \geq \sum_{i=1}^{n(s')} \frac{u(s'_i)}{n(s')}. \tag{2}$$

An ordering satisfying this property *may* therefore be thought of as resulting from the comparison of the *average advantage* achieved by individuals in the various societies. Note that the individual advantage function that appears in this formula is the same for all individuals, who are therefore treated symmetrically. Of course, if one adopts the welfarist paradigm in which the situation of an individual is described by a single attribute (utility), then $k = 1$ and the ordering defined by (2) corresponds to what is called "generalized average utilitarianism" by Blackorby et al. (1999). Note that (2) defines a *family* of social criteria, with as many members as there are logically conceivable continuous and monotonically increasing advantage functions. We shall discuss below how could one could restrict this family by imposing additional axioms on the social ranking. We refer to any ranking that satisfies (2) for some function u as an *Average Advantage* (AA) ranking.

We now introduce five axioms that, as we shall show, characterize the AA family of social rankings.

The first axiom combines the assumption that the attributes that matter for normative appraisal are positively valued by the social planner with a Pareto-like condition that says that it is a social improvement when all members of society experience an increase in their attribute bundles. This axiom is stated formally as follows.

Monotonicity. For all societies $s, s' \in \cup_{l\in\mathbb{N}_{++}}\mathbb{R}^{lk}$ for which $n(s) = n(s') = n$ for some $n \in \mathbb{N}_{++}$, if $s_i \geq s'_i$ for all $i = 1, \ldots, n$, then $s \succ s'$.

This axiom can be seen as an adaptation to the current multidimensional setting of the axiom called Weak Pareto by Blackorby et al. (2005). Of course, their axiom applies only to the case in which there is only one attribute – welfare, while our formulation applies to any number of attributes. In our view, this monotonicity axiom is natural if the attributes can be interpreted as primary goods à la Rawls (1982) or, using the terminology of Sen (1987), as things that "people have reasons to value," provided of course that the social planner is minimally concerned about improving the situations of individuals.

The second axiom requires the social ranking to satisfy what Blackorby et al. (2005) have called *Same People Anonymity*. That is, the names of the individuals who receive the attributes do not matter for normative evaluation when comparing societies with the same number of people. In other words, all societies that distribute the same list of attributes among the same number of people are normatively equivalent. This axiom is also natural in the setting we are considering, especially in view of the discussion made above. We state this axiom formally as follows.

Same People Anonymity. For every society $s \in \cup_{l \in \mathbb{N}_{++}} \mathbb{R}^{lk}$ and all $n(s) \times n(s)$ permutation matrices π, one has $\pi \cdot s \sim s$.

The third axiom is a continuity condition. It is weaker than most related continuity conditions because it applies only to sets of attribute bundles that are considered to be weakly better than, or weakly worse than, a given society if they are received by a single individual. It says that if a converging sequence of such bundles are considered weakly better (resp. weakly worse) than a given society, then the point of convergence of this sequence should also be considered weakly better (resp. weakly worse) than the considered society.

Continuity. For every society $s \in \cup_{l \in \mathbb{N}_{++}} \mathbb{R}^{lk}$, the sets $B(s) = \{x \in \mathbb{R}^k : x \succsim s\}$ and $W(s) = \{x \in \mathbb{R}^k : s \succsim x\}$ are both closed in $\mathbb{R}^k$.

While weak, this axiom rules out rankings such as the Leximin one, which compare ordered lists of bundles by first defining a continuous utility function on those bundles and by then ranking vectors of the utilities associated with these bundles by the usual lexicographic ordering of $\cup_{l \in \mathbb{N}_{++}} \mathbb{R}^l$ (generalized to account for the different dimensions of the vectors being compared). It is clear that such a ranking violates Continuity because it is possible to consider a sequence of bundles that are ranked weakly above a bundle that is worse for a given society and that converges to the latter bundle. Yet, contrary to what is required by Continuity, a society containing only one individual endowed with this bundle is considered strictly worse than the original many-individual society by the Leximin criterion.

The next axiom plays a crucial role in our characterization theorem and captures the very idea of averaging numbers for comparing societies. We call it, for this reason, the *Averaging* axiom. This axiom says that merging two distinct societies generates a (larger) society that is worse than the best of the two societies and better than the worst of the two societies. It also says, conversely, that if a society loses (gains) from bringing in members with specific attribute endowments, then this can only be because the distribution of attributes that is brought in is worse (better) than that already present in the original society. Using the language of population ethics, this axiom says that bringing in new members with specific endowments of attributes is worth doing if and only if the added distribution of endowments is better than the original one. This axiom is stated formally as follows.

Averaging. For all societies $s, s' \in \cup_{l \in \mathbb{N}_{++}} \mathbb{R}^{lk}$, $s \succsim s' \Leftrightarrow s \succsim (s, s') \Leftrightarrow (s, s') \succsim s'$.

When applied to an ordering, Averaging implies some other properties that have been considered in the literature on population ethics. One of them is the axiom called Replication Equivalence by Blackorby et al. (2005, p. 197). This axiom states that, for societies in which everyone gets the same attribute bundle, the *number* of members in the society does not matter. This property clearly rules out social preferences of the type "small is beautiful" or, conversely, the biblical "be fertile and multiply." We state this property formally as follows.

Replication Equivalence. For every attribute bundle $x \in \mathbb{R}^k$ and all societies $s \in \cup_{l \in \mathbb{N}_{++}} \mathbb{R}^{lk}$ for which $s_i = x$ for all $i = 1, \ldots, n(s)$, one has $s \sim x$.

This condition is implied by Averaging if $\succsim$ is reflexive. The proof of this claim is left to the reader.

The next, and last, axiom is an axiom that we call *Same Number Existence Independence*, extending the terminology of Blackorby et al. (2005). This axiom says that the comparisons of two societies with the same number of individuals should only depend upon the distribution of the attribute bundles that differ between the two societies. Individuals who do not experience any change in their attribute bundles, and who are therefore "unconcerned" by the change, should not matter for the normative comparison of the two societies. As a consequence, the existence, or non-existence, of these individuals should not affect the ranking of the societies. We state this axiom formally as follows.

Same Number Existence Independence. For all societies $s, s', s'' \in \cup_{l \in \mathbb{N}_{++}} \mathbb{R}^{lk}$ for which $n(s) = n(s')$, $(s, s'') \succsim (s', s'') \Leftrightarrow s \succsim s'$.

It can be easily checked that any AA ranking that uses a continuous and monotonically increasing advantage function u satisfies Monotonicity, Same People Anonymity, Continuity, Averaging, and Same Number Existence Independence. In the next section, we establish the converse proposition that any ordering of $\cup_{l \in \mathbb{N}_{++}} \mathbb{R}^{lk}$ that satisfies these five axioms must be an AA ranking.

3 The Main Result

The main result established here relies heavily on a companion article, Gravel et al. (2010) (GMS in the sequel), that characterizes a *uniform expected utility* criterion in the somewhat different – but formally close – setting of choice under complete uncertainty. In GMS, the objects that are compared are finite sets of consequences instead of vectors of attribute bundles.

The first step in establishing our result consists in showing that if a social ordering $\succsim$ satisfies our five axioms, then it also satisfies the following condition.

Existence of Critical Levels. For every society $s \in \cup_{l \in \mathbb{N}_{++}} \mathbb{R}^{lk}$, there exists an attribute bundle $x(s) \in \mathbb{R}^k$ for which $x(s) \sim s$.

In words, this condition says that, for every society s, it is always possible to find an attribute bundle that, if given to a single individual, would be socially equivalent to s. For obvious reasons, this condition was called Certainty Equivalence in our article on uncertainty. Given Averaging, Existence of Critical Levels is equivalent to the requirement that, for every society, there exists an attribute bundle that will make the social planner indifferent between adding an individual endowed with this bundle to the society and not bringing this individual into existence. If the "bundle" is one-dimensional and is interpreted as utility, then this requirement corresponds to what Blackorby et al. (2005, p. 160) call Existence of Critical Levels in their welfarist framework. In this case, the attribute bundle is, in fact, a number that is called the "critical level of utility" by these authors.

We now show that Existence of Critical Levels is implied by Monotonicity, Same People Anonymity, Continuity, and Averaging. (Same Number Existence Independence is not needed to establish this result.)

Proposition 1. *Let $\succsim$ be an ordering of $\cup_{l\in\mathbb{N}_{++}}\mathbb{R}^{lk}$ that satisfies Monotonicity, Same People Anonymity, Continuity, and Averaging. Then $\succsim$ satisfies Existence of Critical Levels.*

Proof. Consider any society $s \in \cup_{l\in\mathbb{N}_{++}}\mathbb{R}^{lk}$. Recall that $B(s) = \{x \in \mathbb{R}^k : x \succsim s\}$ and $W(s) = \{x \in \mathbb{R}^k : s \succsim x\}$. By Continuity, both of these sets are closed. By Same People Anonymity, we may without loss of generality write s as $s = (s_1, \ldots, s_{n(s)})$ with $s_h \precsim s_{h+1}$ for $h = 1, \ldots, n(s) - 1$. By Averaging, $s_{n(s)} \succsim s_{n(s)-1}$ implies $(s_{n(s)}, s_{n(s)-1}) \succsim s_{n(s)-1}$. Because $s_{n(s)-1} \succsim s_{n(s)-2}$, it follows from the transitivity of $\succsim$ that $(s_{n(s)}, s_{n(s)-1}) \succsim s_{n(s)-2}$. Averaging then implies $(s_{n(s)}, s_{n(s)-1}, s_{n(s)-2}) \succsim s_{n(s)-2}$. Repeating this argument a finite number of times, we conclude that $(s_{n(s)}, \ldots, s_1) \succsim s_1$. Hence, by Same People Anonymity, we have $s \succsim s_1$. A similar argument can be used to show that $s_{n(s)} \succsim s$. Therefore, $s_{n(s)} \in B(s)$ and $s_1 \in W(s)$. Because $\succsim$ is complete, $B(s) \cup W(s) = \mathbb{R}^k$. The arc connectedness of $\mathbb{R}^k$ implies that there exists a continuous function $f : [0, 1] \to \mathbb{R}^k$ such that $f(0) = s_1$ and $f(1) = s_{n(s)}$. Because $B(s)$ and $W(s)$ are both closed, by Continuity, there must exist an $\alpha \in [0, 1]$ such that $f(\alpha) \in B(s) \cap W(s)$. That is, $f(\alpha) \sim s$, which shows that $\succsim$ satisfies Existence of Critical Levels. □

Endowed with this result, we are equipped to state and prove the main result of this article.

Theorem 1. *Let $\succsim$ be an ordering of $\cup_{l\in\mathbb{N}_{++}}\mathbb{R}^{lk}$ that satisfies Monotonicity, Same People Anonymity, Continuity, Averaging, and Same Number Existence Independence. Then $\succsim$ is an AA social ordering. Furthermore, the u function in the definition of an AA social ordering is unique up to a positive affine transformation and it is a continuous and increasing function of its k arguments.*

Proof. Suppose that $\succsim$ is an ordering of $\cup_{l\in\mathbb{N}_{++}}\mathbb{R}^{lk}$ that satisfies Monotonicity, Same People Anonymity, Continuity, Averaging, and Same Number Existence Independence. Let $\mathscr{P}(\mathbb{R}^k)$ denote the set of all finite non-empty subsets of $\mathbb{R}^k$ with representative elements A, B, C, etc. For any set $C \in \mathscr{P}(\mathbb{R}^k)$, write it as $C = \{c_1, \ldots, c_{\#C}\}$ and define the society $s^C \in \cup_{l\in\mathbb{N}_{++}}\mathbb{R}^{lk}$ by letting $s^C = (c_1, \ldots, c_{\#C})$.

Define the binary relation $\widehat{\succsim}$ on $\mathscr{P}(\mathbb{R}^k)$ by:

$$A \mathrel{\widehat{\succsim}} B \Longleftrightarrow s^A \succsim s^B$$

and denote the asymmetric and symmetric factors of this binary relation by $\widehat{\succ}$ and $\widehat{\sim}$ respectively. It is clear that $\widehat{\succsim}$ is an ordering of $\mathscr{P}(\mathbb{R}^k)$ if $\succsim$ is an ordering of $\cup_{l\in\mathbb{N}_{++}}\mathbb{R}^{lk}$.

We now show that $\widehat{\succsim}$ is continuous in the sense that the sets $\{x \in \mathbb{R}^k : \{x\} \mathrel{\widehat{\succsim}} A\}$ and $\{x \in \mathbb{R}^k : A \mathrel{\widehat{\succsim}} \{x\}\}$ are closed in $\mathbb{R}^k$ for any A in $\mathscr{P}(\mathbb{R}^k)$. That is, we show that $\succsim$ satisfies the axiom called Continuity in GMS. We provide the argument for the set $\{x \in \mathbb{R}^k : \{x\} \mathrel{\widehat{\succsim}} A\}$ (the argument for the set $\{x \in \mathbb{R}^k : A \mathrel{\widehat{\succsim}} \{x\}\}$ is similar). Consider a sequence $x^1, x^2, \ldots$ of elements of $\mathbb{R}^k$ converging to some element x of $\mathbb{R}^k$ for which one has $\{x^t\} \mathrel{\widehat{\succsim}} A$ for every t. By the definition of $\mathrel{\widehat{\succsim}}$, one has $x^t \succsim s^A$ for every t and, because x^t converges to x, it follows from the continuity of $\succsim$ that $x \succsim s^A$. But this implies, given the definition of $\mathrel{\widehat{\succsim}}$, that $\{x\} \succsim s^A$, which shows that the set $\{x \in \mathbb{R}^k : \{x\} \mathrel{\widehat{\succsim}} A\}$ is closed in $\mathbb{R}^k$.

We next show that for any *disjoint* non-empty finite sets $A, B \in \mathscr{P}(\mathbb{R}^k)$, one has $A \mathrel{\widehat{\succsim}} B \Leftrightarrow A \mathrel{\widehat{\succsim}} A \cup B \Leftrightarrow A \cup B \mathrel{\widehat{\succsim}} B$. That is, we show that $\mathrel{\widehat{\succsim}}$ satisfies the axiom called Averaging in GMS. Let A and B be two disjoint non-empty finite sets in $\mathscr{P}(\mathbb{R}^k)$ for which $A \mathrel{\widehat{\succsim}} B$. By the definition of $\mathrel{\widehat{\succsim}}$, $s^A \succsim s^B$. Because the ordering $\succsim$ satisfies Averaging, it follows that $s^A \succsim (s^A, s^B)$. Because $A \cap B = \varnothing$, it also follows that there exists an $\#(A \cup B) \times \#(A \cup B)$ permutation matrix π such that $\pi \cdot (s^A, s^B) = s^{A \cup B}$. By Same People Anonymity and the transitivity of $\succsim$, one has $s^A \succsim (s^A, s^B) \sim s^{A \cup B}$. By the definition of $\mathrel{\widehat{\succsim}}$, this implies that $A \mathrel{\widehat{\succsim}} A \cup B$. Averaging also implies that one has $(s^A, s^B) \succsim s^B$ and, as a result of what has just been established, it follows that $A \cup B \mathrel{\widehat{\succsim}} B$. Hence, we proved that $A \mathrel{\widehat{\succsim}} B \Rightarrow A \mathrel{\widehat{\succsim}} A \cup B \mathrel{\widehat{\succsim}} B$. For the other direction, assume that A and B are two disjoint non-empty finite sets in $\mathscr{P}(\mathbb{R}^k)$ for which $A \mathrel{\widehat{\succsim}} A \cup B$. By the definition of $\mathrel{\widehat{\succsim}}$, one has $s^A \succsim s^{A \cup B}$. Because A and B are disjoint, there exists an $\#(A \cup B) \times \#(A \cup B)$ permutation matrix π such that $\pi \cdot s^{A \cup B} = (s^A, s^B)$. By Same People Anonymity and the transitivity of $\succsim$, one has $s^A \succsim s^{A \cup B} \sim \pi \cdot s^{A \cup B} = (s^A, s^B)$. By Averaging, $s^A \succsim s^B$, which implies, given the definition of $\mathrel{\widehat{\succsim}}$, that $A \mathrel{\widehat{\succsim}} B$. The argument for establishing the same conclusion starting from the assumption that $A \cup B \mathrel{\widehat{\succsim}} B$ is similar.

The final property of $\mathrel{\widehat{\succsim}}$ that we show is that for any three finite and non-empty sets A, B, and C in $\mathscr{P}(\mathbb{R}^k)$ for which $A \cap C = B \cap C = \varnothing$ and $\#A = \#B$, one has $A \mathrel{\widehat{\succsim}} B \Leftrightarrow A \cup C \mathrel{\widehat{\succsim}} B \cup C$. That is, we show that $\mathrel{\widehat{\succsim}}$ satisfies the axiom called Restricted Independence in GMS. Let A, B, and C be three finite and non-empty sets in $\mathscr{P}(\mathbb{R}^k)$ for which $A \cap C = B \cap C = \varnothing$ and $\#A = \#B$. Assume first that $A \mathrel{\widehat{\succsim}} B$ and, therefore, that $s^A \succsim s^B$. By Same Number Existence Independence, one has $(s^A, s^C) \succsim (s^B, s^C)$. Because $A \cap C = B \cap C = \varnothing$, there are permutation matrices π and π' such that $\pi \cdot (s^A, s^C) = s^{A \cup C}$ and $\pi' \cdot (s^B, s^C) = s^{B \cup C}$. By Same People Anonymity and the transitivity of $\succsim$, one has $s^{A \cup C} = \pi \cdot (s^A, s^C) \sim (s^A, s^C) \succsim (s^B, s^C) \sim \pi' \cdot (s^B, s^C) = s^{B \cup C}$, which implies, given the definition of $\mathrel{\widehat{\succsim}}$, that $A \cup C \mathrel{\widehat{\succsim}} B \cup C$. For the other direction, assume now that $A \cup C \mathrel{\widehat{\succsim}} B \cup C$ and, therefore, that $s^{A \cup C} \succsim s^{B \cup C}$. Because $A \cap C = B \cap C = \varnothing$, there are permutation matrices π and π' such that $\pi \cdot s^{A \cup C} = (s^A, s^C)$ and $\pi' \cdot s^{B \cup C} = (s^B, s^C)$. By Same People Anonymity and the transitivity of $\succsim$, one has $(s^A, s^C) = \pi \cdot s^{A \cup C} \sim s^{A \cup C} \succsim s^{B \cup C} \sim \pi' \cdot s^{B \cup C} = (s^B, s^C)$. It then follows from Same Number Existence Independence that $s^A \succsim s^B$ and, by the definition of $\mathrel{\widehat{\succsim}}$, that $A \mathrel{\widehat{\succsim}} B$, as required.

We have shown that $\mathrel{\widehat{\succsim}}$ is an ordering of $\mathscr{P}(\mathbb{R}^k)$ that satisfies the axioms of Continuity, Averaging, and Restricted Independence of GMS. Moreover, $\mathbb{R}^k$ is clearly a separable and connected topological space. Hence, Theorem 4 of GMS applies to $\widehat{\succsim}$, so there exists a continuous function $u: \mathbb{R}^k \to \mathbb{R}$ such that, for every A and $B \in \mathscr{P}(\mathbb{R}^k)$, one has

$$A \mathrel{\widehat{\succsim}} B \iff \frac{\sum_{a\in A} u(a)}{\#A} \geq \frac{\sum_{b\in B} u(b)}{\#B}. \tag{3}$$

We need to show that this function u also represents the ordering $\succsim$ of $\cup_{l\in\mathbb{N}_{++}} \mathbb{R}^{lk}$. That is, we need to show that for any $s, s' \in \cup_{l\in\mathbb{N}_{++}} \mathbb{R}^{lk}$,

$$s \succsim s' \Longrightarrow \frac{\sum_{i=1}^{n(s)} u(s_i)}{n(s)} \geq \frac{\sum_{i=1}^{n(s')} u(s'_i)}{n(s')}$$

and (thanks to the completeness of $\succsim$) that

$$s \succ s' \Longrightarrow \frac{\sum_{i=1}^{n(s)} u(s_i)}{n(s)} > \frac{\sum_{i=1}^{n(s')} u(s'_i)}{n(s')}.$$

We only provide the proof for the first implication.

By way of contradiction, assume that $s \succsim s'$ and

$$\frac{\sum_{i=1}^{n(s)} u(s_i)}{n(s)} < \frac{\sum_{i=1}^{n(s')} u(s'_i)}{n(s')}. \tag{4}$$

Using Proposition 1, let $x(s)$ and $x(s')$ be the critical-level bundles that correspond to s and s' respectively. Because $x(s) \sim s \succsim s' \sim x(s')$, it follows from the transitivity of $\succsim$ and the definition of $\widehat{\succsim}$ that $\{x(s)\} \mathrel{\widehat{\succsim}} \{x(s')\}$, so that $u(x(s)) \geq u(x(s'))$. Clearly, this inequality is compatible with (4) only if at least one of the following two inequalities hold:

$$u(x(s)) > \frac{\sum_{i=1}^{n(s)} u(s_i)}{n(s)} \tag{5}$$

or

$$\frac{\sum_{i=1}^{n(s')} u(s'_i)}{n(s')} > u(x(s')).$$

We show that (5) cannot hold (the proof for the other inequality being similar). Consider the sequence of societies s^t defined, for any positive integer t, by:

$$s_i^t = \left(s_i + \frac{i}{t}\right).$$

By Monotonicity, one must have $s^t \succ s$ for all t. Using Proposition 1, let $x(s^t)$ be the critical-level bundle that corresponds to the society s^t. Hence, one has

$$x(s^t) \sim s^t \succ s \sim x(s).$$

By the transitivity of $\succsim$ and the fact that s^t is such that $s_i^t \neq s_{i'}^t$ for all $i, i' \in \{1, \ldots, n(s)\}$ for which $i \neq i'$, it follows from the definition of the ordering $\widehat{\succsim}$ that

$$\{x(s^t)\} \widehat{\sim} \{s_1^t, s_2^t, \ldots, s_{n(s)}^t\} \widehat{\succ} \{x(s)\}$$

for all t or, using the numerical representation of $\widehat{\succsim}$ provided by (3):

$$u(x(s^t)) = \frac{\sum_{i=1}^{n(s)} u\left(s_i + \frac{i}{t}\right)}{n(s)} > u(x(s)) \tag{6}$$

for all t. But, given the continuity of u, inequality (6) is clearly incompatible with inequality (5) because the sequence of numbers $u(x(s^t))$ converges to $u(x(s))$ while the sequence of numbers $\left[\sum_{i=1}^{n(s)} u\left(s_i + \frac{i}{t}\right)\right]/n(s)$ converges to $\left[\sum_{i=1}^{n(s)} u(s_i)\right]/n(s)$.

It is straightforward to verify that the u function in the definition of an AA social ordering is unique up to a positive affine transformation and that it is a continuous and increasing function of its k arguments. □

We conclude this section by establishing, in Remark 1, that when applied to an ordering of $\cup_{l\in\mathbb{N}_{++}}\mathbb{R}^{lk}$ that satisfies Same People Anonymity, the Monotonicity, Continuity, Averaging, and Same Number Existence Independence axioms are independent. We do not provide an example of an ordering of $\cup_{l\in\mathbb{N}_{++}}\mathbb{R}^{lk}$ that satisfies all of our five axioms except Same People Anonymity because considering non-anonymous orderings would lead one to consider a somewhat different domain than $\cup_{l\in\mathbb{N}_{++}}\mathbb{R}^{lk}$, one in which all conceivable individuals, whether alive, dead, or not yet born, would be given an identity.

Remark 1. *When imposed on an ordering of $\cup_{l\in\mathbb{N}_{++}}\mathbb{R}^{lk}$ that satisfies Same People Anonymity, the axioms of Monotonicity, Continuity, Averaging, and Same Number Existence Independence are independent.*

Proof. An AA ranking of $\cup_{l\in\mathbb{N}_{++}}\mathbb{R}^{lk}$ that uses a non-increasing function u (for example, $u(x) = \prod_{j=1}^{k} x_j - \sum_{j=1}^{k} x_j$) satisfies Same People Anonymity, Continuity, Averaging, and Same Number Existence Independence, but it obviously violates Monotonicity.

As an example of an ordering of $\cup_{l\in\mathbb{N}_{++}}\mathbb{R}^{lk}$ satisfying Same People Anonymity, Monotonicity, Continuity, and Averaging, but violating Same Number Existence Independence, let $k = 1$ and define $\succsim$ by:

$$s \succsim s' \iff \frac{\sum_{i=1}^{n(s)} s_i}{\sum_{i=1}^{n(s)} \frac{1}{s_i}} \geq \frac{\sum_{i=1}^{n(s')} s'_i}{\sum_{i=1}^{n(s')} \frac{1}{s'_i}}. \tag{7}$$

It is not hard to check that this ordering satisfies Same People Anonymity, Monotonicity, Continuity, and Averaging. To show that $\succsim$ violates Same Number Existence Independence, consider the societies $s = (1,7)$, $s' = (2,3)$, and $s'' = (4,12)$. Using (7), we have $s \succsim s'$ because

$$\frac{1+7}{1+\frac{1}{7}} = 7 \geq \frac{2+3}{\frac{1}{2}+\frac{1}{3}} = 6.$$

However, contrary to what is required by Same Number Existence Independence, one has $(s, s'') \prec (s', s'')$ because

$$\frac{1+4+7+12}{1+\frac{1}{4}+\frac{1}{7}+\frac{1}{12}} = \frac{24 \times 84}{84+21+12+7} = \frac{6 \times 84}{31} < \frac{2+3+4+12}{\frac{1}{2}+\frac{1}{3}+\frac{1}{4}+\frac{1}{12}} = 6 \times 3.$$

As an example of an ordering of $\cup_{l \in \mathbb{N}_{++}} \mathbb{R}^{lk}$ that satisfies all of the five axioms except Continuity, let $k = 2$ and define $\succsim$ by:

$$s \sim s' \iff \frac{\sum_{i=1}^{n(s)} s_{i1}}{n(s)} = \frac{\sum_{i=1}^{n(s')} s'_{i1}}{n(s')} \text{ and } \frac{\sum_{i=1}^{n(s)} s_{i2}}{n(s)} = \frac{\sum_{i=1}^{n(s')} s'_{i2}}{n(s')}$$

and

$$s \succ s' \iff \begin{cases} \dfrac{\sum_{i=1}^{n(s)} s_{i1}}{n(s)} > \dfrac{\sum_{i=1}^{n(s')} s'_{i1}}{n(s')} \text{ or} \\ \dfrac{\sum_{i=1}^{n(s)} s_{i1}}{n(s)} = \dfrac{\sum_{i=1}^{n(s')} s'_{i1}}{n(s')} \text{ and } \dfrac{\sum_{i=1}^{n(s)} s_{i2}}{n(s)} > \dfrac{\sum_{i=1}^{n(s')} s'_{i2}}{n(s')}. \end{cases}$$

We leave to the reader the easy task of verifying that this lexicographic ordering violates Continuity, but satisfies Same People Anonymity, Monotonicity, Averaging, and Same Number Existence Independence.

As an example of an ordering of $\cup_{l \in \mathbb{N}_{++}} \mathbb{R}^{lk}$ that violates Averaging but satisfies Same People Anonymity, Monotonicity, Continuity, and Same Number Existence Independence, consider the Classical Utilitarian ranking $\succsim^{CU}$ of societies defined, for every pair of societies s and s', by

$$s \succsim^{CU} s' \iff \sum_{i=1}^{n(s)} u(s_i) \geq \sum_{i=1}^{n(s')} u(s'_i)$$

for some increasing and continuous real valued function u having $\mathbb{R}^k$ as its domain. It is straightforward to check that $\succsim^{CU}$ violates Averaging but satisfies the other four axioms. □

4 Inequality Aversion

The social orderings characterized in Theorem 1 do not exhibit specific attitudes toward attribute inequality. It is easy to incorporate such attitudes in our framework if they are deemed appropriate. From a technical point of view, requiring a social ordering to exhibit a specific form of inequality aversion leads to additional restrictions on the advantage function whose average defines the social ordering, as in (2).

For instance, a widely discussed concept of inequality aversion in a multidimensional context is that underlying the principle of progressive transfers. See, for example, Ebert (1997), Fleurbaey et al. (2003), Fleurbaey and Trannoy (2003), and, in this volume, Gravel and Moyes (2011). According to this principle, which applies to societies of identical size, any transfer of attributes between two individuals must be seen as a social improvement if:

1. The person from which the transfer originates initially has a weakly larger endowment of every attribute than the beneficiary of the transfer.
2. For each attribute, the amount transferred does not exceed the difference between the donor's and the recipient's endowment of this attribute.

This kind of transfer, illustrated in Fig. 1, can be seen as a generalization to several attributes of the conventional Pigou–Dalton transfer used to define one-dimensional inequality. We should note that the kind of transfer that is defined here permits the amount of an attribute to be transferred between two individuals to be as large as the difference between them in this attribute. For instance, if Mary has three units of attribute 1 and two units of attribute 2 while Kumar has one unit of each, then transferring two units of attribute 1 from Mary to Kumar is considered to be equalizing here. Yet, after giving two units of attribute 1 to Kumar, Mary is poorer than Kumar in attribute 1 (even though she remains richer than Kumar in

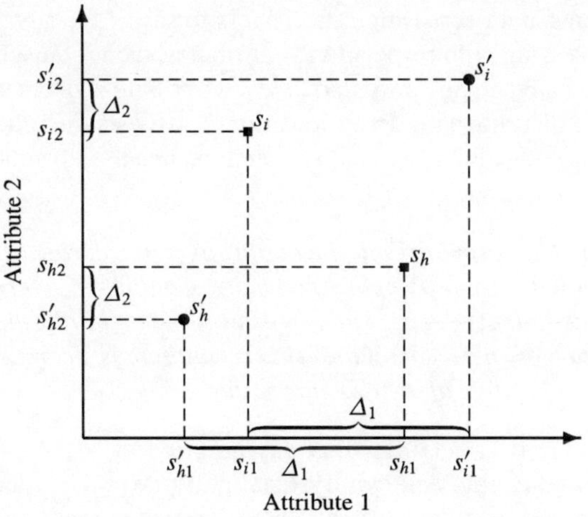

Fig. 1 A progressive transfer from i to h

attribute 2). For this reason, our definition of a progressive transfer embodies what is called a favorable permutation in Gravel and Moyes (2011) and a correlation decreasing transfer in Tsui (1999).

We define formally this concept of a progressive transfer as follows.

Definition. For societies s and s' with $n(s) = n(s') = n$, society s is obtained from society s' by a *progressive transfer* if there exist individuals h and i and, for $j = 1, \ldots, k$, real numbers $\Delta_j \geq 0$ (not all zero) such that:

1. $s_g = s'_g$ for all $g \neq h, i$,
2. $s_{hj} = s'_{hj} + \Delta_j \leq s'_{ij}$ and $s_{ij} = s'_{ij} - \Delta_j \geq s'_{hj}$ for all $j = 1, \ldots, k$, and
3. s is not a permutation of s'.

These kinds of transfers are used to define *attribute-inequality aversion* for $\succsim$.

Definition. An ordering $\succsim$ of $\cup_{l \in \mathbb{N}_{++}} \mathbb{R}^{lk}$ exhibits *attribute-inequality aversion* if it always ranks a society s strictly above a society s' when s has been obtained from s' by a progressive transfer.

It is of interest to identify the restriction on the advantage function u in formula (2) that is implied by the requirement that the social ordering $\succsim$ exhibits inequality aversion. As it happens, the property of the advantage function that is implied by this concept of inequality is that of *decreasing increasingness*. This property, also known as ALEP substitutability in the literature (see, e.g., Chipman 1977), is formally defined as follows.

Definition. A function $\Phi: \mathbb{R}^k \to \mathbb{R}$ is *decreasingly increasing* if Φ is increasing in each of its arguments and if for all $x, x' \in \mathbb{R}^k$ for which $x \geq x'$ and every strictly positive real number Δ, one has $0 < \Phi_j^{\Delta}(x) < \Phi_j^{\Delta}(x')$ for all $j = 1, \ldots, k$ for which $x_j \neq x'_j$, where Φ_j^{Δ} is as defined in (1).

In words, a decreasingly increasing function is a function that is increasing in all of its arguments at a decreasing rate. That is to say, if the advantage function is decreasingly increasing with respect to the attributes, then it must have the property that the "marginal advantage" provided by each attribute is decreasing with respect to the amount of that attribute. In Proposition 2, we establish that if $\succsim$ is an AA ordering that exhibits attribute-inequality aversion, then the advantage function must be decreasingly increasing.

Proposition 2. *Let $\succsim$ be an attribute-inequality averse ordering of $\cup_{l \in \mathbb{N}_{++}} \mathbb{R}^{lk}$ that satisfies Monotonicity, Same People Anonymity, Continuity, Averaging, and Same Number Existence Independence. Then $\succsim$ is an AA social ordering and the u function in the definition of an AA social ordering is continuous, decreasingly increasing, and unique up to a positive affine transformation.*

Proof. From Theorem 1, we know that any ordering of $\cup_{l \in \mathbb{N}_{++}} \mathbb{R}^{lk}$ that satisfies Monotonicity, Same People Anonymity, Continuity, Averaging, and Same Number Existence Independence is an AA social ordering that is represented, as in (2), by some increasing and continuous advantage function that is unique up to a positive affine transformation. We show that if the ordering is further required to exhibit aversion to attribute inequality, then the advantage function must be decreasingly increasing.

By contraposition, assume that the advantage function is increasing but not decreasingly increasing and, therefore, that there are attribute bundles $x, x' \in \mathbb{R}^k$ with $x \geq x'$ for which, for some attribute j and some strictly positive real number Δ, one has $0 < u_j^{\Delta}(x') \leq u_j^{\Delta}(x)$. Consider then two societies $s, s' \in \mathbb{R}^{nk}$ for some $n \in \mathbb{N}_{++}$ with $n \geq 2$ for which there exists two individuals h and i such that:

1. $s_g = s'_g$ for all $g \neq h, i$,
2. $s_{hj} = x'_j + \Delta$, $s'_{hj} = x'_j$, $s_{ij} = x_j$, and $s'_{ij} = x_j + \Delta$, and
3. $s_{he} = s'_{he} = x'_e$ and $s_{ie} = s'_{ie} = x_e$ for all $e \neq j$.

From the definition given above, s has been obtained from s' by a progressive transfer of attributes (in fact only attribute j has been transferred from i to h). Note that

$$\begin{aligned}
\frac{1}{n}\sum_{i=1}^{n} u(s_i) - \frac{1}{n}\sum_{i=1}^{n} u(s'_i) \\
&= \frac{1}{n}[u(x'_1, \ldots, x'_j + \Delta, \ldots, x'_n) - u(x'_1, \ldots, x'_j, \ldots, x'_n)] \\
&\quad - \frac{1}{n}[u(x_1, \ldots, x_j + \Delta, \ldots, x'_n) - u(x_1, \ldots, x_j, \ldots, x_n)] \\
&< 0
\end{aligned}$$

because $u_j^{\Delta}(x') < u_j^{\Delta}(x)$. Hence, the AA ranking does not exhibit attribute-inequality aversion because it ranks s strictly below s'. □

5 Conclusion

This article has provided an axiomatic justification for using, when ranking societies described by finite lists of attribute bundles, a ranking that can be thought of as resulting from a comparison of the average advantage achieved by individuals from their attribute bundles for some advantage function. While our approach applies to the welfarist case in which the only normatively relevant individual attribute is taken to be utility, its main interest is, in our view, that it can be applied to multidimensional and non-welfarist contexts where many individual attributes may matter for normative evaluation. To that extent, the advantage function that appears in the representation of the social ordering should not be interpreted as a measure of an individual's well-being but should, instead, be thought of as the valuation of the attributes made by the theoretician of justice. We have also shown that our approach is flexible and that it can incorporate important normative considerations like, for instance, attribute-inequality aversion.

It seems to us that requiring the social ordering to be anonymous, monotonic, and continuous is quite natural. Anonymity is a mild requirement here because it says that individual names do not matter for normative evaluation once the list of attributes that describes an individual's situation is sufficiently comprehensive. This justification of Anonymity is, of course, reminiscent of the one made famous by Kolm (1972) to justify his concept of "fundamental preference." If there is something in an individual's name that matters for normative evaluation, then we should put this "something" in the list of relevant attributes so that, ultimately, the name of this individual should not matter. Monotonicity is also a very natural requirement if we view attributes as "primary goods" or as things that "any reasonable person" would desire, and if we believe that a theory of justice should value, at least minimally, individual achievements. Continuity is probably not as natural a requirement because, among other things, it rules out lexicographic rankings of societies such as the Leximin one that have been advocated by Kolm (1972), among others. Yet, we contend that an ability to make continuous trade-offs between individuals when making collective decisions has clear practical advantages and is, after all, quite defensible from an ethical point of view.

If we accept this line of reasoning, and we therefore agree to restrict ourselves to the class of anonymous, monotonic, and continuous orderings of societies, then there are only two axioms that single out the AA family of social orderings in this class: Averaging and Same Number Existence Independence. Any reservation about agreeing to rank societies on the basis of their average advantage, for some advantage function defined on the set of all attribute bundles, must come from a reservation about accepting either, or both, of these axioms.

AA rankings and their generalized counterparts have been criticized in the welfarist population ethics literature for the fact that they may fail to recommend the enlargement of a society even when the new individuals that are added will have a "valuable" existence (see, e.g., Blackorby et al. 2005). This criticism rests on the existence of an "absolute" norm for what constitutes a "valuable" existence. The existence of such a norm may be plausible in a welfarist context in which an individual's utility is given a cardinally meaningful significance. Yet, we believe that it is much more difficult to come up with an absolute norm for a valuable existence in a multidimensional and non-welfarist context. The average advantage family of rankings examined in this article adopts the "relativist" point of view that it is worth adding a new individual to a society when, and only when, we can provide this individual with an attribute bundle that gives him or her an advantage level at least as large as that achieved on average in the society. The value of adding an individual to a society is therefore relative to the society to which the individual is added.

Of course, the AA family of ordering of societies, described as vectors of attribute bundles, is not the only conceivable class of social orderings. It is our hope that further work in this area will provide us with other social orderings whose axiomatic properties could then be usefully compared with those identified here.

Acknowledgements We are pleased to dedicate this work to Serge-Christophe Kolm. While we are not sure that he will find the proposal for comparing societies with variable population that is examined in this article attractive, we are certain that our discussions with him on many related issues and our reading of his work has been incredibly influential in shaping our views on the subject. We are also indebted, with the usual disclaiming qualification, to David Donaldson, Maurice Salles, John Weymark, and an anonymous referee for their helpful comments. The work leading to this research was initiated during a stay of Thierry Marchant at the Indian Statistical Institute, which he thanks for its warm hospitality.

References

Arrow, K. J. (1950). A difficulty in the concept of welfare. *Journal of Political Economy, 58*, 328–346

Blackorby, C., Bossert, W., & Donaldson, D. (1999). Information invariance in variable-population social-choice problems. *International Economic Review, 40*, 403–422

Blackorby, C., Bossert, W., & Donaldson, D. (2005). *Population issues in social choice theory, welfare economics, and ethics*. Cambridge: Cambridge University Press

Broome, J. (2004). *Weighing lives*. Oxford: Oxford University Press

Chipman, J. S. (1977). An empirical implication of Auspitz–Lieben–Edgeworth–Pareto complementarity. *Journal of Economic Theory, 14*, 228–231

Ebert, U. (1997). Sequential generalized Lorenz dominance and transfer principles. *Bulletin of Economic Research, 52*, 113–122

Fleurbaey, M., & Trannoy, A. (2003). The impossibility of a Paretian egalitarian. *Social Choice and Welfare, 21*, 243–264

Fleurbaey, M., Hagneré, C., & Trannoy, A. (2003). Welfare comparisons with bounded equivalence scales. *Journal of Economic Theory, 110*, 309–336

Gravel, N., & Moyes, P. (2011). Bidimensional inequalities with an ordinal variable. In M. Fleurbaey, M. Salles, & J. A. Weymark (Eds.), *Social ethics and normative economics: Essays in honour of Serge-Christophe Kolm* (pp. 101–127). Berlin: Springer

Gravel, N., Marchant, T., & Sen, A. (2010). Uniform expected utility criteria for decision making under ignorance or objective ambiguity. Unpublished manuscript, IDEP, Ghent University, and Indian Statistical Institute

Kolm, S.-C. (1972). *Justice et équité*. Paris: Editions du CNRS

Kolm, S.-C. (2005). *Macrojustice: The political economy of fairness*. Cambridge: Cambridge University Press

Parfit, D. (1984). *Reasons and persons*. Oxford: Oxford University Press

Rawls, J. (1982). Social unity and primary goods. In A. Sen & B. Williams (Eds.), *Utilitarianism and beyond* (pp. 159–185). Cambridge: Cambridge University Press

Sen, A. (1985). *Commodities and capabilities*. Amsterdam: North-Holland

Sen, A. (1987). *The standard of living*. Cambridge: Cambridge University Press

Tsui, K.-Y. (1999). Multidimensional inequality and multidimensionnal generalized entropy measures: An axiomatic derivation. *Social Choice and Welfare, 16*, 145–157

On Kolm's Use of Epistemic Counterfactuals in Social Choice Theory

John A. Weymark

1 Introduction

In a series of writings, Serge Kolm has examined the conceptual foundations of Arrovian social choice theory (see Kolm 1993, 1994, 1995, 1996, 1997). In its choice-theoretic formulation, an Arrovian social choice correspondence specifies the socially best alternatives from each admissible feasible set of alternatives as a function of the individual preferences over the universal set of alternatives. An issue that needs to be addressed when constructing a social choice correspondence is: For what feasible sets of alternatives and for what preference profiles are social decisions required? The rationale for the choice of this domain is one of the issues that Kolm discusses at some length. When considering resource allocation problems, social alternatives are meant to be complete descriptions of all the features of a social state relevant to choice, including future allocations of resources. It would then seem to follow that there is only one choice situation for which a social choice is required, the situation characterized by the actual feasible set and the actual preference profile. However, Arrow's famous impossibility theorem (see Arrow 1951, 1963) requires the domain of a social choice correspondence to be reasonably rich. Indeed, many of Arrow's axioms are vacuous if there is only one feasible set and one preference profile. Arrow (1951, p. 24) appeals to uncertainty about what the actual choice environment is at the time social decisions are being made to justify having a non-singleton domain. Kolm (1996), however, believes that it is difficult to reconcile this rationale for the choice of domain with the adoption of the axioms Arrow proposes for relating choices in different choice environments.

Kolm (1993, 1995, 1996, 1997) has proposed a different rationale for considering more than one choice situation in the domain of an Arrovian social choice correspondence – his "epistemic counterfactual" principle. In this rationale, a social choice only needs to be made from the actual feasible set given the actual profile

J.A. Weymark
Department of Economics, Vanderbilt University, VU Station B #35189, 2301 Vanderbilt Place, Nashville, TN 37235-1819, USA
e-mail: john.weymark@vanderbilt.edu

M. Fleurbaey et al. (eds.), *Social Ethics and Normative Economics*, Studies in Choice and Welfare, DOI 10.1007/978-3-642-17807-8_12,

of preferences, but in order for this choice to be justified, good reasons must be provided for this choice. These reasons involve comparing the choice that is actually made with what would have been justifiably chosen in appropriate counterfactual feasible sets with appropriate counterfactual preference profiles. In other words, we need to consider a social choice rule that specifies what is chosen in a range of test situations in order to determine if the choice in the actual choice situation is justified. Thus, the process of justification involves a thought experiment in which hypothetical choice situations are envisaged, and the choices that are recommended in these situations provide grounds for regarding the choice in the actual situation as being justifiable. Together with the actual feasible set and the actual preference profile, these hypothetical choice situations constitute the domain for the social choice correspondence.[1]

Kolm's epistemic counterfactual principle provides a rationale for including preference profiles and feasible sets in the domain of a social choice correspondence in addition to the actual profile and the actual feasible set. However, this principle does not provide any guidance as to what these alternative choice situations should be. The purpose of this article is to consider this issue. In my investigation, I shall simply take the premises of Kolm's argument (i.e., that there is only one actual social decision to be made, but this decision must be justified by the choices that would have been made in appropriate counterfactual choice situations) as given and focus on what his principle implies for the domain of a social choice correspondence.

The choice of an appropriate set of counterfactual choice situations, and hence the choice of an appropriate domain for the social choice correspondence, depends on the purpose for which the choice is being made. Kolm is interested in theories of justice and fairness in the allocation of resources. Impartiality is an essential feature of all such theories.[2] Here, I shall suppose that the objective is to make an impartial social choice. Different concepts of impartiality impose different constraints on choice, and so will result in the consideration of different sets of counterfactual choice situations. For example, impartiality might be with respect to personal identity, generation, or conception of the good. The theory of justice proposed by Rawls (1971, 1993) is impartial in all three of these senses, while the ethical theories of Harsanyi (1953, 1955, 1977), Vickrey (1945, 1960, 1961), and Hare (1952, 1963, 1981) are only impartial with respect to personal identity.[3]

---

[1] Epistemic counterfactuals should be distinguished from counterfactual conditionals, which are if-then statements that specify what would be the case if the antecedent were false. With an epistemic counterfactual of the kind considered here, it is not a question of what *would* be chosen in the counterfactual feasible set, but what can be *justifiably* chosen. The best-known account of counterfactual conditionals is the possible worlds semantics of Lewis (1973).

[2] Kolm argues that impartiality is implied by the requirement that a social choice should be rational (i.e., justifiable). See, for example, Kolm (1996, p. 185). My arguments do not depend on the validity of this claim.

[3] For an approach to fair allocation that employs the ordinality of the Arrovian framework, see Fleurbaey and Maniquet (2008). Impartiality in their model is captured by an anonymity axiom that requires the identities of individuals not to matter.

The restrictions that impartiality places on collective decisions can be determined directly using a particular concept of impartiality. Alternatively, these restrictions can be identified by investigating how impartiality is embodied in an ethical theory. For example, devices like a veil of ignorance or an ideal observer can be used to ensure impartiality. Largely for heuristic reasons, I consider how different ways that have been proposed for incorporating impartiality into an ethical theory can be used to identify an appropriate domain for an Arrovian social choice correspondence in order to justify the claim that the actual social decision has been made impartially, rather than determining this domain directly from a concept of impartiality. Specifically, I consider (a) the Harsanyi–Vickrey and Rawlsian veils of ignorance, (b) ideal observer theories, and (c) Hare's universal presecriptivism.

Harsanyi, Rawls, and Vickrey all make use of a veil of ignorance to help determine substantive principles of justice and social ethics. A veil characterizes the information that is morally relevant for making social decisions, with different conceptions of impartiality resulting in different specifications of the veil. Harsanyi and Vickrey have a "thin" veil of ignorance because personal identity is the only morally irrelevant information in their theories. Rawls has a thicker veil because his principles are not only required to be impartial with respect to personal identity, they are also required to be impartial with respect to generation and with respect to conception of the good. Here, I show how a veil of ignorance can be used to generate the set of counterfactual choice situations required by Kolm's epistemic counterfactual principle when the objective is to make an impartial social choice. The relevant Arrovian domain is the set of all choice situations that a moral agent behind a veil of ignorance thinks might be the actual choice situation outside the veil. The size of this domain is positively related to the thickness of the veil. Thus, my argument supplements Kolm's principle by providing an account of how the appropriate domain for a social choice correspondence can be determined, at least when the objective is to justify the actual social choice impartially. Once this domain has been identified, one can then ask if it is rich enough for all of Arrow's axioms to be nonvacuous. I shall argue that this is the case when the domain is generated by a Rawlsian veil, but not when it is generated by a Harsanyi–Vickrey veil.

Ideal observer theories and Hare's universal presecriptivism share with the Harsanyi–Vickrey veil of ignorance the idea that the relevant impartiality is with respect to personal identity. As a consequence, these theories generate the same set of counterfactuals as is obtained with a Harsanyi–Vickrey veil.

In the next section, I describe Arrow's formulation of the social choice problem and the choice-theoretic version of his impossibility theorem. In Sect. 3, I consider a number of rationales that have been proposed for including more than one choice situation in the domain of a social choice correspondence. In Sect. 4, I discuss Kolm's epistemic counterfactual principle. Section 5 sets out in a preliminary way my procedure for using a veil of ignorance to generate the set of counterfactual choice situations required by Kolm's principle. The following two sections examine the Harsanyi–Vickrey and Rawlsian veils. In Sect. 8, I discuss ideal observer theories and Hare's universal prescriptivism. In Sect. 9, I consider the relative merits of using a concept of impartiality directly to identify the relevant counterfactual choice situations instead of using those features of a normative theory that embody the requirements of impartiality to do so. Section 10 offers some concluding remarks.

2 Arrow's Theorem

Arrow's Theorem demonstrates that it is impossible for any procedure for making collective decisions to satisfy a number of properties that a priori one might think any reasonable collective decision-making procedure should satisfy. Arrow's Theorem can be formulated in terms of either a social welfare function or a social choice correspondence. A *social welfare function* assigns a social ordering (i.e., a reflexive, complete, and transitive binary relation) of the alternatives to each admissible profile of individual preference orderings of the alternatives. A *social choice correspondence* specifies, for each admissible feasible set of alternatives and each admissible profile of individual preferences on the universal set of alternatives, a subset of the feasible alternatives – the *social choice set*. For brevity, I often refer to a feasible set of alternatives as an *agenda* and refer to a combination of an agenda and a preference profile as a *choice situation*. The original versions of Arrow's Theorem, as found in Arrow (1951, 1963), were expressed in terms of social welfare functions, but it is a straightforward exercise to restate Arrow's Theorem in terms of social choice correspondences. Formal statements of both the welfare-theoretic and choice-theoretic versions of Arrow's Theorem may be found in Donaldson and Weymark (1988) and Le Breton and Weymark (2011).

The two approaches are closely related. A social welfare function can be used to construct a social choice correspondence as follows. For any choice situation, the social welfare function is first used to determine which social ordering of the universal set of alternatives is assigned to the profile of individual preferences. Then the social choice set is determined by maximizing this social ordering on the feasible set of alternatives. This is the procedure Arrow (1951, p. 26) uses to determine the social choice set in any admissible choice situation. While it is possible to generate a social choice correspondence in this fashion, it is not necessary to do so; one could instead determine the social choice set directly from knowledge of the choice situation without the intermediary of a social welfare function. This direct approach to making social choices is more general than the two-step procedure outlined above because there exist social choice correspondences for which the choices made from the various agendas for a given profile of preferences are not rationalizable by any ordering of the alternatives.

My concern is with social choice, not the social ranking of alternatives, and so I use the social choice formulation of Arrow's problem. The *domain* of a social choice correspondence is the collection of admissible choice situations; that is, the combinations of preference profiles and agendas for which a social choice is to be made. Arrow's impossibility theorem assumes that the domain of the social choice correspondence is quite rich. In standard choice-theoretic versions of this theorem, the domain includes (a) all conceivable profiles of individual preference orderings as possible profiles and (b) all nonempty finite subsets (or at least all two- and three-alternative subsets) of the set of alternatives as possible agendas. Arrow (1963, p. 97), however, noted that his preference domain assumption is "unnecessarily strong."

Kolm (1993, 1994, 1995, 1996, 1997) has been particularly critical of the assumption that there is an unrestricted domain of preference profiles, arguing that this results in "absurd" preferences being considered. For example, he notes that such a domain would require the consideration of preferences in which it is always preferable to have less of every good. However, it has been shown that the social welfare function version of Arrow's Theorem holds on quite restricted domains, including domains that satisfy the kinds of assumptions normally made in economic models. For social choice correspondences, the inconsistency of Arrow's axioms is less robust than in the welfare-theoretic case. On some natural domains, Arrow's axioms are consistent, whereas on some other natural domains, they are either inconsistent or only consistent with rather undesirable choice rules (see Le Breton and Weymark 2011). While these results demonstrate that one does not need to consider absurd choice situations to establish versions of Arrow's Theorem, they show that a reasonably rich domain is required if the properties Arrow proposed for a social choice correspondence are to have much force.

Given the domain assumptions described above, the choice-theoretic version of Arrow's Theorem shows that it is not possible to jointly satisfy Weak Pareto, Independence of Infeasible Alternatives, Arrow's Choice Axiom, and Nondictatorship.

Weak Pareto applies to each choice situation in the domain separately. This axiom says that a feasible alternative must not be chosen if there is another feasible alternative that everyone strictly prefers.

Independence of Infeasible Alternatives applies to pairs of choice situations that share a common agenda and in which both preference profiles agree on this agenda (but may differ on nonfeasible alternatives). This axiom requires the social choice set to be the same whenever the two choice situations are related in this fashion. Informally, the chosen alternatives only depend on the individual preferences for feasible alternatives.

Arrow's Choice Axiom, first introduced in Arrow (1959), requires that, holding the preference profile fixed, if the feasible set shrinks and some alternative that was originally chosen is still feasible, then any of the originally chosen alternatives that remain feasible must continue to be chosen and no alternative that was originally rejected should now be chosen. Arrow's Choice Axiom is an example of what is known as a collective rationality assumption.[4]

An individual is a *dictator* if for every choice situation, each alternative in the social choice set is one of this individual's most-preferred choices on the agenda. If the dictator has more than one best choice on an agenda, it is permissible (but not

[4] On some domains, Arrow's Choice Axiom is equivalent to the Weak Axiom of Revealed Preference. This axiom requires that if there is a situation in which one alternative is chosen and a second is rejected, then the latter alternative should never be chosen when the former is available. See, for example, Le Breton and Weymark (2011, p. 259).

required) to select among them. *Nondictatorship* requires that no such individual exists.

Whether these axioms are reasonable or desirable constraints on social choice is not my concern here.[5] Kolm, in the works cited above, has expressed reservations about many features of Arrow's formulation of the social choice problem, including the axioms.

3 Rationales for Non-Singleton Domains

In both its choice-theoretic and welfare-theoretic formulations, Arrow's Theorem supposes that every conceivable profile of individual preference orderings is included in the domain. In the choice-theoretic version of the theorem, it is also supposed that choices must be made from all possible finite agendas (or all those agendas containing two or three alternatives). In one of his earliest contributions, Kolm (1969, p. 168) says that

> ... the object of a normative theory is to define and to determine the optimum (i.e., to point out the right public action) under the given, and unique, set of constraints (which may be uncertain, dated for the future, etc.); what should be done *if* there are other constraints is simply irrelevant to the problem.

Expressed in terms of a social choice correspondence, his point is that there is only one choice situation – the actual one – and this is the only relevant choice situation. Accepting this view would imply that the domain of the social choice correspondence should only contain the actual choice situation, in which case both Arrow's Choice Axiom and Independence of Infeasible Alternatives would be vacuous.

As we shall see in the next section, Kolm now believes that the domain should contain more than one choice situation. However, before presenting the details of Kolm's argument, it is useful to see how the domain issue is dealt with in Bergson (1938)–Samuelson (1947) welfare economics and in Arrovian social choice theory.

Little (1952), Samuelson (1967), and others have suggested that a fundamental difference between a Bergson–Samuelson social welfare function and an Arrovian social welfare function is that the former is defined for only a single preference profile, whereas the latter is defined for all conceivable profiles.[6] A Bergson–Samuelson social welfare function is a function that represents an ordering of the social alternatives.[7] Bergson and Samuelson use their kind of social welfare function

---

[5] Formal statements and a discussion of these axioms may be found in Le Breton and Weymark (2011).

[6] See also Bergson (1954, p. 247). Little (1952, p. 423) acknowledges that he is indebted to Samuelson (in conversation) for this observation. Kemp and Ng (1976), Parks (1976), and Pollak (1979), among others, have established versions of Arrow's Theorem in its social welfare function formulation for a domain consisting of a single preference profile. These versions of the impossibility theorem utilize an intraprofile independence condition that Samuelson (1977) finds quite unreasonable.

[7] See Bergson (1938, p. 312) and Samuelson (1947, p. 221).

to characterize the optimal choice from a given agenda when the alternatives are allocations of economic goods. Thus, they use the two-step procedure described above to determine the social choice correspondence. From their writings, it is not very clear whether a Bergson–Samuelson social welfare function is meant to be used to determine the social choice for different agendas or for just the current feasible set. In the subsequent literature, the ordering of alternatives given by a Bergson–Samuelson social welfare function is used to determine the social choice set from alternative agendas.[8] Thus, a Bergson–Samuelson social welfare function is the foundation for a social choice correspondence that has more than one choice situation in its domain, but each of these choice situations only differs in the agenda being considered, not in the preference profile.

This approach does not preclude considering different preference profiles. As Little (1952, pp. 423–424), defending the Bergson–Samuelson approach, puts it:

> If tastes change, we may expect a new ordering of all the conceivable states; but we do not require that the difference between the new and the old ordering should bear any particular relation to the changes of taste which have occurred. We have, so to speak, a new world and a new order; and we do not demand correspondence between the change in the world and the change in the order.[9]

Furthermore, Little (1952, p. 423) says that:

> If, for a given set of tastes, the environment varies we expect that the choices will be consistent in the sense that the choice function is derivable from a weak ordering of all social states.

Thus, each profile defines a new Bergson–Samuelson social welfare function that is used to determine the choices from the admissible agendas. Piecing together these choices for the alternative profiles and the alternative agendas, we obtain an Arrovian social choice correspondence (on a possibly restricted domain).[10]

Kolm (1996, p. 180) has suggested that one possible reason for considering more than one choice situation is that there is a single set of individuals, each with preferences that are temporally independent, facing a sequence of undated agendas (so that the universal set of alternatives is the same in each of the choice situations). With the further proviso that individual preferences do not change from period to period, we have the kind of situation Bergson–Samuelson social welfare functions were designed to handle. Different agendas arise through time as technologies and, hence, feasible sets change.[11]

[8] Little (1952, p. 423) is explicit on this point.

[9] For further discussion of this point, see Fleurbaey and Mongin (2005, Sect. 2).

[10] The passages quoted above appear as part of Little's critique of Arrow's independence axiom. As is clear from these quotations, Little does not believe that this axiom is compelling, whereas he does believe that a collective rationality axiom that places cross-agenda restrictions on choice for a given preference profile, such as Arrow's Choice Axiom, is justifiable. His rationale for this position may be found in Little (1952, p. 424). For critical discussions of Little's arguments, see Kolm (1993, Sect. 13), Mongin and d'Aspremont (1998, p. 423), and Pattanaik (2005, Sect. 3.3).

[11] It is possible to interpret the rationale proposed by Little (1952, p. 423) for considering different agendas in this manner. Kolm (1993, Sect. 6) notes that this kind of rationale is inappropriate with dated alternatives.

It is also possible to regard the various possible agendas as arising not because there is a sequence of agendas, but because there is uncertainty about what the actual agenda will be at the time social decisions are made. Restated in terms of preference profiles, this is the rationale Arrow used to justify the presence of alternative profiles in the domain of his social welfare function.

> If we do not wish to require any prior knowledge of the tastes of individuals before specifying our social welfare function, that function will have to be defined for every logically possible set of individual orderings. ... However, we may feel on some sort of a priori grounds that certain types of individual orderings need not be admissible. (Arrow 1951, p. 24)

Implicit in Arrow's argument (as applied to social choice correspondences) is the assumption that while the social choice correspondence must be specified before the uncertainty is resolved, the actual implementation of the choice does not occur until the actual choice situation is known.[12]

4 Kolm's Epistemic Counterfactual Principle

The epistemic counterfactual principle proposed by Kolm (1993, 1995, 1996, 1997) provides a further rationale for considering a non-singleton domain. In contrast to Arrow, Kolm assumes that the actual choice situation is known when any decision must be made. Nevertheless, while it is only necessary to make a choice in the actual choice situation, this choice needs to be justified by the choices that would have been made in certain counterfactual choice situations. There must be a good reason that justifies the actual choice and it is the choices that would have been made in these hypothetical choice situations that provide this reason.

A natural way of interpreting Kolm's principle is as follows. To see whether the choice made in the actual choice situation is justified, we need to consider a social choice correspondence defined on an appropriate domain of choice situations. If, for example, our objective is to choose among the alternatives impartially, then we need to determine if the choice in the actual choice situation is consistent with making impartial decisions in a range of choice situations in which the roles of individuals are interchanged in some way. More generally, it is by testing our intuitions about what choices are reasonable in a range of choice situations that we can determine whether the actual choice is justified or not. In effect, the social choice correspondence provides the reasons for making the choices, both actual and hypothetical. Thus, we need to determine if the social choice correspondence conforms with the principles that we want to govern the collective decision-making process and, if so, whether these choices are consistent with our considered judgments. If

[12] Kolm believes that using Arrow's argument for having more than one choice situation in the domain makes it difficult to justify the adoption of the Arrovian axioms that place restrictions on how choices from different choice situations are related to each other. See, for example, Kolm (1996, Sect. 4.2) or Kolm (1997, Sect. 15.2).

they are, then this social choice correspondence provides a good reason for making the prescribed choice in the actual choice situation.

According to Kolm's epistemic counterfactual principle, the need to justify the actual social decision provides a reason for not restricting the domain of a social choice correspondence to the actual choice situation, but it does not, by itself, provide guidance as to which counterfactual choice situations should be considered. In other words, there remains the question of determining the appropriate domain for the social choice correspondence. Kolm (1993, Sect.12) raises this issue, but does not provide a specific proposal for its solution. Without specifying the criteria by which the actual choice should be judged, it is not possible to determine the set of counterfactual choice situations that are needed to apply Kolm's principle. In order to show how Kolm's principle can be used to determine an appropriate domain for a social choice correspondence when the actual choice situation is known, in subsequent sections I shall suppose that the objective is to choose alternatives impartially. Different concepts of impartially will be seen to lead to different specifications of this domain.

It should be emphasized that the application of Kolm's epistemic counterfactual principle to justify the actual social decision involves two distinct steps. First, the domain of the social choice correspondence must be specified. In other words, we first need to determine the set of "test" choice situations that should be considered in order to justify the choice in the actual choice situation. Second, we must determine if a social choice correspondence on this domain can be constructed that (a) chooses the actual social choice set in the actual choice situation and (b) embodies the principle or principles that the decision-making procedure is meant to conform to. If this is possible and the choices that the social choice correspondence recommends are consistent with our considered judgments, then the choice made in the actual choice situation has been justified. My concern here is with identifying the domain needed to apply Kolm's epistemic counterfactual principle when choices are to be made impartially, and not with whether a social choice correspondence satisfying the properties specified in the second step can be constructed. According, I focus on the first step in this procedure.

Kolm has argued that his epistemic counterfactual principle should take a more specific form than I have described above (see, for example, Kolm 1996, p. 180). To justify the choice of x when the agenda is X, he argues that there must exist another agenda Y containing x in which some other alternative y is chosen. Presumably, it is permissible to vary the profile as well as the agenda in this thought experiment, although Kolm is not very clear on this point. One can adopt the general version of the epistemic counterfactual principle without committing oneself to this specific version, and that is what I shall do here. The reason why I only adopt the general, and not the particular, features of Kolm's counterfactual argument can be illustrated with the following example.

Suppose that there are two individuals who differ in their productive abilities and that there are two goods, jam and leisure. For concreteness, let person one be the low productivity individual and person two be the high productivity individual. A social alternative specifies how much of each of the two goods each person consumes. Both individuals have the same preferences for jam and leisure (which is a normal good), but person two earns more than person one if they both work the same number of hours. While the government knows that one person has a high productivity, it does not know which individual is the more productive. As a consequence, to pursue its redistributive goals, the government is not able to use personalized lump-sum taxes and transfers. Instead, the government chooses a single tax schedule that determines the tax paid (or the transfer received) by any individual as a function of the income earned.

The model I have just described is the two-person version of the Mirrlees (1971) optimal income taxation problem, as presented in Stiglitz (1982). In this model, any feasible alternative has the property that the jam consumption of person one does not exceed the jam consumption of person two.[13] Let me further suppose that the unique social choice, call it x, involves giving person two strictly more jam consumption than person one (which turns out to also require that person two earns more than person one), perhaps because doing so results in both individuals consuming more jam than would be possible if jam consumption were equalized. Stiglitz (1982, p. 220) refers to this outcome as the "normal" case.

Assuming that one of our objectives is to treat individuals impartially, a natural counterfactual to this choice situation is obtained by permuting the individuals in this example. This involves not only permuting who has which preference and productivity, but also permuting who gets what consumption bundle in each feasible allocation. Symmetry considerations suggest that the social choice in the new choice situation, call it y, should be the allocation that is obtained by permuting the consumption bundles in x. This symmetry argument provides a counterfactual justification for choosing x in the actual choice situation – the choice of x is justified because if the roles of the individuals had been reversed, the symmetric allocation y would have been chosen. While this justification for choosing x conforms to the general form of the Kolm's epistemic counterfactual principle, it does not satisfy Kolm's more specific desiderata because x is not in the counterfactual agenda. Person two has more jam consumption in x than person one, but in the counterfactual situation person two has the lower productivity and so, as a consequence of the incentive constraints in this problem, cannot receive a higher jam consumption.

5 A Veil of Ignorance as a Source of Counterfactuals for Impartial Social Choice

Kolm (1993, 1995, 1996, 1997) is interested in determining the extent to which the Arrovian paradigm can contribute to social ethics. Kolm is particularly concerned with problems of distributive justice – how to reconcile the conflicting claims of the individuals in society. While it is commonly held that impartiality is an essential feature of all theories of morality and normative collective decision-making, including theories of justice and theories of fair allocation, there is considerable disagreement

[13] This is only a necessary, and not a sufficient, condition for an alternative to be feasible.

about what exactly is meant by impartiality and about how impartiality should be incorporated into such theories. In this and the subsequent three sections, I consider how different thought experiments that have been proposed for incorporating impartiality into a normative theory can be used to identify an appropriate domain for an Arrovian social choice correspondence in order to justify the claim that the actual social choice set has been chosen impartially.

I first consider the ways in which impartiality is incorporated into the original position theories of Harsanyi (1953, 1955, 1977), Rawls (1971, 1993), and Vickrey (1945, 1960, 1961). In each of these theories (as well as in many other ethical theories), principles of morality or justice are the principles that would be proposed by an individual who adopts an impartial perspective when making his or her recommendations. In the subsequent discussion, I shall refer to such an impartial individual as a *moral agent*. Following Kolm, I suppose that there is only one actual choice situation, but the choice made in this situation must be justified by the choices that would have been made in certain counterfactual choice situations. The devices that have been used by Harsanyi, Rawls, and Vickrey to derive substantive principles of morality and justice are instead used here to generate the domain for an Arrovian social choice problem.

The original position theories of Harsanyi, Rawls, and Vickrey suppose that principles of morality or justice are embodied in the decision rules that would be adopted in certain idealized *individual* choice problems. In these theories, social decisions are made by a rational moral agent. An *original position theory* supposes that a social decision (or the principle that is to be appealed to when making social decisions) is justified if it would be recommended by a rational, self-interested individual who is deprived of certain information, including the decision-maker's identity. An *original position* is simply any hypothetical decision problem with these features. The informational constraints facing a moral agent in an original position describe what Rawls calls a "veil of ignorance." The idea of an original position (although not the terminology) has its origin in the work of Harsanyi (1953, 1955) and Vickrey (1945), who independently proposed what is essentially the same description of an original position. Interest in original position theories became much more widespread with the appearance of Rawls' *A Theory of Justice* (Rawls 1971). While sharing with Harsanyi and Vickrey the device of an original position, Rawls' description of an original position differs markedly from that of Harsanyi and Vickrey.[14]

Barry (1973, p. 10) has observed that the features characterizing an original position are of two kinds: "... those which concern knowledge and those which concern motivation." In Barry (1989, Chap. 9), theories of justice in which the substantive principles of justice are determined by the choices made by moral agents (whether or not the moral agents are self-interested or operate behind a veil of ignorance) are

[14] In describing Rawls' original position in terms of a single moral agent choosing principles of justice from behind a veil of ignorance, I am following the description found, for example, in Rawls (1971, p. 139).

classified along these two dimensions.[15] In an original position theory, the moral agent pursues his or her own self-interest to the extent that this is possible given the information available and does so rationally in the sense of choosing appropriate means to achieve his or her objectives. Further, the moral agent is stripped of all morally irrelevant information, including his or her own identity, but is provided with all morally relevant information. Alternative original position theories differ in what they regard as morally relevant information.

Original position theories have been used to justify the choice of principles of justice, moral rules, social institutions, and particular social alternatives. Here, the device of a veil of ignorance is used to generate the set of counterfactual choice situations required to justify the actual social decision made in an Arrovian social choice problem when this decision must be made impartially. Because I am only concerned with identifying the domain needed to apply Kolm's epistemic counterfactual principle, and not with specifying the social choice correspondence on this domain that is used in the justificatory process, the motivations ascribed to a moral agent behind the veil of ignorance are irrelevant, although, of course, these motivations play a fundamental justificatory role in original positions theories. The relevant domain for the problem I am considering depends only on the informational constraints that characterize the veil of ignorance. The veil of ignorance specifies the morally relevant information and it is the description of the veil, not the motivational assumption, that distinguishes the original position of Harsanyi and Vickrey from that of Rawls. Harsanyi and Vickrey disagree with Rawls as to which information is morally relevant for choice in the original position, with Harsanyi and Vickrey endowing moral agents with much better information about the particulars of the world outside the veil than does Rawls. These differences in what is viewed as morally relevant information largely account for the substantially different principles advocated by Harsanyi and Vickrey on the one hand and Rawls on the other.[16]

It is now possible to describe more precisely my veil-of-ignorance procedure for generating the Arrovian domain needed to justify an impartial social choice. In this procedure, this domain consists of all the choice situations one might think could be the actual choice situation given the information available behind the veil of ignorance. The use of a veil is compatible with quite different notions of impartiality, and so with quite different ethical theories. The size of the domain obtained in this fashion depends on what is considered to be morally relevant information; the thicker is the veil of ignorance, the larger is the set of possible counterfactual choice situations. If, as in Harsanyi's and Vickrey's theories, there is a "thin" veil of ignorance, then the domain is not very rich. On the other hand, if, as in Rawls' theory, there is a "thick" veil of ignorance, then a rather large set of counterfactuals is obtained. In the

[15] Barry (1989) refers to all such theories as "original position theories," but it is more usual to use this term in the more restricted way that I do here.

[16] Rawls (1971, p. 121) conjectures that for all of the major theories of justice, it is possible to specify an original position that would lead to the choice of its principles.

next two sections, this general procedure is used to construct the domains implied by the Harsanyi–Vickrey and the Rawlsian veils.

Barry (1989, Sect. 41), Kolm (1996, Sect. 3), and Kolm (1997, Chap. 8) have argued that no original position theory – not just the original position theories of Harsanyi, Rawls, and Vickrey – can provide a satisfactory basis for determining principles of justice because the use of an original position necessarily results in the choice of principles that permit the sacrifice of some people's interests for the interests of others without at the same time providing a compelling reason for anyone to accept such sacrifices as being morally justified. Even if one finds their arguments compelling, one can consistently use original position arguments as I have done here. My argument only makes use of one part of the description of an original position – the veil of ignorance. It is the veil, not the assumption that a moral agent is self-interested, that is needed to identify my set of counterfactual choice situations. Once these counterfactual choice situations have been identified, the veil can be lifted before making the choices. I escape the criticisms of original position arguments advanced by Barry and Kolm because I do not require that the choices proposed by a moral agent are the ones that would have been chosen by pursuing *self-interest* behind a veil of ignorance.

6 A Harsanyi–Vickrey Veil

The first original position arguments were developed independently by Vickrey (1945) and Harsanyi (1953, 1955). The basic features of their original positions are similar, although they do differ in some respects, including the kinds of social alternatives that they consider.[17]

A moral agent behind the Harsanyi–Vickrey veil of ignorance chooses without knowing his or her actual identity, but with full knowledge of all other features of the social alternatives. For Harsanyi and Vickrey, personal identities are morally irrelevant, but everything else about social alternatives is morally relevant information. More precisely, when considering a social alternative, a moral agent imagines that he or she has an equal chance of being any particular person in society when the veil is lifted.[18] Thus, the thought experiment replaces an actual social alternative with an uncertain prospect in which the moral agent has an equal chance of occupying any position in society.

[17] Because Vickrey believes that interpersonal comparisons of utility are problematic, for the most part he assumes that all individuals share the same utility function. Harsanyi has written extensively on the nature of interpersonal utility comparisons (see, for example, Harsanyi 1955), and so heterogeneity of preference plays a prominent role in his writings. More complete statements of their theories may be found in Harsanyi (1977) and Vickrey (1960, 1961).

[18] In different alternatives, the same individuals (or even the same number of individuals) need not be alive. While it is not difficult to deal with this complexity, for simplicity, in the subsequent discussion I restrict attention to a fixed group of individuals.

To evaluate one of these uncertain prospects, the moral agent must empathize with each individual in turn, considering the worth of the underlying social alternative from each person's point of view. When imagining being person i in social alternative x, the moral agent evaluates the social alternative from person i's perspective, complete with i's tastes and objective circumstances. Harsanyi and Vickrey assume that the moral agent is self-interested. Although self-interested, because the moral agent does not know his or her identity, he or she must promote the interests of all individuals, and must do so impartially because it is equally likely that the agent will be any particular person when the veil is lifted. Harsanyi and Vickrey also assume that the moral agent ranks uncertain prospects in accordance with the principles of expected utility theory. Because uncertain prospects assign equal probability to each of the outcomes (i.e., to which position the moral agent occupies when the veil is removed), Harsanyi and Vickrey argue that different prospects, and hence different social alternatives, will be ranked by the average of the utilities obtained by each of the individuals. In this way, or so they argue, the Harsanyi–Vickrey original position results in a form of average utilitarianism.[19]

In order to identify the set of counterfactual choice situations that can be used to justify the social choice from the actual agenda given the actual preference profile, I borrow from the Harsanyi–Vickrey construction (a) the idea that personal identities are morally irrelevant and (b) the idea that this irrelevance can be operationalized by supposing that a moral agent is ignorant of his or her true identity. Adapting the first of these ideas to choice situations leads one to the view that who has which preference in the actual preference profile is morally irrelevant and that it is also morally irrelevant who occupies which position in the various alternatives that make up the actual agenda. Rather than introducing uncertain prospects to capture the ignorance imposed on a moral agent, I instead include in the domain of the social choice correspondence all of the choice situations one might think could be the actual choice situation if one were ignorant of one's true identity. This domain, excluding the actual choice situation, is the set of counterfactual choice situations that are used to justify the actual social choice when the relevant impartiality is with respect to personal identity.

In constructing one of these counterfactual choice situations, the identities of the individuals are permuted in a particular way. For example, the identities of individuals one and two could be permuted, with all other identities unchanged. In this example, the preferences of the first two individuals in the actual preference profile are interchanged. In each of the alternatives that make up the actual agenda, the roles of these two individuals are also switched; person one takes on two's objective circumstances and two's tastes and values in each alternative and vice versa for person two. More generally, a counterfactual choice situation is obtained by applying the same permutation of individuals to the actual preference profile and to all alternatives in the actual agenda.

---

[19] Whether Harsanyi's utilitarian conclusions follow from his assumptions is a matter of considerable controversy. See Weymark (1991, 2005).

The domain constructed in this way is not very rich. In general, no two admissible choice situations share a common preference profile, nor do they share a common agenda. For example, if the circumstances of each individual are unique, as in my jam-leisure example, then any nontrivial permutation of an agenda differs from the original agenda. It would then not be possible to find two choice situations with a common agenda, and so Independence of Infeasible Alternatives would be vacuous.[20] Because all agendas have the same number of alternatives, it is not possible to shrink the set of alternatives holding the profile fixed. As a consequence, Arrow's Choice Axiom is necessarily vacuous on the domain generated using this thought experiment. So while the need to justify the actual social choice in an impartial way provides an argument for considering a domain that includes hypothetical choice situations, it does not justify the choice of a rich enough domain for Arrow's independence and collective rationality assumptions to have any force if the relevant impartiality only concerns personal identity.

7 A Rawlsian Veil

In Rawls (1971, 1993), a moral agent in his version of an original position is charged with designing principles of justice that are to apply to the basic institutions in society. Compared with a moral agent behind the Harsanyi–Vickrey veil of ignorance, a Rawlsian moral agent is endowed with much less information. As is the case with Harsanyi and Vickrey, Rawls believes that personal identities in the distribution of advantages are morally irrelevant. Further, each person's particular conception of the good (comprehensive doctrine for ordering one's life) is morally irrelevant in Rawls' theory – in part because conceptions of the good are not independent of the institutions that help shape people's lives and in part because in each society "... there is a diversity of comprehensive doctrines, all perfectly reasonable." (Rawls 1993, p. 24) Instead, Rawls argues that what is morally relevant is that there are certain basic goods – primary goods and liberties – that are known to facilitate the advancement of any conception of the good and that the more of these goods one has, the better one is able to fulfill one's life plans. More particularly, a moral agent does not know the features of his or her psychology that determine the content of his or her interests or that determine his or her willingness to take risks to promote these interests. Rawls also argues that the actual point in history at which social decisions are being made is morally irrelevant, for otherwise particular generations could use this information to the detriment of subsequent generations. In addition,

[20] If there are two individuals who share the same preference over the feasible alternatives in the actual profile and if these same two individuals are in exactly the same circumstances in each of the alternatives that make up the actual agenda, then permuting these two individuals will result in a new choice situation that can only differ from the actual choice situation in the preferences over nonfeasible alternatives. It is only in such very special circumstances that the independence axiom has any role to play on this kind of domain.

Rawls does not provide a moral agent with the information needed to determine the relative likelihood of the various social outcomes.[21]

Thus, in the Rawlsian theory, impartiality with respect to personal identity is extended to include impartiality with respect to particular conceptions of the good and impartiality with respect to generations. All individuals are to have equal status as moral beings, regardless of one's natural advantages, one's social circumstances, or one's conception of the good.

As in Harsanyi's and Vickrey's description of an original position, Rawls supposes that a moral agent is self-interested (in the sense of wanting to advance his or her particular conception of the good whatever it should turn out to be when the veil is lifted). He argues that a moral agent with these interests situated behind his veil will choose principles of justice that (a) give priority to the equality of basic liberties, (b) arrange social and economic advantages so as to maximize the interests of the most disadvantaged group in society as measured by an index of primary goods (the *difference principle*), and (c) have positions and offices open to all individuals under conditions of fair equality of opportunity.[22] As is the case with the Harsanyi–Vickrey original position, the only relevant feature of Rawls' theory for my argument is his description of the veil of ignorance (and not his principles of justice or the motivations he ascribes to a moral agent).

Because Rawls has a much thicker veil than do Harsanyi and Vickrey, there are many more possibilities for what the world looks like outside the veil. Hence, my veil-of-ignorance procedure for determining the domain of a social choice correspondence generates a much richer set of counterfactual choice situations when the Rawlsian veil is used instead of the Harsanyi–Vickrey veil. To facilitate comparison with the domain generated by the Harsanyi–Vickrey veil, I adapt the Rawlsian veil to deal with the problem of impartial resource allocation for a fixed population (over the history of the world), rather than the more general problem of determining principles of justice for regulating the structure of social institutions.

For concreteness, let me suppose that social alternatives are allocations of public and private goods. The actual choice situation is described by the preferences of individuals over allocations and by the set of allocations that are feasible given the endowment of resources and given the technologies available for producing goods and services. Information that is morally irrelevant for Harsanyi and Vickrey is also morally irrelevant for Rawls, so each of the choice situations obtained by permuting individuals in the actual choice situation is also a choice situation that must be

[21] This description of the information available behind the veil of ignorance is largely drawn from the account given in Rawls (1971, p. 137). While information relating to particular individuals outside a Rawlsian veil is restricted behind the veil as described above, Rawls provides a moral agent with general information about human societies, such as principles of individual behaviour and social interaction.

[22] The derivation of Rawls' principles from his formulation of an original position is widely held to be problematic, as is the use of the difference principle to regulate social and economic affairs. See, for example, Barry (1973, 1989). The appropriateness of Rawls' formulation of the veil is also the subject of some controversy. See, for example, Hare (1973) and Nagel (1973).

included in the domain of the social choice correspondence. In other words, the domain generated by the Rawlsian veil must include the domain generated by the Harsanyi–Vickrey veil. Because the detailed conceptions of the good are morally irrelevant, but increases in primary goods are known to advance anyone's goals, it is reasonable to suppose that the domain of possible preference profiles for the counterfactual justification procedure includes (but may not be limited to) all profiles of preferences that are increasing in the personal consumption of all private and public goods. Because the state of development is morally irrelevant, any feasible set of allocations that can be obtained from some conceivable technologies using resources that do not exceed the earth's (or perhaps the universe's) initial endowment is an agenda that should be included in the domain.

Essentially the same domain was considered by Donaldson and Weymark (1988), but for different reasons. Donaldson and Weymark were interested in determining the consistency of the Arrovian axioms when natural economic restrictions are placed on the admissible preference profiles and on the admissible agendas. With minor and unimportant differences, the domain I have identified using a Rawlsian veil is the domain considered in their Theorem 1.[23] This domain is rich enough for both Arrow's Choice Axiom and Independence of Infeasible Alternatives to play substantive roles. By holding preferences fixed, but changing the technologies available to firms, it is possible to shrink the agenda in such a way that Arrow's Choice Axiom is nonvacuous. Because a counterfactual preference profile does not need to be a permutation of the actual profile, it is possible to change preferences (while holding the agenda fixed) in such a way that Independence of Infeasible Alternatives is nonvacuous. Thus, the domain considered by Donaldson and Weymark can be interpreted as being the domain generated by a Rawlsian veil, and this domain is rich enough for the Arrovian independence and collective rationality conditions to restrict the kind of social choice correspondences that can be considered.

8 Ideal Observer Theories and Hare's Universal Prescriptivism

Ideal observer theories and Hare's universal prescriptivism share with the Harsanyi–Vickrey version of an original position the idea that the relevant impartiality is with respect to personal identity. While these theories differ from the Harsanyi–Vickrey original position in the thought experiments used to achieve impartiality on the part

[23] Formally, Donaldson and Weymark's universal set of alternatives is the nonnegative orthant in a Euclidean space. Each component of this space corresponds either to the consumption of a public good or to some individual's consumption of a private good. Any subset of the orthant that is compact, comprehensive (i.e., satisfies free disposal), and has a nonempty interior is a feasible agenda. An agenda can be interpreted as being the set of all feasible allocations for an economy, with different agendas resulting from different resource endowments and/or different production technologies. Various preference domains satisfy Donaldson and Weymark's assumptions, including domains in which standard economic restrictions on preferences are assumed.

of a moral agent, because these theories all share the same concept of impartiality, they all identify the same set of counterfactual choice situations as the ones that should be used to justify the social choice in the actual choice situation as being impartial.

Hare (1972, p. 168) characterizes an *ideal observer theory* as follows:

> The ideal observer theory ... holds that in considering what we ought to do, we have to conform our thought to what would be said by a person who had access to complete knowledge of all the facts, was absolutely clear in his thinking, was impartial between all the parties affected by the action, and yet equally benevolent to them all.

In an ideal observer theory, the moral agent is a perfect altruist, giving each person's interests equal consideration. There is no veil of ignorance in an ideal observer theory. On the contrary, an ideal observer knows the interests of all individuals and knows his or her own identity. However, the ideal observer's full knowledge of personal identities is not something that is taken advantage of for personal gain because of the observer's benevolence.

Ideal observer theories have been used to justify classical utilitarianism – the principle that holds that alternatives are to be ordered in terms of the sum of individuals' utilities. Classical utilitarianism follows from the requirement that the observer is equally benevolent to the interests of each individual. Because of this fact, Hare (1972, p. 169) has argued that original position theories of the sort advocated by Harsanyi and Vickrey are essentially equivalent to an ideal observer theory, at least for fixed population problems. So we see that utilitarian conclusions emerge from either the combination of self-interest with ignorance about one's own identity or the combination of perfect benevolence with full knowledge of each person's identity. The Harsanyi–Vickrey original position and the ideal observer are simply two different devices for incorporating impartiality with respect to personal identity into a moral theory.

Hare's universal prescriptivism received its first statement in *The Language of Morals* (Hare 1952). This theory has been further developed and refined in many of Hare's later writings, most notably in Hare (1963, 1981). Hare obtains substantive moral principles – in particular, a form of classical utilitarianism – by elucidating the meaning of moral words and the nature of moral reasoning.

Gorr (1985, p. 116) provides a nice summary of Hare's theory:

> To sincerely affirm a moral judgment is, on Hare's view, to prescribe acting in accordance with a universal moral principle from which, in conjunction with statements specifying one's beliefs concerning the relevant facts, the judgment can be derived. To in turn determine whether one can prescribe acting in accordance with a universal principle is to determine whether one would actually choose to perform that action if one knew that one would have to play, in a series of possible worlds otherwise identical to the actual world, the role of *each* person (including oneself) who would be affected. Moreover, it is not enough that one simply imagines oneself, with one's *own* interests, in the place of those other persons – rather, one must imagine oneself as being in their place while having, in turn, *their* interests and desires.

Hare's moral agent is not ignorant of what role he or she occupies, as is the case behind a veil of ignorance; rather, this is information that is known, but it is morally irrelevant information, and so ignored. As a consequence, each person's interests are given equal weight. In order to promote each person's interests, it is necessary to know what these interests are. The moral agent obtains this knowledge by empathetic identification, imagining what it is like to be each person in turn (see Hare 1981, Chap. 5).

In Hare's theory, impartiality is achieved by the requirement that moral prescriptions be universalizable to all situations, both actual and hypothetical, that share with the situation under consideration the same universal features. The interests of all are advanced because in promoting one's own interests, one is constrained by the principle of universality to promote everyone else's interests as well. Because the thought experiment that underlies universal prescriptivism embodies the impartiality, equal benevolence, and knowledge of an ideal observer theory, Hare (1972, p. 171) argues that these two theories are for all practical purposes the same in their consequences. The idea of empathetically identifying with each individual and then giving each person's interests equal weight when aggregating is conceptually similar to the procedure used behind a Harsanyi–Vickrey veil, the main difference being that utilities are added in Hare's theory, but are averaged in the theories of Harsanyi and Vickrey. For a fixed population, classical and average utilitarianism order alternatives in the same way. Thus, Hare's universal prescriptivism, like the Harsanyi–Vickrey original position and the ideal observer, is a device for incorporating impartiality with respect to personal identity into a moral theory.

9 Direct Versus Indirect Approaches to Generating Impartial Consideration

The kind of impartiality required by a normative theory of collective decision-making can also be used directly (a) to identify the appropriate set of counterfactual choice situations and (b) to place restrictions on how the choices made in the admissible choice situations so identified are related to each other without the need for special devices, such as a veil of ignorance, which force a moral agent to adopt an impartial perspective. For example, when impartiality is with respect to personal identity, one could simply say that this kind of impartiality requires that the choice(s) in any hypothetical choice situation that is obtained from the actual choice situation by permuting the identities of the individuals must be the permuted alternative(s) corresponding to the actual choice(s). In this argument, the very concept of "impartiality with respect to personal identity" identifies the relevant set of counterfactual choice situations, independent of how this concept is embodied in the normative theory. As in Hare's theory, we are guided by the meaning of moral words, in this case, the meaning of "impartiality with respect to personal identity." Similarly, other notions of impartiality, such as impartiality with respect to generations or with respect to conceptions of the good, can be used to identify different sets of counterfactual choice situations without appealing to devices like a veil of ignorance.

Implicit in the preceding discussion is the view articulated by Kymlicka (1991) that the devices used to ensure impartiality are less important than the purpose for which they are adopted. As Kymlicka (1991, p. 194) observes:

> Impartial consideration can also be generated without any special devices at all, just by asking agents to give equal consideration to others notwithstanding their knowledge of, and ability to promote, their own good.[24]

Even if one endorses Kymlicka's position, using a device such as a veil of ignorance to generate impartial consideration serves a useful heuristic purpose.

If for heuristic or other reasons, one chooses not to directly use a particular concept of impartiality to identify the appropriate epistemic counterfactuals, then the veil-of-ignorance procedure is particularly appealing because, behind a veil, it is natural to think in terms of alternative choice situations – all the choice situations compatible with the information allowed by the veil. In contrast, with an ideal observer theory or with Hare's universal prescriptivism, the moral agent *knows* what the actual choice situation is. As a consequence, neither an ideal observer theory nor the idea of a moral agent arriving at universal prescriptions by a process of empathetic identification leads naturally to the consideration of alternative hypothetical *choice situations*. While an impartial observer or one of Hare's moral agents imagines him- or herself in the hypothetical circumstance of being someone else, this is not a hypothetical choice situation; that is, it is not a combination of a preference profile and an agenda. Hence, while the Harsanyi–Vickrey original position, an ideal observer theory, and Hare's universal prescriptivism utilize the same notion of impartiality and could in principle be used to identify the same set of counterfactuals, it is the veil argument that most simply and naturally leads one to think in terms of counterfactual choice situations.

10 Concluding Remarks

According to Kolm's epistemic counterfactual principle, the actual social choice must be justified by the choices that would have been made in appropriate counterfactual choice situations. Together with the actual choice situation, these hypothetical choice situations constitute the domain for an Arrovian social choice correspondence. I have argued that Kolm's principle needs to be supplemented by an account of how the relevant set of counterfactual choice situations is to be determined. I have suggested that an investigation of the constraints imposed on choice by the need to be impartial provides such an account when the objective is to make collective decisions impartially. This can be done either by directly using a concept of impartiality or by instead employing those features of a normative theory that embody the requirements of impartiality, such as has been done here with my use of veil-of-ignorance arguments to generate the relevant epistemic counterfactuals.

[24] Ackerman (1994, p. 369) makes a similar point in his critique of the Rawlsian veil.

Kolm's epistemic counterfactual principle can also be applied to any social choice axiom that places restrictions across choice situations. Arrow (1997, pp. 4–5) appeals to essentially the same principle in a discussion of the axiomatic approach to elections, arguing that when there is only a single election, the application of his independence and collective rationality axioms requires the use of counterfactuals. Kolm's principle does not provide support for the use of any particular axiom. Rather, it is concerned with what is needed in order to support the claim that what is chosen in a single choice situation is in fact justified by this axiom. With different axioms, different counterfactual choice situations are needed to apply Kolm's principle, just as here the choice of the domain needed to support the claim that the actual choice is impartial depends on the concept of impartiality that is employed.

Acknowledgements This article develops some ideas that were only briefly sketched in Weymark (1996). I have benefitted from comments received from Ken Binmore, Marc Fleurbaey, Nicolas Gravel, the late Jean Hampton, Andrew Irvine, Serge Kolm, Philippe Mongin, Maurice Salles, Peter Vallentyne, and the participants in the Conference on Social Ethics and Normative Economics held in honour of Serge Kolm at the Université de Caen, May 18–19, 2007. I am particularly grateful to Nicolas Gravel and Peter Vallentyne for their extensive written comments on previous drafts of this article. Research support from the Social Sciences and Humanities Research Council of Canada, the Hampton Fund of the University of British Columbia, and the College of Arts and Science at Vanderbilt University is gratefully acknowledged.

References

Ackerman, B. (1994). Political liberalisms. *Journal of Philosophy, 91*, 364–386

Arrow, K. J. (1951). *Social choice and individual values.* New York: Wiley

Arrow, K. J. (1959). Rational choice functions and orderings. *Economica, 26*, 121–127

Arrow, K. J. (1963). *Social choice and individual values* (2nd ed.). New York: Wiley

Arrow, K. J. (1997). The functions of social choice theory. In K. J. Arrow, A. K. Sen, & K. Suzumura (Eds.), *Social choice re-examined* (Vol. 1, pp. 3–9). London: Macmillan

Barry, B. (1973). *The liberal theory of justice.* Oxford: Clarendon

Barry, B. (1989). *A treatise on social justice. Volume 1: Theories of justice.* Berkeley and Los Angeles: University of California Press

Bergson, A. (1938). A reformulation of certain aspects of welfare economics. *Quarterly Journal of Economics, 52*, 310–334

Bergson, A. (1954). On the concept of social welfare. *Quarterly Journal of Economics, 63*, 233–252

Donaldson, D., & Weymark, J. A. (1988). Social choice in economic environments. *Journal of Economic Theory, 46*, 291–308

Fleurbaey, M., & Maniquet, F. (2008). Utilitarianism versus fairness in welfare economics. In M. Fleurbaey, M. Salles, & J. A. Weymark (Eds.), *Justice, political liberalism, and utilitarianism: Themes from Harsanyi and Rawls* (pp. 263–280). Cambridge: Cambridge University Press

Fleurbaey, M., & Mongin, P. (2005). The news of the death of welfare economics is greatly exaggerated. *Social Choice and Welfare, 25*, 381–418

Gorr, M. (1985). Reason, impartiality and utilitarianism. In N. T. Potter & M. Timmons (Eds.), *Morality and universality* (pp. 115–138). Dordrecht: D. Reidel

Hare, R. M. (1952). *The language of morals.* Oxford: Clarendon

Hare, R. M. (1963). *Freedom and reason.* Oxford: Clarendon

Hare, R. M. (1972). Rules of war and moral reasoning. *Philosophy and Public Affairs, 1*, 166–181
Hare, R. M. (1973). Rawls' theory of justice–I and II. *Philosophical Quarterly, 23*, 144–155 and 241–251
Hare, R. M. (1981). *Moral thinking*. Oxford: Clarendon
Harsanyi, J. C. (1953). Cardinal utility in welfare economics and in the theory of risk-taking. *Journal of Political Economy, 61*, 434–435
Harsanyi, J. C. (1955). Cardinal welfare, individualistic ethics, and interpersonal comparisons of utility. *Journal of Political Economy, 63*, 309–321
Harsanyi, J. C. (1977). *Rational behavior and bargaining equilibrium in games and social situations*. Cambridge: Cambridge University Press
Kemp, M. C., & Ng, Y.-K. (1976). On the existence of social welfare functions, social orderings and social decision functions. *Economica, 43*, 59–66
Kolm, S.-C. (1969). The optimal production of social justice. In J. Margolis & H. Guitton (Eds.), *Public economics: An analysis of public production and consumption and their relations to the private sector* (pp. 145–200). London: Macmillan
Kolm, S.-C. (1993). What sense social choice? Unpublished manuscript, Conseil Général des Ponts et Chausées, Paris
Kolm, S.-C. (1994). Rational normative economics vs 'social welfare' and 'social choice'. *European Economic Review, 38*, 721–730
Kolm, S.-C. (1995). Meanings and rationality in social choice theory. In D. Andler, P. Banerjee, M. Chaudhury, & O. Guillaume (Eds.), *Facets of Rationality* (pp. 79–103). New Dehli: Sage
Kolm, S.-C. (1996). Rational just social choice. In K. J. Arrow, A. K. Sen, & K. Suzumura (Eds.), *Social choice re-examined* (Vol. 2, pp. 167–196). London: Macmillan
Kolm, S.-C. (1997). *Modern theories of justice*. Cambridge, MA: MIT Press
Kymlicka, W. (1991). The social contract tradition. In P. Singer (Ed.), *A companion to ethics* (pp. 186–196). Oxford: Basil Blackwell
Le Breton, M., & Weymark, J. A. (2011). Arrovian social choice theory on economic domains. In K. J. Arrow, A. K. Sen, & K. Suzumura (Eds.), *Handbook of social choice and welfare* (Vol. 2, pp. 191–299). Amsterdam: North-Holland
Lewis, D. K. (1973). *Counterfactuals*. Cambridge, MA: Harvard University Press
Little, I. M. D. (1952). Social choice and individual values. *Journal of Political Economy, 60*, 422–432
Mirrlees, J. A. (1971). An exploration in the theory of optimum income taxation. *Review of Economic Studies, 38*, 175–208
Mongin, P., & d'Aspremont, C. (1998). Utility theory and ethics. In S. Barberà, P. J. Hammond, & C. Seidl (Eds.), *Handbook of utility theory. Volume 1: Principles* (pp. 371–481). Boston: Kluwer
Nagel, T. (1973). Rawls on justice. *Philosophical Review, 82*, 220–234
Parks, R. P. (1976). An impossibility theorem for fixed preferences: A dictatorial Bergson–Samuelson welfare function. *Review of Economic Studies, 43*, 447–450
Pattanaik, P. K. (2005). Little and Bergson on Arrow's concept of social welfare. *Social Choice and Welfare, 25*, 369–379
Pollak, R. A. (1979). Bergson–Samuelson social welfare functions and the theory of social choice. *Quarterly Journal of Economics, 93*, 73–90
Rawls, J. (1971). *A theory of justice*. Cambridge, MA: Harvard University Press
Rawls, J. (1993). *Political liberalism*. New York: Columbia University Press
Samuelson, P. A. (1947). *Foundations of economic analysis*. Cambridge, MA: Harvard University Press
Samuelson, P. A. (1967). Arrow's mathematical politics. In S. Hook (Ed.), *Human values and economic policy* (pp. 41–51). New York: New York University Press
Samuelson, P. A. (1977). Reaffirming the existence of "reasonable" Bergson–Samuelson social welfare functions. *Economica, 44*, 81–88
Stiglitz, J. E. (1982). Self-selection and Pareto efficient taxation. *Journal of Public Economics, 17*, 213–240

Vickrey, W. (1945). Measuring marginal utility by reactions to risk. *Econometrica, 13*, 319–333
Vickrey, W. (1960). Utility, strategy, and social decision rules. *Quarterly Journal of Economics, 74*, 507–535
Vickrey, W. (1961). Risk, utility, and social policy. *Social Research, 28*, 205–217
Weymark, J. A. (1991). A reconsideration of the Harsanyi–Sen debate on utilitarianism. In J. Elster & J. E. Roemer (Eds.), *Interpersonal comparisons of well-being* (pp. 255–320). Cambridge: Cambridge University Press
Weymark, J. A. (1996). Discussion of Kolm's paper. In K. J. Arrow, A. K. Sen, & K. Suzumura (Eds.), *Social choice re-examined* (Vol. 2, pp. 197–201). London: Macmillan
Weymark, J. A. (2005). Measurement theory and the foundations of utilitarianism. *Social Choice and Welfare, 25*, 527–555

Optimal Redistribution in the Distributive Liberal Social Contract

Jean Mercier Ythier

1 Introduction

The liberal social contract introduced in Kolm (1985, 1987a,b) and further developed in Kolm (1996, Chap. 5) and Kolm (2004, Chap. 3) is a normative construct corresponding to the unanimous agreement of individuals derived from the sole consideration of their preferences and rights, while abstracting from all conceivable impediments to the achievement of this agreement or implementation of its contents. These impediments are, notably, informational and other obstacles to the elaboration of the clauses of the social contract, and difficulties with their enforcement.[1] It differs from alternative normative theories such as Harsanyi's (1955) derivation of utilitarianism or Rawl's *A Theory of Justice* (1971) by deducing the normative content of the theory from *actual* individual preferences and rights.

Harsanyi and Rawls use the fiction of the veil of ignorance in an original position for abstracting from all possible sources of partiality in the individual judgments that may follow from an individual's actual position in society, his "interests" in an all-inclusive sense, including not only material wealth (the rich and the poor), but also human wealth (the sick and the healthy, the smart and the dull), social status, interpersonal relations, etc. Individuals, so abstractly placed in a position of objectivity, form their impartial judgments over social states by means of acts of imaginative sympathy, which consist of imagining themselves successively occupying all of the actual positions in society. The norms of justice are unanimous agreements of such individual impartial judgments, obtained from rational deliberation and bargaining

[1] Kolm's liberal social contract and the construct of Nozick (1974) share some important common features, notably in the method of derivation of a consistent system of individual rights, including property rights as a central feature. They also differ in several important respects, notably in the emphasis they place on market failures and other contract failures, which are essential in the former and almost absent from the latter.

J. Mercier Ythier
Université Panthéon-Assas, ERMES, and IDEP, 12 place du Panthéon, 75005 Paris, France
e-mail: jean.mercier-ythier@u-paris2.fr

M. Fleurbaey et al. (eds.), *Social Ethics and Normative Economics*,
Studies in Choice and Welfare, DOI 10.1007/978-3-642-17807-8_13,

in the construct of Rawls, and from the axioms of rational decision-making under uncertainty in the construct of Harsanyi.

The liberal social contract, in contrast, is a unanimous agreement of individuals in their actual positions in society. It is a *positive* theory in that respect. It becomes normative, hence a theory of justice, only insofar as the process of contracting and subsequent implementation of agreements takes place in idealized circumstances. The operation of abstraction that is performed at this level consists of extending, as an "as if" or *ceteris paribus* proviso, the abstract characteristics of perfectly competitive market exchange (notably costless information, bargaining, and enforcement) to the whole space of social contracting. The norm of justice is the unanimous agreement that obtains in these ideal conditions of perfect social contracting. It defines the (ideal) objective of collective action.

Actual collective action inspired by the liberal social contract fills the gap between the norm of the social contract and the reality of society by means of actual contractual arrangements, or institutional substitutes for them, which permit the achievement, partial or complete, of some of its ideal objectives subject to the constraints associated with the actual costs of the corresponding action. These modalities of collective action include state intervention, but do not reduce to the latter, in principle at least. In other words, the liberal social contract is mute, by construction, on the modalities of its implementation, as the costs of the latter proceed from circumstances (information, transaction, and enforcement costs) that are assumed away for its derivation.

We are specifically interested, in this article, in the *distributive* aspects of the liberal social contract (Kolm 1985, Chap. 19). We provide a formal interpretation of the concept of the distributive liberal contract and analyze some of its basic properties within the framework of the theory of Pareto-optimal redistribution developed using the contributions of Kolm (1968, 1969) and Hochman and Rodgers (1969).[2] This framework is particularly suitable for these purposes, notably for the following three reasons.

First, individuals have preferences over the distribution of wealth (in short, distributive preferences). An individual's concern about another's wealth can be of the benevolent type, also called an altruistic concern, or of the malevolent type, in situations of envy or of an ill-intended gift.[3] Altruistic concerns, in particular if they are strong or widespread enough, induce a willingness to give. If the gifts are

[2] See Mercier Ythier (2006, especially Sects. 4.1 and 6.1) for a comprehensive review of this literature.

[3] Envy is defined by economic theory as a situation in which an individual prefers another's position (here, another's wealth) to his own. Envy in this sense does not imply malevolence; nor does malevolence imply envy. They can be associated, though, in the psychological attitudes of someone relative to the wealthy, as when the consideration of wealthy positions creates both dissatisfaction with one's own situation and subsequent resentment for the source of this painful comparison. A malevolent distributive concern does not reduce to the case of envy, although the latter certainly is of great practical importance. Another important case is an ill-intended gift. See Kolm (2006, Sect. 4.2) for a comprehensive classification of gift motives, including the types of malevolent gift giving.

properly oriented and intended, they can be accepted by the beneficiaries. Subject to the same conditions, they may also arouse no frustration and cause no objection from those who do not take part in the gift-giving relationship as donor or beneficiary. They may, therefore, meet with unanimous agreement (the latter understood in the wide, or *weak*, sense that includes indifference as a case of agreement); that is, they may produce a legitimate (Pareto-improving) redistribution according to the ethical principles of the liberal social contract.

Second, individual distributive preferences make distribution a public good, as an object of common concern of the individual members of society (Kolm 1968, 1969). Any individual wealth, likewise, is a public good (or bad) for the set of individuals who feel concerned about it, whenever this set does not reduce to the wealth owner himself. Pareto-improving redistribution confronts, consequently, the general problems of individual and collective action in the presence of public goods, such as free-riding or preference revelation problems (e.g., Musgrave 1970) and difficulties of coordination (Warr 1983). The distributive liberal social contract yields a first-best Pareto-optimal solution to these problems, that is, a Pareto optimum relative to individual distributive preferences determined in the ideal conditions of perfect social contracting (no costs of information, transaction, and enforcement).

Third, the theory of Pareto-optimal redistribution suitably articulates competitive markets and Pareto-optimal redistributions. Competitive markets are in some sense implied by the normative reference to perfect contracting in the definition of the (norm of the) liberal social contract. Further, the first and second fundamental theorems of welfare economics extend to the case of non-paternalistically interdependent utilities, provided that malevolence, if any, is not so strong as to imply Pareto-optimal disposal of aggregate resources. (See notably Winter (1969), Archibald and Donaldson (1976), and Rader (1980).) That is, in this setup, a Pareto-optimal distribution achieves a competitive market equilibrium.

This article situates the liberal social contract in the theory of Pareto-optimal redistribution in the following way. We first retain the basic assumptions of the latter theory, that is, essentially, non-paternalistic utility interdependence, competitive markets, and private property. We next define a hypothetical initial position of the social system, which consists of the actual (pre-transfer) distribution of individual endowments and associated Walrasian equilibrium. In other words, the initial position corresponds to the allocation of resources by the (competitive) market prior to social contract redistribution. This hypothetical situation plays the same instrumental role, in the version of the social contract considered here, as the original position in the version of Rawls or the state of nature in the theory of the social contract of the eighteenth century.[4]

[4] Note, in particular, that the anteriority of the initial position relative to the social contract solution is *logical*, not *chronological*. Time is abstracted from in this rational reconstruction of the distributive institution. The redistributive transfers of the social contract are a thought experiment by construction, and hence reversible, as are, more generally, any individual or collective acts derived using the norm of the liberal distributive social contract "before" or "after" social contract redistribution.

The (norm of the) distributive liberal social contract relative to an initial position then consists of *a set of lump-sum transfers achieved from the endowment distribution of the initial position and of some associated Walrasian equilibrium such that the latter is a strong Pareto optimum relative to individual non-paternalistic preferences that is unanimously weakly preferred to the Walrasian equilibrium of the initial position.*

This definition embodies two sets of voluntary transfers. First, there are the transfers of market exchange, which result in an allocation that is both Pareto efficient relative to individual *consumption* preferences (e.g., Debreu 1954, Theorem 1) and also unanimously preferred to the *endowment distribution* relative to these same preferences (Debreu and Scarf 1962, Theorem 1). Second, there are the transfers of the social contract, which result in an allocation that is both Pareto efficient relative to individual *distributive* preferences and unanimously preferred to the *market equilibrium distribution* of the initial position relative to the latter preferences.[5]

It differs in this second respect (unanimous preference relative to the initial market equilibrium distribution) from the Pareto-efficient solutions of Foley (1970) and Bergstrom (1970). The core solution of Foley implies unanimous preference relative to the initial endowment distribution, but it does not imply, in general, unanimous preference relative to the market equilibrium with no provision of public goods (see the example in Sect. 5 below). The Lindahl equilibrium of Bergstrom neither implies unanimous preference relative to the initial endowment distribution,[6] nor unanimous preference relative to the market equilibrium with no redistribution (see Sect. 5).[7]

To sum up, the distributive liberal social contract considers Pareto-optimal redistribution *within an already constituted and functioning market economy*. Consequently, and consistently, it values a Pareto improvement in the distribution of wealth relative to a hypothetical initial position of market equilibrium with no redistribution.

---

[5] Although atemporal, as noted above in footnote 4, the logical sequence of market transfers improving upon the endowment distribution and social contract transfers improving upon the market equilibrium distribution somehow matches the historical sequence of the economic revolution from the late eighteenth century and the welfare state revolution from the late nineteenth century. The first type of argument synthesizes the economist's view about the contribution of market exchange to economic development. The second one is the liberal social contract rationale for the building up of a redistributive welfare state in developed market economies.

[6] This claim is established by Example 3 in Mercier Ythier (2004). See Mercier Ythier (2006, pp. 311–314) for a general analysis of the relations between the distributive liberal social contract, Bergstrom's Lindahl equilibrium, and Foley's core solution when there is only one consumption commodity (and therefore no market exchange).

[7] Note that, symmetrically, the distributive liberal social contract solutions need not, in general, be unanimously preferred to the (pre- or even post-social contract) endowment distribution for individual *distributive* preferences. Following the interpretation in historical terms in footnote 5, it is conceivable that some individuals express (for some reason, sentimental or otherwise) a preference for autarky (where the latter corresponds to an egalitarian state of nature à la Jean-Jacques Rousseau, for example) relative to the distributive and market efficiency of the equilibrium allocation of the liberal social contract.

To conclude this introductory section, it should be noted that the concept defined in the statement above captures only one part of the general concept of Kolm (1985, Chap. 19) because it ignores the process of bargaining and social communication, which is supposed, in Kolm's construct, to yield a *unique* social contract solution (i.e., a unique allocation and associated distribution of wealth) from any pre-contractual social state. The concept of a social contract, such as specified above, typically covers a large number of solutions from a given pre-contractual social state (see Fig. 1 in Sect. 4 below). One and only one of these numerous solutions is *the* distributive liberal social contract in the sense of Kolm. The definition above should be viewed, in other words, as a set of fundamental *necessary* conditions for the distributive features of the liberal social contract, rather than as a full characterization of it.

In the rest of this article, we: (1) provide formal definitions of the concepts and assumptions discussed above (Sect. 2), (2) introduce and interpret the differentiability and convexity assumptions that we employ (Sect. 3), (3) derive and analyze the fundamental property of separability between allocation and distribution (Sect. 4), and (4) situate the distributive liberal social contract relative to the comparable solutions of Bergstrom and Foley (Sect. 5). We provide some concluding remarks in Sect. 6. An Appendix summarizes some useful fundamental properties of differentiable Walrasian economies and collects the proofs of the theorems in Sect. 4.

2 Formal Definitions and Fundamental Assumptions

We consider the following simple society of individual owners of resources who consume, exchange, and redistribute commodities.[8]

There are n individuals denoted by an index i in the set $N = \{1, \ldots, n\}$ and l goods and services denoted by an index h in the set $L = \{1, \ldots, l\}$. We assume that

[8] We abstract from production for simplicity. The introduction of privately owned, price-taking, profit-maximizing firms with well-behaved (notably convex) production sets does not result in any significant change in our analysis. "Private utility"-maximizing owners of firms unanimously prefer, in particular, that the firms they own maximize their profits. This also holds true for "social utility"-maximizing owners endowed with non-paternalistic interdependent utilities (because social utility maximization presupposes private utility maximization for such individuals). This conformity of views for any individual in his different economic and social positions and in his roles as firm owner, consumer, and (potential) donor presupposes that exchange is perfectly competitive; that is, there is price-taking behavior on the part of individuals and firms and there are complete markets (with or without uncertainty). This conformity of views does not hold, in general, when there is imperfect competition or incomplete markets. But, in the latter case, we are outside the enchanted world of an Arrow–Debreu economy (Arrow and Debreu 1952) which, as we have argued in Sect. 1, is an essential part of the more general concept of perfect social contracting that underlies the norm of the distributive liberal social contract. Note, finally, that the types of activities that are really essential for the functioning of the distributive liberal social contract are the transfer activities of market exchange and social contract gift giving. Production, consumption, and disposal activities are only subsidiary in this respect.

$n \geq 2$ and $l \geq 1$ in the sequel; that is, we consider social systems with at least two agents and at least one commodity.[9]

The final destination of goods and services is individual consumption. A consumption bundle for individual i is a vector $x_i = (x_{i1}, \ldots, x_{il})$ of quantities of his consumption of commodities. The entries of x_i are nonnegative by convention, corresponding to demands in the abstract exchange economy described below. An allocation is a vector $x = (x_1, \ldots, x_n)$.

Individuals exchange commodities on a complete system of perfectly competitive markets. There is, consequently, for each commodity h, a unique market price, denoted by p_h, which agents take as given (i.e., as independent from their consumption, exchange, or transfer decisions, including their collective transfer decisions if any). We let $p = (p_1, \ldots, p_l)$.

Transfer decisions are made by coalitions of individuals, formally defined as any nonempty subset I of N. The set I could be a single individual. A transfer of commodity h from individual i to individual j is a nonnegative quantity t_{ijh}. We let $t_{ij} = (t_{ij1}, \ldots, t_{ijl})$ denote i's commodity transfers to j and $t_i = (t_{ij})_{j:j \neq i}$ denote the collection of i's transfers to other individuals (viewed as a row vector in $\mathbb{R}_+^{l(n-1)}$). A collection of transfers for the grand coalition N is denoted by t, that is, $t = (t_1, \ldots, t_n)$.

We make the following assumptions about commodities: (1) they are perfectly *divisible* and (2) the total quantity of each commodity is given once and for all, which, without loss of generality, is set equal to 1 (the latter is a simple choice of units of measurement); that is, there is an *exchange economy* with *fixed total resources*. An allocation x is *attainable* if it satisfies the aggregate resource constraint of the economy specified as follows: $\sum_{i \in N} x_{ih} \leq 1$ for all h. Note that this definition of attainability implies *free disposability*.

The vector of total initial resources of the economy is $\rho = (1, \ldots, 1) \in \mathbb{R}^l$. The set of attainable allocations is $A = \{x \in \mathbb{R}_+^{ln} : \sum_{i \in N} x_i \leq \rho\}$.

The society is a *society of private property*. In particular, the total resources of the economy are owned by its individual members. The initial ownership or endowment of individual i of commodity h is a nonnegative quantity ω_{ih}. The vector $(\omega_{i1}, \ldots, \omega_{il})$ of i's initial endowments is denoted by ω_i. By assumption, $\sum_{i \in N} \omega_i = \rho$. The initial distribution $(\omega_1, \ldots, \omega_n)$ is denoted by ω.

Individuals have preference preorderings over *allocations* that are reflexive, transitive, and complete. The allocation preferences of every individual i are assumed to be *separable* in his own consumption; that is, i's preference preordering induces a unique preordering on i's consumption set for all i. We suppose that preferences can be represented by utility functions. In particular, the preferences of individual i over his own consumption, as induced by his allocation preferences, are represented by the ("private" or "market") utility function $u_i : \mathbb{R}_+^l \to \mathbb{R}$, which we will sometimes also call an ophelimity function by reference to Pareto (1913, 1916). The product function $(u_1 \circ \mathrm{pr}_1, \ldots, u_n \circ \mathrm{pr}_n) : (x_1, \ldots, x_n) \to (u_1(x_1), \ldots, u_n(x_n))$, where pr_i

[9] The special case $l = 1$ is studied in Mercier Ythier (1998c), several results of which are subsumed in the results of the present study, notably in Theorem 2.

denotes the ith canonical projection $(x_1, \ldots, x_n) \to x_i$, is denoted by u. Finally, we suppose that individual allocation preferences satisfy the following hypothesis of *non-paternalistic utility interdependence*: For all i, there exists a ("social" or "distributive") utility function $w_i: u(\mathbb{R}_+^n) \to \mathbb{R}$, increasing in its ith argument, such that the product function $w_i \circ u: (x_1, \ldots, x_n) \to w_i(u_1(x_1), \ldots, u_n(x_n))$ represents i's allocation preferences. Let w denote the product function $(w_1, \ldots, w_n): \hat{u} \to (w_1(\hat{u}), \ldots, w_n(\hat{u}))$, which is defined on $u(\mathbb{R}_+^n)$.

If i's distributive utility is increasing in j's ophelimity, then i endorses j's consumption preferences within his own allocation preferences ("non-paternalism"). Note, nevertheless, that non-paternalistic utility interdependence does not imply *distributive benevolence* in the sense of individual distributive utilities increasing in some other individuals' ophelimities. It is compatible, in particular, with the *distributive indifference* of any individual i relative to any other individual j, that is, the constancy of i's distributive utility in j's ophelimity in some open subset of the domain $u(\mathbb{R}_+^n)$ ("local" distributive indifference of i relative to j) or on the whole of it ("global" indifference). It is also compatible with local or global *distributive malevolence*, in the sense of individual distributive utilities decreasing in some other individuals' ophelimities, and, naturally, with any possible combination of local benevolence, indifference, or malevolence of any individual relative to any other. For the sake of clarity, we reserve the terms"individual distributive utility function" for functions of the type w_i and "individual social utility function" for functions of the type $w_i \circ u$. The terms "individual distributive preferences" and "individual social preferences," on the contrary, are used synonymously, and designate individual preference relations over allocations – in short, individual allocation preferences.

Individual private utilities are normalized so that $u_i(\mathbf{0}) = 0$ for all i, where $\mathbf{0}$ denotes a vector whose components are all 0. Naturally, this choice is without loss of generality due to the ordinal character of allocation preferences.

We use as synonyms the following pairs of properties of a preference preordering and any of its utility representations: (1) C^1 preordering and C^1 utility representation, (2) *monotonic* (resp. *strictly monotonic*) preordering and *increasing* (resp. *strictly increasing*) utility representation, and (3) *convex* (resp. *strictly convex*) preordering and *quasi-concave* (resp. *strictly quasi-concave*) utility representation. Their definitions for utility representations are provided in footnote 11 below.

A social system is a list (w, u, ρ) of the individuals' distributive and private utility functions and of the aggregate initial endowments of the consumption commodities. A social system of private property is a list (w, u, ω). In such a social system, the total resources of society are owned by individuals and initially distributed between them according to the distribution ω.

For the purposes of this article, it is not necessary to develop a fully explicit concept of social interactions, synthesized in a formal model of social equilibrium such as those of Debreu (1952), Becker (1974), or Mercier Ythier (1993, 1998a,b) for example.[10] The following informal description and set of partial definitions will suffice.

---

[10] See Mercier Ythier (2006, Sects. 3.1.1, 4.2.1, and 6.1.1) for a review of such models.

Market exchange is operated by individuals, who interact "asympathetically" (Edgeworth 1881) or "nontuistically" (Wicksteed 1910) on anonymous markets through ophelimity-maximizing demands determined on the sole basis of market prices and individual wealth.

Sympathetic or altruistic interactions take place in the redistributive process. They may proceed, in principle, from a whole range of moral sentiments on the part of individuals, from individual sentiments of affection between relatives to individual moral sentiments of a more universal kind, such as philanthropy or an individual sense of distributive justice. They may, likewise, find their expression in a large variety of actions, from individual gift giving to family transfers, charitable donations, and public transfers. We concentrate, in this article, on *lump-sum redistributions that receive the (weak) unanimous agreement of the grand coalition*, that is, redistributions of initial endowments that are approved by some individual members of society (one of them at least) and are disapproved by none.

These various forms of social functioning are summarized in the following formal definitions of a *competitive market equilibrium* and a *distributive liberal social contract*. They are complemented by the two concepts of Pareto efficiency naturally associated with them, that is, respectively, Pareto efficiency relative to individual private utilities (in short, *market efficiency* or a *market optimum*) and Pareto efficiency relative to individual social utilities (in short, *distributive efficiency* or a *distributive optimum*).

Definition 1. A pair (p, x) such that $p \geq 0$ is a *competitive market equilibrium with free disposal* of the social system of private property (w, u, ω) if (i) x is attainable, (ii) $p_h(1 - \sum_{i \in N} x_{ih}) = 0$ for all h, and (iii) x_i maximizes u_i in $\{z_i \in \mathbb{R}^l_+ \colon \sum_{h \in L} p_h z_{ih} \leq \sum_{h \in L} p_h \omega_{ih}\}$ for all i.

Definition 2. An allocation x is a *strong* (resp. *weak*) *market optimum* of the social system (w, u, ρ) if it is attainable and if there exists no attainable allocation x' such that $u_i(x'_i) \geq u_i(x_i)$ for all i, with a strict inequality for at least one i (resp. $u_i(x'_i) > u_i(x_i)$ for all i). The set of weak (resp. strong) market optima of (w, u, ρ) is denoted by P_u (resp. $P^*_u \subset P_u$).

Definition 3. An allocation x is a *strong* (resp. *weak*) *distributive optimum* of the social system (w, u, ρ) if it is attainable and if there exists no attainable allocation x' such that $w_i(u(x')) \geq w_i(u(x))$ for all i, with a strict inequality for at least one i (resp. $w_i(u(x')) > w_i(u(x))$ for all i). The set of weak (resp. strong) distributive optima of (w, u, ρ) is denoted by P_w (resp. $P^*_w \subset P_w$).

Definition 4. Let (p, x) be a competitive market equilibrium with free disposal of the social system of private property (w, u, ω). The pair $(\omega', (p', x'))$ is a *distributive liberal social contract* of (w, u, ω) relative to the market equilibrium (p, x) if (p', x') is a competitive market equilibrium with free disposal of (w, u, ω') such that (i) x' is a strong distributive optimum of (w, u, ρ) and (ii) $w_i(u(x')) \geq w_i(u(x))$ for all i.

For the sake of brevity, a competitive market equilibrium with free disposal (Definition 1) will often be referred to as a Walrasian equilibrium or even simply as a "market equilibrium" in the sequel. Likewise, we will often refer to a distributive liberal social contract simply as a "social contract."

If a pair $(\omega', (p', x'))$ is a distributive liberal social contract of (w, u, ω) relative to the market equilibrium (p, x), we also refer to ω' as a distributive liberal social contract of (w, u, ω) relative to (p, x) and to x' as a *distributive liberal social contract solution* of (w, u, ω) relative to (p, x).

3 Differentiable Convex Social Systems

In this section, we first present our maintained convexity and differentiability assumptions, summarized in Assumption 1 below. The definitions of the corresponding standard properties of utility functions, such as differentiability, quasi-concavity, strict quasi-concavity, etc., are recalled in the footnote accompanying Assumption 1. We next discuss the general significance of and justifications for the non-technical aspects of parts (ii) and (iii) of this assumption (which apply to individual social preferences). We omit a similar discussion of part (i) because it corresponds to a set of conditions on private preferences that are standard in the study of differentiable exchange economies.

We use the following notation. Let $z = (z_1, \dots, z_m)$ and $z' = (z'_1, \dots, z'_m)$ be elements of $\mathbb{R}^m$, $m \geq 1$. We use the following conventions for vector inequalities: $z \geq z'$ if $z_i \geq z'_i$ for all i, $z > z'$ if $z \geq z'$ and $z \neq z'$, and $z \gg z'$ if $z_i > z'_i$ for all i. The inner product $\sum_{i=1}^m z_i z'_i$ is denoted by $z \cdot z'$ and the transpose (column) vector of z by z^T.

Let $f = (f_1, \dots, f_q)\colon V \to \mathbb{R}^q$, defined on an open set $V \subset \mathbb{R}^m$, be the Cartesian product of the C^1 real-valued functions $f_i\colon V \to \mathbb{R}$, $i = 1, \dots, q$. Let ∂f denote its first derivatives. Viewed in matrix form, $\partial f(x)$ is the $q \times m$ (Jacobian) matrix whose generic entry $(\partial f_i / \partial x_j)(x)$, also denoted by $\partial_j f_i(x)$ (or, sometimes, by $\partial_{x_j} f_i(x)$), is the first partial derivative of f_i with respect to its jth argument at x. The transpose $[\partial f_i(x)]^T$ of the ith row of $\partial f(x)$ is the gradient vector of f_i at x.

Assumption 1 (Differentiable Convex Social System).

(i) For all i, u_i is (a) continuous, strictly increasing, and unbounded above, (b) C^1 on $\mathbb{R}^l_{++}$, (c) strictly quasi-concave on $\mathbb{R}^l_{++}$, and (d) such that $x_i \gg \mathbf{0}$ whenever $u_i(x_i) > 0\ (= u_i(\mathbf{0}))$.

(ii) For all i, w_i is (a) increasing in its ith argument and continuous, (b) C^1 on $\mathbb{R}^n_{++}$, (c) quasi-concave, and (d) such that $w_i(\hat{u}) > w_i(\mathbf{0})$ if and only if $\hat{u} \gg \mathbf{0}$.

(iii) For all i, $w_i \circ u$ is quasi-concave.[11]

Assumption 1 will be maintained throughout the sequel.

[11] Recall that u_i is defined on $\mathbb{R}^l_+$, the nonnegative orthant of $\mathbb{R}^l$. We say that such a function is *increasing* (resp. *strictly increasing*) if $x_i \gg x'_i$ (resp. $x_i > x'_i$) implies $u_i(x_i) > u_i(x'_i)$. It is *continuously differentiable* (or C^1) on $\mathbb{R}^l_{++}$ if it is differentiable and has a continuous first

The convexity of individual social preferences admits a natural interpretation and justification in terms of inequality aversion because it implies a "preference for averaging" (in the sense that if z and z' are indifferent for the preference relation, then $\alpha z + (1-\alpha)z'$ is weakly preferred to both z and z' for any $\alpha \in [0,1]$).

The boundary condition Assumption 1.(ii).(d) on distributive utilities is a substantial assumption. In combination with Assumption 1.(i).(d) (the standard, technically convenient analogue for private utilities), it implies that all individuals strictly prefer allocations in which every individual enjoys positive wealth and welfare to allocations in which any individual is starving or freezing to death.

The monotonicity and convexity assumptions on individual social preferences are narrowly conditioned by the object of these preferences and, notably, by their large-scale character (the allocation of resources in society as a whole).

We only assume that an individual's distributive utility is increasing in his *own* private utility (see Sect. 2). This assumption follows from the basic hypothesis that individual allocation preferences are separable in own consumption, which can be interpreted as being a simple consistency requirement that stipulates that an individual's "social" view on his own consumption, as induced by his allocation preferences, must coincide with his "private" view on the same object, as represented by his private utility function.

We mentioned in Sect. 2 that our formulation of the hypothesis of non-paternalistic utility interdependence is compatible with distributive malevolence or indifference on the part of any individual relative to any other in a local or in a global sense. Casual observation of social life suggests that no such psychological attitude can be excluded on a priori grounds. It is also a commonplace of the stylized psychological theory of economists, elaborately expressed in Adam Smith's *The Theory of Moral Sentiments* (1759), that individuals should, in most circumstances of ordinary life, be more sensitive to their own welfare (in the sense of their ophelimity) than to the welfare of other individuals (at least "distant" others). The basis for this view is that the psychological perception of other individuals' welfare proceeds, to a large extent, from acts of imaginative sympathy (imagining oneself

---

derivative on this domain. It is *quasi-concave* if $u_i(x_i) \geq u_i(x_i')$ implies $u_i(\alpha x_i + (1-\alpha)x_i') \geq u_i(x_i')$ for any $1 \geq \alpha \geq 0$ and *strictly quasi-concave* if $u_i(x_i) \geq u_i(x_i')$, $x_i \neq x_i'$, implies $u_i(\alpha x_i + (1-\alpha)x_i') > u_i(x_i')$ for any $1 > \alpha > 0$. Note that in the special case of a single market commodity (i.e., $l = 1$), we can let $u_i(x_i) = \log(1 + x_i)$ without loss of generality (because "C^1 strictly quasi-concave" degenerates, in this simple case, into "C^1 strictly increasing").

Suppose, next, that the utility representation u_i is bounded above, but satisfies the other parts of Assumption 1.(i). Let $\sup u_i(\mathbb{R}^l_+) = b > a > u_i(\rho)$. Note that $a \in u_i(\mathbb{R}^l_+) = [0, b)$ because u_i is continuous and increasing. Define $\xi: [0, b) \to \mathbb{R}_+$ by setting $\xi(t) = t$ if $t \in [0, a)$ and $\xi(t) = t + (t-a)^3 \exp(1/(b-t))$ if $t \in [a, b)$. One can verify by simple calculations that ξ is strictly increasing and that $\xi \circ u_i$ is C^1 and unbounded above. Therefore, $\xi \circ u_i$ represents the same preordering as u_i and satisfies Assumption 1.(i). Thus, there is no loss of generality in supposing that u_i is unbounded above.

Assumption 1.(i) notably implies that $u: \mathbb{R}^{ln}_+ \to \mathbb{R}^n_+$ is onto (because u_i is a continuous, increasing, and unbounded from above function for all i), so that the domain $u(\mathbb{R}^l_+)$ of individual distributive utility functions coincides with the nonnegative orthant of $\mathbb{R}^n$. The preceding definitions readily extend to the functions w_i and $w_i \circ u$.

in another's shoes), which tend to be associated with less powerful affects in terms of frequency and average intensity, and hence to produce less vivid and enduring perceptions, than the perception of one's own welfare through one's own senses.[12]

Considered from this elaborate theoretical perspective, or from flat factual evidence, individual social preferences should be expected to exhibit wide ranges of indifference, distributive or otherwise, due to the large-scale character of their object. It seems natural to expect, for example, that an individual will ordinarily feel indifferent between reallocations among individuals with similar observable characteristics (for instance, similar ways of life) if these characteristics are very different from his own and if he has no personal acquaintance with them. Such indifference is inconsistent, in general, with strictly monotonic or strictly convex preferences. We chose, therefore, to keep to a minimum the monotonicity and convexity assumptions on social preferences at the individual level.

4 The Separability of Allocation and Distribution

A fundamental property of the abstract social systems outlined in Sect. 2 is the separability of allocation and distribution. This property states, essentially, that the redistribution of the social contract does not alter the fundamental features of the allocation of resources through the market that follow from the role of market prices in the coordination of individual supplies and demands, namely, the existence of market equilibrium, the Pareto efficiency of equilibrium allocations relative to private utilities ("market efficiency"), and the price-supportability of market optima.

The existence of market equilibrium, and the so-called first and second fundamental theorems of welfare economics (i.e., respectively, in our terms, the market efficiency of an equilibrium allocation and the price-supportability of market optima), are well-known consequences of Assumption 1.(i). Social contract redistribution was characterized, in Sect. 2, as a redistribution of individual endowments yielding a market equilibrium that is both Pareto efficient relative to the individual social utilities and unanimously (weakly) preferred to the initial market equilibrium. The separability property readily follows, therefore, from the concept of a distributive liberal social contract itself, provided that the latter is consistently defined. That is, provided that there always exists a market equilibrium that is a distributive optimum which is unanimously preferred to the initial market equilibrium for the individual social preferences.

In the rest of this section, we first establish the inner consistency of the definition of the distributive liberal social contract and characterize the set of social contract solutions in Sect. 4.1. Next, we provide a useful characterization of distributive optima as the maxima of averages of the individual social utility functions

[12] See Lévy-Garboua et al. (2006) for a comprehensive review of the literature, and also for their original views, on the formation of the social preferences of individuals primarily, but not exclusively, from an economic perspective.

in Sect. 4.2. We then proceed in Sect. 4.3 to the elicitation of an important consequence of separability, namely, the equivalence of cash and in-kind transfers for Pareto-efficient redistribution. We conclude this section with an analysis of the significance and scope of separability. The proofs of our theorems are presented in the Appendix.

4.1 Existence of a Distributive Liberal Social Contract

The inner consistency of the definition of the distributive liberal social contract is a simple consequence of the well-known fact that distributive optima are necessarily also market optima provided that: (1) utility interdependence is non-paternalistic and (2) the Pareto partial preordering associated with the distributive utilities satisfies an appropriate nonsatiation property.[13] Theorem 1 below first situates this basic property into the differentiable setup of the present article and then draws its consequences for the existence and characterization of distributive liberal social contract solutions.

The strong (resp. weak) Pareto partial preordering relative to the distributive utilities (in short, the strong (resp. weak) distributive Pareto preordering), denoted by $\succ_w$ (resp. $\succ_w^*$), is defined on the set $u(\mathbb{R}_+^n)$ of ophelimity distributions by setting $\hat{u} \succ_w \hat{u}'$ (resp. $\hat{u} \succ_w^* \hat{u}'$) if $w(\hat{u}) \gg w(\hat{u}')$ (resp. $w(\hat{u}) > w(\hat{u}')$). The weak (resp. strong) ophelimity distributions associated with the distributive optima of (w, u, ρ) are, by definition, the maximal elements of $\succ_w$ (resp. $\succ_w^*$) in the set $u(A)$ of attainable ophelimity distributions, that is, the elements $\hat{u}$ of $u(A)$ such that there exists no $\hat{u}'$ in $u(A)$ for which $\hat{u}' \succ_w \hat{u}$ (resp. $\hat{u}' \succ_w^* \hat{u}$).

Note that weak and strong distributive efficiency are not equivalent, in general, under Assumption 1. We will therefore maintain the distinction between the weak and strong concepts of a distributive optimum throughout this article. On the contrary, as is well-known, weak and strong market efficiency are equivalent under Assumption 1.(i) (see Theorem 4 in the Appendix). Therefore, we shall not distinguish between them in the sequel.

For any integer $m \geq 2$, we denote by S_m the unit-simplex of $\mathbb{R}^m$, that is, the set $\{z = (z_1, \ldots, z_m) \in \mathbb{R}_+^m : \sum_{i=1}^m z_i = 1\}$.

The following assumption of *differentiable nonsatiation of the weak distributive Pareto preordering* is maintained throughout the sequel.

Assumption 2. For all $\mu \in S_n$ and all $\hat{u} \in u(A) \cap \mathbb{R}_{++}^n$, $\sum_{i \in N} \mu_i \partial w_i(\hat{u}) \neq 0$.

Theorem 1. *Suppose that* (w, u, ρ) *satisfies Assumptions 1 and 2. Then:*

(i) *Any distributive optimum is a market optimum.*
(ii) *There exists a distributive liberal social contract for any initial distribution* ω *relative to any market equilibrium of* (w, u, ω).

[13] See notably Rader (1980) and Lemche (1986). A detailed account of this literature is provided in Mercier Ythier (2006, Sect. 4.1.2).

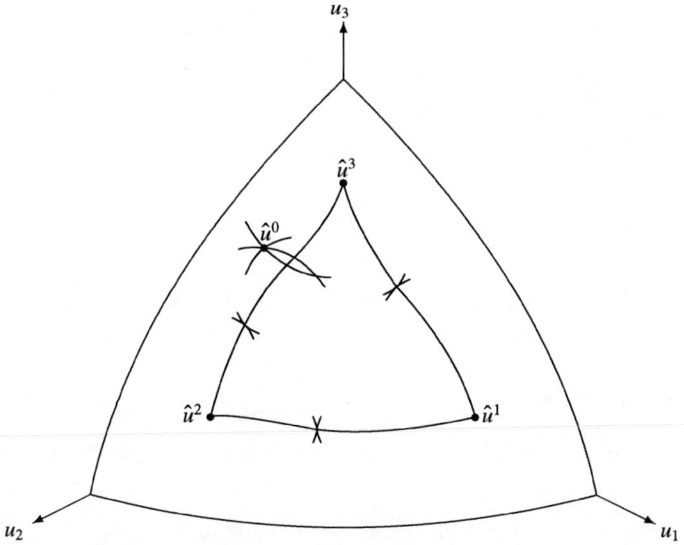

Fig. 1 Separability and the set of liberal social contracts

(iii) *The set of distributive liberal social contract solutions of* (w, u, ω) *relative to the Walrasian equilibrium* (p, x^0) *is the set* $\{x \in P_w^*\colon w(u(x)) \geq w(u(x^0))\}$.

Figure 1 provides a graphical illustration of the intuitions underlying Theorem 1. We consider a three-agent social system. We denote by $\hat{u}^i$ the maximum of w_i on the set $u(P_u)$ of ophelimity distributions corresponding to the market optima of the social system and by $\hat{u}^0$ the ophelimity distribution associated with some market equilibrium allocation $x^0 \notin P_w$. We suppose that $P_w = P_w^*$ (this will necessarily be the case, for example, if w_i is strictly quasi-concave for all i). The set $u(P_w)$ of ophelimity distributions corresponding to the distributive optima of the social system is the subarea of the surface $u(P_u)$ delimited by the continuous curves $\hat{u}^i\hat{u}^j = \arg\max\{(w_i(\hat{u}), w_j(\hat{u}))\colon \hat{u} \in P_u\}$ for all pairs $\{i, j\}$ of distinct individuals in $N = \{1, 2, 3\}$. The ophelimity distributions of $\{\hat{u} \in u(P_w^*)\colon w(\hat{u}) \geq w(u^0)\}$ that correspond to the distributive liberal social contract solutions relative to x^0 constitute the subarea of $u(P_w)$ delimited by the indifference curves of w_2 and w_3 through $\hat{u}^0$.

4.2 Distributive Efficiency as the Aggregation of Individual Social Preferences

An important by-product of the proof of Theorem 1 is the characterization provided in Theorem 2 below of distributive optima as maxima of weighted averages of individual social utilities. Theorem 2 extends to distributive optima and utilities the familiar characterization (using similar arguments) of market optima as maxima of weighted averages of individual private utilities.[14]

The Pareto-efficient redistribution of the distributive liberal social contract, in particular, implicitly assumes a process of identification of socially desirable allocations by (1) first aggregating "individual-social" utilities into a "social-social" utility function $\sum_{i \in N} \mu_i (w_i \circ u)$ by means of an arbitrary vector of weights $\mu \in S_n$ and (2) then maximizing these "social-social" utility functions on the set of attainable allocations unanimously weakly preferred to some initial equilibrium position (see our constructive proof of the existence of a distributive liberal social contract, in part (ii) of the proof of Theorem 1). Note, however, that the distributive liberal social contract, as defined in Sect. 2, does not itself implement the distributive optimum. It only redistributes endowments and leaves to the market the task of achieving the equilibrium allocation.[15]

Theorem 2. *Suppose that (w, u, ρ) satisfies Assumptions 1 and 2. Then, the following two propositions are equivalent.*

(i) *The allocation x is a weak distributive optimum of the social system (w, u, ρ).*
(ii) *There exists a weight vector $\mu \in S_n$ such that x maximizes $\sum_{i \in N} \mu_i (w_i \circ u)$ on A.*

4.3 Equivalence of Cash and In-Kind Pareto-Efficient Redistribution

The third aspect of separability considered in this section is the equivalence of cash and in-kind Pareto-efficient redistribution.[16] We first introduce the concept of a price-wealth distributive optimum, patterned on the price-wealth equilibrium

---

[14] A related property is the supportability of distributive optima by systems of Lindahl and market prices. Bergstrom (1970, Lemmas 3 and 5) shows that supportability holds for non-malevolent convex preferences. Mercier Ythier (2010) establishes the same property for social systems satisfying Assumption 1 that are differentiable and allow for malevolence.

[15] Except, of course, in the special case in which, as in part (ii) of the proof of Theorem 1, the endowment redistribution achieves a market equilibrium. This special case is theoretically interesting because it is always available in theory (by the second fundamental theorem of welfare economics). It therefore provides an easy and simple way for establishing the existence of a distributive liberal social contract. The corresponding market equilibrium is the autarkic equilibrium, that is, a market equilibrium in which each individual demands and consumes his own endowment. This equilibrium is unique in a regular differentiable exchange economy (Balasko 1988, Sect. 3.4.4). This observation implies, in particular, that social contract redistribution fully crowds out market exchange in this case. This case, therefore, is vacuous on practical grounds because actual economies hardly reach or even approach any state of reasonable economic efficiency without large market exchanges.

[16] For an analogous demonstration of the equivalence of cash and in-kind transfers in a general equilibrium set-up with non-cooperative altruistic transfers, see Mercier Ythier (2006, Theorem 5).

of market equilibrium theory, and then establish its equivalence with distributive efficiency.

We use standard definitions and properties of demand and indirect utility functions that hold when Assumption 1.(i) is satisfied. Notably, there exists, for each individual i, a continuous demand function $f_i \colon \mathbb{R}^l_{++} \times \mathbb{R}_+ \to \mathbb{R}^l_+$, that is, a continuous function such that for any price-wealth vector $(p, r_i) \in \mathbb{R}^l_{++} \times \mathbb{R}_+$, $f_i(p, r_i)$ is the (unique) consumption bundle that maximizes the private utility of individual i subject to his budget constraint $p \cdot x_i \leq r_i$. The (private) indirect utility function of individual i, defined as $v_i = u_i \circ f_i$, is a continuous function $v_i \colon \mathbb{R}^l_{++} \times \mathbb{R}_+ \to \mathbb{R}_+$. Demand functions are positively homogeneous of degree 0 (i.e., $f_i(\alpha p, \alpha r_i) = f_i(p, r_i)$ for all $(p, r_i) \in \mathbb{R}^l_{++} \times \mathbb{R}_+$ and all $\alpha \in \mathbb{R}_{++}$) and such that $p \cdot f_i(p, r_i) = r_i$ for all $(p, r_i) \in \mathbb{R}^l_{++} \times \mathbb{R}_+$ (the so-called additivity property of Walrasian demand). Indirect utility functions are positively homogeneous of degree 0 and strictly increasing with respect to wealth.

Because the money wealth of an individual reduces, in our set-up, to the market value of his endowment $r_i = p \cdot \omega_i$, we obtain $\sum_{i \in N} p \cdot f_i(p, p \cdot \omega_i) = \sum_{i \in N} p \cdot \omega_i = p \cdot \rho$ as the expression for Walras' Law for aggregate demand, which is satisfied for any system of positive market prices $p \gg 0$ and any distribution of initial endowments $\omega \in \{z \in \mathbb{R}^{ln}_+ \colon \sum_{i \in N} z_i = \rho\}$. From Walras' Law and the homogeneity properties of individual demands, a system of equilibrium market prices is defined only up to an arbitrary positive multiplicative constant. In the sequel, market prices are normalized so that $p \in S_l$ (i.e., we replace p by the equivalent $p / \sum_{i \in L} p_i$). This is always possible because $\sum_{i \in L} p_i$ is necessarily positive in equilibrium with our definitions and assumptions. With this normalization, $p \cdot \rho = 1$ for any p; that is, the market value of the aggregate resources of the economy is always equal to 1 using normalized market prices.

We let the distribution of money wealth $(r_1, \ldots, r_n)$ be denoted by r. The product function $(p, r) \to (f_1(p, r_1), \ldots, f_n(p, r_n))$ is denoted by f and the product function $(p, r) \to (v_1(p, r_1), \ldots, v_n(p, r_n))$ is denoted by v.

We now provide a formal definition a price-wealth market equilibrium for a social system.

Definition 5. A *price-wealth market equilibrium* of the social system (w, u, ρ) is a pair $(p, r) \in S_l \times S_n$ such that $\sum_{i \in N} f_i(p, r_i) = \rho$.

In differentiable economies, there is a well-known one-to-one correspondence between market optima $x \in P_u$ and the systems of price-wealth pairs (p, r) that are price-wealth market equilibria of the corresponding social system. Precisely, under Assumption 1.(i): For any $x \in P_u$, there exists a unique $p \in S_l$ such that the pair $(p, r) = (p, (p \cdot x_1, \ldots, p \cdot x_n))$ is a price-wealth market equilibrium (and the equilibrium p is strictly positive) and, conversely, if (p, r) is a price-wealth market equilibrium, then $x = f(p, r)$ is a market optimum, $p \gg 0$, and $r = (p \cdot x_1, \ldots, p \cdot x_n)$ (see Theorem 4 in the Appendix).

The concept of a price-wealth market equilibrium yields a natural alternative definition of a distributive optimum as a price-wealth market equilibrium that is not

Pareto-dominated relative to the individual social utilities by any other price-wealth market equilibrium.

Definition 6. A pair $(p, r) \in S_l \times S_n$ is a (weak) *price-wealth distributive optimum* of the social system (w, u, ρ) if (i) (p, r) is a price-wealth equilibrium of (w, u, ρ) and (ii) there exists no price-wealth equilibrium (p', r') of (w, u, ρ) such that $w(v(p', r')) \gg w(v(p, r))$.

Theorem 3. *Suppose that (w, u, ρ) satisfies Assumptions 1 and 2. Let x be a market optimum of (w, u, ρ) and $(p, r) \in S_l \times S_n$ be the unique price-wealth market equilibrium such that $x = f(p, r)$. Then, the following two propositions are equivalent.*

(i) *The allocation x is a weak distributive optimum.*
(ii) *The pair (p, r) is a weak price-wealth distributive optimum.*

4.4 Meaning and Scope of the Separability of Allocation and Distribution

To conclude this section, we very briefly return to the meaning and scope of the separability of allocation and distribution in our framework.[17]

The separability property has two components. First, the redistribution of endowments by the distributive liberal social contract and the allocation of resources by competitive markets are two autonomous processes. Second, these autonomous processes articulate consistently in the sense that the allocation that they jointly produce (they do produce one, which is unanimously preferred to the initial market equilibrium) is Pareto efficient relative to both the private and the social preferences of individuals.

The separability property relies upon a set of four main conditions: (1) Walrasian equilibrium, (2) non-paternalistic utility interdependence, (3) lump-sum endowment transfers, and (4) nonsatiation of the distributive Pareto preordering. Each of them can be considered as being essential for the property, independently of the other three. Taken together, they delineate the scope and the limits of the property.

Condition (1) is a basic hypothesis about the (ideal) organization and functioning of market exchange. Conditions (2) and (3) ensure that the design of a redistributive institution is perfectly compatible with the preceding hypothesis. Condition (4) embodies the hypothesis that civil peace is a common foundation and/or joint consequence of market exchange and social contract redistribution.

[17] See also Mercier Ythier (2006, Sect. 2.2) for further discussion of this issue.

5 A Comparison of Alternative Solutions for the Pareto-Efficient Provision of Public Goods

The example presented in this section supports the following claim of Sect. 1. For individual distributive preferences, Foley's core solutions and Bergstrom's Lindahl equilibrium solutions are not, in general, unanimously preferred to a Walrasian equilibrium with no provision of public goods.

Our example illustrates the following general ideas. The introduction of a public sector to an initial Walrasian equilibrium with no provision of public goods generally induces changes in the system of equilibrium market prices. These changes in the terms of trade might have adverse effects on the wealth and private welfare of some individuals. Public good provision is vetoed by an individual whenever the gain in her social welfare from this provision does not compensate for her loss in private welfare (more precisely, for the loss in terms of her individual social welfare that the latter induces). This is precisely what happens with the "egoistic rich" person in the example below. She has no taste for the public good (redistribution to the poor) and suffers adverse consequences, in terms of her private welfare, from any departure from the market equilibrium of the initial position.

Example. We consider the following simple social system, compatible with the present framework and those of Bergstrom (1970) and Foley (1970) simultaneously. There are two market commodities ($l = 2$) and four individuals ($n = 4$). The first commodity is the numeraire ($p_1 = 1$). Individuals have identical quasi-linear private utility functions of the form $u_i(x_i) = x_{i1} + \log x_{i2}$. Individual 4 is "poor": He has no initial endowment of resources ($\omega_4 = \mathbf{0}$). Individuals 1, 2, and 3 are "rich": Individual 1 owns the economy's endowment of the numeraire good ($\omega_{11} = \rho_1 = 1$) and each of individuals 2 and 3 owns one half of the economy's endowment of the second commodity ($\omega_{22} = \omega_{32} = \rho_2/2 = 1/2$). Rich individual 1 and poor individual 4 are egoistic, that is, $w_i(u(x)) = u_i(x_i)$ for all x, for $i = 1, 4$. Rich individuals 2 and 3 have identical distributive utility functions of the form $w_i(u(x)) = u_i(x_i) + u_4(x_4)$. This functional form implies that these two individuals express indifference towards the private welfare of the other rich person and non-paternalistic altruism towards the poor person. The private welfare or individual wealth of the poor person is a public good in this social system; it is an object of common concern for the poor and the altruistic rich individuals. This public good is "produced" from transfers of market commodities by means of the concave transfer "technology" $\rho - \sum_{i:i \neq 4} x_i \to u_4(\rho - \sum_{i:i \neq 4} x_i)$.

It is straightforward to show that the demand functions are $f_i(p, p \cdot \omega_i) = (\omega_{i1} + p_2\omega_{i2} - 1, 1/p_2)$ for all $i \neq 4$. Naturally, $f_4(p, p \cdot \omega_4) = (0, 0)$. Thus, in the Walrasian equilibrium of the initial position, the rich consume the same quantity of commodity 2, which must therefore be equal to 1/3 by the market equilibrium condition. The associated equilibrium price of this good is $p_2 = 3$. Hence, the equilibrium demands of the rich are (0,1/3) for individual 1 and (1/2,1/3) for individuals 2 and 3. The equilibrium distributive utility levels are $-\log 3$ for $i = 1$ and $-\infty$ for the other three individuals.

Any market optimum that induces social utility levels for the altruistic rich individuals that exceed $-\infty$ must have a positive consumption of commodity 2 by the poor individual. The same type of calculations as above then yield a supporting market price of 4 for commodity 2 and associated equal individual demands of 1/4. Individual 1's distributive utility level is $-\log 4$, which is less than $-\log 3$. That is, the egoistic rich individual strictly prefers the Walrasian equilibrium of the initial position to any market optimum that yields a social utility level that exceeds $-\infty$ for everyone. In particular, the set of distributive liberal social contracts of this social system reduces to the Walrasian equilibrium of the initial position.

Each of the two altruistic individuals by acting alone and using only her own endowment can obtain a distributive utility of

$$\max\{u_i(x_i) + u_4(x_4) \colon x \geq \mathbf{0} \text{ and } x_i + x_4 \leq (0, 1/2)\},$$

which is attained when $x_i = x_4 = (0, 1/4)$, yielding a distributive utility of $-2\log 4$, which exceeds $-\infty$. Any allocation in which the poor person has no consumption of commodity 2 is therefore blocked, in the sense of Foley (1970), by any of the coalitions $\{2\}$, $\{3\}$, and $\{2, 3\}$. Consequently, individual 1 strictly prefers the Walrasian equilibrium of the initial position to any allocation in the Foley core. A fortiori, this individual strictly prefers the Walrasian equilibrium of the initial position to Bergstrom's Lindahl equilibrium because it belongs to the Foley core as a consequence of Foley (1970, Sect. 6).[18]

[18] The following minor adjustments must be made in order for the frameworks of this example, Bergstrom (1970), and Foley (1970) to be exactly comparable.

First, we must account for the fact that the public good in the example is the private welfare of an individual who can, in principle, be included in the blocking coalitions of Foley, while there is no such possibility in Foley's set-up. This difficulty is resolved very easily using the following observations. It follows immediately from the definition of a Foley core that this set expands if the admissible coalitions are restricted to the nonempty subsets of $\{1, 2, 3\}$ (instead of $N = \{1, 2, 3, 4\}$). Conversely, if an allocation is unblocked by a coalition $I \subset \{1, 2, 3\}$, then it is unblocked by $I \cup \{4\}$ because $\omega_4 = (0, 0)$ (hence, adding individual 4 leaves unchanged the coalition's set of alternatives). That is, the Foley core is the same whether the admissible coalitions are the nonempty subsets of $\{1, 2, 3\}$ or the nonempty subsets of all of N.

Second, there is a slight and inconsequential difference in the formal definitions of a Lindahl equilibrium of Bergstrom and Foley, namely, the introduction in the latter of value-maximizing firms for the production of public goods. Foley's definition requires, in our example, the introduction of a firm (or a charity) who maximizes the net value $(\sum_{i:i\neq 4} \pi_i) u_4(x_4) - p \cdot x_4$, where π_i denotes the Lindahl price of the public good for individual i. This can be done without changing the equilibrium because the equilibrium value of $\sum_{i:i\neq 4} \pi_i$ coincides with the inverse of the marginal utility of wealth of individual 4 and, hence, the first-order conditions $(\sum_{i:i\neq 4} \pi_i) \partial u_4(x_4) = p$ for the maximization of the firm's value is automatically satisfied in equilibrium.

The Lindahl equilibrium for the example can be computed very easily by noting that it requires a positive consumption of commodity 2 by the poor person and, therefore, an equilibrium market price $p_2 = 4$ and equal individual demands of 1/4 for commodity 2. We have $\pi_1 = 0$, so that the equilibrium demand of egoistic individual 1 for market commodities is (0,1/4). That is, she exchanges her endowment of the numeraire good for commodity 2 purchased from the altruistic rich individuals. Because the distributive utility of an altruistic rich person is invariant to transfers

6 Conclusion

Kolm's distributive liberal social contract is a normative construct that is concerned with the Pareto-optimal redistribution of wealth within a functioning market economy. It derives its norm of wealth redistribution from an idealized assumption of perfect private and social contracting. We have analyzed this concept using the formal framework of the theory of Pareto-optimal redistribution. The distributive liberal social contract consists of a competitive market equilibrium that is both Pareto efficient relative to the individual distributive preferences and Pareto-improving relative to the initial competitive market equilibrium (that is, the competitive market equilibrium with no redistribution) for these preferences. These conditions are essential necessary characteristics of the distributive liberal social contract in this framework. However, they are not sufficient, in general, for a full characterization of it.

The distributive liberal social contract exhibits a fundamental property of separability of allocation and distribution. Social contract redistribution, performed by means of lump-sum transfers from initial individual endowments, preserves the basic existence and efficiency properties of competitive market equilibria. Such in-kind social transfers are essentially equivalent to monetary transfers. Social contract wealth distribution maximizes a weighted average of the individual social utility functions on the set of market equilibria that Pareto dominate the initial market equilibrium relative to the individuals' social preferences.

Appendix

In this Appendix, we first summarize in Theorem 4 some useful standard results about competitive equilibria of differentiable exchange economies that satisfy Assumption 1.(i). We then provide the proofs of our theorems.

Theorem 4. *Suppose that (u, ρ) satisfies Assumption 1.(i). Then, the following five propositions are equivalent.*

(i) *The allocation x is a weak market optimum of (u, ρ).*
(ii) *The allocation x is a strong market optimum of (u, ρ).*
(iii) *The allocation $x \in A$ is such that $\sum_{i \in N} x_i = \rho$ and there exists a price system $p \gg \mathbf{0}$ such that, for all i, either (a) $x_i = \mathbf{0}$ or (b) $x_i \gg \mathbf{0}$ and $\partial u_i(x_i) = \partial_{r_i} v_i(p, r_i)p$.*
(iv) *There exists a price system $p \gg \mathbf{0}$ such that $(p, (p \cdot x_1, \ldots, p \cdot x_n))$ is a price-wealth market equilibrium of (u, ρ).*
(v) *The allocation x is a market price equilibrium of (u, ρ).*

---

of the numeraire good to the poor person, strong distributive efficiency requires, then, that the total endowment of the numeraire good be transferred to the poor person and consumed by her. Therefore, the Lindahl equilibrium allocation is $((0, 1/4), (0, 1/4), (0, 1/4), (1, 1/4))$.

Proof of Theorem 1. (i) A distributive optimum x is by definition a local weak maximum of the product function $(w_1 \circ u, \ldots, w_n \circ u)$ on the set of attainable allocations A. Assumptions 1.(i).(d) and 1.(ii).(d) readily imply that $x \gg \mathbf{0}$ and $u(x) \gg \mathbf{0}$. The first-order necessary conditions (f.o.c.) for this smooth optimization problem (e.g., Mas-Collel 1985, Chap. 1, Sect. D.1) then state that there exists $(\mu, p) \in \mathbb{R}^n_+ \times \mathbb{R}^l_+$ such that (i) $(\mu, p) \neq \mathbf{0}$, (ii) $p \cdot (\rho - \sum_{i \in N} x_i) = 0$, and (iii) $\sum_{i \in N} \mu_i \partial_j w_i(u(x)) \partial u_j(x_j) - p = \mathbf{0}$ for all $j \in N$. We must have $\mu > \mathbf{0}$, for otherwise $p = \mathbf{0}$ by f.o.c. (iii), which contradicts f.o.c. (i). Because $\mu > \mathbf{0}$, (μ, p) can be replaced by $(\mu / \sum_{i \in N} \mu_i, p / \sum_{i \in N} \mu_i)$ in the first-order conditions; that is, we can suppose from now on that $\mu \in S_n$. Thus, f.o.c. (iii) is equivalent to requiring that $[\sum_{i \in N} \mu_i \partial_j w_i(u(x))] \partial u_j(x_j) = p$ for all j. Differentiable nonsatiation of the Paretian preordering and strictly increasing private utilities then imply that $p \gg \mathbf{0}$ and $\sum_{i \in N} \mu_i \partial_j w_i(u(x)) > \mathbf{0}$ for all j. The necessary first-order conditions reduce therefore to the following equivalent proposition: $x \gg \mathbf{0}$ is such that $\sum_{i \in N} x_i = \rho$ and there exists $(\mu, p) \in S_n \times \mathbb{R}^l_{++}$ for which, for all $j \in N$, $\sum_{i \in N} \mu_i \partial_j w_i(u(x)) > \mathbf{0}$ and $\partial u_j(x_j) = [1 / \sum_{i \in N} \mu_i \partial_j w_i(u(x))] p$. The latter system of conditions characterizes a market optimum of (w, u, ρ) under Assumption 1.(i) by the application of standard results on the characterization of Pareto optima of differentiable economies (see Theorem 4).

(ii) Let (p, x) be a competitive market equilibrium with free disposal for (w, u, ω). The set $A(x) = \{z \in A : w_i(u(z)) \geq w_i(u(x)) \text{ for all } i \in N\}$ of attainable allocations unanimously weakly preferred to x is nonempty (it contains x) and compact (as a subset of the compact set A, which is closed by the continuity of $w_i \circ u$ for all i). The continuous function $\sum_{i \in N} \mu_i (w_i \circ u)$ therefore has at least one maximum on $A(x)$ for any given $\mu \in S_n$. Let ω' be such a maximum. That is, suppose that $\sum_{i \in N} \mu_i w_i(u(\omega')) \geq \sum_{i \in N} \mu_i w_i(u(z))$ for all $z \in A(x)$ for a given $\mu \in S_n$. We suppose moreover that $\mu \gg \mathbf{0}$. We want to prove that there exists a price system p' such that $(\omega', (p', \omega'))$ is a distributive liberal social contract of (w, u, ω) relative to (p, x).

If $z \in A(x)$ is not a strong distributive optimum, that is, if there exists a $z' \in A$ such that $w(u(z')) > w(u(z))$, then $z' \in A(x)$ and $\sum_{i \in N} \mu_i w_i(u(z')) > \sum_{i \in N} \mu_i w_i(u(z))$ (because $\mu \gg \mathbf{0}$). Hence, z does not maximize $\sum_{i \in N} \mu_i (w_i \circ u)$ on $A(x)$. Therefore, ω' is a strong distributive optimum of (w, u, ρ) that is unanimously weakly preferred to x by construction. To complete this part of the proof, it suffices to establish that there exists a price system p' such that (p', ω') is a competitive market equilibrium with free disposal of (w, u, ω'). But this readily follows from the first-order conditions near the end of part (i) of this proof (recall that $P^*_w \subset P_w$) by application of standard results on the characterization of competitive equilibria of differentiable economies.

(iii) Theorem 1.(iii) is a simple consequence of Theorem 1.(i) and the properties of Walrasian exchange economies recalled in Theorem 4. □

Proof of Theorem 2. The proof of Theorem 2 is a simple extension of an argument in the proof of Theorem 1.(i), where we have already established that (i) implies the following set of necessary first-order conditions: $x \gg \mathbf{0}$ is such that

$\sum_{i \in N} x_i = \rho$ and there exists $(\mu, p) \in S_n \times \mathbb{R}^l_{++}$ for which, for all $j \in N$, $\sum_{i \in N} \mu_i \partial_j w_i(u(x)) > 0$ and $\partial u_j(x_j) = [1/\sum_{i \in N} \mu_i \partial_j w_i(u(x))]p$.

We now prove the following: If x satisfies the first-order conditions, then it maximizes $\sum_{i \in N} \mu_i (w_i \circ u)$ on A. Note that the first-order conditions imply the necessary first-order conditions for a local maximum of $\sum_{i \in N} \mu_i (w_i \circ u)$ on A (apply to the latter program the argument developed in the proof of Theorem 1 for the derivation of the first-order conditions for a weak distributive optimum). It will suffice, therefore, to establish that these necessary conditions for a local maximum of $\sum_{i \in N} \mu_i (w_i \circ u)$ on A are also sufficient conditions for a global maximum of the same program. But this readily follows from our assumptions and Theorem 1 of Arrow and Enthoven (1961), notably their conditions (b) or (c), which are both satisfied with our assumptions.

We have established at this point that (i) implies (ii). To complete the proof, we establish the converse. Suppose that x is not a weak distributive optimum. That is, suppose that either (a) $x \notin A$ or (b) $x \in A$ and there exists $x' \in A$ such that $w(u(x')) \gg w(u(x))$. Then, clearly, x is not a maximum of $\sum_{i \in N} \mu_i (w_i \circ u)$ on A for any $\mu \in S_n$. Therefore, (ii) implies (i). □

Proof of Theorem 3. Suppose, first, that part (ii) of Theorem 3 is not satisfied. That is, suppose that the unique $(p, r) \in S_l \times S_n$ for which $x = f(p, r)$ is not a price-wealth distributive optimum. Definitions 3 and 6 then imply that x is not a weak distributive optimum. Therefore, (i) implies (ii).

We now prove the converse. Suppose that the market optimum $x = f(p, r)$ is not a distributive optimum. Let x' denote some attainable allocation for which $w(u(x')) \gg w(u(x))$. From part (ii) of the proof of Theorem 1, there exists a strong distributive optimum x'' such that $w(u(x'')) \geq w(u(x'))$. From Theorem 1.(i), x'' also is a market optimum. From Theorem 4, there exists a price-wealth market equilibrium (p'', r'') such that $x'' = f(p'', r'')$. Therefore, (p, r) is not a price-wealth distributive optimum. □

Acknowledgements This article has benefited from the comments of Serge Kolm, Marc Fleurbaey, an anonymous referee, and the participants in the conference in honor of Serge Kolm at the University of Caen, May 18–19, 2007.

References

Archibald, G. C., & Donaldson, D. (1976). Non-paternalism and the basic theorems of welfare economics. *Canadian Journal of Economics*, *9*, 492–507

Arrow, K. J., & Debreu, G. (1952). Existence of an equilibrium for a competitive economy. *Econometrica*, *22*, 265–290

Arrow, K. J., & Enthoven, A. C. (1961). Quasi-concave programming. *Econometrica*, *29*, 779–800

Balasko, Y. (1988). *Foundations of the theory of general equilibrium.* San Diego: Academic Press

Becker, G. S. (1974). A theory of social interactions. *Journal of Political Economy*, *82*, 1063–1093

Bergstrom, T. C. (1970). A "Scandinavian consensus" solution for efficient income distribution among non-malevolent consumers. *Journal of Economic Theory*, *2*, 383–398

Debreu, G. (1952). A social equilibrium existence theorem. *Proceedings of the National Academy of Sciences, 38*, 886–893

Debreu, G. (1954). Valuation equilibrium and Pareto optimum. *Proceedings of the National Academy of Sciences, 40*, 588–592

Debreu, G., & Scarf, H. (1962). A limit theorem on the core of an economy. *International Economic Review, 4*, 235–246

Edgeworth, F. Y. (1881). *Mathematical psychics*. London: C. Kegan Paul

Foley, D. K. (1970). Lindahl's solution and the core of an economy with public goods. *Econometrica, 38*, 66–72

Harsanyi, J. C. (1955). Cardinal welfare, individualistic ethics, and interpersonal comparisons of utility. *Journal of Political Economy, 63*, 309–321

Hochman, H. M., & Rodgers, J. D. (1969). Pareto optimal redistribution. *American Economic Review, 59*, 542–557

Kolm, S.-C. (1968). La production optimale de justice sociale. In J. Margolis & H. Guitton (Eds.), *Economie Publique* (pp. 109–177). Paris: Editions du Centre National de la Recherche Scientifique

Kolm, S.-C. (1969). The optimal production of social justice. In J. Margolis & H. Guitton (Eds.), *Public economics: An analysis of public production and consumption and their relations to the private sector* (pp. 145–200). London: Macmillan

Kolm, S.-C. (1985). *Le contrat social libéral: Philosophie et pratique du libéralisme*. Paris: Presses Universitaires de France

Kolm, S.-C. (1987a). The freedom and consensus normative theory of the state: The liberal social contract. In P. Kolowski (Ed.), *Individuelle freiheit und demokratische entscheidung: Ethische, ökonomische und politische theorie der demokratie (Individual liberty and democratic decision-making: The ethics, economics and politics of democracy)* (pp. 97–127). Tübingen: J. C. B. Mohr (Paul Siebeck)

Kolm, S.-C. (1987b). Public economics. In J. Eatwell, M. Milgate, & P. Newman (Eds.), *The new Palgrave: A dictionary of economics* (pp. 1047–1055). London: Macmillan

Kolm, S.-C. (1996). *Modern theories of justice*. Cambridge, MA: MIT Press

Kolm, S.-C. (2004). *Macrojustice: The political economy of fairness*. Cambridge: Cambridge University Press

Kolm, S.-C. (2006). Reciprocity: Its scope, rationales, and consequences. In S.-C. Kolm & J. Mercier Ythier (Eds.), *Handbook of the economics of giving, altruism and reciprocity. Volume 1: Foundations* (pp. 371–541). Amsterdam: North-Holland

Lemche, S. Q. (1986). Remarks on non-paternalism and the second theorem of welfare economics. *Canadian Journal of Economics, 19*, 270–280

Lévy-Garboua, L., Meidinger, C., & Rapoport, B. (2006). The formation of social preferences: Some lessons from psychology and biology. In S.-C. Kolm & J. Mercier Ythier (Eds.), *Handbook of the economics of giving, altruism and reciprocity. Volume 1: Foundations* (pp. 545–613). Amsterdam: North-Holland

Mas-Collel, A. (1985). *The theory of general equilibrium: A differentiable approach*. Cambridge: Cambridge University Press

Mercier Ythier, J. (1993). Equilibre général de dons individuels. *Revue Economique, 44*, 925–950

Mercier Ythier, J. (1998a). The distribution of wealth in the liberal social contract. *European Economic Review, 42*, 329–347

Mercier Ythier, J. (1998b). Existence of an equilibrium of property rights. *Mathematical Social Sciences, 35*, 261–272

Mercier Ythier, J. (1998c). First order conditions for distributive efficiency. Document de Travail No. 98A39, GREQAM

Mercier Ythier, J. (2004). A limit theorem on the dual core of a distributive social system. *Social Choice and Welfare, 22*, 147–174

Mercier Ythier, J. (2006). The economic theory of gift-giving: Perfect substitutability of transfers and redistribution of wealth. In S.-C. Kolm & J. Mercier Ythier (Eds.), *Handbook of the economics of giving, altruism and reciprocity. Volume 1: Foundations* (pp. 227–339). Amsterdam: North-Holland

Mercier Ythier, J. (2010). Regular distributive efficiency and the distributive liberal social contract. *Journal of Public Economic Theory*, *12*, 943–978.

Musgrave, R. A. (1970). Pareto optimal redistribution: Comment. *American Economic Review*, *60*, 991–993

Nozick, R. (1974). *Anarchy, state, and utopia*. New York: Basic Books

Pareto, V. (1913). Il massimo di utilità per una colletività. *Giornale degli Economisti*, *13*, 337–341

Pareto, V. (1916). *Traité de sociologie générale*. Genève: Droz

Rader, T. (1980). The second theorem of welfare economics when utilities are interdependent. *Journal of Economic Theory*, *23*, 420–424

Rawls, J. (1971). *A theory of justice*. Cambridge, MA: Harvard University Press

Smith, A. (1759). *The theory of moral sentiments*. D. D. Raphael & A. L. Macfie (Eds.) 1976. Oxford: Clarendon

Warr, P. G. (1983). The private provision of a public good is independent of the distribution of income. *Economics Letters*, *13*, 207–211

Wicksteed, P. H. (1910). *The common sense of political economy*. London: Macmillan

Winter, S. G. (1969). A simple remark on the second optimality theorem of welfare economics. *Journal of Economic Theory*, *1*, 99–103

Reciprocity and Norms

Jon Elster

Why should I care about posterity? What's posterity ever done for me? (Groucho Marx)

Always go to other people's funerals, otherwise they won't come to yours. (Yogi Berra)

1 Introduction

For over a quarter of a century or more, Serge Kolm (see Kolm 1984, 2006, 2008) has made a number of contributions to the study of reciprocity. This article is intended to supplement his writings by addressing a topic that Kolm discusses mostly (but frequently) in passing: the relation between reciprocity and norms. I shall also consider the relation between Kolm's work and the recent work by Ernst Fehr and his collaborators. The paper is organized as follows. In Sect. 2, I consider the structure of two-party reciprocity, and in Sect. 3 the relation between norms and reciprocity. In Sect. 4, I discuss third-party reciprocity as "the cement of society."

In doing so, I shall consider:

- Two kinds of reciprocity: positive and negative.
- Three kinds of third-party reciprocity: the "Descartes effect," altruistic punishment, and third-party punishment.
- Four kinds of norms: legal norms, moral norms, quasi-moral norms, and social norms.

J. Elster
Collège de France, 11, Place Marcelin Berthelot, 75231 Paris, Cedex 05, France
and
Department of Political Science, Columbia University, 7th Floor, IAB, 420 West 118th Street, New York, NY 10027, USA
e-mail: je70@columbia.edu

M. Fleurbaey et al. (eds.), *Social Ethics and Normative Economics*, Studies in Choice and Welfare, DOI 10.1007/978-3-642-17807-8_14,

2 Two-Party Reciprocity

In this section, I assume that when people reciprocate, return good with good, and bad with bad, they do so because they think it is *right* or morally required. They do not do so to gain advantage. A normative question then arises immediately: *how much* should you return? The answer might seem obvious: return a good or a bad equal to what you received. This answer turns out to be ambiguous however. In the case of positive reciprocity, consider the following possibilities:

My utility from your gift	= A
Your utility from my gift	= B
Your disutility from your gift	= C
My disutility from my gift	= D

Equal reciprocity could mean any of the following: A = B, or C = D, or A = D, or B = C. I shall consider them in turn. Before I do so, note that the principles A = B and C = D presuppose interpersonal comparisons of utility. Although this operation cannot be done rigorously, it is one that we perform all the time.

Consider first the principle A = B. This principle of *equality of output*, independently of the burden, is probably what we mostly have in mind when we talk about returning good for good. In the choice among many possible return favors, all of which benefit you as much as your favor benefited me, I might choose the one that costs me the less, but that is a matter of simple rationality, not of norms.

Consider next the principle C = D. This principle of *equality of input* or equality of burden is sometimes observed in the exchange of gifts among friends. I compensate you for the time you spent looking for the perfect gift for me by spending an equal amount of time, independently of how much I value the gift. In friendship, sacrificing can be more important than benefiting.

Consider now the principle A = D. This is a principle of "no loss, no gain." The subjective costs of rendering a gift should equal the subjective value of the gift to oneself. This idea of equal reciprocity can, however, be a source of asymmetry, because of loss aversion (Kahneman and Tversky 1979). In a typical experiment demonstrating the "endowment effect," the subject is prepared to pay up to \$3 for a beer mug. Once it is in his possession, he is not prepared to sell it for less than \$7. Hence when you give me an object worth \$10, my utility gain from this windfall equals the utility loss I experience when I have to spend \$4 or \$5 out my own pocket on a return gift.

Consider finally the principle B = C. This is also a principle of "no loss, no gain" applied to the person who initiates the exchange. Gratitude might indeed seem to dictate this principle. Once again, however, loss aversion might induce an asymmetry. If you give me an object worth \$10, your utility loss can be offset only by a return gift worth \$20 or \$25. Unlike the previous principles, however, this one is unlikely to have a big impact on behavior. Since loss-averse people do not impute loss-aversion to others (Van Boven et al. 2001), those who are motivated by gratitude will typically fail to make good the loss of their benefactor.

La Rochefoucauld thought these asymmetries were a self-serving effect of *amour-propre*:

> What makes false reckoning, as regards gratitude, is that the pride of the giver and that of the receiver cannot agree as to the value of the benefit. (de La Rochefoucauld 2007, Maxim 225)

In many cases, there may indeed be a motivational mechanism of this kind at work. The endowment effect itself might seem to reflect amour-propre: I value the beer mug I bought more highly because it is *mine* and because *I* bought it. Yet the more general mechanism of loss aversion also applies to cases that involve only monetary gains or losses, in which this motivational mechanism is implausible. In the beer-mug case, loss aversion and amour-propre may both be at work.

In the case of negative reciprocity, the *Lex talionis* dictates equality of output: "an eye for an eye, a tooth for a tooth." The appearance of equality and symmetry may, however, be misleading. It seems possible that the *Lex talionis* served to limit the extent of revenge rather than (or only to) create an obligation to take revenge (Parisi 2008). It forbids the taking of two eyes for one or an eye for a tooth. The *Koran*, too, says that "If you want to take revenge, the action should not exceed the offense." (*Koran*, Sura XVI) In this perspective, the *Lex talionis* would serve to counteract a spontaneous tendency to excessive revenge.

Is there such a tendency? According to Seneca "A wrong not exceeded is not revenged." (Nisard 1844, *Thyestes*, p. 27, line 95) Other ancient literary sources point in the same direction (Gildenhard and Sissos 2007). Kalyvas (2006, p. 59) cites one example of "two for one" from the American Civil War and two from contemporary Lebanon. Sometimes, punitive damages are cited as a legal expression of this tendency. I shall not try to assess the empirical importance of excessive retaliation, but only make a distinction between two ways in which it might happen. In the first, corresponding to Seneca's statement and some of the examples cited by Kalyvas, the avenger will not be satisfied unless he *knows* that he has exceeded the wrong to him. In the second, the subjective desire is to "restore the moral balance of the universe," but in the calculation of the equilibrium losses loom larger than gains. I shall limit myself to the second case.

There is some neurophysiological evidence for the second mechanism (Shergill et al. 2003). When instructed to apply the same force on another participant as the latter had applied to them, subjects escalated on average 38% in each round. The explanation is that the perception of force is attenuated when the force is self-generated. Although this mechanism may well explain, as the authors suggest, escalation in fighting among children, it would not apply to less direct forms of interaction.

Loss aversion might also be at work. In the following passage, I have transposed an argument by Kahneman and Tversky (1995, p. 56) about negotiated disarmament to the case of revenge. Bold-faced statements in parenthesis indicate the transpositions.

> Loss aversion, we argue, could have a significant impact on conflict resolution. Imagine two countries negotiating the number of missiles that they will keep and aim at each other (**two**

> **clans involved in a long-standing conflict**). Each country derives security from its own missiles and is threatened by those of the other side. (**Each clan finds security in numbers and is threatened by numbers on the other side.**) Thus, missiles (**persons**) eliminated by (**on**) the other side are evaluated as gains, and missiles (**persons**) one must give up (**killed on one's own side**) are evaluated as losses, relative to the status quo. If losses have twice the impact of gains, then each side will require its opponent to eliminate (**lose**) twice as many missiles (**persons**) as it eliminates (**loses**).

Hence the psychology of reciprocity harbors several complexities. For both cognitive and motivational reasons, my gains and losses and yours are not assessed by the same standards. A further complexity arises when A's gift to B is put to a productive use by B, as in the Trust Games studied in experimental economics. Moral intuition suggests that the trustee should return the whole invested amount to the investor plus half the profit on the investment. Self-interest (in a one-shot interaction) would tell the trustee to return nothing. Instead, the general finding is that the trustee returns more or less exactly the amount invested. Although some writers (Dufwenberg and Gneezy 2000) explain this fact by assuming that the trustee is altruistic, I believe it is more plausible to assume that he does not care to think of himself as being exploitative or to be thought by the investor to be exploitative. The findings by Dana et al. (2006) are relevant here.

3 Reciprocity and Norms

I now move on to a discussion of norms. First, however, let me distinguish between norms and equilibria. Some forms of reciprocation do not stem from a desire to do the right thing, but from the desire to gain an advantage. They are forward-looking, not backward-looking. As an example, a government might refrain from opening the archives of its predecessor in the expectation that when the opposition comes into power again it will do the same, for the same reason. Although the work of Ernst Fehr and his collaborators (see Fehr et al. 2009) shows that reputation-building concerns and the concern for pure reciprocity can reinforce each other, they remain analytically distinct.

Legal norms are written in the law books and subject to vertical enforcement by specialized agents. *Moral norms* include utilitarianism and its weaker cousin altruism, the norm of equal sharing, the norm of "everyday Kantianism" – do what would be best if everyone did the same – and others. For my purpose here, their distinguishing feature is that they do not require, for their motivational efficacy, the presence of other agents. *Social norms* include norms of etiquette, norms of revenge, norms regulating the use of money, and many others. They are subject to horizontal enforcement by other agents, notably through the expression of disapproval and ostracism. What I shall call *quasi-moral norms* include the two-party norms of positive and negative reciprocity and the norm of conditional cooperation, which tells us to cooperate if others do, but allows us not to cooperate if others don't.

Both social norms and quasi-moral norms are conditional, in the sense that they are triggered by the presence or behavior of other people. Social norms are triggered when other people can observe what the agent is doing, and quasi-moral norms when the agent can observe what other people are doing. The two can reinforce each other, when the agent can observe what the observers are themselves doing. If I see you littering, I may not mind you watching me doing the same. But if I see you carefully putting your ice cream wrapper in your pocket, fairness and fear of disapproval may combine to produce conformity. As we shall see shortly, however, social and quasi-moral norms need not go together. Moral norms, by contrast, are unconditional. They are pro-active rather than reactive.

Let me clarify these categories through a couple of examples: voluntary restriction of water consumption and philanthropic donations. In times of water shortage, the municipal council may impose bans on watering lawns and refilling swimming pools, and enforce them by sending out inspectors. Even when there are no legal restrictions, however, neighbors may monitor each other's consumption and express their disapproval of excessive use. Indoors consumption can be monitored by visitors, who may and do express their disapproval if the toilet bowl is clean. Small children, who are notoriously moralizing, can give their parents a hard time if they do not turn off the water when brushing their teeth or when soaping themselves in the shower. These cases illustrate the operation of social norms.

The operation of quasi-moral norms may be illustrated by the handling of water shortages in Bogotá, under the imaginative mayorship of Antanas Mockus. In that city, the traditional method for recurring water crises involved shutting off the water some hours every day, affecting essential as well less essential usages. The mayor encouraged them to use water for essential purposes only. Although individual monitoring was not feasible, the aggregate water consumption in the city was shown in real time on TV, so that people could know whether others were for the most part complying. It appears that enough people did so to sustain the conditional cooperation. People were saying to themselves, "Since other people are cutting down on their consumption, it's only fair that I should do so as well."

By contrast, nobody has to observe others or be observed by them in order to abide by moral norms. For the everyday Kantian, limiting consumption to essential uses is of course mandatory. For the altruist or the utilitarian, the issue is a bit more complicated. For simplicity, I limit myself to those with a utilitarian motivation, but a similar argument applies to those who attach some weight to the welfare of others, although less than the weight they attach to their own.

If the technology of collective action (Oliver et al. 1985; Elster 1989, Chap. 1) has linear costs and benefits, a utilitarian will always choose to cooperate. In many cases, however, it is more plausible to assume that the benefit curve is S-shaped. Costs may be linear, increasing or decreasing; I assume here that they are linear. Under these assumptions, the decision of a utilitarian to contribute to the public good will depend on the number of other cooperators, *but only indirectly*. If many others are contributing (for whatever motives) his contribution makes so little difference that it is likely to exceed to the cost to himself of contributing.

We may see this last point even more clearly using the example of philanthropic donations. There can of course be no legal norms mandating charity, or rather: they are called taxes. In some social circles, there are social norms mandating donations to good causes, be they museums, universities, or alleviation of inner-city poverty. Among the very rich, those who do not engage in conspicuous giving are apparently ostracized (Posner 2000, p. 61).

Quasi-moral norms come into operation when I can observe that others are giving. After the 2004 Tsunami, everybody could read in the newspapers about the large-scale donations that were coming in to support the devastated populations. Many may have said to themselves, "Since others are donating so much, it is only fair that I should do so too." Although they could not be observed by others, their observation of what others were doing, collectively even though not individually, may have triggered their generosity. Similarly, some good causes may never gain enough publicized support to get the snowball rolling.

If I have a utility-based norm of charity, how much I will give depends on how much good I can do. Assuming decreasing marginal utility in the recipients, how much good I can do depends on how much others are giving. I am not here referring to a Nash-equilibrium, but to a *process* in which each person takes as given the donations of his predecessors but do not anticipate that of his successors. Therefore, if others give much, I may decide to give little and vice versa. The norm itself, however, makes no reference to other donors, only to the recipients. *Conditionality is not the same thing as reciprocity*. In fact, if I thought that the good in question had increasing marginal utility for the recipients, I wouldn't bother to find out whether others were giving.

In practice, it may be hard to distinguish moral norms from quasi-moral norms and quasi-moral norms from social norms. Cooperation in the first round of a public-good experiment is not conditional on the actual behavior of others, since under the usual conditions subjects make their decisions simultaneously and anonymously. Positive contributions might seem, therefore, to be motivated by pro-active altruism. They are more likely, however, to be triggered by an *expectation* that others will make a contribution, together with the reactive quasi-moral norm of positive reciprocity.

Reciprocity as a quasi-moral norm is usually insufficient to trigger cooperation by itself. As illustrated by the Groucho Marx quote, if someone else has not taken the first step, there is nothing to reciprocate. A group is more likely to generate cooperation, therefore, if it contains, along with conditional reciprocators motivated by quasi-moral norms, some unconditional ones (Weber and Murnighan 2008).

4 Third-Party Reciprocity

Some might consider this phrase to be a misnomer, since the idea of reciprocity suggests a relation between two agents only. Maybe the phrase "third-party quasi-moral norms" would have been more appropriate. But it does not really matter what we call them. I shall consider one form of positive third-party reciprocity and two forms of negative third-party reciprocity.

It is an interesting fact that Descartes is at the origin of both positive and negative third-party reciprocity. Many readers will be familiar with the famous text that states what Kolm (1984) called "the Descartes effect":

> The reason that makes me believe that those who do nothing save for their own utility, ought also, if they wish to be prudent, work, as do others, for the good of others, and try to please everyone as much as they can, is that one ordinarily sees it occur that those who are deemed obliging and prompt to please also receive a quantity of good deeds from others, *even from people who have never been obliged to them*; and these things they would not receive did people believe them of another humor; and the pains they take to please other people are not so great as the conveniences that the friendship of those who know them provides. For others expect of us only the deeds we can render without inconvenience to ourselves, nor do we expect more of them; but it often happens that deeds that cost others little profit us very much, and can even save our life. It is true that occasionally one wastes his toil in doing good and that, on the other hand, occasionally one gains in doing evil; but that cannot change the rule of prudence that relates only to things that happen most often. As for me, the maxim I have followed in all the conduct of my life has been to follow only the grand path, and to believe that the principal subtlety [finesse] is never to make use of subtlety. (Descartes 1978, p. 176–177; my italics; translation modified)

The structure of the situation is that an act by A benefits B, and that C, observing this interaction, acts to benefit A. (A non-paradoxical reading of the Yogi Berra quote illustrates this case: If I see you going to someone's funeral, I will go to yours.) Descartes suggests that this might provide a selfish reason for A to benefit B. He is not denying that people sometimes help for non-selfish motives, but arguing that such motives are not necessary. In rewarding A, C could also act either from a selfish or a non-selfish motive. As noted by Kolm (2006, p. 415), however, a non-selfish C might not reward A's gift to B if C believes it to be have been motivated by A's self-interest. The only stable combinations may be that both A and C are non-selfish or that both are selfish.

The idea of third-party punishment also goes back to Descartes. "The harm done by others, when it does not concern ourselves, only causes indignation; when it concerns ourselves, it causes anger." (*The Passions of the Soul*, Art. 65, in Cottingham et al. 1985) Elsewhere (*The Passions of the Soul*, Art. 201), Descartes adds that when the first party loves the third party, the emotional reaction is anger rather than indignation. In experiments, subjects are surprisingly willing to punish, at some cost to themselves, those who have behaved unfairly towards third parties. A stylized fact seems to be that indignation triggers punishments that cost the punisher around two thirds of what they are willing to spend when they punish in anger (Fehr and Fischbacher 2004).

There two are reasons to believe that two-party negative reciprocity may be insufficient to sustain cooperation. First, to the extent that punishment takes the form of ostracism and avoidance, it may not matter much to the defector. Because ostracism results in a gain forgone, loss aversion implies that it is felt less heavily than a punishment that involves a direct loss. In fact, the ostracism may not even be noticed. Also, even if the defector is not able to take advantage of a particular victim again, there are plenty of other victims he can exploit. As the saying goes, there's a sucker born every minute.

Second, to the extent that punishment and ostracism are costly for the punisher, as they typically are, it is not clear why people would choose to carry out these sanctions. What's in it for them? In a public goods situation, people are tempted to free ride by imposing negative externalities on each other. If the solution requires their willingness to impose positive externalities on each other (by punishing free riders), isn't the original problem just recreated at a higher level? This conundrum is usually referred to as "the second-order free-rider problem."

Fehr's work suggests answers to these two puzzles. He argues that third-party punishment can provide a powerful supplement to second-party punishment. Suppose that A defects in an interaction with B, in the presence of C, D, E, etc. Although A's loss from B's ostracism of him may be small compared to the gains from the defection, the sum-total of the costs that follow from being ostracized by C, D, E, etc. may exceed those gains. Although third-party punishments are weaker than second-party retaliations, there can be many more of them.

The physical presence of C, D, etc. on the scene is not necessary; what matters is that they somehow gain knowledge about A's defection. I believe this is the proper perspective in which to see the relation between gossip and social norms: gossip acts as a *multiplier* on punishment. Suppose A engages in norm-violating behavior towards B, e.g., by letting his cattle trespass on B's land, and that B tells C, D, etc. about the trespass. The diffusion of information about the trespass adds a group of potential third-party punishers (C, D, etc.) to the original second-party punisher (B). In fact, B may deliberately pass on information about A's trespass in order to increase the social pressure on A to reform his behavior. Knowing this, A may be deterred from defecting in the first place. Many writers on norms assert that gossiping is *costly* for the gossiper. This seems wrong. Casual observation as well as a reading of the French moralists suggest that people gossip because of the direct benefits it provides – it's *fun*.

Concerning the second-order free rider problem, Fehr and his co-authors offer two responses. One is that cooperation is more likely to emerge and persist "when punishment of non-cooperators *and non-punishers* is possible" (Fehr and Fischbacher 2003, p. 790; my italics). This appeal to the punishment of non-punishers seems, however, empirically unfounded and theoretically weak. Empirically, the phenomenon seems to be rare. In everyday social interactions people rarely shun those do not shun defectors. Theoretically, the appeal to the punishment of non-punishers seems arbitrary, for who would punish the non-punishers of non-punishers? It is not only more parsimonious but also empirically more plausible to argue that people *spontaneously* punish defectors.

This is in fact, I believe, Fehr's main line of argument. The bulk of his work is indeed oriented to showing that even when they are completely unobserved and hence invulnerable to sanctions, people are willing to spend resources on punishing defectors. This spontaneous willingness to punish offers a simple solution to the second-order free-rider problem. It may even offer a plausible mechanism for the operation of *group selection*. The main objection to group selection, namely the vulnerability of a population of cooperators to invasion by free riders, does not hold if free riders are liable to be punished for attempts to exploit the cooperators.

Consider next altruistic punishment. In experiments, one subject A has the option of punishing another subject B for non-cooperative behavior, at some cost to himself. There is no face-to-face interaction and the two subjects will never meet again. Yet many subjects use the punishment option, causing B to be more cooperative in his later dealings with a third party C. The phrase "altruistic punishment" reflects the fact that the punishment *could* spring from altruistic motivations, namely if A anticipates, and is motivated by, the benefit that his punishment of B confers on C. In reality, it is more likely to be motivated by a desire for revenge.

There are many instances of such behavior outside the laboratory. Here is an example from the Great Fear of 1789. Referring to vagrants in the countryside, Georges Lefebvre writes that:

> These travelers, even if they were not beggars in the proper meaning of the word, would even so stop at a farmhouse and ask for food and a bed for the night. They were not turned away, any more than genuine beggars were. This was not through charity or good nature: the farmer cursed furiously behind their backs. "Begging slowly and subtly undermines us all and brings us to destruction," says the *cahier* of Villamblain, near Patay. But the farmers were afraid. Afraid of a direct attack, naturally, but even more afraid of anonymous vengeance, trees and fences mysteriously cut down, cattle mutilated and, worst of all, fire. (Lefebvre 1973, p. 17)

These acts of vengeance were clearly costly, since they involved a risk of being caught and punished, and brought no benefits to the particular vagrant who carried them out. Yet they did bring a benefit to future vagrants by making it more likely that their requests would be granted. Similarly, grain rebellions in pre-industrial England were invariably unsuccessful in their immediate objectives and their leaders often punished harshly. Yet as Thompson (1971) argues, by virtue of their nuisance value the rebellions had a long-term success in making farmers behave more moderately than they would have done otherwise.

Cooperation among genetically unrelated individuals may owe its explanation to the combination of the Descartes effect, altruistic punishment, and third-party punishment, at least in part. Reputation effects may bring cooperation to even higher levels (Rockenbach and Milinski 2006). Although Kolm (2006) does refer to reputation effects, they are not central to his argument. Although I cannot claim to have read all his numerous writings on positive reciprocity, the idea that it needs to be sustained by negative reciprocity seems to be even less central. He does discuss revenge and retaliation as negative forms of reciprocity, but unless I have missed something he does not claim that we would be worse off without them.

Pure positive reciprocity is fragile, however, since without the possibility of punishment, the egoists would drive out the conditional cooperators. Consider the Public Goods Game shown in Table 1. In this four-person society, there is one egoist who contributes nothing and three conditional cooperators who contribute 10 in the first round and in each later round contribute the average of the preceding round. After ten rounds, the contributions are close to zero. One rotten apple spoils the barrel. If, as seems plausible, real societies contain a substantial share of egoists, something is needed to keep them in line. The punishment option seems to solve the problem.

Table 1 Public goods game

Period	Subject 1	Subject 2	Subject 3	Subject 4	Mean
1	10	10	10	0	7.5
2	7.5	7.5	7.5	0	5.6
3	5.6	5.6	5.6	0	5.6
4	4.2	4.2	4.2	0	3.1
5	3.1	3.1	3.1	0	2.4
⋮	⋮	⋮	⋮	⋮	⋮
10	0.4	0.4	0.4	0	0.3

There is, however, a seemingly unresolved puzzle: What would prevent a population of cooperating punishers from being invaded by non-punishing cooperators, who could in turn by invaded by free riders? To my knowledge, the issue was first raised by Henrich and Boyd (2001). The short version of their answer is that tendency to punish will be robust, because it will be protected by *conformism* – a tendency to copy the most frequent behavior in the population. If this idea is correct, it adds a new dimension to the debate. The tendency to do as your neighbors do can in some cases be explained by positive reciprocity, in the form of quasi-moral norms. Conformism as a tendency to imitate the majority, either as a means of avoiding ostracism or as a cognitive heuristic, is orthogonal to reciprocity. Either can exist without the other.

References

Cottingham, J., Stoothoff, R., & Murdoch, D. (Eds.) (1985). *The philosophical writings of Descartes* (Vol. 1). Cambridge: Cambridge University Press

Dana, J., Cain, D. M., & Dawes, R. M. (2006). What you don't know can't hurt me: Costly (but quiet) exit in dictator games. *Organizational Behavior and Human Decision Processes, 100*, 193–201

de La Rochefoucauld, F. (2007). *Collected maxims and other reflections* (E. H. Blackmore, A. M. Blackmore, & F. Giguère, Trans.). Oxford: Oxford University Press

Descartes, R. (1978). *Descartes: His moral philosophy and psychology* (J. J. Blom, Trans.). Hassocks, Sussex: Harvester

Dufwenberg, M., & Gneezy, U. (2000). Measuring beliefs in an experimental lost wallet game. *Games and Economic Behavior, 30*, 163–182

Elster, J. (1989). *The cement of society*. Cambridge: Cambridge University Press

Fehr, E., & Fischbacher, U. (2003). The nature of human altruism. *Nature, 425*, 785–791

Fehr, E., & Fischbacher, U. (2004). Social norms and human cooperation. *Trends in Cognitive Sciences, 8*, 185–190

Fehr, E., Brown, M., & Zendher, C. (2009). On reputation: A microfoundation of contract enforcement and price rigidity. *Economic Journal, 119*, 333–353

Gildenhard, I., & Sissos, A. (2007). Barbarian variations: Tereus, Procne and Phiomela in Ovid (*Met.* 6.412–674) and beyond. *Dictynna, 4*, 1–25

Henrich, J., & Boyd, R. (2001). Why people punish defectors: Weak conformist transmission can stabilize costly enforcement of norms in cooperative dilemmas. *Journal of Theoretical Biology, 208*, 79–89

Kahneman, D., & Tversky, A. (1979). Propect theory: An analysis of decision under risk. *Econometrica, 47*, 263–291

Kahneman, D., & Tversky, A. (1995). Conflict resolution: A cognitive perspective. In K. Arrow, R. H. Mnookin, L. Ross, A. Tversky, & R. Wilson (Eds.), *Barriers to conflict resolution* (pp. 44–61). New York: W. W. Norton

Kalyvas, S. N. (2006). *The logic of violence in civil war*. Cambridge: Cambridge University Press

Kolm, S.-C. (1984). *La bonne économie: La réciprocité générale*. Paris: Presses Universitaries de France

Kolm, S.-C. (2006). Reciprocity: Its scope, rationales and consequences. In S.-C. Kolm & J. Mercier-Ythier (Eds.), *Handbook of the economics of giving, altruism and reciprocity. Volume 1: Foundations* (pp. 371–541). Amsterdam: North-Holland

Kolm, S.-C. (2008). *Reciprocity: An economics of social relations*. Cambridge: Cambridge University Press

Lefebvre, G. (1973). *The great fear of 1789: Rural panic in revolutionary France* (J. White, Trans.). New York: Pantheon Books

Nisard, M. (Ed.) (1844). *Théâtre complet des Latins comprenant Plaute, Térence et Sénèque le Tragique*. Paris: Dubochet

Oliver, P., Marwell, G., & Teixeira, R. (1985). A theory of the critical mass: I. Interdependence, group heterogeneity, and the production of collective action. *American Journal of Sociology, 91*, 522–556

Parisi, F. (2008). The genesis of liability in ancient law. *American Law and Economics Review, 3*, 1340–1353

Posner, E. A. (2000). *Law and social norms*. Cambridge, MA: Harvard University Press

Rockenbach, B., & Milinski, M. (2006). The efficient interaction of indirect reciprocity and costly punishment. *Nature, 444*, 718–723

Shergill, S. S., Bayes, P. M., Firth, C. D., & Wolpert, D. M. (2003). Two eyes for an eye: The neuroscience of force escalation. *Science, 301*, 187

Thompson, E. P. (1971). The moral economy of the English crowd in the eighteenth century. *Past and Present, 50*, 76–136

Van Boven, L., Dunning, D., & Loewenstein, G. (2001). Egocentric empathy gaps between owners and buyers: Misperceptions of the endowment effect. *Journal of Personality and Social Psychology, 79*, 82–123

Weber, J. M., & Murnighan, J. K. (2008). Suckers or saviors? Consistent contributors in social dilemmas. *Journal of Personality and Social Psychology, 95*, 1340–1353

Scientific Publications of Serge-Christophe Kolm

List of Acronyms

ADRES Association pour le Développement de la Recherche en Economie et en Statistique
CEPREMAP Centre d'Etudes Prospectives d'Economie Mathématique Appliquées à la Planification
CERAS Centre d'Enseignement et de Recherche en Analyse Socio-Economique
CGPC Conseil Général des Ponts et Chaussées
CNRS Centre National de la Recherche Scientifique
CORDES Comité d'Organisation des Recherches Appliquées sur le Développement Economique et Social
CREME Centre de Recherche en Economie Mathématique et Econométrie
ECINEQ Society for the Study of Economic Inequality
EHESS Ecole des Hautes Etudes en Sciences Sociales
IDEP Institut d'Economie Publique
MAUSS Mouvement Anti-Utilitariste dans les Sciences Sociales
OCDE/OECD Organisation de Coopération et de Développement Economiques/ Organisation for Economic Co-operation and Development
PEGS Committee on the Political Economy of the Good Society
PSU Parti Socialiste Unifié
SEDEIS Société d'Etudes et de Documentation Economiques, Industrielles et Sociales
UNITAR United Nations Institute for Training and Research

Updates to this bibliography will be posted on Serge Kolm's website: http://ehess.fr/kolm/. This site also lists a selection of his journalistic writings.

M. Fleurbaey et al. (eds.), *Social Ethics and Normative Economics*,
Studies in Choice and Welfare, DOI 10.1007/978-3-642-17807-8,

1 Normative Economics, Theory of Justice, Equalities, Inequalities

Books

Justice et Equité. CEPREMAP, Paris, 1971 and Editions du CNRS, Paris, 1972. Translated by H. F. See into English as *Justice and Equity* with a new foreword, MIT Press, Cambridge, MA, 1998.

Modern Theories of Justice. MIT Press, Cambridge, MA, 1996. Translated into Portuguese as *Teorias Modernas do Justiça*, Martins Fontes, São Paulo, Brazil, 2000.

Macrojustice: The Political Economy of Fairness. Cambridge University Press, Cambridge, 2004.

Articles

La production optimale de justice sociale. In *Economie Publique*, Editions du CNRS, Paris, 1968, pages 109–177. French version of the proceedings of the International Economic Association Conference on Public Economics, Biarritz, France, 1966.

The optimal production of social justice. In J. Margolis and H. Guitton, editors, *Public Economics: An Analysis of Public Production and Consumption and Their Relations to the Private Sector*, Macmillan, London, 1969, pages 145–200. English version of the proceedings of the International Economic Association Conference on Public Economics, Biarritz, France, 1966. Reprinted in K. J. Arrow and G. Debreu, editors, *Landmark Papers in General Equilibrium Theory, Social Choice and Welfare Selected by K. J. Arrow and G. Debreu*, The Foundations of 20th Century Economics, Volume 3, Edward Elgar, Cheltenham, UK, 2001, pages 606–653. Excerpts reprinted with an editorial introduction by P. J. Lambert in *Journal of Economic Inequality*, **5**, 2007, 213–234.

La théorie démocratique de la justice sociale. *Revue d'Economie Politique*, **79**, 1969, 138–141.

Super-équité. *Kyklos*, **26**, 1973, 841–843.

Sur les conséquences économiques des principes de justice et de justice pratique. *Revue d'Economie Politique*, **84**, 1974, 80–107.

Unequal inequalities. I. *Journal of Economic Theory*, **12**, 1976, 416–442.

Unequal inequalities. II. *Journal of Economic Theory*, **13**, 1976, 82–111.

Multidimensionnal egalitarianisms. *Quarterly Journal of Economics*, **91**, 1977, 1–13.

Marx maintenant. In *Actualité du Marxisme*, Proceedings of the Colloquium of Villeneuve d'Ascq, 1981.

Au 2e siècle après Marx. *Commentaire*, **6**, 1983, 521–525.

The normative economics of unanimity and equality: Equity, adequacy and fundamental dominance with applications to matchings and wages. In K. J. Arrow, editor, *Issues in Contemporary Economics. Volume 1: Markets and Welfare*,

Macmillan, London, 1991, pages 243–286. Proceedings of the Ninth World Congress of the International Economic Association, Athens, Greece, 1989.

Distributive justice. In R. E. Goodin and P. Pettit, editors, *A Companion to Contemporary Political Philosophy*, Blackwell, Oxford, 1993, pages 438–461.

The impossibility of utilitarianism. In P. Koslowski and Y. Shionoya, editors, *The Good and the Economical: Ethical Choices in Economics and Management*, Springer, Berlin, 1993, pages 30–66.

Rational normative economics vs 'social welfare' and 'social choice'. *European Economic Review*, **38**, 1994, 721–730.

The meaning of 'fundamental preferences'. *Social Choice and Welfare*, **11**, 1994, 193–198.

Rejoinder to John Broome. *Social Choice and Welfare*, **11**, 1994, 203–204.

L'égalité de la liberté. *Recherches Economiques de Louvain*, **60**, 1994, 81–86.

Rational justice and equality. In W. Eichhorn, editor, *Models and Measurement of Welfare and Inequality*, Springer, Berlin, 1994, pages 970–992.

Review of *Egalitarian Perspectives: Essays on Philosophical Economics* by J. E. Roemer. *Journal of Economics*, **60**, 1994, 210–214.

The economics of social sentiments: The case of envy. *Japanese Economic Review*, **46**, 1995, 63–87.

Economic justice: The central question. *European Economic Review*, **39**, 1995, 661–673.

The modern theory of justice. *L'Année Sociologique*, **5**, 1995, 297–315.

Moral public choice. *Public Choice*, **87**, 1996, 117–141.

The theory of justice. *Social Choice and Welfare*, **13**, 1996, 151–182.

Playing fair with fairness (A comment on Arnsperger's 'Envy-freeness and distributive justice'). *Journal of Economic Surveys*, **10**, 1996, 199–215.

Risk, justice, and social policy. In P. Koslowski and A. Føllesdal, editors, *Restructuring the Welfare State: Ethical Issues of Social Policy in an International Perspective*, Springer, Berlin, 1996, pages 287–318.

The values of liberty. *Nordic Journal of Political Economy*, **23**, 1996, 25–46.

La théorie de la justice. In H. Brochier, editor, *Economie Normative*, Economica, Paris, 1997.

The values of freedom. In J.-F. Laslier, M. Fleurbaey, N. Gravel, and A. Trannoy, editors, *Freedom in Economics: New Perspectives in Normative Analysis*, Routledge, London, 1997, pages 17–44.

Macrojustice. In *Les Avancées Théoriques en Economie Sociale et Leurs Applications, Tome 1*, Editions du CNRS, Paris, 1997, pages 3–28. Proceedings of XVIIèmes Journées de l'Association d'Economie Sociale.

La théorie moderne de la justice. In *Les Avancées Théoriques en Economie Sociale et Leurs Applications, Tome 1*, Editions du CNRS, Paris, 1997, pages 29–52. Proceedings of XVIIèmes Journées de l'Association d'Economie Sociale.

Review of *The Political Economy of Fairness* by E. E. Zajac. *Journal of Economics*, **66**, 1997, 90–91.

Review of *Economic Rights* edited by E. F. Paul, F. D. Miller, and J. E. Paul. *Journal of Institutional and Theoretical Economics*, **153**, 1997, 587–589.

Chance and justice: Social policies and the Harsanyi–Vickrey–Rawls problem. *European Economic Review*, **42**, 1998, 1393–1416.

Rational foundations of income inequality measurement. In J. Silber, editor, *Handbook of Income Inequality Measurement*, Kluwer Academic Publishers, Boston, 1999, pages 19–94.

A historical introduction to normative economics. *Social Choice and Welfare*, **17**, 2000, 707–738.

Unequal thinking. Review of *Thinking about Inequality: Personal Judgments and Income Distributions* by Y. Amiel and F. Cowell and *Economic Inequality and Income Distribution* by D. Champernowne and F. Cowell. *Journal of Economics*, **73**, 2001, 96–107.

Quelques souvenirs de John Rawls. *Revue de Philosophie Economique*, **7**, 2003, 21–31.

Logique et usage du contrat social. *Revue de Philosophie Economique*, **8**, 2003, 3–17.

Liberty and distribution: Macrojustice from social freedom. *Social Choice and Welfare*, **22**, 2004, 113–145.

Taxes and Justice. Review of *The Myth of Ownership: Taxes and Justice* by L. Murphy and T. Nagel. *Archives Européennes de Sociologie/European Journal of Sociology*, **44**, 2003, 271–272.

Les théories du contrat social. In R. Boudon and F. Bourricaud, editors, *Dictionnaire Critique de la Sociologie*, Presses Universitaires de France, Paris, 2004.

Review of *Classical Utilitarianism from Hume to Mill* by F. Rosen. *Journal of Economics*, **84**, 2005, 211–216.

Macrojustice. In A. Leroux and P. Livet, editors, *Leçons de Philosophie Economique. Tome II : Economie Normative et Philosophie Morale*, Economica, Paris, 2006, pages 487–521.

Liberté, justice et efficacité: Distribution, impôts et transferts optimaux. *Revue Economique*, **57**, 2006, 55–84.

Macrojustice: Distribution, impôts et tranferts optimaux. *Revue d'Economie Politique*, **117**, 2007, 61–89.

Qu'est-ce qu'un impôt juste? Interview de Serge-Christophe Kolm. *Regards Croisés sur l'Economie*, No. 1, 2007, 37–50.

Economic inequality. In D. S. Clark, editor, *Encyclopedia of Law and Society: American and Global Perspectives, Volume 2*, Sage Publications, Thousand Oaks, CA, 2007, pages 738–742.

Equal liberties and the resulting optimum income distribution. In J. Bishop and B. Zheng, editors, *Inequality and Opportunity: Papers from the Second ECINEQ Society Meeting. Research on Economic Inequality, Volume 16*, Emerald Group Publishing, Bingley, UK, 2008, pages 1–36.

Inequality. In J. Peil and I. van Staveren, editors, *Handbook of Economics and Ethics*, Edward Elgar, Cheltenham, UK, 2009, pages 267–275.

Justice. In J. Peil and I. van Staveren, editors, *Handbook of Economics and Ethics*, Edward Elgar, Cheltenham, UK, 2009, pages 292–300.

A response to Erik Schockkaert on *Macrojustice*. *Economics and Philosophy*, **25**, 2009, 85–98.
Défiscalisation des heures supplémentaires: La théorie. *Raisons Politiques*, **33**, 2009, 45–55.
On real economic freedom. *Social Choice and Welfare*, **35**, 2010, 351–375.
General presentation. In C. Gamel and M. Lubrano, editors, *On Kolm's Theory of Macrojustice: A Pluridisciplinary Forum of Exchange*, Springer, Berlin, 2011, pages 35–67.
Economic macrojustice: Fair optimum income distribution, taxation and transfers. In C. Gamel and M. Lubrano, editors, *On Kolm's Theory of Macrojustice: A Pluridisciplinary Forum of Exchange*, Springer, Berlin, 2011, pages 69–130.
Macrojustice in normative economics and ethics. In C. Gamel and M. Lubrano, editors, *On Kolm's Theory of Macrojustice: A Pluridisciplinary Forum of Exchange*, Springer, Berlin, 2011, pages 343–372.
Inequality, new directions: Full ethical foundations and consequences. *Journal of Economic Inequality*, forthcoming.
Equality. In B. Badie, D. Berg-Schlosser, and L. Morlino, editors, *International Encyclopedia of Political Science*, Sage Publications, Thousand Oaks, CA, forthcoming.
Review of *Against Injustice* edited by R. Gotoh and P. Dumouchal. *Economica*, forthcoming.
On health and justice. In C. J. L. Murray and D. Wikler, editors, *Fairness and Goodness: Ethical Issues in Health Resource Allocation*, World Health Organization, Geneva, forthcoming.

Government Report

La théorie des transferts sociaux et son application. Final Report, Commissariat Général du Plan, Paris, 2002.

Unpublished Manuscripts

More equal distribution of bundles of commodities. CEPREMAP, Paris, 1973.
Measuring inequality. CEPREMAP, Paris, 1973.
Rectifiances et dominances intégrales de tous degrés. CEPREMAP, Paris, 1974.
Multidimensional inequality comparisons. CEPREMAP, Paris, 1975.
La société bien ordonnée: La justice comme justesse. Document de Recherche No. 31, CERAS, Paris, 1984.
Le raisonnement d'éthique sociale. Document de Recherche No. 41, CERAS, Paris, 1985.
Adequation, equity and fundamental analysis. Document de Recherche No. 59, CERAS, Paris, 1987.
Adequation. Document de Recherche No. 69, CERAS, Paris, 1987.
Adequate or equitable. Document de Recherche No. 73, CERAS, Paris, 1988.
Adequacy, equity and fundamental dominance: Unanimous and comparable allocations in rational social choice, with applications to marriage and wages. Document de Recherche No. 76, CERAS, Paris, 1989.

The General Theory of Justice. Document de Recherche: Volume de Résultats, CERAS, Paris, 1990.

The ethical economics of envy. Document de Recherche No. 90, CERAS, Paris, 1991. German Bernacer Lecture, University of Alicante.

Axioms of fairness. Document de Recherche No. 91, CERAS, Paris, 1991.

Super-equity. Document de Recherche No. 98, CERAS, Paris, 1991. German Bernacer Lecture, University of Alicante.

Philosophical reasons for equity. Document de Recherche No. 99, CERAS, Paris, 1991.

The impossibility of utilitarianism. CGPC, Paris, 1992.

Fundamental analysis. CGPC, Paris, 1992.

Equal liberty. CGPC, Paris, 1993.

Inequalities and super equity. CGPC, Paris, 1993.

Efficient economic justice. CGPC, Paris, 1993.

The economics of envy. CGPC, Paris, 1993.

Income justice: Its reason and optimal policy. CGPC, Paris, 1995. Presented at the Eleventh World Congress of the International Economic Association, Tunis, Tunisia, 1995.

Risk and justice: Harsanyi's enigmas and social policy. CGPC, Paris, 1995.

The comparison of pairwise preferences and its normative consequences. CGPC, Paris, 1995.

Intermediate measures of inequality. CGPC, Paris, 1996.

Freedom justice. Cahier de Recherche No. 99-5, CREME, Université de Caen, Caen, 1999.

To each according to her work? Just entitlement from action: Desert, merit, responsibility and equality of opportunity. A review of John Roemer's *Equality of Opportunity*. Document de Travail No. 01-07, IDEP, Marseille, 2001.

Vox populi, vox dei: Endogenous social choice and the rational original position. Document de Travail No. 01-08, IDEP, Marseille, 2001.

Normative Economics. Paris, 2002.

The freedom ordering of budget sets: Volume or pointed distance? Document de Travail No. 05-07, IDEP, Marseille, 2005.

The rational, recursive original position. A fully determined impartial endogenous social welfare function. Prepared for the Grand Colloque de l'ADRES, New Developments in Social Choice and Welfare Theories: A Tribute to Maurice Salles, Université de Caen, 2009.

Social ethics and rationality, new directions for the optimum production of social justice: Meaningful welfare, equal liberties, social solidarity. Prepared for the Conference on Inequality: New Directions, Cornell University, 2009.

Théories Modernes de l'Exploitation. No date.

2 Public Economics

Books

Introduction à la Théorie du Rôle Economique de l'Etat: Les Fondements de l'Economie Publique. Institut Français de Presse, Paris, 1963.
La Théorie Economique Générale de l'Encombrement. SEDEIS, Paris, 1968.
L'Etat et le Système des Prix. Volume 1: La Valeur Publique. CNRS and Dunod, Paris, 1970.
L'Etat et le Système des Prix. Volume 2: Prix Publics Optimaux. CNRS and Dunod, Paris, 1970.
L'Etat et le Système des Prix. Volume 3: La Théorie des Contraintes de Valeur and Ses Applications. CNRS and Dunod, Paris, 1970.
Le Service des Masses. CNRS and Dunod, Paris, 1970.

Articles

Décisions et concernements collectifs. *Analyse et Prévision*, **6**, 1967.
L'économie des services publics. *Economie Appliquée*, **18**, 1965, 557–582.
Le déficit optimal des transports en commun. *Revue d'Economie Politique*, **78**, 1968, 658–663.
Le rôle social ambigü des prix publics. *Economie Appliquée*, **21**, 1968, 417–516.
Les consommations collectives. *Revue d'Economie Politique*, **79**, 1969, 619–649.
La vérité des prix dans un monde imparfait. *Revue Economique*, **20**, 1969, 727–740.
Les politiques dynamiques optimales d'investissement. *Revue Economique*, **20**, 1969, 753–782.
L'encombrement pluridimensionnel. *Revue Economique*, **20**, 1969, 954–967.
Le juste prix des services publics. *Analyse et Prévision*, **8**, 1969, 737–742.
L'économie normative des services de masse. *Revue d'Economie Politique*, **80**, 1970, 61–84.
Service optimal d'une demande variable et prix de l'incertitude. *Revue Economique*, **21**, 1970, 243–271.
L'économie de la santé publique. *Analyse et Prévision*, **9**, 1970.
L'inégalité des valeurs des vies humaines. *Cahiers du Séminaire d'Econométrie*, **12**, 1970, 40–62.
Footnotes to Marcel Boiteux's value-constrained second best. *Journal of Economic Theory*, **3**, 1971, 341–344.
La taxation de la consommation ostentatoire. *Revue d'Economie Politique*, **81**, 1971, 65–79.
A note on optimum tax evasion. *Journal of Public Economics*, **2**, 1973, 265–270.
Sur les conséquences des principes de justice et de justice pratique. *Revue d'Economie Politique*, **84**, 1974, 80–107.
Public safety. *American Economic Review*, **66**, 1976, 382–387. Reprinted in A. Sandmo, editor, *Essays in Public Economics: The Kiryat Anavim Papers*, Lexington Books, D. C. Heath and Co., Lexington, MA, 1978, pages 1–11.

Public economics. In J. Eatwell, M. Milgate, and P. Newman, editors, *The New Palgrave: A Dictionary of Economics*, Macmillan, London, 1987, pages 1047–1055.

L'économie publique fondée sur la liberté. In J. Bidet and G. Labica, editors, *Libéralisme et Etat de Droit*, Méridiens Klincksieck, Paris, 1992, pages 127–168.

Sens ou nonsens du calcul économique public: Le principe de compensation. *Entreprise Ethique*, **2**, 1995, 1–9.

History of public economics: The historical French school. *European Journal of the History of Economic Thought*, **17**, 687–718.

Unpublished Manuscripts

Alternative ethical foundations of fiscal systems. Document de Recherche No. 50, CERAS, Paris, 1986.

Liberty-based public economics: Its foundations, principle, method, application and structural results. Document de Recherche No. 60, CERAS, Paris, 1987.

Freedom and public goods. Document de Recherche No. 62, CERAS, Paris, 1987.

Free-riding and voluntary contributions in large numbers. Document de Recherche No. 63, CERAS, Paris, 1987.

Freedoms, cores and public goods. Document de Recherche No. 66, CERAS, Paris, 1987.

Freedom and the provision of public goods with all degrees of exclusion. Document de Recherche No. 67, CERAS, Paris, 1987.

Freedom, core, efficiency with public goods in general interdependence. Document de Recherche No. 68, CERAS, Paris, 1987.

Liberty-based public economics. International Monetary Fund, Washington, DC, 1992.

Full process liberalism. CGPC, Paris, 1992.

On the historical significance of a Public Economic Theory meeting in Paris. Prepared for the Third International Conference on Public Economic Theory, Paris, 2002.

3 Liberalisms

Books

Le Libéralisme Moderne: Analyse d'une Raison Economique. Presses Universitaires de France, Paris, 1984.

Le Contrat Social Libéral: Philosophie et Pratique du Libéralisme. Presses Universitaires de France, Paris, 1985.

Articles

Laissez faire quand même. *Revue d'Economie Politique*, **83**, 1973, 348–356.

Problèmes du libéralisme économique. *Commentaires*, **6**, 1982, 49–56.

Libres, égaux et fraternels: La logique profonde de la morale républicaine. *Revue Française de Science Politique*, **35**, 1985, 639–653.

L'allocation des ressources naturelles et le libéralisme. *Revue Economique*, **37**, 1986, 207–241.

The freedom and consensus normative theory of state: The Liberal Social Contract. In P. Koslowski, editor, *Individual Liberty and Democratic Decision-Making: The Ethics, Economics and Politics of Democracy*, J. C. B. Mohr (Paul Siebeck), Tübingen, 1987, pages 98–126.

Libres, égaux et fraternels: Problèmes et pièges logiques dans la définition et la réalisation des valeurs modernes. *Revue Européenne des Sciences Sociales*, **74**, 1987, 195–216.

Libéralismes classiques et renouvelés. In P. Ory, editor, *Nouvelle Histoire des Idées Politiques*, Hachette, Paris, 1987, pages 575–587.

Free and equal in rights: The philosophies of the 1789 Declaration of the Rights of Man and of the Citizen. *Journal of Regional Policy*, **11**, 1991, 5–62. Presented at the session in honour of the bicentennial of the Declaration at the Annual Meeting of Canadian Political Science Association, Québec City, 1989. An Italian translation appears in the Italian edition of this journal, *Mezzogiorno d'Europa*.

Free and equal in rights: The philosophies of the Declaration of 1789. *Journal of Political Philosophy*, **1**, 1993, 158–183.

Unpublished Manuscripts

Marx et Locke. No date.

Liberté et exploitation. No date.

4 The Economics of Altruism and Reciprocity

Books

La Bonne Economie: La Réciprocité Générale. Presses Universitaires de France, Paris, 1984.

The Economics of Reciprocity, Giving and Altruism (co-edited with L.-A. Gérard-Varet and J. Mercier Ythier). Macmillan, London, 2000. Proceedings of the International Economic Association Conference on the Economics of Reciprocity, Giving, and Altruism, Marseille, France, 1997.

Handbook of the Economics of Giving, Altruism and Reciprocity. Volume 1: Foundations (co-edited with J. Mercier Ythier). North-Holland, Amsterdam, 2006.

Handbook of the Economics of Giving, Altruism and Reciprocity. Volume 2: Applications (co-edited with J. Mercier Ythier). North-Holland, Amsterdam, 2006.

Reciprocity: An Economics of Social Relations. Cambridge University Press, Cambridge, 2008. Revised version of the Federico Caffè Lectures delivered at the Università degli Studi di Roma "La Sapienza", Rome, Italy, 2003.

Articles

Réciprocité et autogestion. In J.-L. Dallemagne and A. Dumas, editors, *L'Autogestion, un Système Economique?*, Dunod, Paris, 1981, pages 45–62.

Efficacité et altruisme: Les sophismes de Mandeville, Smith et Pareto. *Revue Economique*, **32**, 1981, 5–31.

Efficacité et altruisme: Le sophisme de Rousseau. *Social Science Information*, **20**, 1981, 293–344.

Altruism and efficiency. *Ethics*, **94**, 1983, 18–65. Reprinted in S. Zamagni, editor, *The Economics of Altruism*, Edward Elgar, Cheltenham, UK, 1995.

Introduction à la réciprocité générale. *Social Science Information*, **22**, 1983, 569–621.

Théorie de la réciprocité et du choix des systèmes économiques. *Revue Economique*, **35**, 1984, 871–910.

Is only egoism productive? *Development*, **3**, 1986.

Le devoir général de réciprocité. *Revue d'Ethique et de Théologie Morale. Le Supplément: Les devoirs de l'homme. De la réciprocité dans les droits de l'homme*, No. 168, 1989, 135–146.

Reciprocity. *The Newsletter of PEGS*, **2**(2), 1992, 1, 5–6.

The theory of reciprocity and of the choice of economic systems: An introduction. *Investigaciones Económicas*, **18**, 1994, 67–95.

Une introduction à la théorie de la réciprocité et du choix des systèmes économiques. In F.-R. Mahieu and H. Rapoport, editors, *Altruisme: Analyses Economiques*, Economica, Paris, 1998, pages 17–50.

Introduction: The economics of reciprocity, giving and altruism. In L.-A. Gérard-Varet, S.-C. Kolm, and J. Mercier Ythier, editors, *The Economics of Reciprocity, Giving and Altruism*, Macmillan, London, 2000, pages 1–44. Proceedings of the International Economic Association Conference on the Economics of Reciprocity, Giving, and Altruism, Marseille, France, 1997.

The theory of reciprocity. In L.-A. Gérard-Varet, S.-C. Kolm, and J. Mercier Ythier, editors, *The Economics of Reciprocity, Giving and Altruism*, Macmillan, London, 2000, pages 115–141. Proceedings of the International Economic Association Conference on the Economics of Reciprocity, Giving, and Altruism, Marseille, France, 1997.

The logic of good social relations. *Annals of Public and Cooperative Economics*, **71**, 2000, 171–189.

The logic of good social relations. In B. Gui and R. Sugden, editors, *Economics and Social Interaction: Accounting for Interpersonal Relations*, Cambridge University Press, Cambridge, 2005, pages 174–189. Revised version of the preceding entry.

Introduction to the economics of altruism, giving, and reciprocity. In S.-C. Kolm and J. Mercier Ythier, editors, *Handbook of the Economics of Giving, Altruism and Reciprocity. Volume 1: Foundations*, North-Holland, Amsterdam, 2006, pages 1–122.

Reciprocity: Its scope, rationales and consequences. In S.-C. Kolm and J. Mercier Ythier, editors, *Handbook of the Economics of Giving, Altruism and Reciprocity. Volume 1: Foundations*, North-Holland, Amsterdam, 2006, pages 371–541.

Unpublished Manuscripts

La réciprocité générale. CEPREMAP, Paris, 1975 and 1979.

Systèmes sociaux et choix individuels. CEPREMAP, Paris, 1979.

The perplexing joint giving theorem: Public transfers, charity, morality, efficiency. Presented at the Sixth International Conference on Public Economic Theory, Marseille, 2005.

Paradoxes of the war on poverty: Warm-glows and efficiency. Document de Travail No. 08-07, IDEP, Marseille, 2008.

The theory of rules and the moral provision of public goods. EHESS, Paris, 2008.

On the public good of fighting poverty: Paradoxes of solidarity. Presented at the joint Eleventh International Conference on Public Economic Theory and the Public Goods, Public Policy, Externalities Closing Conference, Istanbul, 2010.

5 Social Choice

Book

Les Elections Sont-Elles la Démocratie? Editions du Cerf, Paris, 1978.

Articles

Choix social, choix collectif, optimum social. *Revue d'Economie Politique*, **90**, 1980, 246–254.

Meanings and rationalities in social choice theory. In D. Andler, P. Banerjee, M. Chaudhury, and O. Guillaume, editors, *Facets of Rationality*, Sage Publications, New Delhi, 1995, pages 79–103.

Rational just social choice. In K. J. Arrow, A. Sen, and K. Suzumura, editors, *Social Choice Re-Examined, Volume 2*, Macmillan, London, 1996, pages 167–196. Proceedings of the International Economic Association Conference on Social Choice Re-Examined, Schloss Hernstein, Austria, 1994.

Unpublished Manuscript

What sense social choice? CGPC, 1993. Presented at the International Economic Association Conference on Social Choice Re-Examined, Schloss Hernstein, Austria, 1994.

6 Economics of the Environment

Book

L'Economie de l'Environnement. Economica, Paris, forthcoming.

Articles

La croissance et la qualité de l'environnement. *Analyse et Prévision*, **8**, 1969, 445–452.

Politiques anti-pollution optimales en présence d'incertitude. *Kyklos*, **24**, 1971, 281–304.

La pollution des lieux publics. *Recherches Economiques de Louvain*, **37**, 1971, 3–20.

La macro-économie de l'environnement. *Revue d'Economie Politique*, **81**, 1971, 595–598.

Possibilités et limites d'une régulation de l'environnement par entente directe. *Consommation*, **3**, 1971, 85–116.

Les pollueurs doivent-ils être les payeurs ? *Canadian Journal of Economics/Revue Canadienne d'Economique*, **4**, 1971, 506–523.

Instruments et critères d'une politique d'environnement. *Analyse et Prévision*, **12**, 1971.

Restriction sans discrimination. *Kyklos*, **25**, 1972, 140–142.

Le plus mauvais modèle du monde. *Nuisance et Environnement*, 1972.

Introduction à l'économie de l'environnement. *Revue Suisse d'Economie Politique et de Statistique*, **108**, 1972. Reprinted in *Bulletin des Ingénieurs des Ponts et Chaussées et des Mines*, 1972.

Une économie écologique. *Revue Politique et Parlementaire*, Supplément au No. 838, 1973, 19–27.

Les pollués doivent-ils payer? *Kyklos*, **26**, 1973, 322–336.

'Taxing pollutees': A response. *Kyklos*, **27**, 1974, 888.

Principes de règlement des externalités internationales. In *Problèmes de la Pollution Transfrontière*, OCDE/OECD, Paris, 1974. French version of the proceedings of the Seminar on Economic and Legal Aspects of Transfrontier Pollution, Paris, 1972.

Guidelines for the guidelines on the question of physical international externalities. In *Problems in Transfrontier Pollution*, OCDE/OECD, Paris, 1974. English version of the proceedings of the Seminar on Economic and Legal Aspects of Transfrontier Pollution, Paris, 1972.

Foundations of an optimum environment policy. In R. Mundell and B. E. van Snellenberg, editors, *Policy Formation in an Open Economy*, University of Waterloo, Waterloo, Canada, 1974.

Qualitative returns to scale and the optimum financing of environment policies. In J. G. Rothenberg and I. G. Heggie, editors, *The Management of Water Quality and the Environment*, Macmillan, London, 1974. Proceedings of the International

Economic Association Conference on the Management of Water Quality and the Environment, Lyngby, Denmark, 1972.
Connaissance des coûts et valeurs d'environnement. In *Mesures des dommages d'environnement*, OCDE/OECD, Paris, 1974.
Information on environmental values. In *Pollution Damage Functions*, OCDE/OECD, Paris, 1974.
Ascertaining environmental costs and benefits. In R. E. Wyzga, editor, *Environmental Damage Costs*, OCDE/OECD, Paris, 1974.
Rendement qualitatif et financement optimal des politiques d'environnement. *Econometrica*, **43**, 1975, 93–113.

Government Report

Estimation de la valeur des biens publics. Report for CORDES, Commissariat Général du Plan, Paris, 1973.

Unpublished Manuscript

Le moindre mal en politique d'environnement. CEPREMAP, Paris, 1974.

7 Macroeconomics, Macroeconomic Policy, Unemployment, Inflation

Book

Sortir de la Crise. Hachette, Collection Pluriel, Paris, 1984.

Articles

La théorie de la courbe inflation-chômage. *Revue Economique*, **21**, 1970, 295–309.
Note sur l'inflation de productivité. *Revue Economique*, **21**, 1970, 1006–1011.
L'avenir du capitalisme américain. *Revue d'Economie Politique*, **81**, 1971.
Apprivoiser l'inflation. *Preuves*, 1971. Portuguese translation published in Brazil.
L'exploitation par l'inflation. *Les Temps Modernes*, No. 303, 1971.
Inflation, stagflation et relation inflation-chômage induits par les incertitudes de la politique économique. *Revue d'Economie Politique*, **85**, 1975.
L'âge des Keynes aux Etats-Unis et sa fin dans le monde. *Annales. Economies, Sociétés, Civilisations*, **30**, 1975, 1263–1276.
Fondements de l'économie monétaire normative: Seigneuriage, liquidité externe, impossibilité de rémunérer les espèces. *Revue Economique*, **28**, 1977, 1–35.
La grande crise de 1974. *Annales. Economies, Sociétés, Civilisations*, **32**, 1977, 815–823.
Les économistes avaient prévu la crise. *La Recherche*, 1979.
Discussion. In E. Malinvaud and J.-P. Fitoussi, editors, *Unemployment in Western Countries*, Macmillan, London, 1980. Proceedings of the International Economic Association Conference on Unemployment in Western Countries, Bischenberg, France, 1978.

Cinq ans pour redresser l'économie française, stratégie de sortie de la crise et de fin de l'inflation. *Revue Politique et Parlementaire*, 1981.

Labor market and employment policies for France. In *Labor Market Policies*, Washington, DC, 1981.

La politique du chômage. *Libertés*, 1981.

La politique économique socialiste française. *Critique Socialiste, Revue Théorique du PSU*, 1981.

Comment gagner malgré deux ans d'erreurs. *Intervention*, 1983.

Une alternative à l'austérité. *Critique*, 1983, 433–434.

On inflation and the crisis. In L. Lindberg and C. S. Maier, editors, *The Politics of Inflation and Economic Stagnation: Theoretical Approaches and International Case Studies*, Brookings Institution, Washington, DC, 1985.

La cause de la crise. *Annales. Economies, Sociétés, Civilisations*, **40**, 1985, 563–577.

La stratégie macro-économique pour l'emploi. *Inter Régions*, 1985. Livre Blanc du 33ème congrès des économies régionales.

Mensonge et vérité dans la communcation gouvernementale. In M. Le Net, editor, *La Communication Gouvernementale*, Institut de la Communication Sociale, Paris, 1985, pages 197–204.

Les explications de la crise d'inspiration marxiste. *Annales. Economies, Sociétés, Civilisations*, **40**, 1985, 1453–1461.

Les explications de la crise d'inspiration marxiste: Une vue critique. In A. Grjebine, editor, *Théories de la Crise et Politiques Economiques*, Editions du Seuil, Paris, 1986, pages 101–114. A more technical version of the preceding entry.

Sortir de la crise? In P. Pascallon, editor, *Pour Sortir la France de la Crise*, Cujas, Paris, 1986, pages 244–249.

La dynamique mondiale de l'inflation et du chômage. In A. Grjebine, editor, *Théories de la Crise et Politiques Economiques*, Editions du Seuil, Paris, 1986, pages 145–159.

Logique et politique économique: Les sophismes fauteurs de crise. *Revue Politique et Parlementaire*, No. 923, 1986.

Monsieur Chirac peut-il le faire? *Politique Economique*, 1986.

Unemployment resulting from preferences on wages and prices. In O. Hamouda and J. Smithin, editors, *Keynes and Public Policy After Fifty Years. Volume II: Theories and Method*, Edward Elgar, Cheltenham, UK, 1988, pages 102–118.

Chômage et politique résultant des rôles de norme, de statut ou de signe des salaires. In A. Monfort, Y. Younes, J. Mairesse, G. Laroque, J.-J. Laffont, C. Henry, R. Guesnerie, J. M. Grandmont, M. Deleau, and P. Champsaur, editors, *Mélanges Economiques. Essais en l'Honneur d'Edmond Malinvaud*, Economica and Editions EHESS, Paris, 1988.

Employment and fiscal policies with a realistic view of the social role of wages. In A. Monfort, Y. Younes, J. Mairesse, G. Laroque, J.-J. Laffont, C. Henry, R. Guesnerie, J. M. Grandmont, M. Deleau, and P. Champsaur, editors, *Essays in Honor of Edmond Malinvaud. Volume 2: Macroeconomics*, MIT Press,

Cambridge, MA, 1990, pages 226–286. English translation of the preceding entry.

La crise. In Y. Afanassiev and M. Ferro, editors, *50 Idées qui Ebranlent le Monde: Dictionnaire de la Glasnost*, Payot, Paris, 1989, pages 267–279.

Unpublished Manuscripts

Première leçon de macro-économie moderne. CEPREMAP, Paris, 1971.

Plan monétaire de sortie de la crise et de fin de l'inflation. CEPREMAP, Paris, 1978.

L'Etat doit-il avoir des politiques de l'emploi, de stabilisation, macro-économique? Document de Recherche No. 48, CERAS, Paris, 1986.

Chômage et inflation comme résultant des effets de norme et de statut des salaires et des prix. Document de Recherche No. 51, CERAS, Paris, 1986.

Unemployment and policy with wage preference. Prepared for the Ninth World Congress of the International Economic Association, Athens, Greece, 1989.

Unemployment and policies resulting from the norm, status or sign effects of wages. Prepared for the Ninth World Congress of the International Economic Association, Athens, Greece, 1989.

La crise des économies nationales. No date.

La crise, Marx et le taux de profit. No date.

8 Monetary Economics

Book

Les Choix Financiers et Monétaires: Théorie et Technique Modernes. Dunod, Paris, 1966.

Articles

L'économie monétaire normative: Sous-liquidité et pleine liquidité. *Revue d'Economie Politique*, **81**, 1971.

Le monétarisme et la nouvelle macro-économie. *Chroniques d'Actualité*, **4**, 1971. Reprinted in *Problèmes Economiques*, No. 1227, 1971.

External liquidity. In G. P. Szegö and K. Shell, editors, *Mathematical Methods in Investment and Finance*, North-Holland, Amsterdam, 1972, pages 190–206.

Notes sur les leçons monétaires de l'histoire. *Annales. Economies, Sociétés, Civilisations*, **30**, 1975, 1477–1482.

9 International Economics

Articles

La monétisation américaine du capital français. *Revue Economique*, **18**, 1967, 1038–1057.

Sur la structure optimale de la division internationale du travail: Une généralisation de la théorie de l'avantage comparatif. *Revue Economique*, **20**, 1969, 536–539.
De l'union douanière sans intégration monétaire. *Revue d'Economie Politique*, **79**, 1969.
L'exploitation des nations par les nations. *Revue Economique*, **20**, 1969, 851–872.
Les Etats-Unis bénéficient-ils du 'droit de seigneur'? *Kyklos*, **23**, 1970, 425–445.
Positions de classe sur les variations de prix ou effets de l''Europe verte' ou du 'Kennedy Round' sur la distribution du revenu. *Revue Economique*, **22**, 1971, 306–330.
La politique du franc d'équilibre. *Revue Politique et Parlementaire*, No. 920, 1985.
Dollars et crises. *Commentaire*, 1985.
Le nouveau système monétaire international. *Politique Economique*, 1986.

Unpublished Manuscripts

Elements of the theory of international coordination. CERAS, Paris, 1989.
Cooperative-game properties of international coordination. Document de Recherche No. 77, CERAS, Paris, 1989.

10 Theory of Production

Articles

Note sur la division du travail. *Revue Economique*, **20**, 1969, 337–350.
Structures méta-homogènes des productions et préférences. *Canadian Journal of Economics/Revue Canadienne d'Economique*, **9**, 1976, 1–44.
Technical progress, neutral inventions, and Cobb-Douglas (with W. Eichhorn). In W. Eichhorn, R. Henn, O. Opitz and R. W. Shephard, editors, *Production Theory*, Lecture Notes in Economics and Mathematical Systems, Vol. 99, Springer, Berlin, 1974, pages 21–33.
Pétrole: Le tentacule caché. *Review*, **8**, 1985, 319–334.

11 Economic Systems and Transformations

Books

La Transition Socialiste: La Politique Economique de Gauche. Editions du Cerf, Paris, 1977. Translated into Italian by B. Liverani as *La Transizione Socialista: La Politica Economica di Sinistra*, Edizioni Boria, Rome, 1979.
Solutions Socialistes: A Propos de 'La Transition Socialiste' (editor). Editions Ramsay, Paris, 1978.

Articles

Structuration informationnelle centralisée et hiérarchisée: Une contribution à la théorie des organisations. *Revue Economique*, **20**, 1969, 455–467.

Pour une nouvelle planification française. *Revue Economique*, **21**, 1970, 918–928. Reprinted in *Problèmes Economiques*, No. 1244, 1971.

Chili-Portugal: Vers une théorie économique des révolutions modernes. *Annales. Economies, Sociétés, Civilisations*, **31**, 1976, 1245–1261.

Portugal: Quelle révolution, vers quelle société? Dynamique du changement des structures de propriété dans le Portugal actuel. *Futuribles*, 1976.

L'économie politique du socialisme. In S.-C. Kolm, editor, *Solutions Socialistes: A Propos de 'La Transition Socialiste'*, Editions Ramsay, Paris, 1978, pages 17–84.

Autogestion ou réciprocité. *Autogestion et Socialisme. Etudes, Débats, Documents*, **40**, 1978, 67–76.

A general theory of socialist failures. In B. Persson, editor, *Surviving Failures: Patterns and Cases of Project Mismanagement*, Almqvist & Wicksell International, Stockholm and Humanities Press, Atlantic Highlands, NJ, 1979, pages 61–70.

Possibilities of socialist transition in freedom and peace. In *Alternative Development Strategies and the Future of Asia, Conference Papers*, UNITAR, New York, 1980. Proceedings of the UNITAR Conference on Alternative Development Strategies and the Future of Asia, New Delhi, 1980.

Los condicionamientos de una repuesta de izquierda a la crisis. In *La Izquierda Ante la Crisis Economica Mundial*, Fundación Pablo Iglesias, Madrid, 1980, 104–116.

Liberal transition to socialism: Theory and difficulties. *Review (Fernand Braudel Center)*, **5**, 1981, 205-218.

Μακρο-οσκονομικη πολιτικη (Political macroeconomics). In *Μεταβαση στο Σοσιαλισμο (Transition to Socialism)*, Athens, 1981 (in Greek).

La crise de l'Etat. *CPA Management*, 1986.

Review of *Authority and Inequality Under Capitalism and Socialism* by B. Moore. *Annales. Economies, Sociétés, Civilisations*, **44**, 1989, 1178–1180.

Economic development and the theory of social ethics. *Journal of Regional Policy*, **11**, 1991, 427–432.

Review of *The Origin and Evolution of Cultures* by R. Boyd and P. Richerson. *Journal of Economics*, **88**, 2006, 205–207.

Government Report

Les Hommes du Fouta-Toro. Bulletin No. 121, Division Socio-Economique, Mission d'Aménagement du Fleuve Sénégal, Saint-Louis, Sénégal, 1960. A slightly revised version of this report was issued as a book.

Unpublished Manuscript

Preface to *Why Has Japan 'Succeeded'?* by M. Morishima. Document de Recherche No. 56, CERAS, Paris, 1986.

12 Philosophy of Economics, Epistemology, Methodology

Book

Philosophie de l'Economie. Editions du Seuil, Paris, 1986.

Articles

Léon Walras' correspondence and related papers: The birth of mathematical economics. A review article. *American Economic Review*, **58**, 1968, 1330–1341.

A quoi sert la science économique? *Annales. Economies, Sociétés, Civilisations*, **30**, 1975, 123–136.

Sur la méthode de l'économie. *Annales. Economies, Sociétés, Civilisations*, **33**, 1978, 602–622.

Science économique et position politique. *Revue Economique*, **29**, 1978, 605–654.

Dix ans de science économique. *Bulletin de la Maison des Sciences de l'Homme*, 1979.

Sur la théorie économique. In *Relations Internationales, Politique Economique et Méthodologie: Essais en l'Honneur de Jacques L'Huillier*, Georg Verlag, Geneva, 1987, pages 274–285.

Where is economic science, where must it go? (in Italian). *Rassegna Economica*, **52**, 1988.

Economics in Europe and in the U.S. *European Economic Review*, **32**, 1988, 207–212.

L'économie comme science et comme politique. In Y. Michaud, editor, *Université de Tous les Savoirs. Volume 3: Qu'est-ce que la Société*, Odile Jacob, Paris, 2000, pages 52–64.

The human person in normative economics. In E. Malinvaud and M. A. Glendon, editors, *Conceptualization of the Person in Social Sciences*, Pontifical Academy of Social Sciences, Vatican City, 2006, pages 369-413. Proceedings of the Eleventh Plenary Session of the Pontifical Academy of Social Sciences, Vatican City, November 18–22, 2005.

Unpublished Manuscripts

The epistemic predicament of economics, its causes, consequences and general solutions. Document de Recherche No. 64, CERAS, Paris, 1987.

L'ouverture de la science économique: Les perles (ou épines) de la couronne de la reine des sciences sociales, CERAS, Paris, 1990.

Méta-économie: Propositions d'auto-méthodologie de la science économique. Document de Recherche No. 88, CERAS, Paris, 1990.

13 Theory of Man, Psychologies, Oriental Philosophy

Books

Le Bonheur-Liberté: Bouddhisme Profond et Modernité. Presses Universitaires de France, Paris, 1982. Second edition, 1984. Third revised edition, 1994.

L'Homme Pluridimensionnel: Bouddhisme, Marxisme, Psychanalyse pour une Economie de l'Esprit. Editions Albin-Michel, Paris, 1987.

Articles

La philosophie bouddhiste et les 'hommes économiques'. *Social Science Information*, **18**, 1979, 489–588.

Psychanalyse et théorie des choix. *Social Science Information*, **19**, 1980, 269–339. Reprinted in *Revue de Psychologie Economique*, actes du 5ème congrès de psychologie économique, 1981.

De l'individualisme. *Commentaires*, 1981.

Essence et utilité du bouddhisme. *Esprit*, 1981.

La théorie bouddhique de la liberté. *Critique*, 1982.

Le bouddhisme et les 'hommes économiques'. *Bulletin du MAUSS*, No. 6, 1983, 52–83.

Marxisme et Bouddhisme. *Cahiers Internationaux de Sociologie*, No. 77, 1984, 339–360.

Must one be Buddhist to grow? An analysis of the cultural basis of Japanese productivity. In P. Koslowski, editor, *Economics and Philosophy*, J. C. B. Mohr (Paul Siebeck), Tübingen, 1985, pages 221–243.

The Buddhist theory of 'no-self'. In J. Elster, editor, *The Multiple Self*, Cambridge University Press, Cambridge, 1986, pages 233–263.

Bouddhisme. *Le Temps Stratégique*, 1988.

The psychology of happiness and of liberty. *Journal of Oriental Studies*, **2**, 1989, 11–20. A Japanese translation appears in the Japanese edition of this journal, *Toyo Gakujutsu Kenkyu*, **28**, 1989. Also issued as a booklet in English in the series *Buddhism Today*, The Institute of Oriental Philosophy, Tokyo, 1989.

Le bouddhisme, l'Occident et la nouvelle situation du monde. The Institute of Oriental Philosophy, Tokyo, 1990.

La philosophie bouddhiste et les 'hommes économiques'. *Dalhousie French Studies*, **46**, 1999, 125–148.